슈퍼그라운드 SUPERGROUND

서울
새로운 *땅의 풍경*

SEOUL
NEW *GROUNDSCAPES*

언더그라운드 UNDERGROUND

CURATED BY YOUNG JOON KIM AND MANUEL GAUSA

차 례

CONTENTS

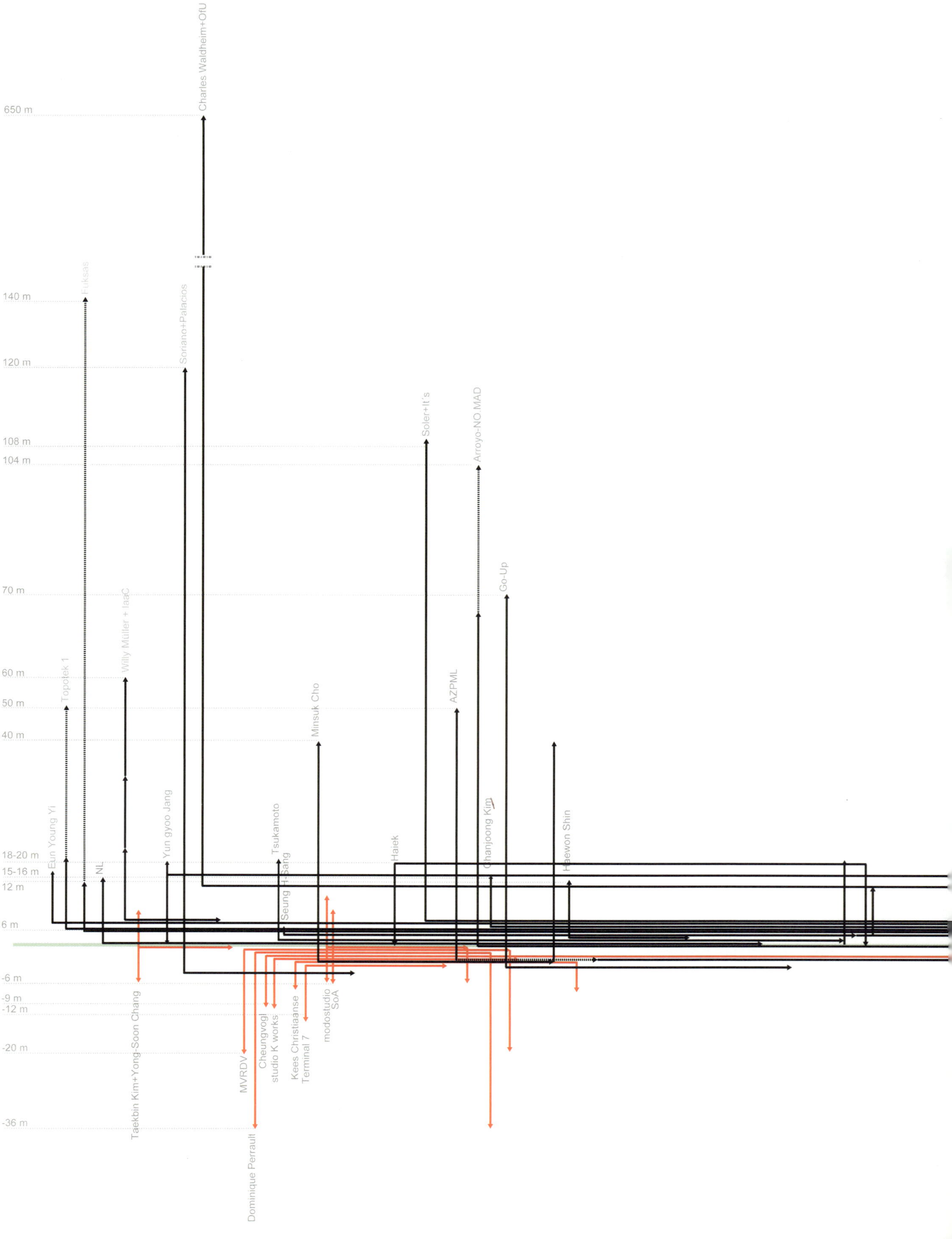

650 m
140 m
120 m
108 m
104 m
70 m
60 m
50 m
40 m
18-20 m
15-16 m
12 m
6 m
-6 m
-9 m
-12 m
-20 m
-36 m
Charles Waldheim+OfU
Fuksas
Soriano+Palacios
Soler+It's
Arroyo-NO MAD
Go-Up
Willy Müller + IaaC
Topotek 1
AZPML
Minsuk Cho
Eun Young Yi
NL
Yun gyoo Jang
Tsukamoto
Seung H-Sang
Haiek
Chanjoong Kim
Haewon Shin
Taekbin Kim+Yong-Soon Chang
MVRDV
Dominique Perrault
Cheungvogl
studio K works
Kees Christiaanse
Terminal 7
modostudio
SoA

5

1

발간사
PREFACE

박원순
Won-soon Park

안녕하세요 서울특별시장 박원순입니다.

매년 700여만 명이 방문하는 서울은 세계적인 글로벌 도시입니다. 이 책은 글로벌 도시 미래서울의 비전과 위상을 알리고 새로운 서울의 도시 건축정책의 전략적 방향 설정에 도움을 주기 위해 제작되었습니다.

이 책에서 소개하는 서울의 지상과 지하의 27개 장소의 건축기본 구상안은 하천, 도로, 유수지 등 이제껏 개발의 사각지대에 있었던 다양한 유휴공간을 재조명하여 미래서울이 직면한 도시문제 해결과 글로벌 도시 서울의 가치를 높이기 위해 국내외 건축가들의 노력과 헌신으로 수립되었습니다. 서울의 도시공간이 단순한 미학적 상상력의 장소로 머물기보다는 국제도시 서울이 반드시 갖추어야 할 주거, 상업, 업무, 공원, 교통, 휴식 등의 다양한 도시기능이 복합적으로 어우러진 미래도시 비전을 실현하는 새로운 시도가 될 것입니다.

미래서울의 모습은 지금까지 와는 전혀 다른 공간적·사회적·환경적 여건을 가지게 되며 도시발전의 패러다임과 사회구조적 변화 속에 서울은 4차 산업혁명 중심지, 스마트팩토리 구축, 세계 최고 수준의 관광과 MICE산업의 중심지로 각광받는 새로운 국제도시로서 서울이 여러분 앞에 펼쳐지게 될 것입니다.

미래서울의 주인은 서울에 애정과 관심을 가지고 계신 전 세계인들이며 그들의 참여로 미래서울의 모습은 완성될 수 있으며, 모든 사람의 사랑을 받는 서울을 만들기 위해 서울시도 더욱 노력하겠습니다.

감사합니다.

This is Seoul Mayor Park Won-soon.

Visited by 7 million people every year, Seoul is a world-famous global city. This book aims to promote the vision and status of global Seoul and help it to establish strategies for its urban development policy.

This book introduces preliminary design proposals for 27 sites above ground or underground across Seoul. They are the outcome of the efforts and commitment of domestic and foreign architects who shed new light on various types of underused spaces, such as streams, roads or reservoirs, which used to be outside the area of development, with an aim to resolve urban problems emerging across Seoul and add value to this global city. These urban spaces in Seoul will open up a new opportunity to build a futuristic city in which different urban features, such as residences, retails, offices, parks, transportations and resting areas, are intertwined with each other in various ways, rather than simply becoming a place for promoting aesthetics and imagination.

In the future, Seoul will provide totally different spatial, social and environmental conditions compared to the past, and, in tandem with the changes in urban development paradigms and social structures, it will evolve into a new cosmopolitan city renowned as an epicenter of the fourth industrial revolution, incubator for smart factories and world-class hub for tourism and MICE Industry.

The owner of future Seoul is the cosmopolitans who have affection and interest in Seoul, and their participation will help the city to complete its transformation. The Seoul Metropolitan Government also will put much more effort into making Seoul into a city loved by all.

Thank you.

슈퍼그라운드 언더그라운드
SUPERGROUND UNDERGROUND

김영준
Young Joon Kim

마뉴엘 가우사
Manuel Gausa

근대 이후 세계 곳곳 많은 도시에서 도시화의 여정이 마무리되고 있습니다. 서울 역시 1960년대 이후 급격한 팽창의 시대를 거쳐 이제는 안정의 시대로 접어들었습니다. 그간의 결과로 서울은 이전부터 존재하던 산과 강의 거대한 자연을 품으면서, 대규모의 개발 패턴과 역사가 만들어낸 과거의 패턴이 공존하는 도시로 정착되고 있습니다.

안정의 시대를 맞이하면서, 서울에서는 여러 다른 도시와 마찬가지로 이제 급격한 재개발보다는 사람을 중심에 두고 도시의 재생을 실행하고 있습니다. 그간 성장의 시대를 겪으면서 파생된 여러 가지 부조화를 다듬어야 하는 과제도 함께 다루고 있습니다. 그러면서 안정된 체계 내에서 새로운 시대가 요구하는 내부 성장을 도모하고 있습니다.

많은 도시에서 고민하듯, 교통 수단의 혁신에서 파생된 도시의 변화가 서울에도 상당한 영향을 주고 있습니다. 결과로 드러나듯, 이민, 관광, 노인 인구의 급격한 증대는 여지껏 겪어보지 못한 새로운 도전입니다. 도시의 주인이 과거의 정의를 벗어난다면 어떤 미래를 예상해야 하는지 모든 도시들과 함께 고민하고 있습니다.

안정된 도시에서는 이전의 도시계획적인 수법이 아니라 건축적인 대안을 동원하여 도시의 미래를 대비하는 수법을 검토하게 됩니다. 건축적 제안을매개로 도시적인 목표를 가늠하는 수법입니다. 도시를 바라보는 관점 속에서 건축의 역할이 정립되어야 하는 수법이기도 합니다. 건축을 고립된 조형으로 바라보지 않는 기본 가정에서 출발합니다.

일단의 기본 리서치를 바탕으로 여러 건축가를 초청하여 언더그라운드, 슈퍼그라운드 프로젝트를 전개하였습니다. 그간 단일 목적으로만 구분하였던 도시의 여러 체계들을 재검토하는 프로젝트입니다. 도시의 구성에서 소외되었던 지하공간과 인프라 공간을 주목하여 도시의 체계를 보완하면서 미래를 대비하려는 프로젝트입니다. 다양한 논의 속에서 서울의 특정한 영역을 대상으로 하고 있지만, 전 세계 다른 도시에서도 적용 가능한 일반해를 목표로 삼았습니다.

총 27인의 건축가들이 건축적 상상력으로 서울의 특정 영역에 새롭고 대담한 대안을 제시하였습니다. 과거의 도시계획에서 소외되었던 남겨진 영역들이 이제 도시 삶의 중요한 공간으로 치환되는 대안을 보실 수 있습니다. 이들 스터디가 던져주는 미래 실현의 가능성을 주목하고 싶습니다.

Since the dawn of the modern era, cities around the world have gone through urbanization. Seoul also has experienced an era of dramatic expansion since the 1960s. But now it has reached a plateau. The outcome of such a processis transforming Seoul into a city which embraces its pre-existing, spectacular natural scenery of mountains and riversand allows new large-scale development patterns and outdated ones, a remnant of history, to exist together.

Adapting itself to this era of stability, Seoul, like many other cities, is promoting human-centered urban regeneration projects rather than pursuing rapid redevelopment. At the same time, it's trying to settle various conflicts that have emerged during its growth process. Also, under its well-established system, it's cultivating internal growth to meet the needs of a new era.

Like many cities in a challenging situation, Seoul is also being significantly affected by urban changes brought about by innovations in transportation.As these situations have shown, issues around immigration, tourism and rapidly aging population areposing a new challenge that we have never experienced before. Therefore, in tandem with other cities, Seoul is trying to figure out how it should shape its future when urban dwellers are no longer bound by outdated definitions.

Settled cities adopt architectural solutionsinstead of old-fashioned urban planning approaches when they seek preparation measures for their future. This method uses architectural proposals as a medium to assess urban objectives. It's effective only when the role of architecture is defined from the perspective of urban design. It's based on the premise that an architecture is not an isolated sculpture.

In the light of a series of preliminary researches, a number of architects are invited for our 'Underground' and 'Superground'projects.These projects reexamine various urban systems which used to be regarded as monofunctional. They look into underground spaces and infrastructures which were isolated from urban structures, with an aim to complement existing urban systems and prepare for the future. Though their discussions are around specific sites in Seoul, the ultimate goal is to find a universal solution applicable to other cities around the world.

A total of 27 architects stretched their architectural imagination and came up with innovative and bold solutions for specific sites in Seoul. Here you can see how their solutions convert leftover areas excluded from urban development in the past into an essential space for city life. The feasibility of various future scenariosexplored in these studies is what we should pay our attention to.

서울의 그라운드스케이프 :
SEOUL *GROUNDSCAPES:*

비장소가 아닌 노드 플레이스
NODE-PLACES MORE THAN NO-PLACES

마뉴엘 가우사
Manuel Gausa

김영준
Young Joon Kim

I– 슈퍼와 비욘드

2018년 10월에 선보인 도시의 전망을 담은'서울 슈퍼그라운드" 라는 전시 제목은 서울의 새로운 대지 공간이 갖고 있는 보다 복잡하고, 혼성적이며, 다층적인 조건을 의미할 뿐만 아니라 (위–above, supra라는 측면에서 super) 동시에 도시의 혁신과 질적 가치의 측면에서 창조성, 혁신, 리더쉽을 시험하려는 새로운 정치적 의미를 내포한다.(초월–beyond, meta라는 의미로 super)

이러한 미래를 전망하는 야심 찬 작업은 슈퍼 그라운드 이전 2018년 5월 '서울 언더그라운드' 작업을 통해 이미 진행된 바 있는데, 새로운 유형의 땅의 풍경을 만들어 내려는 서울시의 의지를 표현하고자 하는 또 다른 시도였다.

서울은 오늘날 전 세계에서 가장 중요한 대도시 중 하나이자 도시를 방문하는 사람들이 두 번째로 많은 곳으로서 다른 대도시들이 갖고 있는 현안과 도전들을 모두 지니고 있다.

서울의 새롭고 위대한 기회는 기존 고밀 상황을 새로 재구성하는 재도시화와 결합하는 데 있으며, 이는 마크 오제가 이야기한 비장소를 넘어서는 거점 장소로서 전략적이면서도 정확한 거점 장소들을 연결시키고 활성화시키는 것이다.

서울의 새로운 기회는 기존 고밀 도시 위에 새로운 리–세팅(Re-Setting) 또는 *재 도시(Re–Citying)* 전략을 결합하는 것이며, 이는 마크 오제가 언급한 비장소를 넘어서 전략적으로 정밀한 거점이 될 장소들을 활성화하고 이들 사이의 네트워크를 만들어 기존 도시와 결합하여 *혼성도시와 시민성*–도시 개발, 혼성 프로그램, 인프라와 공공공간, 조경의 결합 등–을 활용할 수 있으며, 새로운 극들이 만들어내는 매트릭스 안에서 혁신적인 도시 유도체이자 매력요소로 인지될 것이다.

지난 몇십 년 동안 도시에서 우리의 삶과 교류의 공간을 정의하는 스케일과 패러다임에 있어서 놀랄만한 변화들이 있었다. 교통과 장거리 통신, 교환의 탈장소화, 우리의 환경을 변화시키는 기술적 역량 등이 관련되어 있다. 또한 전 세계적으로 동시에 엮여 있는 정보 변수들을 다룰 수 있는 디지털 역량이 있다.

현대의 *다원도시*는 점점 더 역동적이고 복잡한 상황 속에서 영역과 정보 시스템을 그 본질로 하고 있다. 놀라운 도시의 변이 양상과 점점 증가하는 복잡한 상황에 대응하는 전통적인 원칙의 혼란 앞에서 도시 문화와 도시정부는 두 세기에 걸쳐서 여러 가지 모델을 실험해 왔다.

I– SUPER AND BEYOND

The title of the *Seoul Superground* urban prospection and exhibition, presented on October 2018, wants to express a more complex, mixed and multi-layering condition of the new Seoul land-space (*super* as *supra*, above), but also refers to a new politic will that wants to punt on the creativity, the innovation and the leadership in terms of urban innovation and qualitative value (*super* as *meta*, a "beyond" condition).

This set of ambitious prospective works completed the anterior research –Seoul Underground–, presented on May 2018, conjugating a double proposal able to express the new will of the city, oriented to formulate a new type of *groundscapes.*

Seoul is today one of the must important metropolis in the word (the second in number of visitors) with all the current problems and the main challenges of a global megalopolis.

Its new – and great – bet is to combine its existing high agglomeration with a new re-setting (or *re-citying*) reformulation based in the networked reactivation of strategic precise and qualitative nodal sites (node-places more than the no-places of Marc Augé). Sites able to conjugate *mixicity* and *civility* – urban development, mixed programs, integrated infrastructures and public and relational spaces (and landscapes) – in an articulated matrix of new polarities conceived as new innovating urban inductors… and attractors.

The last few decades have confirmed the evidence of a spectacular change of scale (and paradigms) in the definition of our spaces of live and sociability – of our own habitats and our cities – linked with the accelerated increase in mobility and long-distance communication, the delocalization of exchanges, and the technological and material capacity of transformation of our environment.

A global process connected, also, with the digital rising capacity to combine overlapped and simultaneous parameters of information.

The contemporary *multi-city* evidences, more and more, its dynamic and complex condition, that is the nature of a territorial and informational system.

In front of the impressive urban mutations and in front of the perplexity of the traditional disciplines for answering to all the implications of the new complex conditions, the urban cultures and governments of the cities in-between centuries have experimented different models:

- 첫 번째로 수정주의 모델은 특히 70년대와 80년대에 등장했는데 역사와 과거의 회복에 기반을 두고 있다. 반동적이고 역사주의적인 모델은 도시의 재창조와 포스트모더니즘 문화가 제시했던 형태적인 환기에 바탕을 두고 있다. "전통적인 도시로 되돌아가기"는 이 같은 접근방식이 내세웠던 구호이다.

- 두 번째는 구조주의 모델로서 20세기 말, 즉 80년대와 90년대에 매우 중요했던 개념으로 물질적이고 발전에 기반한 도시의 확장과 연결에 바탕을 둔다. '네오 모더니즘' 모델은 도시의 상위계획, 관계항의 표준화, 물리적인 교통망의 효율화 등에 기반을 두고 있다. "대도시의 꿈을 향하여"는 이와 같은 접근방식의 구호이다.

- 세 번째는 대상주의 또는 중상주의 모델로서 최근인 90년대와 2000년대 도시 마케팅과 도시 관리에 기반들 두고 있으며, 상징적인 대상을 이벤트화하는 데서 발견할 수 있다. 포스트모더니즘과 네오모더니즘, 파라모더니즘 모델은 아이콘처럼 목적을 가진 디자인, 대기업의 도입, 브랜딩, 건축적 화려함, 그리고 그 중요성을 쉽게 인지할 수 있는 형태로 연결시킨다. "브랜딩의 기호로서의 도시"는 이 같은 접근방식의 구호이다.

이와 같은 수정주의 혹은 구조주의, 대상주의 혹은 중상중의, 상징적 혹은 수사적인 모델들은 모두 오래된 도시 형태나 법칙의 자기참조적인 소용돌이에 갇혀서 디지털 혁명과 관련된 새로운 정보시대의 도전 및 새로운 다층 관계의 열린 환경으로 이해되는 오늘날의 n-시티의 다중적이고 복잡한 논리들에 대응할 수 없음을 스스로 보여주었다.

— a first model (*Revisionistic),* specially present in the 70´and 80´, based in the recuperation of the history and the past. A retroactive and historicist model based in the urban recreation and the formal evocation of the postmodern cultures. "*Coming back to the traditional city*" would be the slogan of this kind of approach.

— a second model (*Structuralistic*), very important at the end of the XXI century (80´and 90´) based in the materialistic and developistic extension of the cities and its arterial netting articulation. A "neo-modern" model based in the urban (super)planning, the standardisation of the referents and the efficiency of the traffic physical nets.
"*Towards a Metropolitan Dream*" would be the second slogan of this kind of approach.

— a third model (*Objectualistic / Mercantilistic),* more recent (90´ and 2000´) based in the urban marketing and urban management of the cities, founded in the *event* positioning of iconic objects. A Post, Neo & Para-modern model, associated to the objectual design (iconic), the importation of big firms, the branding, the architectural glamour, and its to signification by the (same) implantation recognizable elements.
"*The city as a branding-mark*" would be the slogan of this third of approach.

All these models (*revisionistic or structuralistic, objectualistic or mercantilistic, iconic or rhetoric*) have revealed themselves as closed in a self-referential spiral of old urban forms and formulas not able to confront the challenges of a new informational time associated to the digital revolution and the multiple and complex logics of the today´s *n-City* understood as a new multi-relational and open environment.

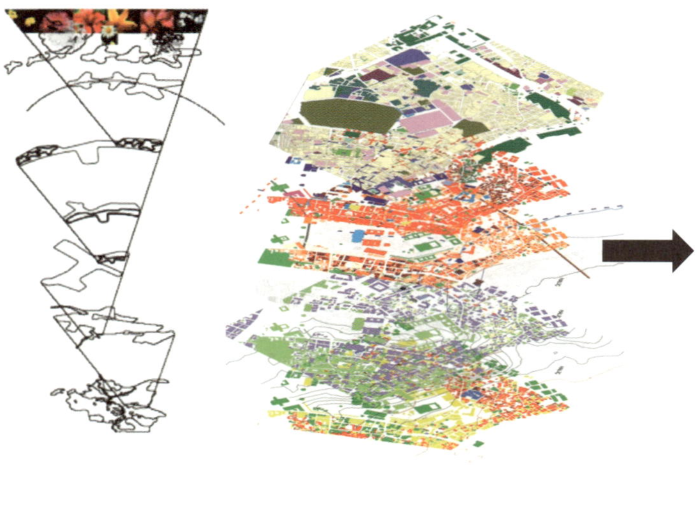

ADVANCED URBAN PROSPECTION
Multi-scalar (transversal) & Multilayer (complex) strategic approach
COMPLEX ANALYSIS > INTENTIONAL SYNTHESIS

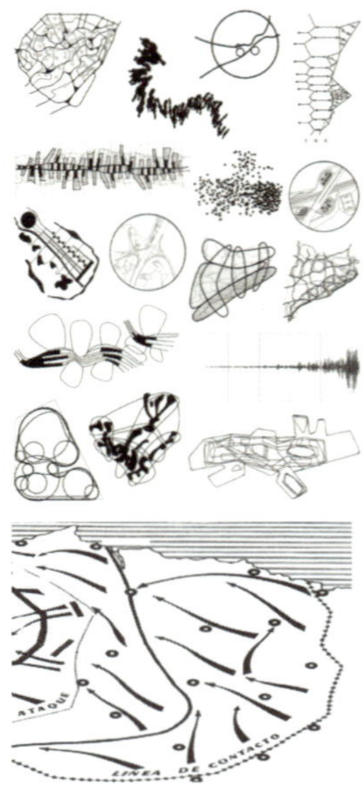

LAYERS & VECTORS

이제는 새로운 모델, 혹은 행동의 기준을 찾아내야 할 것으로 보이는 데이는 도시를 진화하면서 계속 발전하는 과정과 연결된 역동적이고 다중적인 체계로 이해할 수 있는 미래적인 모델이다.
21세기 초부터 새로운 정보와 컴퓨터 시대의 혁명이 우리 도시 환경의 복잡성과 이질성을 증가시켜 왔다면, 혁신적인 연구와 탐구에 기반을 둔 새로운 선진적인 도시 논리가 더욱 필요해 보인다.

향상된 논리는 동시적인 현실의 다양한 층을 결합시킬 수 있는 이전의 전체론적 인식, 혹은 통찰력 있는 연구와 관련된 새로운 도시 전략의 등장을 선호하고, 새롭고 더욱 감정이입이 되어 반응하고 적극적인 해답 가운데 데이터의 조건, 방향, 시각화 등을 통합하면서 이원적 정보 및 상호작용과 협력해야 한다.
과거의 회복, 구조적인 표준화 혹은 관계 항들의 상징적인 도입을 넘어서 현대적인 접근법에서 중요한 점은 관계 항들의 새로운 작동방식에 있다.
"새로운 다층 및 다중적으로 상호작용하는 환경 전략의 탐구"는 이 같은 앞선 관점에서 제시하는 구호이다.

우리는 안정적인 형태의 도시를 떠나서 변화하는 시스템, 즉 관계와 상호작용의 역동적이면서 비선형적인 시스템이라는 도시로 넘어왔다. 이는 현실이자 가상이며, 물질적이면서 비물질적이다.
도시의 새로운 방법론적 접근법이 가져온 획기적인 조언들은 다양하면서도 서로 상호연결된 행동의 세 가지 발달된 체계와 연관 지을 수 있는데, 이는 패러다임의 변화뿐 아니라 새로운 체계, 기구적이면서 기술적인 도구의 적용과 실험적인 결과에 문을 열어 놓고 있다.

A new model (or better, criterion of action) seems today necessary to be explored: a prospective model able to understand the city as a dynamic and plural system linked with evolutionary and in-progress processes.

If, from the beginnings of the XXI Century, the revolutions of the new informational and computational era have increased the complexity and heterogeneity of our urban environments, a new advanced urban logic (based in the innovative research and prospection), seems more and more necessary.

An advanced logic called to work with the duality Information + Interaction, favouring the emergence of new urban strategies connected with the research of anticipatory holistic recognitions – and visions – able to combine multiple layers of simultaneous realities, integrating data-conditions, data-orientations and data-visualisations in new more empathic and responsive and proactive answers.

Beyond the past recuperation, the structural standardisation or the iconic importation of referents, the important of this contemporary approach would be the generation of new operational referents

"*Exploring new multi-layering and multi-interactive environmental strategies*" could be the slogan of this advanced gaze.

From the city as a stable form we have passed to the city as a fluctuant system:
— a dynamic and non-linear system of relations and interactions.
— ... real and virtual... material and immaterial...

The innovative inputs of new methodological urban approaches can be associated to three advanced lines of action, diverse but interconnected in-between them, that are opening the door not only to different changes of paradigms but also to new frameworks, instrumental and technological tool-applications and experimental outputs:

A- **디지털 및 데이터 처리 기술의 혁신**으로서 정보관리, 오픈소스 프로그램과 실시간 데이터, 스마트 시티 변수화 및 센서화의 새로운 역학관계와 연결되어 있다.

B- **통합적이고 환경 시스템의 혁신**으로서 과거의 토지이용계획부터 새로운 토지 네트워크 전략으로 이동하며 패러다임의 중요한 변화를 표현한다. 새로운 네트워크를 갖춘 관계망과 실행에 기반한 시나리오와 시스템에서 복잡한 층위와 구조를 통합할 수 있다.

C- **사회적이자 상향식의 창조적 혁신**으로서 새로운 형태의 참여 및 공동생산과 연결되어 있고 새로운 종류의 사회적인 '도시 시설' 및 집합적인 행동에 관련된다. 다중적이고 상호반응하는 경험을 선호할 수 있는 새로운 종류의 관계에 기반한 공간과 구조에서 공유되고 있다. 이들은 새롭게 가능한 발전된 도시론과 관련하여 개념적 방향들 중 하나이다.

정확한 데이터와 전체론적 전망을 결합해야 하는 새로운 도시론.

이와 같은 "정보+통찰력"의 조합(처리능력과 가능성 있고 전략적이며 연관시키는 능력)에는 오늘날 참고하기에 적절한 지역과 여러 분야 사이에 교류하는 원대한 프로그램이 부족하다.

이 점에서 현실과 조건 및 정보 사이의 상호작용을 증가시키기 위해서 이와 같은 새로운 정보시대의 과제들과 연계하여 새로운 도시적 사고에 관련된 새로운 논리와 능력을 우리가 이해한다면, 우리는 데이터 변수나 데이터 지표로서뿐 아니라 새롭고 더 개방적이며 융통성 있는 현대 도시 시스템에서 결합될 수 있는 다른 유사한 주요 용어들과 연계된 확장된 개념으로서의 "정보"를 어떤 용어로 정의할지 이해해야 한다.

A – A digital (& data-processing) technological innovation linked with the informational management and the new dynamics of open-source programs, real time data and smart-cities *parametrisation* and *sensorisation.*

B – An integrative ands eco-systemic innovation who expresses an important change of paradigms –from old land-uses planning to new land-networked strategies– able to integrate complex layers and structures in new networked, relational (and operational) scenarios and systems.

C – A social (& bottom-up) creative innovation connected with new forms of participation and co-production –and with a new kind of social "civilities" and collective behaviours– shared in a new kind of relational spaces (and structures) able to favour multiple interactive experiences. These are some of the new conceptual orientations in relation with a new possible Advanced Urbanism.

A new urbanism that must to combine *Precise DATAS & holistic VISIONS.*

Such combination "information + vision" (processing capacity and prospective, strategic and relational capacity) lacks today of suitable reference areas and ambitious programs of inter-disciplinary exchange.

If we understand the new logics – associated to a new urban thinking – in relation with the challenges of these new informational era – and the capacity, in this one, to multiply the interactions between realities and conditions and information(s) – we need to understand also in what terms we define "information", not only as a data-parameter or a data-indicator but as a more enlarge concept associated to other assimilated key-terms (programs, solicitations, messages, patterns, identities, matters, cultures, types, behaviours, senses, networks, natures, morphologies and metabolic contexts) able to be combined in (and from) new –and more– open, flexible and contemporary urban systems.

II- 새로운 도시적 과제

새로운 시대의 도시계획가는 인구, 에너지, 환경, 식량, 물, 보안, 주거, 건강, 교통 등과 관련된 복잡한 문제들에 대한 해답을 찾아야 하는 과제에 직면해 있다. 그러나 새로운 전략적 시나리오가 더 이상 생산이나 재생에 관한 것이라기보다는 "공동 생산"에 관한 것이라면 이것은 새로운 합리적인 토지이용과 공공 도시 공간이라는 새로운 종류의 개념과 연결된 지속가능한 발전 및 도시기반시설 개발에 대한 해답이기도 하다. 이 시나리오는 개방적이고 똑똑한 해답을 만들어낼 수 있고, 방향성이 있으면서도 조정이 가능하고, 오늘날 우리와 동시대의 가장 중요한 패러다임을 따르는 것으로 보이는 새로운 세계적인 주요 과제 및 주제와 연결되어 있다.

- 새로운 환경 감수성과 관련된 구조적인 요소로서의 풍경의 재귀화 및 새로운 가치화라는 새로운 요구에 대한 지역과 도시의 새로운 장소적이며 대지의 표현 및 해석
- 기능적이면서도 상관관계가 있는 공간으로서 공공공간의 새로운 활동적인 차원. 컴퓨터로 조종되며 반응하는 데이터 활용과 새로운 재귀화의 도시적 요구에 연관된 새로운 유형의 상호작용하는 공공 인터페이스와의 관계 증가
- 효율적이고 빠르면서도 느린 이동성에 대한 새로운 개념과 새로운 통합된 모델에서 여러 가지 사회기반시설에 대한 개념
- 도시적 재활용과 기존시설 재사용의 중요성

II- NEW URBAN CHALLENGES

The new generation of urban planners is challenged to find solutions to complex problems related to population, energy, environment, food, water, security, housing, health, and transportation. But also to a new rational land-use, a sustainable growth and infrastructural development linked with a new kind of conception of the public and civic space, providing new strategic scenarios no longer productive or reproductive but "co-productive": scenarios capable of generating open and intelligent solutions, orientated and adaptable at a time, connected with the new main global challenges and topics that seem to conform, today, the must substantial paradigms of our contemporaneity:

— The new *territorial* and land-articulations of the region-city and their translation in new demands of re-naturalisation and a new valorisation of the landscape as a structural factor associated to a new environmental sensibility in the land-use developments.

— The new active dimension of the public space as an operational and relational space at a time. The increase of smart and responsive data applications and its relationship with a new kind of interactive public "interfaces associated, at a time, with a new re-naturalisation urban demand.

— The new conception of the mobility (efficient, speed and slow at time) and the conception of the different infrastructures in new integrated models.

— The importance of the urban recycling and the reuse of the pre-existences.

- 3차원적으로 지어진 레퍼토리와 몇 배로 밀도를 높인 혼합 유형에서 용도, 기능, 프로그램을 혼합할 수 있는 새로운 용량
- 활기찬 자급자족, 자원의 지능적인 관리 등과 같은 새로운 지속가능한 안건과 새로운 형태의 친환경 거주지로의 변환
- 새로운 유동적이고 조정할 수 있는 전략에서 도시의 회복 가능 능력
- 해변 및 수변 생활의 중요성에 대한 고려와 이 점에서 수변공간 처리의 중요성
- 새로운 레저 및 지식사회에서 여행의 증가와 그에 대한 영향 및 도시적 유인요소의 관련성
- 문화와 혁신, 유산과 전통 가치, 창조적이면서 생산적인 플랫폼과 공간 사이의 결합 중요성

특히 서울의 경우 화두와 과제는 새로운 관계 시나리오에 연관된 다섯 개의 이항으로 된 핵심적인 벡터로 합성할 수 있다.

- 통합된 사회기반시설과 새롭게 상호작용하는 공공 공간, 즉
  - 다중의 중심과 연결성: 새로운 여러 개의 다양한 이동 시스템에서 대지의 흐름과 느린 사회기반시설의 결합
  - 새로운 활동적인 인터페이스로 이해되는 공공공간을 위한 새로운 종류의 상호작용 네트워크의 구상
- 도시적 재귀화 및 경관 요소, 즉
  - 자연적인 도시 회랑과 촘촘한 녹색 구조물
  - 경관의 상호작용: 여러 층으로 된 경계(강의 수변공간, 산지)와 다양한 지형

— The new capacities to mix uses, functions and programs in a new kind of tri-dimensional built repertories and n-densified hybrid typologies.

— The new sustainable agendas (energetic (self)sufficiency, intelligent management of resources, etc.) and their translation into new types of eco-habitats.

— The resilient capacity of the cities in new flexible and adaptable strategies.

— The importance of the coastal and river-rives consideration and, in this sense, the importance of the water-fronts treatments.

— The increase of the tourism and its incidence in the new society of leisure and knowledge and the relevance of the urban attractors.

— The importance of the combination between culture and innovation, heritage and patrimonial values and creative and generative platforms and spaces.

Topics and challenges that –specially in the case of Seoul– can be synthetized in five binomial *key-vectors* involved in and with new relational scenarios:

— Integrated infrastructures and new interactive public spaces, that is:
—— Multi-centrality and connectivity: integration of land flow and slow infrastructures in new plural and diversified systems of mobility.
—— Conception of a new type of interactive networks for public spaces understood as new active interfaces

— Urban re-naturalization and landscape factor, that is:
—— Natural urban corridors and meshed green-structures.
—— Landscape interaction: multi-layered borders (river waterfronts, mountain frictions) and diversified *topos*.

- 도시적 재활용과 새로운 삼차원적 밀도와 복합도시, 즉:
  - 도시와 사회기반시설의 재활용: 전통적인 기존 도시와 그 상위시설 및 기반시설을 재생 및 재가동하기 위한 과정
  - 주거지를 위한 새로운 형태의 삼차원적 혼합 유형에서 용도, 기능, 프로그램의 다양화

- 친환경 시스템의 관리와 회복가능한 적응성, 즉:
  - 지속가능한 안건: 새로운 공동 참여적이고 호응하는 과정과 연관된 지속가능하면서 공간적인 복지 환경
  - 회복력: 적응력 있는 도시적 생태환경

- 관광 개발, 도시 지식 유인자, 문화적인 가치(유산과 혁신), 즉:
  - 관광업: 시민들 간 새롭고 오래된 관광 유인요소의 교류
  - 유산과 지식: 역동적이고 문화적이면서도 창조적이고 혁신적인 지식

여러 도시 사이의 수 세기에 걸친 도시적 변형과 경쟁이라는 복잡한 과정을 통해 이러한 변화 혹은 도전의 패러다임 앞에서 새로운 도시의 리더십은 지속 가능하고 진보적이며 혁신적인 방식으로 과정들을 수행하고 방향을 설정할 수 있는 질적인 발전이라는 새로운 벡터를 통해서 효율성과 상상력, 실용주의와 창조성, 스스로의 문화와 넓게 걸쳐진 세계주의를 통합할 것을 요구한다. 새로운 기술의 디지털 능력, 혁신적인 개념과 탐구의 새로운 과정은 야심만만한 서울의 새로운 도시 프로그램에서 도시의 데이터 처리와 창조적 전망을 새로운 전체론적 전략으로 결합시키려는 목적으로 구체적으로 연관된 핵심 기능에 놓여있다. 새로운 압축 및 농축된 시나리오는 전 세계 도시의 새로운 과제를 지역의 대상지와 그 조건에 결합시킬 수 있다.

세계의 도시 도전 패러다임 (시민도시 서울 연구: 마뉴엘 가우사, 신혜원, 니콜라 카네사)

Global Urban Challenges Paradigms (Research Civic Seoul: Manuel Gausa, Haewon Shin, Nicola Canessa)

— Urban Recycling and new tri-dimensional density and mixicity, that is:
—— Urban and infrastructural recycle: reviving and reactivating processes for the traditional and/or existing city (and its super and infra structures).
—— Diversity of uses, functions and programs in a new kind of tri-dimensional hybrid typologies and/for habitats.

— Eco-systemic management and resilient adaptability, that is:
—— Sustainable agenda: sustainable and spatial welfare environments associated to new co-participatory and responsive processes.
—— Resilience: adaptable urban ecosystems.

— Touristic development, urban knowledge attractors, cultural values (heritage and innovation), that is:
—— Tourism: citizen exchange in touristic old (and new) attractors
—— Heritage & knowledge: dynamic cultural, but also creative and innovative knowledge.

In front of these *cha(lle)nge-paradigms* (associated the complex processes of urban mutations – and competitions – in-between cities… and centuries) the new urban leaderships require to combine efficiency and imagination, pragmatism and creativity, own culture and transversal cosmopolitism, trough new vectors of qualitative developing able to conduct and orientate the processes in a sustainable, progressive and innovative way: new technological and digital capabilities and new processes of innovative conception and prospection, aimed to combine urban data-processes and urban creative-visions in new holistic strategies, landed – in the case of a new ambitious Seoul urban program– in referential and concrete key-operations: new *compressing* – and *condensing* – scenarios, able to integrate new urban global challenges and local sites (and situations).

서울의 변환된 도시 도전 패러다임. 이디오그램 (시민도시 서울 연구: 마뉴엘 가우사, 신혜원, 니콜라 카네사)

Seoul Local Urban Challenges Transferred Paradigms. Ideograms (Research Civic Seoul: Manuel Gausa, Haewon Shin, Nicola Canessa)

복합서식지
Urban and Natural Multi-Habitat

참여형 시민도시
Participatory Civic City

다중심·소통형 기반시설
Multicentered-Communicative Infrastructures

지속가능한 공간 생태계
Sustainable Spatial Ecosystems

도시 살리기
Reviving the City

응축·공유 도시
Condensed-Common City

manner.

자생력 있는 도시환경
Resilient Urban Environments

다층적 경계
Multilayered Borders

시민 중심 관광
Citizen-Centered Tourisms

역동적 문화유산
Dynamic Cultural Heritage

서울의 변환된 도시 도전 패러다임. 계획 (시민도시 서울 연구: 마누엘 가우사, 신혜원, 니콜라 카네사)

Seoul Local Urban Challenges Transferred Paradigms. Schemes. (Research Civic Seoul: Manuel Gausa, Haewon Shin, Nicola Canessa)

III-서울:생활 도시기반시설, 압축적 도시시설

서울이 갖고 있는 흥미롭고 특별한 특징, 특히 잠재적으로 새로운 대도시의 참조점의 측면에서 볼 때, 오늘날 현대 다중도시를 정의하는 이러한 새로운 도시 패러다임들을 복합적인 현실에서 결합하고 관리할 수 있는 능력이다. 현대의 다중도시는 도시의 밀도와 상호작용하는 시민성을 활용하여 새로운 도시의 성찬들(도시 공유, 도시 통합, 도시 관계, 도시 상호작용 등) 속에서 도전들을 응축할 수 있다.
이 시민 인자들은 기존의 구조들(과 인프라 공간들)을 사회적 환경이나 프로그램에 있어서 재설정하여, 새로운 고밀 시민도시로 서울의 새로운 방향을 제시한다.
실제 서울의 큰 잠재성은 거대한 인프라 네트워크, 간선도로망이나 결절점 등에 있으며, 새로운 도시 정치 속에서 이들은 다시 연결되거나 새로운 방향이 필요하다. 다층적인 인프라 네트워크는 오늘날 도시가 새로운 리셋을 경험할 수 있는 기회의 핫 포인트가 될 수 있다.

이러한 도시적인 벡터는 지난 시간 동안 서울을 새로운 밀집한 도시로 만든 도시개발을 서울의 새로운 방향으로 설정하는데, 이는 서울의 오래된 구조와 사회기반시설을 사회-환경적이고 계획에 따라 방향을 재설정하는 것과 직접 연관되어 있다.

사실, 서울의 거대한 잠재력은 도처에 깔려 있는 사회기반시설의 매트릭스, 망, 주요 관 및 연결점에 놓여 있으며, 이들은 새로운 도시의 정치학에서 새로 진행하여 방향을 다시 잡도록 요구된다. 다중의 사회기반시설 네트워크는 오늘날 서울을 새로 재정비하는 실험을 할 수 있는 가능성 있는 지역과 사회적 운용성, 즉 핫 포인트를 감지할 수 있는 곳이다.
이제 오래된 인프라와 연결되어 있는 장소들은 새로운 내부구조로 재해석된다.

III- SEOUL: LIVING INFRASTRUCTURES, CONDENSING CIVILITIES

The interest and singular specificity of Seoul –as a potentially new metropolitan referential context– is the capacity for the city to combine and manage all these new urban paradigmatic challenges that are defining our contemporary multi-cities, in a mixed reality able to condense all them in a new kind of urban conviviality (urban sharing, urban integration, urban relationship, urban interaction, etc.) called to conjugate urban density and interactive civility.

This civil vector marks the new orientation of the Seoul last years urban development where the city appears as a new *dense civic-city,* directly associated to the socio-environmental and programmatic reorientation of its old structures (and infrastructures).

In fact, the big potential of Seoul is based in its infrastructural immanent network of matrixes, meshes, arterial lines and nodes that, in the new urban politics of the city, are called to be re-conduced and re-orientated. A multi-infrastructural network where is possible, today, to detect *hot-points*, areas of opportunity (and social operability) where the city can experiment a new reset.

Spaces linked with old infrastructures re-interpreted, today, as *new intra-structures.*

Eco, info and *meta* structures, also, that express this super-grounding dimension for a new SeYoul (a "you-city", convivial, collective and connected)

에코, 인포, 메타 구조는 또한 새로운 서울(SeYoul, 스페인어로 "너-도시", 생기있고 집합적이며 연계된 도시)을 위한 슈퍼 그라운드를 표현한다.
새로운 도시와 인프라 공간에 조성된 특정 활동을 위한 특정 공간들은 혼합 도시 프로그램들을 목적으로, 주거와 생활, 관계와 교류, 생산과 교환, 여가와 지식 등 각 부분별로 서로 다른 강도와 역량으로 결합되어 개발될 수 있다.
대상지들은 참고한 클러스터의 특징에 따라 네 종류로 나눌 수 있다.[1]

도로, 철도, 지하 공간의 다층 복합 연결

서울이 확장하면서 간선도로와 철도들은 서울을 관통하며, 도시의 내부로 파고들었다. 소음을 차단하기 위하여 세워진 거대한 벽이나 고가구조물들은 도시의 경관을 바꾸어 놓았으며, 강을 따라 놓인 간선도로들은 수변 공간을 도시로부터 분리시켜, 그 가치를 찾지 못하고 있다. 도시를 가로지르는 거대한 도로들은 생활 공간을 분리시키고, 보행을 어렵게 만들고 있다.

1. 대상지의 여러가지 유형에 대한 설명에 실려 있는 글은 서울 슈퍼그라운드 프로젝트의 코디네이터인 신은기가 처음 작성한 글에서 가져왔다.

Singular spaces for singular operations linked with these new urban and infrastructural targets of mixed urban programs able to be developed in each sector, housing and living, relational and convivial, productive and exchanging, leisure and knowledge spaces, combined with different degrees of intensity and capacity of growing and evolution.

Sites that can be synthesized in 4 families of cluster points referred to[1]:

MIX-MULTILAYER CONNECTORS OF ROADS, RAILWAYS AND UNDERGROUND AREAS

As Seoul expanded, the main arterial roads, highways and railways – and underground networks – penetrated the center of the city. Large walls for blocking noise, elevated structures and subway lines, have significantly changed the urban scenery, and expressways aligned with the river separated the city and the riverfront for good. Wide roads unnecessarily cut across urban centers and make it difficult for pedestrians to travel. Certain main roads including the Gyeongbu Expressway and railways are being planned to go underground.

1. The text that accompanies the description of the different typologies of sites comes from a first version developed by Eungee Cinn, assistant coordinator of the Seoul Superground project.

A B C D

인프라스트럭쳐 대지의 서로 다른 유형들 (신은기, 슈퍼그라운드 서울 코디네이터)

Different typologies of infrastructural sites (Eungee Cinn, coordinator of the Seoul Superground project).

A– 도로, 철도, 지하 공간의 다층 복합 연결
Mix-multilayer connectors of roads, railways and underground areas

B– 오래된 고가 구조물과 하부 구조물의 프로그램 재가동과 재활성화
Program reactivation and revitalization of old elevated and lower-level structure

C– 물, 유수지의 복합적 활용
Water, mix-use of reservoir sites

D– 단절된 도시 섬과 교차로의 회복
Recovery of urban island-sectors and crossing points

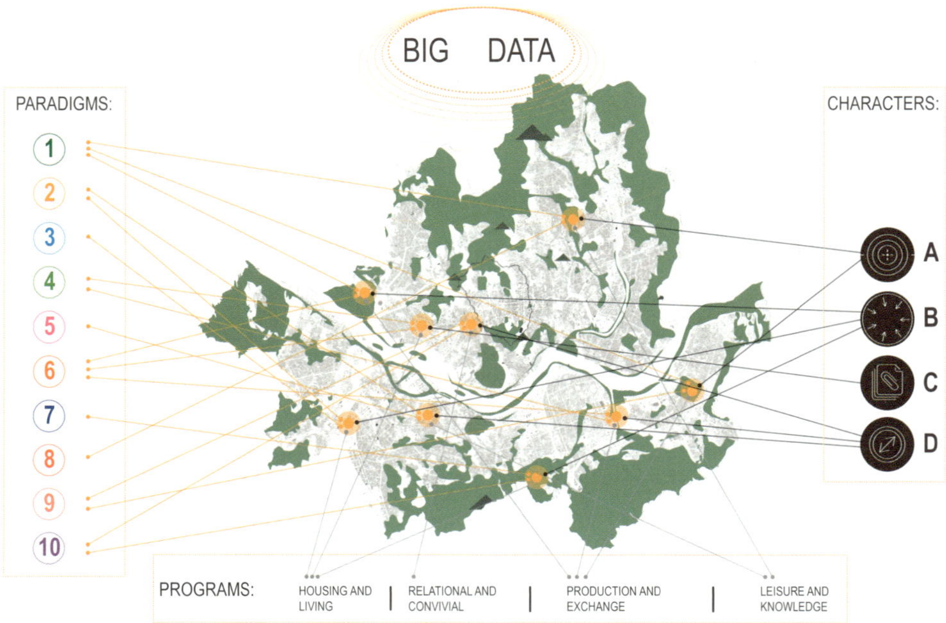

서울-새로운 전망. 개념 지도-교차 전략: 패러다임, 유형, 프로그램과 데이터 (시민도시 서울 연구: 마뉴엘 가우사, 신혜원, 니콜라 카네사)

Seoul-New Prospection. Conceptual Map - Crossing Strategies: Paradigms, Typologies, Programs and Data. (Research Civic Seoul: Manuel Gausa, Haewon Shin, Nicola Canessa)

서울 인프라스트럭쳐 지도. 녹지/그리드의 해석. 슈퍼그라운드 서울 조사 (시민도시 서울 연구: 마뉴엘 가우사, 신혜원, 니콜라 카네사)

Seoul infrastructural map. Green/Grid interpretation. Preparation for the Seoul-Superground Prospective Survey (Research Civic Seoul: Manuel Gausa, Haewon Shin, Nicola Canessa)

서울 인프라스트럭쳐 지도. 슈퍼그라운드 서울 조사 (서울특별시 도시공간개선단)

Seoul infrastructural map. Preparation for the Seoul-Superground Prospective Survey (Seoul Metropolitan Government, Urban Space Improvement Bureau)

이제 경부고속도로를 비롯하여 몇몇 간선도로와 철도들의 지하화를 검토하고 있다. 도로와 철도를 위한 공간과 사람을 위한 공간이 입체화될 때, 도시의 조각난 부분들이 연결되고, 서울의 산과 하천과 같은 자연 자원과 도시가 만나고, 보행자들을 위한 새로운 오픈 스페이스가 생성된다. 슈퍼그라운드를 통해서 도로와 철도의 지하화뿐만 아니라 다양한 입체화, 복합화 비전을 제시하고, 이들이 만드는 새로운 도시 공간을 발견한다.

프로그램의 재가동과 오래된 고가구조물과 지하 구조물의 재활성화

도시 곳곳에 자리 잡은 고가구조물들은 원활한 교통 흐름을 위하여 건설되었다. 하지만 이 구조물들은 그 본래의 목적에만 충실하여 도시의 주변 공간들과 유리되어 있으며, 구조물의 하부 공간은 어둡고 방치된 공간이 되어, 지역 경관을 악화시키고 있다.

오늘날 노후화되어 생명을 다한 고가구조물들은 철거되기도 하지만, 공원과 보행가로처럼 주변에 활력을 불어넣는 새로운 역할들을 부여받고 있다. 앞으로 철도나 간선도로가 지하화되면서 기존 통과교통의 역할을 잃어버린 고가구조물들 역시 이들이 놓인 상황과 맥락에 따라 지금과 다른 모습과 역할을 가질 것이다.
또한 기존 역할을 그대로 유지하는 고가구조물들의 경우에도, 구조물 자체와 구조물의 하부 공간 등 고가구조물이 만들어 내는 다양한 3차원의 공간들을 활용하여 새로운 도시 공간을 만들어낼 수 있는 가능성을 탐색한다.

물, 유수지 공간의 복합용도

서울은 여름철 짧은 시기에 일 년 강수량의 대부분이 집중된다. 이 시기 하천의 범람과 침수를 막기 위하여 한강을 비롯한 주요 하천 주변에는 52곳의 유수지를 비롯하여 저류조, 제방들이 지어졌다.
유수지와 저류조의 경우, 집중 호우 기간 외는 거의 사용되지 않음에도 불구하고 도시 내에서 넓은 면적을 차지하고 있으며, 유수지 주변으로 청소차고지, 자원재활용처리장 등 도시 혐오시설들이 밀집해있어 도시 하천 주변의 경관을 악화시키고 있다. 하천을 따라 형성된 제방은 거대한 벽이 되어 도시에서 하천으로의 접근을 가로막고 있다.
최근 들어 유수지와 저류조가 차지하는 공간을 효율적으로 활용하기

The vertical separation of space for pedestrians and space for transportation will lead to the connection among the city's isolated pieces, between the city and the nature such as mountains and rivers, and for the pedestrians to new open spaces. Hence, the roads and railways will not only go underground but also be more layered and made complex to offer new urban spaces.

PROGRAM REACTIVATION AND REVITALIZATION OF OLD ELEVATED AND LOWER-LEVEL STRUCTURES

Throughout the city, elevated structures were originally constructed to enable smooth traffic flows. While faithfully fulfilling their duty, these structures however have remained aloof from surrounding spaces, made obsolete the spaces underneath them, and damaged the local sceneries.

Nowadays, while deteriorated structures are duly demolished, remaining structures are often given a new purpose by being transformed into park spaces or pedestrian pathways. As roads and railways become underground, the elevated structures are likely to lose their traffic function and need to adjust to new circumstances and contexts.

For structures that maintain their original function, various possible ways to utilize all sections of spaces of the structures will need to be explored.

WATER, MIX-USE OF RESERVOIR SITES

For Seoul, most of rainfall is concentrated during a short period of time in the summer. To prevent the overflowing of the river and streams and the subsequent inundations, 52 sites of reservoirs and embankments were strategically chosen and developed along the waterways.

Although rarely used outside of the monsoon season, the reservoir sites occupy very large plots of land in Seoul, and around them are garbage processing and recycling centers that render the surrounding area rather unpleasant. In the case of embankments, they act as large walls that prevent easy access to the water bodies.

위하여, 체육공원이나 주차장으로 사용하는 사례들이 있다. 하지만 아직까지는 이들이 갖고 있는 3차원 가능성을 충분히 활용하지 못하고 있다. 범람과 침수를 막는 본래의 취지를 유지하면서도 동시에 이 시설들이 매력적인 도시의 수변 공간이 될 수 있는 방법을 모색한다.

도시의 외딴 섬 구역과 교차점의 회복

서울에는 철도차량기지, 물재생센터와 같이 도시의 기능을 유지하기 위하여 필요하지만, 접근이 차단된 거대한 시설들이 존재한다. 이들은 도시 맥락에서 하나의 거대한 섬으로 남아 있으며, 주변에 다른 혐오시설들을 끌어들이며 점점 그 면적을 키워간다. 하지만 최근 들어 차량기지 이전, 물재생센터 현대화 사업 등을 추진하며 이 거대한 면적의 부지들이 갖고 있는 잠재성에 주목하고 있다.
폐쇄된 것이 아니라 도시를 향해 개방된 대지이지만, 도로와 철도의 흐름으로 가로막혀 접근이 어려운 도시 섬들도 존재한다. 간선도로와 철도 옆에 위치한 완충 녹지를 비롯하여 지하철 환기구가 점거한 지역 내 작은 유휴필지에 이르기까지 다양한 목적과 스케일로 도시 내 곳곳에 있다. 이러한 섬들이 주변의 도시적 조건과 만나서 만들어내는 다양한 가능성이 있다.

IV- 여러 층의 전망 - 슈퍼그라운드와 언더그라운드

교류와 동시성이라는 다수의 시나리오로서 영역을 인식하는 것은 사실 대지를 계획하고 개발하는 전통적인 도구를 새로운 시각, 즉 과거의 공식들을 재평가하려는 시각으로 바라보는 것이다. 오늘날 복합적인 도시(현재 그 해석, 활동, 삶의 차원에서 중첩에 대응하는)는 더 이상 2차원적인 조닝이나 단일 기능 분류(주거, 공업, 녹지 등)에 기반한 토지의 “평가”가 아니라 “다차원(n-dimensional)”에 기준을 지향해야 한다. 이는 용도와 프로그램의 레벨 및 층위를 새로 통합된 입체적인 혼합기능과 결합하면서 여기에 자연과 인공, 풍경과 건축, 주거-생산-휴식, 주거와 시설 등과 같이 전통적으로 나눠진 분류 사이의 상호작용의 새로운 영역을 구축하는 것이며, 이들은 단순한 연결만이 아니라 상호연결과 서로 엮어진 관계를 통해서 활성화된다.

Increasing number of contemporary examples demonstrate how the reservoir sites embrace other programs such as sports centers and parking garages. However, most of them do not show the full extent to which the sites can be utilized three-dimensionally. While preserving the function of preventing flood, the sites have much potential to turn into attractive places.

RECOVERY OF URBAN ISLAND-SECTORS AND CROSSING POINTS

There exist in Seoul many large facilities such as railroad car stations and water re-use center that run the city's infrastructural system but are mostly inaccessible. These facilities remain as large islands within urban contexts and continuously grow by absorbing other smaller infrastructural structures. They are now being examined as new sites of intervention for their large sizes and potential shifts in functions.

Though inherently open in orientation, certain urban islands exist due to the formation of road and railway networks. Such islands vary in size and nature, ranging from greenbelts alongside expressways and railways to small idle plots occupied by infrastructural pipes. These islands may also create new possibilities when connected to the existing city fabric.

IV- MULTILAYER PROSPECTION UPER AND UNDER GROUNDS

To conceive the territory as a multiple scenario of interchange and simultaneity would, in fact, refer to a new look at the traditional tools of planning and development of the ground, a look destined to re-evaluate its old formulations. A more complex city (subject to responding to the current overlapping of levels of interpretation, activity and life) should be faced, preferably, through different levels of use and definition, starting from a “qualification” of the land based no longer on two-dimensional zonning and monofunctional classifications (residential areas, industrial zones, green areas, etc.), but rather on “n-dimensional” criteria; combining levels and layers of use and programming with and in new integrated three-dimensional mixed operations where to establish new areas of interaction between traditionally separate categories (natural and artificial, landscape and architecture, residence-production-recreation, housing and equipment, etc.) activated not only through simple connections but interconnections and/or interweaving relationships.

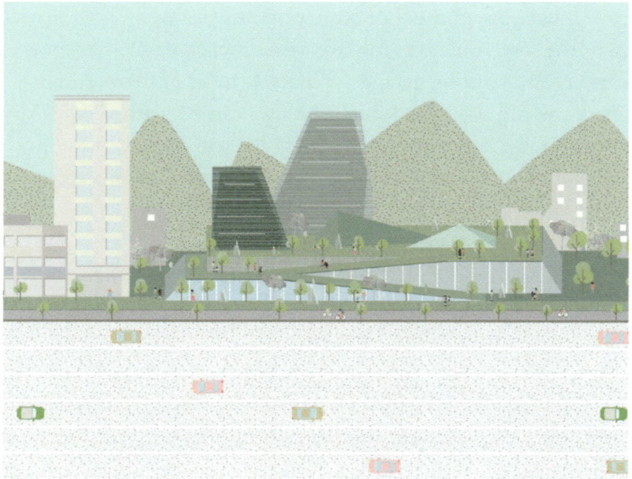

CITY-CITY
도시-도시

CITY-WATER
도시-물

CITY-INFRASTRUCTURE
도시-인프라스트럭쳐

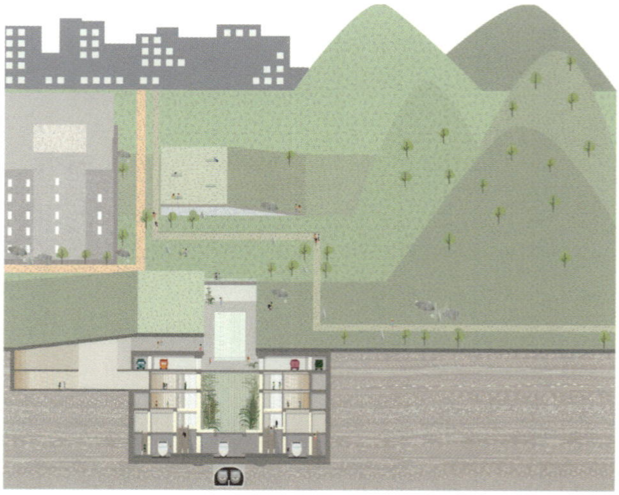

CITY-NATURE
도시-자연

복잡한 프로그램의 단면들로 만들어진 새로운 입체적인 시각에서 표면과 볼륨, 수평성과 수직성, 지면과 지반을 결합하고 합성할 수 있는 하이브리드 디자인의 접근법과 관련된 새로운 최신 기술적 도구의 가능성에 관심을 갖는 새로운 3차원 시각과 시간을 역동적인 요소로 결합시키는 4차원 시각을 위해서 2차원적 평면과 바닥 높이에 바탕을 둔 전통적인 시각의 관성을 극복하는 것은 앞에서 언급했듯이 적절하게 재활용되고 "다시 도입된" 어떤 전략적인 도시기반시설 부지를 창조적이고 질적으로 재평가하는 것을 지원하고자 한다.

슈퍼그라운드나 언더그라운드와 같은 n개의 대지 혹은 다중대지의 개념은 이 같은 기준에 부합하지만 이것은 전통적인 도시를 '지속'시키거나 '재창조'하려는 의도는 아니다. 무엇을 부여하거나, 위치시키거나, 변형시키는 것이 아니며, 도시 필지 위에 어떤 기계나 사물들을 만드는 것이 아니다. 대신 새로운 조밀한 바닥을 중첩(덮거나 겹치거나 침투하거나 미끄러지거나 배치하는 등의 유사한 활동들)시키는데 이것은 그 위나 내부나 안에서 생활과 관계에 대한 새로우면서도 오래된 프로그램, 용도, 행동을 발전시킬 수 있는 새로운 지형이 된다.

프로그램의 두께를 지탱할 수 있고 새로운 형태의 부조나 플랫폼이 될 수 있는 새로운 바닥은 길이나 높이에서 수평 혹은 수직적으로 드러난다. 새로운 바닥은 현재의 도시나 환경의 조건에 따라 변하거나 맞출 수 있는 새로운 형태의 시스템 혹은 장치에서 풍경 및 인프라, 빌딩을 결합시킬 수 있다.
확실히 아직 운영 중이거나, 구식이 되거나 폐기된 몇몇 오래된 인프라라는 새로운 가능성 있는 영역으로서 이같이 때로는 실제적이고 때로는 가상의 새로운 층을 지탱하거나 통합 또는 구조화하는 이상적인 공간으로 드러난다.

Overcoming the inertia of traditional vision, based on 2D plans and +0 levels, for a new 3D vision (and 4D, incorporating the time dynamic factor) attentive to the potential of recent technological tools associated to with a new "hybrid" designing approach capable to couple – and synthesize – surfaces and volumes, horizontality and verticality, soils and subsoils in a new three-dimensional-vision made of complex programmatic sections aimed at favoring, as mentioned, the creative and qualitative revaluation of certain strategic and infrastructural sites, appropriately recycled and "re-informed".

The concept of *n-ground* or *multi-ground* (*Superground* or *Underground*) responds to these criteria: it does not intend to "continue" or "recreate" the traditional city. Nor impose or positionate, transforming it, built machines or objects (re-objectualizing the urban plot) but superimpose (with all associated synonyms, cover, overlap, infiltrate, slide, interspersed ...) a new dense floor (container and articulator at the same time) that becomes a new topos *on, inside, in, where* and *through which* to develop new/old programs, uses and activities of life and relationship.

A new floor able to maintain a programmatic thickness and also become a new type of relief, platform or revea in length and height, horizontally and vertically at the same time: a new floor capable of merging landscapes, infrastructure and building in a new type of systems/devices variable and adaptable to the current urban and environmental conditions.
Obviously the opportunity areas of the old infrastructures (some in operation, others obsolete or in disuse) are revealed as the ideal spaces to support (to incorporate and to structurate) these new floors, real and virtual at time.

VI–벡터와 전망

서울 슈퍼그라운드 전시회에서 선보인 프로젝트들은 신념과 상상력, 사실주의와 이상주의, 창조성과 운용성, 감각과 감수성 등을 결합할 수 있는 엄선된 건축가들이 만들어낸 것으로 전략적인 시나리오를 표현하고 때로는 극한까지 몰아가면서 정확한 데이터와 전략적인 벡터와 전체론적인 전망을 결합하면서 각 대상지의 여러 가지 가능성을 추론해보고자 한다.

서울을 다시 알리려는 목적을 가지고 과정과 목표에서 결과의 질과 모든 팀의 영향을 뒷받침했던 이 선택 때문에 도시의 책임을 생각해보는 것이 중요하다.
매우 정확하고 구체화된 시나리오 안에서 몇몇 기본적인 전략적 변수에 바탕을 둔 채 운영사항은 즉각적으로 변경될 수 있다.

– 메쉬 메커니즘
새로운 도시적 연결성을 우선시하는 다중 연결 기제를 조립할 것을 요청
– 적극적인 지형학
새로운 도시 지질학을 우선시하는 새롭게 작동하는 경관을 만들어낼 것을 요청
– 복합 다중 프로그램
새로운 도시적 다중 교류를 우선시하는 복합 프로그램과 활동들을 즐길 것을 요청
– 연속적인 결과
새로운 도시 진동을 우선시하면서 다중 스칼라의 사회의 율동적인 결합을 합칠 것으로 요청
– 통합된 기술
새로운 도시 생태시스템을 우선시하면서 새로운 환경 기술을 동원할 것을 요청
그리고 진화하는 정보의 시대
우리 도시의 단계별 진화의 중요성을 이해하는 발전적인 시간요소를 고려할 것을 요청

VI– VECTORS AND VISIONS

The projects presented in the exhibition *Seoul Superground* –produced by a selection of architects able to combine conviction and imagination, realism and idealism, creativity and operability, sense and sensibility– wants to extrapolate the multiple capacities of each site expressing strategic scenarios, often taken to the limit, combining *precise DATAS, strategic VECTORS and holistic VISIONS.*

It´s important to thanks the responsables of the city for this bet that has favoured the quality of the results and the implication of all the teams in the process and in the goals, oriented to aid to re-inform Seoul.

Operations that can be immediately transformed in very precise and concretized scenarios and based in some basic strategic parameters:

MESH MECHANISMS
Called to assemble multi-connective mechanisms prioritizing *new urban connectivities.*

ACTIVE TOPOGRAPHIES
Called to model new operational landscapes prioritizing *new urban geologies.*

MIXED MULTI-PROGRAMS
Called to enjoy mixed programs and activities prioritizing *new urban multi-exchanges.*

SERIAL SEQUENCES
Called to combine multi-scalar social rhythmic combinations prioritizing *new urban vibrations.*

INTEGRATED TECHNOLOGIES
Called to mobilise new environmental technologies prioritizing new *urban eco-systems.*

AND... EVOLVING INFORMATIONAL TIME
Called to take account of evolutionary time-factor understanding the importance of the own *urban phased evolution.*

처리 용량과 장래의 전략적, 상관적 용량인 "정보+방향+전망"을 결합할 수 있는 프로젝트와 디자인은 학제간, 차원간, 사회간 교류라는 원대한 프로그램만이 아니라 오늘날 새로운 적합한 참조용 모델과 도시적 정치를 되찾고자 한다.

다른 팀들의 해답은 어떤 경우에도 다른 요소들 사이의 발생적인 연결로부터 해결되었다. 이러한 해답은 접근한 장소나 대상지의 성격으로부터 유추하거나 보다 도시적이거나 영역에 관련되거나 체계적 혹은 특수하기도 한 운영 그 자체의 차원에서 나오기도 하고 활성화된 여러 가지 표현하는 매개변수에 주어진 우선 사항을 통해서 개념적일 뿐만 아니라 운영상의 전략적인 논리 자체에서 나온다. 그러나 그 해답은 특히 그러한 메커니즘이 놓여있는 높이나 깊이에 관련되어 있고 특별한 장치의 배치에서 그들이 제안하거나 이루어낸 높이나 깊이에도 상관이 있다. 앞의 세 가지 기준을 섞은 마지막 기준은 출판이나 제안의 지표를 분명히 보여준다. 이 책의 페이지에 소개한 주석이 달린 매트릭스 테이블은 대응하는 전략적인 매개변수와 도시나 조경 요소들의 분석적이고 종합적인 교차점에서 여러 가지 프로젝트들을 요약하고 있다.

새로운 종류의 여러 층위의 n섹션으로 만들어지기를 원하는 새로운 복잡한 서울 n시티를 위한 복합적인 해답.
새로운 압축된 사회적, 환경적인 도시시설을 위한 다층의 연결
상징적인 대상이기보다는 연관성이 있는 시나리오.
함께 맞물려 있는 슈퍼그라운드, 언더그라운드, 멀티그라운드.

Projects and designs able to combine "information + orientation + vision" (processing capacity and prospective, strategic and relational capacity) reclaming today new suitable referential models and urban politics as well as ambitious programs of inter-disciplinary, inter-dimensional (and inter-social) exchanges.

The answers of the different teams are solved, in any case, from the generative crossing between different factors: those that would derive from the nature of the placeor site approached; those of the own dimension of the operation (more urban or more territorial, more systemic or more particular); and those of the strategic logic itself (not only conceptually but also operationally) through the priority given to the various formulating parameters activated.

But also, and that would be particularly relevant, the height and depth at which such mechanisms are "disposed" and the height and/or depth that they propose or attain in their particular device deployment. This last criterion (crossed with the previous three) articules the index of the publication and proposals. The commented matrix-table that is presented in these pages also summarizes the various projects in these analytical and synthetic intersection of strategic parameters and urban (and landscape) factors to which they respond.

Complex answers for a new complex *Seoul n-city* that wants to be traduced in a new kind of multilevel *n-sections*.

Multilayer links for a new condensed, social and environmental, ci(vili)ty.

Relational scenarios more than iconic objects.

Super-grounds, undergrounds (and multi-grounds), meshed together.

서울 슈퍼그라운드 언더그라운드 서울 조사. 지역과 높이를 함께 전체적으로 보여주는 다이어그램 (마뉴엘 가우사, 마틸드 피탄티)

Seoul Seoul-Superground and Underground Prospective Surveys. Superposition of localisations and Level-scanning diagrams (Manuel Gausa with Matilde Pitanti).

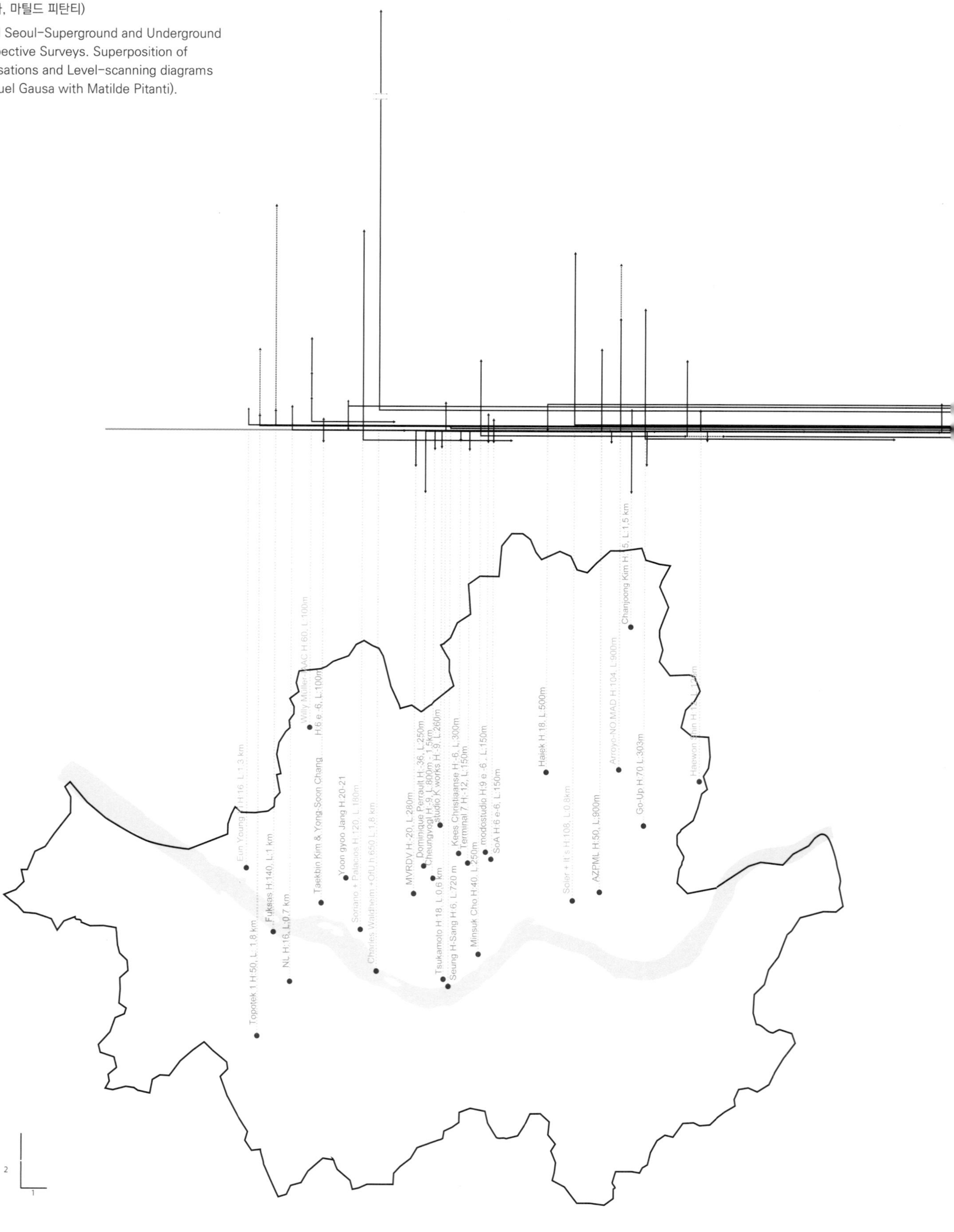

서울 슈퍼그라운드 언더그라운드 서울 조사. 지역과 높이를 함께 전체적으로 보여주는 다이어그램 (마뉴엘 가우사, 마틸드 피탄티)

Seoul Seoul-Superground and Underground Prospective Surveys. Superposition of localisations and Level-scanning diagrams (Manuel Gausa with Matilde Pitanti).

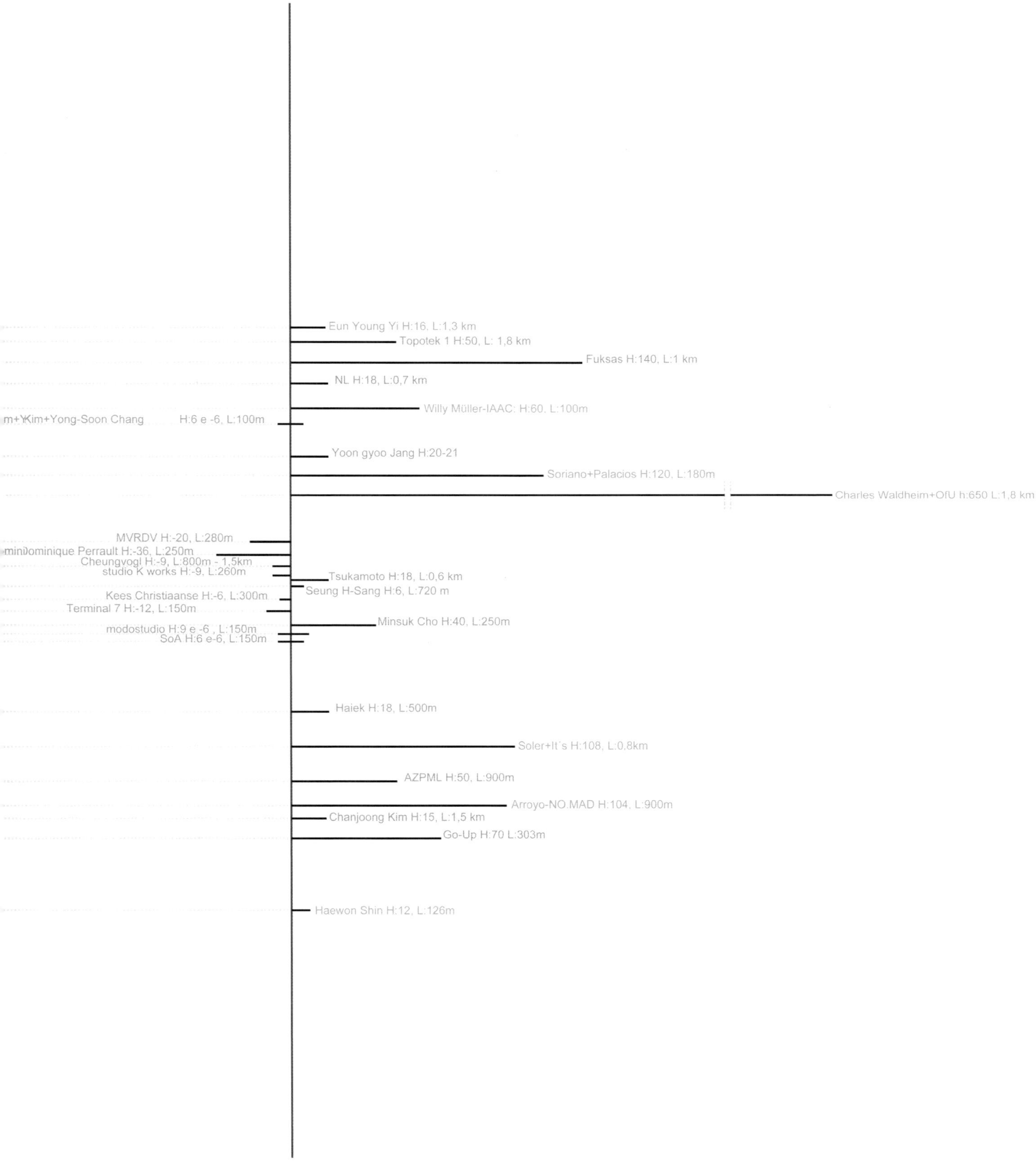

Eun Young Yi H:16, L:1,3 km
Topotek 1 H:50, L: 1,8 km
Fuksas H:140, L:1 km
NL H:18, L:0,7 km
Willy Müller-IAAC: H:60, L:100m
m+Kim+Yong-Soon Chang H:6 e -6, L:100m
Yoon gyoo Jang H:20-21
Soriano+Palacios H:120, L:180m
Charles Waldheim+OfU h:650 L:1,8 km
MVRDV H:-20, L:280m
Dominique Perrault H:-36, L:250m
Cheungvogl H:-9, L:800m - 1,5km
studio K works H:-9, L:260m
Tsukamoto H:18, L:0,6 km
Seung H-Sang H:6, L:720 m
Kees Christiaanse H:-6, L:300m
Terminal 7 H:-12, L:150m
Minsuk Cho H:40, L:250m
modostudio H:9 e -6 , L:150m
SoA H:6 e-6, L:150m
Haiek H:18, L:500m
Soler+It's H:108, L:0,8km
AZPML H:50, L:900m
Arroyo-NO.MAD H:104, L:900m
Chanjoong Kim H:15, L:1,5 km
Go-Up H:70 L:303m
Haewon Shin H:12, L:126m

서울 슈퍼그라운드 언더그라운드 서울 조사. 지역과 높이를 함께 전체적으로 보여주는 다이어그램 (마뉴엘 가우사, 마틸드 피탄티)

Seoul Seoul–Superground and Underground Prospective Surveys. Superposition of localisations and Level–scanning diagrams (Manuel Gausa with Matilde Pitanti).

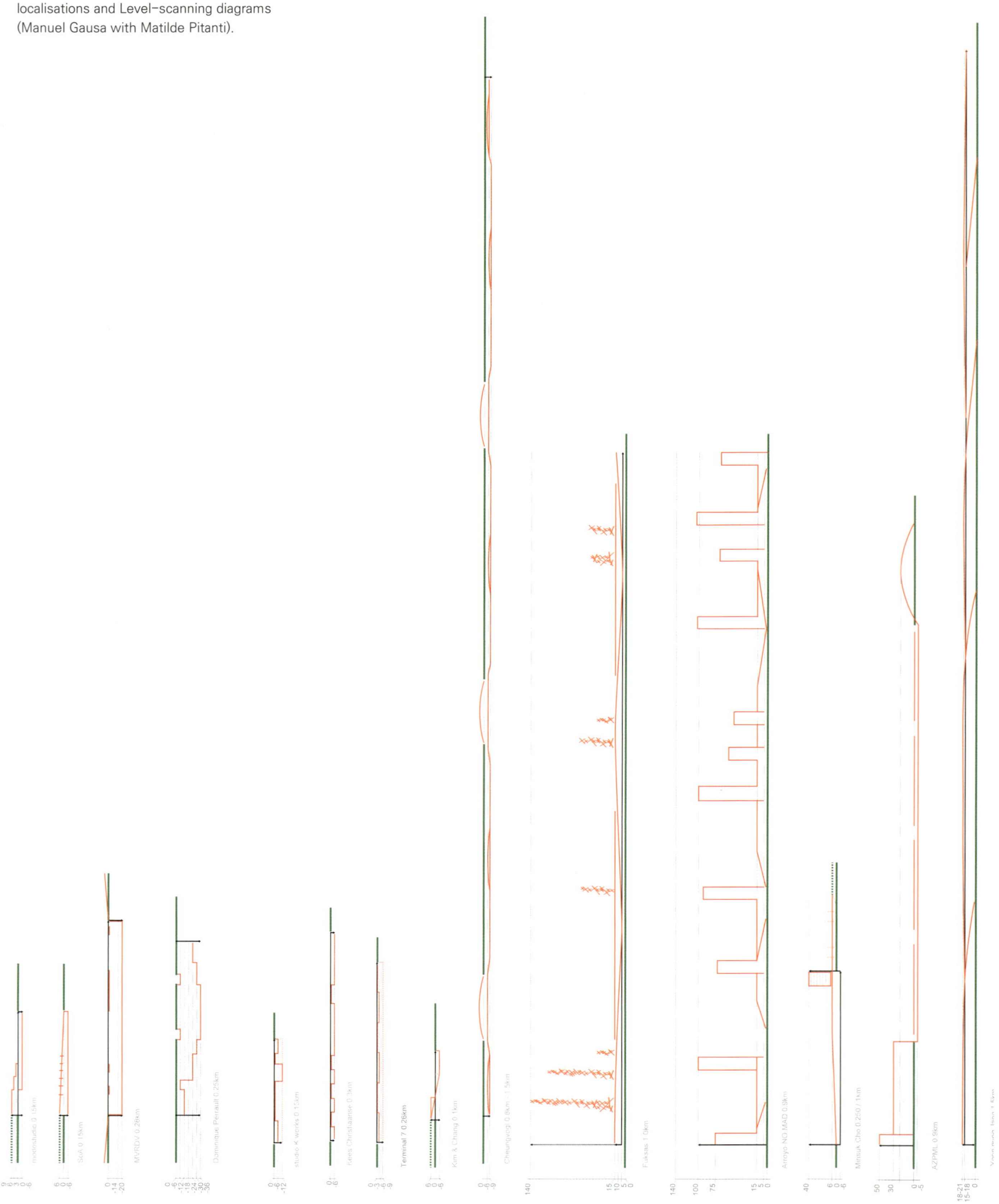

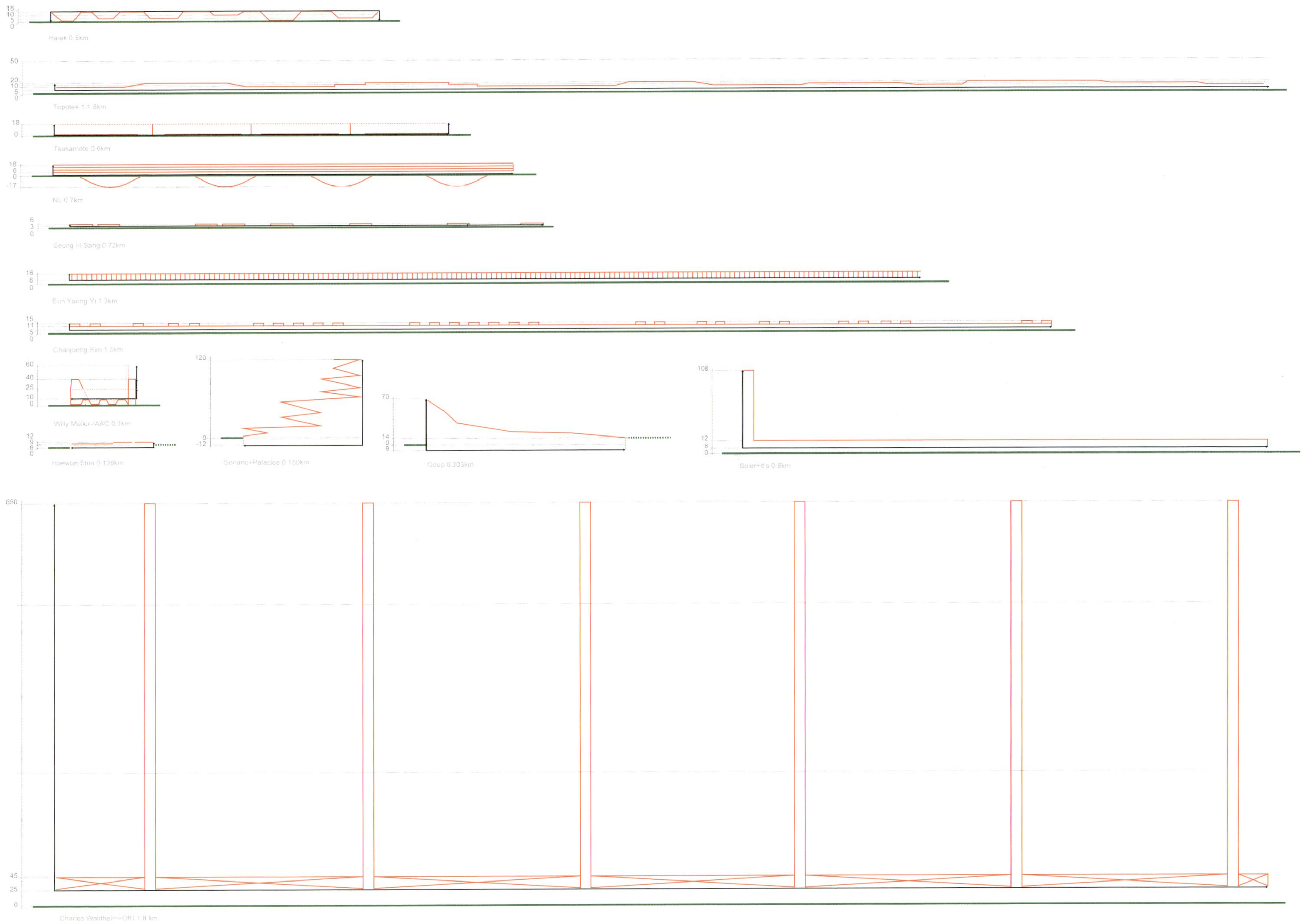

Hajek 0.5km
Topotek 1 1.8km
Tsukamoto 0.6km
NL 0.7km
Seung H-Sang 0.72km
Eun Young Yi 1.3km
Chanjoong Kim 1.5km
Willy Müller-IAAC 0.1km
Haewon Shin 0.126km
Soriano+Palacios 0.180km
Gouo 0.303km
Soler+it's 0.8km
Charles Waldheim+OfU 1.8 km

PROJECT STRATEGIES: DEGREE OF PREVALENCE FROM LIGHTNES (YELLOW) TO DARKNESS (BROWN)
프로젝트 전략: 관련된 정도에 따라 밝은 색(노랑)에서 어두운 색(갈색)으로 변화

SUPERGROUND UNDERGROUND	SITE / TITLE 대지/제목	TEAM 참여자	ABSTRACT 내용 요약

PROGRAM RE-ACTIVATION AND REVITALISATION OF OLD ELEVATED AND LOWER-LEVEL STRUCTURES
오래된 고가 및 하부 구조물의 재활성화

SUPERGROUND	Hangang Cheolgyo HELIOMORPHIC SEOUL: BIOPRODUCTIVE MODELS FOR TRAVERSING THE HAN	Charles Waldheim + Office for Urban-ization	A qualitative change of the traditional infrastructural "bridge" dimension, orientated to perform with a new eco-urban and environmental scale, where a sequence of twelve new bio-productive and residential towers traverse the Han river, proposing a new sustainable and technological approach based in energy optimization and solar orientation, absorption, and reflection; façade panels that use biomass to filter air and fog-harvesting screens that capture precipitations, conform substantial parts of the proposition. 12개의 생물 생산 및 주거용 타워가 한강을 가로지르는 새로운 도시 생태 및 환경에 맞춘 전통적 기반시설 '다리'의 질적 변화를 만든다. 이를 위해 에너지 최적화, 태양광의 추적, 흡수, 반사, 바이오매스로 공기를 여과하는 입면 패널, 빗물 수집용 수분 흡수 스크린 등 지속가능하며 기술적인 접근을 제안한다.
SUPERGROUND	Line 2 (Shindorim-Sillim) YONG, THE SERPENTINE GALLERIES	Topotek 1	A new linear neighborhood (and lineal park also) imagined to house the world's largest collection of art and creative industry programs and facilities – the snaking metro line turned creative mega-block associ-ated to the Korean artistic production and talent – otherwise known as Young, The Serpentine Galleries. 세계 최대 규모의 예술 및 창의산업 프로그램과 시설을 위한 새로운 선형 공간이자 공원이다. 구불구불 이어진 지하철 노선은 한국의 예술 작품과 인재를 아우르는 창의적인 초대형 블록 즉, 용, 서펜타인 갤러리로 다시 태어난다.
SUPERGROUND	Kyeongui Jungang Line (Yonsei Univ) URBAN CONNECTOR	Yoon gyoo Jang	A subtle and soft relief model the cover of the old infrastructure for a new public space perforated by multiple hosting-holes that rhythm the structure, permeate to illuminate the ground under the cover and host different functional programs and activities. 오래된 기반시설을 가볍고 유연한 구조물로 덮어 새로운 공공공간을 조성한다. 여러 개의 구멍을 뚫어 구조에 율동감을 부여하고 덮개 아래 지상에 빛이 스며들게 하며, 다양한 기능 프로그램과 활동을 수용한다.
SUPERGROUND	Naebu Expressway (Jongam) SEOUL ECO-CONDENSER	Alejandro Haiek Coll	A rich inventory, a neat catalogue of uses and treatments, below, beside and on top of the viaduct, always associated with social exchange and a light and, mostly, reversible treatment of a space, converted into a diversified multi-programmatic and multi-activated linear park. 고가 하부와 측면, 상부에 풍성한 자원과 잘 정리된 기능 및 구성 전략을 제안하여 사회적 교류와 채광, 다양한 프로그램과 활동을 채워진 원상회복이 가능한 선형공간을 조성한다.
SUPERGROUND	North of Dongjak Bridge YONGSAN BODY CULTURE CLUB	Yoshiharu Tsuka-moto	An expressive and subtle sequence of enjoying spaces and public facilities, treated as plastic and diversified surfaces marks a combinatory lineal system of three open and ambivalent sectors where light facilities, sports and resting areas can be identified and mixed at time. 유연하고 다양한 표면은 일련의 풍성하고 절묘한 즐거운 공간들과 공공시설들로 구성된다. 개방적이며 양면적인 세 부분들로 이루어진 선형 복합체로서, 각 부분들은 조명 시설들과 체육 및 휴게 공간들이 혼합되어 있다.
SUPERGROUND	Yeongdeungpo Rotary YEONGDEUNGPO FREE WAYS	NL Architects	A qualitative multilevel "remix" of the road Seoul system in a way able to liberate valuable space at ground level and, specially in the Yeoeuido Square Bridge, able to create a useful public multi-pro-gram lineal space as a connector between the two important adjacent neighborhoods. 서울 도로망의 질적, 다층적 '재구성'을 통해 귀중한 지상 공간을 자유롭게 한다. 특히, 여의도광장다리는 기능적이며 열린 선형 다중 프로그램 공간을 담는 중요한 두 인접 지역 사이의 연결 고리가 된다.
UNDERGROUND	Hoehyeon Underground Shopping Center SHINSEOUL, THE PUBLIC LAYERS OF SEOUL	Cheungvogl	The underground system connects, drills and opens on the surface, in its central nodes, creating places of urban, cultural and social relevance that result in a transformation of the city into sections of/with ambiguous landscapes (natural and artificial) between levels: urban landscapes between urban layers that depend, to a great extent, on the simultaneous activation between vertical surfaces, plans and public spaces. 지하공간의 연결, 구성, 지상 개방을 통해 주요 결절점에 도시적, 문화적, 사회적 공간을 조성하여 도시를 다양한 층위 사이에서 추상적 풍경(자연 또는 인공)을 빚어내는 여러 영역으로 분할한다. 도시 조직 사이의 도시 경관은 수직면과 평면, 공공영역의 동시적 활성화 양상에 따라 크게 달라진다.
UNDERGROUND	Jongro 4-ga Junction JONGRO CONNECTOR	Kees Christiaanse	The potential of an extended three-dimensional use from the subway to the pedestrian networks defines the proposal. Four residual crossing spaces become new three-dimensional and creative spaces: one forms a collection of skylights of different shapes, a diurnal sculpture under the floor; the second a spherical source from which the water flows into a public underground basin; the third, a fiberglass daytime tree; the fourth, a patio with a small quiet garden in the full effervescence of the metro fluxes. 지하철에서 보행자 네트워크로 이어지는 입체적 기능 확장 가능성에 주목한다. 네 교차로의 자투리 공간은 입체적, 창의적 공간으로 변화한다. 첫 번째 공간은 바닥 아래의 빛 조형물이 되는 다양한 형태의 천창으로 구성되고, 두 번째 공간은 지하 수조로 물을 흘려 보내는 구형 구조물이 된다. 세 번째 공간은 유리 섬유 소재로 된 나무가 되고, 네 번째 공간은 지하철의 역동성을 머금은 파티오와 작고 조용한 정원이 된다.
UNDERGROUND	Jeongdok Public Library ROOF GARDEN SCAPE FOR READING	studio_K_works	A platform-park perforated by courtyards at various levels favor the exchange of uses oriented to the book-culture and the residence. The level of the roof rises slightly above the original level and favors a large surface of panoramic views. Sunken spaces and level games in section allow filling this underground space with natural light, lighting, ventilation and connection between circulations. 다양한 레벨에서 마당을 형성하는 다공성의 플랫폼 공원은 책 문화와 지역 주민의 교류 역할을 한다. 지붕 레벨은 기존 레벨 위로 완만하게 솟아올라 전망 좋은 넓은 터가 된다. 선큰 공간과 단면의 레벨 변화는 지하공간에서의 자연 채광과 환기 그리고 동선 연계를 가능하게 한다.

	SIZE XL/L/M/S HIGHNESS OR DEPTHNESS 크기 X/L/M/x 높이 또는 깊이	MIXED PROGRAMS 혼합 프로그램	MESH MECHANISMS 그물 메커니즘	ACTIVE TOPOS 적극적인 지형	INTEGRATED TECHNOLO-GIES 상호통합된 기술	SERIAL SEQUENCES 연속적 경험	EVOLVING TIME 시간에 따른 변화
	XL. > 1,8 kms +25mts > + 650 mts						
	XL. > 5,8 kms +15mts > + 50 mts						
	L. > 0,6 KMS +15mts > + h 3 mts (18mts)						
	L. > 0,6 kms +0mts > + h 18mts						
	L. > 0,6 kms +0mts > + h 18 mts						
	L. > 0,6 KMS – 0/mts (–17 mts) > + h 18mts						
	L/M/ > 800mts / 1,5 Kms +0 > -3mts / -6mts/ -9 mts						
	S/M > 300mts 0 > -6 mts						
	S/M > 260mts 0 > -3 mts / - 9 mts						

SUPERGROUND UNDERGROUND	SITE / TITLE 대지/제목	TEAM 참여자	ABSTRACT 내용 요약

MIX-MULTILAYER-CONNECTORS OF ROADS, RAILWAYS AND UNDERGROUND AREAS
도로와 철도, 지하공간을 잇는 다층 복합 커넥터

SUPERGROUND	**South of Yanghwa bridge** URBAN QUANTUM	**STUDIO FUKSAS + Ramon Prat Homs**	A topologic new germinal battle-field able to growth and evolve through different formats of densities and high-low textures, open to future Seoul developing forces transformed in light and bright, dynamic and variable geometries. 성장과 진화가 가능한 새로운 지형은 다양한 형식의 밀도와 높낮이의 변화를 만들어내며, 가볍고 밝으며, 역동적이고 가변적인 형태로 구현된 미래 서울의 발전 동력을 향해 열려 있다.
SUPERGROUND	**Hannam-Daero** FROM MOUNTAIN TO RIVER	**Minsuk Cho**	A precise set of different connective and transfer “inter-devices”, associated to a clear sequence of hybrid topo-structural, eco-structural and infra-structural mechanisms of urban articulation and assemblage. 정밀도 높은 일련의 연결 구조와 ‘내부 장치’를 적용하여, 도시의 요소들과 집합에서 만들어지는 지형구조적, 생태구조적, 기반구조적 체계가 혼합된 명료한 흐름과 연계한다.
SUPERGROUND	**Line 4 (Changdong-Danggogae)** SEOUL LAPUTA: SELF-DEVELOPING LINEAR CITY	**Chanjoong Kim**	A profuse system of use of the infrastructural covers able to propitiate a public, commercial, ludic and productive use of the aerial floor based on the linear succession of varied and diversified micro-elements/events. 기반시설 상부를 활성화하기 위한 여러 시스템은 떠 있는 바닥면의 공공과 상업, 유희와 생산적 활용을 강화할 수 있으며, 이는 다채로운 미세 인자와 이벤트의 선적 연속성에 기반한다.
SUPERGROUND	**Jeungsan-Ro** SUPERCOLONNADE SEOUL: URBAN COLONNADE VS GROUND ENGRAVING	**Eunyoung Yi**	The creation of a pedestrian cover pathway that links the Han River with the newly railroad recuperated landscape, permits to articulate a slow equilibrated vibration in the site associated to a light structure close to the thin pavilion-structures of Korean tradition. A strong horizontal presence capable of absorbing programs, and framing land surfaces and movements around it, filtering them into a contemporary spirit not indifferent to a certain sense of proportion. 한강과 새롭게 회복된 풍경을 연결하는 보행로 구축은 한국의 전통적인 파빌리온과 같은 경량 구조물과 연계를 통해 대지에 느리고 균형 잡힌 움직임을 생성한다. 프로그램 흡인력이 뛰어나며 강렬한 수평적 존재는 대지와 주변 움직임을 감싸고, 그것을 균형 감각을 잃지 않은 현시대의 정서로 풀어낸다.
SUPERGROUND	**Hangang Pedestrian Bridge** HABITABLE BRIDGE, Domestic Landscape of Seoul	**Seung H-Sang**	The 29th bridge over the Han River, proposed to complete the river connections, will be the first footbridge linking Yongsan in the north and Banpo's cap park in the south. A no-car bridge, a green linear-path, but a habitable bridge also, studded with multiple facilities for relax, rest and enjoy: slow surfaces, small yards, mini theatres and galleries, small shops and so on, where people can spend their daily lives. 수변 연결망 완성을 위해 제안한 한강의 29번째 다리는 북쪽의 용산과 남쪽의 반포 덮개공원을 연결하는 첫 번째 보행교가 된다. 차 없는 다리, 선형 녹색 길, 거주 가능한 다리 사이사이에는 일상의 삶을 영위할 수 있는 느림의 공간, 작은 마당, 소극장과 갤러리, 소형 상점 등 각종 휴식 및 오락 시설이 들어서 있다.
UNDERGROUND	**Dongdaemun Gate Area** UN-INTERRUPTED CITY	**modostudio**	The proposal addresses the possibility of redefining the urban pattern of linking, preserving the valuable elements of the area. Namsan Park preserves the green surface, acting at the same time not only as an urban green space but as an important element of reconnection for the area, through its new multi-layered definition: the new volumes of the wall museum and the design foundation and the new underground spaces activate the transformation of the district, restoring the idea of an interrupted Continuum. 도시 연결 패턴의 재정의와 지역 가치 요소의 보존이 주는 가능성에 주목한다. 남산공원은 녹지 보존 기능을 하고, 새롭게 정의된 다층 구조를 통해 지역을 위한 도심 녹지 공간이자 중요한 연결 회복 장치 역할을 한다. 전쟁박물관 신관과 서울디자인재단 건물, 새 지하공간은 지역의 변화를 촉진하며 단절된 연속성 개념을 회복한다.
UNDERGROUND	**Park of Seoul Hunlyunwon (Euljiro 5-ga Junction)** VESSELS	**SoA**	Huge circular “vessels” developed from the level +0 to the subway, define areas of varied sizes, and a large park with circular hollows. The longitudinal pattern expands the area from east to west and favors the continuity of vertical exterior space at different levels, from the Euljiro underground shopping center to the Pyeonghwa and Cheonggyecheon market. 레벨 +0에서 지하철까지 이어지는 거대한 원형 ‘베셀’이 다양한 크기의 영역 그리고 순환로를 품은 대형 공원을 형성한다. 을지로 지하상가에서 평화시장, 청계천시장까지 이어지는 종적 패턴은 동에서 서로 대지를 확장하고, 다양한 레벨의 수직 외부 공간의 연속성을 강화한다.
UNDERGROUND	**Baekbeom Plaza (Namsan Park Area)** KNITTING TOPO-HISTORY	**Taekbin Kim + Yong-Soon Chang**	Restore the interrupted: topography, old castle and urban continuity. Two large sunken gardens provide a place for people to feel signs and traces of the past, of history, in a quiet environment. Restoring topography and history, the proposal aims to create a three-dimensional structure in which past and present, artificial and natural, soil and subsoil are crossed. 단절된 지형과 옛 성곽, 도시 연속성을 회복한다. 두 개의 대형 선큰 가든은 조용한 분위기 속에서 과거와 역사의 자취와 흔적을 느낄 수 있는 공간을 제공한다. 지형과 역사의 회복을 위한 본 설계안은 과거와 현재, 인공과 자연, 지하와 지상이 교차하는 입체적 구조물 구축을 목표로 한다.

	SIZE XL/L/M/S HIGHNESS OR DEPTHNESS 크기 X/L/M/x 높이 또는 깊이	MIXED PROGRAMS 혼합 프로그램	MESH MECHANISMS 그물 메커니즘	ACTIVE TOPOS 적극적인 지형	INTEGRATED TECHNOLO-GIES 상호통합된 기술	SERIAL SEQUENCES 연속적 경험	EVOLVING TIME 시간에 따른 변화
	L.> 1 KM +6 /15 mts > +h 40 / 140mts						
	L (XL) > 5,8 kms (sectors of 1 KM) +6 mts > +h 40mts						
	L (XL) > 1,5 kms +6/11mts > +h 14 mts						
	L > 1,3 KMS +6 mts > +h 15/16mts						
	L > 0,7 KMS +3 mts > +h 6mts						
	S/M > 150 mts 0 > +9 mts / - 6 mts						
	S/M > 150 mts 0 > +6 mts / - 6 mts						
	SM > 800mts / 1,5 Kms +0 > -3mts / -6mts/ -9 mts						

SUPERGROUND UNDERGROUND	SITE / TITLE 대지/제목	TEAM 참여자	ABSTRACT 내용 요약

WATER– MIX-USE OF RESERVOIR SITES
유수지 시설을 위한 복합적 물 연계 활용 방안

SUPERGROUND	**Mapo Basin** MAPO STACKEDSCAPE MACHINE	**Soriano+Palacios**	An exuberant and expressive creative and operative landscape (multi-active) open to the joyous profusion of programs and activities for the citizen, foreseeable and – still – unforeseen: infrastructures and water-control deposit appear hybridized with public productive uses, transforming the site into a natural device-field of enjoying functions –swimming pools, parks, botanical gardens, water bars, etc.–, as well as profit-based uses: hospitality, spas, shared housing for the young and elderly, etc. 즐겁고 다채로운 시민 프로그램 및 활동을 향해 열린, 예측 가능하지만 아직 규명되지 않은, 생기 넘치고 풍성하며, 창의적이고 기능적인 풍경을 제안한다(다중 활성화). 기반시설과 유수지는 생산적인 공적기능과 어우러져 대지를 수영장, 공원, 수목원, 워터바 등 다양한 오락 기능과 젊은이와 노인 모두를 위한 숙박 및 휴양시설, 공유주택 등 수익 기반 기능으로 채워진 자연친화적 장치로 변화시킨다.
SUPERGROUND	**Myeonmok Basin** URBAN MOUNTAIN PARK: A WALKABLE SKIN	**Go-Up Architects**	A multi-layered and multi-programmatic topography called to be used and traversed by different functional paths and able to qualify the site through a new natural-artificial connective landscape; a relief of variable densities orientated to mesh neighboring frames and urban rhythms. 다양한 기능을 가진 길로 활용될 수 있는, 횡단 가능한 다층적이고 다목적인 지형은 자연과 인공이 결합된 새로운 풍경으로 대지를 풍성하게 한다. 이는 그물망처럼 얽혀 있는 지역 맥락과 도시 리듬을 지향하는 다양한 밀도의 구조물이다.
SUPERGROUND	**Mangwoo Reservoir Park** URBAN AND NATURAL MULTI-HABITAT: DESIGNING THE COMPLEXITY OF LIFE	**Hae Won Shin**	Understood as a new "multi-habitat" capable of condensing the mixed-use nature of the large Seoul metropolitan condition, the new Mangwoo reservoir site appears as a pad-park located on the Korea's first large public cemetery site: the work with a subtle section of overlapped uses and platforms allows to configure a millefeuille topography: a sensible multilayer space slipped in the site. 대도시 서울의 복합 기능적 특성이 압축되어 있는 '복합서식지'로 재해석한 망우저류조 일대는 한국 최초의 대형 공동묘지 터에 자리잡은 공원이 된다. 중첩된 기능과 플랫폼의 모호한 단면은 밀푀유 지형 즉, 대지에 살며시 끼어든 감각적 다층 공간을 조성한다.

RECOVERY OF URBAN ISLAND-SECTORS AND CROSSING POINTS
도시 속 섬과 교차로의 회복

SUPERGROUND	**Songjeong Embankment** SHOEMAKERS' ISLAND	**Francis Soler + It's, Michel Desvigne**	An unexpected change of gaze and conventions, in which the long and uniform existing linear green slope, of fluvial edge, becomes (in its final stretch) a rich large sheet of water parallel to the river and open to the city and to the south. A new built ground over the motorway road (with well-oriented and low density social housing and workshops, and a large mixed-use emergent tower, as a vertical high point) completes a new operational geology, where landscape and urbanity, topography and polis, work together. 선형으로 길고 단조롭게 이어지는 기존의 녹색 수변 경사지가 (그 흐름의 끝에서) 도시와 남쪽으로 열린 강과 평행한 풍성하고 거대한 수공간이 되면서 예기치 못한 풍경과 맥락의 변화를 만든다. (향이 좋은 저밀 공공주택과 공방, 수직 랜드마크가 되는 신축 다목적 타워와 함께) 고속도로 위에 새로 조성된 공간은 풍경과 도시 맥락, 지형과 도시가 어우러진 새롭고 기능적인 지형을 완성한다.
SUPERGROUND	**Imun Train Depot** ENTROPYTECTURE	**Eduardo Arroyo-NO.MAD**	A differential an elastic pattern of hybrid block-towers that create a new meshed needlework in the area, combining variable densities and hatched open and public spaces in a new "knick-knot" scenario where the revision of old typologies (reconverted in a new networked landscape) reactivates all the sector. 혼성 블록 타워의 차별화되고 탄력적인 패턴은 지역 내에 촘촘히 짜인 새로운 맥락을 엮어 낸다. 옛 지형을 새로운 그물망 같은 풍경으로 전환하고 모든 부분들을 재활성화시키는 새로운 "매듭" 시나리오 안에서 다양한 밀도를 결합하며 열린 시민공간을 조성한다.
SUPERGROUND	**Yeonsinnae Station** SUPERCROSSING SEOUL	**Willy Müller-IAAC**	A mechanism of urban tables and suspended boards able to mesh and to "staple" different urban tissues through a new multi-programmatic connective and civil device able, also, to be adapted to different sites and scenarios. 도시 그리드 및 공중 플랫폼은 새로운 다중 프로그램 연결체와 다양한 환경과 맥락에 적용 가능한 공적 장치로서 여러 도시 조직을 그물망처럼 연결하거나 '접합'할 수 있다.
SUPERGROUND	**Jungnang Water Reuse + Gunja Train Depot** HIGH-INTENSITY PARK JUNGNANG	**AZPML**	A new set of dense perimeters on the north edge and slow margins on the borders of the river that surround a large central park treated as a large field of cultivation(s) based on large circles-pergolas next to agricultural irrigation and plowing and environmental technologies. 북쪽의 새로운 고밀 경계와 커다란 중앙 공원을 에워싸는 강둑의 느린 여백은 거대한 경작지로 활용되는 중앙공원을 에워싼다. 이 경작지는 농업용 관개수로와 경작 및 환경 관련 장치와 결합한 거대한 원형의 구조물들로 구성된다.
UNDERGROUND	**Euljiro 4-ga Junction** SEOUL CHRONICLE: VEINS	**Terminal 7 Architects**	The process of the printing industry itself is closely linked to the proposal that restores the connection between levels, between moles and underground spaces: a large traffic island is used to introduce natural light: a roundabout at ground level that allows centrality to be restored and to create a public square in the underground network. 서로 다른 레벨, 지점, 지하공간 사이의 연계 회복을 위한 본 설계안은 인쇄산업의 공정 과정과 밀접하게 연관되어 있다. 대형 교통섬을 활용해 자연광을 끌어들이고, 지상에 로터리를 설치해 중심성을 회복하고 지하 네트워크에 열린 광장을 조성한다.
UNDERGROUND	**Seoul Station Area** WELCOME TO SEOUL!	**MVRDV**	The proposal for the old Seoul station reorganizes its underground space in a three-dimensional way. Train tracks, automobile and metro roads coincide on the same level. Level +0 makes up Seoul's new central park: a transparent roof brings daylight to the large underground station-plaza that hosts several programs (theater, library, restaurants, gyms, shops, etc.) and is formulated as a symbol for a new landscape inside-outside, up and down. 옛 서울역사를 위한 본 설계 안은 서울역사의 지하공간을 입체적으로 재구성한다. 철도와 자동차 도로, 지하철 노선이 같은 레벨에서 만나고, 레벨 +0은 서울의 새 중앙 공원이 된다. 투명한 지붕은 다양한 프로그램을 수용하고, 새로운 내부와 외부, 지상과 지하 풍경의 상징이 되는 대형 지하 역사와 광장으로 햇빛을 끌어들여준다.
UNDERGROUND	**City Hall Underground** SEOUL GROUNDSCAPE PLAZA	**Dominique Perrault**	A huge circular "piazza", worked as a counter-platform in depth development, from the level +0 to the subway, defines an iconic and expressive space of varied sizes, in front of the City Hall, and a sequence of circular and descending plateaux. 거대한 원형의 "광장"은 레벨 0에서부터 지하철에 이르는 깊이의 개발에서 이루어지는 카운터 플랫폼으로 작동하며, 시청 앞에서 다양한 크기의 상징적이고 표현적인 공간이자 원형의 연속적인 장면, 아래로 경사진 고원이다.

	SIZE XL/L/M/S HIGHNESS OR DEPTHNESS 크기 X/L/M/x 높이 또는 깊이	MIXED PROGRAMS 혼합 프로그램	MESH MECHANISMS 그물 메커니즘	ACTIVE TOPOS 적극적인 지형	INTEGRATED TECHNOLO-GIES 상호통합된 기술	SERIAL SEQUENCES 연속적 경험	EVOLVING TIME 시간에 따른 변화
	S/M. 180 mts > 30.600 m2 +0mts / – 12 mts >> + h 120mts						
	S/M. 300 mts // 92.000 m2 – 7 mts > + h 70mts						
	S/M. 126 mts // 14.500 m2 – 5 mts > + h 12mts						
	L > 0,5 KMS +6 mts > +h 108mts						
	L > 900mts > 210.000 mts2 +6 mts > +h 40/ 104mts						
	L / SM > 100mts a 0,5 kms> 100.000/10.800 mts2 +6 /+ 12 mts > +h 60 mts						
	L > 900 mts // 990.000 mts2 +0mts / – 5 mts > + h 30/ 50mts						
	S/M > 150mts 0 > -6 mts / - 12 mts						
	S/M/L > 150mts 0 > -6 mts / - 12 mts						
	S/M > 250 mts 0 > -12mts / - 36 mts						

슈퍼그라운드

서울
새로운 땅의 풍경

SUPERGROUND

SEOUL
NEW *GROUNDSCAPES*

14
Supercrossing Seoul /
Willy Müller –IaaC Urban Science Lab
2
URBAN CONNECTOR /
Yoon Gyoo Jang
7
SUPERCONLONNADE SEOUL /
Eunyoung Yi
17
SE
Ale
Mapo S
8
Urban Quantum /
Massimiliano Fuksas +Ramon Prat Homs
11
Yeongdeungpo Freeways /
NL Architects
3
용. The Serpentine Galleries /
Topotek 1
1
Heliomorphic Seoul /
Charles Waldheim with Office for Urbanization

Seoul Laputa : Self-Developing Linear City /
4
Chanjoong Kim
ENTROPYTECTURE /
5
Eduardo Arroyo - NO.MAD
ECO-CONDENSER /
Haiek Coll
Urban and Natural Multi-Habitat /
16
Haewon Shin
UNBAN MOUNTAIN PARK /
9
Co-Up Architects
High-Intensity Park Jungnang /
6
AZPML
dscape Machine /
10
Federico Soriano +
Dolores Palacios
SHOEMAKERS' ISLAND /
18
Francis SOLER with It's + Michel Desvigne
From the Mountain to the River /
13
Minsuk Cho
Habitable Bridge /
12
SEUNG H-SANG
Yongsan Body Culture Club /
15
Yoshiharu Tsukamoto - Atelier Bow-Wow+ TokyoTech.Tsukamoto Lab

찰스 왈드하임과 어바니제이션오피스

Charles Waldheim with Office for Urbanization

헬리오모픽 서울 : 한강을 가로지르는 생태적 생산모델

한강은 한국 문화의 상징이다. 수천 년 동안 물과 농작물의 핵심 공급원이었다. 오늘날 도시는 급속한 산업화와 경제 성장에 힘입어 강 너머까지 확장되었다. 한강의 산업화는 심각한 강 주변 생태계 파괴와 생물 다양성 상실로 이어졌다. 헬리오모픽 서울은 생물학적 생산성의 새로운 개념을 제시하며 한강을 관통하는 도시의 발전상을 완전히 새롭게 정의한다. 지형은 인공의 생태계로부터 조성된다. 분산 배치된 인공 구조물들은 물의 흐름을 바꾸고, 대지를 안정시키며, 토양을 축적한다. 헬리오모픽 서울은 태양광의 추적, 흡수, 반사를 통해 열역학 에너지를 활용하는 친환경 에너지 모델을 제안한다. 입면 패널은 바이오매스를 활용해 공기 오염물질을 여과하여 공중의 주거 공간을 지원한다. 안개집수 스크린은 도시의 높은 곳에 있는 수증기를 흡수한다. 헬리오모픽 서울은 한강철교를 생물 다양성을 증대하고 생태 연계성 강화를 위한 플랫폼 구축을 이끄는 역동적, 생산적 풍경으로 재구성한다.

Heliomorphic Seoul: Bioproductive Models for Traversing the Han River

The Han River is a symbol of Korean civilization. It has been a vital source of water and agricultural production for thousands of years. Today, the city extends well beyond the river, spurred by rapid industrialization and economic expansion. The industrialization of the river has led to massive ecological damage and loss of biodiversity along the Han. *Heliomorphic Seoul* produces novel forms of bioproductivity, radically reimagining the city's growth traversing the Han. Landforms emerge from engineered ecological systems. Dispersed engineering structures redirect water flow, stabilize land, and accumulate soil. *Heliomorphic Seoul* proposes sustainable energy models for thermodynamic performance, including solar orientation, absorption, and reflection. Façade panels use biomass to filter air pollutants and support habitats in the sky. Fog-harvesting screens capture precipitation high over the city. *Heliomorphic Seoul* transforms Hangangcheolgy o into a vibrant, productive landscape, increasing biodiversity and establishing a platform for ecological connectivity.

찰스 왈드하임은 캐나다계 미국인 건축가이자 도시연구자이다. 하버드 디자인 대학원 John E. Irving 교수이자 도시설계사무소 소장으로 활동 중이다. 왈드하임의 연구는 조경과 생태, 현대 도시 사이의 관계를 탐구한다.

Charles Waldheim is a Canadian-American architect and urbanist. Waldheim is John E. Irving Professor at the Harvard Graduate School of Design and director in the Office for Urbanization. Waldheim's research examines the relations between landscape, ecology, and contemporary urbanism.

700
160
150
140
130
120
110
100
90
80
70
60
50
40
30
20
10
0 m
-10
-20
-30
-40

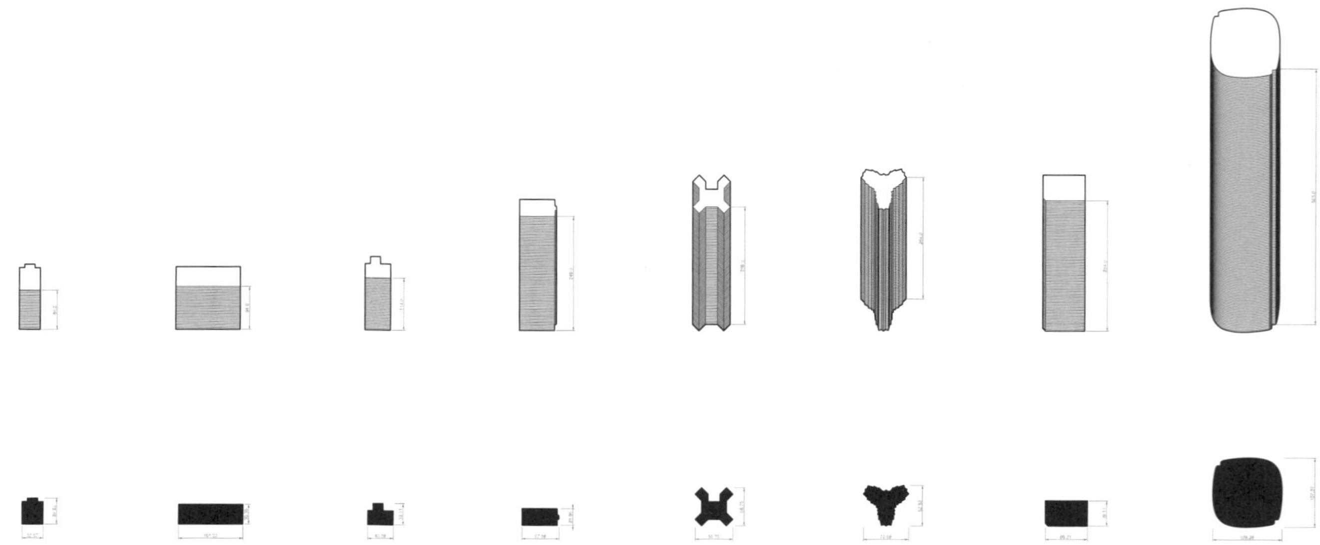

1969	1970	1970	1980	2003	2004	2012	2017
KAL Building	Govt. Complex	31 Building	63 Building	Hyperion	Tower Palace	3 IFC Tower	Lotte Tower
86m	94m	114m	249m	256m	264m	284m	555m
1 : 2.6	1 : 3.1	1 : 3.5	1 : 9.6	1 : 4.4	1 : 4.2	1 : 7.1	1: 5.1

Slenderness Ratio

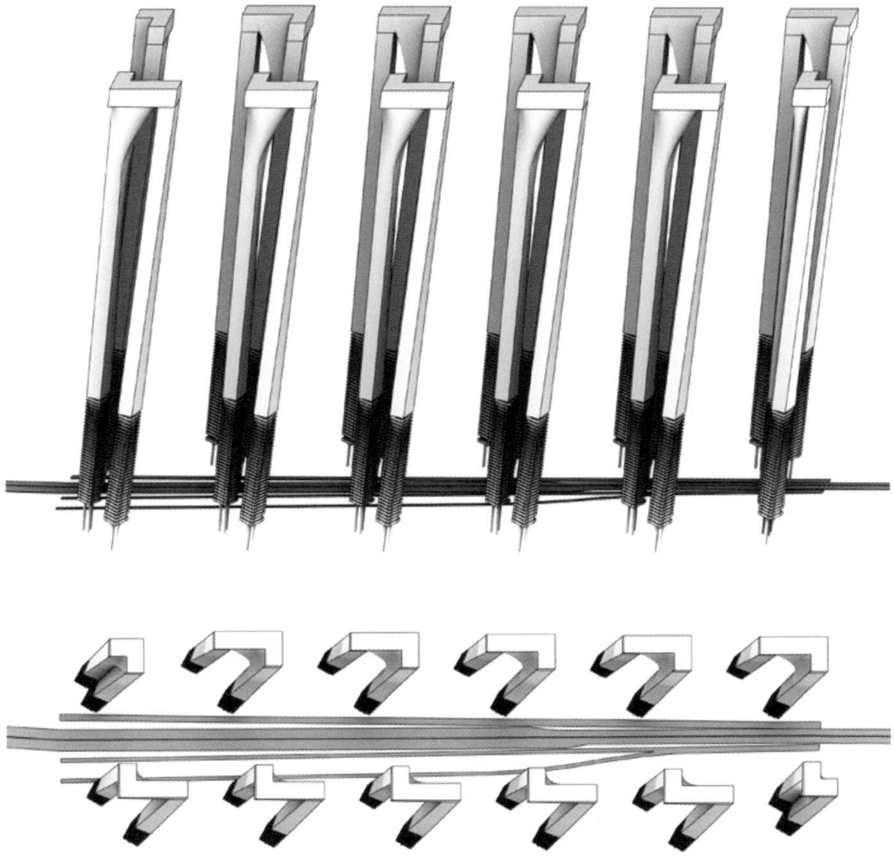

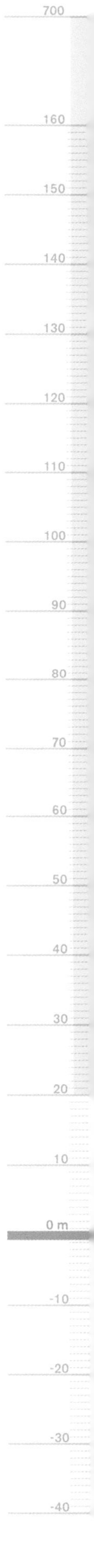

12 towers
650 meters
18.50 degrees
1 : 25 slenderness ratio

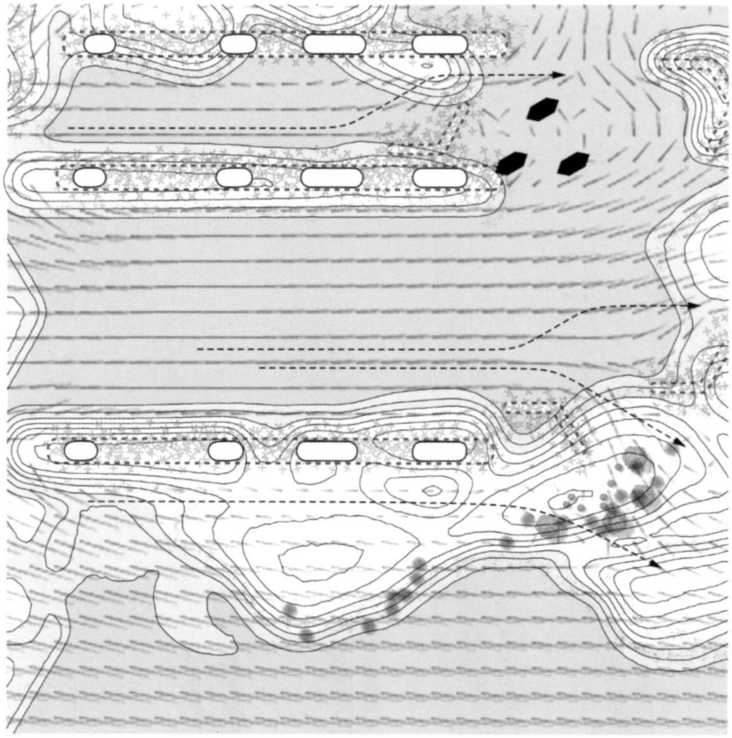

방향설정
Flow Redirection

새로이 형성될 지형을 전략적으로 안배하여 강물의 유속을 낮추고, 수중침식을 방지하며, 철교와 타워를 받치는 교각과 지지대가 보호되도록 물의 흐름을 조율한다.

Landforms are strategically placed in the Han River to slow the current, prevent scouring, and protect structural footings and piers supporting the bridge and towers above.

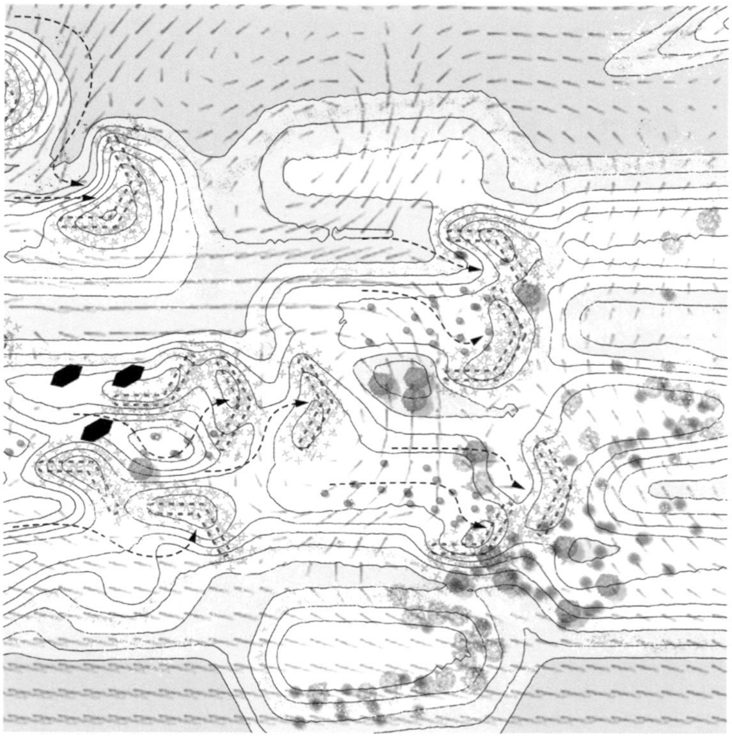

배포
Soil Distribution

지형형성은 가령 면밀한 공학적 과정을 거친 지지대들의 배치와 같은 여러 안정화 테크닉으로부터 도출되며, 수중 생태계를 위한 군도형성을 가능하게 하고, 잠재적인 수중 손상을 미연에 방지한다.

Synthetic landforms, made using stabilization techniques such as the placement of engineered ‘tetrapods’, create archipelagos that support water ecologies and prevent future water damage.

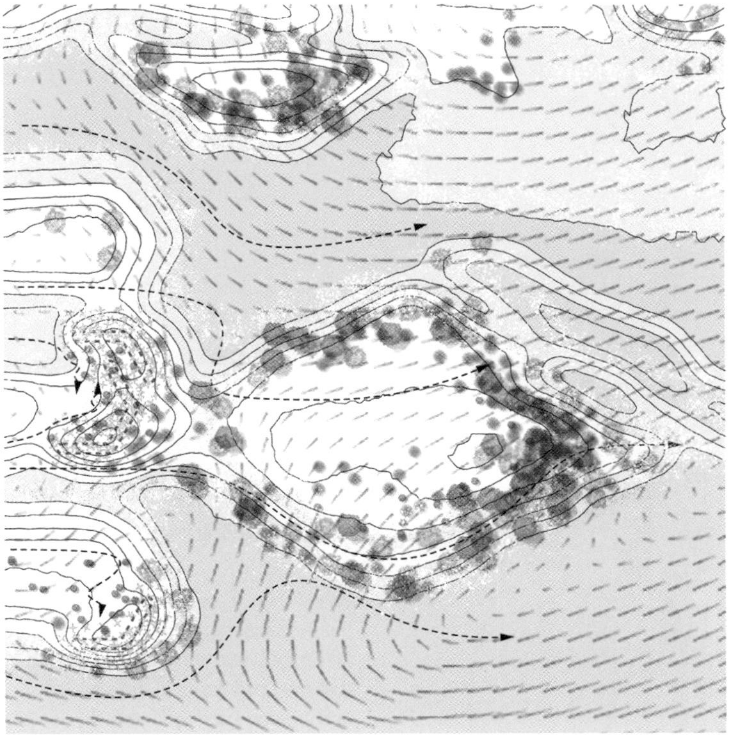

퇴적화
Sediment Accumulation

거듭 진화하는 강가 모서리의 형태들, 군도의 형태, 그리고 수심의 변형은 지형의 퇴적화 과정에서 다양한 생산적 구역을 만들어내고 예측할 수 없는 수많은 생태적이고 공학적인 응용사례를 가능하게 한다.

Evolving river edge patterns, island formations, and changes in water depth and sediment accumulation produce new zones of ecological productivity that allow for unpredictable forms of ecological and engineered applications in the Han River ecosystem.

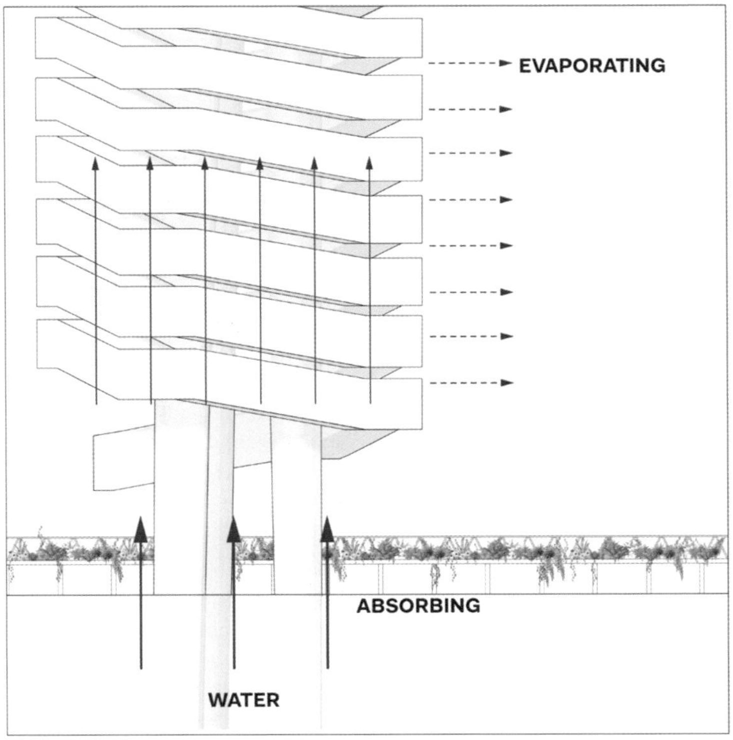

증발 냉각
Evaporative Cooling

150m에서 600m 사이의 높이에 위치한 타워의 외관 패널들은 적절하게 생물군 서식지로 활용될 예정이며 미세먼지로 오염된 공기를 정화시킬 것이다.

Select panels are replaced by biomass inserts, ranging from 150 to 600 meters in elevation, that filter pollutants in the air and support habitats in the sky.

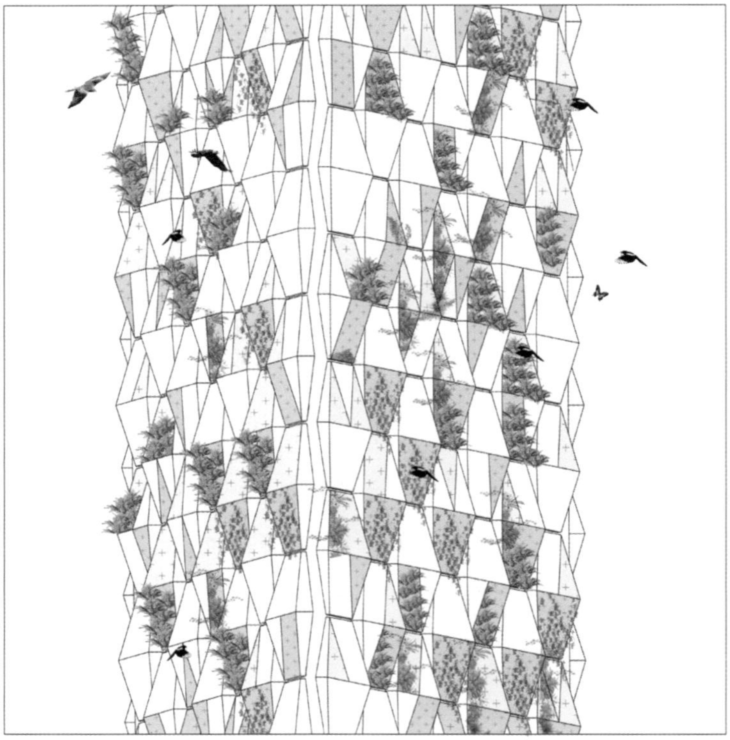

생물군 서식지
Biomass Habitat

150m에서 600m 사이의 높이에 위치한 타워의 외관 패널들은 적절하게 생물군 서식지로 활용될 예정이며 미세먼지로 오염된 공기를 정화시킬 것이다.

Select panels are replaced by biomass inserts, ranging from 150 to 600 meters in elevation, that filter pollutants in the air and support habitats in the sky.

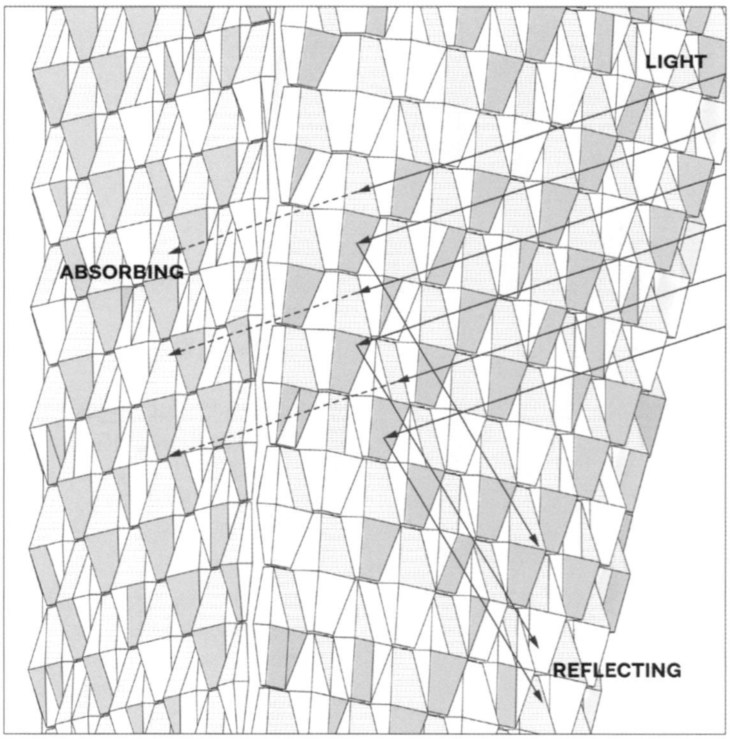

태양열 기능
Solar Performance

태양광이 많이 비치는 표면에는 광전지 패널이 설치되어 에너지를 생산해내기도 하고 빛을 많이 반사하는 패널이 설치되어 음지로 빛을 유도하기도 한다.

Surfaces with high solar exposure are lined with photovoltaic panels to generate energy, along with highly reflective panels that shine light into shaded regions.

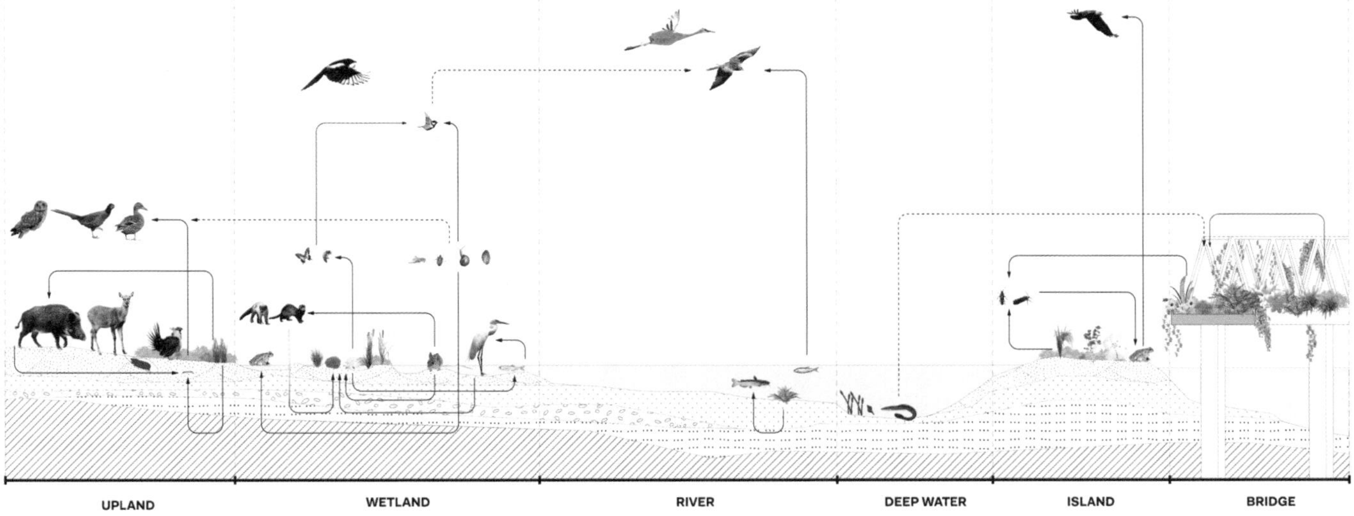

점진적 지형
Evolutionary Landform

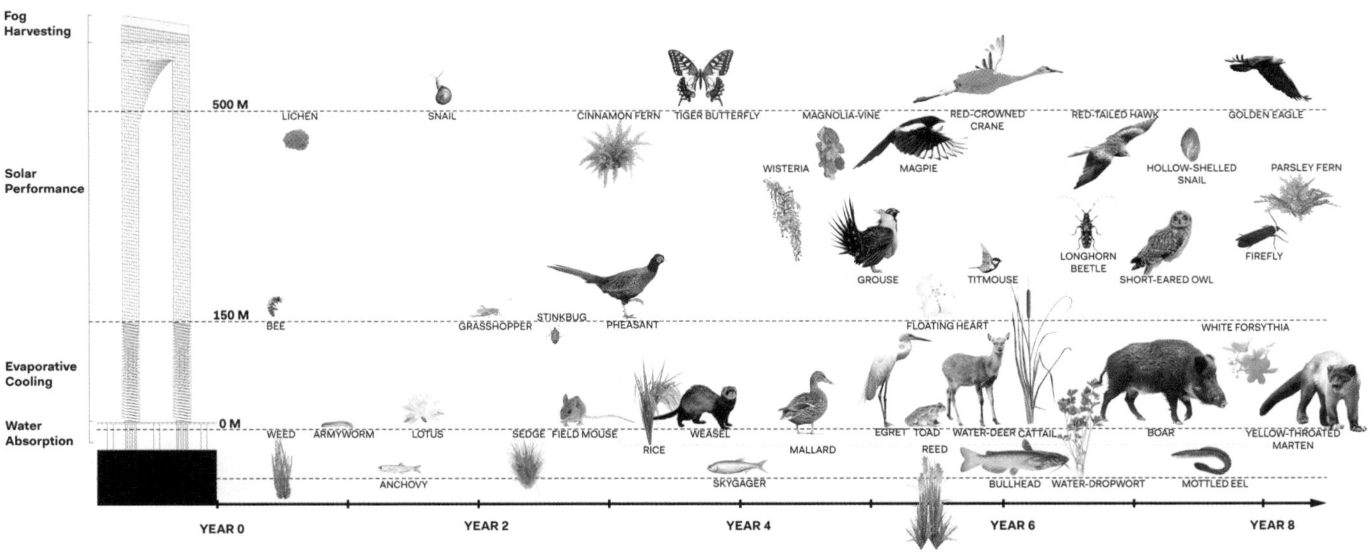

700
160
150
140
130
120
110
100
90
80
70
60
50
40
30
20
10
0 m
-10
-20
-30
-40

700
160
150
140
130
120
110
100
90
80
70
60
50
40
30
20
10
0 m
-10
-20
-30
-40

700
160
150
140
130
120
110
100
90
80
70
60
50
40
30
20
10
0 m
-10
-20
-30
-40

토포텍 1

Topotek 1

용, 서펜타인 갤러리

5.2km의 길이, 용 서펜타인 갤러리는 길쭉한 형태의 도시 경관을 만든다. 이 지역에서 선형의 공간은 기존 선로를 예술을 위한 거대 블록으로 탈바꿈시킴으로써 세계 최대의 예술 프로그램의 집합체로 다시 태어난다.
이 파빌리온의 대부분은 도림천 강변공원의 고가 선로 위에 위치하며, 약 174,000 제곱미터의 공간 안에서 62개의 서로 다른 건물들로 이루어져 있다. 새로운 프로그램으로 재탄생될 기존의 지하철역들과 연동하여 각 구조물들은 독특하고 상징적인 모습을 가지지만 하나의 커다란 상징적이며 눈길을 끄는 선형의 모습을 이룰 것이다. 파빌리온 안의 컬렉션들은 다양한 예술 프로그램으로 구성될 것이다. 화랑이나 미술관의 고전 미술, 조각, 회화, 설치미술, 미디어아트 전시 등 장르를 아우르는 한국 예술품 및 국제 예술품들이다.
이 프로젝트는 이 지역을 도시 내외의 상징적인 특징과 장소로서 어필할 수 있는 건축적, 예술적 의도를 모두 제공한다. 어쩌면 거대하고 무분별하게 보이는 야심 찬 비전일지라도 이 프로젝트가 갖는 가능성과 지역 사회 및 서울시의 미래에 미치는 영향을 상상해보기 위해 여러분을 초대한다,

Yong, The Serpentine Galleries

5.2km in length, *Young, The Serpentine Galleries* is a snaking cityscape on stilts. The linear neighbourhood within a neighbourhood is imagined to house the world's largest collection of cultural program – a former metro line turned artistic mega-block. Nearly the entirety of the elevated structure, the pavilion sits above an existing linear river park. With approximately 174,000sqm of space, the proposal is composed of 62 distinct buildings. Interlocked with the existing and reprogrammed metro stations, each structure is imagined individually as unique and emblematic, yet en masse to form an iconic and eye catching linear cluster. Housed within the pavilions, the collection is envisioned as an assortment of artistic programming. The programmatic proposal includes galleries and museums that would span genera's from classical art, sculpture, 2d arts, installations and multi-media exhibitions with a focus on Korean as well as international works. The proposal offers both architectural and artistic intentions that would catapult the neighbourhood as an iconic location in the city and beyond its borders. While perhaps a colossal and indiscreetly ambitious vision, as a provocation we invite viewers to imagine the possibilities of our proposal and its impact on the future of the community and Seoul at large.

토포텍 1은 21년 전 설립되었으며, 이후 조경, 도시 디자인, 최근에는 건축에 이르기까지 지속적으로 광범위한 디자인 스펙트럼을 개발해 왔다. 크거나 작기도 하고, 형식적이거나 예측할 수 없으며, 이상적이거나 합리적이며, 논쟁적이거나 합리적이고, 화려하거나 섬세한 디자인이다. 극단적인 표현들처럼 디자인 접근 방식은 솔직하고 직접적이다. 재료 활용의 다양함 속에서 다양한 유형의 프로젝트들은 한결같은 아름다움에 대한 믿음, 과장된 표현, 예리해지고자 하는 욕망, 주어진 현실에 대한 의문, 그리고 결정적이지만 상황에 맞춘 것과 같은 접근 방식들을 보여준다.

Since our launch 21 years ago, Topotek 1, as a landscape, urban design and more recently an architecture firm, we have consistently developed a broad design spectrum: large and small, formal and unpredictable, dreamy and sensible, controversial and harmonious, glitzy and subtle. An array of expressive extremes – our design approach is unapologetic, frank and decisive from the get go. A typological mixed bag, varied in material execution, consistency resides in our unshaken faith in the beautiful, in our loyalty to hyperbolic statements, in the desire to sharpen, skew and question given realities and in an approach that is decisive yet tailor made.

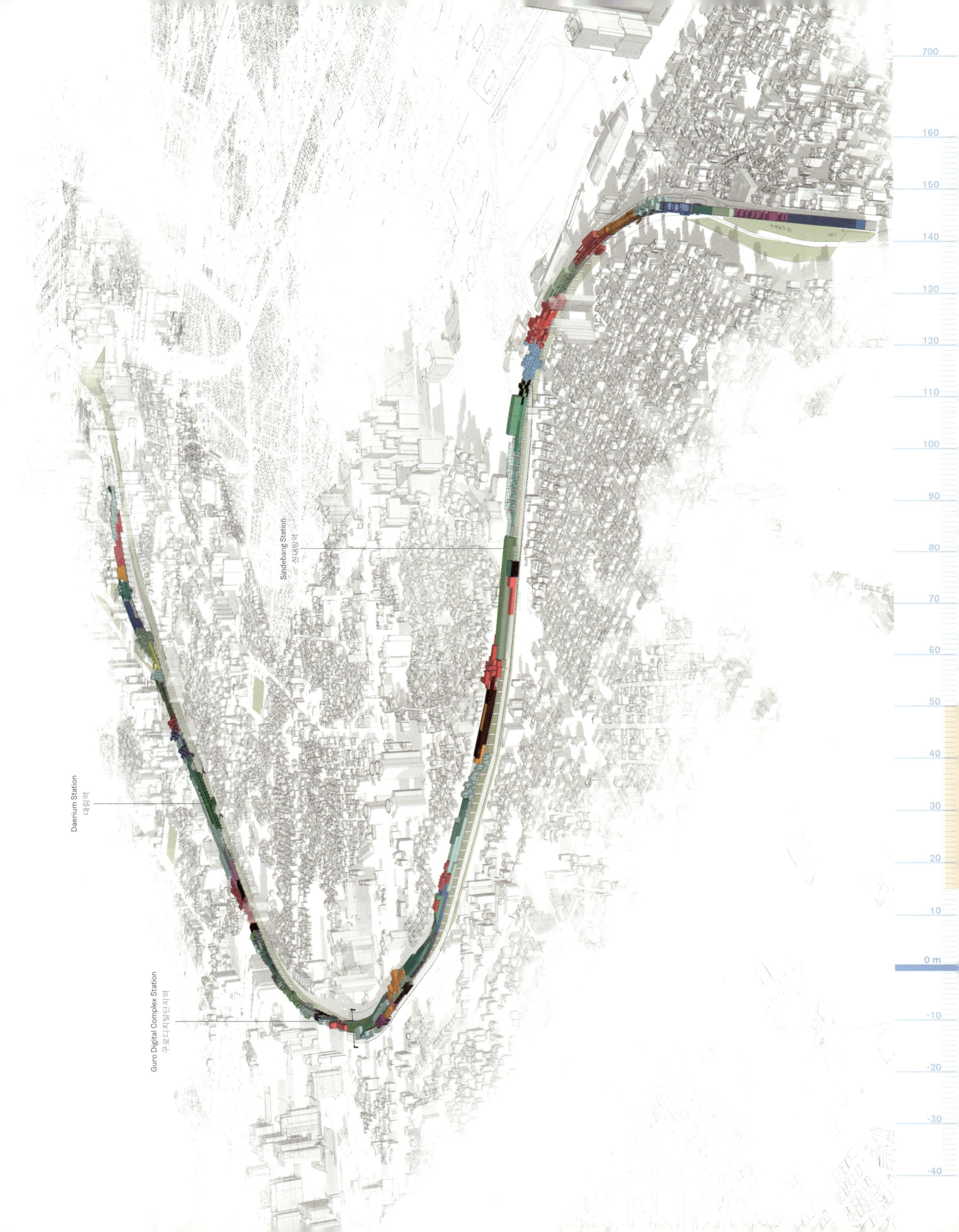

Sindebang Station
신대방역
Daerium Station
대림역
Guro Digital Complex Station
구로디지털단지역
700
160
150
140
130
120
110
100
90
80
70
60
50
40
30
20
10
0 m
-10
-20
-30
-40

제안안 / THE PROPOSAL

이 분야에서 가장 뛰어난 미술품 수집가와 존경받는 현대 한국 예술가들이 있어서 서울은 국제무대에서 선도적인 예술도전자이다. 그러나 역동적이며 실질적인 예술적인 시도들은 풍부하지만, 관련 프로젝트와 프로그램들은 강남이나 종로에 집중되어 있다.

이러한 상황에서 서울시의 문화지도를 재구성하기 위한 시도로써 우리는 서울의 예술 에너지를 이 프로젝트 지역으로 이끌고 오려고 한다. 예술이 문화적 촉매제로서 한국계 중국인으로 대표되는 이민자들의 활기를 북돋우며 지역사회의 발전과 사회 통합을 추진하는 도구로 사용될 수 있는 것에 주목하였다.

이 제안은 문화적이며 건축적인 방향으로 탐구되었으며, 5.2km의 길이에 이르는 도시 내 고가블록이 예술적인 도시 경관으로 탈바꿈될 수 있는 모든 가능성을 활용하는 방향으로 이루어졌다. 용과 같은 형태의 지하철 선로를 예술적인 메가 블록으로 탈바꿈시킴으로써 세계 최대의 예술 프로그램들의 집합체의 형태로 용, 서펜타인 갤러리로 다시 태어날 것이다.

Supported by some of the most prominent art collectors in the field and by well-respected contemporary Korean artists, Seoul is thus a leading art contender on the international stage. While certainly dynamic and rich in substance the majority of such artistic ventures, projects and programming is however concentrated in the Gangnam and Jonglo-Gu areas.

Tapping into this rich asset, in an attempt to reorient the culture map of Seoul, the proposal seeks to channel and mobilize Seoul's artistic energy to stimulate the area. Art as a catalyst of culture was of particular interest in invigorating the immigrant, largely Chinese community, as a tool for community building and social integration.

As such, our proposal ventured in a surprisingly cultural and architectonic direction that explores the possibilities of an elevated city block 5.2km in length as an artistic cityscape on stilts. The new linear neighbourhood within a neighbourhood is imagined to house the world's largest collection of artistic program - the snaking metro line turned artistic mega-block - otherwise known as Young, The Serpentine Galleries.

REVENUE FROM DIFFERENT ART TYPES (2016)

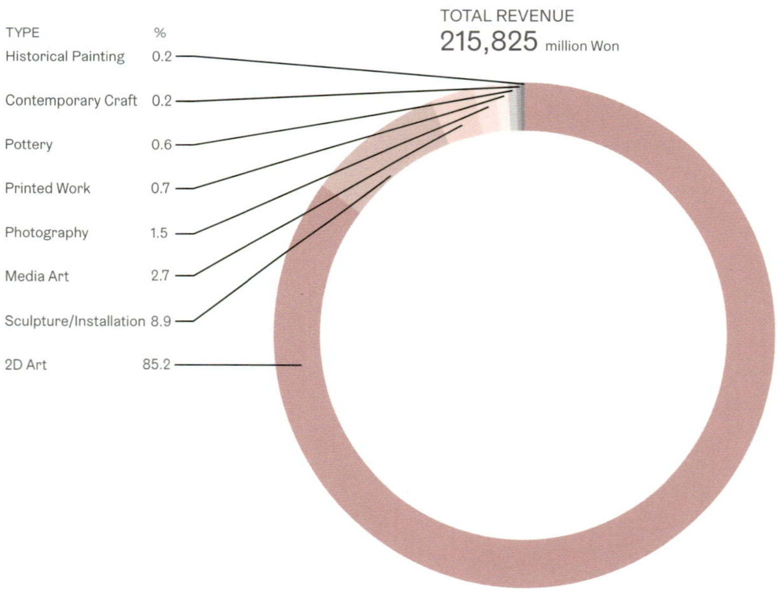

NUMBER OF PIECES TRADED (2016)

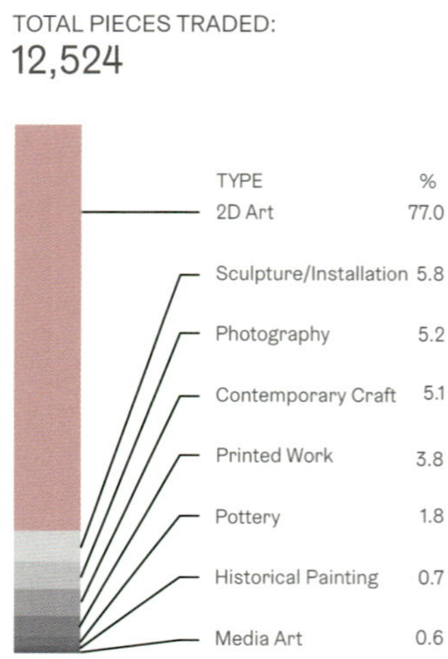

Source : Survey on the art market, 2017
Source : Private art museum report, Larrys list, 2016

TOTAL AMOUNT OF ART TRADED (2016)

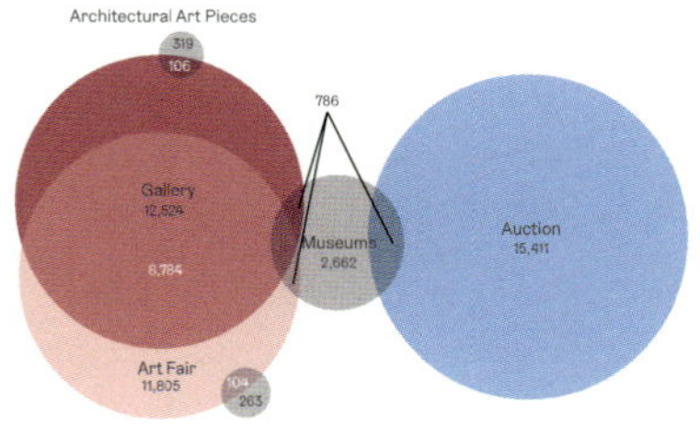

ART TRADE REVENUE DISTRIBUTION (2016)

Total Revenue:
230,604 million Won

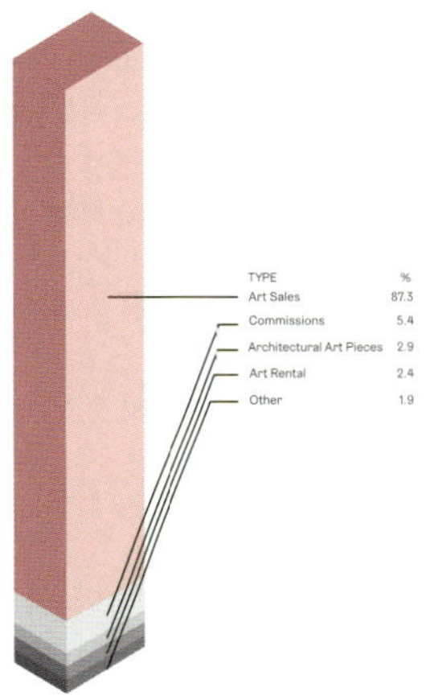

COUNTRIES WIHT THE MOST MUSEUMS

CITIES WITH THE MOST MUSEUMS

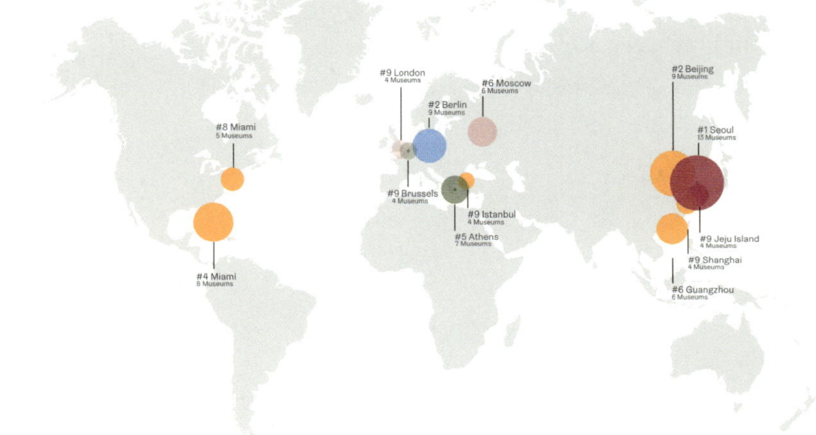

SEOUL GALLERIES

TOTAL: 437

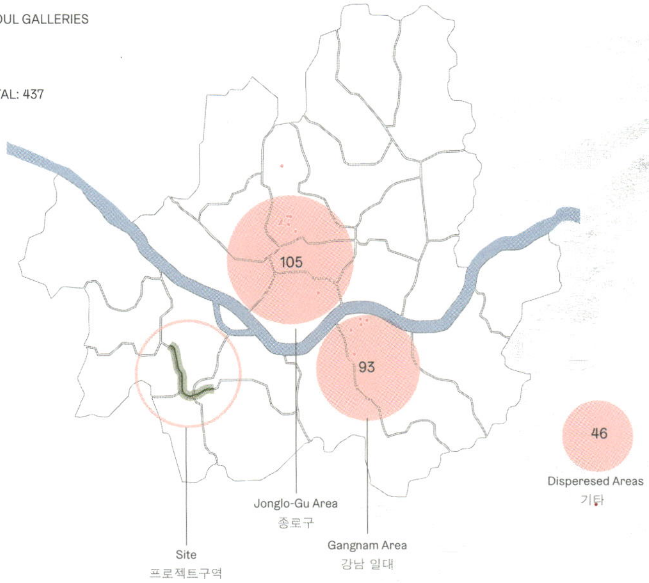

SEOUL PUBLIC/PRIVATE MUSEUMS

TOTAL: 39

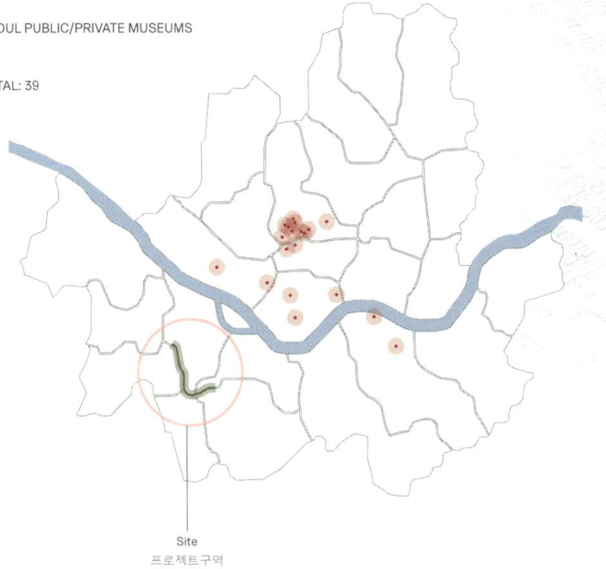

파빌리온 / PAVILLIONS

길이 약 5.2km, 약 174,000 제곱미터의 공간, 용, 서펜타인 갤러리는 62개의 서로 다른 건물들로 이루어져 있다. 새로운 프로그램으로 재탄생될 기존의 지하철역들과 연결되며, 각각의 구조는 독특하고 상징적인 모습을 갖지만 전체적으로 상징적이며 눈길을 끄는 하나의 거대한 선형을 이룰 것이다.

약 10.5m의 좁은 폭의 기존 철로의 진행 방향을 따라 파빌리온은 틀어지거나 커브를 이루며, 순간적으로 공간이 확장되는 곳에서는 더 큰 내부 공간이 생기거나 높은 플랫폼에서 주변의 동네나 공원까지 내려갈 수 있다. 동시에 수직적 연결은 빈번하게 이루어지지만 공원에 매우 중요한 채광을 확보하기 위하여 연결 부분의 면적은 제한을 두었다. 녹지의 성격을 더하기 위하여, 높은 고가 구조물로부터 공원까지 덩굴들이 내려와 폭포수 같은 초록색 커튼을 이루도록 했으며, 이들은 두 평행한 공간 사이의 시각적, 물리적 연결을 담당한다.

고가도로가 만나는 구로디지털단지역과 신대방역에서는 구조가 확장되어 중요한 허브와 통로들을 만든다. 전체적으로 보았을 때, 최종적으로는 많은 부분이 단계적으로 실현될 수 있는 유연성을 가질 것이다. 아마도 시간의 흐름에 따라 지하철역을 중심으로 개발이 확장되거나, 북쪽에서 남쪽 또는 남쪽에서 북쪽으로 선형적으로 개발이 이루어질 것이다.

5.2 km long with approximately 174,000 sqm of space, Young, The Serpentine Galleries is composed of 62 distinct buildings. Interlocked with the existing and reprogrammed metro stations, each structure is imagined individually as unique and emblematic, yet en masse to form an iconic and eye catching linear cluster.

Typically a narrow 10.5 m in width, the pavilions twist and bend with the direction of the winding former railway infrastructure, at moments however, the proportions expand to accommodate greater interior spaces or to reach down from the elevated platform to the neighbourhood and park below. Ensuring sunlight to the much-valued park, connections are frequent but limited in coverage. As a supplementary green feature, vines hang from the elevated infrastructure cascading as a green curtain to the park beneath, making a visual and physical connection between the parallel worlds.

At the locations where the raised highway meets the Guro Digital Complex and Sindebang stations the structures multiply and expand to greater proportions to create important hubs and gateways to the development. Visualized here in its entirety, as many parts to a final whole, the development has the flexibility however to be realized in stages, perhaps growing out from station hubs or linearly from north to south or south to north over time.

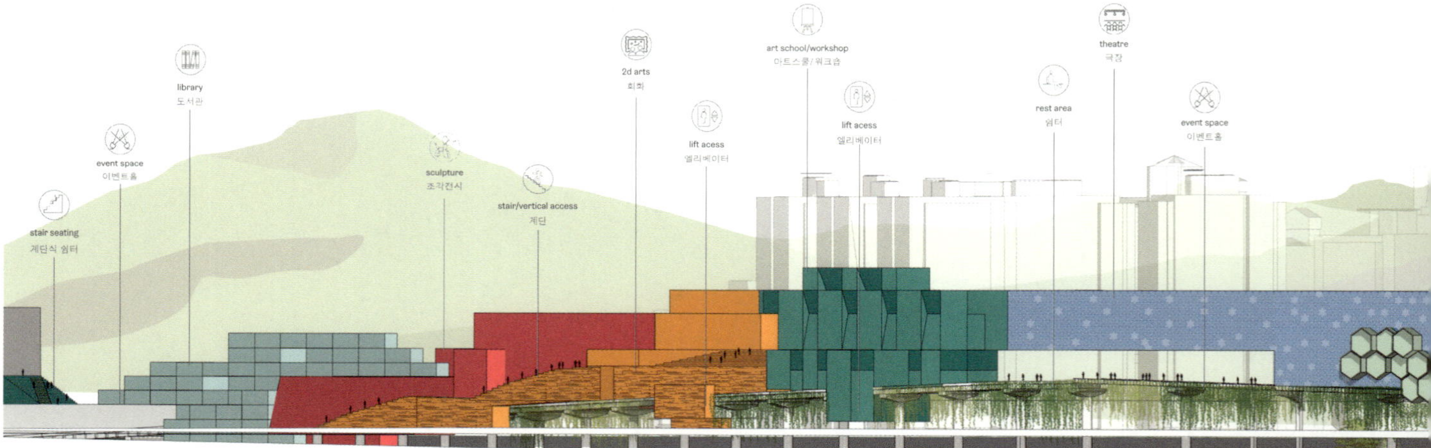

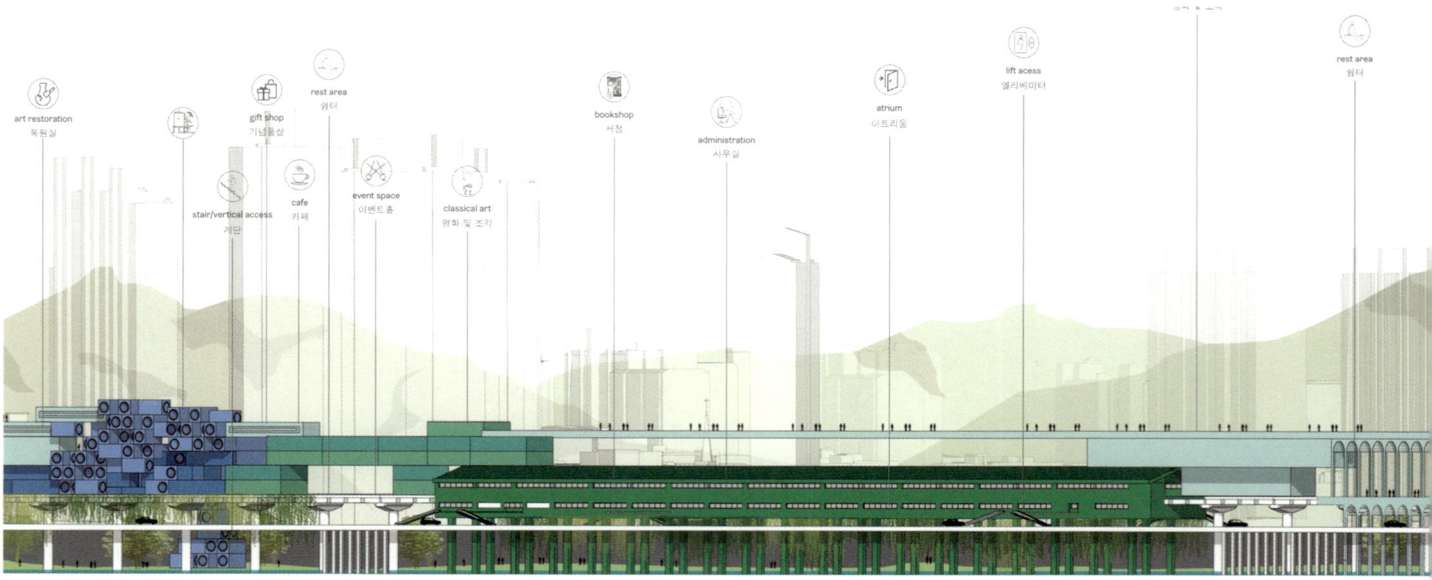

프로그램 / PROGRAM

전시관 안의 컬렉션들은 다양한 예술 프로그램으로 구성될 것이다. 이 프로그램은 한국 예술품 및 국제 예술품 등을 중심으로 고전 미술, 조각, 회화, 설치미술, 미디어아트 전시 등 장르를 아우르는 갤러리나 미술관을 포함한다. 이 중 대다수는 현재 서울의 개인 컬렉터들의 전시들을 따를 것으로 예상한다.

부가적인 프로그램으로는 예술 학교/워크숍, 예술가들의 주거공간/호텔, 아티스트 스튜디오, 미술 복원실, 도서관, 서점, 카페, 레스토랑, 선물 가게, 극장, 행사장, 조각 정원, 공공 모임 장소, 녹색 지역 및 예술 놀이 공간이 있다.

Housed within the pavilions, the collection is envisioned as an assortment of artistic programming. The programmatic proposal includes galleries and museums that would span genera's from classical art, sculpture, 2d arts, installations and multi-media exhibitions with a focus on Korean as well as international works. The majority of these are imagined to follow the existing art scene trajectory in Seoul of private collection exhibition.

Additional programmatic elements include art school/ workshops, artist in residencies/hotels, artist studios, art restoration, libraries, bookstores, cafés, restaurants, gift shops, theatres, event spaces, sculpture gardens, public gathering spaces, green areas and art playgrounds.

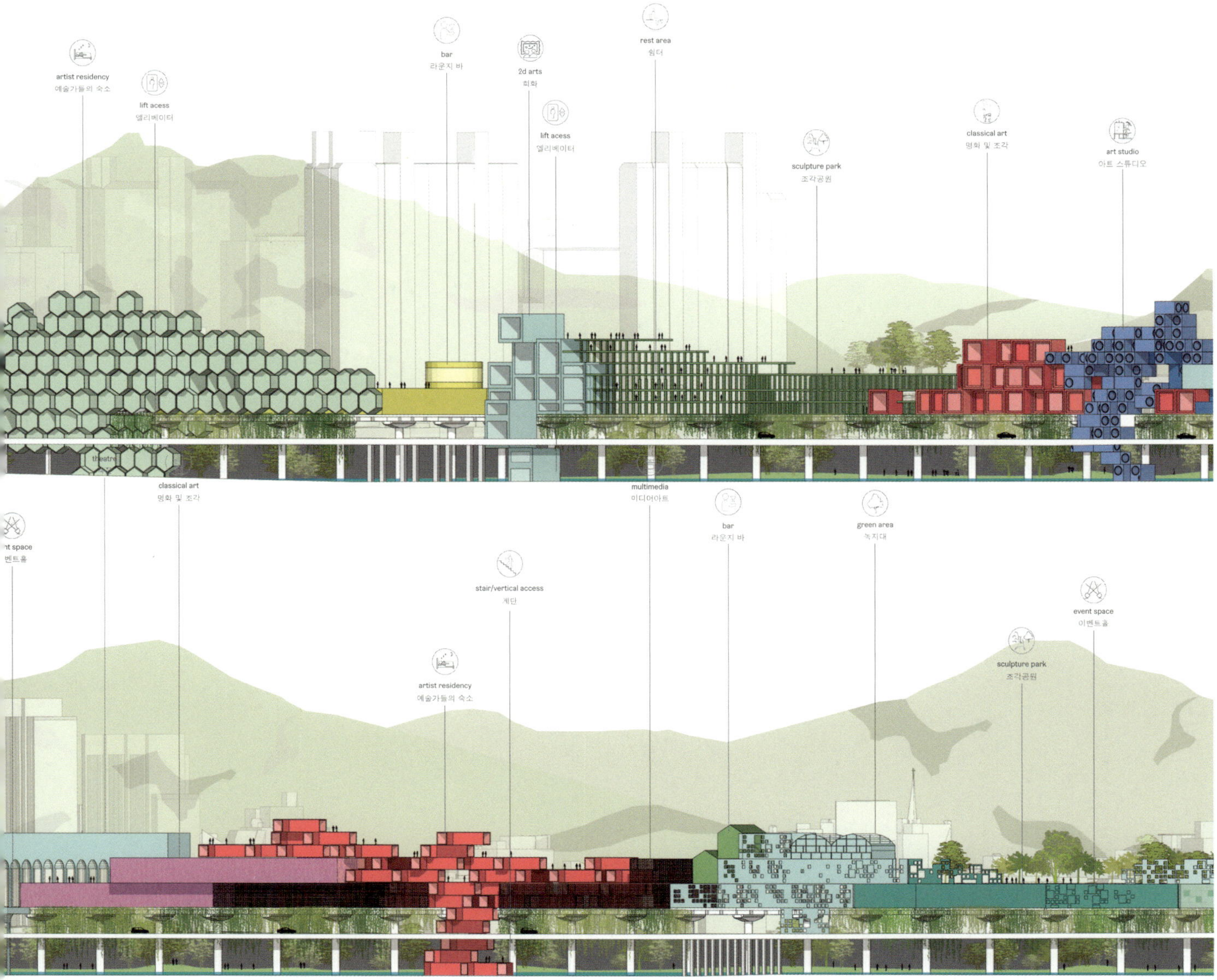

프로그램 / PROGRAM

내부 프로그램을 반영하여 건물 형태는 다양한 기능을 수용하도록 바뀔 수 있다. 예를 들어, 폭이 좁은 철도 구간에는 예술가들의 숙소 및 호텔을 위하여 일본 도쿄의 캡슐 호텔의 개별 유닛들이 조합된 형태를 참조할 수 있다. 또한 아티스트 스튜디오의 경우에도 이런 치수들을 적용해 모듈식 유닛을 개별적으로 쌓아 구성할 수 있다. 한편, 극장이나 조명에 민감한 컬렉션들의 경우 불투명한 외벽이 있는 구조물에 전시되며, 야외 조각 컬렉션의 경우 야외 조각 정원이 전시 장소로 제공될 수 있다.

이 공간들의 사이 공간이나 윗부분은 큰 계단들로 이루어진 앉을 수 있는 공간, 녹지 공간, 넓은 통로, 그늘이 있는 정원, 경매나 아트 페어 및 기타 예술 행사 또는 인근 주민들과 관련된 행사 등을 개최할 수 있는 이벤트 공간 등 다양한 열려있는 공공장소가 될 수 있다.

Reflecting the interior program, the building forms adapt according to the variety of functions. For example, capitalizing on the narrow railway structure dimensions, artist in residencies and hotels emulate the small individual units of capsule hotels in Tokyo, Japan. Artist studios also mimic these floor plan dimensions with individually stacked and modular units. Meanwhile, theatres and light sensitive collections are housed in structures with impervious facades while outdoor sculpture collections are provided open-air sculpture gardens.

Dotted between and on top of these spaces are open public spaces including large staircase seating areas, green spaces, spacious passageways, shaded pavilions and numerous event spaces to house fairs, markets and other art or neighbourhood related events.

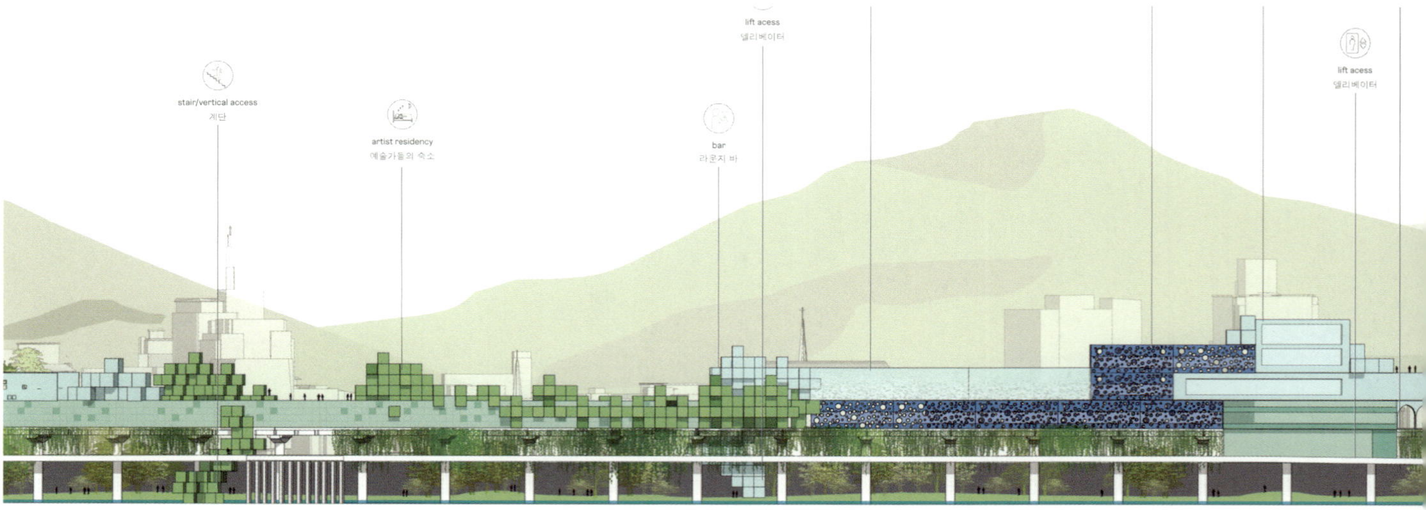

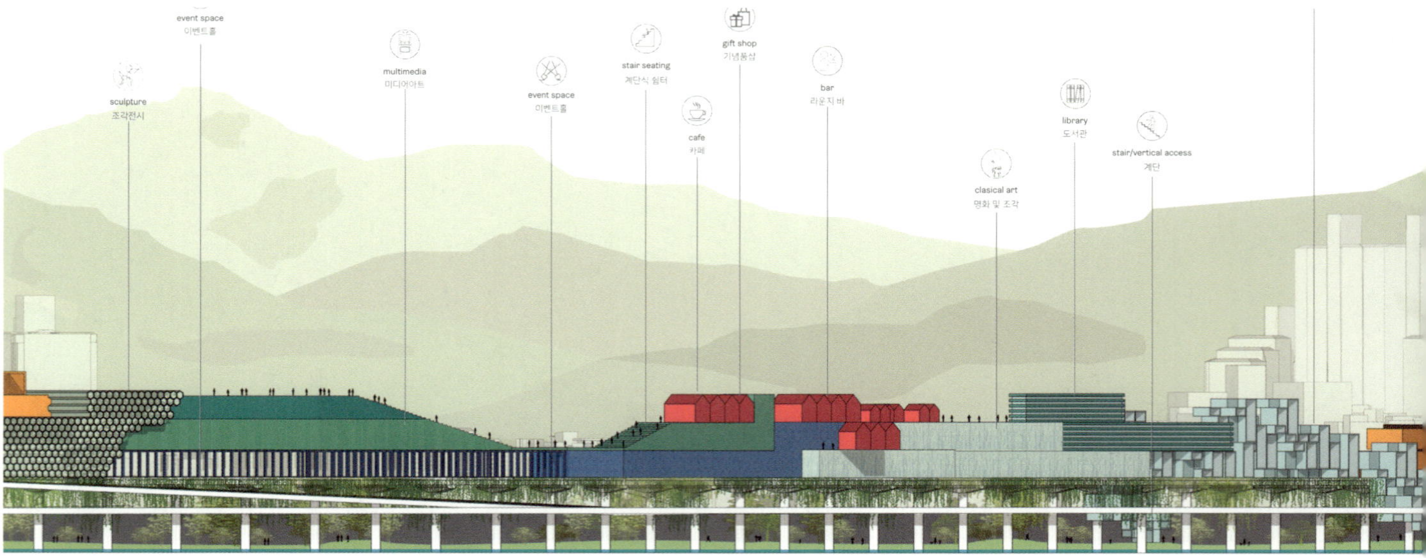

연결 / CONNECTION

용, 서펜타인 갤러리는 기존의 3개의 지하철역들을 연결하며, 이 역들 플랫폼 높이는 인접한 건물들의 층 높이를 결정한다. 기존의 대림역, 구로디지털단지역, 신대방역은 지하철과 연결을 유지하며, 사무실, 아트리움, 인포센터 및 연결통로로 활용될 수 있다.

모든 역은 지하철 2호선과 대림역의 경우 7호선과도 연결되어, 이 복합적인 공간으로 바로 접근할 수 있어서 대도시 서울의 시민들이 편리하고 쉽게 이용할 수 있도록 한다. 또한 이 역들은 이미 주변 환경과 잘 연결되어 있어서, 서로 다른 동네로 쉽게 접근할 수 있다.

역과 역 사이 건물들에 (최대 100m 간격으로) 지면, 도로면 또는 강변까지 이어지는 계단이나 엘리베이터를 설치하여, 주변 지역들과 연결, 구조물 아래에 위치한 강변 공원과의 연결, 그리고 적어도 50m마다 설치해야 하는 비상 대피로를 고려하였다.

The linked structures of Yong, The Serpentine Galleries integrate the three existing metro stations, borrowing the spacious height dimensions of the railway platform to determine the floor height levels of the adjacent buildings. The Daerim, Guro Digital Complex and Sindebang stations are utilized as administrative areas, atriums, information points and main areas of access as connection to the underground metro would be maintained.

The interlinking to the circle Line 2 at all three stations, as well as Line 7 at Daerim station, would provide easy and immediate access to the development by the wider Seoul population linking the complex conveniently to the greater city. In addition, the stations, already well connected to the surrounding context, would offer direct access to the population in the adjacent neighbourhoods.

For further connection to the neighbourhood and directly to the park below, between stations (at a 100m minimum interval to maintain the required 50m exit requirements), further access is granted through the extension of buildings to the ground level roadway or directly to the park beneath, connecting via stairways or elevator.

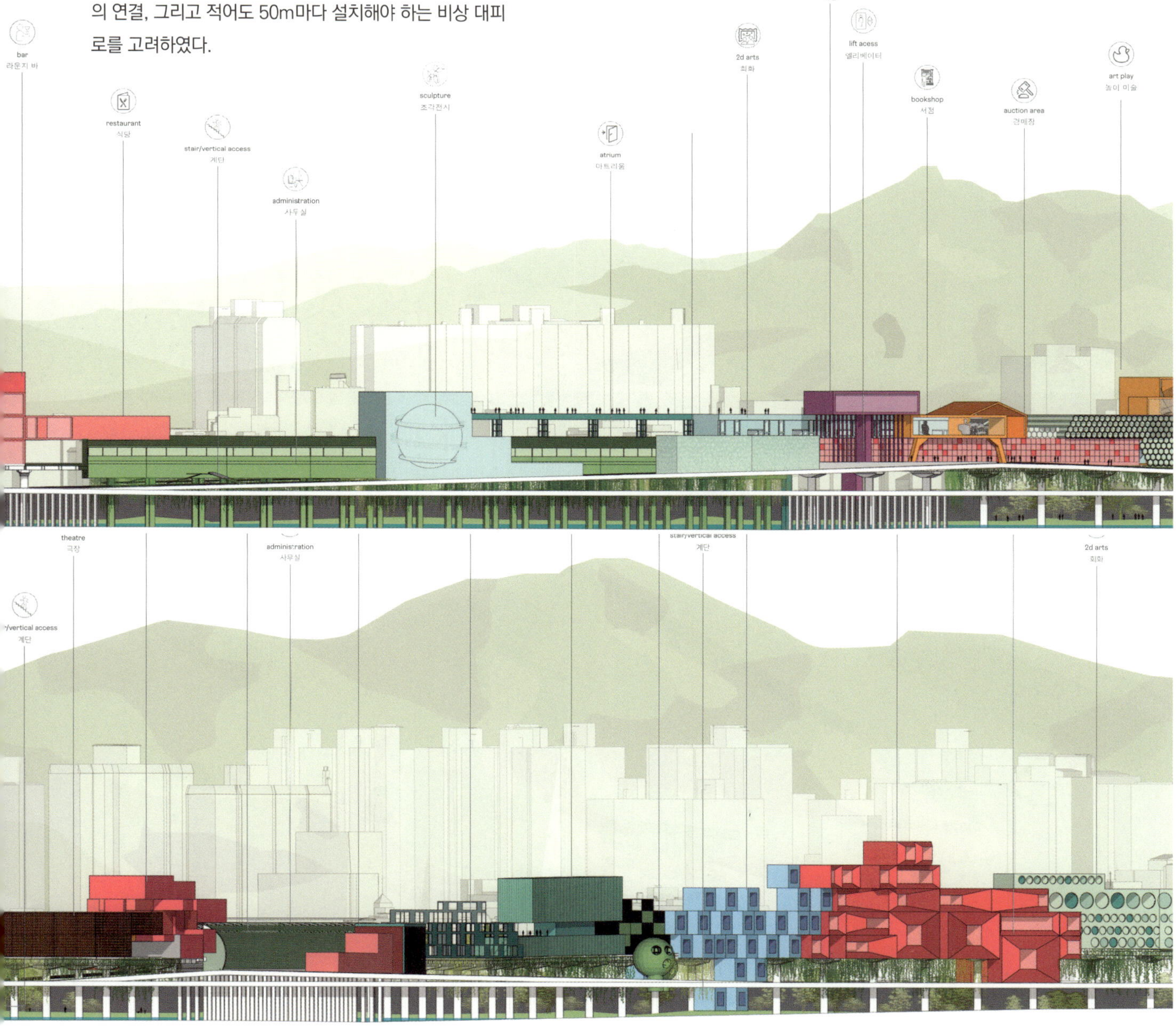

미래 / THE FUTURE

용, 서펜타인 갤러리는 2호선 지상 구간이 사라진 이후 미래에 대한 혁신적인 비전이다. 이 제안은 이 지역을 서울의 상징적인 장소로 만들 수 있는 건축적, 예술적 의도를 모두 가지고 있으며 끊임없이 진화하는 도시 환경 내에서 사용되지 않는 인프라 시설의 예술적, 문화적, 건축적인 재활용 가능성을 국제적으로 보여줄 것이다.

어쩌면 거대하고 무분별하게 보이는 야심 찬 비전일지라도 이 제안의 가능성과 지역 사회 및 서울의 미래에 미치는 영향을 상상해보기 위해 우리는 여러분을 초대하고자 한다.

Young, The Serpentine Galleries is a bold vision for the future of the disused Line 2. The proposal offers both architectural and artistic intentions that would catapult the neighbourhood as an iconic feature and location of Seoul, and further, launch the district and the city into the international conversation on the repurposing of disused infrastructure as well as the possibilities of art, culture and architecture in the constantly evolving urban context.

While perhaps a colossal and indiscreetly ambitious vision, as a provocation we invite viewers to imagine the possibilities of our proposal and its impact on the future of the community and Seoul at large.

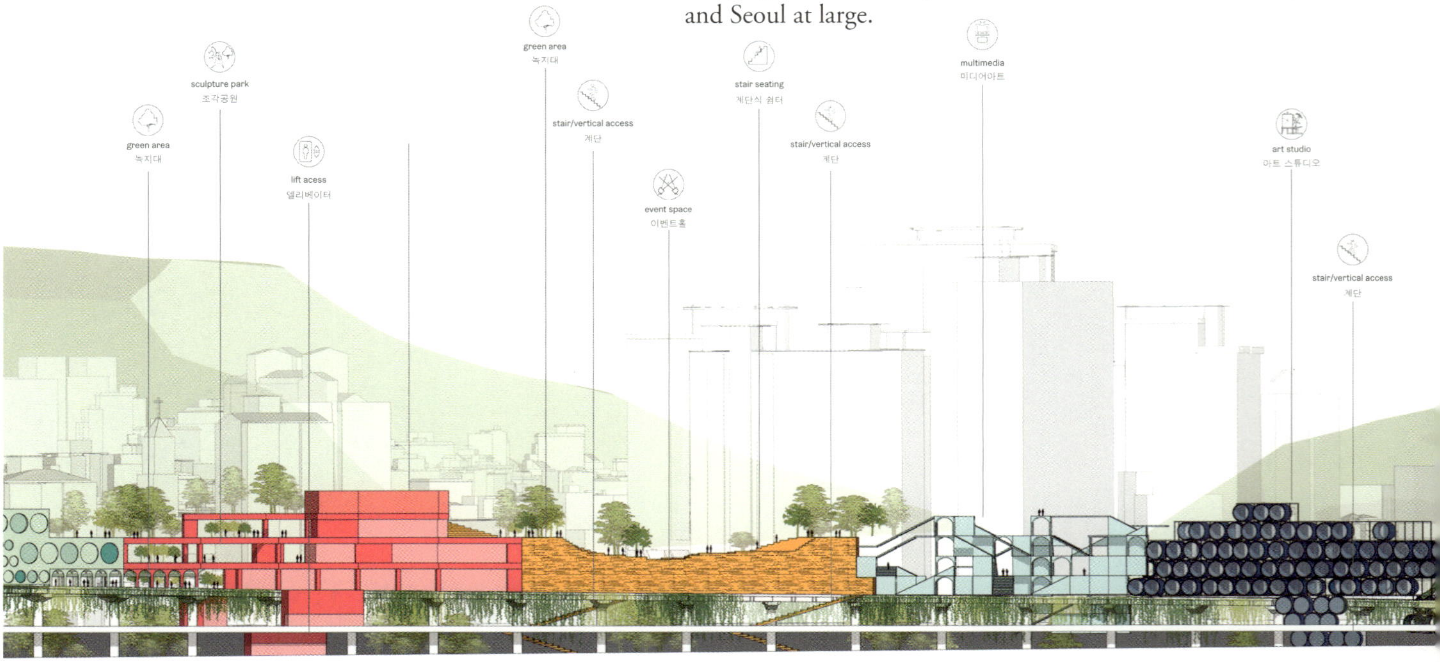

용, SERPENTINE GALLERIES

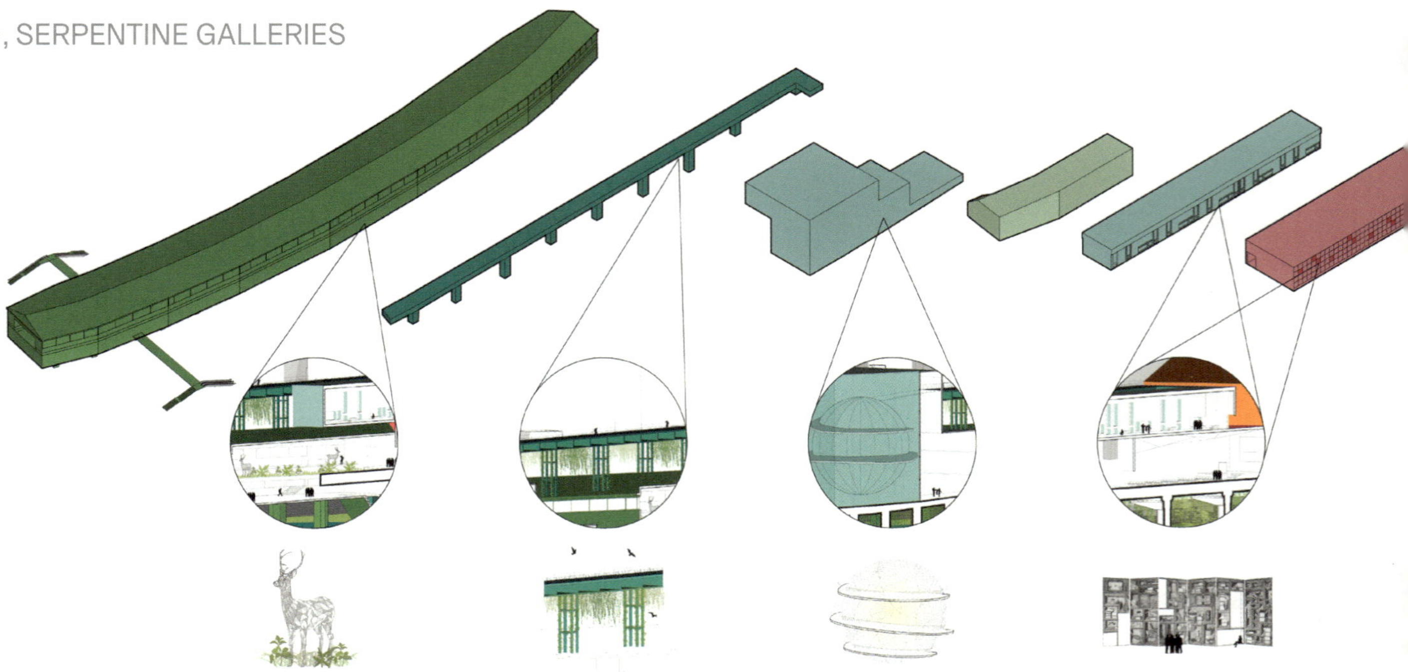

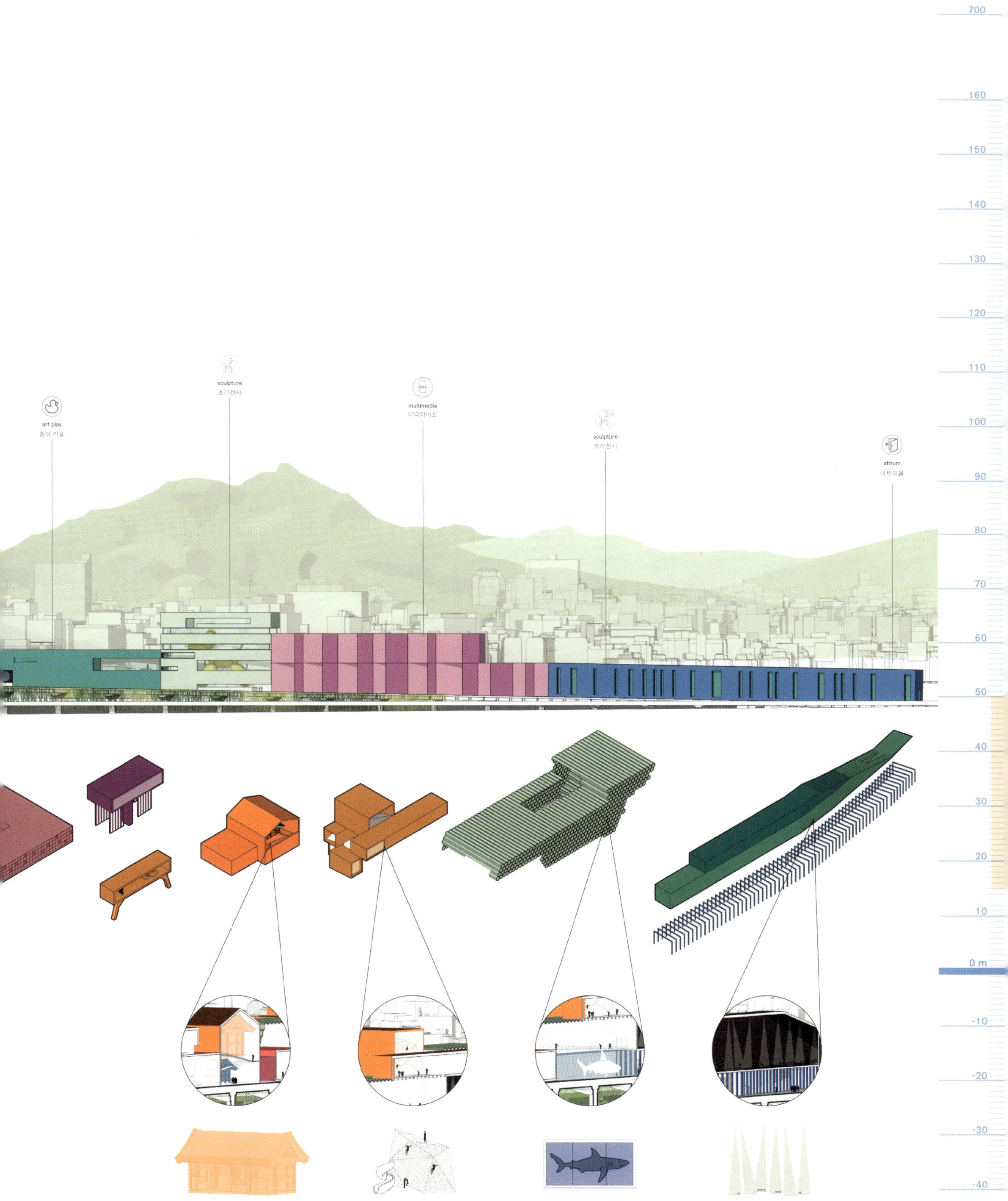
art play
놀이 미술
sculpture
조각전시
multimedia
미디어아트
sculpture
조각전시
atrium
아트리움
700
160
150
140
130
120
110
100
90
80
70
60
50
40
30
20
10
0 m
-10
-20
-30
-40

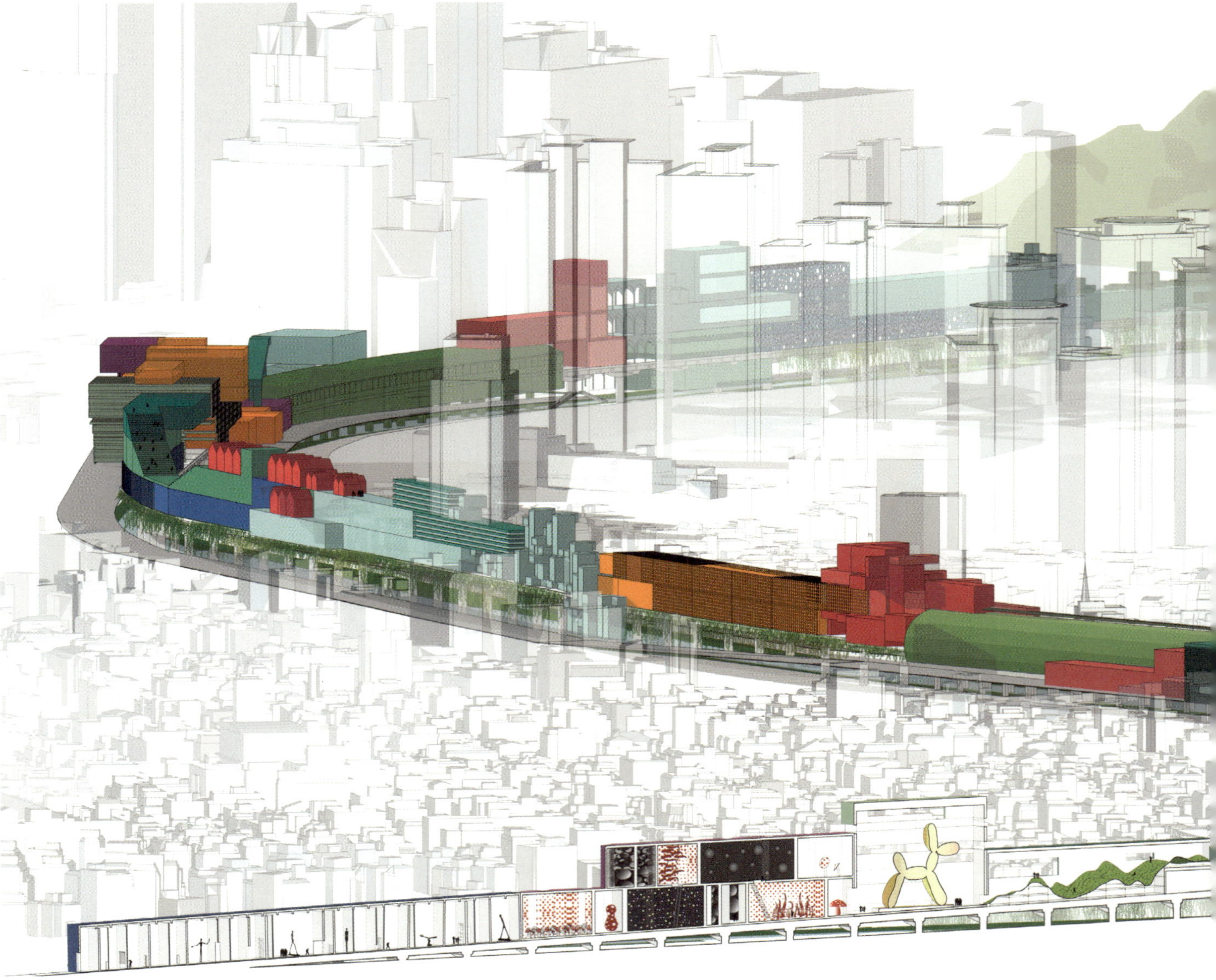

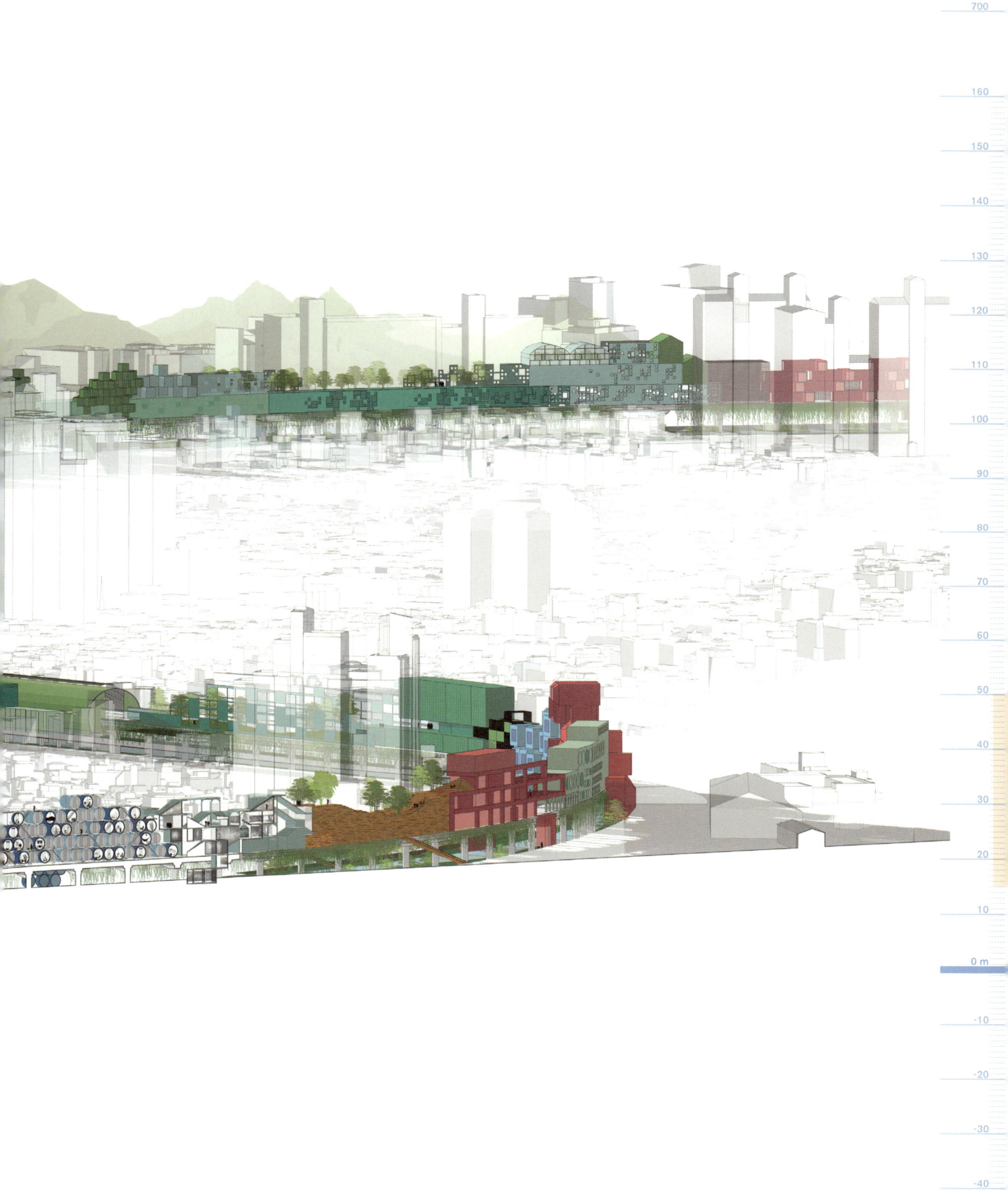

700
160
150
140
130
120
110
100
90
80
70
60
50
40
30
20
10
0 m
-10
-20
-30
-40

장윤규

Yoon gyoo Jang

경의중앙선(연세대 앞 구간) / Kyeongui-Jungang Line (Yonsei Univ.)

어반 커넥터

기존 도시의 단절을 야기하고 있는 연대 앞 굴다리에 소통을 위한 하나의 틀로 프로그램 보이드 시스템을 제안한다. 이 프로그램 보이드는 기존 도시 인프라를 변화시켜 다양한 이벤트와 새로운 문화적인 도시 연결체를 만들어 내는 것을 목표로 한다. 부분적으로 존재하는 연결 굴다리를 도시 조직과 연계 시켜 확장 시킨다. 수평적 연결 굴다리로부터 버려진 폐철로, 공중 데크로 관통하는 프로그램 보이드는 다양한 테마인 휴식, 공원, 상업시설, 공공인프라, 문화, 미디어 등의 프로그램을 수행한다. 보이드는 프로그램적 구분보다는 유연한 도시적 요구를 수용하기 위해 구분 없는 영역과 확장을 만들어 낸다. 열차의 지하화 계획으로 만들어지는 폐철로와 공중보행 데크는 시민에게 열린 공원적 성격을 갖게 되며 프로그램 보이드는 내부적 성격을 갖는다. 이로써 새로운 연대 앞 굴다리는 인공의 외부이벤트 공간을 담은 플랫폼이 겹쳐지며 서로 연결되는 자연적 인공도시로서 기능한다.

Urban Connector

We propose the program void system as the frame for communication in the front railway which causes the disconnection of existing city. The program aims to change existing urban infrastructures to create diverse events and new cultural city connections. Extends a partially existing underway in conjunction with urban organization. Void through the underway, railway and aerial decks performs programs such as resting, parks, commercial facilities, public infrastructure, culture and media. VOID creates delimited areas and extensions to accommodate flexible urban needs rather than programmatic distinctions. The railway track and aerial deck made by the underground plan of the train have the park character which is open to the citizen. And the Program void has the internal character. As a result, the new underway function as natural artificial cities where the platforms containing artificial outer event spaces overlap and connect with each other.

운생동 건축가그룹의 대표인 장윤규는 건축과 예술, 건축과 문화의 통합된 구조를 찾는 건축가이다. "복합체 compound body"라는 자신의 저서를 통하여 "Mythology", "Floating", "Skinscape", "Transprogramming", "Being Animal"이라는 단어로 요약하는 일련의 새로운 건축적 접근들을 제시하였다. 갤러리정미소, 운생동출판, 운생동아트를 동시에 운영하여, 문화적 콘텐츠로서의 가능성을 다각적으로 발현해 내기 위한 소통의 방식을 건축에 적용하려 노력해왔다. 대표작으로 KRING 복합문화센터, 예화랑, 생능출판사, 하이서울패스티벌, 워터스토리, 성동복지문화센터 등이 있다.

Jang Yoon Gyoo is the Principal of Unsangdong Architects Cooperation. Unsangdong Architects is the experimental group organized to realize conceptual architecture with variable possibilities of cultural contents. The main research and project of Unsangdong is based on the diversity of architecture. He has presented a a series of new architectural approaches that summarize through "Mythology", "Floating", "Skinscape", "Transprogramming", "Being Animal" through his book, "Compound body". He has been trying to apply the communication method to manifest various possibilities as cultural contents by operating the galleries JungMiSo, YunGiDong Publishing, and YunGeDong Art simultaneously. Representative works include KRING Complex Cultural Center, Ya Gallery, Sungnyun Publishing House, High Seoul Festivals, Water Story, Seongdong Welfare Cultural Center, etc.

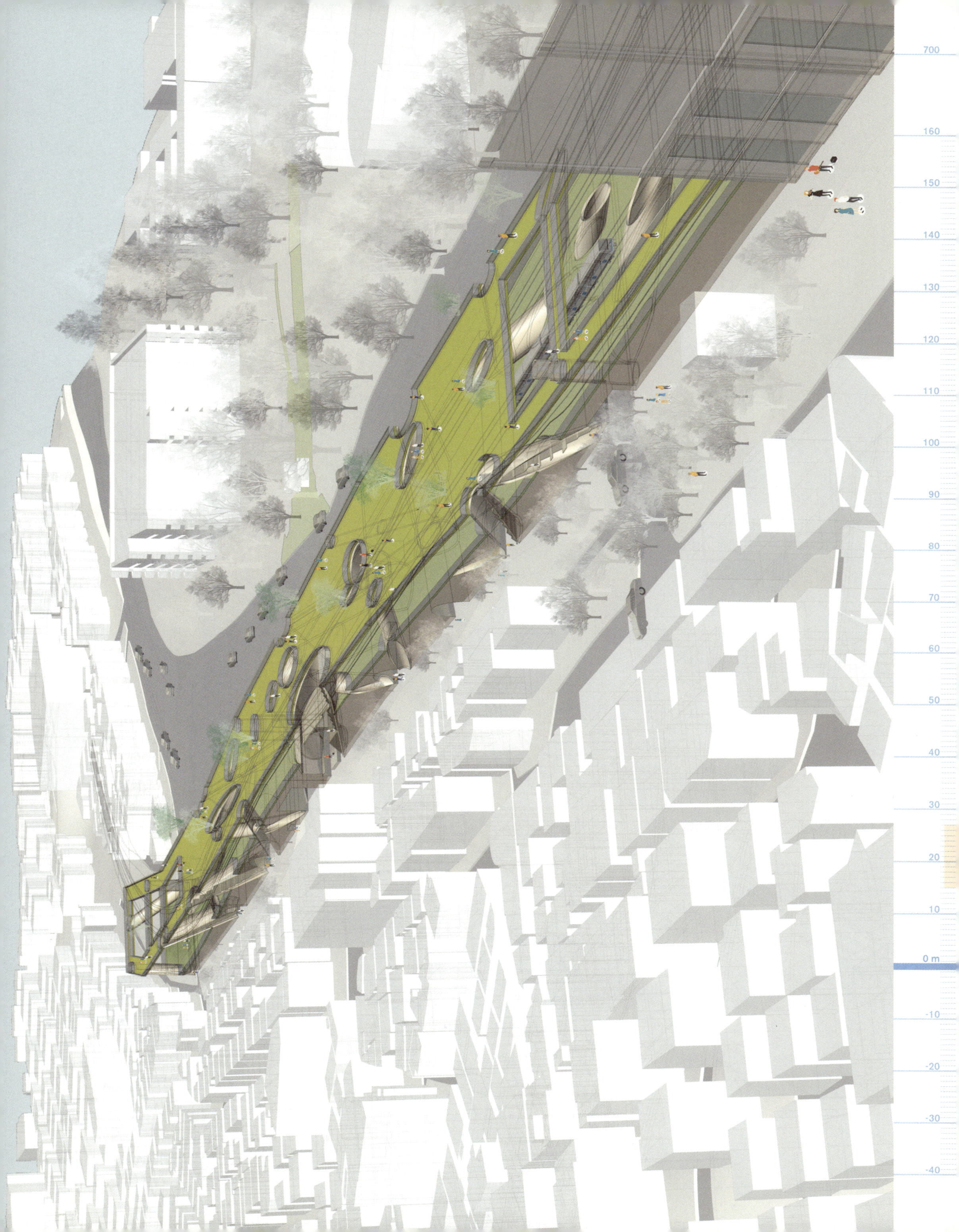
700
160
150
140
130
120
110
100
90
80
70
60
50
40
30
20
10
0 m
-10
-20
-30
-40

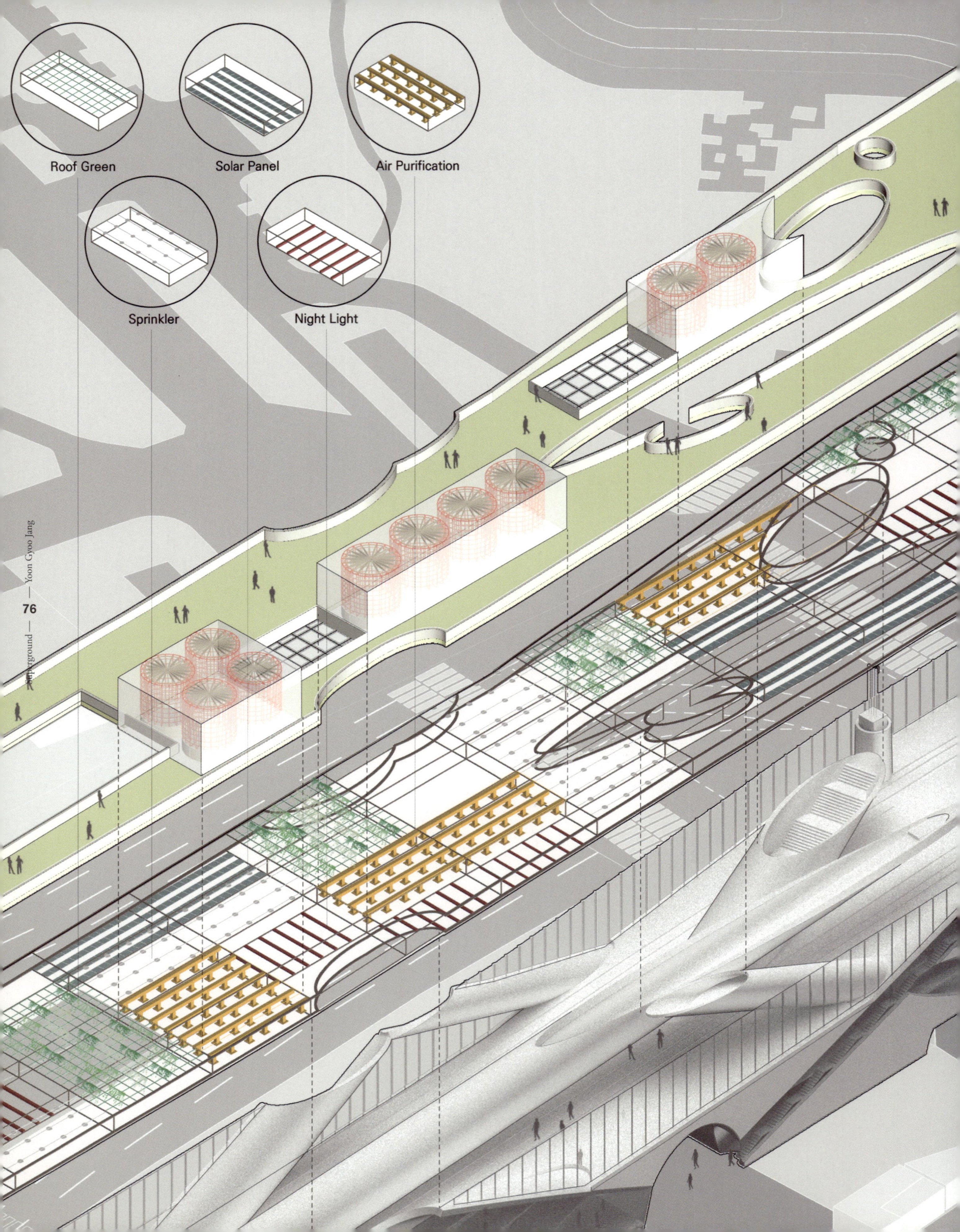
Roof Green
Solar Panel
Air Purification
Sprinkler
Night Light

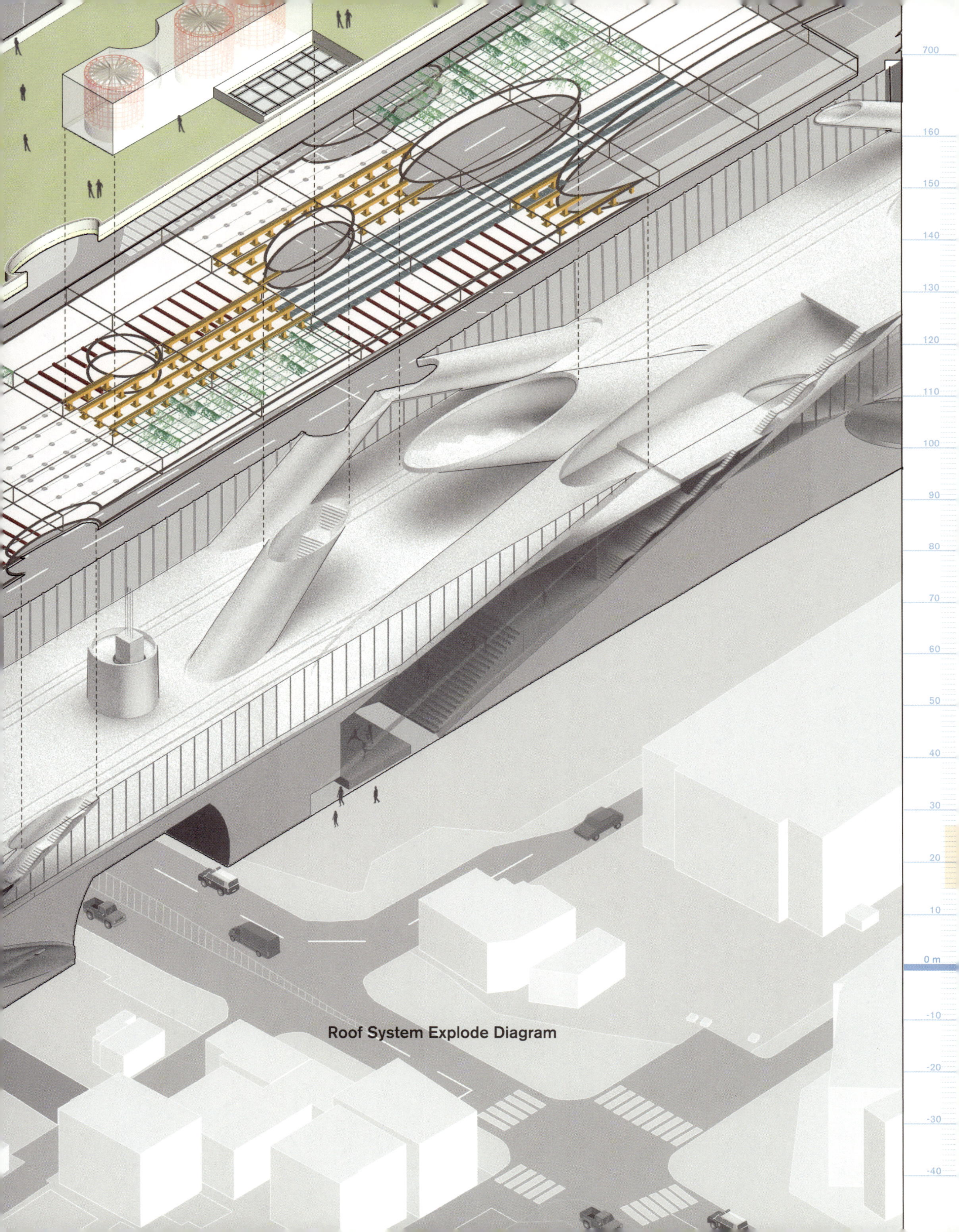

Roof System Explode Diagram

Winter Garden Explode Diagram

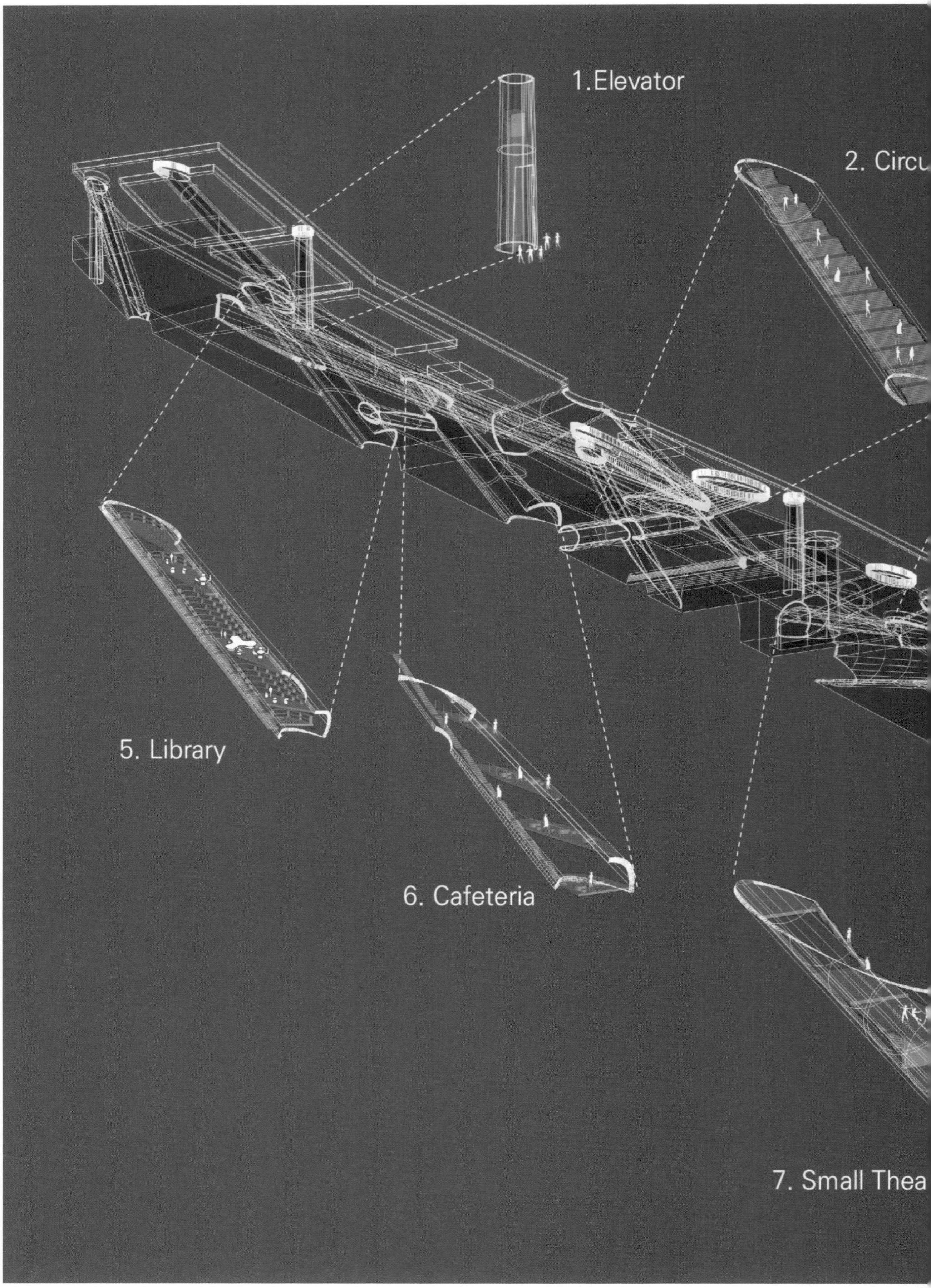
1.Elevator
2. Circu
5. Library
6. Cafeteria
7. Small Thea

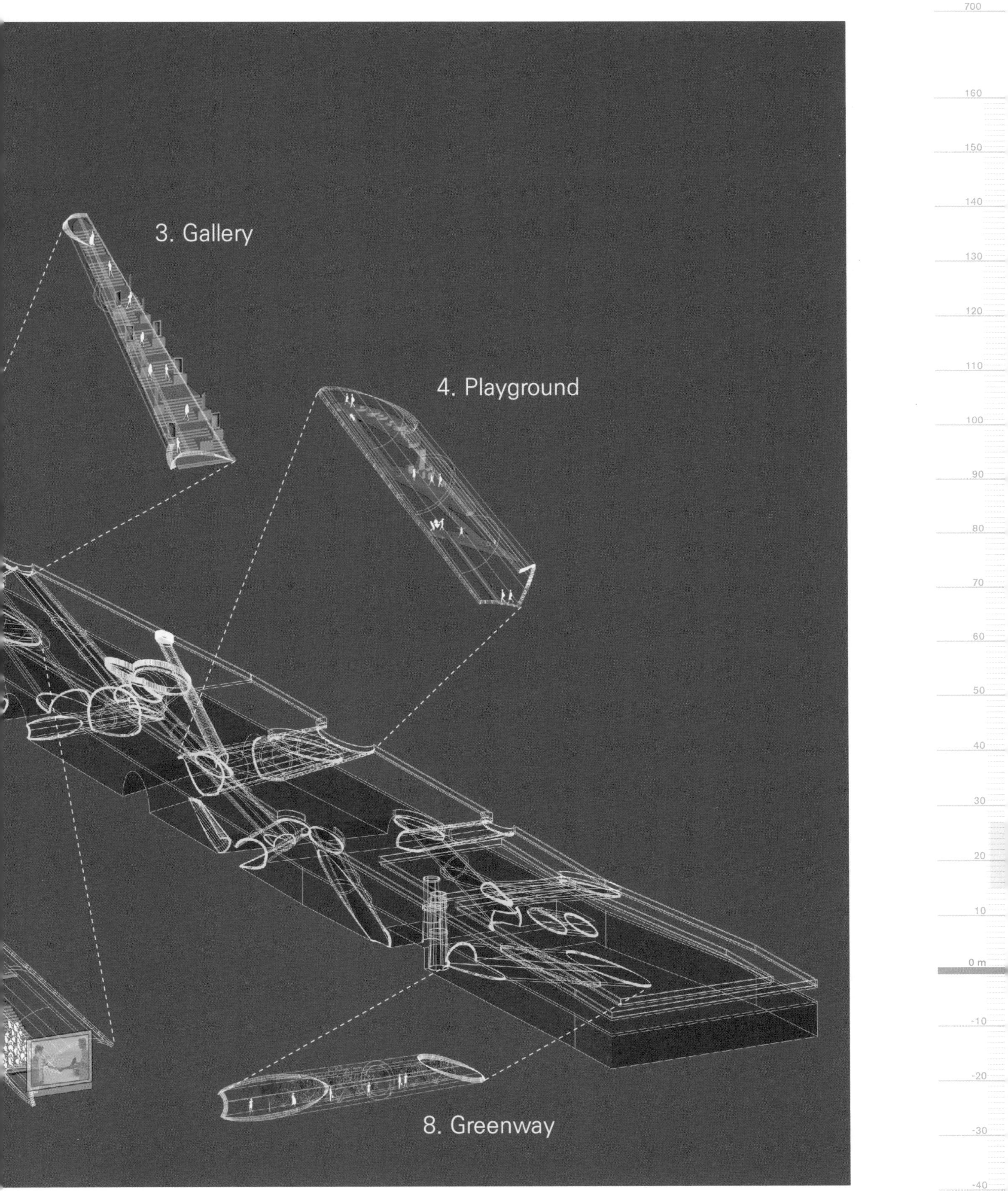
3. Gallery
4. Playground
8. Greenway
700
160
150
140
130
120
110
100
90
80
70
60
50
40
30
20
10
0 m
-10
-20
-30
-40

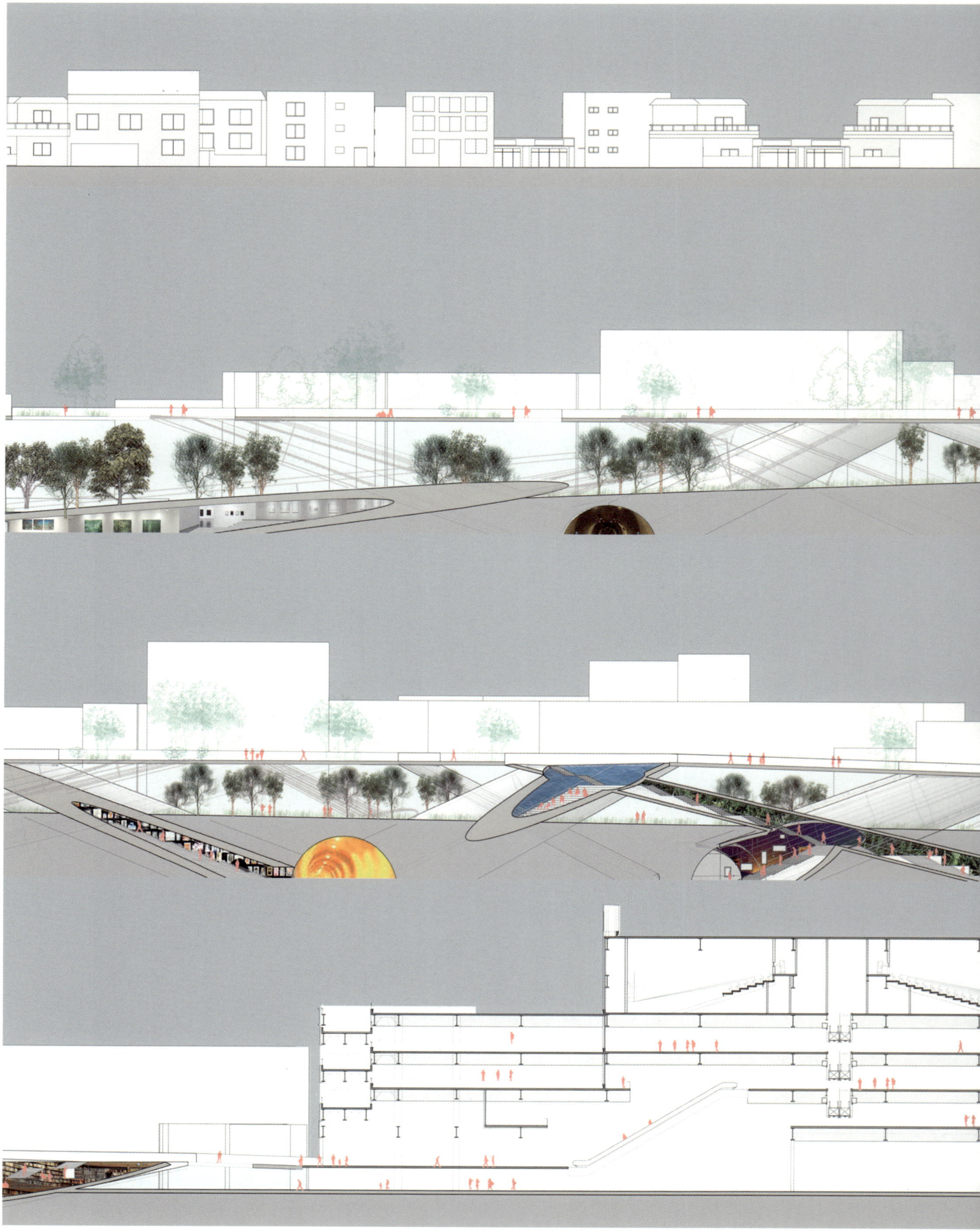

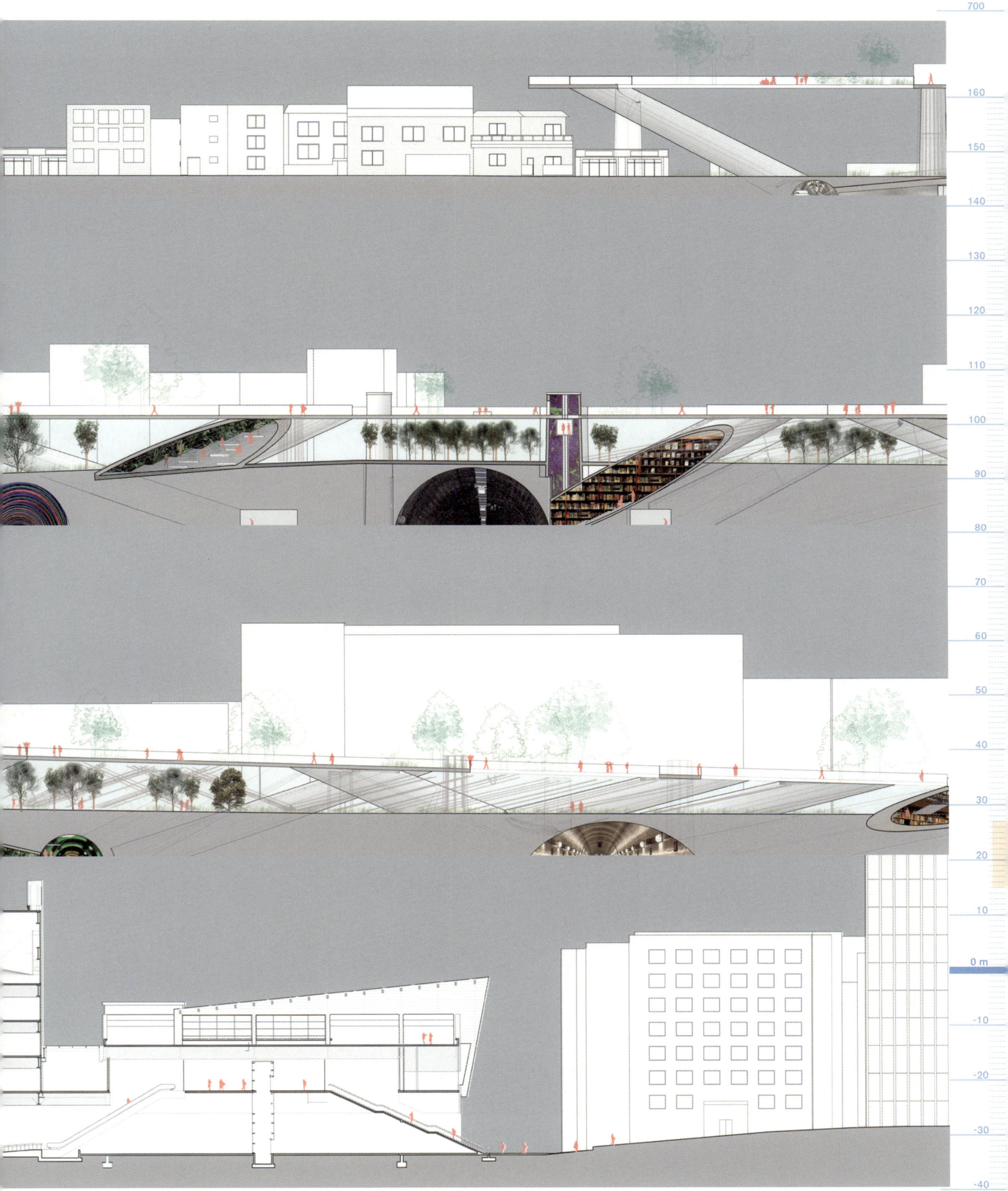

700
160
150
140
130
120
110
100
90
80
70
60
50
40
30
20
10
0 m
-10
-20
-30
-40

700
160
150
140
130
120
110
100
90
80
70
60
50
40
30
20
10
0 m
-10
-20
-30
-40

스튜디오 푹사스 + 라몬 프랫 홈스

Studio FUKSAS + Ramon Prat Homs

어반 퀀텀

어반 퀀텀은 기존의 인프라가 현재 갖고 있는 문제들을 해결하고 더 좋은 법칙으로 도시를 다시 만들 수 있는 치유 역량을 지녔음을 보여주는 새로운 기회이다.
어반 퀀텀은 기존 인프라가 만들어낸 환경적인 불균형 부분을 보완하고자 했다. 예를 들어 인프라 위를 달리는 자동차들이 만들어내는 역동적인 에너지를 새로운 동력을 만들어내거나 자동차들이 발생한 이산화탄소를 정화하기 위하여 활용한다.
어반 퀀텀은 이 새로운 도시 공간을 일단 되찾았다는 점에 가치를 두고자 한다.
"되찾은" 공간을 계획하는 것은 아무것도 없는 것에서 새로 시작할 수 있다는 점을 고려하여, 우리는 보다 복합적인 삼단논리를 사용해야 했다.(지어진 것/지어지지 않은 것/지어진 것) 예를 들어 새로운 완충녹지공간을 구축할 수 있는데, 이 상부에는 주거, 상업, 문화, 스타트 업이나 공유 오피스 등 여러 다른 프로그램을 위한 고밀 건축물을 세우고, 주차장, 이를 지지하기 위한 구조물 하부에는 주차장이나 스포츠 시설을 둘 수 있다.

Urban Quantum

Urban Quantum is a proposal that wants to reflect on how existing infrastructures could become a new opportunity to apply more complex solutions to solve the current conflicts and recover the capability to re-urbanize using better formulas.
Urban Quantum tries to compensate part of the environmental imbalance that the existing infrastructures produces, for example, using all the dynamic energy produced by the vehicles that circulate through it to generate new power or purifying their CO2.
Urban Quantum wants to put in value that once recovered that new urban space, we must use a more complex ternary logic, (built / not built / built), to consider that the planning of that "recovered" space can start almost from scratch, for example, with the build a new buffer green space on the top combined with high density edifications with different programs (housing, shopping and cultural facilities, start-up offices, co-working spaces), and parking and sport facilities located below inside the support structures.

마시밀리아노와 도리아나 푹사스가 이끄는 스튜디오 푹사스는 가장 뛰어난 국제적인 건축사무소들 중 하나이다. 지난 40년간 도시 관련 프로젝트에서부터 공항, 미술관, 문화센터나 음악 공간, 컨벤션 센터, 오피스, 인테리어에 이르는 범위에서 놀랍도록 광범위하고 다양한 프로젝트들을 통해 혁신적인 접근 방법을 발전시켜 왔다. 로마, 파리, 선전에 본사를 두고, 170명의 전문적인 직원들로 구성되어 있으며, 600여 개의 프로젝트를 완성했고, 유럽, 아프리카, 아메리카, 아시아. 오스트레일리아에서 작업을 해왔으며, 많은 국제적인 상을 받았다.

Studio Fuksas, led by Massimiliano and Doriana Fuksas, is one of the most outstanding international architectural firm in the world. Over the past 40 years the company has developed an innovative approach through a strikingly wide variety of projects, ranging from urban interventions to airports, from museums to cultural centers and spaces for music, from convention centers to offices, from interiors to design collections. With headquarters in Rome, Paris and Shenzhen, and a staff of 170 professionals, the practice has completed more than 600 projects and has worked in Europe, Africa, America, Asia and Australia, receiving numerous international awards.

700
160
150
140
130
120
110
100
90
80
70
60
50
40
30
20
10
0 m
-10
-20
-30
-40

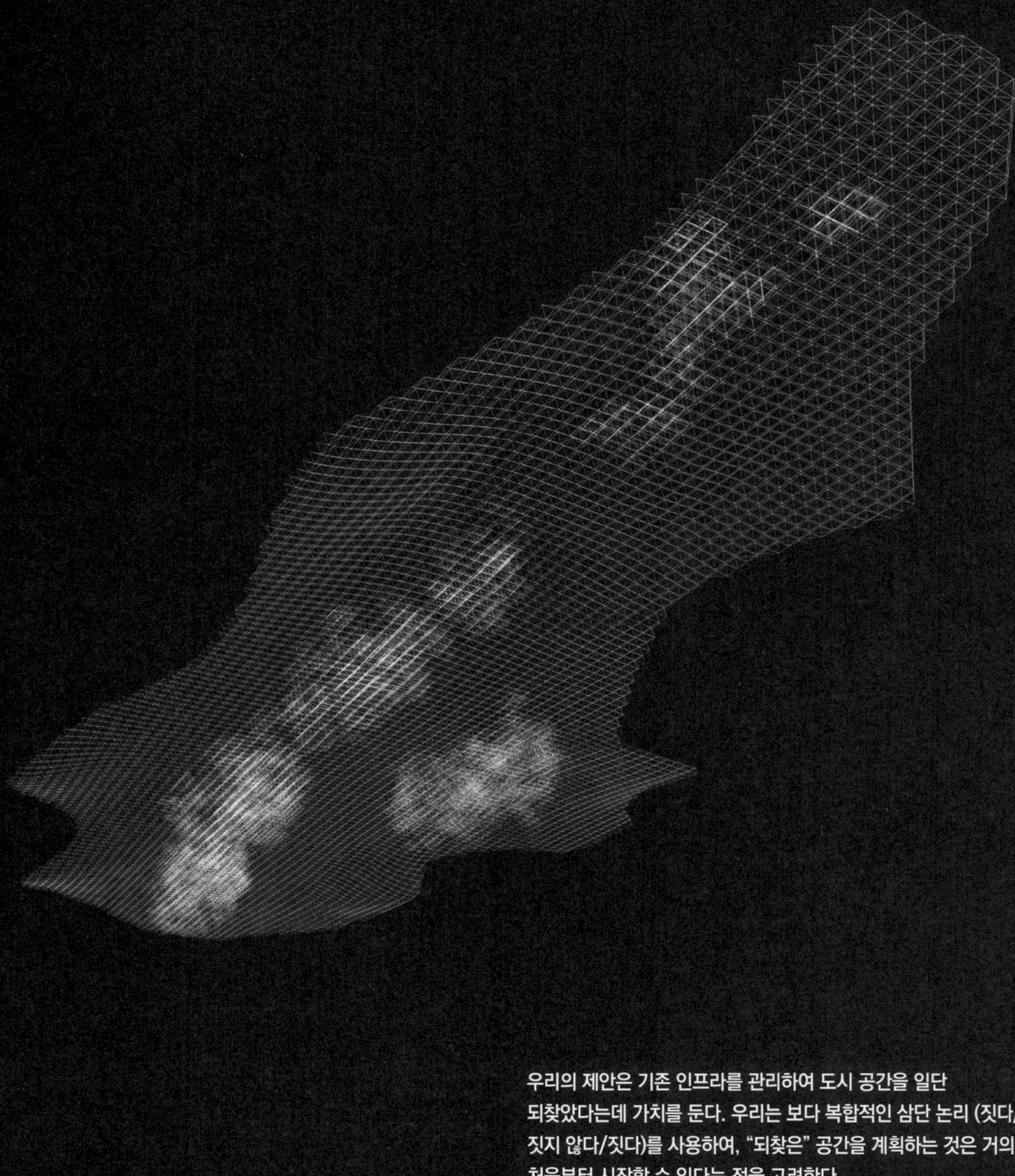

우리의 제안은 기존 인프라를 관리하여 도시 공간을 일단 되찾았다는데 가치를 둔다. 우리는 보다 복합적인 삼단 논리 (짓다/짓지 않다/짓다)를 사용하여, "되찾은" 공간을 계획하는 것은 거의 처음부터 시작할 수 있다는 점을 고려한다.

The proposal wants to put in value that once recovered that urban space, maintaining the existing infrastructures, we must use a more complex ternary logic, (built / not built / built), to consider that the planning of that "recovered" space can start almost from scratch.

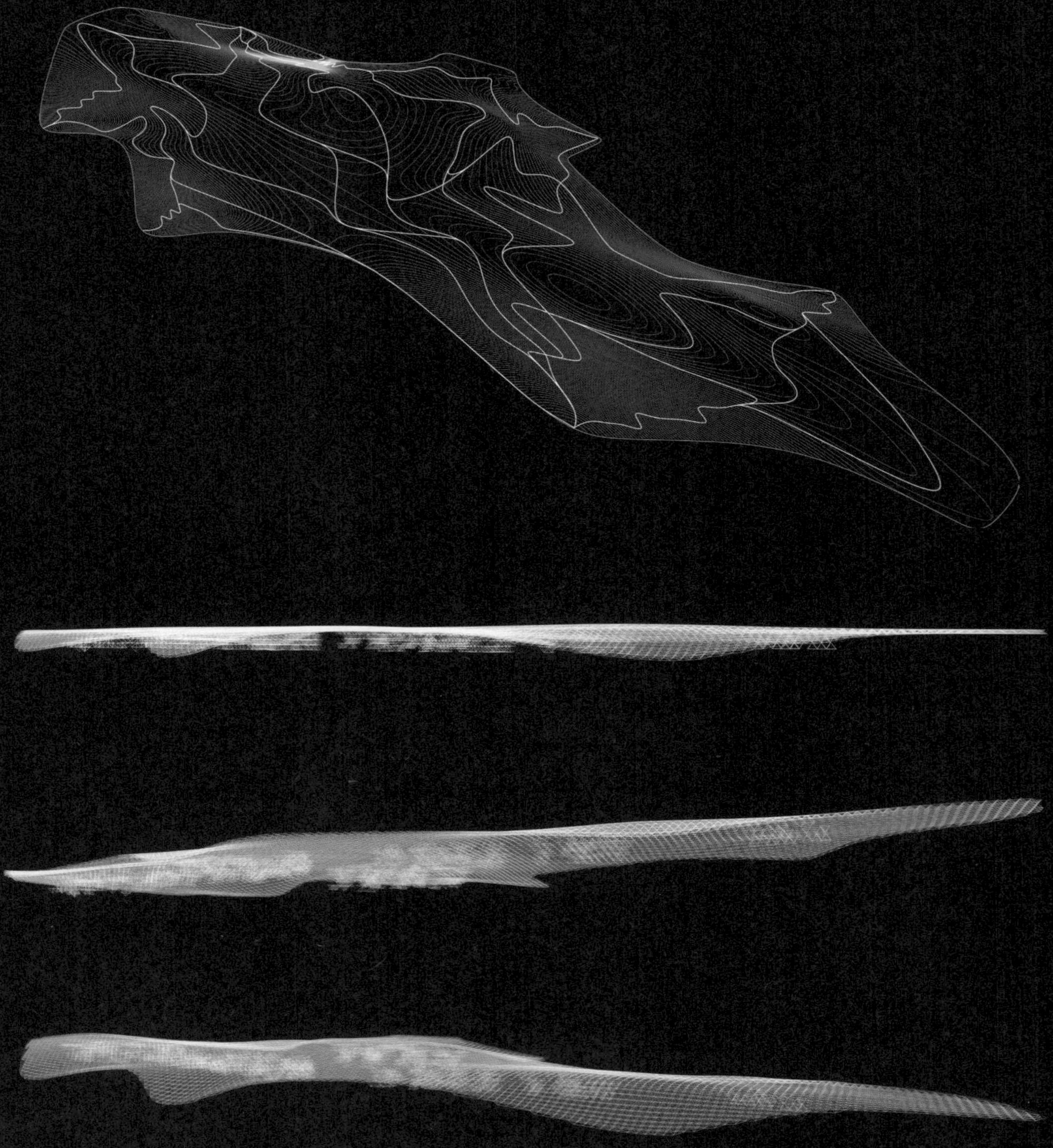

개념 1: 지지 구조의 상부에는 새로운 완충녹지공간, 하부에는 주차장과 스포츠 시설

Concept 1: New buffer green space on the top, and parking and sport facilities located below inside the support structures

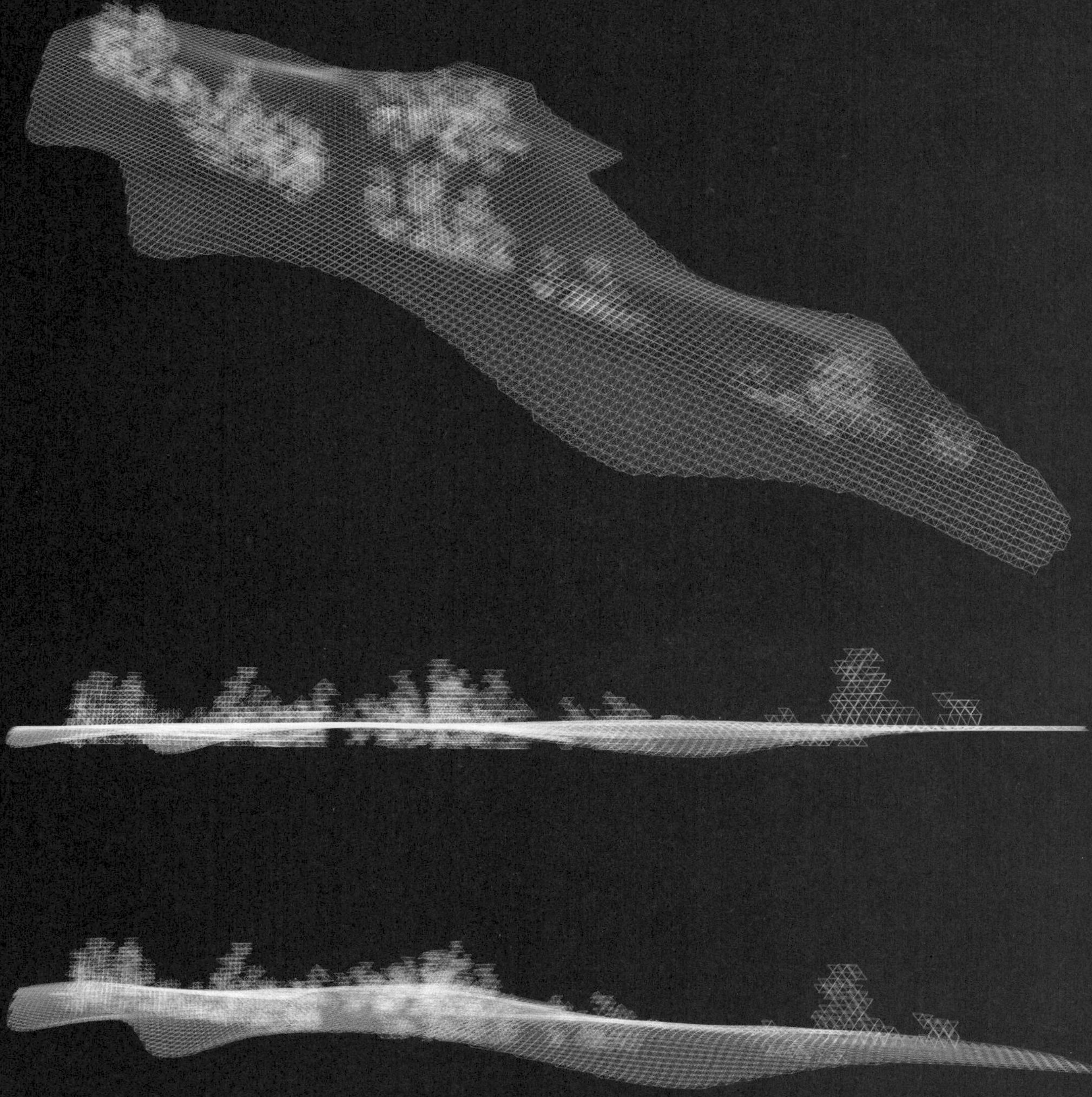

개념 2: 지지 구조의 상부의 새로운 완충녹지공간은 서로 다른 프로그램(스타트업 오피스, 공유사무실)을 담은 낮은 밀도의 건축물과 결합, 하부는 주차장과 스포츠시설

Concept 2: New buffer green space on the top combined with low density edifications with different programs (start-up offices, co-working spaces), and parking and sport facilities located below inside the support structures

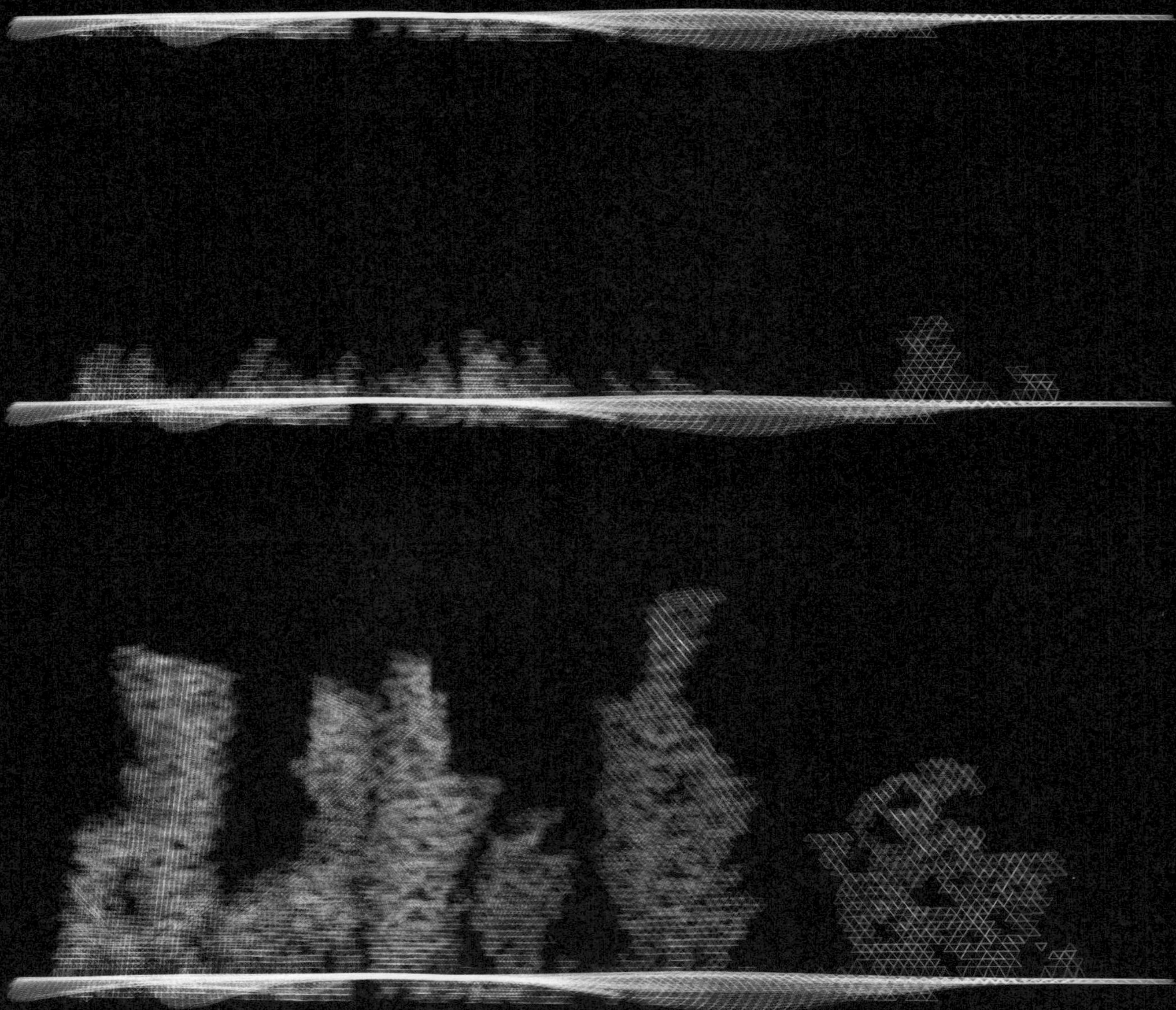

개념 3: 지지 구조의 상부의 새로운 완충녹지공간은 서로 다른 프로그램(주거, 상업, 문화, 스타트업 오피스, 공유사무실 등)을 담은 높은 밀도의 건축물과 결합, 하부는 주차장과 스포츠 시설

Concept 3: New buffer green space on the top combined with high density edifications with different programs (housing, shopping and cultural facilities, start-up offices, co-working spaces), and parking and sport facilities located below inside the support structures

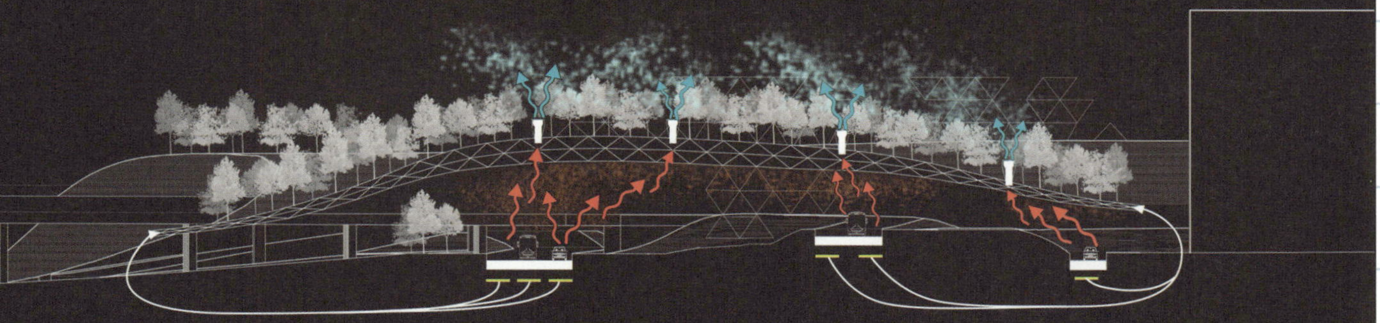

새로운 도시 공간은 기존 인프라가 만든 환경적인 불균형을 보완하고자 한다.

The new urban space tries to compensate part of the environmental imbalance that the existing infrastructure produces.

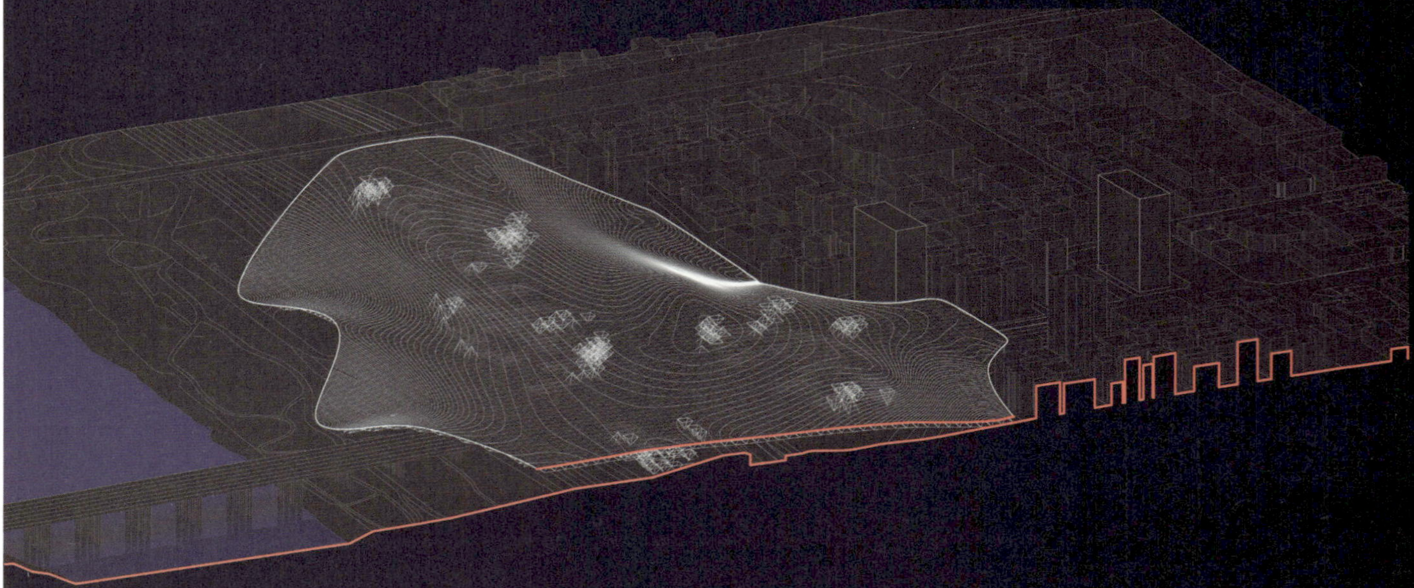

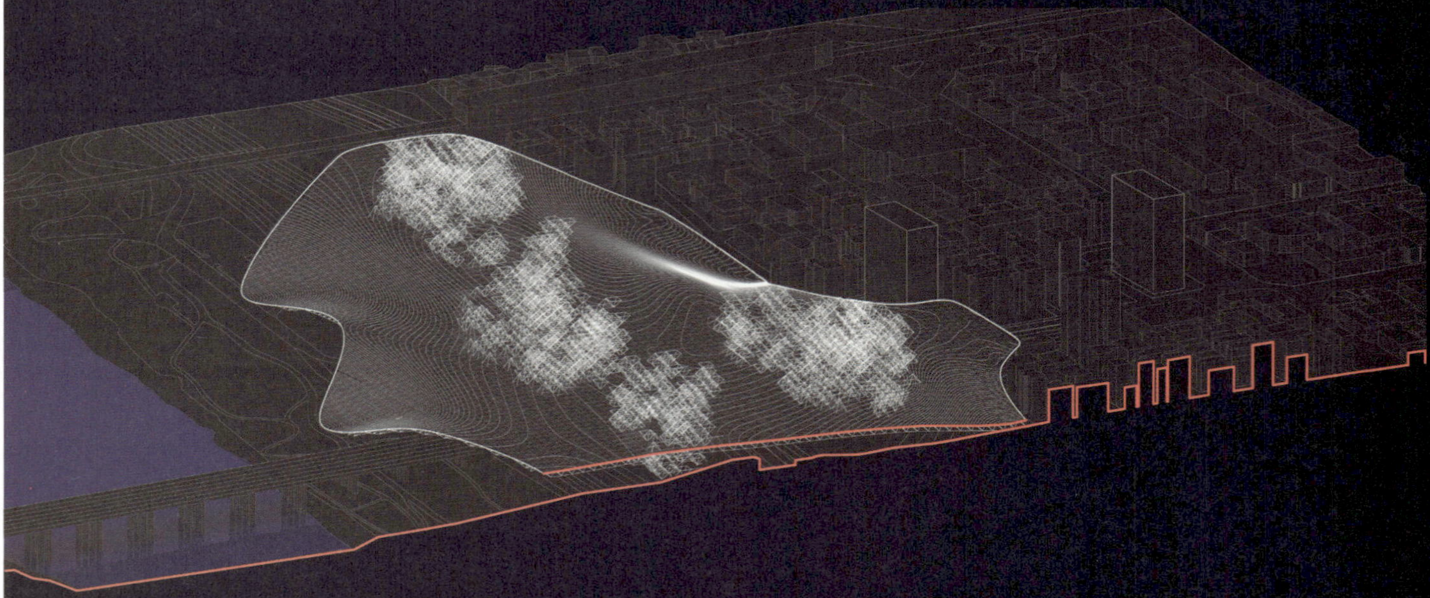

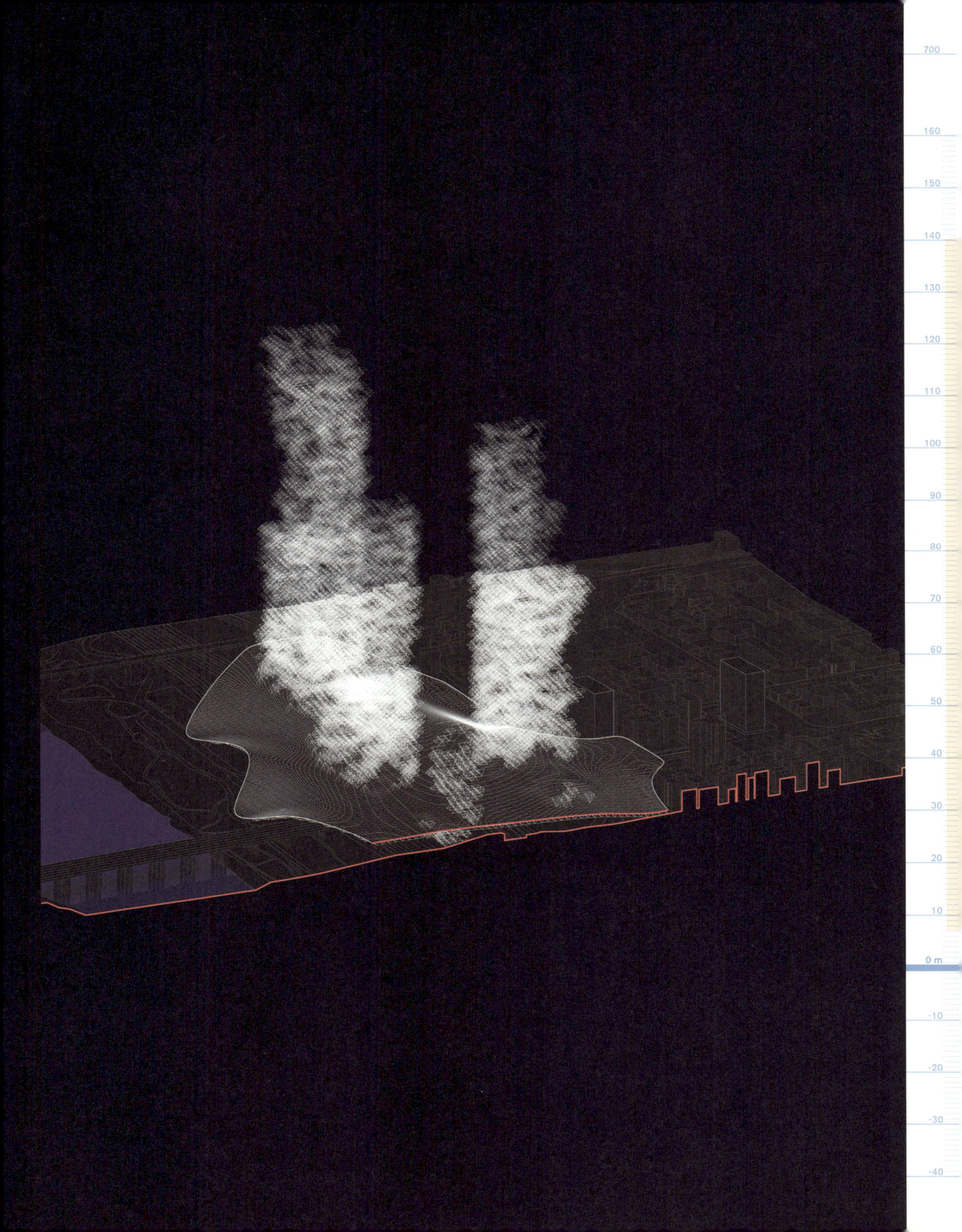
700
160
150
140
130
120
110
100
90
80
70
60
50
40
30
20
10
0 m
-10
-20
-30
-40

700
160
150
140
130
120
110
100
90
80
70
60
50
40
30
20
10
0 m
-10
-20
-30
-40

조민석

Minsuk Cho

산에서 강으로

남산과 한강의 한남대교를 이어주는 2km 길이의 한남대로는 양단에서 82m의 레벨 차이가 나는 변화무쌍한 자연/인공 지형과, 그에 못지않게 복합적인 도시적 요소들로 구성되어 있다. 이 한남대로에 대한 고찰을 기반으로 하는 건축적 제안인 〈산에서 강으로〉는 보행자 문화를 중심으로 하는 서울의 도시 재생에 대한 공명이자, 이 도시 조직의 뿌리는 풍부한 자연 환경임을 환기시키고자 하는 시도이다. 급격한 성장이 야기한 혼잡하고도 파편화된 도시풍경은 자연을 전면으로 내세운 다음의 5가지 개입을 통해 더욱 매력적으로 일구어질 것이다. 또한 도시 인프라스트럭처의 언어와 문화공간 사이의 동시다발적인 교류를 통해 공공 영역의 생성을 꾀하고자 한다.

1--- 브릿지 게이트 - 남산으로 직접 이어지는 새로운 보행자 다리는 하부의 번잡한 교차로와는 독립된 산책로로써 보행자들을 이태원 방향의 도시조직으로 이끈다.

2--- 점유 가능한 차음벽 - 한남대로의 여분의 폭은 실내외가 점유 가능한 선형 구조물로 전환되어 내부로는 상업 및 문화기반 시설이, 외부로는 한남대로를 따라 도심 속 산책을 가능케 할 옥상 정원이 사회적 활동들을 촉발시킨다.

From Mountain to River

From Mountain to River endeavors to reciprocate the urban regeneration of Seoul's pedestrian culture along a 2 km stretch of Hannamdaero with an 82m level change – from Namsan Mountain to the Han River waterfront at the Hannam Bridge. The highly exaggerated natural/artificial topography of its municipality is unequivocally a vital root to the urban fabric. An incarnation of five distinct interventions cultivates to re-fascinate the nature to the foreground of post chaotic and fragmented landscapes of sudden growths. The simultaneous exchange between the language of infrastructure and production of cultural artifacts synthesize the public realm of the project.

1— Bridge Gate - a new pedestrian bridge provides direct access to Namsan Mountain and marks the gateway into the urban fabric of Itaewon above a vast, intimidating intersection.

2— Inhabitable Sound Barrier – the extraneous width of Hannamdaero is turned into a 750m long occupiable linear building with commercial and cultural functions and a roof park that utilizes road space, widens sidewalks and triggers social activities.

조민석은 2003년 서울에서 매스스터디스 건축사무소를 설립했다. 사회 문화 및 도시 연구를 통해 새로운 건축적 담론을 제시하는 그의 대표작으로는 픽셀 하우스, 실종된 매트릭스, 다발 매트릭스, 상하이 엑스포 2010: 한국관, 다음 스페이스 닷 원, 티스톤/이니스프리, 사우스케이프, 돔-이노, 대전대학교 기숙사 등을 꼽을 수 있고, 최근에는 서울 시네마테크 국제공모전에서 당선되었다. 2011년 광주디자인비엔날레 전시를 공동기획했고, 2014년 베니스 비엔날레 한국관 커미셔너/큐레이터로 황금사자상 수상하였다. 2014년 삼성 플라토 미술관에서 〈매스스터디스 건축하기 전/후〉 개인전 등 다수의 전시와 강의를 통해 전 세계적으로 활동하고 있다.

Minsuk Cho founded the Seoul-based firm Mass Studies in 2003. He has been committed to the discourse of architecture through socio-cultural and urban research, and mostly built works, which have been recognized globally. Representative works include the Pixel House, Missing Matrix, Bundle Matrix, Shanghai Expo 2010: Korea Pavilion, Daum Space.1, Tea Stone/Innisfree, Southcape, Dome-ino, the Daejeon University Student Dormitory, and was recently selected to design the new Seoul Cinematheque. Active beyond his practice, he co-curated the 2011 Gwangju Design Biennale, and was the commissioner and co-curator of the Korean Pavilion for the 14th International Architecture Exhibition - la Biennale di Venezia, which was awarded the Gold Lion for Best National Participation. In late 2014, PLATEAU Samsung Museum of Art, Seoul, held their first ever architecture exhibition, highlighting his works in a solo exhibition titled "Before/After: Mass Studies Does Architecture." Cho is an active lecturer and speaker at symposiums worldwide.

FROM MOUNTAIN
TO RIVER
1 BRIDGE GATE
2 INHABITABLE SOUND BARRIER
3 LEISURE VAULTS
4 PARK'N'PARK & LINEAR BLOCK
5 RIVERSIDE BAZAAR
-40
-30
-20
-10
0 m
10
20
30
40
50
60
70
80
90
100
110
120
130
140
150
160
700

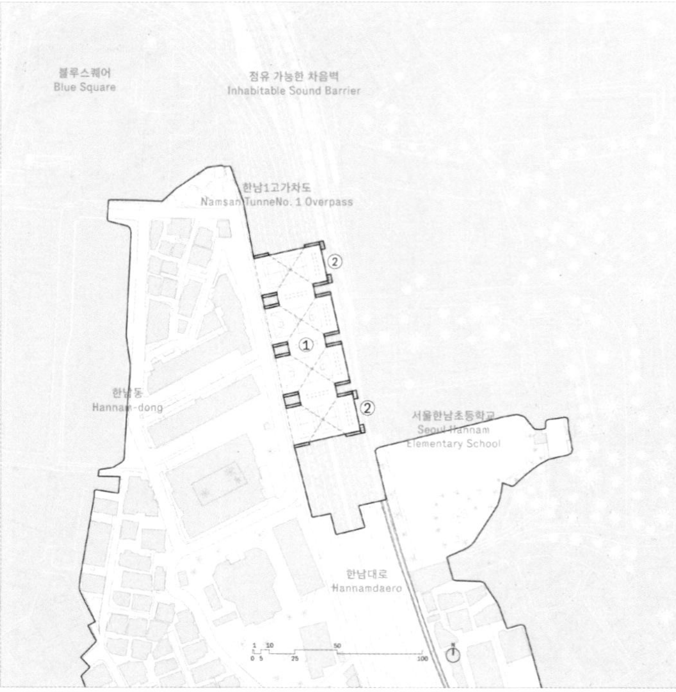

1. 레저 볼트
2. 레저 볼트에서 점유 가능한 차음벽으로의 접근을 위한 수직 동선

1. Leisure Vaults
2. vertical access to the Inhabitable Sound Barrier from the Leisure Vaults

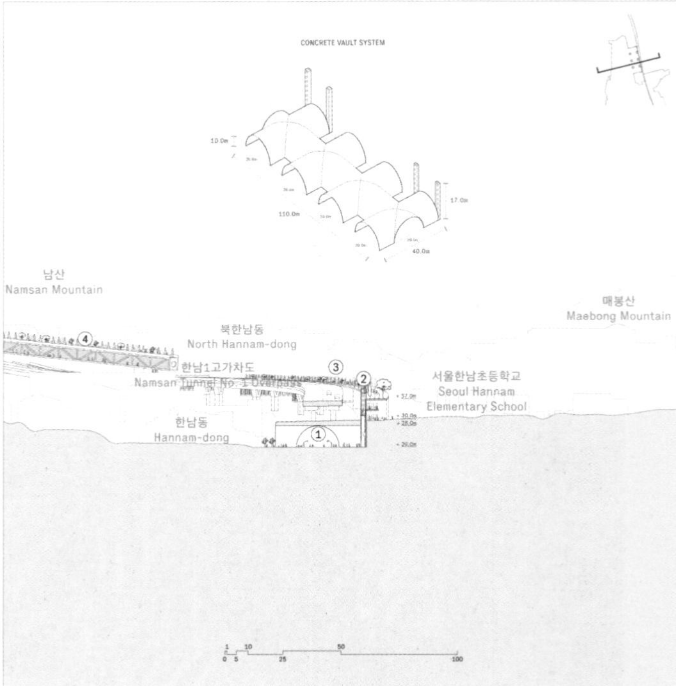

1. 레저 볼트
2. 레저 볼트에서 점유 가능한 차음벽으로의 접근을 위한 수직 동선
3. 점유 가능한 차음벽
4. 브릿지 게이트

1. Leisure Vaults
2. vertical access to the Inhabitable Sound Barrier from the Leisure Vaults
3. Inhabitable Sound Barrier
4. Bridge Gate

3--- 레저 볼트 - 한남대로의 급격한 레벨 차이로 인해 생겨난 10~15m 높이의 옹벽 뒤편으로 볼트 지붕으로 덮인 실내 공간을 파내어 공공 참여가 가능한 새로운 지하 레저공간을 제공한다.

4--- Park'n'Park와 선형 블록 - 현재 개발되지 않은 채 남아 있는 빈 땅은 32,450㎡의 넓은 공원으로 다시 탄생한다. 공공주차장과 이를 에워싼 상업공간들로 이루어진 이 공원은 부유하는 주거/업무 선형 블록 아래를 통과하여 매봉산의 숨겨진 입구로 연결된다. 이 새로운 복합체는 추후 버스중앙차선 정류장의 지붕으로도 활용된다.

5--- 한강 시민장터 - 기존 한남 고수부지로 향하는 지하 공간에는 연속된 볼트 모듈을 사용하여 부분적으로 땅에 덮인 공간을 연출하여 한강으로의 접근성을 향상시키며 시민장터와 같은 공공 공간으로 활용된다. 또한 교외 통근열차로 사용되는 한남역을 한남대교와 수직적으로 연결시킴으로써 출·퇴근자들의 통행에 도움이 되고자 한다.

3— Leisure Vaults - at the northern bend of the southbound Hannamdaero is a 10-15m tall retaining wall created by the drastic level difference from the road, and is an opportunity to re-sculpt the man-made mound into a series of internal vaults for public engagement.

4— Park'n'Park and Linear Block - an undeveloped empty plot of land reorganized as a large 32,450m² park consists of a two-levels of public parking below and is enclosed by retail spaces. The surface of the park continues below a 'floating,' 9-story linear block for office and residential use, and crosses over Hannamdaero to link to the hidden entrance to Maebong Mountain Park. This new complex will also umbrella the future bus median lane on Hannamdaero.

5— Riverside Bazaar - at a close distance to the remote commuter rail, Hannam Station, the existing, isolated river access point is upgraded into a series of prefabricated sail vault modules generating a wide opening and passage for a fluent approach to the waterfront and public gatherings, such as a marketplace, along the Han River. Access to Hannam Station is also improved by the addition of a vertical entity from Hannam Bridge.

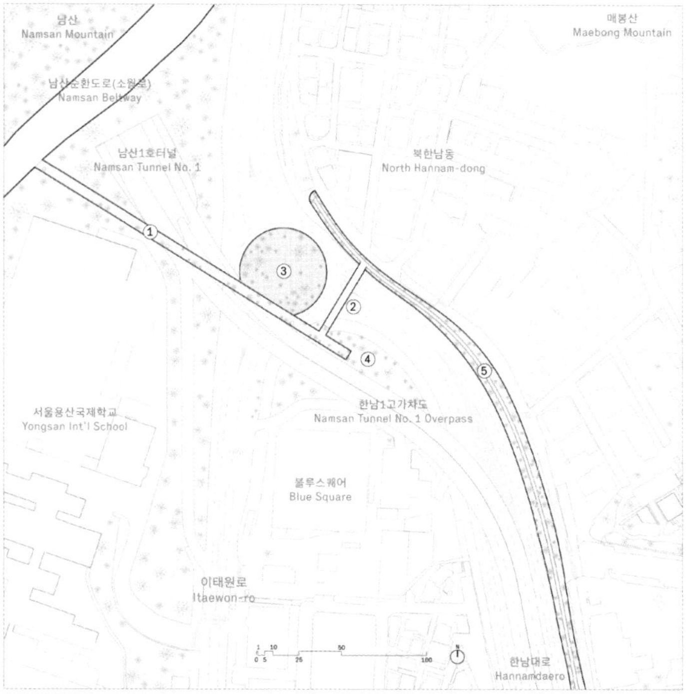

1. 브릿지 게이트
2. 연결로
3. 녹색 회전교차로
4. 터널 고가도로 아래의 공원
5. 점유 가능한 차음벽

1. Bridge Gate
2. connecting bridge
3. green traffic circle park
4. park below tunnel overpass
5. Inhabitable Sound Barrier

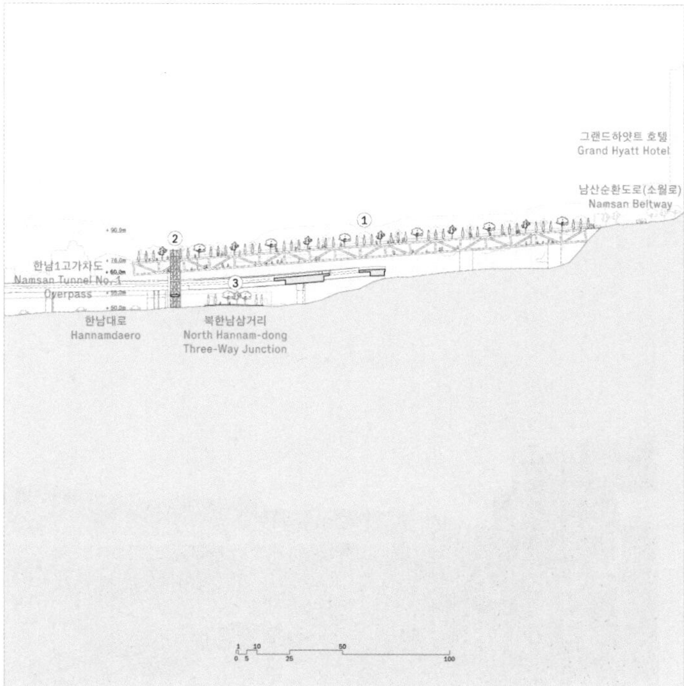

1. 브릿지 게이트
2. 브릿지 게이트로의 수직 동선
3. 녹색 회전교차로

1. Bridge Gate
2. vertical connection to Bridge Gate
3. green traffic circle park

1. 750m 길이의 점유 가능한 차음벽
2. 한남대로 아래의 레저 볼트
3. Park'n'Park 연결
4. 버스 중앙 차선
5. 브릿지 게이트
6. 녹색 회전교차로
7. Park'n'Park와 선형 블록

1. 750m long Inhabitable Sound Barrier
2. Leisure Vaults below Hannamdaero
3. connection to Park'n'Park
4. bus median lane
5. Bridge Gate
6. green traffic circle park
7. Park'n'Park & Linear Block

BEFORE: 북행 7차선 남행 3차선으로 구성되어 차선 불균형을 이루는 북한남동삼거리 부근의 한남대로

An imbalanced Hannamdaero with seven-lanes Northbound and three-lanes Southbound near the North Hannam-dong Three-way Junction

AFTER: 점유 가능한 차음벽

Inhabitable Sound Barrier

점유 가능한 차음벽 - 한남대로의 여분의 폭은 실내외가 점유 가능한 선형 구조물로 전환되어 내부로는 상업 및 문화기반 시설이, 외부로는 한남대로를 따라 도심 속 산책을 가능케 할 옥상 정원이 사회적 활동들을 촉발시킨다.

INHABITABLE SOUND BARRIER - the extraneous width of Hannamdaero is turned into a 750m long occupiable linear building with commercial and cultural functions and a roof park that utilizes road space, widens sidewalks and triggers social activities.

BEFORE: 남산1호터널 시작지점 아래 위치한 높이 10-15m, 길이 205m의 옹벽

10-15m tall, 205m long retaining wall below Hannamdaero at the start of the the Namsan Tunnel No. 1 Overpass

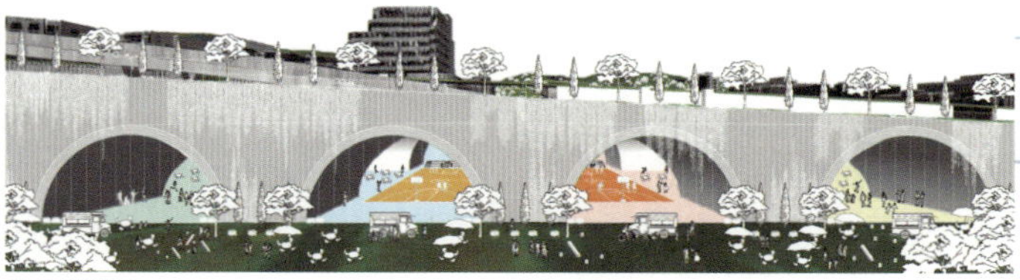

AFTER: 레저 볼트

Leisure Vaults

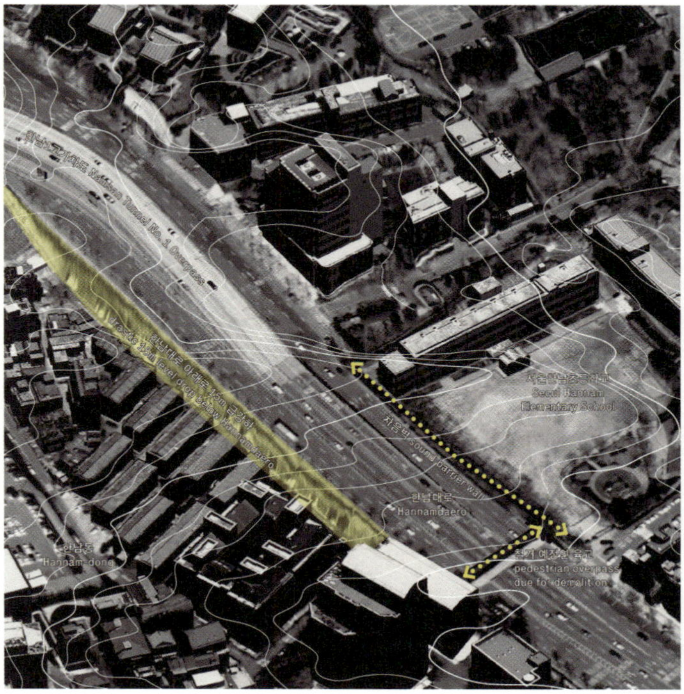

레저 볼트 – 한남대로의 급격한 레벨 차이로 인해 생겨난 10-15m 높이의 옹벽 뒤편으로 볼트 지붕으로 덮인 실내 공간을 파내어 공공 참여가 가능한 새로운 지하 레저공간을 제공한다.

LEISURE VAULTS - at the northern bend of the southbound Hannamdaero is a 10-15m tall retaining wall created by the drastic level difference from the road, and is an opportunity to re-sculpt the man-made mound into a series of internal vaults for public engagement.

BEFORE: 한남오거리 북쪽의 순천향대학교 병원 버스 정류장과 육교

The Soon Chung Hyang University Hospital bus stop and pedestrian bridge on Hannamdaero immediately north of Hannam Ogeori

AFTER: Park'n'Park

Park'n'Park

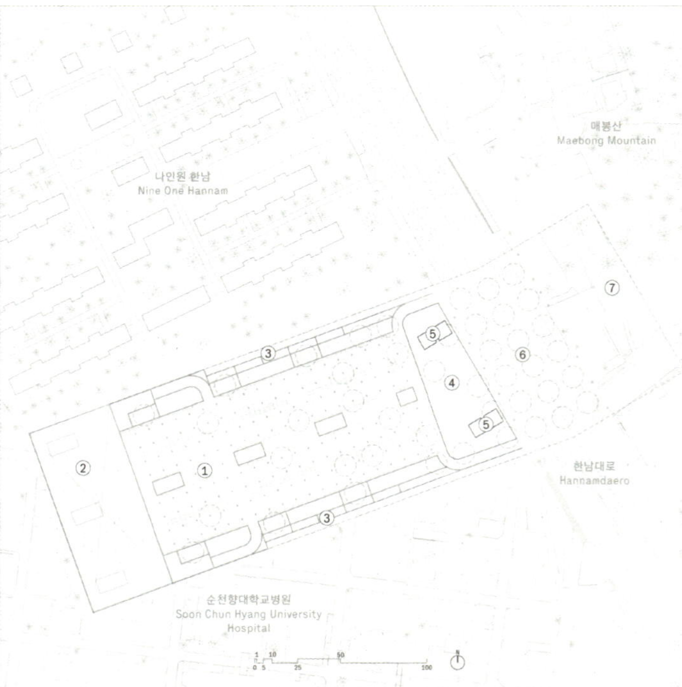

1. 1층 주차장
2. 지하1층 주차장
3. 1층 상점
4. 1층 중앙 마켓
5. 선형 블록의 코어
6. 중앙버스전용차로
7. 매봉산과의 연결

1. 1F parking
2. B1 parking
3. 1F retail
4. 1F central market
5. Linear Block Cores
6. bus median lane on Hammandaero
7. direct connection to Maebong Mountain

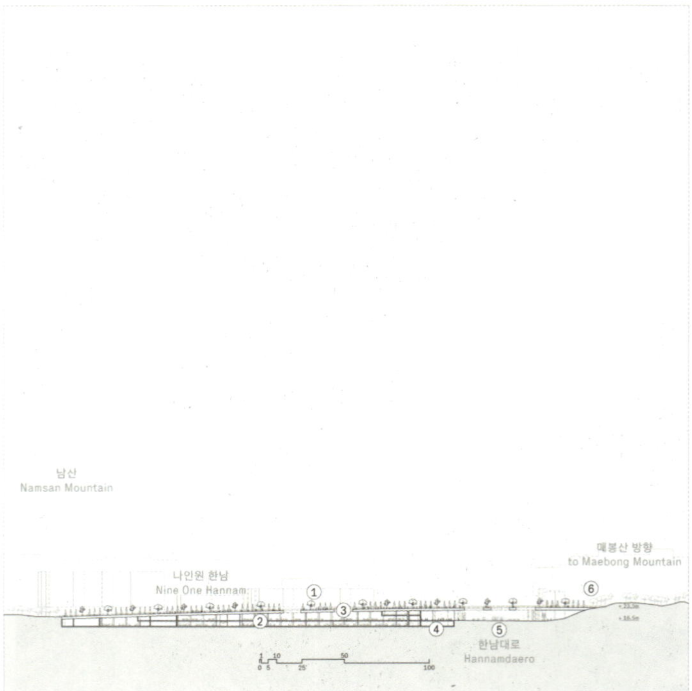

1. 공원
2. 1층 주차장 및 상점
3. 공원 천공
4. 중앙 마켓
5. 중앙버스전용차로
6. 매봉산과의 연결

1. park
2. 1F parking and retail
3. perforated park surface
4. 1F/B1 central market
5. bus median lane on Hammandaero
6. direct connection to Maebong Mountain

AFTER: Park'n'Park

Park'n'Park

AFTER: Park'n'Park와 선형 블록

Park'n'Park & Linear Block

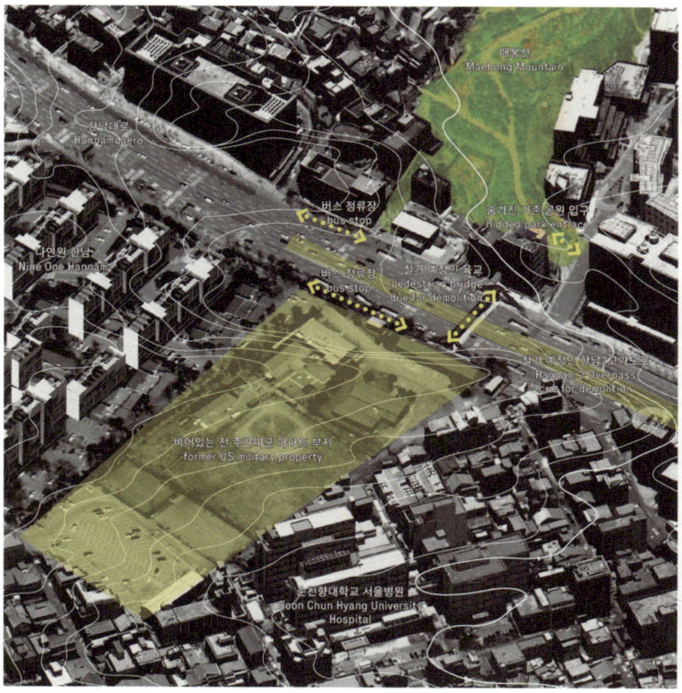

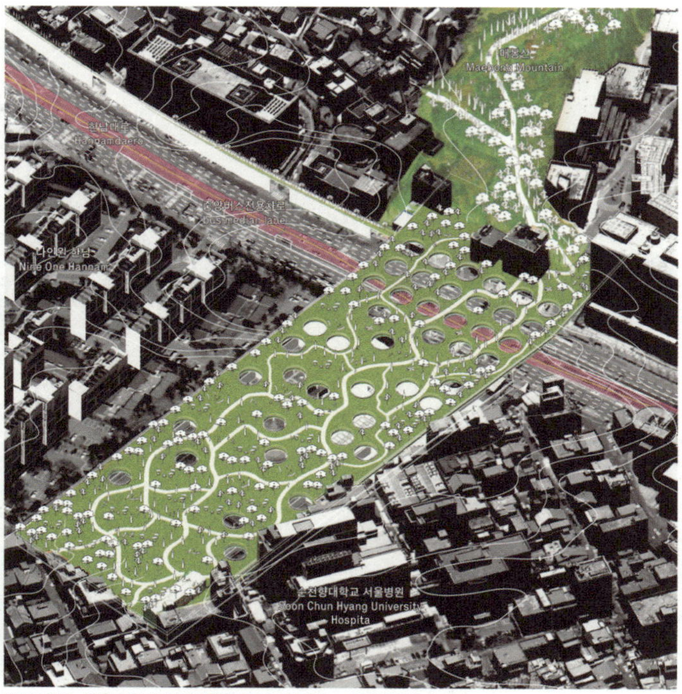

PARK'N'PARK - 2개층의 주차장이 마련되어있어 약 1,000대의 차량이 머무를수 있으며, 32,450m²의 옥상공원, 그리고 도로에 면한 12개의 상점과 중앙시장이 배치된다.

PARK'N'PARK - a parking structure, a rooftop park, retail and dining to liven up the disengaged pedestrian and commuters flow in the area and is essentially a significant bridge structure that connects the surrounding

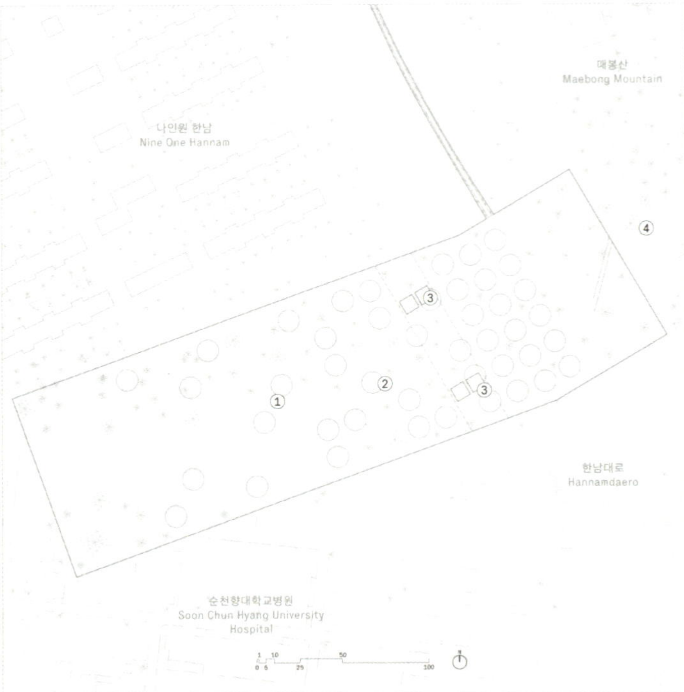

1. 공원
2. 공원 천공
3. 선형 블록의 코어
4. 매봉산과의 연결

1. park
2. perforated park surface to 1F/B1 parking below
3. Linear Block Cores
4. direct connection to Maebong Mountain

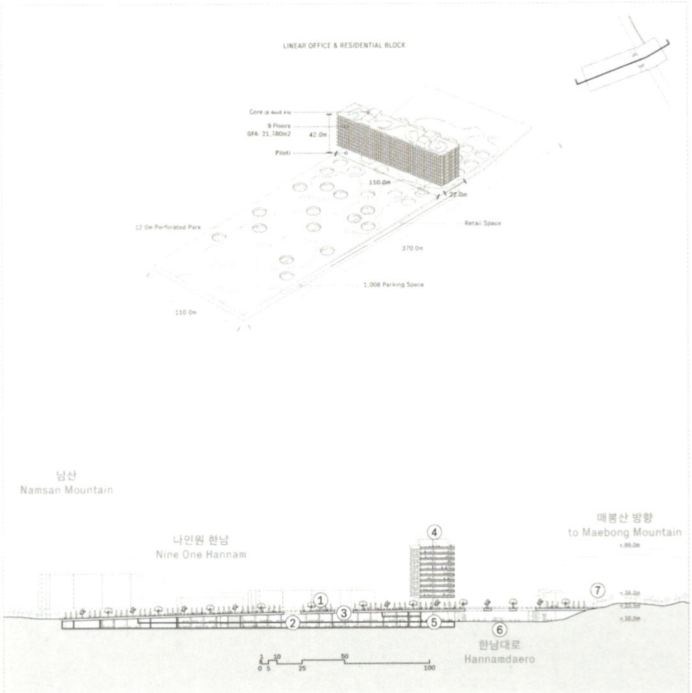

1. 공원
2. 주차장 및 상점
3. 빛과 환기를 위한 공원 천공
4. 9층 선형 블록
5. 중앙 마켓
6. 중앙버스전용차로
7. 매봉산과의 연결

1. park
2. 1F-B1 parking and 1F retail
3. perforated park surface for light and ventilation
4. 9-story Linear Block
5. central market
6. bus median lane
7. direct connection to Maebong Mountain

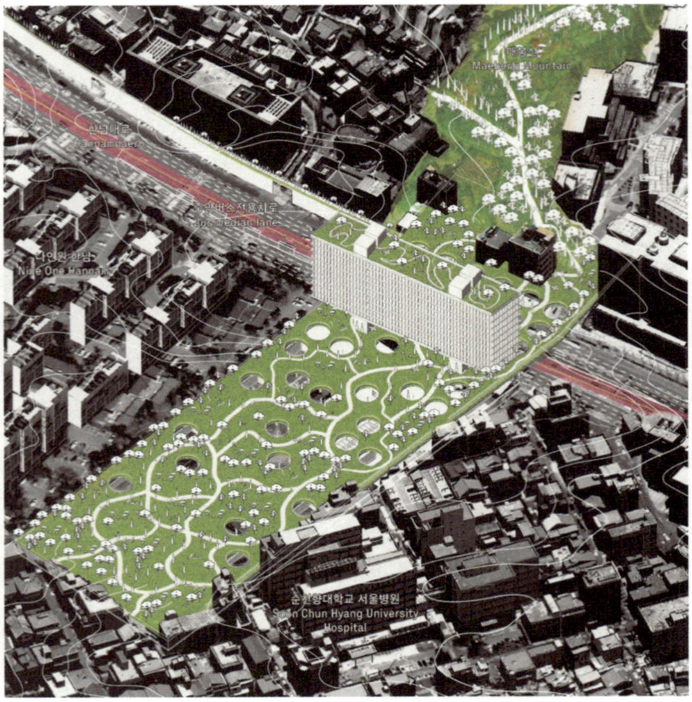

PARK'N'PARK와 선형 블록 – 공동개발로 이뤄질 9개층의 오피스: 높이 52.5m, 너비 22m, 길이 110m의 선형 블록은 코어들로 지탱되어 옥상공원으로부터 10.5m 더 높은 공간에 위치하게 된다.

PARK'N'PARK & LINEAR BLOCK - a 'floating,' nine-story office: 52.5m tall, 22m wide, and 110m long linear block is elevated 10.5m from the surface of the park on cores and direct connection to Maebong Mountain.

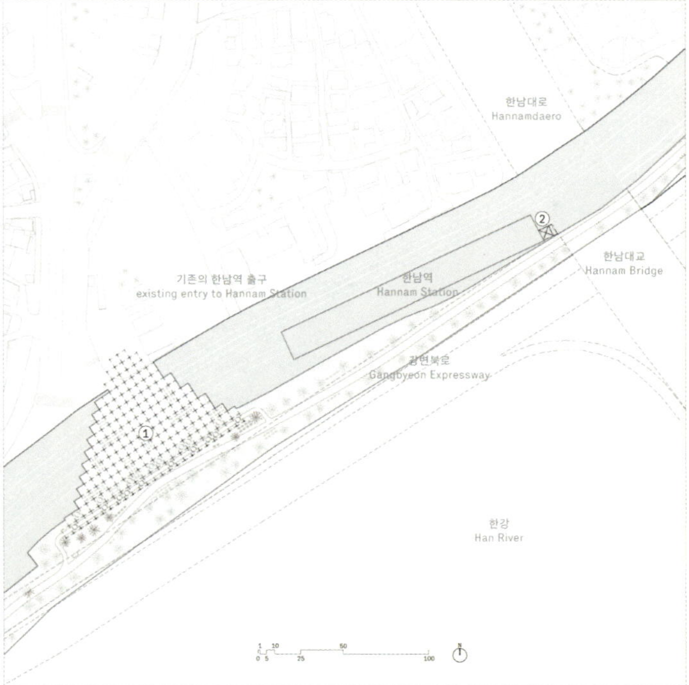

1. 한강 시민장터
2. 한남역과 한남대교의 수직 연결

1. Riverside Bazaar
2. new vertical access to Hannam Station from Hannam Bridge

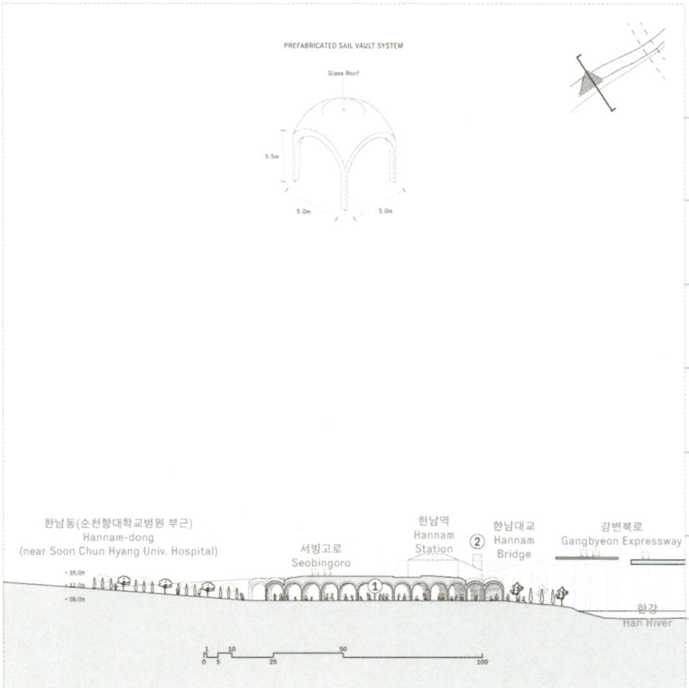

1. 한강 시민장터
2. 한남역과 한남대교의 수직 연결

1. Riverside Bazaar
2. new vertical access point to Hannam Station from Hannam Bridge

BEFORE: 강변북로 아래의 한남역과 한강공원

Hannam Station and the Han River Park below the Gangbyeon Expressway

AFTER: 한강 시민장터

Riverside Bazaar

700
160
150
140
130
120
110
100
90
80
70
60
50
40
30
20
10
0 m
-10
-20
-30
-40

프란시스 솔러 + It's, 미셸 드빈

Francis Soler + It's, Michael Desvigne

구두장이의 섬

성수동의 변화는 안에 숨겨진 무언가를 표현한 생텍쥐페리의 『어린 왕자』에 나오는 코끼리를 삼킨 보아뱀 같다. 여기 성동교와 장안교 사이에 강둑 위를 달리는 고속도로를 흡수하여 구두장이의 섬의 도시와 사회를 삼켜버린 보아뱀을 그렸다. 마치 코끼리처럼 고속도로는 움직일 수 없는 것처럼 보여서, 강으로 접근성을 만들기 위하여 고속도로 위에 거대한 수평판을 덮어서 이 고속도로를 약 800미터 길이와 도로 폭을 가진 섬으로 만들었다. 구두장이 섬의 실루엣은 200미터 높이의 가늘고 긴 수직 구조물로 완성되는데, 이는 새로 만들어진 이 지역의 존재감을 보여주는 서울의 스카이라인이 될 것이다.
고속도로 아래를 지난 물은 광나루로로 흘러 조용한 호수를 만들며, 새로운 건물을 만들어낸 수평판을 비춘다. 기존의 도시는 이제 장소를 만든다. 남쪽으로부터 태양의 빛을 받아 장인들의 이야기로 물들인 곳. 그들의 원래 영역이 사라지는 곳에서 만들어진 화해의 장소이다.
파리의 세인트루이스 섬처럼 구두장이의 섬은 양쪽으로 물이 있어, 섬의 입면을 만드는 건축물들 아래로 흐른다. 섬의 중앙은 도시와 섬을 연결하기 뻗어 나간 우아한 선형의 골목들이 만나는 비워진 곳이다.
수평판은 확장이 가능한 열린 시스템이지만, 동시에 불완전하지 않다. 성수동과 같이 강을 따라 지나가는 고속도로로 고통받는 유사한 지역인 동쪽과 서쪽 방향으로 무한히 확장할 수 있다. 새로운 도시의 첫 번째 조각이자 슈퍼그라운드 서울의 경계를 유용하게 다시 만들 수 있는 잠재성을 갖고 있다.

Shoemakers' Island

The story of the transformation of the district of SEONGSU-DONG is a bit like that of Saint Exupéry's Little Prince, when he shows a boa digesting an elephant as the hidden basis of his picture.
Here, on the banks of the river, between the bridges of SEONGDONG-GYO and JANGAN-GYO, we absorbed the impressive highway that ran along the embankment of the river to draw a new boa swallowing the urban and social fabric of Shoemakers' Island. The highway seemed to us as immovable as an elephant so, in order to link up with the river, we isolated it from beneath and from the surrounding spaces by laying a slab on top of it, along its full length, turning it into an island about 800m long and the width of the lanes. The silhouette of Shoemaker's Island was completed by a slender, 200m high vertical construction, marking, in the skyline of SEOUL the presence of the new district that we are constructing.
The water passed under the highway and reached the river GWANGNARU-RO, creating a calm water basin in which the reflected slab formed a new building. Thus we rotated the existing urban scheme (which turned its back on the city) to give the place - receiving the full light of the sun from the south and tinged with stories of artisans - all the power of a reconciliation of men with the erased footprint of their home territory.
Isle Saint Louis, in PARIS, has some of the same characteristics as Shoemakers 'island in SEOUL, with water on each side, flowing directly beneath the facades of buildings that shape the flanks of the island. Equally, in its centre, you find a porous territory of converging alleys from which elegant strips spread to connect the island to the city.
The slab is built as a system open to territorial expansion and yet it does not leave the city incomplete. It can extend indefinitely, towards the east as well as the west, over neighbouring lands of the same nature as those of SEONGSU-DONG, suffering the same constraint of motorways along the river. It is potentially this first fragment of a new city that can usefully reformat the inner boundaries of SEOUL-SUPERGROUND.

프란시스 솔러는 프랑스 건축가로 1985년 사무소를 시작했다. 사무소의 활동들은 작은 시설에서부터 주거까지, 스튜디오에서부터 도시개발 프로젝트까지 매우 다양하다. 프랑스 및 해외의 주요 다양한 설계 공모들에 참여해왔다. 연구와 혁신에 중점을 둔 로마, 제네바, 파리에서 Alessandro Cambi, Francesco Marinelli, Paolo Mezzalama가 2016년에 설립한 이탈리아 스튜디오 It's와 협업 예정이며 광장이나 조경에서부터 도시계획에 이르기까지 다양한 영역에서 활동하고 있는 프랑스 도시계획가이자 조경가인 Michel Desvigne와도 함께 작업할 예정이다.

Francis Soler is a French architect who set up his private practice in 1985. Its activities are extremely varied: from facilities to housing and from studios to urban development. The office takes part in major competitions for public projects both in France and abroad. He will be working with It's, Italian architecture studio that focuses on research and innovation, founded in 2016 by Alessandro Cambi, Francesco Marinelli and Paolo Mezzalama with branches in Rome, Geneva and Paris, and with Michel Desvigne, French urban planner and landscape architect, internationally renowned for his rigorous and contemporary work that covers many different fields: from public squares and gardens to large-scale landscape strategy and city planning.

700
160
150
140
130
120
110
100
90
80
70
60
50
40
30
20
10
0 m
-10
-20
-30
-40

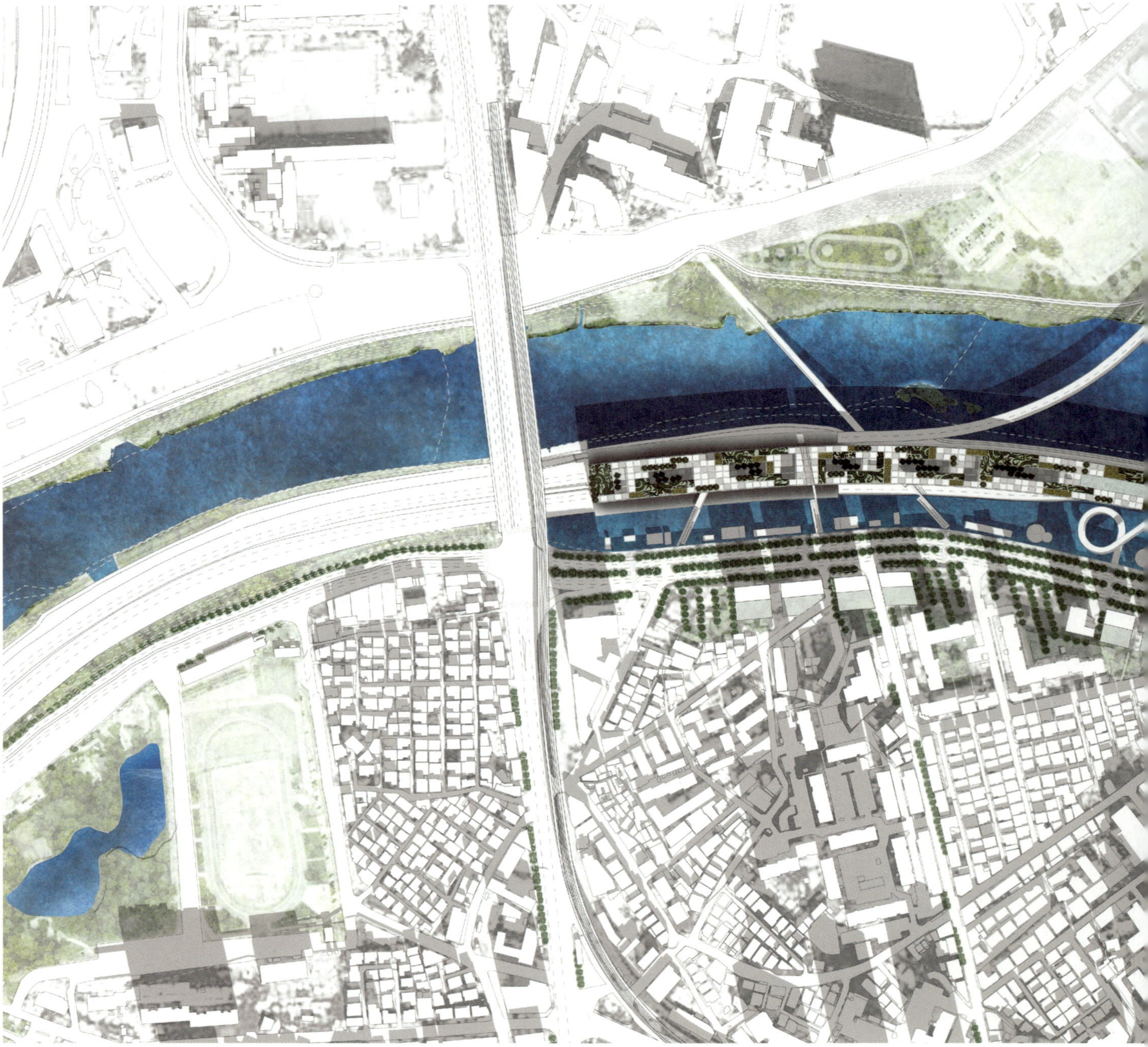

Masterplan

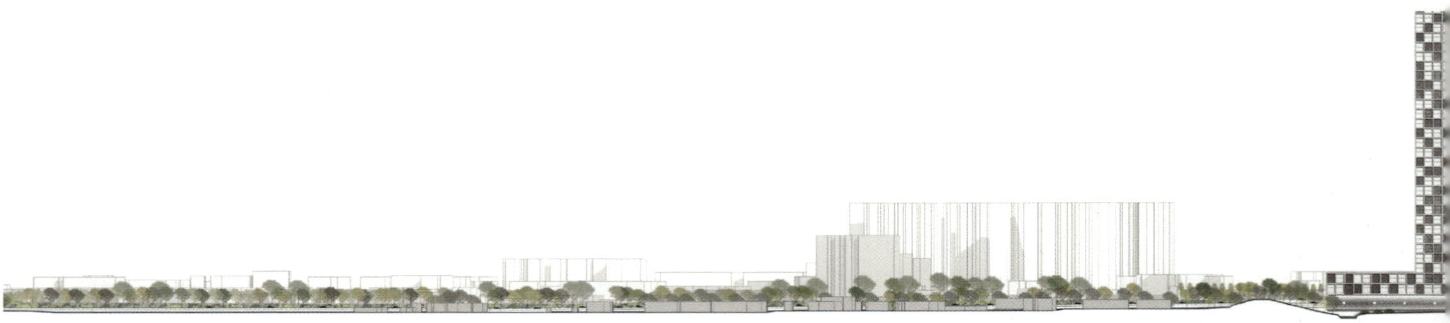

Urban section

0 10 20 50 100 m

0 10 20 50 100 m

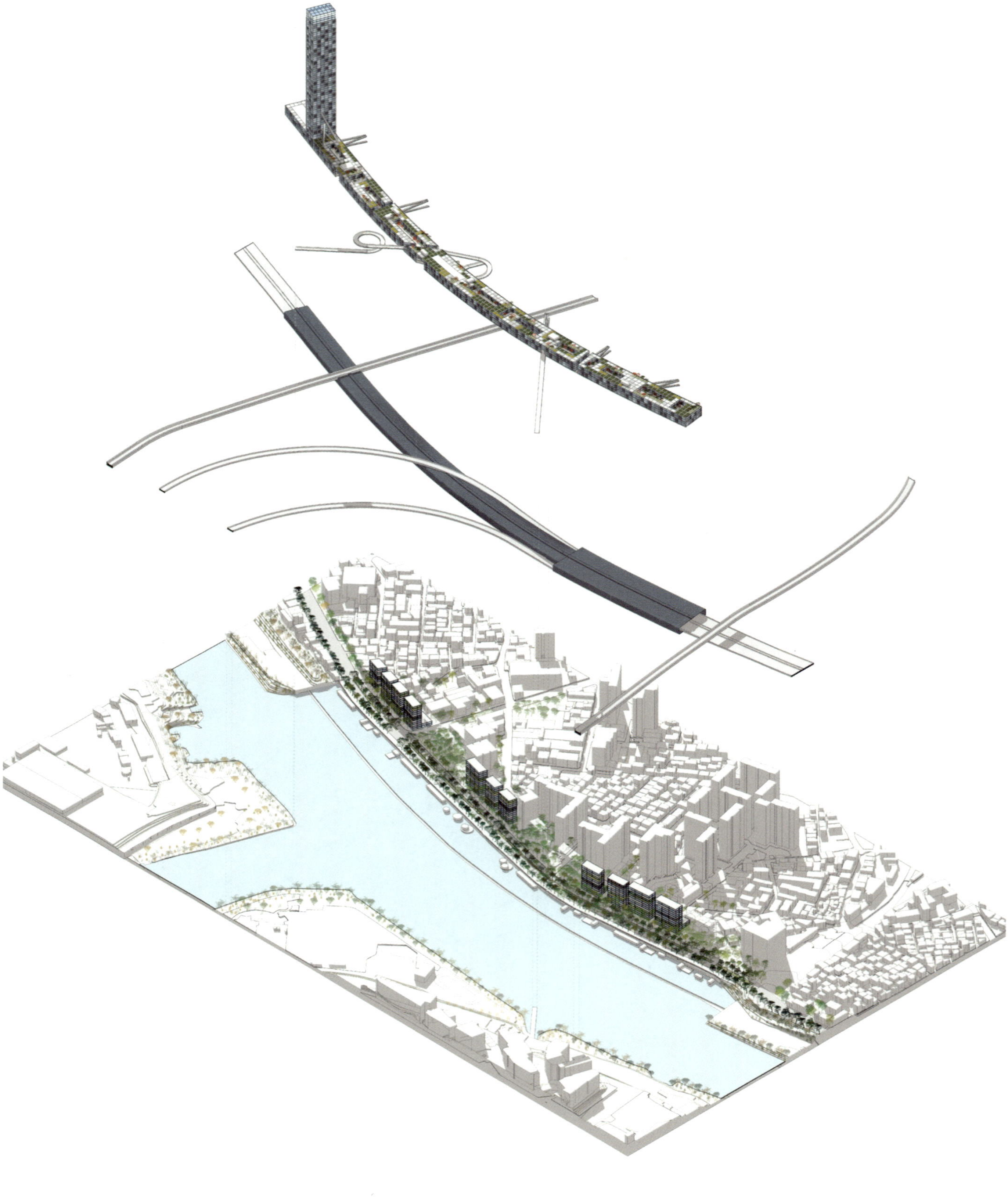

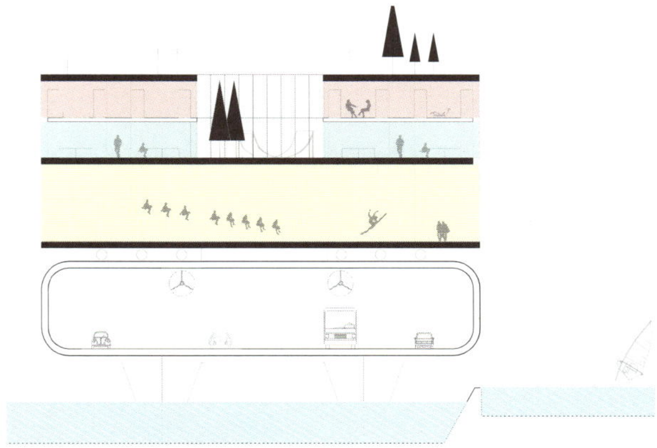

RESIDENTIAL

OFFICES

CULTURE

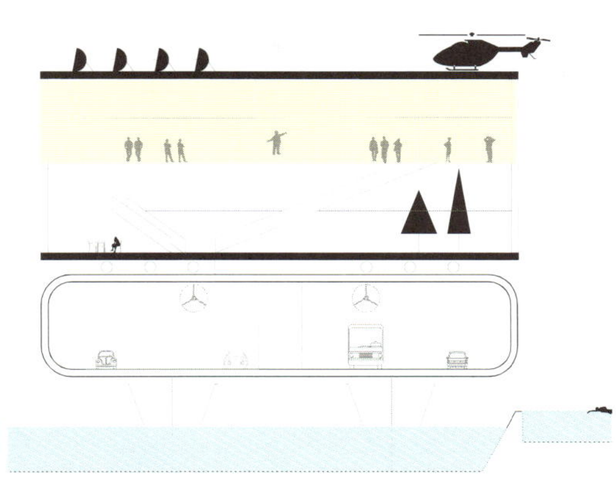

CULTURE

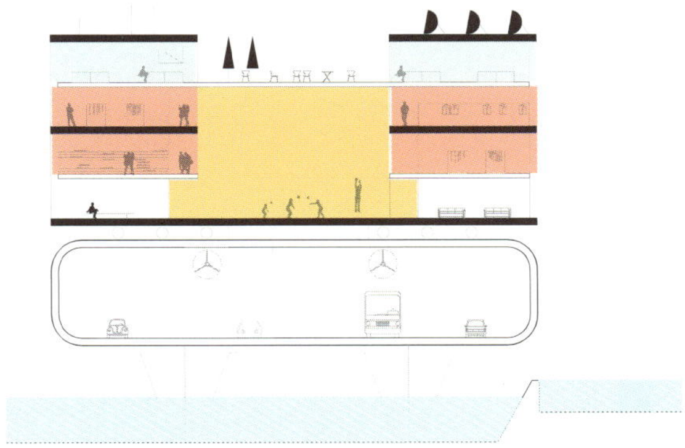

OFFICES

SPORT

SHOE MAKERS

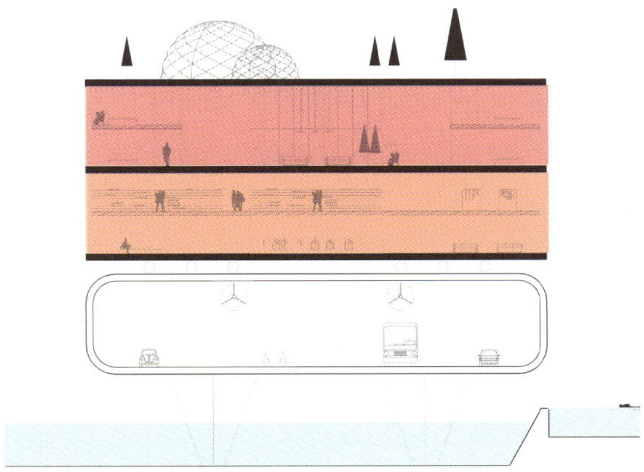

HOTEL & SPA

SHOE MAKERS

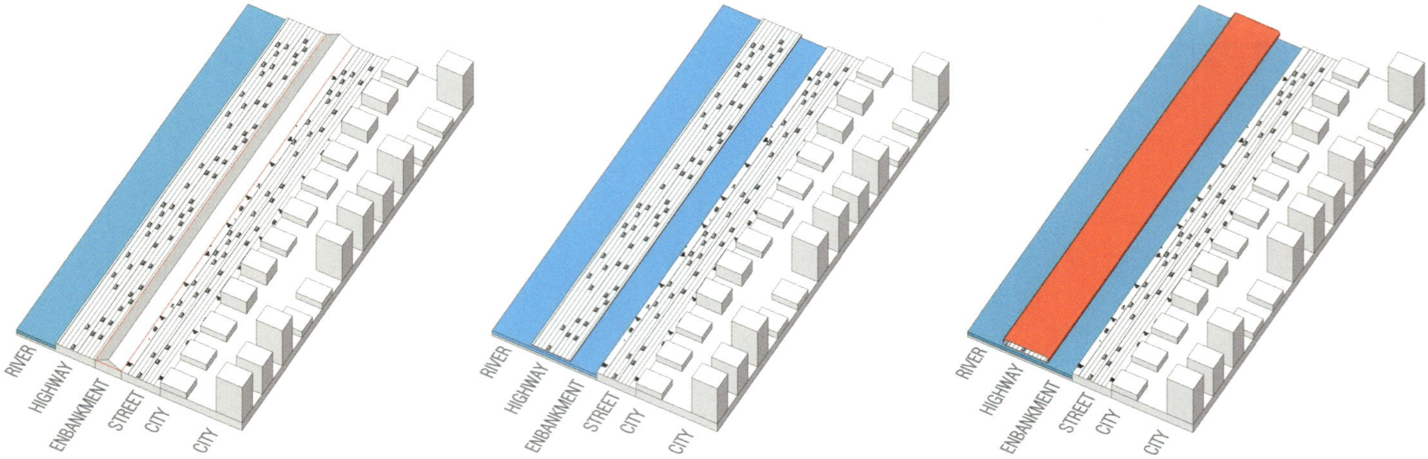

.1

CURRENT STATE

.2

PUSHING THE RIVER
TOWARDS THE CITY

.3

INTUBATING
THE HIGHWAY

Level 0

Level 1

Level 2/3
op.1

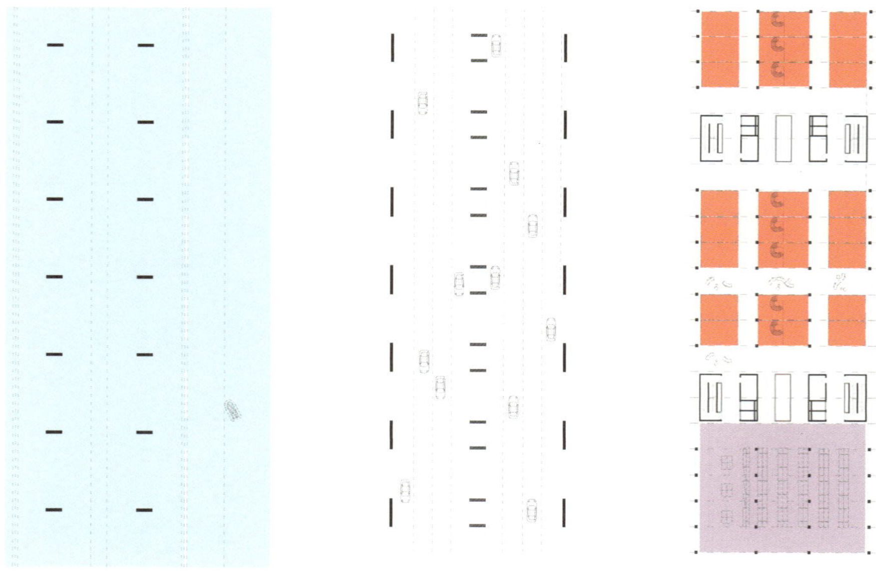

SHOE MAKERS

RETAIL

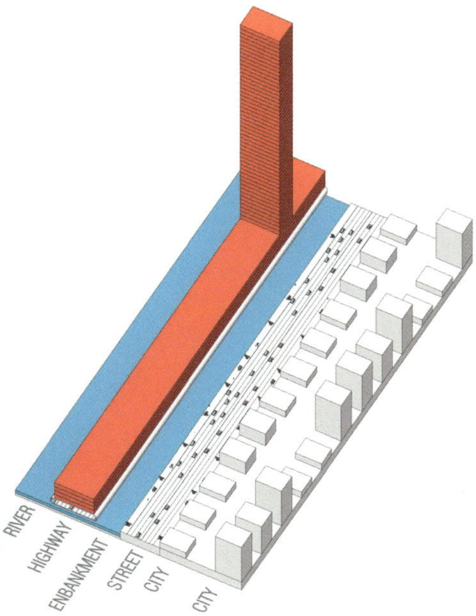

.4

CREATING A NEW LIVING INFRASTRUCTURE

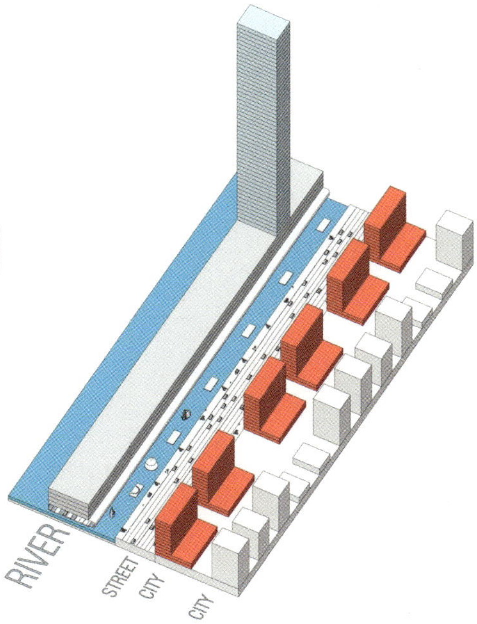

.5

RE-SHAPING THE URBAN FRONT

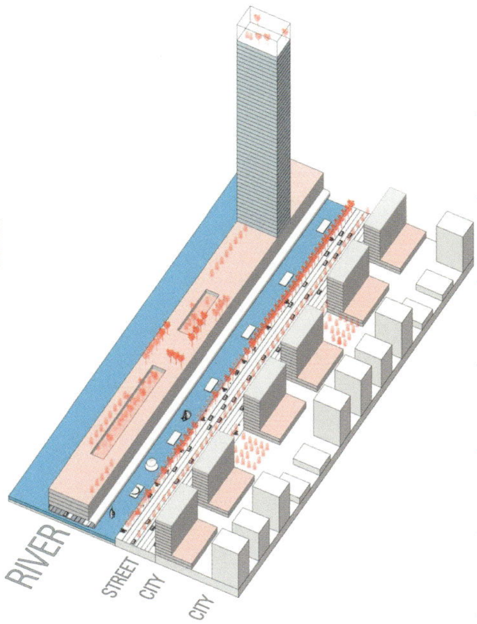

.6

TRACKING A NEW PUBLIC SEQUENCE OF GREEN AREAS

Level 2/3
op.2

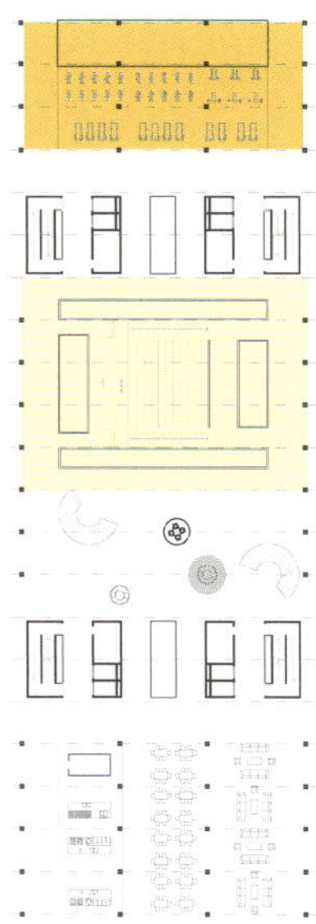

Level 4/5
op.1

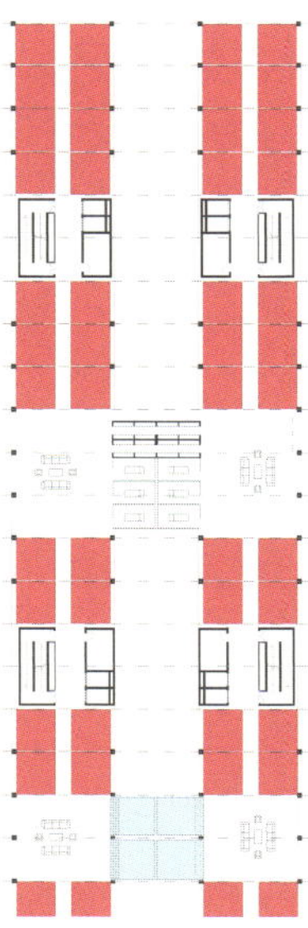

Level 4/5
op.2

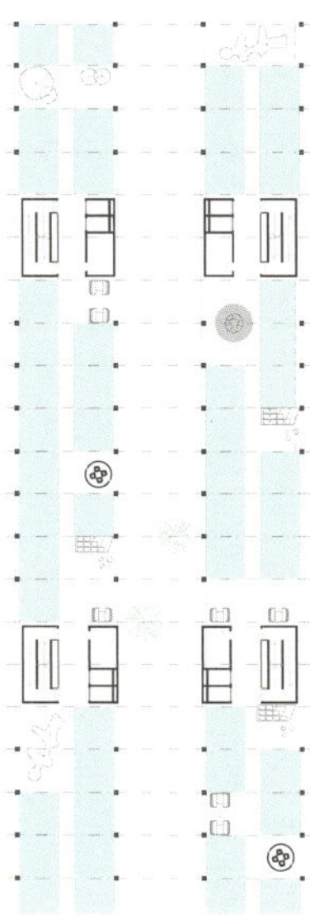

Level 4/5
op.3

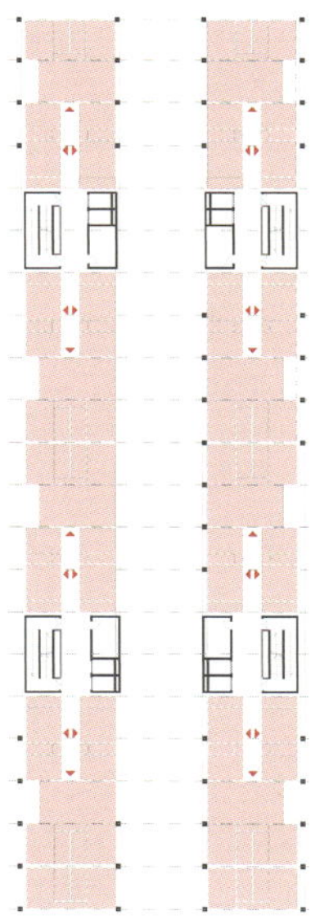

AUDITORIUM

SPORT

RESTAURANT

HOTEL & SPA

OFFICES

RESIDENTIAL

OFFICES

HOTEL & SPA

THE ROOFTOP *The Pool*

THE RIVERSIDE

700
160
150
140
130
120
110
100
90
80
70
60
50
40
30
20
10
0 m
-10
-20
-30
-40

700
160
150
140
130
120
110
100
90
80
70
60
50
40
30
20
10
0 m
-10
-20
-30
-40

에두아르도 아로요-NO.MAD

Eduardo Arroyo-NO.MAD

엔트로피텍쳐

인류는 허상에 사로잡혀 버린 듯하다. 친환경 기술, 연계성, 에너지 절감, 재활용, 생태, 지속가능성, 순환 경제 등이 정책적 담론을 주도하고 있지만 도시에서 공간에 대한 경험이나 소속감을 주는 데 실패하고 있다. 따라서 거주 공간이 비현실적 담론으로 만들어지는 것이 아니라는 점을 알리기 위하여 실체가 있는 건축이 도시 개발의 주축으로 돌아와야 한다.

엔트로피텍쳐는 느리게 움직이며 도시와 다양한 공적인 층들을 만드는 방법을 찾는 도시 설계 도구다. 4차원 연속체 속에 자유로운 공간과 다양한 감각의 혼합물을 만들어낸다. 또한 다양한 유형의 공공공간을 형성하는 건축 복합체들을 조합하여 군락을 만든다. 희미해진 도시성은 공간적 발견으로 가득 차 있고, 뚜렷한 질서가 없는 매력적이고 모호한 분위기 속을 가로지를 때 그 모습을 드러낸다. 이러한 건축은 지상에서 건물 꼭대기까지 이어지는, 광장, 숲, 경관로, 강변이 어우러진 모습을 보여준다.

그 결과 탄생한 도시 구조는 전통적 도시와 암시적으로 나타나는 거대함 사이에 최적의 밀도를 구현해낸다. 새로운 도시는 자급자족이 가능해 주거, 업무, 상업, 설비 시설 사이에서 균형을 유지할 수 있어야 한다. 이는 기능에 따른 구분이 없이 유사한 기능들을 흥미롭게 결합한다. 유동적인 체계로서 이 도구는 기존 도시와 앞으로 다가올 미래 사이의 결합을 마련하는 여러 다양한 대안을 예시해준다.

Entropytecture

It seems that humanity has sunken into the virtual: green technology, connectivity, energy saving, recycling, ecology, sustainability or circular economy guide political agendas but they fail to provide a sense of urban space and a feeling of belonging. Architecture tangibility must then fully come back as the main actor structuring the city to convey the idea that living space is no longer arranged by virtual interests. Entropytecture is an urban design tool seeking to generate slow movement cities with diverse public levels. It provides a mix of informal space and variable perception within a four dimensional continuum. It develops an act of colonization based on the combination of architectural hybrids that give shape to a vast catalogue of public spaces. Its blurred urban character is full of spatial discoveries, unveiled as we traverse and intriguing fuzzy atmosphere with an apparent lack of order. This topology displays a unity of plazas, forests, panoramic paths, and river banks from the ground level to the top of the buildings.

The resulting urban structure shows an optimal density in-between a traditional city and the speculative massiveness. The new urbanity is meant to be selfsufficient so it keeps the equilibrium between housing, offices, shopping and equipment facilities. It reveals an exciting mixture of functions close to each other but without zoning. As a fluctuant system, this projective tool exemplifies an ample range of responsiveness to guarantee the absorption and integration of the existing city and of any future contingency.

에두아르도 아로요는 건축가로, 1988년 마드리드 건축학교(ETSAM)에서 건축 도시설계 석사와 박사 학위를 받았다. 졸업 후에는 세계 여러 곳에서 학생들을 가르쳤다. 1989년 암스테르담에 NO.MAD를 설립했고, 1996년 마드리드로 본사를 이전했다. 많은 상을 받은 NO.MAD의 작품들은 여러 나라와 지역에서 출판 및 전시되었다. 가장 많이 알려진 작품으로는 바라칼도의 Lasesarre Stadium, Plaza Desierto, 손디카의 Nursery school, 마드리드의 Levene, Zafra-Uceda Houses, 빌바오의 Arquia Bank, 빈의 University of Economics 등이 있다. NO.MAD의 작품과 생각들은 "CREATE!"라는 책에 수록되어 있다. 이들의 작품은 정밀성, 가능성, 필요성의 결합을 추구하며, 늘 미지의 것을 탐구한다.

Eduardo Arroyo is an Architect, PhD and Master in Architecture and Urbanism since 1988 by the ETSAM in Madrid. Since then he has taught and lectured around the world. He founded NO.MAD in Amsterdam in 1989 and has its main headquarters in Madrid since 1996. Awarded in many occasions the office work has been published and exhibited in many countries and languages. Some of the most recognized are the Lasesarre Stadium and the Plaza Desierto in Barakaldo, the Nursery school in Sondika, the Levene and the Zafra-Uceda Houses in Madrid, the Arquia Bank in Bilbao and the University of Economics in Vienna. The office work and thought production are gathered in the book "CREATE!" NO.MAD work combines precision, chance and necessity, always in search of the unknown.

HOW CAN ENTROPYTECTURE ABSORB THE UNEXPECTED?

This projective tool exemplifies an ample range of responsiveness towards the existing or any future contingency.
As a fluctuant system, any mutating order can be implemented to guarantee the absorption and integration of unexpected factors.
This master plan shows a desired moment of the project but anything added into the area will be absorbed by a modified arrangement.

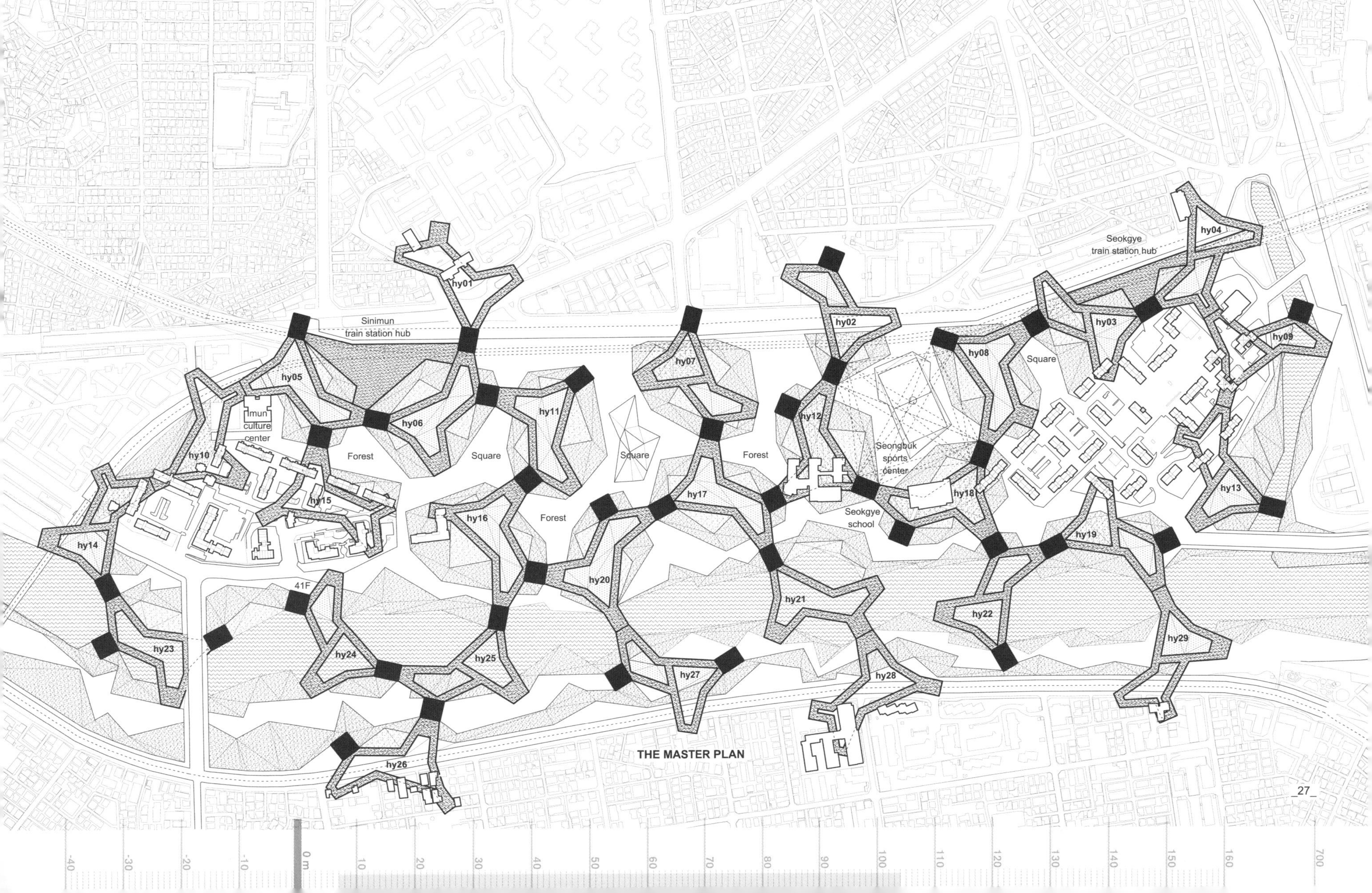

THE MASTER PLAN

도시를 만드는 것은 무엇인가?

도시는 자연과 인공의 요소가 결합된 시스템이다.
역사적으로 기능, 형태, 재료 측면에서 많은 변화가 있었지만 질서의 감각을 주는 기본 단위로 계속 남아 있다.
이들은 공공공간 조성에 큰 영향을 미치는 건축의 주요 조각이라고 할 수 있다.

WHAT ARE CITIES TRULY MADE OF?

Visible cities are systems that combine natural and artificial essentials.
They vary throughout history in terms of function, form or material but they remain the quantum used to provide a sensation of order.
They are fundamental pieces of architecture with a strong power to influence and create public spaces.

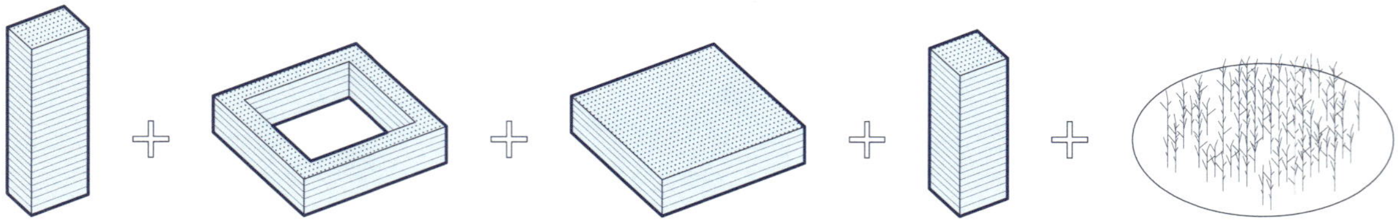

도시의 기본요소

역사적으로 도시 조직을 구성하는 데 쓰이던 여러 기본 요소가 존재한다. 밀도, 중력, 공공공간이 대표적이다.
이들은 서로 다른 형태나 구조, 소재, 내부 배치, 색상, 기능을 취하고 있지만 몇 가지 근본적인 개념으로 압축된다.

CITY ESSENTIALS

There are some basic properties that cities have used throughout history to build urban tissues, mainly density, gravity or public space.
They might take different forms, structures, materials, interior arrangements, colours, and functions but they come down to a few essential concepts.

도시에 강한 영향을 미치는 건축 혼성체는 어떻게 구축하는가?

건축의 기본 요소들은 자신의 다양한 힘을 결합해 더 복잡하고 영향력 있는 도시 구성물을 재창조할 수 있다.
의도적이고 다양한 방향성을 지닌 기하학적 형태는 어떤 영역을 복제하거나 퍼뜨릴 수 있는 수많은 방법을 제시해준다.
다양한 기능이나 행위, 자가변형을 수행할 수 있는 능력은 주변에 미치는 영향력을 높여주고, 기존 맥락에 대한 대응을 구체화할 것이다.

HOW TO CREATE AN ARCHITECTURE HYBRID OF POWERFUL URBAN INFLUENCE?

The essentials of architecture may combine their diverse powers to re-create a more complex and more influential urban object.
An intentional and multi directional geometry guarantees an extensive catalogue of ways to replicate and colonize any kind of territory.
The ability to perform different functions, behaviours and self transformations will enhance its influence on its surroundings and specify its reaction to the existing.

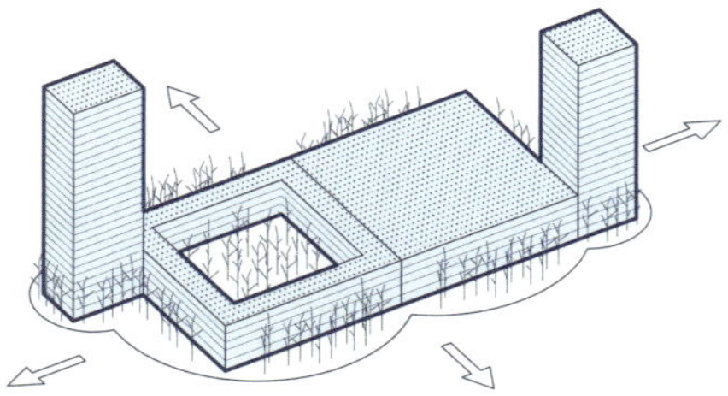

데카르트적 혼성

여러 도시 기본요소의 조합은 플라톤적이면서 데카르트적인 혼성체로 귀결된다.
이 혼성체의 외부 세계와의 관계나 도시 공간을 만드는 능력은 2개의 방향성을 띠거나 매우 제한적이다.

CARTESIAN HYBRID

The combination of the city essentials gives birth to a Platonic-Cartesian object of hybrid character.
Its relation to the outer world and capacity to create urban spaces remains bidirectional and quite restricted.

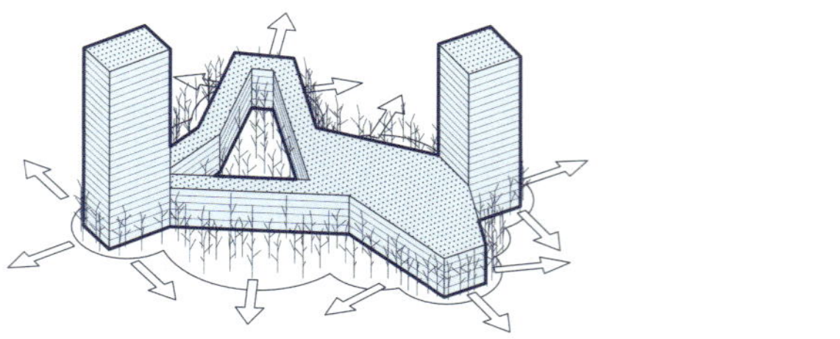

유클리드적 혼성

건축을 통한 풍성한 도시 연계성 구축에 목적을 둔 주요 도시 구성물의 전략적 조합은 유클리드적 혼성체를 만들어낸다. 이 혼성체의 가변적인 형태는 제한을 덜 받는 활동을 지원하며 자신의 도시적 역량을 배가한다.

EUCLIDEAN HYBRID

An intentional mix of fundamental objects, directed to enrich the urban relationships through architecture, creates a Euclidean hybrid.
Its variable geometry provides a less restricted behaviour multiplying its urban power.

보편적 프로젝트 메커니즘은 어떻게 개발하는가?

혼성체는 최대의 유연성과 적용성을 지닌 다양한 행위와 변형을 통해 정의된다.
이때 변형은 메스 밀도, 볼륨, 연계성, 내부 기능, 형태 측면에서 다양한 방식으로 일어나는데 기존 도시나 환경에 대한 온전한 대응력을 확보해준다.

HOW TO DEVELOP A UNIVERSAL PROJECTIVE MECHANISM?

The hybrid is defined through a vast catalogue of behaviors and mutations reaching the maximum flexibility and capacity of adaptation.
These transformations vary in terms of mass density, volume, connectivity, internal use, and form providing full reactivity to any existing city or environment.

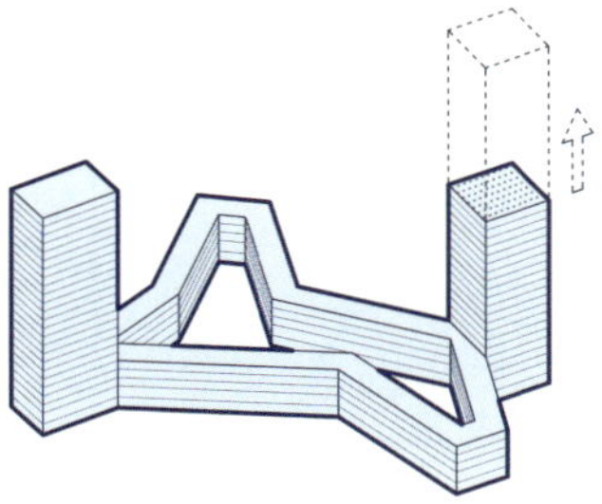

다양한 높이

혼성체 타워는 높이가 다양하게 변화하며
자유롭고 도시적인 건축 풍경을 조성한다.

VARIABLE HEIGHT

Hybrid towers height may vary creating a sense of building designing freedom and urban adaptation.

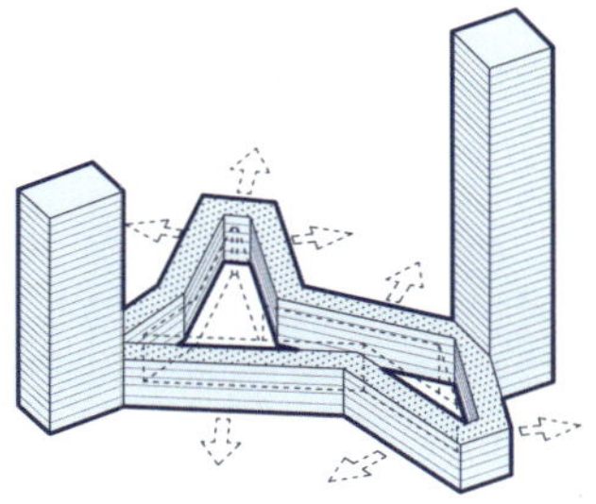

주변부

혼성체의 기단부는 기능이나 주거 유형에 따라
다양한 깊이를 수용할 수 있다.

PERIMETER BAY

Hybrid base structures can adapt their depths depending on the function or housing type.

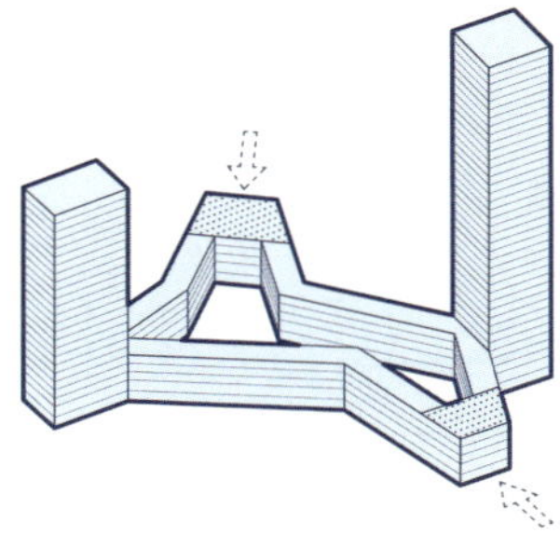

견고한 경계

혼성체의 경계부는 두꺼워지며 접근성이 뛰어난
공공 프로그램을 담는다.

SOLID EXTREMITY

Hybrid extremities thicken to easily hold accessible public programs.

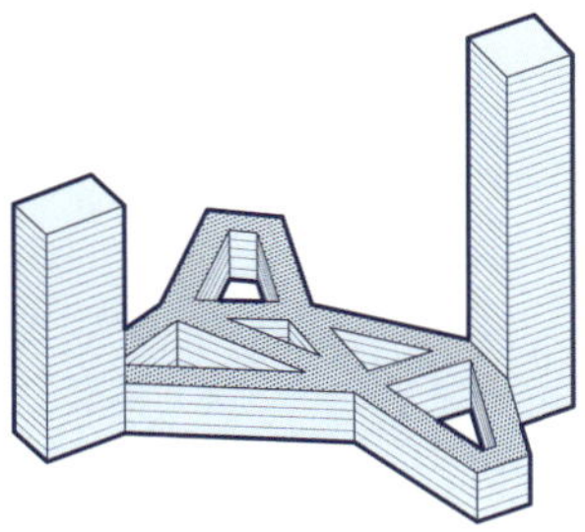

중정의 분절

내부 공간은 연결 구조물을 추가해
응집력을 강화할 수 있다.

COURTYARD FRAGMENTATION

Inner spaces can be condensed through the addition of connecting structures.

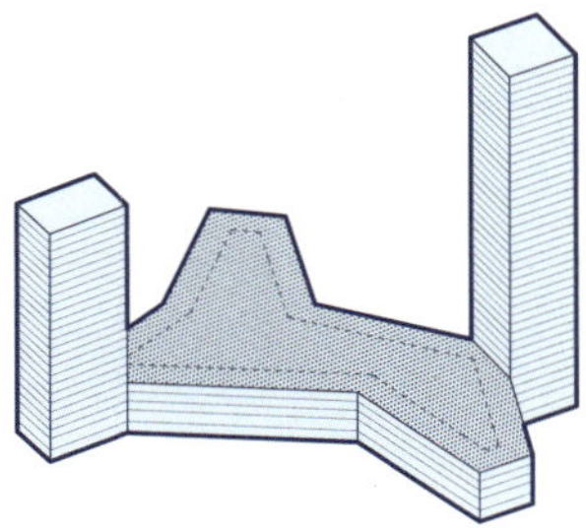

육중한 코어

내부 중정을 완전히 채워 쇼핑센터 같은
큰 스케일의 프로그램을 수용한다.

MASSIVE CORE

The complete filling of inner courts may hold large scale functions like shopping centers.

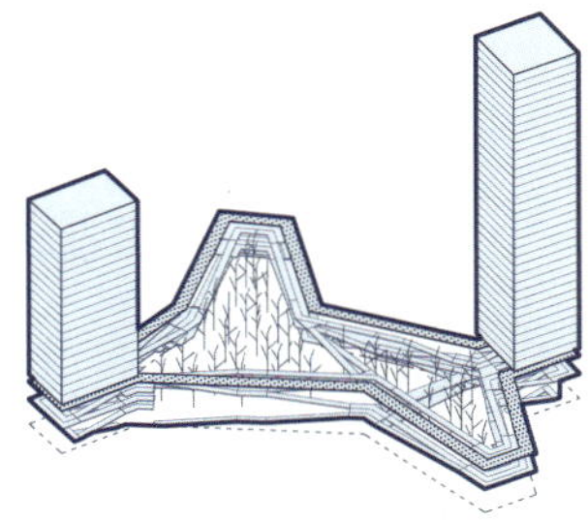

경사로 지형

주요 프로그램이 사라지는 지점에서 혼성체는 경사
구조물 형태의 수직 공공공간 속으로 사라진다.

RAMP CONTOUR

Where the main functions disappear, the hybrid vanishes into a vertical public space shaped as an inclined structure.

시스템 외부와의 연속성은 어떻게 구축하는가?

혼성체를 결합해 구현한 도시 구조는 복잡한 공공공간 네트워크를 형성한다.
혼성체의 변형은 지상과 지하 모든 레벨에서 선형 시스템을 통해 공공 기능의 연속성을 강화한다.
이 연속성은 공간과 시간 사이에 느리게 움직이는 도시의 형태를 띤 연결 고리를 만든다.

HOW TO PROVIDE CONTINUITY OUTSIDE THE LINEAR SYSTEM?

The structure of the city provided by the hybrid coupling system generates a complex public space network.
The hybrid transformations intensify public continuity at all levels, under or above, throughout the linear system.
This continuum shows a direct link between space and the perception of time in the form of a decelerated urban atmosphere.

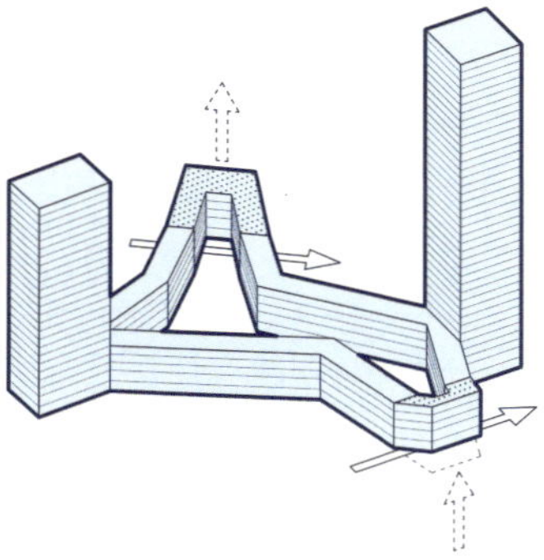

외부 투과성
혼성체의 끝 부분을 들어올려 주요 공공 오픈 스페이스를 통과하거나 연결할 수 있도록 한다.

EXTERNAL PERMEABILITY

The extremities of the hybrid lift up allowing to pass through and to connect the main public open spaces.

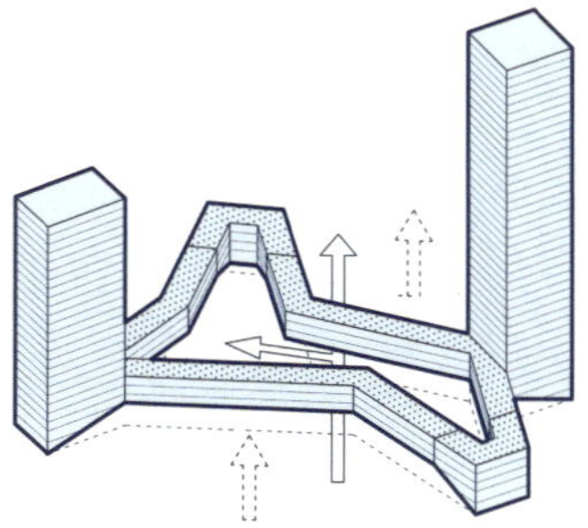

내부 투과성
혼성체의 기단부를 들어올려 공공 및 독립 오픈 스페이스들을 연결한다.

INTERNAL PERMEABILITY

The base of the hybrid lifts up providing connections between public and private open spaces.

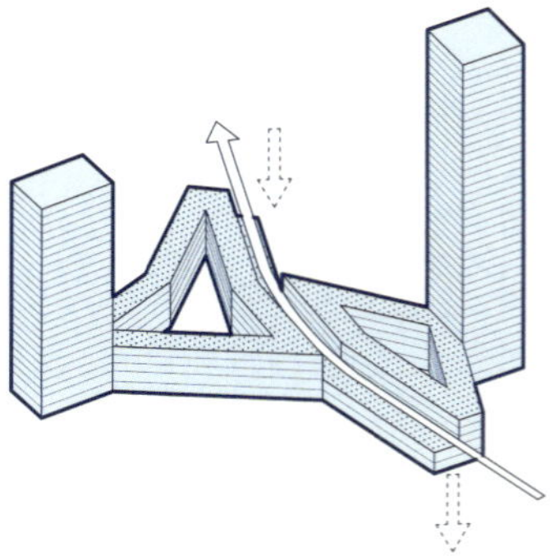

지상부 투과성
혼성체의 형태에 변화를 줘 연속성을 확보하고 동시에 상부의 느린 길과 대지 레벨을 연결한다.

ABOVE GROUND PERMEABILITY

The hybrid mutates in shape providing continuity while connecting the upper slow path and the ground level.

기존 맥락에는 어떻게 대응하는가?

혼성체는 몇 가지 대응 법칙에 따라 기존 도시와의 상호작용을 통해 형태나 용도를 적용하거나 변경한다.
이러한 시스템은 다양한 수준의 유연성을 발휘해 기존 맥락과 어우러질 수 있도록 혼성체에 특정한 기능을 선사해준다.
그리고 혼성체 내외부에는 기존 건물, 하천, 철도, 지형 등과의 상호작용의 결과로 변형이 일어난다.

HOW TO REACT TO WHAT EXISTS?

The hybrids carry some reactivity rules, being able to adapt and mutate in form and use with the existing city interaction.
The system provides the hybrid with a specific behavior so it adapts to anything existing with several degrees of flexibility.
The internal and external mutations occur then as a result of the interactions with existing buildings, rivers, railways or topography.

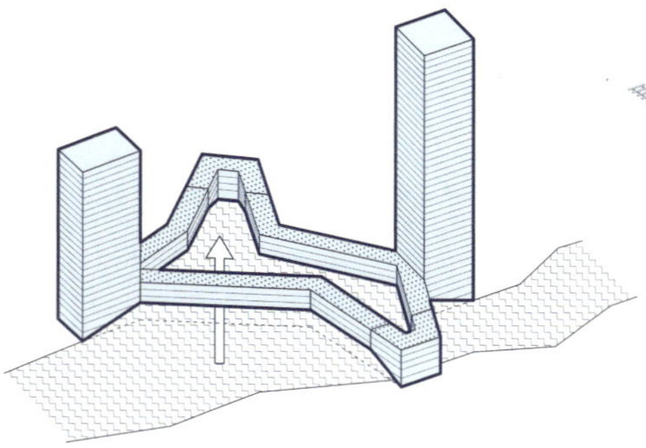

강둑
혼성체는 선착장 또는 강둑 형태로 강을 흡수한다.

RIVER BANKS

The hybrid absorbs the river presence in the form of open marinas and banks.

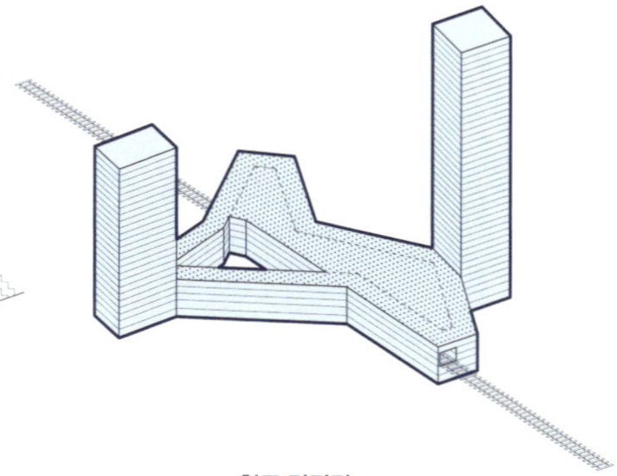

철도 결절점
혼성체는 기차역과 쇼핑센터가 결합된 거대 허브 시설로 철도를 흡수한다.

RAILWAY NODES

The hybrid absorbs the railway presence through massive hubs mixing the railway stations and shopping centers.

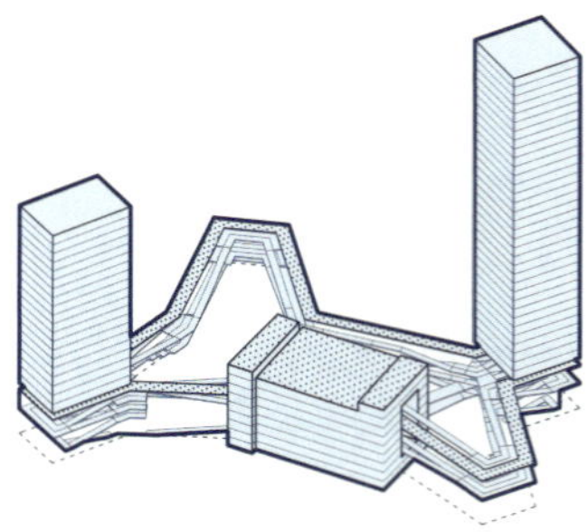

건물 흡수
혼성체는 다양한 레벨의 연결 경사로를 통해 기존 스포츠 관련 시설들을 흡수한다.

ABSORBED BUILDINGS

The hybrid absorbs the existing sport buildings by means of several ramps at multi level connections.

연결 네트워크는 어떻게 발전시키는가?

혼성체의 체계적 결합은 연속성을 보장하는 비데카르트적 공간 구성을 낳는다.
이러한 군집화 과정을 통해 다방향성과 다중 연계성을 강조하는 여러 레벨에 연속적인 도시 공간이 형성된다.
이때 이동성은 도시 도로망과 연계된 선형 시스템 하에 빠른 교통 노선을 보유한 도시를 조성할 때 기준이 된다.

HOW TO DEVELOP A CONNECTIVE NETWORK?

The systematic coupling of the hybrids provides a non-Cartesian spatial organization which generates continuity.
This act of colonization creates a continuum of urban space in several levels focused on the multi-directionality and connectivity.
Movement then becomes the guideline to structure the city with a traffic fast track under the linear system connected to the city road network.

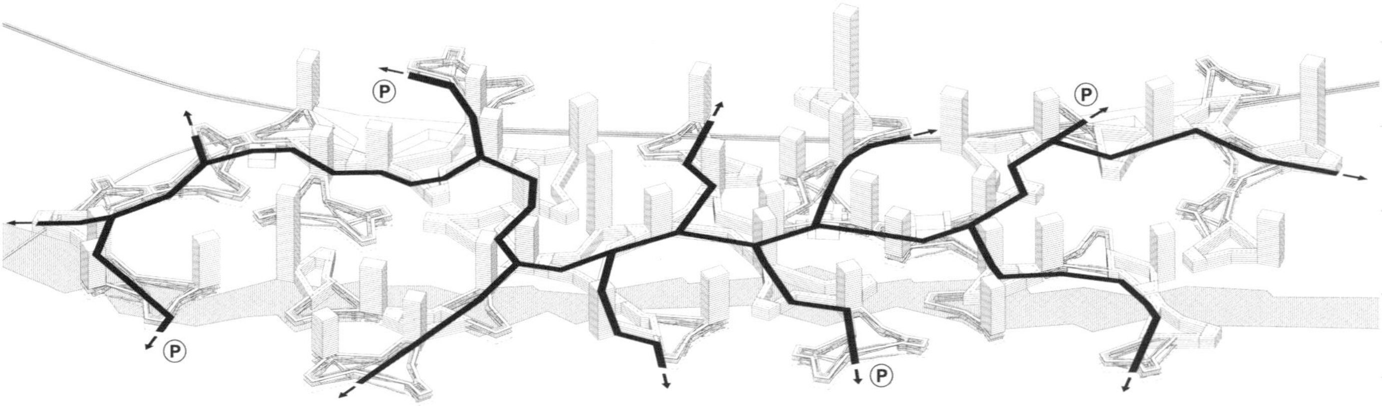

빠른 길 연결

혼성체 프로그램은 대지의 모든 주요 출입구를 연결하는 구조물 아래 빠른 교통 노선을 조성한다.
주차장은 빠른 길의 끝부분에 두어 내부로의 차량 진입을 막는다.

FAST PATH CONNECTIONS

The hybrids program replicate composing a traffic fast track under built structures that links all the main entrances to the site.
Parking plots are placed underground at some endings of the fast track to prevent most vehicles from entering the area.

어떻게 강렬하고도 느리게 움직일 수 있는가?

선형 시스템은 영역을 가로질러 아래쪽으로 느리게 움직이는 3차원 보행로가 된다.
이는 지상에서 휴식을 취하거나 스포츠를 즐길 수 있는 건물 옥상까지 이어지는 연속적인 보행로를 형성한다.
느린 교통 네트워크로의 접근성은 탁 트인 도시 전망을 즐길 수 있는 여러 개의 경사로를 활용해 확보한다.

HOW TO MOVE INTENSELY BUT SLOWLY?

The linear system performs a three dimensional pedestrian path directed to slow down movement through the area.
It is shaped as a walking continuum running from the ground level to the top of the buildings in which people may relax or practice sports.
Accessibility to the slow movement network is guaranteed through several ramped streets featuring intense panoramic views of the city.

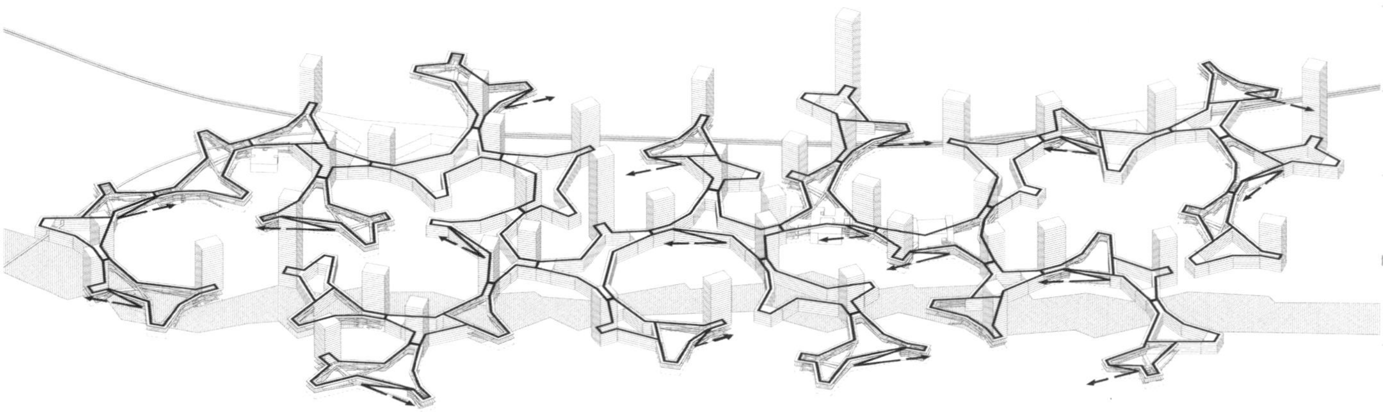

느린 길 연결

혼성체는 구조물 위에 자전거와 보행자를 위한 느린 길을 조성함으로써
자전거 및 보행자 전용 공중 보행로를 만들어낸다.

SLOW PATH CONNECTIONS

The hybrids replicate composing a cycling and pedestrian slow path
over built structures creating an elevated running and walking track.

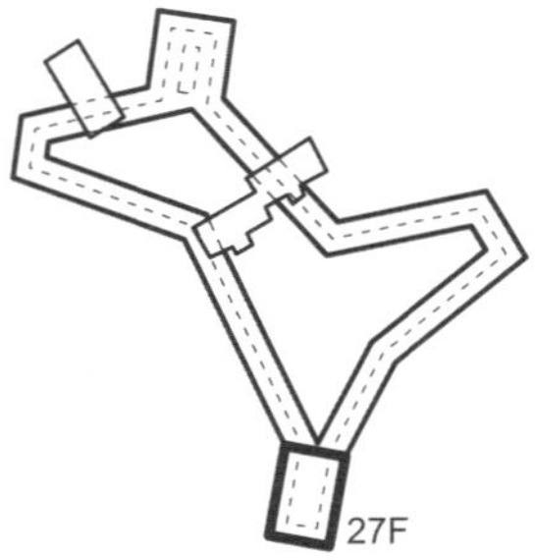

hy01

Ho
14.080
Co
1.860 m²

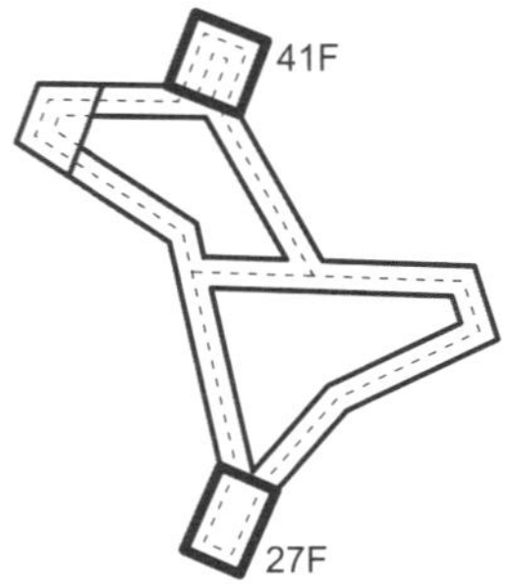

hy02

Eq
2.575 m²
Ho
14.080
Of
34.500 m²

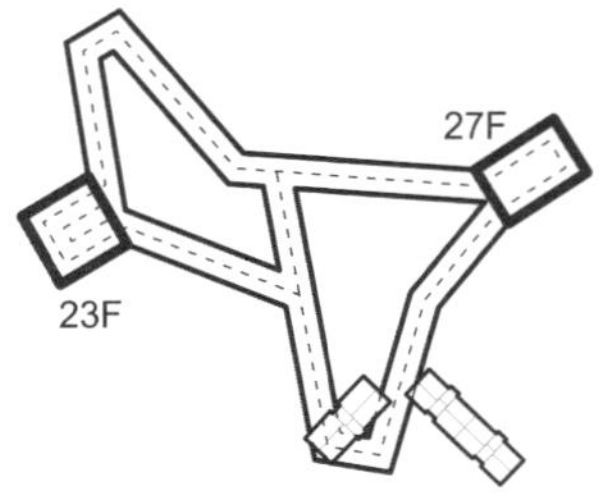

hy03

Eq
3.875 m²
Ho
17.685 m²
Co
26.040 m²

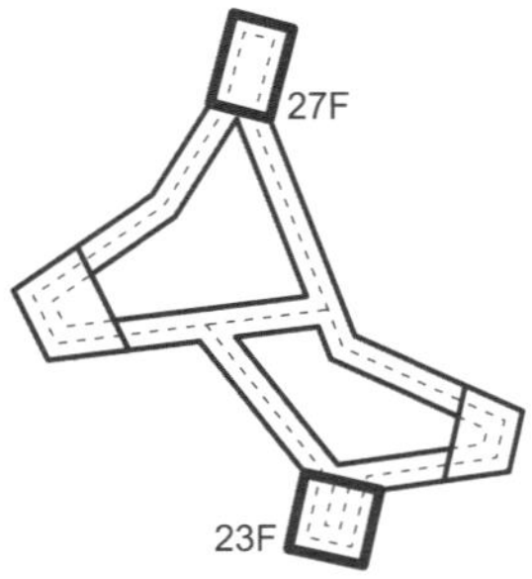

hy07

Eq
4.900 m²
Ho
28.990 m²
Co
3.550 m²

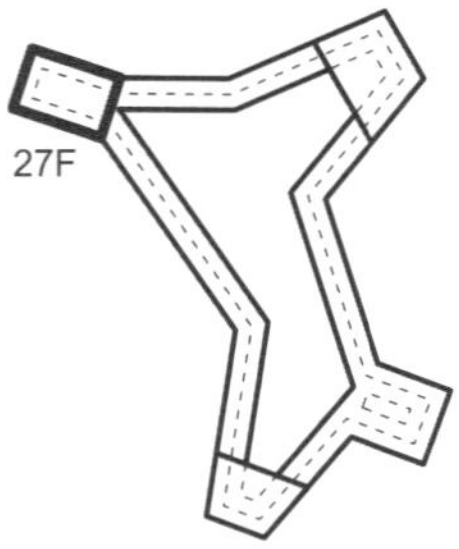

hy08

Eq
3.870 m²
Ho
28.635 m²
Co
7.570 m²

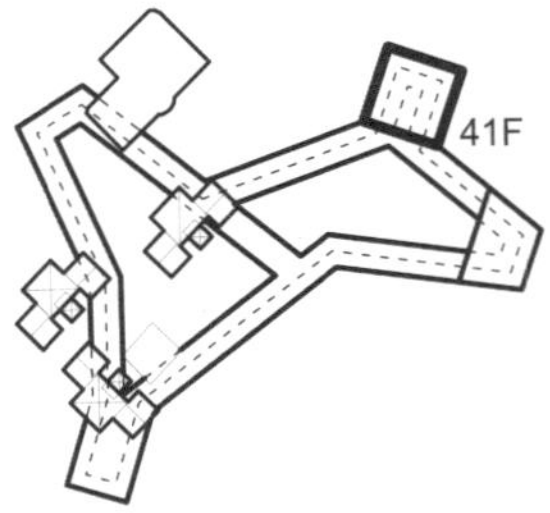

hy09

Eq
2.575 m²
Of
34.500 m²

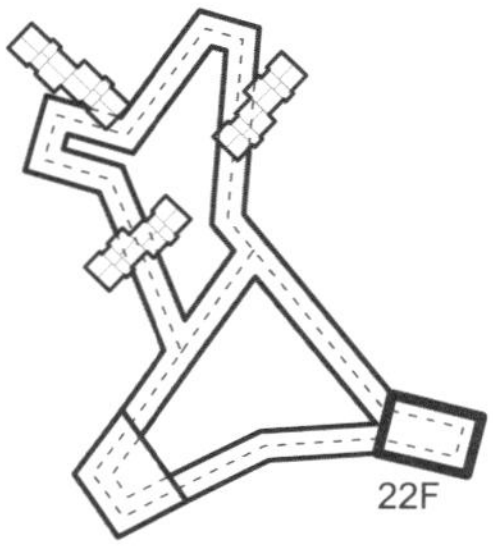

hy13

Eq
3.875 m²
Ho
6.435 m²
Co
21.570 m²

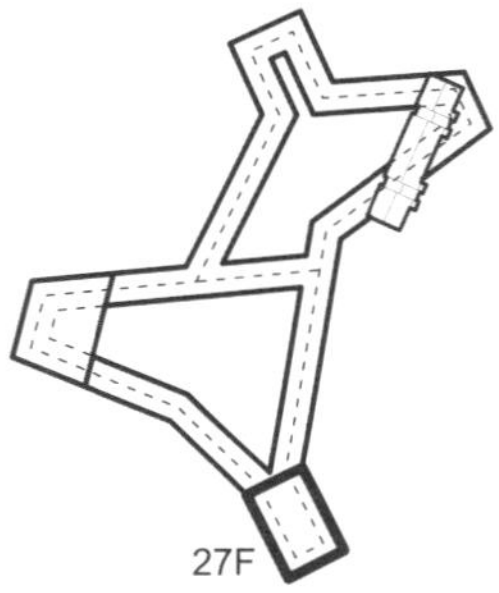

hy14

Eq
3.875 m²
Ho
6.435 m²
Co
21.570 m²

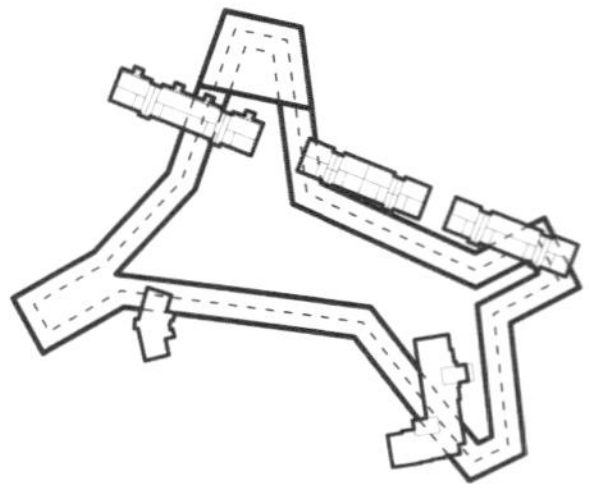

hy15

Eq
2.325 m²
Co
1.860 m²

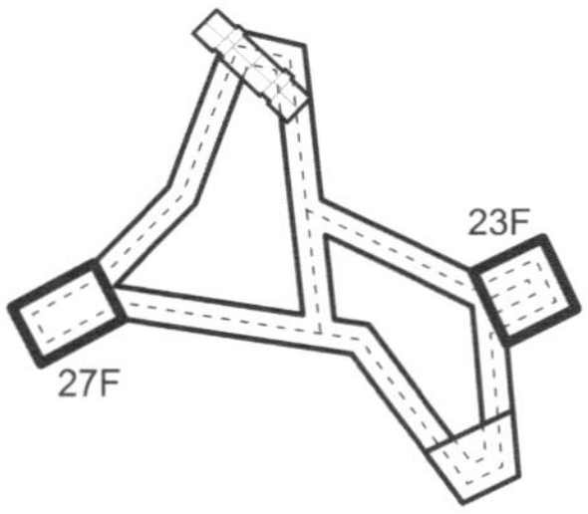

hy19

Eq
1.545 m²
Ho
16.575 m²
Co
3.550 m²

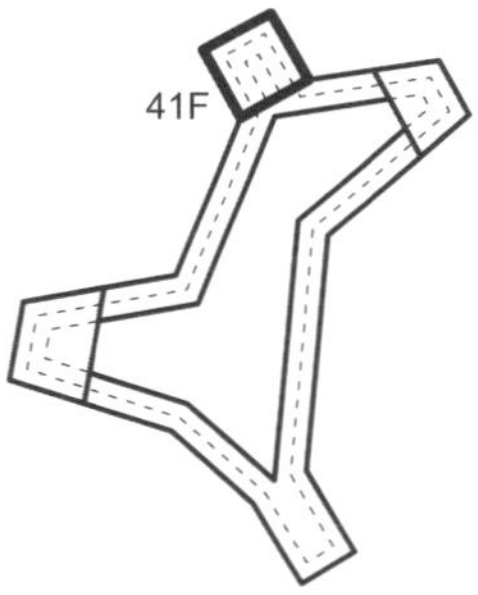

hy20

Eq
3.870 m²
Ho
8.355 m²
Co
4.290 m²
Of
34.500 m²

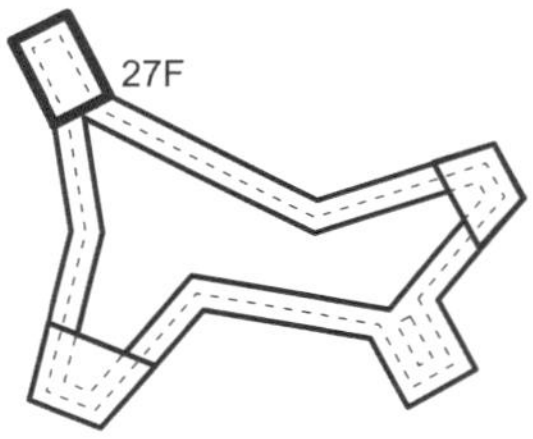

hy21

Eq
2.575 m²
Ho
41.135 m²
Co
6.320 m²
Ls
3.875 m²

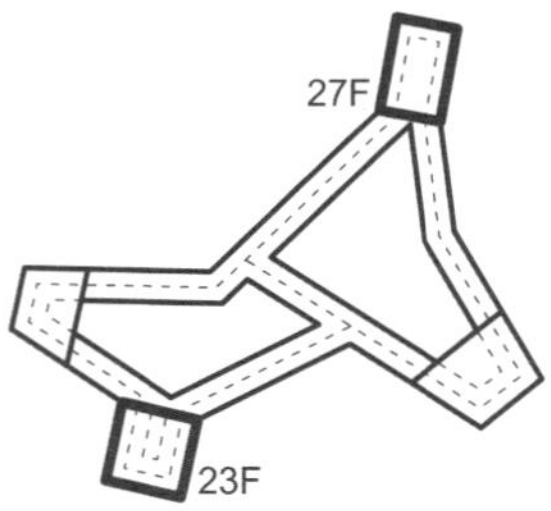

hy25

Eq
5.420 m²
Ho
33.780 m²
Co
3.550 m²

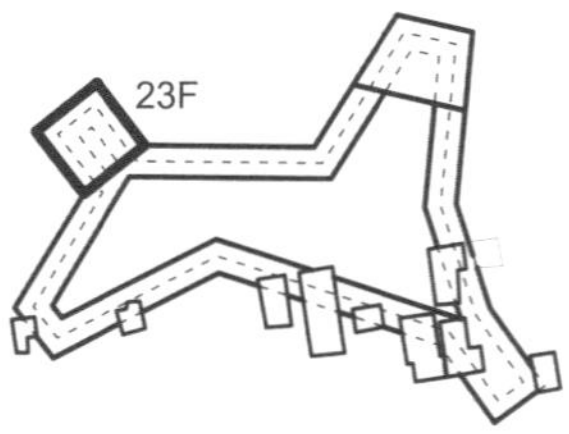

hy26

Eq
2.325 m²
Ho
11.250 m²
Co
1.860 m²

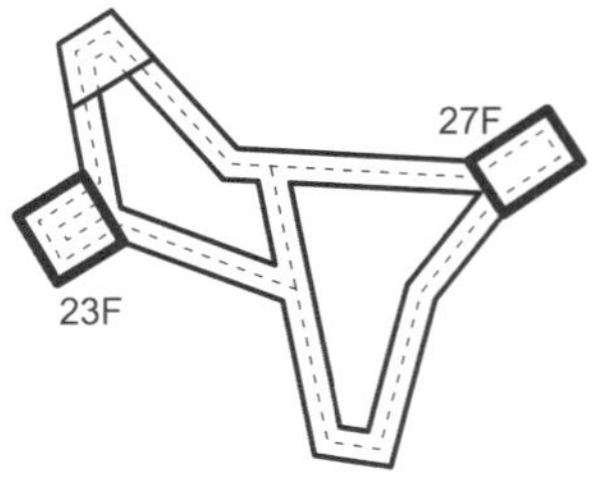

hy27

Eq
1.545 m²
Ho
33.780 m²
Co
3.550 m²

혼성체 매트릭스
각 혼성체는 저마다 특별한 성격을 지니는데 이는 경계 여건에 따라 수정 가능한 프로그램 구성과 연결되어 있다.
전체 체계 안에서 각 혼성체가 지닌 상대적 위치는 그들의 최종적 물성과 순환 구조를 결정한다.

THE HYBRIDS MATRIX
Each hybrid holds a specific character related to its program composition that can be modified by border conditions.
Their relative positions in the system also qualifiy their final materialization and circulation system.

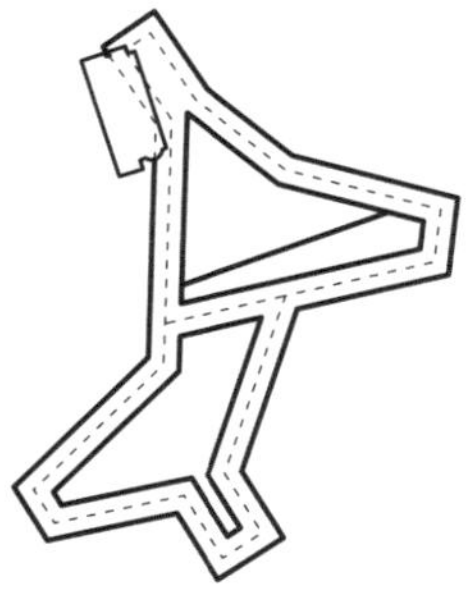

hy04

Eq
1.545 m²
Ho
5.325 m²
Co
6.570 m²

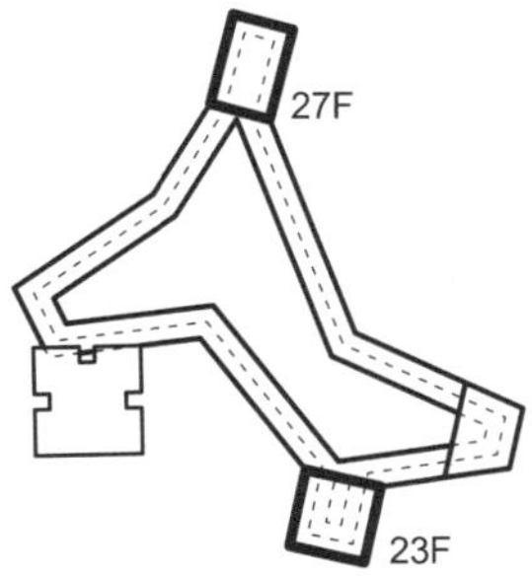

hy05

Eq
2.575 m²
Ho
23.780 m²
Co
6.570 m²

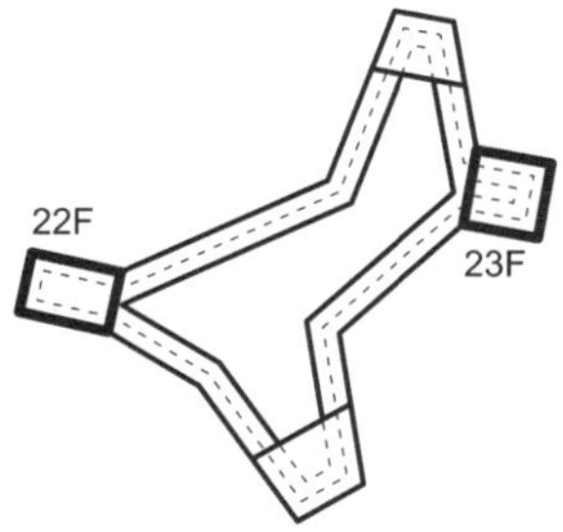

hy06

Eq
5.420 m²
Ho
13.855 m²
Co
31.500 m²

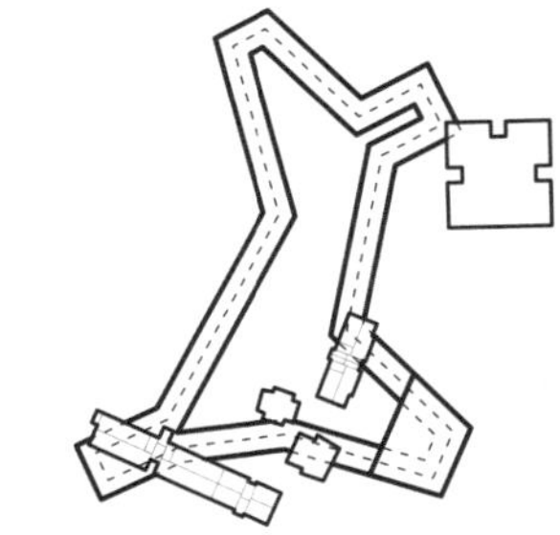

hy10

Eq
2.325 m²
Co
1.860 m²

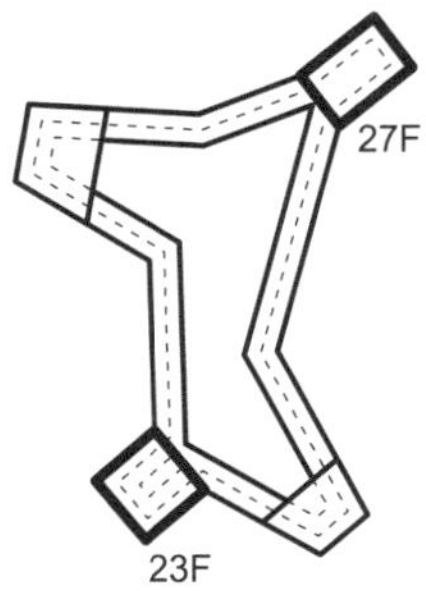

hy11

Eq
4.900 m²
Ho
41.135 m²
Co
6.320 m²

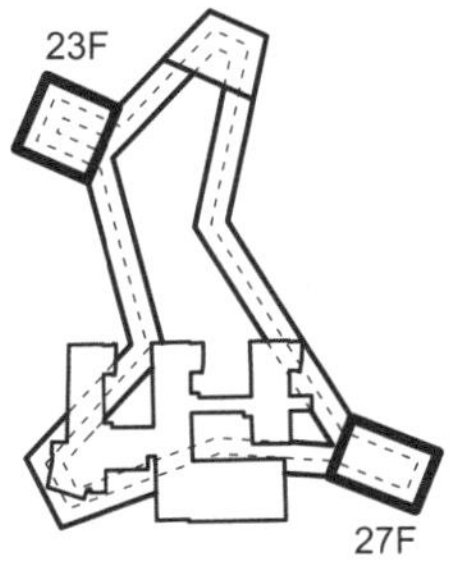

hy12

Eq
1.545 m²
Ho
25.330 m²

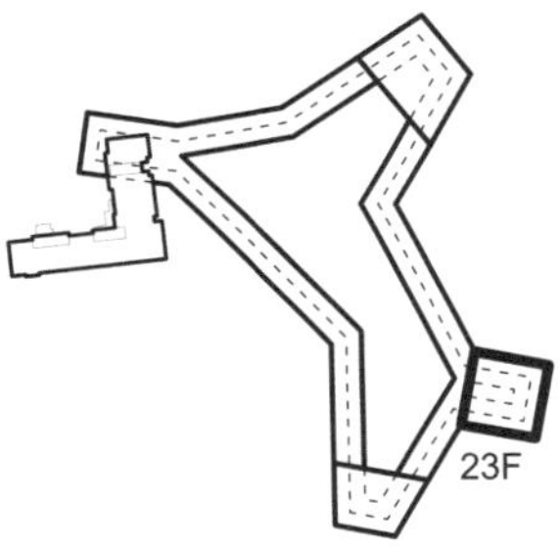

hy16

Eq
2.325 m²
Ho
25.775 m²
Co
7.600 m²
Ls
2.575 m²

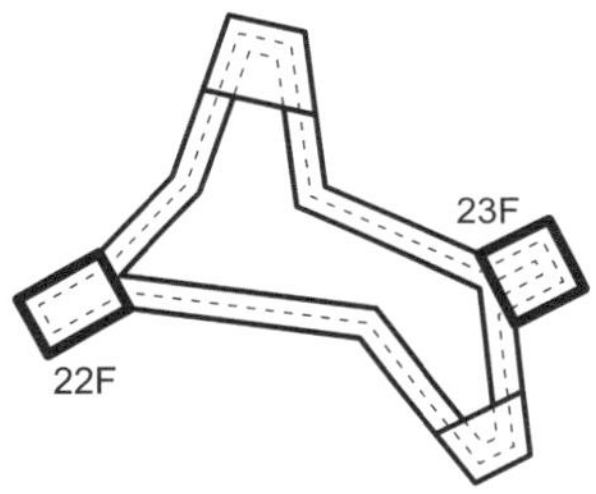

hy17

Eq
3.870 m²
Ho
23.855 m²
Co
20.695 m²

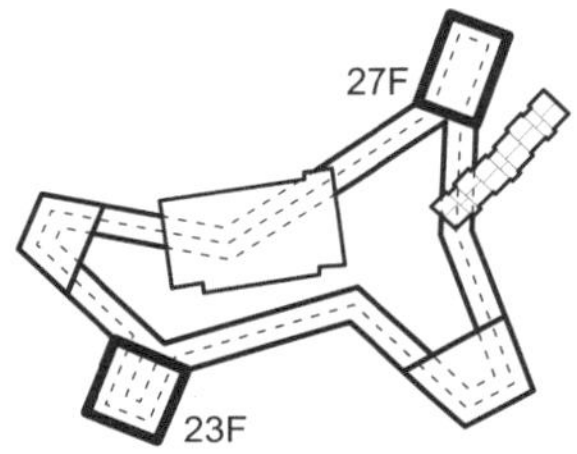

hy18

Eq
3.870 m²
Ho
11.250 m²
Co
14.080 m²

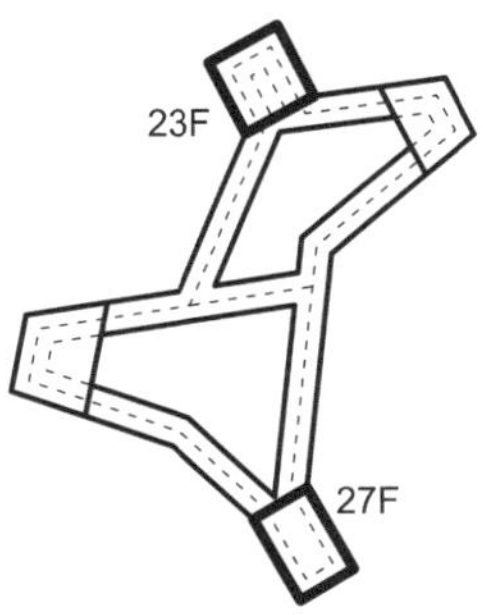

hy22

Eq
2.325 m²
Ho
33.780 m²
Co
3.550 m²
Ls
2.575 m²

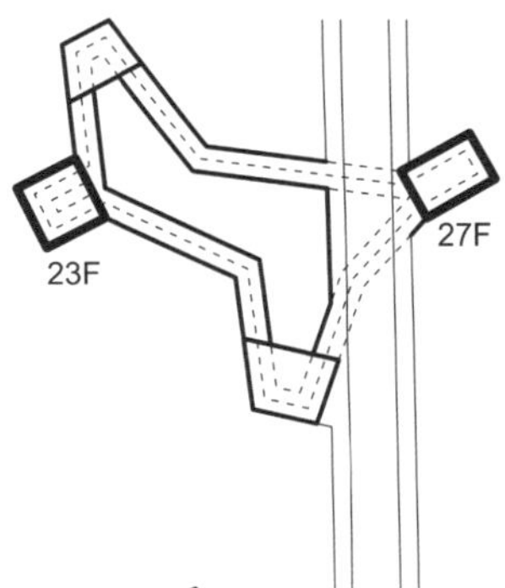

hy23

Eq
3.870 m²
Ho
25.330 m²

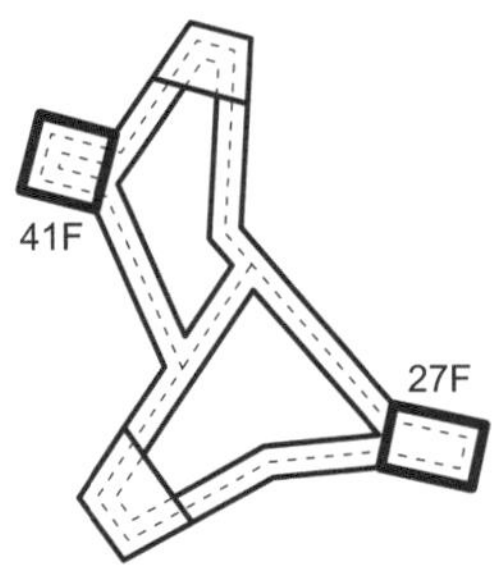

hy24

Eq
2.575 m²
Ho
14.080 m²
Of
34.500 m²
Ls
3.875 m²

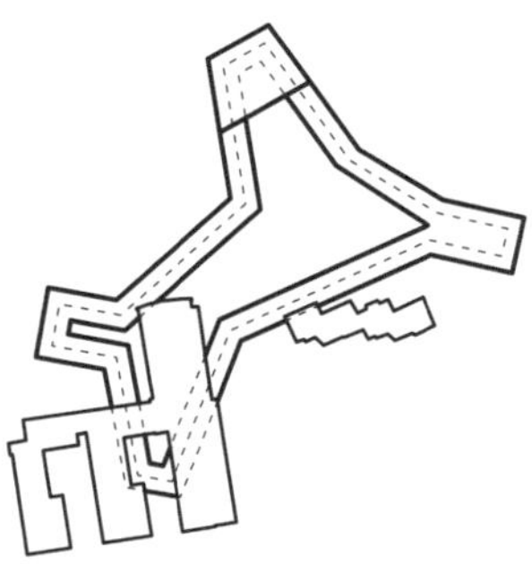

hy28

Eq
2.325 m²
Co
1.860 m²

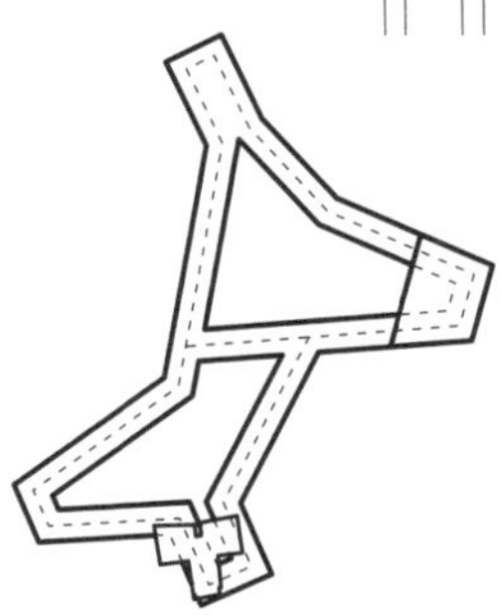

hy29

Eq
3.875 m²
Ho
6.435 m²
Co
4.290 m²

hy00	Hybrid name
Eq	Public equipment
Ho	Housing
Co	Commercial
Of	Office
Ls	Leisure and sports
00F	Floor number

Total built area:	**962.575 m²**
Public equipment:	88.495 m²
Housing:	511.145 m²
Commercial:	212.035 m²
Office:	138.000 m²
Leisure and sports:	12.900 m²

비연역적 도시 구조 안에서 기능은 어떻게 드러나는가?

제안된 도시는 전통적 도시성과 사변적 거대함 사이에 머무는 최적의 밀도를 보여준다.
배치가 완료된 혼성체는 전체 체계 안에서 자신이 지닌 상대적 위치를 기존 도시에 대응하며 자신의 기능과 형태를 변경한다.
이 새로운 도시 공간은 자족적이고 따라서 주거, 업무, 상업 기능과 설비 시설 사이에서 균형을 유지한다.
또한 혼성체의 결합을 다양하게 해석한 결과물로서 조닝을 적용하지 않은, 다양한 기능의 흥미로운 조합을 보여준다.

HOW TO UNVEIL USABILITY IN A NON APRIORISTIC URBAN STRUCTURE?

The resulting city shows an optimal density in-between a traditional urbanity and the speculative massiveness.
Once located, the hybrids vary their functions and morph as they confront their relative position in the system with the existing city.
This new urbanity is meant to be self sufficient and so it keeps the equilibrium between housing, offices, commercial functions and equipment facilities.
It reveals an exciting mixture of functions without any zoning as a result of the diverse interpretations of the hybrids combination.

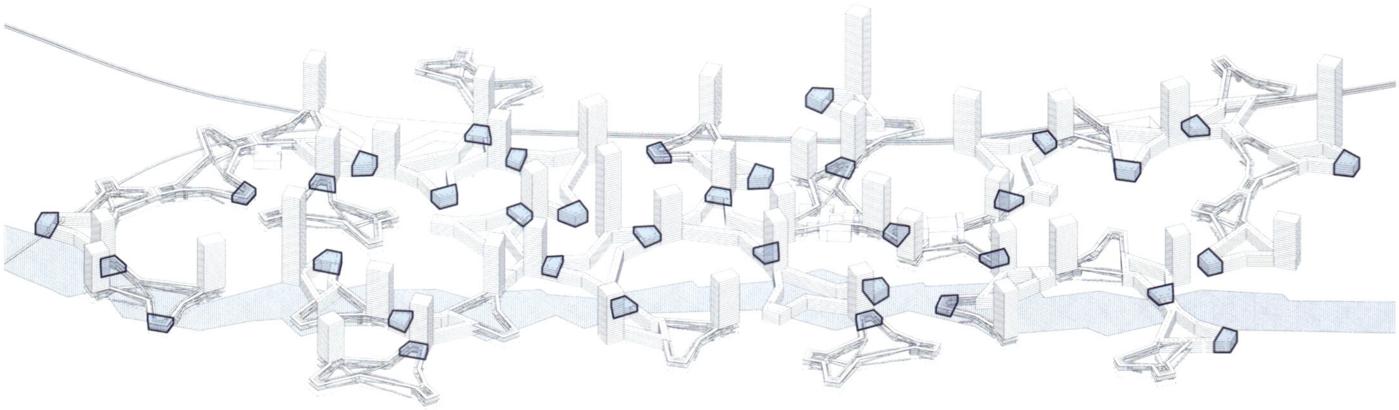

공공시설 (88,495 m2)

의료 센터, 학교를 비롯한 공공시설은 혼성체 경계부에
전략적으로 배치해 접근을 쉽게 한다.

PUBLIC EQUIPMENT (88.495 m²)

Public services such as health centers or schools are strategically located in
the extremities of the hybrids to provide prominent and easy access.

혼성체 시스템은 어떻게 기존 맥락을 흡수하는가?

철도, 역, 강을 비롯한 기존 기반 요소들은 혼성체의 프로그램과 그 순환 체계에 변화를 일으킨다.
동시에 혼성체의 결합 형태는 다양한 레벨과 형태 안에 공공공간을 형성하며 도시에 연속성을 부여해준다.
공간과 시간은 공공 교통에 대한 4차원적 이해를 바탕으로 옛 것과 새 것을 융합하는 데 동참한다.

HOW DOES THE SYSTEM ABSORB WHAT EXISTS?

Existing infrastructures such as train tracks, stations and the river provoke mutations in the hybrids' program and in their circulation system.
At the same time, the hybrids' coupling geometry creates public spaces in diverse levels and forms to provide continuity within the city.
Space and time become then joined melting the old and new on a four dimensional understanding of public movement.

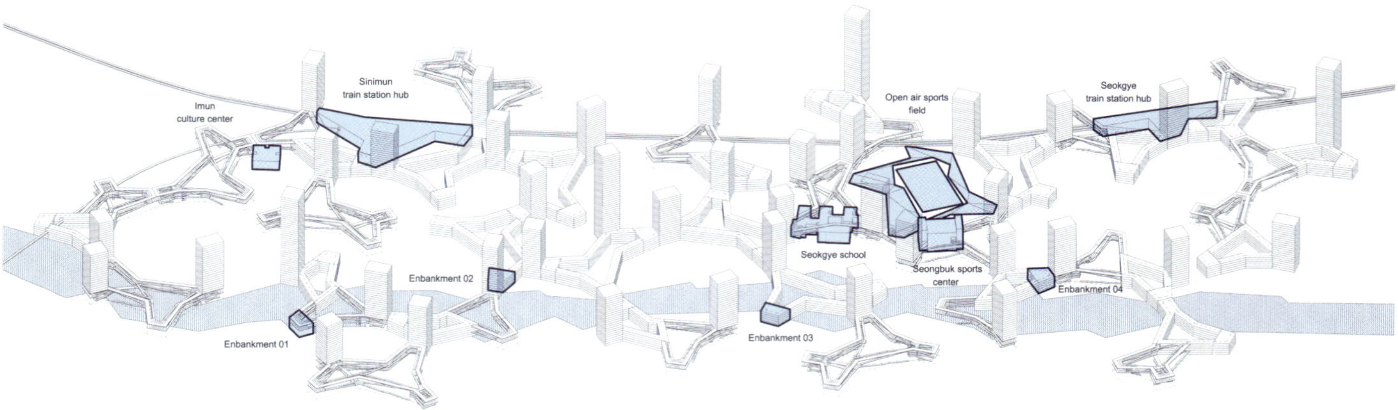

잔존 도시 구조물 흡수

석계역과 신이문역은 새로운 구조물에 통합되어 거대한 지역 상업 및 업무 허브가 된다. 성북과 이문 스포츠 센터는
야외 운동장을 통해 느린 길 시스템과의 연계를 유지한다. 강둑은 보트 정박지와 선착장이 있는 여가 및 스포츠 시설로
재개발해 방치되어 있던 수변 경관을 활용하거나 회복할 수 있도록 한다.

CITY REMAINS ABSORPTION

The Seokgye and Sinimun train stations are incorporated into the new structure becoming large commercial and working hubs for the neighborhood.
Both Seongbuk and Imun sport and cultural centers are kept attaching them to the slow path system in relation to an open air sports field.
The river bank is re-shaped as a leisure and sport area with new boat ports and marinas to enjoy and recover an underused water landscape.

30m atmosphere

300m atmosphere

700
160
150
140
130
120
110
100
90
80
70
60
50
40
30
20
10
0 m
-10
-20
-30
-40
3km atmosphere

윌리 뮐러-IAAC

Willy Müller-IAAC

슈퍼크로싱 서울

오늘날 도시가 당면한 가장 큰 도전은 고밀 조직 속에서 더 많은 공공공간과 도시 활동들을 만들어내는 것이다. 특히 이러한 공간들이 도시의 질서를 정의하고 고밀 기능의 중심이 되는 교차로, 대로, 복합 역과 교통 허브를 재해석하는 것이 중요하다.
도시 안에서 유형, 계층, 크기와 중요성으로 구분되는 교차로들을 따라 도시의 현상이 강화되어 나타난다. 이 장소들은 우리의 집단적인 무의식에서 도시의 코너들을 만든다. 때로는 기념비적이고, 서비스나 장비들이 집적되는 곳, 또는 교통의 흐름이 바뀌는 곳이다, 우리는 새로운 관점에서 서울의 도시 그리드를 다시 만들 수 있는 기회를 얻었다. 더 많은 공간을 만들고, 지하철역과 같이 도시의 연결과 흐름을 이용하는 더 많은 도시의 장치들을 만드는 것이 가능하다. 이러한 새로운 접근은 동시에 단기적, 장기적 관점에서 개별적으로 기존 도시의 현실을 받아들이면서 맞춰갈 수 있다. '슈퍼크로싱 서울'이라는 '적용가능한 유형학적' 연구를 제안한다. 도시의 특정 교차로에 적용된 유형 모델은 공공 공간, 녹지, 도시 활동을 증가시킬 수 있을 만큼 충분히 강력하다. 동시에 중장기적으로 새로운 상업 공간을 만들 수 있으며, 도시의 변화 인자가 될 것이다. 이러한 방식으로 새로운 공공사업, 새로운 부동산 시장, 새로운 상업과 여가 공간을 만들어낼 것이다..
연신내역은 대표적인 미래의 도시 개입을 위한 새로운 전략 계획이다.

Supercrossing Seoul

One of the biggest challenges that cities have to face in our century is to be able to produce more public spaces and urban activities in the middle of such dense tissues. Specifically it's important to reinterpret those spaces that define our urban order and are the center of function's density: crossing streets, boulevards, intermodal stations and public transportations hubs. Along these crossing streets - classified by typology, class, size or importance in the city – is exactly where the phenomenon of urban intensity are happening. The places that belong to our collective unconscious are made of urban corners: sometimes they are monumental, they gather the accumulation of offers of services or equipment, or they amass visible brands in such small space, the changes of directions in the mobility.
We have the opportunity to re-thing the Seoul's urban grid from a new point of view: It's possible to produce more spaces and more urban equipment that take advantage of the connectivity and of the important urban fluxes (metro stations for instance) in order to develop Urban Design Proposals. This new approach would adapt and customize at the same time to each urban existing reality, with a sequence of short-medium and large term.
We propose an "adaptive typological" study that we name "Super-crossing Seoul". These typological models applied on specific crossing-roads of the city could be potentially strong enough to multiply public spaces, green surfaces and urban activities. At the same time in medium –long term, they could create and suggest new spaces of business and they could represent the transformation agents of the city. In this way, it will be created new public works for services and equipment, new real estate market offers, and new retail and urban leisure options.
Yeonsinnae station represents the Pilot Project of a New Strategic Plan for future urban interventions.

윌리 뮐러는 1996년 WMA-Willy Muller Architects를 설립했으며 현재 소장이다. 또한 2000년 Institute of Advanced Architecture in Catalunya (IAAC)를 설립했다. 다양한 전시회, 설계공모 및 프로젝트에서도 여러 국제적인 상을 받았다. Sociopolis, Media House 프로젝트, Metapolis Advanced Architecture 사전, 자급자족 주택 및 한국 DD 시리즈(2008) 등 다양한 작업이 있다. 최근 "21세기를 위한 X 패러다임(IaaC, 2018)"을 출간했다. 바르셀로나 시의회 바르셀로나 지역청 (2011/2015)의 장을 역임했다. 실질적으로 IAAC의 도시 과학 연구소 소장이자 브라질, 리우데 자네이루의 메트로폴리탄 마스터 플랜 총책임자이다.

Willy Müller is a principal and founder of WMA-Willy Müller Architects, and he is founder of the Institute of Advanced Architecture in Catalunya (IAAC) in 2000. He established WMA-Willy Müller Architects in 1996, a recognized architectural firm achieving several international awards in competitions as well as with built projects, featuring his work in numerous exhibitions. He is the author and co-author of several books, including Sociópolis, Media House Project, the Metapolis Dictionary of Advanced Architecture, Self-sufficient Housing, and the monographic about your work, Occupying Structures in Korea DD Series(2008): Recently he published the book X Paradigms for XXI Century (IaaC, 2018) He was a former CEO of Barcelona Regional Agency of the Barcelona City Council (2011/2015) Actually is a Director of Urban Sciences Laboratory at IAAC, and General Manager of Metropolitan Máster Plan of Rio de Janeiro; Brazil.

700
160
150
140
130
120
110
100
90
80
70
60
50
40
30
20
10
0 m
-10
-20
-30
-40

CONCEPTUAL DIAGRAMS OF SUPER-CROSSING

Large scale Urban Agopuncture

1. Tongil Road & Jinheung Road

2. Seooreoung Road & Yeongmal Road

3. Jinheun Road & Seooreoung Road

4. Eunpyeong Road & Seooreoung Road

5. Eunpyeong Road & Jeungsan Road

6. Tongil Road & Bulgwang Road

7. Seooreoung Road & Yeonseo Road

8. Gajwa Road & Eunpyeong Road

CONCEPTUAL DIAGRAMS OF SUPER-CROSSING

Cross Road solution schematic concept:

Conceptual cross-road situation PLAN

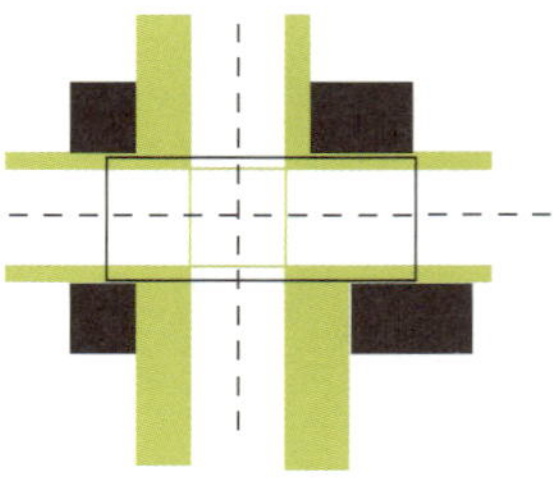

GROUNDFLOOR :
widening the sidewalk enhables citizens to live public space as main reference of the crossroad

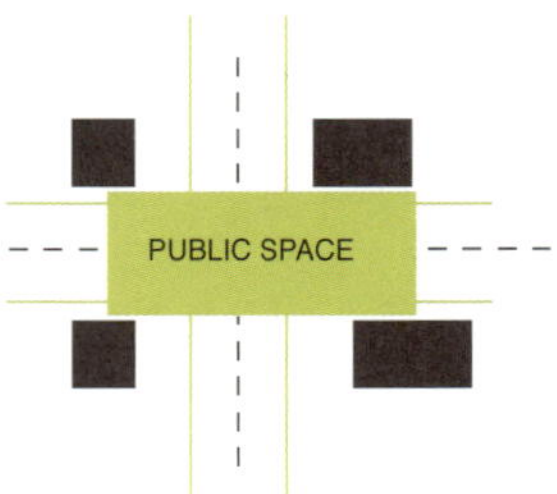

UPPER LEVELS
MULTIFUNCTIONAL PLATFORM:
Lifted Multi-Level plaform from the ground includes series of programs that link local and global activities.
Public spaces and greenery are fundamentals to link the public spaces of the sidewalk and the "island" of the metro with the city.

SECTIONS
variants

"Inverted table " Super-Crossing Option

"Chair" SuperCrossing Option

"Table" SuperCrossing Option

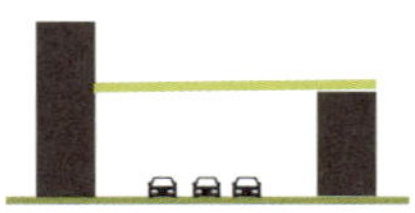

"Green-Chair" SuperCross-ing Option

SUPERCROSSING Typological Options:

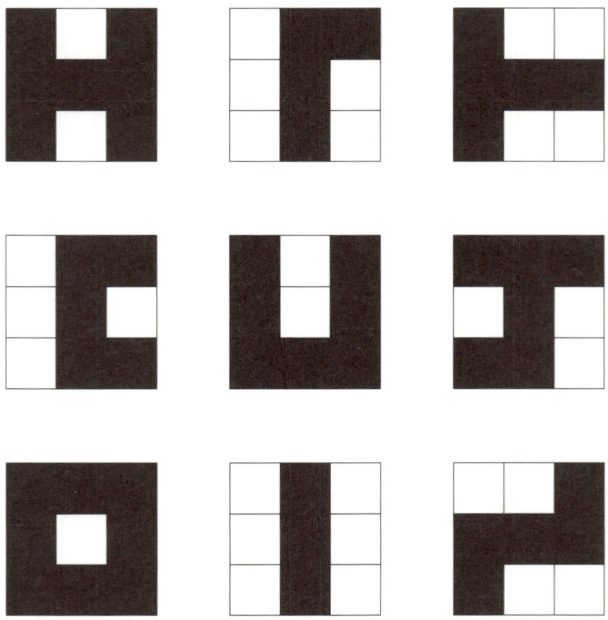

MOBILITY PROPOSAL :

Ground Floor: Exsiting situation

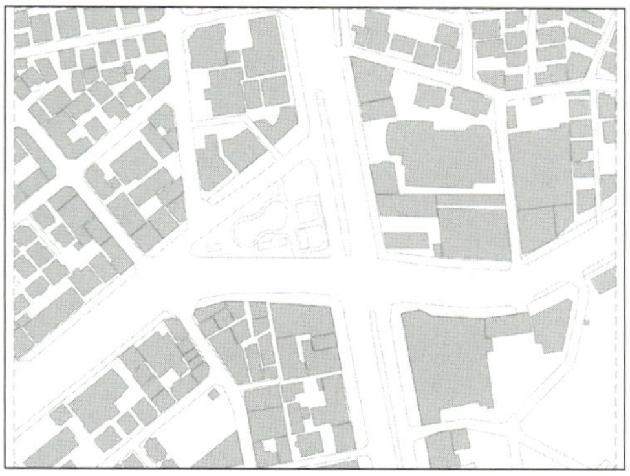

Exsisting Situation

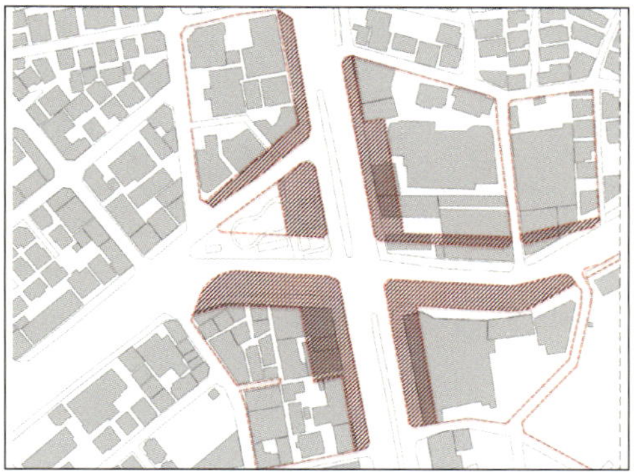

_ new streeet profile
_ new sidewalk

Ground Floor: Project proposal

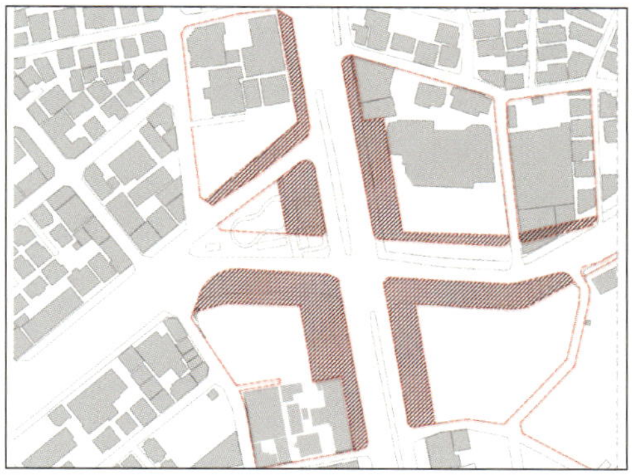

_ new streeet profile
_ new sidewalk
+
_ demolition of exi-
sisting buildings

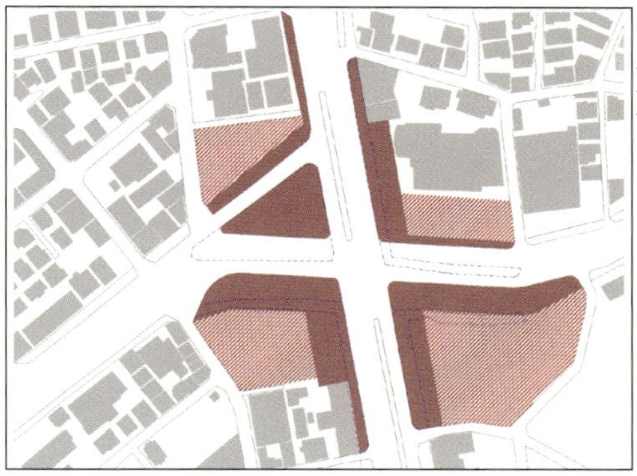

Project proposal:

_ new streeet profile
_ new sidewalk
_ new buildings

FASES OF DEVELOPMENT OF THE DESIGN PROPOSAL

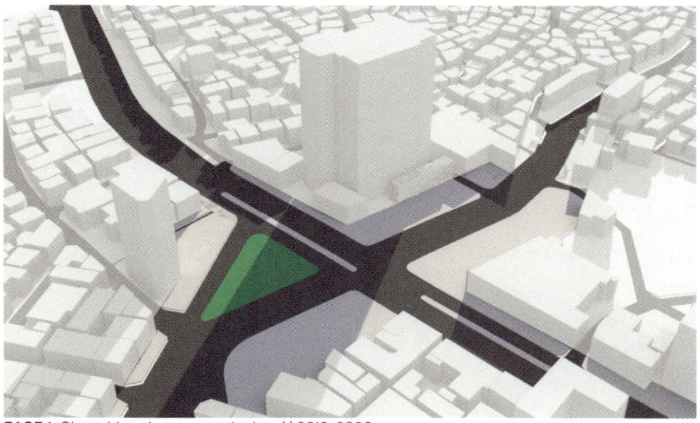

FASE 1: Changhing the streets design // 2019-2020

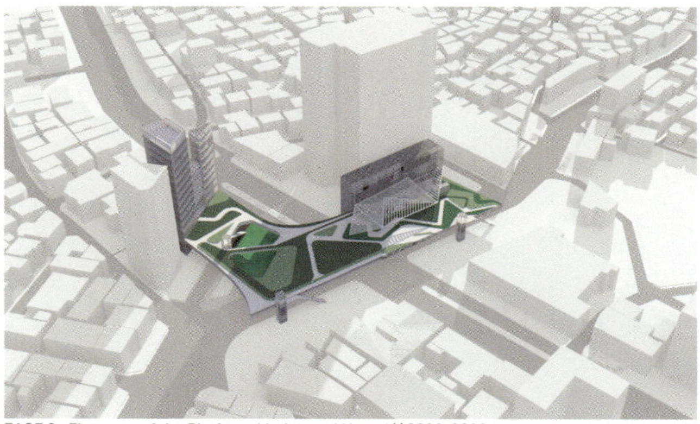

FASE 2: First step of the Platform, Market and Hostel// 2020-2023

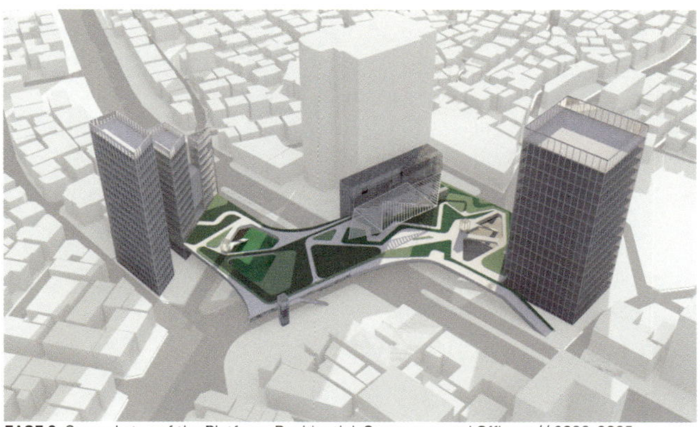

FASE 3: Second step of the Platform, Residential, Commerce and Offices // 2023-2025

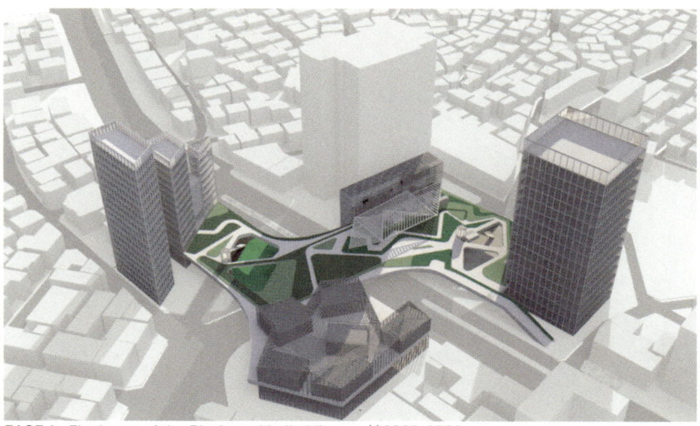

FASE 4: Final step of the Platform, Media Library // 2025-2028

RE-ACTIVATION OF THE NEIGHBORS : ADDED VALUE

Program development according to local citizens age and needs mixed with Glocal activities that attract general public and users of the metro lines and toursist.

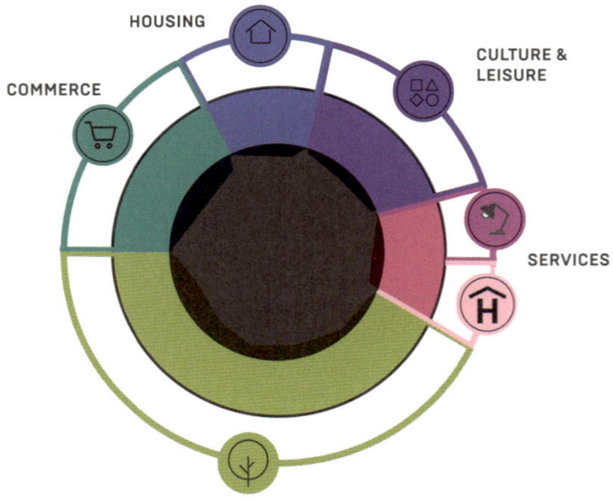

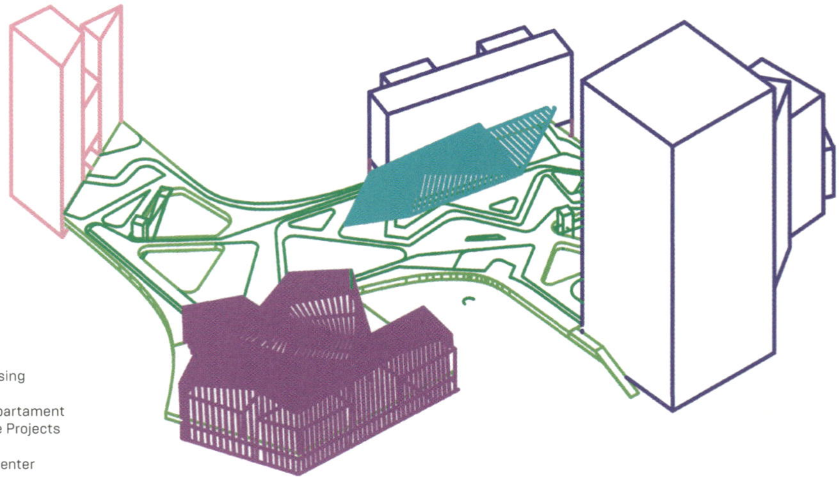

SERVICES
_ Hostel
_ Offices
_ Living working spaces

HOUSING
_ Social Housing
_ Residence
_ Private Appartament
_ Real Estate Projects

CULTURE & LEISURE
_ Cinema
_ Auditorium
_ Mediacenter
_ Civic Center
_ Public Projects

COMMERCE
_Shopping Center
_ Retail
_ Local Market
(Indoor & Outdoor)

PUBLIC SPACES
_ Outdoor activities
_ Green Platform areas
_ Kids playground
_ Bike paths

PROJECT OVERVIEW :

Overview Main Structural Components

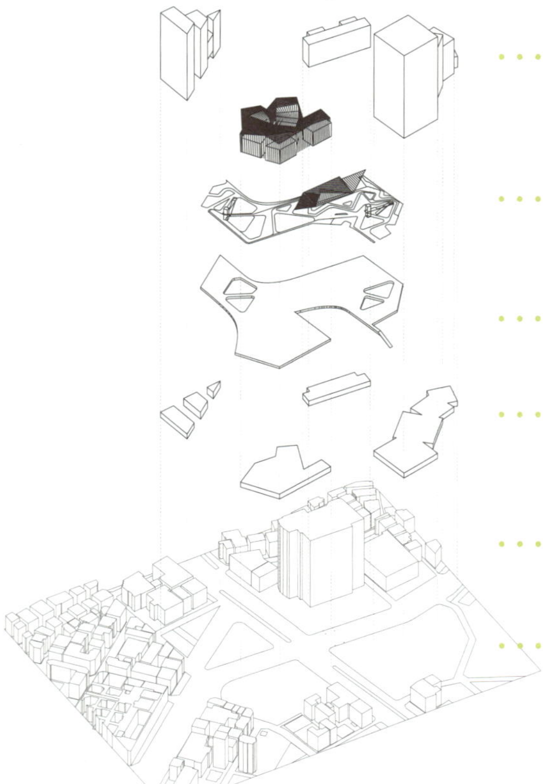

Platform and Buildings Corners' buildings: Buildings at the Cross-Corner are key elements for SuperCross. Their programs help to re-activate the neighbour thanks to their functions and phisical connection with the lifted platform.

Elevated Platform: Public Space. Green areas, Equipped Public Spaces lifted from the ground would be the main program of the Cross-Road SuperSlope project proposal. Green and Pubic spaces would connect the platform with the metro levels and would guarantee playground and enhance the green sustainbility of the Distric.

Platform's Structure: New typology of Urban Design: The Urban False Ceiling. Light Design, sensores etc..

Platform: First Level: The multilevel and multifucntional platform is the connecting tools between the four corners and the two levels of the metro. Commercial activities (the mixture between local market and shopping areas) is the best solution to attract local ctizens and visitors to live the platform.

Cross-road Corners: program development at the cross-corners: Local commerce (local market) and culture activities (such as Civic Center, Mediacenter, Living working spaces) can activate the Cross and the connection with the elevated platform

Street level (Ground Floor): sidewalk widening underground connection between metro and crossreoad with commercial areas

PROJECT OVERVIEW : B

Schematic Plans & Sections

GROUNDFLOOR PLAN

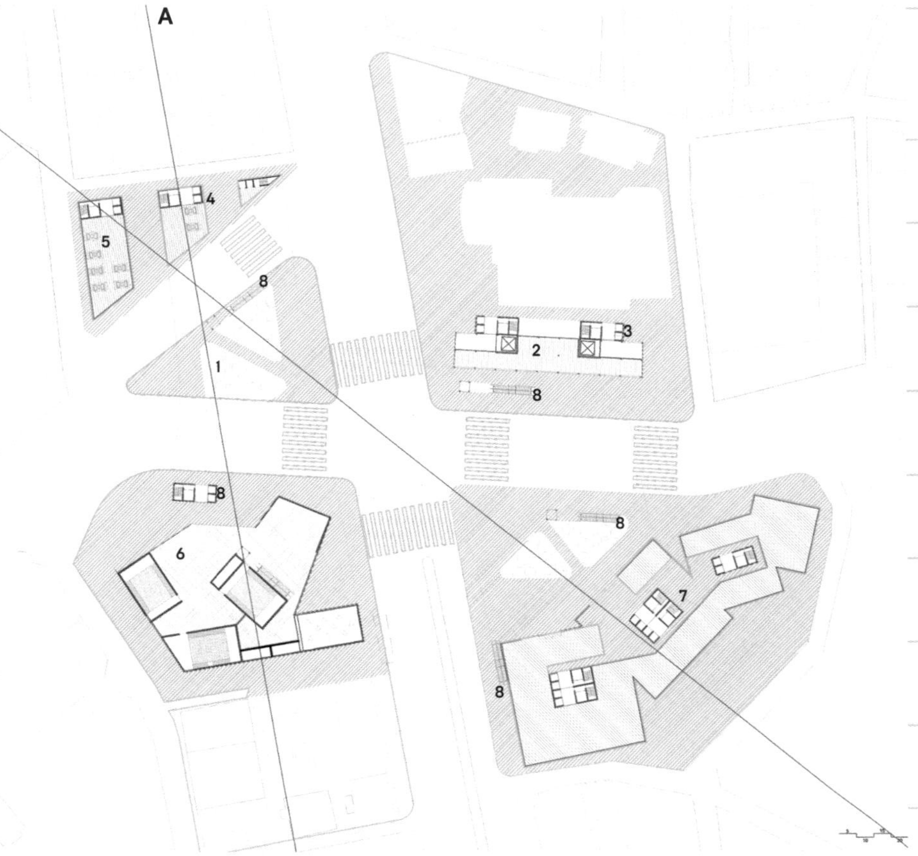

INDEX

1 Yeondimmar Square
2 Market Logistic Area
3 Social Housing Entrance
4 Hostel Access
5 Offices Buildings
6 Media library
7 Residential Commercial and Offices Complex
8 Metro station and Platform Access

PROJECT OVERVIEW : B

Schematic Plans & Sections

PLATFORM PLAN

INDEX

1 Yeonsinnae Elevated Square
2 Market Logistic Area
3 Market Commercial Area
4 Hostel Access
5 Offices Buildings
6 Media library
7 Residential Commercial and Offices Complex
8 Metro station and Platform Access
9 Public Space for events

700
160
150
140
130
120
110
100
90
80
70
60
50
40
30
20
10
0 m
-10
-20
-30
-40

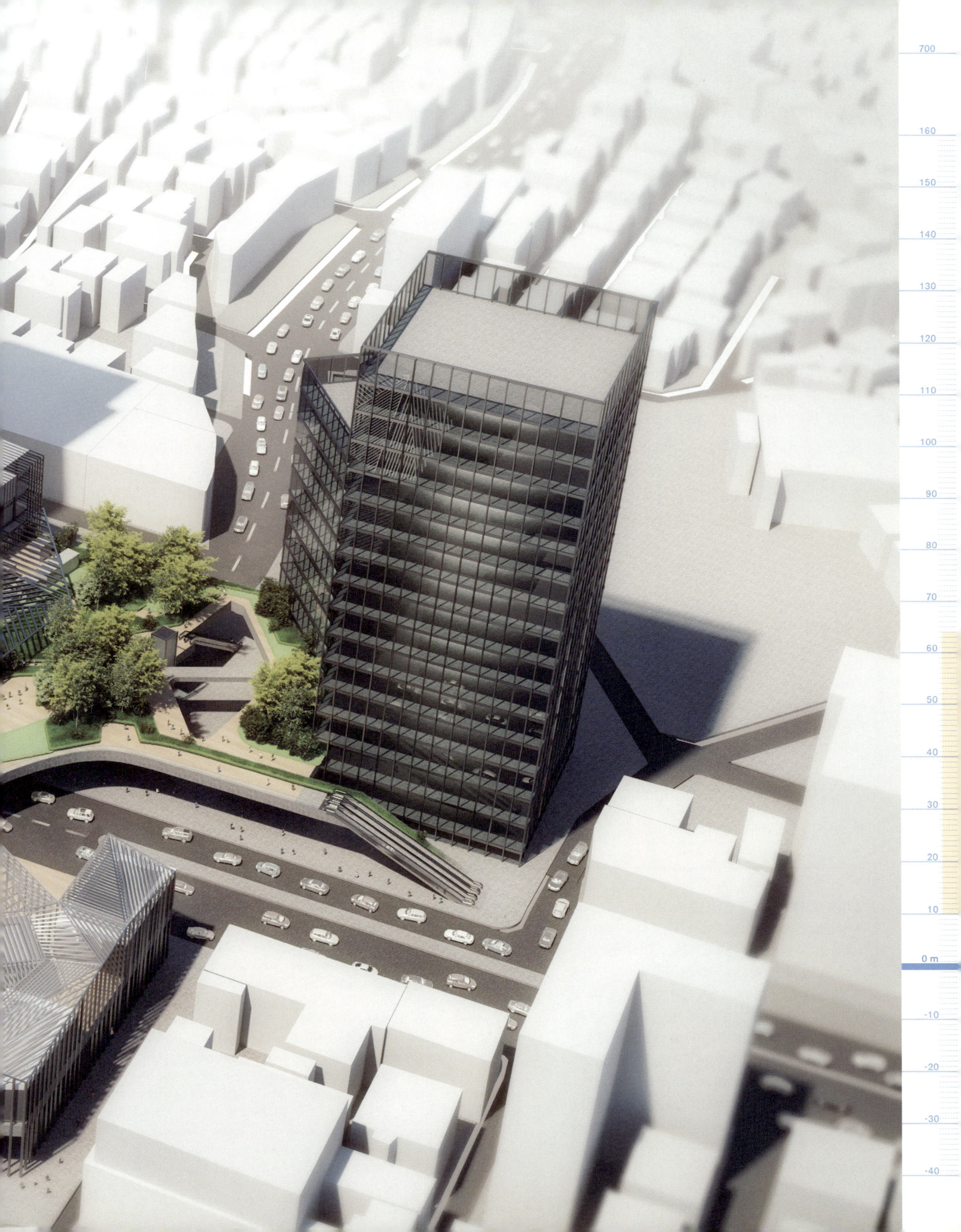
700
160
150
140
130
120
110
100
90
80
70
60
50
40
30
20
10
0 m
-10
-20
-30
-40

김찬중

Chanjoong Kim

4호선(창동역-당고개역) / Line 4(Changdong-Danggogae)

서울 라퓨타: 자율진화 선형도시

현재 창동과 당고개 지하철역 사이에는 거대한 규모의 고가 철도가 있어 마치 떠 있는 섬처럼 보인다. 이 거대한 구조물은 도시의 남과 북을 차단하는 주요 요인이 되고 있다. SEOUL LAPUTA는 민간의 자발적 개발을 장려하고 기존의 인프라 구조를 활용함으로써 도시의 자발적 확장을 장려하는 새로운 접근 방식을 제안한다. 건폐율과 용적률 인센티브와 같은 기존 시스템과는 달리 창동-상계 간에 적용된 새로운 시스템은 대지 영역을 정의하는 수평투영면적을 수직 공간으로 확장시키는 것이다. 기존 인프라를 이용한 새로운 대지 인센티브 시스템은 민간의 개발과 적극적인 투자를 유치할 수 있으며 개발/건설 단계에서 발생할 수 있는 다양한 민원들에 대한 소유주의 적극적인 참여를 장려하여 제동이 가해지는 상황에서도 유연하게 대처할 수 있는 이점이 있다. 또한 철도의 지붕에 모든 수직 동선을 새로 설치하는 것이 아니라 기존 건물의 코어와 연계하여 활용할 수 있으므로 도시와 인접 대지의 경계를 낮추는 좋은 장치가 될 수 있다. 떠 있는 섬 LAPUTA, 서울의 LAPUTA는 시민들에 의해 자생적으로 개발되고 확장되어 도시를 단절하는 것이 아닌 연결하는 매개 공간이 될 것이다.

Seoul Laputa: Self-developing linear city

Between Chang-dong and the Danggogae Station there exists a large elevated railway that looks like a floating island from afar. This monumental structure is one of the main reasons behind the clear division between the north and the south of Seoul. SEOUL LAPUTA proposes a new approach to the city's spontaneous growth by utilizing existing infrastructural structures and encouraging private developments. Unlike typical incentive programs that deal with the building-to-land ratios and FARs, the new system applied to the region between Chang-dong and Sanggye-dong redefines the plot of the site and expands it vertically. This new incentive program that utilize existing infrastructure will attract private capital and investments and by actively involving owners of properties in the development and construction phases be able to flexibly cope with any disturbance factors. Also, not all parts of the roof above railway will need new vertical circulation systems as there can be linkages to the cores of existing buildings along the way, which will further lower the boundary between the city and the site. As a floating island, Seoul's LAPUTA will grow naturally by the citizens and open up to the city as a connective mediating space.

고려대학교 건축공학과를 졸업하고 스위스 연방공과대학에서 수학하였으며 미국 하버드대학에서 건축학 석사학위를 취득하였다. 서울의 한울 건축과 캐임브리지의 Chan Krieger Associates, 보스턴의 KSWA에서 실무를 한 후, 귀국하여 현재까지 경희대 건축대학의 설계 전공 초빙 교수로 재직하면서 THE_SYSTEM LAB의 대표로 활동하고 있다. 2006년 제10회 베니스 비엔날레 한국 대표 건축가로 초청, 같은 해 중국 베이징 국제 건축 비엔날레에서는 주목받는 아시아 젊은 건축가 6인, 2016년 영국 월 페이퍼(wall paper)의 세계의 신진 건축가 20인에 선정되었다. 서울시 건축상 및 건축문화대상, IF Design Award, ICONIC Design Award, Red Dot Award, 한국생태환경건축학회 대상, 코리아 디자인 어워드와 같은 다수의 국내외 수상을 하였다.

Upon graduating from Korea University with a bachelor's degree, Chanjoong Kim studied at the much claimed Swiss Federal Institute of Technology Zurich (ETH). In 2000, he received his master's degree at Harvard University. After working as the senior architect at the Hanwool Architecture Company (Seoul, South Korea), Chan Krieger Associates (Cambridge, USA) and KSWA (Boston, USA), he is currently working as the visiting professor at the Architecture Departement of Kyunghee University while serving as the Principal in charge of THE_SYSTEM LAB in Seoul, South Korea. In 2006, Chan was invited to the Venice Biennale as the representative architect of South Korea. In the same year, he was chosen as one of the six young Asian emerging architects at the Beijing International Architecture Biennale. In 2016, Chan was selected as one of twenty in the Architects' Directory of Wallpaper (UK). His works were recognized domestically by the Seoul Architecture Festival, Korean Architecture Award, Korea Institute of Ecological Architecture and Environment Awards, Korea Design Award; and internationally by ICONIC Awards, IF Design Awards and Red Dot Awards.

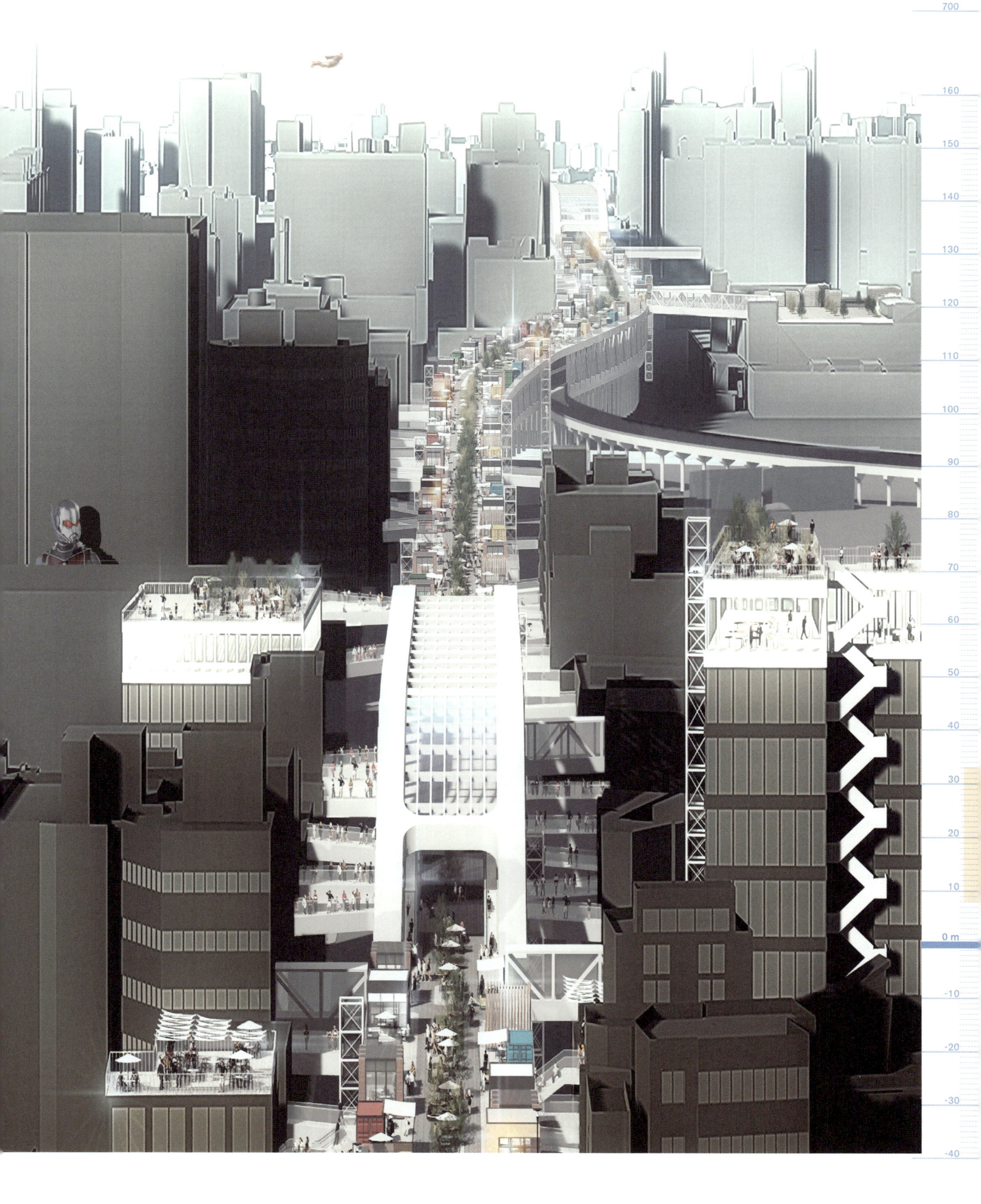
700
160
150
140
130
120
110
100
90
80
70
60
50
40
30
20
10
0 m
-10
-20
-30
-40

Currently, there is an enormous scale of high-railway between Chang-dong and Danggo-gae subway station and it looks like a floating island. This huge structure is becoming a major factor to cut off the north and south of the city. SEOUL LAPUTA proposes a new approach to encourage the voluntary expansion of the city by encouraging private voluntary development and utilizing the existing infrastructure.

The architectural activities that can be performed on the grounded parcels are classified into standard categories: the 'coverage ratio' that regulates the planar density based on the horizontal projection plane 'land area' of the earth, the 'volume ratio' that regulates the spatial and vertical density, and 'the building limit line regulations'. In addition, when the part of the land is opened to the public (such as a public open space), it is encouraged to secure the publicness of individual parcels by alleviating the volume ratio / height restriction. Unlike these existing standards, the incentive applied between Chang-dong and Sang-gye is not simply the reduction of the site coverage and volume ratio standard, but the extension of the horizontal projection, which defines the site area, to a vertical space. For example, if a middle floor is created in a building, a concept similar to a floor area that can be used as a habitable room is applied to the land, which can increase the value of the site and the existing properties. It is the main element of this urban renewal project to give the spatial incentive to the site and utilize the existing rail-highway and the surrounding buildings to the maximum. There are 4 phases to adopt the system on the existing infrastructure.

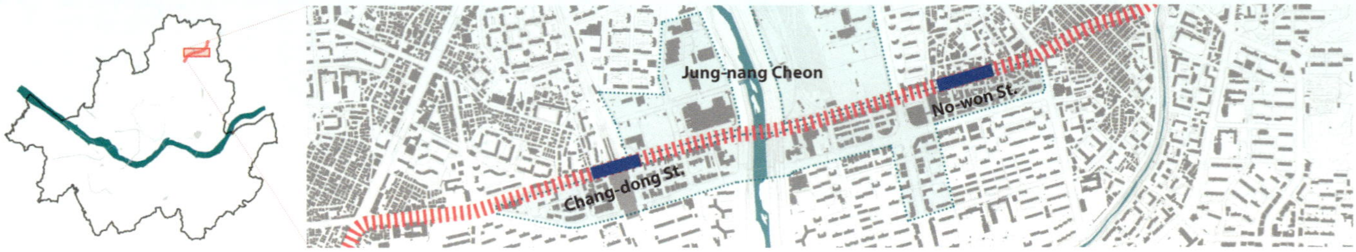

The land-use incentive system that utilizes the existing infrastructure can attract the private development and the active investment of the private sector. In addition, it can reduce the various complaints from owners of surrounding buildings that may arise in the development and construction stage by giving them a permission of occupation and use on the vertically expanded land on the high-railway. In addition, it is possible to utilize it in conjunction with the core of the existing building, not to establish all the new vertical circulation to the roof of the railway. Therefore, it can be a good device to break down the boundary between the city and the individual parcels. Solutions that are not considered deeply can cause an adverse impact on the project, but the new self-expanded incentive system can minimize these impacts. Floating island Laputa, Laputa in Seoul will be developed and expanded by a citizen and become a connecting element rather than a disconnect of the city.

현재 창동과 당고개 지하철역 사이에는 거대한 고가 철도가 놓여 있는데, 마치 공중에 떠 있는 섬처럼 보인다. 이 거대 구조물은 서울의 남북을 차단하는 주요 요인이 되고 있다. 서울 라퓨타는 자발적 민간 개발을 장려하고 기존 기반시설을 활용하여 도시의 자생적 확장을 유도하는 새로운 접근을 제안한다.

실제 필지에서 벌어지는 모든 건축적 활동은 지상 수평투영면적을 기준으로 평면 밀도를 주관하는 '건폐율'과 공간 및 수직 밀도를 주관하는 '용적률' 그리고 '건축한계선'이라는 일반 개념의 지배를 받는다. 특히 (마치 광장처럼) 대지 일부를 시민에게 개방하는 경우 용적률 및 고도 제한을 완화하여 개별 필지의 공공성을 확보하도록 하고 있다. 이러한 기존 방식과 달리 창동-상계 지역에 적용된 우대 정책은 단순히 대지 면적이나 용적률 제한 기준을 낮추는 데 그치지 않고 대지 영역을 정의하는 수평투영면적을 수직 공간으로 확장한다. 예를 들어 어떤 건물에 중간층을 설계한다고 하면 주거 공간에 쓰이는 바닥 면적 개념과 유사한 개념을 대지에 적용할 수 있고, 이는 대지와 기존 부동산의 가치 증대로 이어질 수 있다. 이번 도시재생사업의 주요 사안은 대지에 공간적 인센티브를 부여하고, 기존 고가 철도와 주변 건물을 최대한 활용하는 것이다. 기존 기반시설에 새로운 시스템을 적용하는 작업은 네 단계로 나뉘어 진행된다.

기존 기반시설을 활용하는 대지 인센티브 시스템은 적극적인 민간 개발과 투자를 유도할 수 있다. 아울러 고가 철도 위로 수직 확장된 대지에 대한 소유권이나 사용권을 부여함으로써 개발 및 건설 단계에서 발생할 수 있는 주변 건물주들의 각종 불만을 줄일 수 있다. 또한 철도 지붕까지 새로운 동선을 구성하는 대신 기존 건물의 코어를 연계해 활용할 수도 있다. 결과적으로 이는 도시와 개별 필지 사이의 경계를 허무는 좋은 장치가 될 수 있다. 깊은 고민이 결여된 해결책은 프로젝트에 부정적인 영향을 미칠 수 있다. 그러나 이 새로운 자가 확장적 인센티브 시스템은 그런 영향을 최소화할 수 있다. 천공의 섬 라퓨타 즉, 서울 라퓨타는 시민에 의해 개발되고 확장되며 도시의 단절 요소가 아닌 연결 요소로 자리 잡을 것이다.

PHASE 1. EXISTING CONDITION

> Urban context between Chang-dong and Sang-gye have been separated by High-railway and existing infrastructures because of a linear shape and the huge scale of the structures. Existing buildings have been developed by typical building regulations.

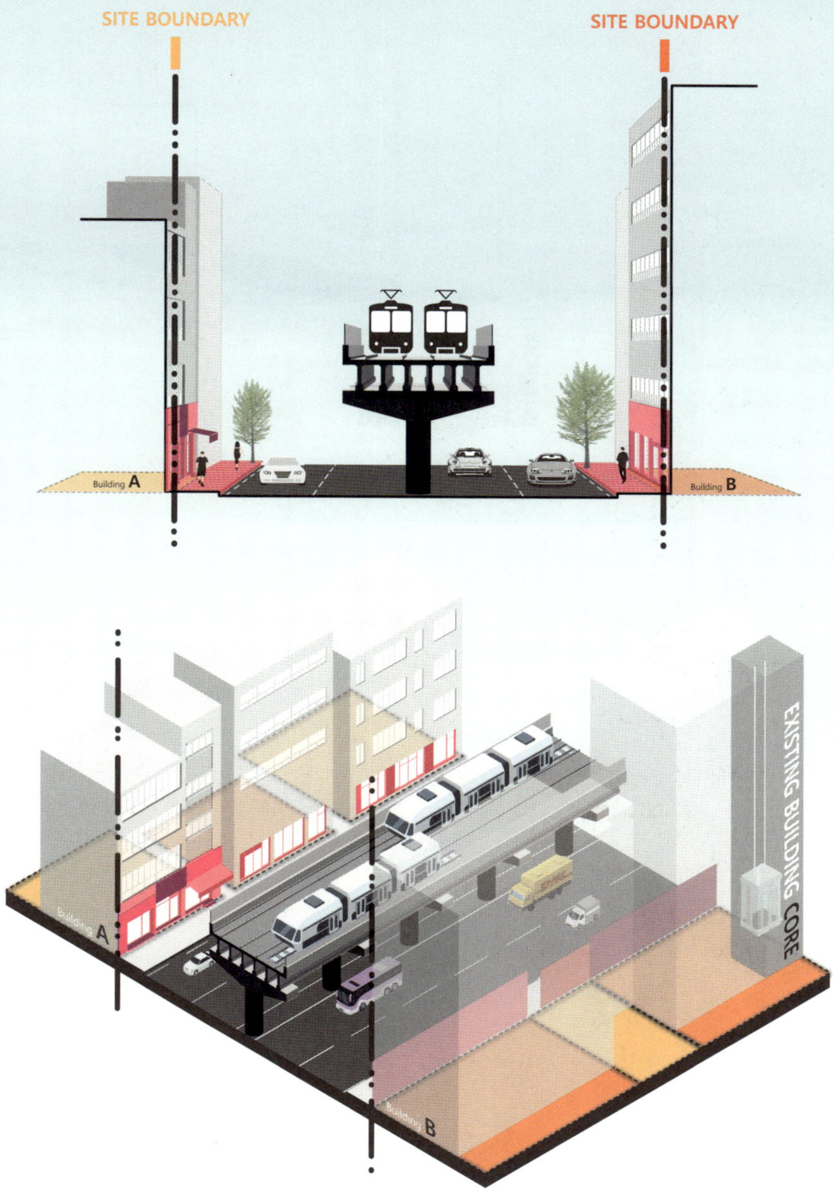

PHASE 1 〉 기존 현황

창동과 상계지역은 거대하고 긴 선형의 고가철로와 남과 북을 가로지르는 중랑천으로 인해 도시적인 맥락이 단절되어 있는 상태이다. 고가철로 주변의 건물들은 정해진 건축법에 맞춰 계획되어 있는 상태이다. 고가철로 하부의 차도는 좁은 인도로 인해 보행환경이 열악하여 보행환경의 개선이 필요한 상황이기도 하다.

PHASE 2. PLATFORM: EXTENSION OF THE SITE BOUNDARY

> Covering the roof of existing rail-highway structure to form a PLATFORM as artificial land and Extension of the existing site boundary to the upper part of the PLATFORM.

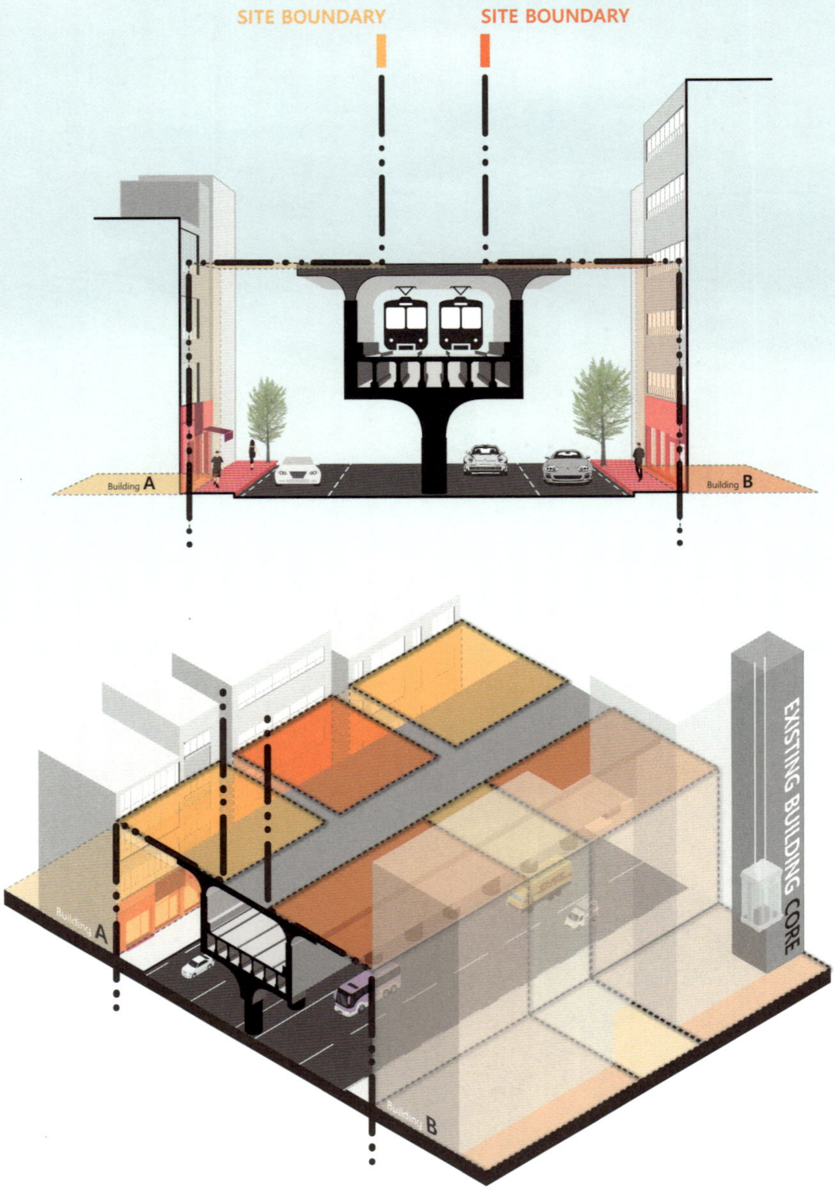

PHASE 2 〉 플랫폼: 대지 경계선의 확장

고가철로 지붕을 활용하여 형성된 PLATFORM의 일정 구간까지 인접 대지들의 대지 경계가 수평적, 수직적으로 확장된다. 확장된 대지 경계의 부분은 해당 부분의 점용권 허용하는 개념으로 시스템을 구축하여 형성한다.

PHASE 3. PERMISSION FOR OCCUPATION AND USE

> Form a connection system from a connected building to a platform such as a bridge or a staircase (should be installed by land or building owners). These connection systems should be a minimum size not to cover skyline. Permission for occupation and use is given to all the consecutive properties allowing to build small facilities and spaces on the expanded site boundary.

PHASE 3 〉 인접 대지의 점용권 부여

인접 건물들로부터 PLATFORM으로 직접 연결되는 다리나 계단과 같은 동선을 설치하여 해당 구간으로의 접근을 용이하게 한다. 이러한 연결구간은 도시의 스카이라인을 고려하여 최소한으로 설치되어야 하며, 기존 건물들의 수직 동선을 활용하는 방안도 함께 고민되어야 한다. 이렇게 연결된 대지에는 해당 영역의 점용권을 부여하여 점용 구간 내 연접건물의 확장으로서 일정 규모 이하 시설물 또는 소형 건축행위를 허용한다.

PHASE 4. SEOUL LAPUTA: SELF-DEVELOPING LINEAR CITY

> These self-development activities should be limited by the criteria for the detailed use of the buildings such as the coverage ratio and maximum possible height of the space. (50% coverage rate, max. 4m average height)

PHASE 4 〉서울 라퓨타: 자율진화 선형도시

이러한 자생적인 개발행위들의 기본적인 건축물의 용도와 건폐율/높이 등의 세부 항목에 대한 기준을 마련하여 무분별한 개발행위는 제한하여 도시확장의 지속가능한 개발을 가능하게 한다.

FRAGILE

STUDIO JHS

700
160
150
140
130
120
110
100
90
80
70
60
50
40
30
20
10
0 m
-10
-20
-30
-40
Shop

이은영

Eunyoung Yi

슈퍼콜로네이드 서울

월드컵경기장, 월드컵공원, 문화비축기지 등 분절된 대형공간들을 하나로 묶고 연계할 수 있는 도시공간을 개입시키고자 한다.
Urban Colonnade 수색차량기지 이전 이후 양질의 도시공간이 생성될 기회의 땅을 기점으로 한강으로 연결되는 보행자 공간을 형성한다. 이동의 시작과 끝점의 동기가 분명하되, 그 공간이 단순한 이동공간이 아닌 머무는 공간으로서의 여유를 가질 수 있도록 회랑의 속성을 넘어 끝없이 연계되어가는 정자와 같은 공간의 속성을 갖도록 하였다. 도시공간에 강렬하게 삽입되는 대형의 수평적 요소로서 어느 시점에서도 시야에 들어오되, 회랑이나 정자가 주는 여유로움과 가벼움이 공간과 형상을 지배케 하여, 부담 없이 주변의 모든 움직임을 흡인하는 힘을 갖도록 한다. 고전적 요소를 극단적으로 추상화하고 비례감을 시대 정서로 여과시켰다.
Ground Engraving 증산로로 분리된 공간들을 땅 위에 새겨지는 음각의 공간으로 자연스럽게 묶어준다. 도시공간을 연결코자 하는 기능적 동기에서 시작한 음각이라는 공간조성기법을 Urban Colonnade를 따라 형성되는 문화적 작업, 주거, 소통공간의 유니트들에도 일관되게 구사한다. 고전에서 전달되어오는 공간의 유형들을 보편화하되 기능과 주어진 대지 조건에 따라 변용하는 과정을 통해, 우리 시대를 담는 새로운 공간 유형의 시퀀스를 땅에 새겨나가는 작업이다.

Supercolonnade Seoul: Urban Colonnade vs Ground Engraving

The project is to inject an urban space that can weave segregated open areas such as the World Cup Stadium, the World Cup Park, and the Oil Tank Culture Park into an interrelated thread. Urban Colonnade: the creation of a pedestrian pathway that links to the Han River with the newly available land created by the transition of a railroad car station as the focal point. With clear motivation that marks a beginning and an end, pedestrians are allowed not only simple progressions in space—a capability provided by the most typical function of a corridor, hallway, and gallery space—but also leisurely lingering in space made possible by the constantly relational spatial characteristic commonly found in the pavilion-like structure in Korean tradition. As a strong horizontal presence that can be seen from anywhere in the surrounding region, the proposed structure and space will maintain the sense of lightness and composure stemming from the colonnade and the pavilion-like natures and be able to absorb any kind of movement around it. The structure radically abstracts any classical element and filters into the contemporary spirit any sense of proportion. Ground Engraving: the consolidation of disparate spaces divided by the Jeungsan Road through the act of engraving. The engraving technique is applied uniformly to repetitive units of cultural, residential, and communicative spaces along the urban colonnade. Types of spaces extended from antiquity are generalized but adjusted to different functions and topographical conditions, which eventually leads to the engraving of a new sequence of spaces that reflects our times.

이은영은 1956년생으로 한양대학교 졸업 후 1990년 아헨공대(RWTH Aachen)에서 석사학위를 받고, O.M. 웅어스, J. 쉬어만 설계사무소에서 근무했으며, 1994년부터 독일 쾰른에서 이 아키텍츠(Yi Architects)를 운영하고 있다. 아헨공대 건축학과에 출강하였으며, 한양대학교 교수로 재직하였다. 대표작품은 1999년 유럽공개설계공모 당선되어 2011년 완공된 슈투트가르트 시립도서관, 니더작센 주의회 의사당 계획안 (2010 유럽공개설계공모 1등당선), 주 프랑크푸르트 대한민국총영사관 (2018 완공 예정) 등이며, 슈투트가르트 시립도서관은 2013년 독일의 휴고해링 건축상을 받았고, Architectural Digest, CNN, Time 지 등에서는 주목할 아름다운 도서관에 선정되기도 하였다.

Yi, Eun Young was born 1956 in DaeJeon, Korea. Undergraduate Hanyang University, Seoul, Korea and Graduate RWTH Aachen, Germany. Worked for O. M. Ungers and J. Schürmann in Cologne. After receiving architects license from Germany, established Yi Architects in Cologne, where he is until now coordinating international projects. He taught in RWTH Aachen and since 2000 until 2011 was a professor in Hanyang University. Major projects include the Public Library in Stuttgart, Germany (Europe open competition 1. Awards,1999 / construction, 2011), the New Parliament of Niedersachsen in Hannover, Germany (Europe open competition 1. Awards, 2010), General Consulate Building of the Republic of Korea in Frankfurt (2014-, under construction, completion 2018). He won the Hugo Häring Awards 2014 in Germany. The Stuttgart City Library is honored by CNN and Time Magazine as '7 of the world's most beautiful libraries' and by Architectural Digest as one of 'the most spectacular libraries around the world'.

-40 -30 -20 -10 0 m 10 20 30 40 50 60 70 80 90 100 110 120 130 140 150 160 700

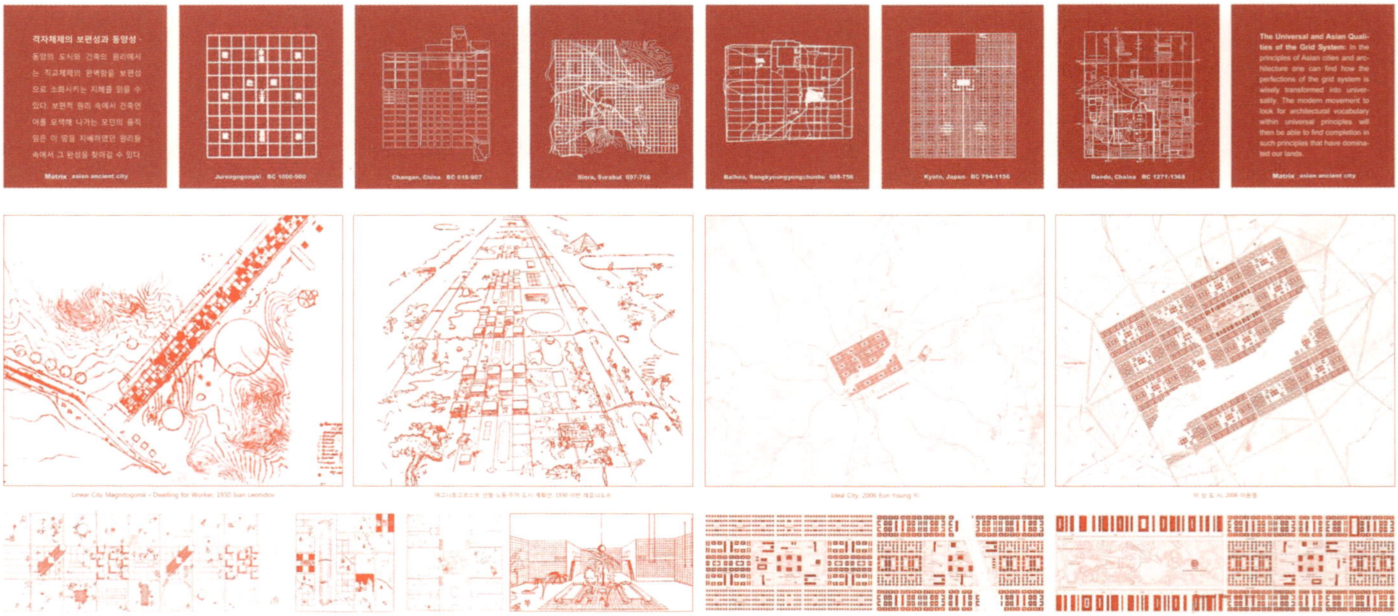

테제

격자체제의 보편성과 동양성·하나의 선과 또 하나의 선이 만날 때 직각처럼 완벽한 형태가 없다. 완벽한 것처럼 시정이 넘치는 것은 없다. 완벽은 신성이기 때문이다. 동양의 도시와 건축의 원리에서는 바로 그러한 완벽함을 보편성으로 소화시키는 지혜를 읽을 수 있다. 보편적 원리 속에서 건축언어를 모색해 나가는 모던의 움직임은 이 땅을 지배하였던 원리들 속에서 그 완성을 찾아 나갈 수 있다. 유형론적 건축·동서를 막론하고 고전 속에서 발견되는 건축의 유형을 우리 시대의 보편적 정서로서 추상화하는 일련의 시도는 수천 년간의 선배들의 지혜 축적과 그 당연한 것들의 완벽한 성취를 향했던 소박한 집념에 대한 최소한의 존경을 바탕으로 하고 있고, 인간 문화의 점진적 승화에 대한 믿음을 바탕으로 하는 것이다. 땅위에 새겨지는 공간·보편적 가치, 본질에 충실한 건축을 통하여서만 우리의 도시도 원시 건축이나 우리가 물려받은 도시가 발하는 그 후광을 우리의 빛깔로 발할 수 있는 것이다. 우리의 정신이 투사되어 응고된 그 물질 덩어리는 대지에 단단히 결합하여, 역사의 무게와 그 끈끈한 생명력의 궤적을 기억하게 될 것이다. 현대건축담론과 메트로폴의 메커니즘 ·길게 보면 약 이백여 년 전 지구의 반대편에서 불이 댕겨진 근대건축의 담론은 시대의 변환기에 도시와 건축에 관한 새로운 정의를 얻고자 하는 절박함에서 시작되었다. 현실에의 열망적인 비전이 차차 퇴색하며 담론이라는 메커니즘이 지성의 엘리티시즘으로 변질되어가고 있는 것을 우리는 체험하고 있다. 본연의 중심에서 벗어나 방향을 잃어버린 현대건축의 담론이 세계 곳곳 메트로폴의 증식 욕망에 결합하며, 우리의 도시에도 그대로 그 힘을 드러내고 있다. 우리의 도시는 더 이상 그 희생물이 되지 않아야 하고, 건강하게 시작한 모던의 담론은 이제 그 빛나는 결실을 맺어내야 한다. 수천 년의 시간 속에서 행해진 건축의 작업 속에서 지혜를 발견하며 그것의 지속적인 완성의 작업을 통하여 진정한 새로운 건축에, 새로운 도시에 다다를 수 있다.

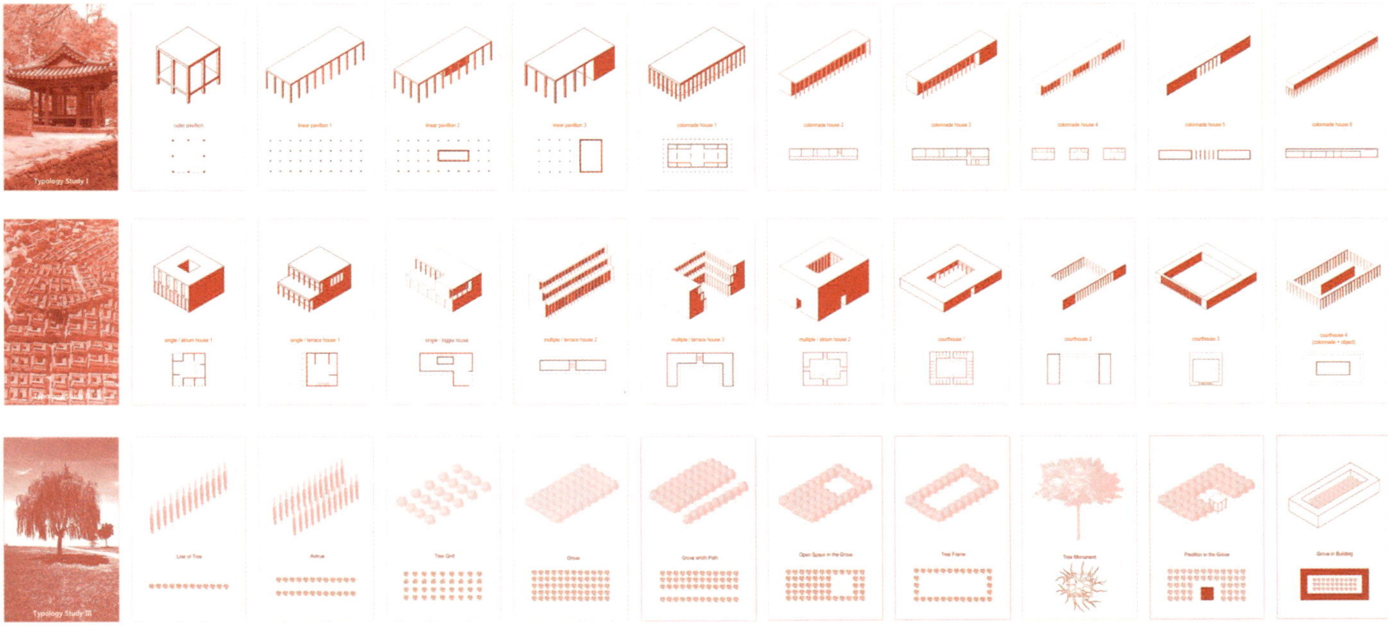

THESE

The Universal and Asian Qualities of the Grid System: There is no form more perfect than the right angle at which one line meets the other. There is no one more poetic as perfection. Indeed, perfection means divinity. In the principles of Asian cities and architecture one can find how such perfection is wisely transformed into universality. The modern movement to look for architectural vocabulary within universal principles will then be able to find completion in such principles that have dominated our lands. Typological Architecture: Ongoing efforts to abstract and universalize the architectural typologies found in the classical worlds of both the East and the West into our current terms are based on firstly the wisdom of the previous architects of thousands of years and the minimum respect for the constant tenacity for that perfect achievement that is now fair and secondly the faith in the gradual progress of humanity's culture. Space Engraved onto the Ground: Only through universal values and architecture faithful to its essence can we give our own color to the reflection of the archaic architecture or of our inherited cities. The coalesced one single mass projected with our spirit will be rooted into the land and remember the weight of its history and the trajectory of its tenacious vitality. Contemporary Architectural Discourse and the Mechanism of Metropole: Modern architecture that was kindled only about two hundred years ago on the other side of the globe was desperately begun to redefine architecture and cities at a turbulent time of change. The fading of aspirational visions rooted in reality led to the rise of discourse as mechanism that is currently being turned into intellectual elitism. The current architecture without orientation far from essence is coupled up with the Metropole's desire for proliferation overall in the world. Such phenomenon is revealed and shows strength in our cities as well. Our cities should no longer be victims to such mechanism, and the modern discourse that started out healthy should now see itself come to fruition. We must seek wisdom in the past architecture of thousands of years and through such effort will be able to reach a new architecture and a new city.

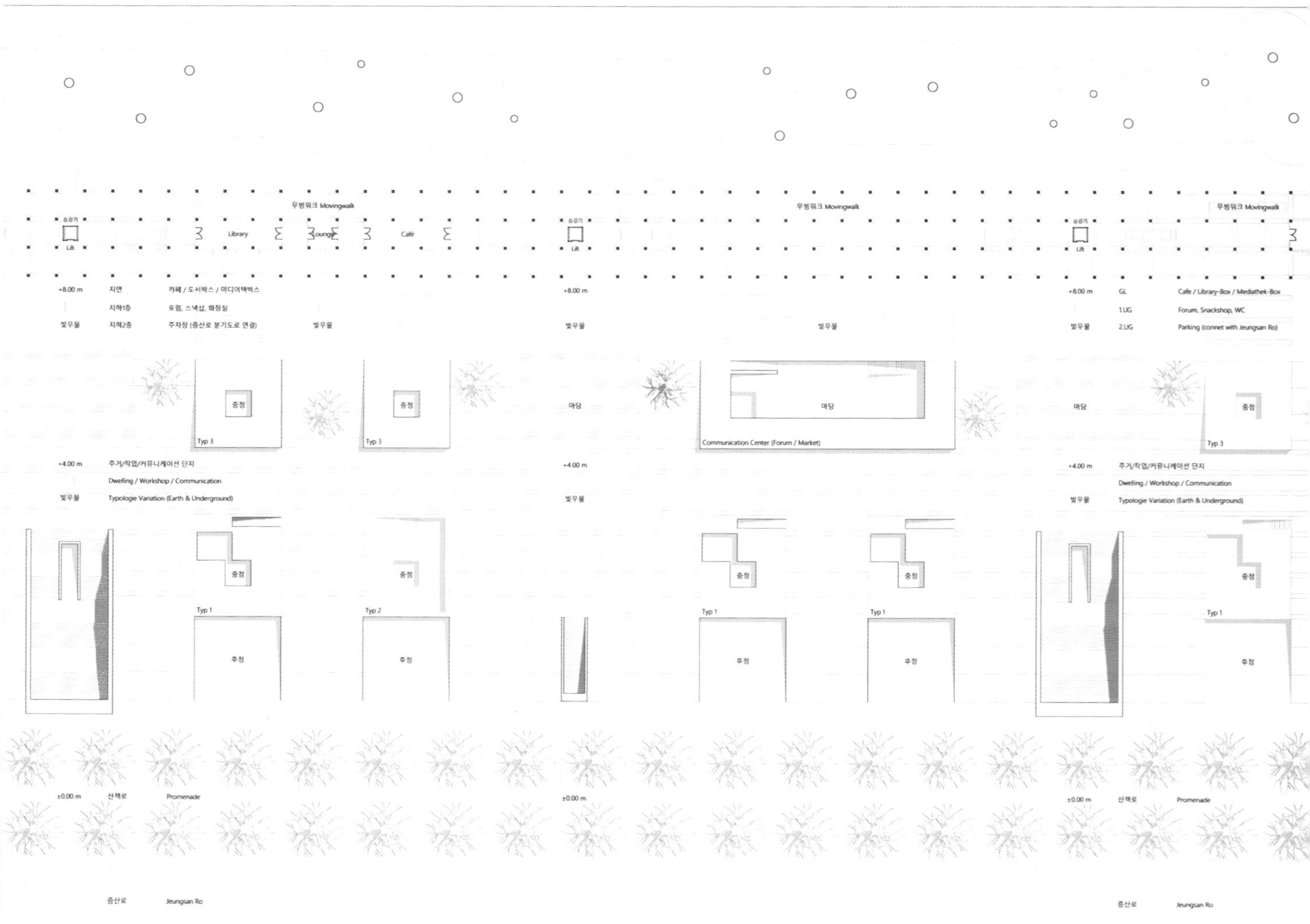

GROUNDPLAN 평면도

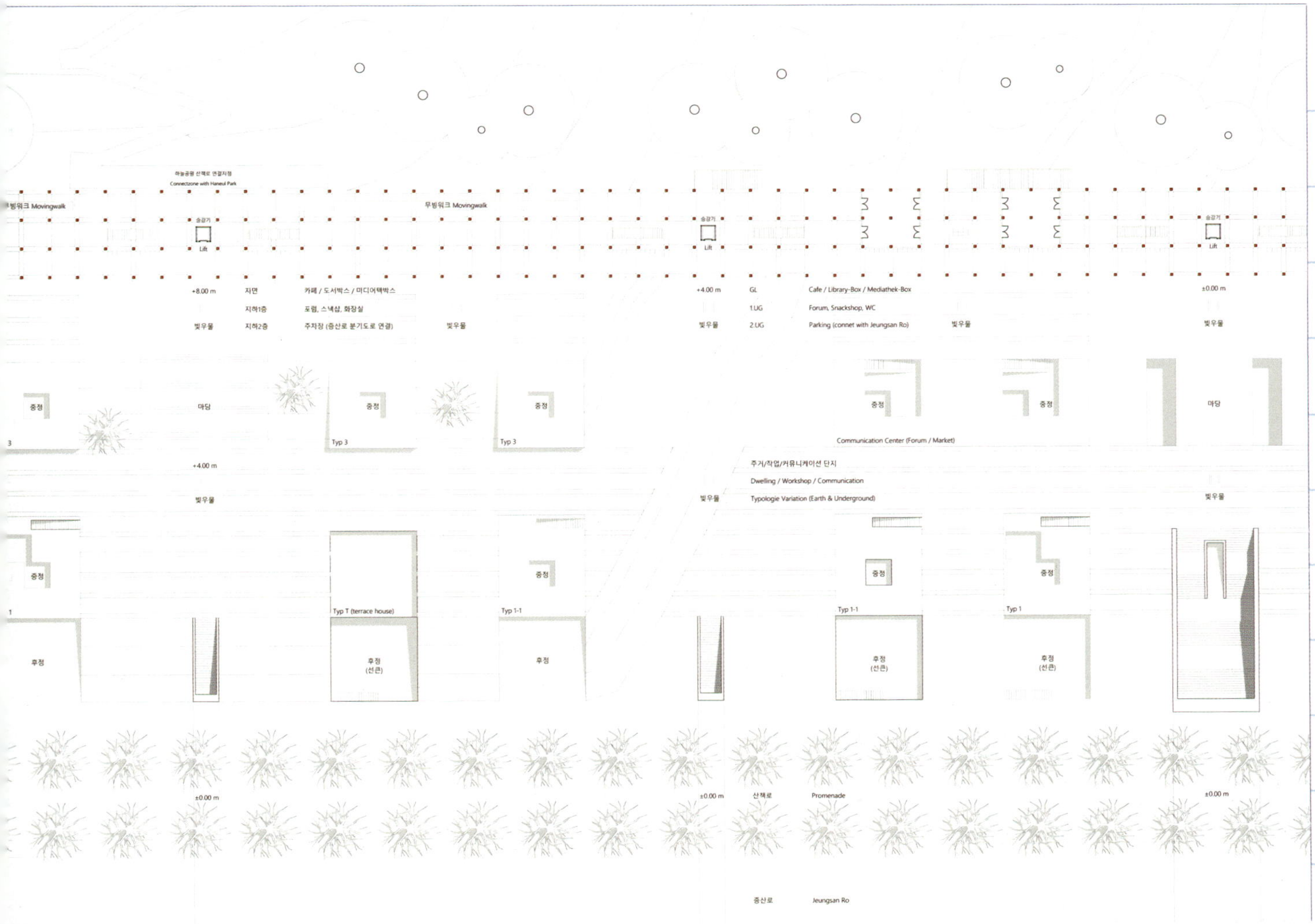

SITEPLAN 배치도

700
160
150
140
130
120
110
100
90
80
70
60
50
40
30
20
10
0 m
-10
-20
-30
-40

700
160
150
140
130
120
110
100
90
80
70
60
50
40
30
20
10
0 m
-10
-20
-30
-40

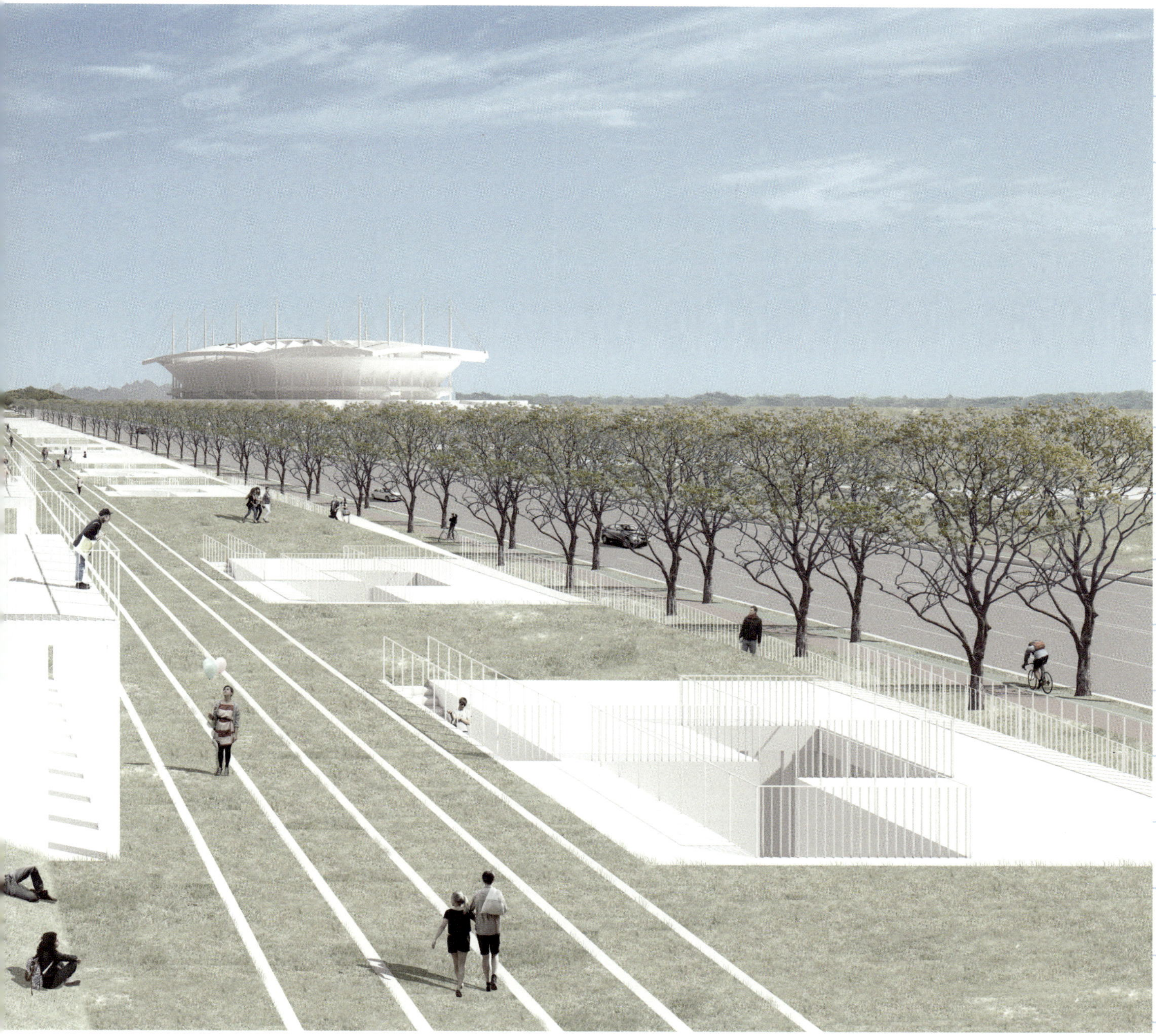

승효상

Seung H-Sang

거주하는 다리

1,000만 인구가 사는 세계의 메가시티 25개 중에서 산을 도시 내부에 품고 있는 곳은 서울이 거의 유일하다. 널리 알려진 대로 서울이 조선의 수도로 정해진 까닭은 산 때문이다. 네 개의 산(북악산·낙산·남산·인왕산)과 이를 둘러싸는 또 다른 네 산(북한산·용마산·관악산·덕양산), 그 사이를 흐르는 물줄기들이 이루는 풍경이 서울의 고유한 지리여서, 산은 말 그대로 랜드마크이며 도시는 그 속에 작은 건축들이 모인 집합체였다.
삼각산에서 발원하여 북악으로 이어지는 산세는 창덕궁과 창경궁, 종묘의 정전을 거쳐 세운상가에 이르러 청계천과 만난다. 계속해서 남쪽으로 목멱을 넘으면 해방촌을 지나 용산공원을 관통하며 마침내 한강에 다다른다. 한강은 서울의 남북을 아우르는 녹지축의 중간이다. 한강을 건너면 녹지는 계속해서 남쪽으로 이어져 마침내 관악으로 치닫는다.
우리가 제안하는 한강의 스물아홉 번째 다리는, 용산에서 동작을 연결하는 새로운 길이다. 다리 위 풍경에는 자동차가 없다. 대신 녹음을 따라 사람만이 오롯이 강을 건널 따름이다. 다리 위의 길은 서울의 골목길을 닮았다. 7.5m의 폭을 절반 이상 녹지에 내어주고 남은 길은 2~3m. 우리 신체 크기에 딱 적합한 이 길들은 통행 기능만 있는 직선이 아니라 좁다가 넓다가 곧게 가다가 휘어지며 드라마틱하게 강물을 넘는다. 길을 따라 걷다 보면 조그만 벤치, 쉬어갈 수 있는 공터, 시끌벅적한 광장, 주전부리를 파는 가판 따위를 마주하게 되는데, 이 또한 골목길의 풍경을 닮아있다. 길옆으로 나란한 녹지들은 서울의 산과 들, 가로를 수놓는 친숙한 꽃나무와 덤불들로 채워질 것이다.
다리의 북쪽 강변으로는 한강이 흐르는 방향을 따라 400m 길이의 새로운 가로가 물 위로 들어설 것이다. 다리를 건너 이곳에 도착한 사람들은 즐길 수 있는 스케일의 강물을 사이에 두고 웃고, 떠들고, 먹고, 마시며 시간을 보낼 것이다. 한강을 유람하던 요트와 유람선 또한 해가 지면 이곳에 와서 정박하며 머문다. 비로소 강물은 손에 닿는 풍경이 되고 서울 시민에게 되돌려진다.
산이 존재하는 서울은 그 고유 풍경을 회복할 원점이 있으므로 아직도 희망적이다. 거주하는 다리는, 풍경의 원점으로의 회귀다.

1952년생으로 서울대학교를 졸업하고 1974년에서 89년까지 김수근 사무실에서 일을 한 후, 1989년에 이로재를 개소하였다. '빈자의 미학(미건사, 1996)'을 비롯한 저서들이 있으며, 북런던대학, 서울대학, 한국예술종합학교, 빈 공과대학에서 강의하였다. 미국 건축가협회에서 2002년 명예상을 수상하였으며, 2002년 국립현대미술관에서 올해의 작가로 선정되었다. 2007년에는 정부로부터 대한민국 예술문화상을 수상하였다. 베니스 비엔날레 한국관 감독 (2008), 광주 디자인 비엔날레 감독 (2011)을 역임하였으며, 서울시 첫 번째 총괄건축가(2014-16)였다. 현재 동아대학교 석좌교수이며, 국가건축정책위원회 위원장이다.

Born in 1952, studied at Seoul National University. Worked for Kim Swoo Geun from 1974 to 1989 and established his office "IROJE architects & planners' in 1989. He published several books including 'Beauty of Poverty(1996 Mikunsa)', and taught at North London University, Seoul National University and at Korea National University of Art, and at TU Wien as visiting professor. The America Institute of Architects invested him with Honorary Fellow of AIA in 2002, and Korea National Museum of Contemporary of Art selected him as 'the artist of year 2002'. In 2007, Korean government honored him with 'Korea Award for Art and Culture', and he was director for Gwangju Design Biennale 2011 after for Korean Pavilion of Venice Biennale 2008, and was the first City Architect of Seoul Metropolitan Government in 2014 and finished its term in 2016. And now he is Chair Professor at Dong-A University and working as Chief Commissioner of Presidential Commission on Architecture Policy.

700
160
150
140
130
120
110
100
90
80
70
60
50
40
30
20
10
0 m
-10
-20
-30
-40

Habitable Bridge, Domestic Landscape of Seoul

Among 25 global megacities with more than one million population, Seoul is almost the only one that embraces mountains within the city, which is the unique identity of Seoul. It has been well-known that mountains were the very reason for Seoul to be selected as the capital of Joseon Dynasty. The unique landscape of Seoul comprises four inner mountains (Bugaksan, Naksan, Namsan and Inwangsan), four outer mountains encompassing these four (Bukhansan, Yongmasan, Gwanaksan and Deokyangsan) and water streams running between these inner and outer mountain groups. Mountains were literally a landmark of Seoul and the city was a collective exhibition of small natural structures.

The mountain range originating from Samgaksan and leading to Bugaksan runs through Changdeokgung Palace, and Jongmyo Shrine, and finally encounters Cheonggyecheon Stream at Seun Sangga. Crossing Namsan to the south leads to Haebangchon, then to Yongsan National Park and finally to the Han River. The river runs through the middle of the green axis embracing northern and southern Seoul. Across the Han River to the south, the green axis could continue to the south and finally rise to Gwanak Mountain.

The proposed 29th bridge over the Han River is a new road linking Yongsan and Dongjak Districts. The landscape on the bridge includes no cars, but instead people cross the river along the greenery built on the bridge. The path on the bridge resembles alleys in Seoul. Over half of the 7.5m-wide street is groomed with greens and the remaining 2~3m-wide path is for pedestrians. The path along the bridge is not just a straight line but sometimes it is narrow, wide or winding, presenting a dramatic journey across the river.

Walking along the streets, we often come across small benches, resting spaces, noisy squares and stalls, which also looks like a landscape along alleys. The green patches along the path on the new bridge will be filled with familiar flowering trees and shrubs that can be easily seen around mountains, fields and roads in Seoul.

On the northern part of the bridge, a 400m-long path will be built on the water along the river. Arriving at this point along the bridge, people will spend some time here in laughing, chatting, eating and drinking. Yachts and cruise ships traveling along the river during the day will spend a night here after dark.

Bridges are not just a functional structure connecting roads but they have become a part of landscape of the city themselves by relating neighboring spaces. The new bridge over the Han River is suggested as a habitable one.

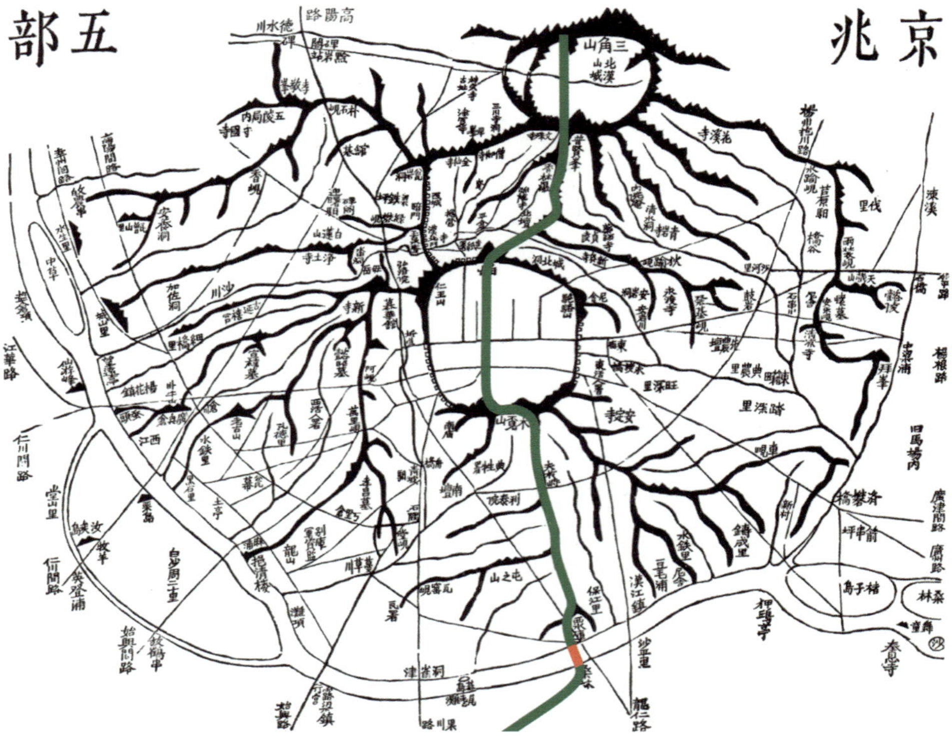

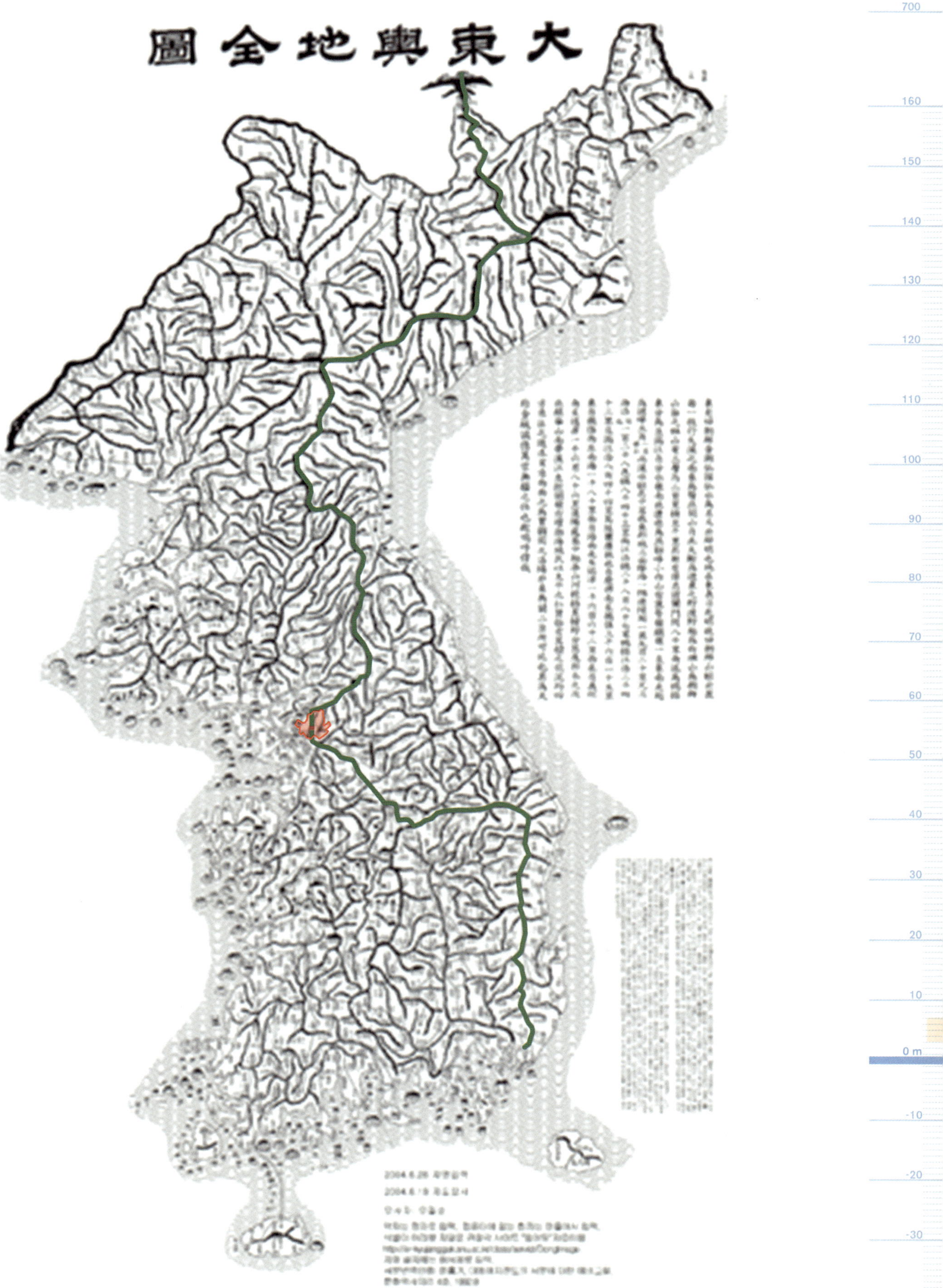
大東輿地全圖
700
160
150
140
130
120
110
100
90
80
70
60
50
40
30
20
10
0 m
-10
-20
-30
-40

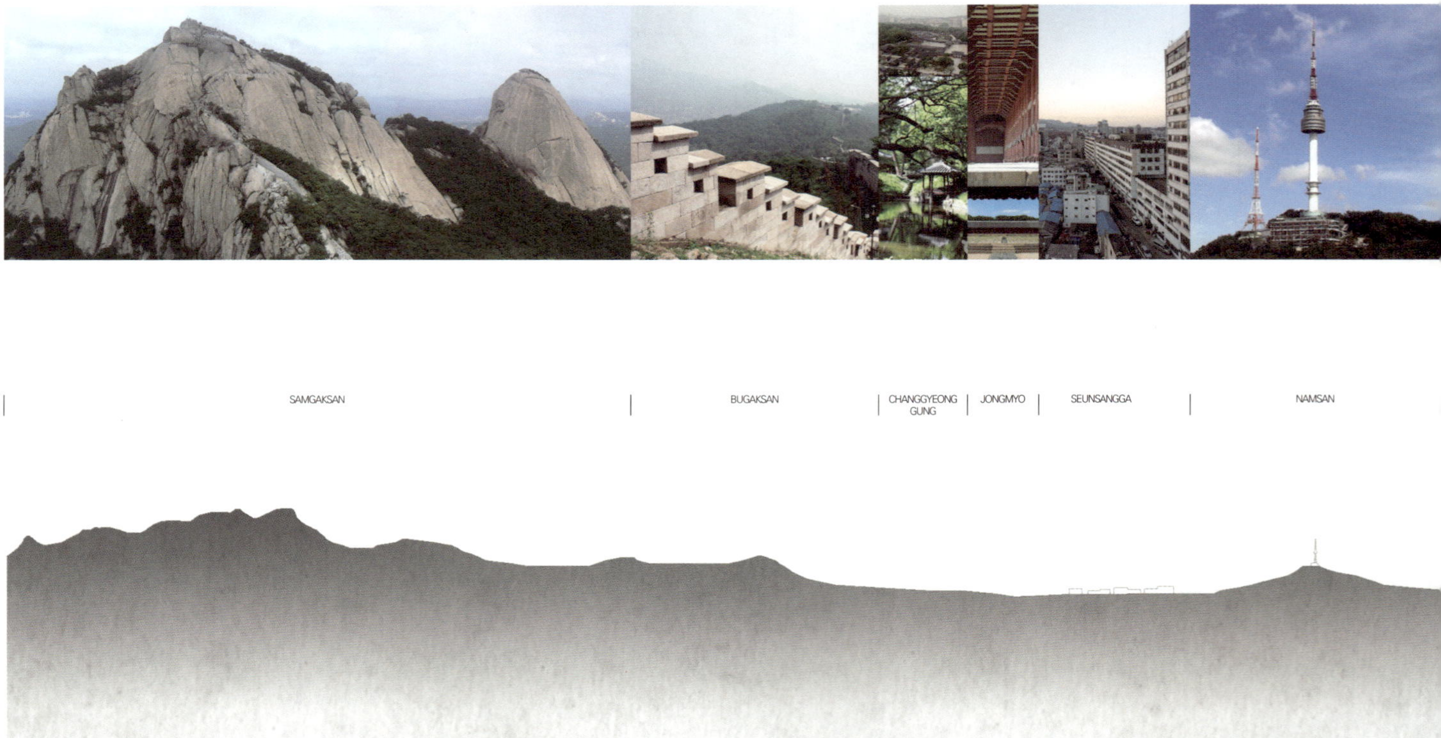
SAMGAKSAN
BUGAKSAN
CHANGGYEONG GUNG
JONGMYO
SEUNSANGGA
NAMSAN

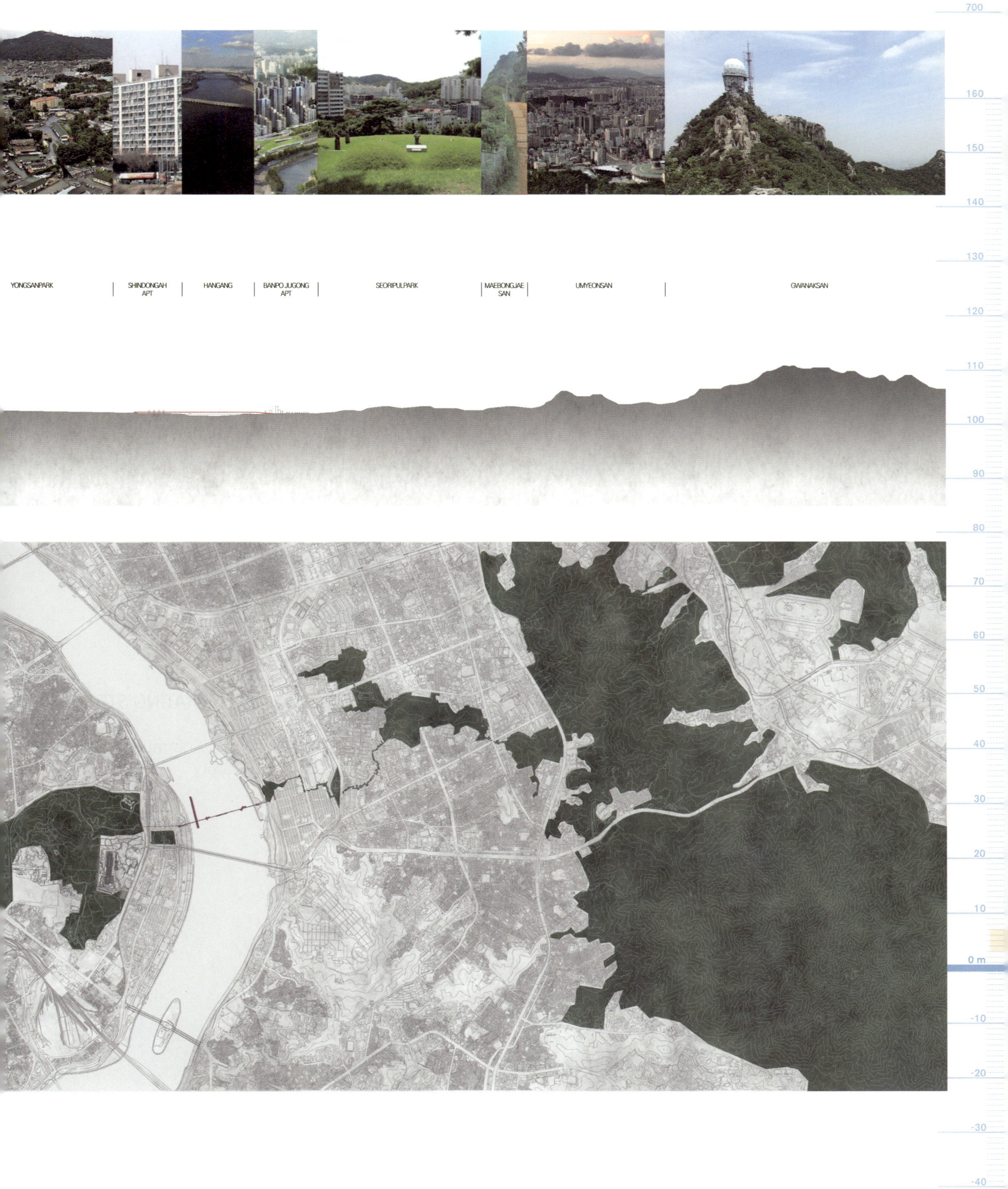
YONGSANPARK
SHINDONGAH APT
HANGANG
BANPO JUGONG APT
SEORIPULPARK
MAEBONGJAE SAN
UMYEONSAN
GWANAKSAN
700
160
150
140
130
120
110
100
90
80
70
60
50
40
30
20
10
0 m
-10
-20
-30
-40

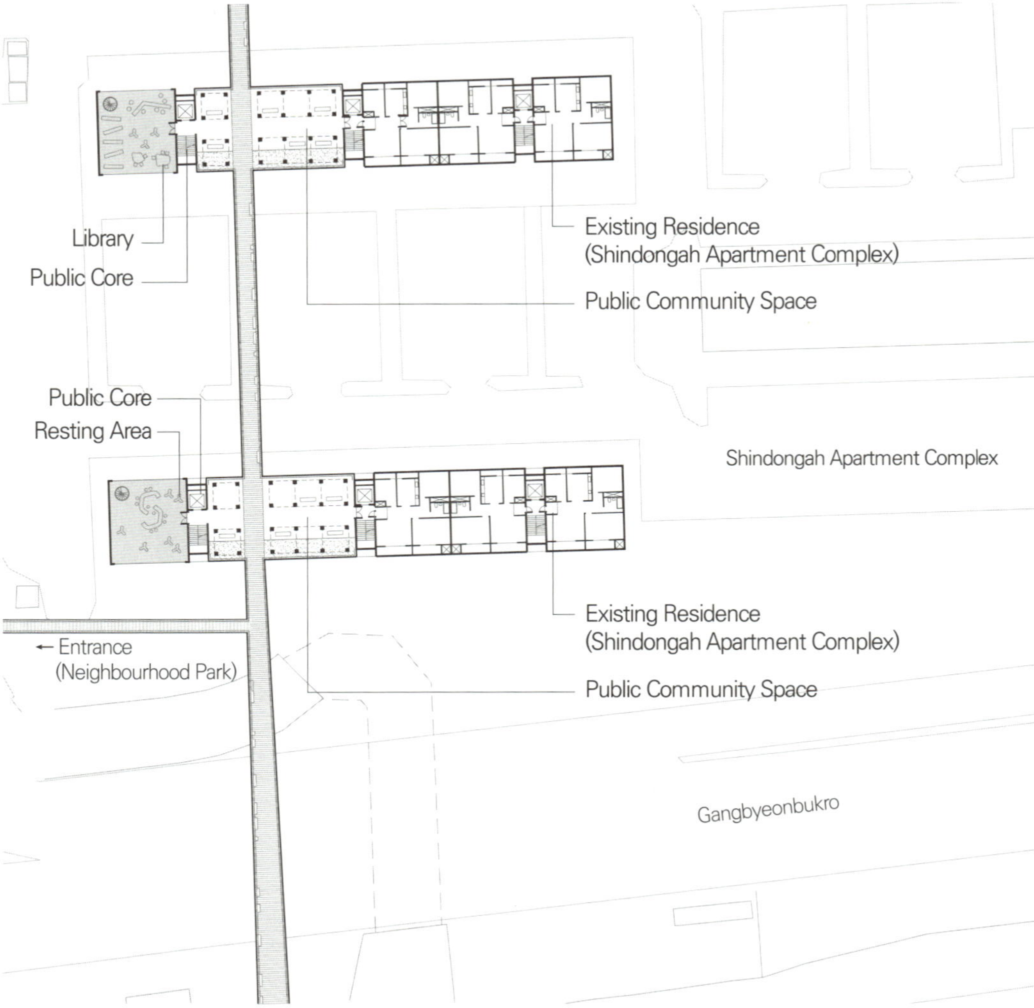

PENETRATING STREET

Public Community Space / Gallery

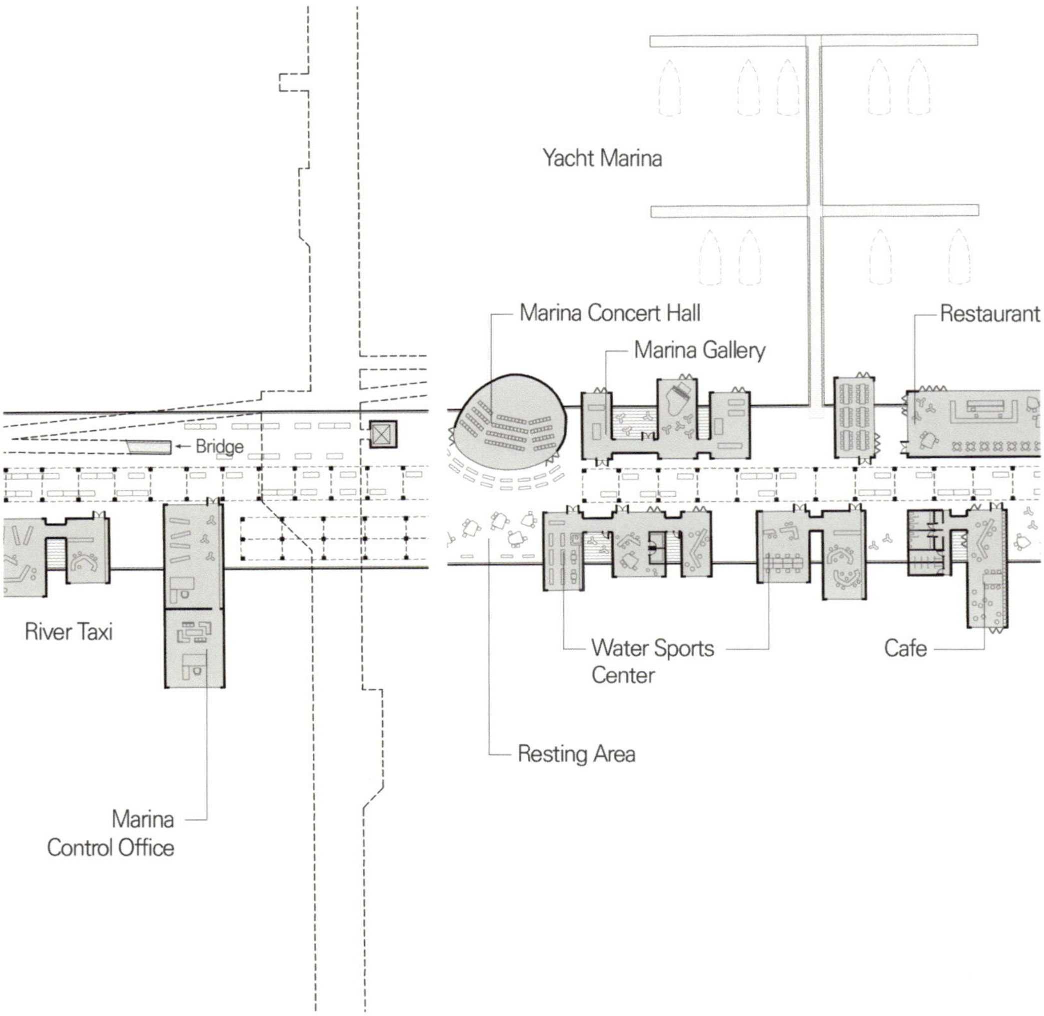

FLOATING LAND

Watersports / River Taxi / Yacht Marina / Concert Hall / Restaurant / Bar / Cafe / Fishing Area

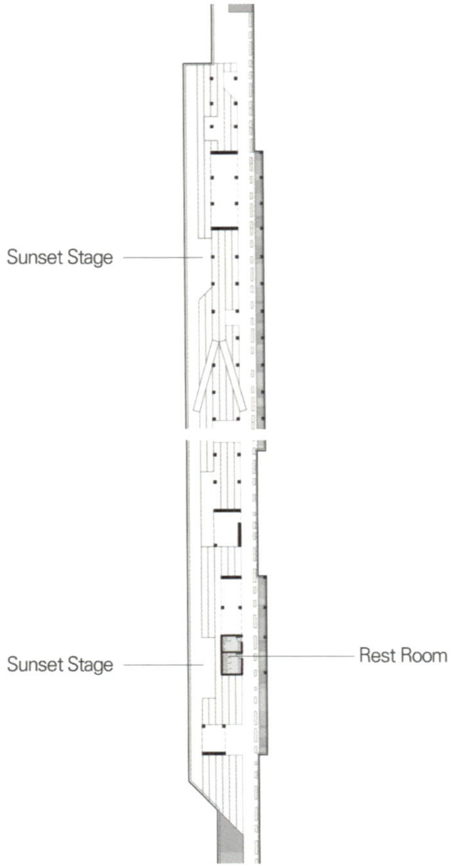

STEPPED DECK

Sunset Pavillion / Sunset Stage / Urban Farming / Cafe / Nursing Room / Kids Room

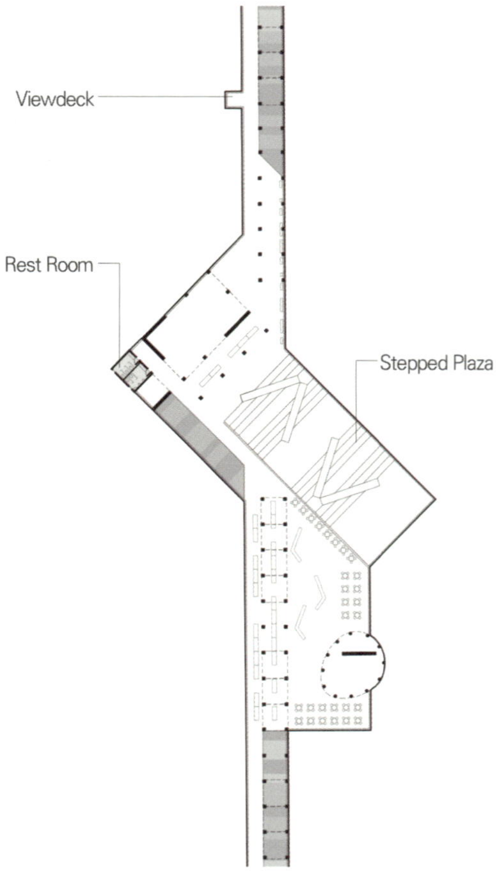

STEPPED PLAZA

Stepped Plaza / Gallery / Cafe / Viewdeck

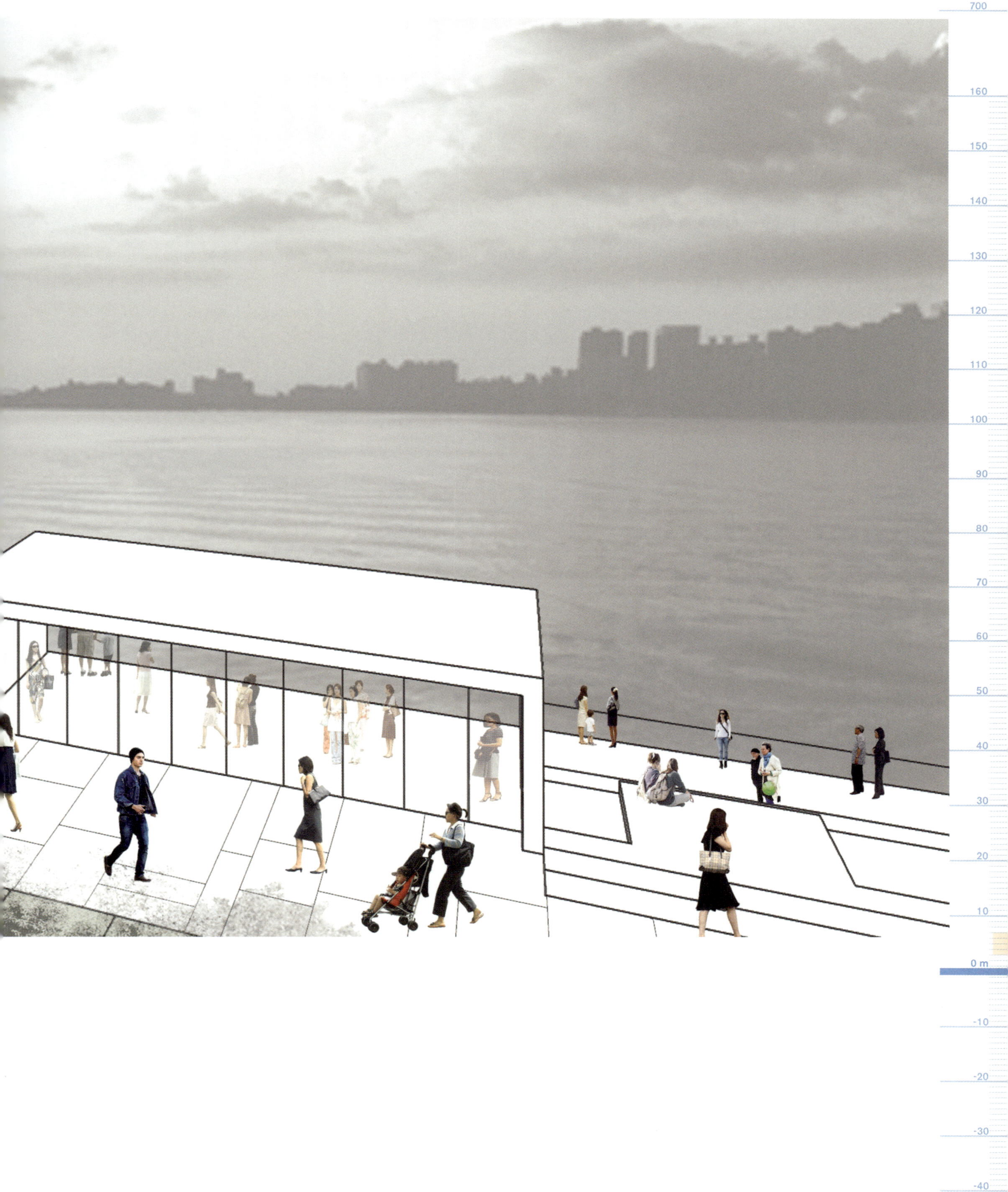
700
160
150
140
130
120
110
100
90
80
70
60
50
40
30
20
10
0 m
-10
-20
-30
-40

알레한드로 하이엑 콜

Alejandro Haiek Coll

내부순환로(종암사거리) / Naebu Expressway (Jongam)

서울 생태 응축기
자급자족 환경 장치: 사회의 지속가능한 경관 인프라로 향하여

공간보다 시간에 대한 개입을 제안한다. 숨어 있는 자연을 되살리고 예전으로 돌아가서 도시 분위기를 만들고자 한다. 이는 혼성적이면서, 일시적/영구적이며 유연한 인프라를 주입하여 문화, 스포츠 및 생산 프로그램을 촉진하는 것으로 가능하다. 기존 교통 네트워크를 다양한 목적과 기능으로 재구성하며, 새로운 공공과 집합적 풍경으로의 접근성을 제공한다. 기존 인프라스트럭쳐를 지속가능한 환경 도구로 만들어 새로운 사회적 활력과 환경을 촉발한다. 새로운 커뮤니티, 미시 경제, 대안적 생산과 소비, 새로운 생태를 활성화하기 위하여 사회적, 기술적, 환경적 전략들을 만든다.
시민 참여, 공공 협의, 지식 민주화, 문화 기술 생산 및 상징적 자본을 통해 이 프로젝트는 도시적 삶을 재구조화하는 새로운 이야기, 새로운 형태를 발견한다. 이런 의미에서 이 프로젝트는 해당 대지에서 다른 캐릭터, 다른 연령대로부터 수집한 '이야기'로 세 가지 시간대를 가로지르며 욕망, 좌절, 기대 그리고 개념적으로 비전들을 기반으로 내레이션을 재구성한다. 이 방법은 집합적인 열망에 접근하여 사회적인 지도를 만들 수 있는 새로운 방법을 발견하게 할 것이다.

Seoul Eco-Condenser Self-Sufficient Environmental Apparatus: Toward a Social Sustainable Landscape Infrastructures

The project proposes to intervene in time more than in space. It focuses on building urban atmospheres by reviving the latent nature and returning to preexisting conditions. This is achieved by injecting a series of hybrid, temporary/permanent and flexible infrastructures in order to promote cultural, sports and productive programs. These tactics reframe the existing mobility network to support multiple uses and function, providing accessibility to new public and collective landscapes. The proposal up to repair existing infrastructures as a eco-sustainable apparatus in order to trigger new social dynamics and environmental conditions. The project distributes a set of social, technological and environmental strategies in order to vitalize the urban land implementing new community micro-economies, alternative production/consumption forms and new ecologies.
Through citizen participation, public consultation, knowledge democratization, cultural-technical production and symbolic capital, the project finds new fiction, new forms of reframing urban life. By this mean, the project crosses three time-laps as a "storytelling" collected on site from different characters and ages, and reconstructs the narration based on their desires, frustrations, expectations and conceptually intermingled visions. This method allows to approach to collective aspirations, finding new ways to developed a social cartography.

건축가이자, 스웨덴 Umea 건축학교에서 가르치고 있다. 베네수엘라 Central 대학을 졸업하였다. 공공 풍경, 후기 산업화 이후 환경, 그리고 네트워크 지배력 정치 사이의 관계를 연구하며, 과학, 문화, 지역 지능을 통합한 사회 혁신을 모색한다. 디자인, 예술, 공학의 교차점 프로젝트 작업을 하며, 하이브리드 기술, 파생 기술, 인적 자원과 물질적 자원을 통한 구성요소 제작에 집중하고 있다. 스페인 카탈루냐 대학과 프랑스 그르노블 대학 국제대학에서 국제협력 에라스무스 프로그램에 초청 교수였으며, 멕시코 그레이엄 재단이 후원하는 도쿄예술대학과 리가의 초청 작가, 호주의 모나쉬 대학, 뉴질랜드 오클랜드 대학의 엘람 미술 학교 레지던시의 작가였다.

Architect. Lecturer at Umeå School of Architecture, Sweden. Receiving honors in Architectural Design Master in Sciences, at the Central University of Venezuela. His research examines the relations between public landscapes, post-industrial ecologies and network governability politics. His work explores social innovations that integrate science, culture and local intelligences. His projects develop at the intersection between design, arts and engineering. Focusing on hybrid techniques, Derived Technologies and building components through human and material resources. He's principles declare architecture as a logistic change of events that eventually transformed in a complex apparatus. A urban choreography as conscious and mindful return to industrialization. Invited professor at the Master of International Cooperation Sustainable Emergency Architecture Erasmus program at Universitat Internacional de Catalunya, Spain and Grenoble University, France. Invited artist at Tokyo University of the Arts, Japan and Liga space for Architecture supported by Graham Foundation, Mexico. Artist in residence at Monash University in Australia and Elam Fine School of Art at Auckland University in New Zealand.

Take I

The project proposes to intervene in time more than in space. It focuses on building urban atmospheres by reviving the latent nature and returning to preexisting conditions. This is achieved by injecting a series of hybrid, temporary/permanent and flexible infrastructures in order to promote cultural, sports and productive programs. These tactics reframe the existing mobility network to support multiple uses and function, providing accessibility to new public and collective landscapes. The proposal up to repair existing infrastructures as a eco-sustainable apparatus in order to trigger new social dynamics and environmental conditions. The project distributes a set of social, technological and environmental strategies in order to vitalize the urban land implementing new community micro-economies, alternative production/consumption forms and new ecologies.

The hub is a support to appropriate the urban soil through diverse activities and multiple and simultaneous programs. Is a proto spatial devices that explore temporality conditions and cultural occupation creating tactical public spaces and mobility strategies.

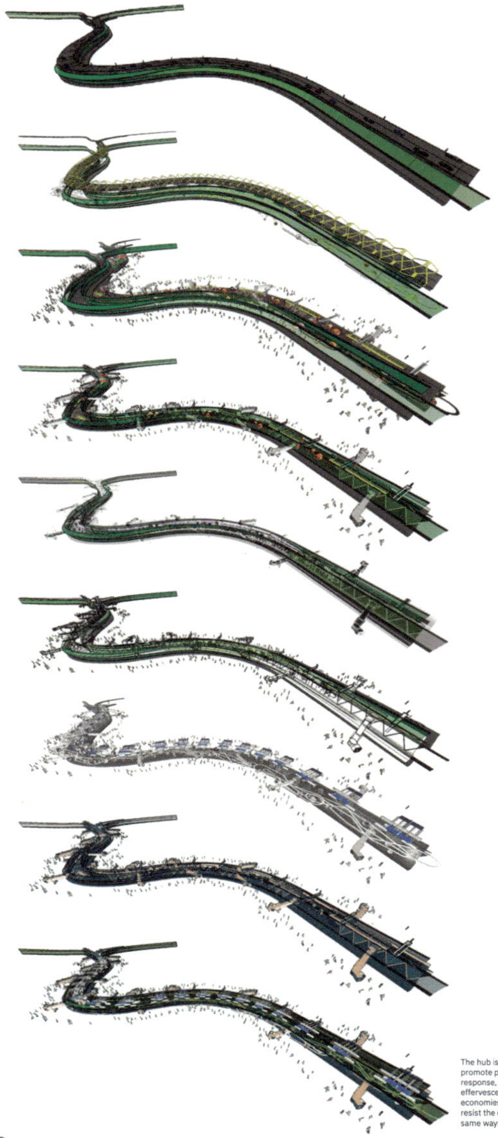

The hub is a infrastructural device that promote political conscious and civic response, transforming the cultural effervescence into alternative jobs and economies, artifacts that aloud citizens to resist the establishment and avoid the same ways of living in the cities context.

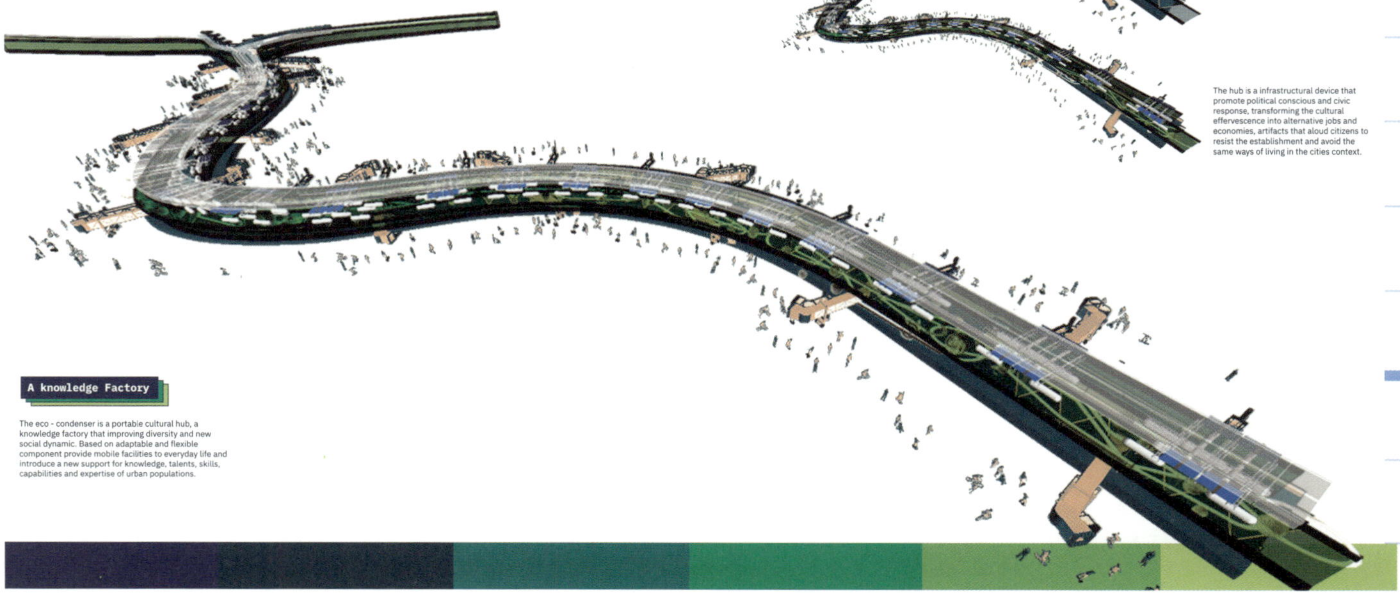

A knowledge Factory

The eco - condenser is a portable cultural hub, a knowledge factory that improving diversity and new social dynamic. Based on adaptable and flexible component provide mobile facilities to everyday life and introduce a new support for knowledge, talents, skills, capabilities and expertise of urban populations.

공연 경관_

사회적 역동성을 활용한 공공영역 활성화

본 프로젝트 1단계는 활성화에 초점을 맞추고 있다. 이는 즉각적이고, 범용적이고, 유연하며, 시노그래피, 무대 디자인, 공연 제작, 한시성 또는 잠정성 공학 등 다양한 전문 분야를 활용한다. 이러한 기술적 장치들은 부지의 체계적 가능성을 보여주는 분리형 시스템을 구성하게 된다. 또한 일상적 체육 활동, 시민 행사, 이동식 극장, 한시적이고 즉각적이거나 자동화된 건축을 비롯한 다채로운 이벤트 구성을 가능하게 한다. 이 즉각적 시스템은 새로운 문화적 지형과 변화 요인, 리더십을 낳을 것이다. 아울러 이 새로운 접근은 공간을 지역 사회에 개방함으로써 시민 참여 및 토론 환경 개선을 위한 공간 구성을 시험해볼 수 있다.

즉각적 장치 구성은 일상 활동, 주말 행사, 월례 시장, 연례 축제 등을 지원해주는 연간 프로그램을 발생시킬 수 있다. 1단계의 성공 여부는 시간을 재료로 사용하는 이벤트를 뒷받침하는 주기성 개념에 달려있다.

자원 경관_

비가시적 천연자원을 활용해 손상된 자연 생태계를 회복하기 위한 도시 확산 역전:

2단계는 환경 통제와 에너지 관리 및 생산을 위한 기술적 시스템을 도입한다. 이는 지역 활성화 촉진에 환경적 현상의 영향을 활용해 중장기적으로 지속가능한 순환 고리 구축을 가능하게 한다. 자원 관리 시스템은 물리적 여건과 기반시설 여건을 활용해 반성의 계기를 마련해준다. 간선도로의 표면 전체는 집수 작업에 활용할 수 있고, 그렇게 공중 탱크에 저장된 물은 중력의 힘에 의해 시설 곳곳으로 퍼져 나가며 작물 농장, 녹화 외장, 울창한 숲, 생산적 조경지역 등에 물을 공급해준다. 간선도로의 기술 및 기계 장비화는 대형 인공 설비로 한강의 흐름을 관리해 에너지 생산과 생산적 조경지의 물 공급을 가능하게 한다.

가상 경관_

가까운 미래, 가능한 미래로의 투영. 욕망의 생태계:

3단계는 사회적 힘과 인공지능을 결합해 에너지를 관리한다. 간선도로는 완전한 기술 장비이자 자연 친화적 장치 즉, 지속가능한 인공 폐가 된다. 이 녹색 인공호흡기는 환경 보전, 청소, 정화 장치가 되어 도시에 자연적 풍경을 되돌려 줄 것이다. 그리고 지식과 새로운 사회적, 도시적, 환경적, 기술적 생태계를 빚어내는 오락 벨트를 구성할 것이다.

3단계는 "가상"에 방점을 찍는다. 이는 기술 설비와 방대한 첨단 장비를 앞세운 급진적 관점으로, 자연계의 통제된 반응 방식을 따른다. 가능한 미래는 새로운 생태와 대안적 미소 생태계에 뿌리를 두고 있을 것이다. 낙관적이고 긍정적인 미래상은 기계 장치가 자주성을 획득하고 인공의 자연을 창조해내는 디스토피아적 도시 시나리오와 결합한다. 결과적으로 이 시나리오는 통제 불능 상태로 귀결되고, 자연은 지배권을 회복한다.

환경 재생의 범위는 도시 내 다른 영역으로의 진출과 지속가능한 선형 공원 체계 안에 그들을 연결하는 것까지 확장된다. 변수를 품은 여러 개의 선은 도시 조직의 새로운 구조적 발전으로 이어지고, 그곳에서 새로운 생태계의 생명력이 보이지 않는 자족적 기술 시스템의 지원을 받는 사회적 역동성과 유기적으로 어우러진다. 인공 환경과 자연 생태계 사이의 경계는 도시를 자신의 구성 요소와 분신의 확장을 위한 움직이는 표면으로 활용해 욕망의 생태계 즉, 순환적 일상으로의 침투를 꾀하는 새로운 하이브리드 도시 환경 속에서 사라진다.

하루하루가 풍경과 기반시설, 자원과 소비 시스템, 일과 여가의 구분 없이 흐른다. 인간 행위, 사회적 패턴, 기계화의 사이. 도시는 인간이 생태계의 중심이 아니라 일부이며 상호작용과 주관성의 네트워크의 구성요소가 되는 복잡한 체제를 이해하고 있는, 생명력을 지닌 유기체다.

Performing landscape_

Activating public domain through social effervescence:

The first phase focuses on activation. It is instantaneous, versatile and flexible, making use of field of expertises, such as the scenographies, set design, production of show and spectacle and temporary or provisional engineering. These technical instruments become demountable systems that shows the programmatic possibilities of the place. This will allow to create a variety of events, ranging from daily sports activities, public scenarios, mobile theaters and a series of devices of ephemeral, instantaneous or automatic architecture. These instantaneous logics will create cultural cartographies, agents of transformation and leadership. This new channels will open space to the community to test configurations that improves participation and public consultation.

The instantaneous devices configuration could generate a year of programmable activities, that will support day-to-day dynamics, weekend events, monthly markets or annual festivals. The success of this phase is based on the notions of periodicity, that implements events using time as a relevant resource.

Resources landscapes_

Reversing urban sprawls to regenerate affected natural ecosystem using invisible natural resources:

The second phase inserts a technical systems of environmental control and energy management production. This will allow to establish medium and long term sustainability cycles, using the force of environmental phenomena to trigger a recovery of the area. The installation of a management resources systems will allow to use the physical infrastructural conditions to create a source of rethinking protocols. The entire surface of the highway could be used for water collections that will be stored in aerial tanks that, by gravity, can be distributed throughout the intervention, feeding crop areas, vegetable skins, immersive forests and productive landscapes. This technification and instrumentation of the highway, as a large scale operational artifact, will also allow to manage the channeling of the River, in order to produce energy and feed the productive landscapes.

Fictional landscapes_

Projecting to near future, possible futures, the ecology of desires:

The third phase will consolidate both social force and an artificial intelligence in order to manage energy. The highway will become a complete technological device, as well as a natural system: a eco-lung. This green respirator will return to the city its natural character as a mechanism of environmental preservation, cleansing and purification. A recreational belt that generates knowledge and new social, urban, environmental and technological ecosystems.

This phase places its speculation in "fiction". It is an extreme perspective from a technical implementations and a vast technological instrumentation, following by a under-control response of the natural world. The possible future will be based on new ecologies and alternative micro-ecosystems. An optimistic and positive vision combine with a dystopian urban scenario, where the technological apparatus takes autonomy and displays an artificial nature. As a result, this scenario get out of control and the domain to the natural is given back.

The limits of an environmental regeneration extends to conquer other territories of the city, and connects them in a system of sustainable linear parks. Several lines of variable became the emerging structural development of the urban fabric, where the vitality of the new ecosystem articulates fluidly with the social dynamics using the invisible self-sufficient technical system as a support. The boundaries between the built environment and natural ecosystems are erased in a new hybrid urban condition that uses the city as a operative surface to extend its embers and branches to infiltrate the ecology of desires: circuits of everyday life. The day to day passes without distinctions between landscape and infrastructure, between resources and the consumption systems, between work and leisure. Between the human behavior, social pattern and the becoming machine. The city as a living organism that understands a complex metabolism where humans are no longer the center of the ecosystem and became a part, a component of a network of interactions and subjectivities.

0 - 1 YEARS (First interventions)

0-1

Temporal /
Activations Steps
Ephemeral scenarios / Ephemeral Devices / Social Engagement

Performing landscape_
Activating public domain through social effervescence:

The first phase focuses on activation. It is instantaneous, versatile and flexible, making use of field of expertises, such as the scenographies, set design, production of show and spectacle and temporary or provisional engineering. These technical instruments become demountable systems that shows the programmatic possibilities of the place. This will allow to create a variety of events, ranging from daily sports activities, public scenarios, mobile theaters and a series of devices of ephemeral, instantaneous or automatic architecture. These instantaneous logics will create cultural cartographies, agents of ransformation and leadership. This new channels will open space to the community to test configurations that improves participation and public consultation. The instantaneous devices configuration could generate a year of programmable activities, that will support day-to-day dynamics, weekend events, monthly markets or annual festivals. The success of this phase is based on the notions of periodicity, that implements events using time as a relevant resource.

Festivals / cultural and sports events / Scenarios / First occupations / Social cartography /Cultural cartography / Participation and consultation process / Community Engagement.

1 - 5 YEARS (Technical and enviromental Transformations)

1-5

Transitional /
Components, systems and technical Installations
Integral Recovering Process

Resources Landscapes_
Reversing urban sprawls to regenerate affected natural ecosystem using invisible natural resources:

The second phase
environmental con
This will allow t
sustainability cy
phenomena to trig
installation of a
to use the physic
source of rethink
highway could be
stored in aerial
throughout the in
skins, immersive
technification an
large scale opera
the channeling of
feed the producti

Self sufficient devic
Social and Environment

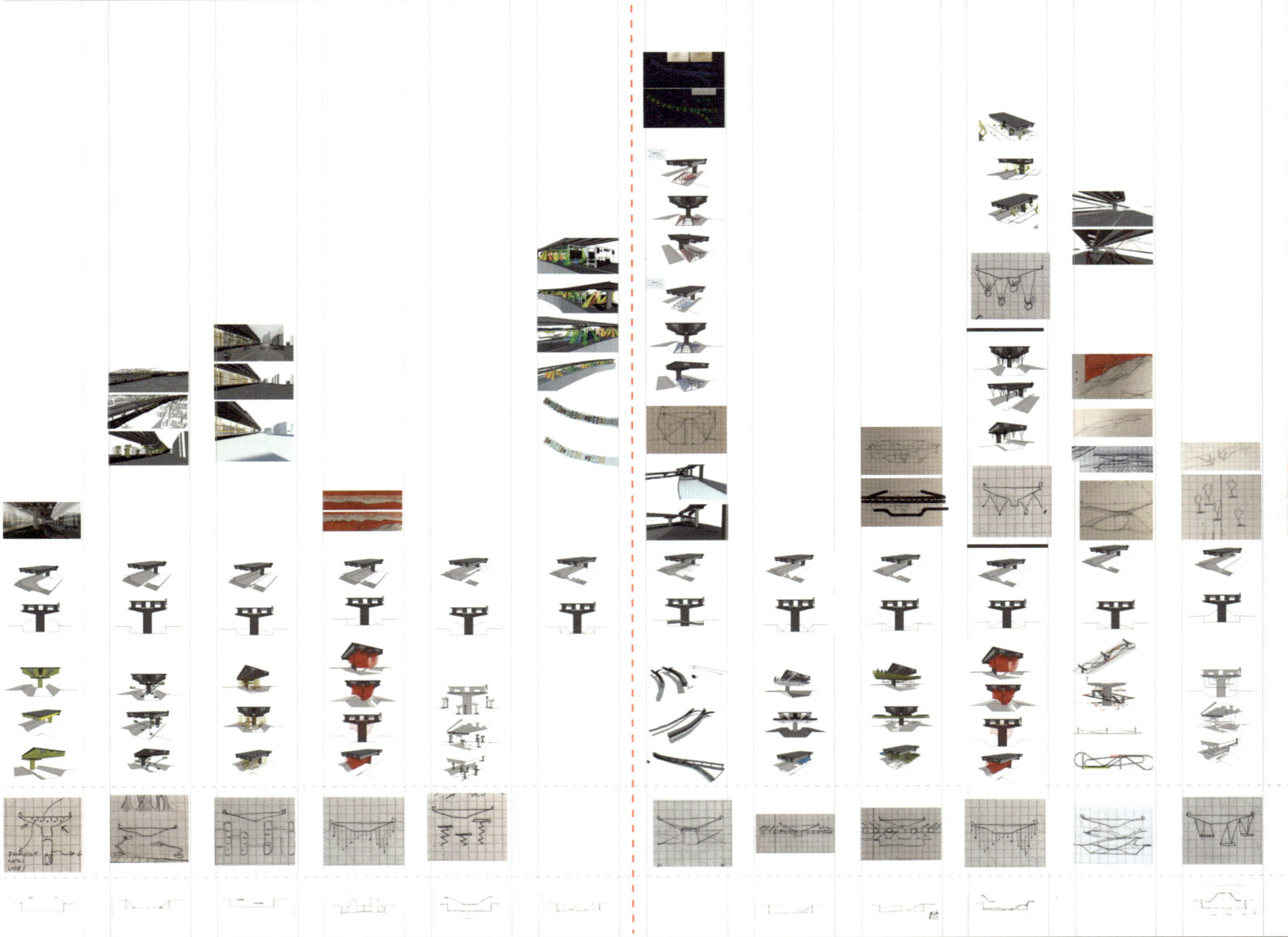

Propuesta 001 | Propuesta 002 | Propuesta 003 | Propuesta 004 | Propuesta 005 | Propuesta 006 | Propuesta 007 | Propuesta 008 | Propuesta 009 | Propuesta 010 | Propuesta 011 | Propuesta 012

systems of
agement production.
and long term
ce of environmental
he area. The
es systems will allow
conditions to create a
entire surface of the
ections that will be
ity, can be distributed
crop areas, vegetable
ive landscapes. This
f the highway, as a
ll also allow to manage
r to produce energy and

cal innovations /
act Control.

5 - 20+ YEARS Possible futures / A New Urban Ecosystem

5-20 Fictional Landscapes_

Permanent /

Utopia - Reallity / Utopia - Fiction

Plant Lung /Ephemeral scenarios / Ephemeral Devices / Social Engagement

Projecting to near future, possible futures, the ecology of desires:

The third phase will consolidate both social force and an artificial intelligence in order to manage energy. The highway will become a complete technological device, as well as a natural system: a eco-lung. This green respirator will return to the city its natural character as a mechanism of environmental preservation, cleansing and purification. A recreational belt that generates knowledge and new social, urban, environmental and technological ecosystems.
This phase places its speculation in ''fiction''. It is an extreme perspective from a techrical implementations and a vast technological instrumentation, following by a under-control response of the natural world. The possible future will be based on new ecologies and alternative micro-ecosystems. An optimistic anc positive vision combine with a dystopian urban scenario, where the technological apparatus takes autonomy ard displays an artificial nature. As a result, this scerario get out of control and the domain to the natural is given back.

The limits of an environmental regeneration extends to conquer other territories of the city, and connects them in a system of sustainable linear parks. Several lines of variable became the emerging structural development of the urban fabric, where the vitality of the new ecosystem articulates fluidly with the social dynamics using the invisible self-sufficient technical system as a support. The boundaries between the built environment and natural ecosystems are erased in a new hybrid urban condition that uses the city as a operative surface to extend its embers and branches to infiltrate the ecology of desires: circuits of everyday life. The day to day passes without distinctions between landscape and infrastructure, between resources and the consumption systems, between work and leisure. Between the human behavior, social pattern and the becoming machine. The city as a living organism that understands a complex metabolism where humans are no longer the center of the ecosystem and became a part, a component of a network of interactions and subjectivities.

New environmental Conditions / Spontaneous Nature Recovering /
New Urban Consolidations / New Urban Scenarios / Alternative ecologies.

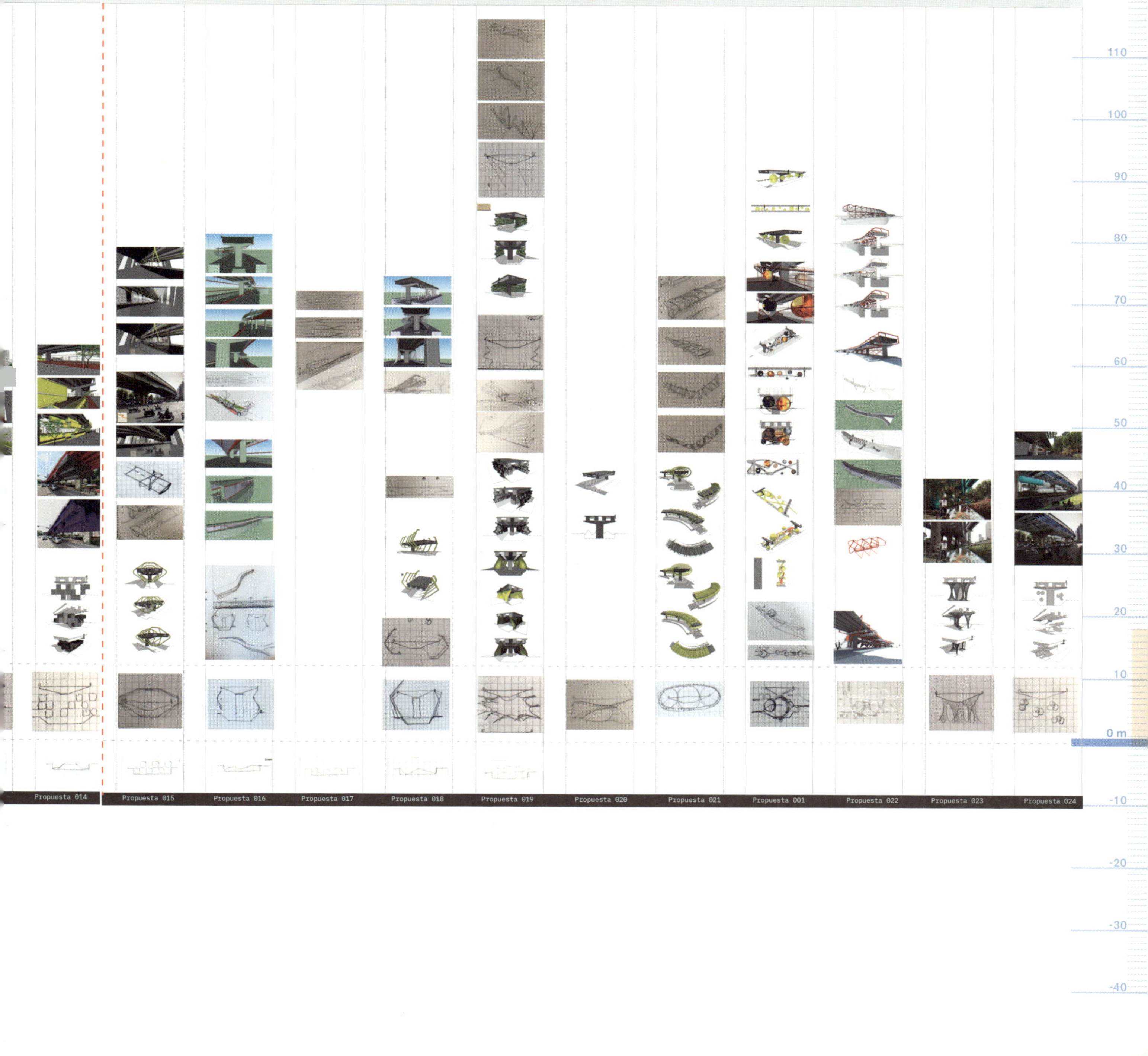

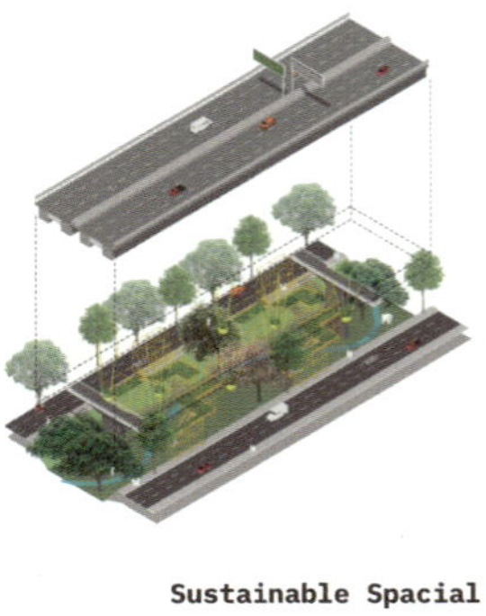

Sustainable Spacial Ecosystem

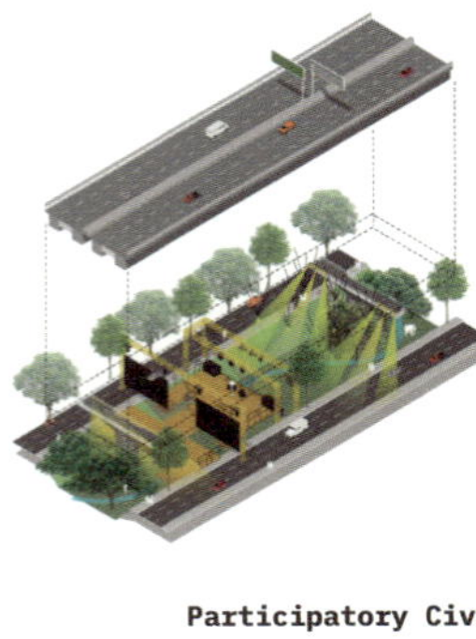

Participatory Civic City

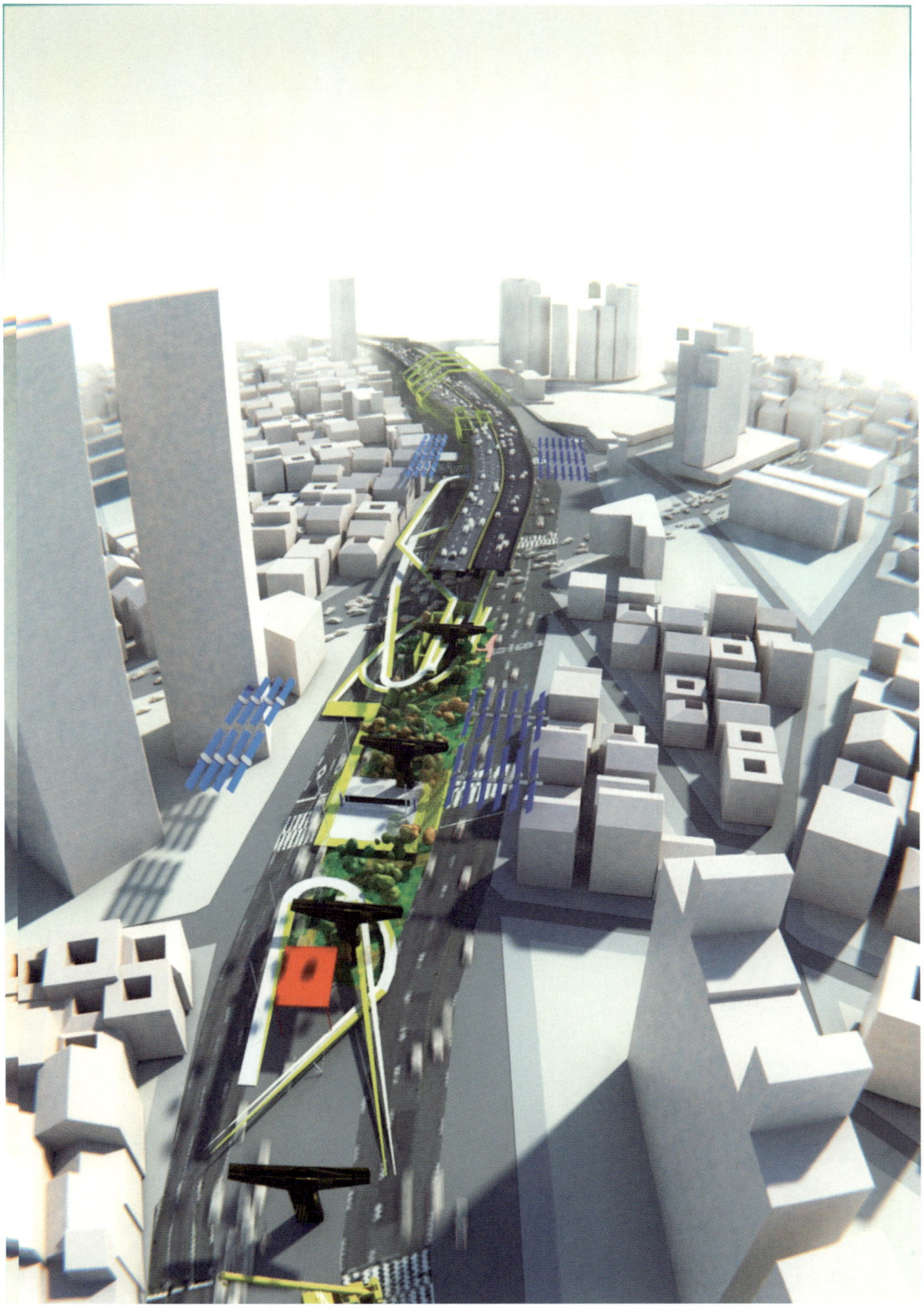

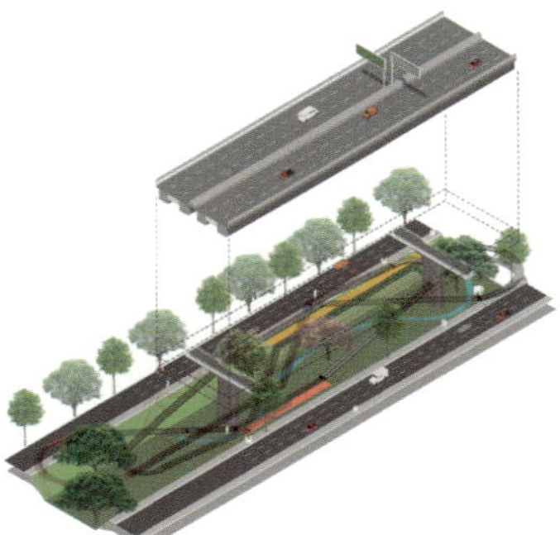

Alternative ecologies

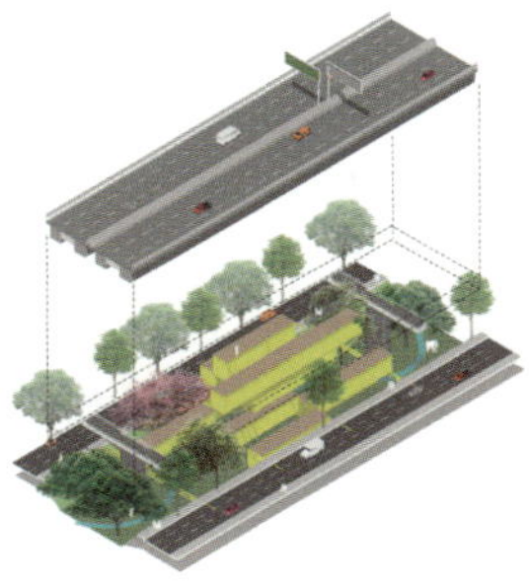

Urban Multi-Habitat

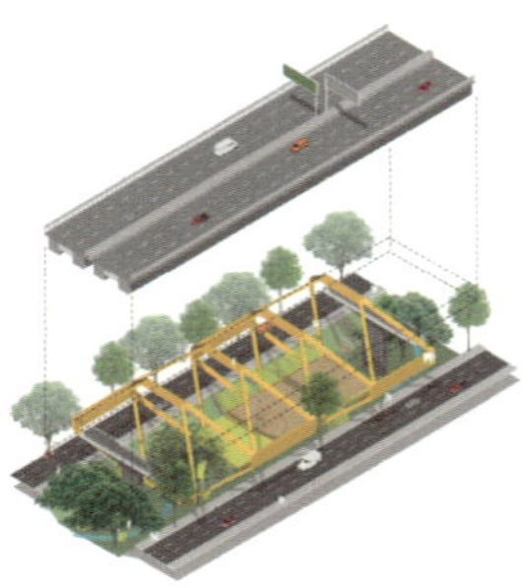

Alternative production/consumption

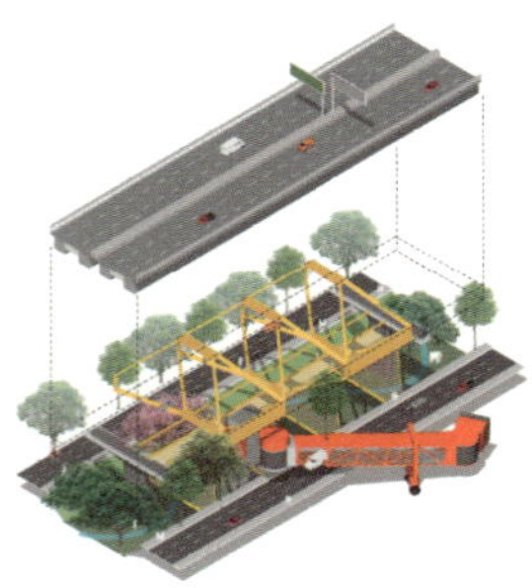

Communicative Infrastructure

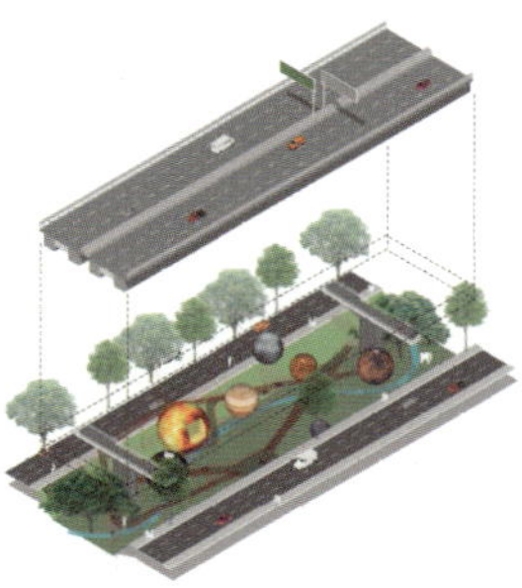

Community Micro-Economies

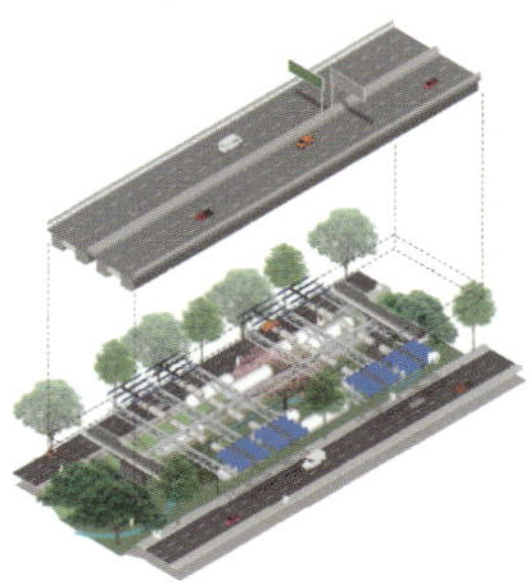

The technocrats infrastructure
is now a social ground

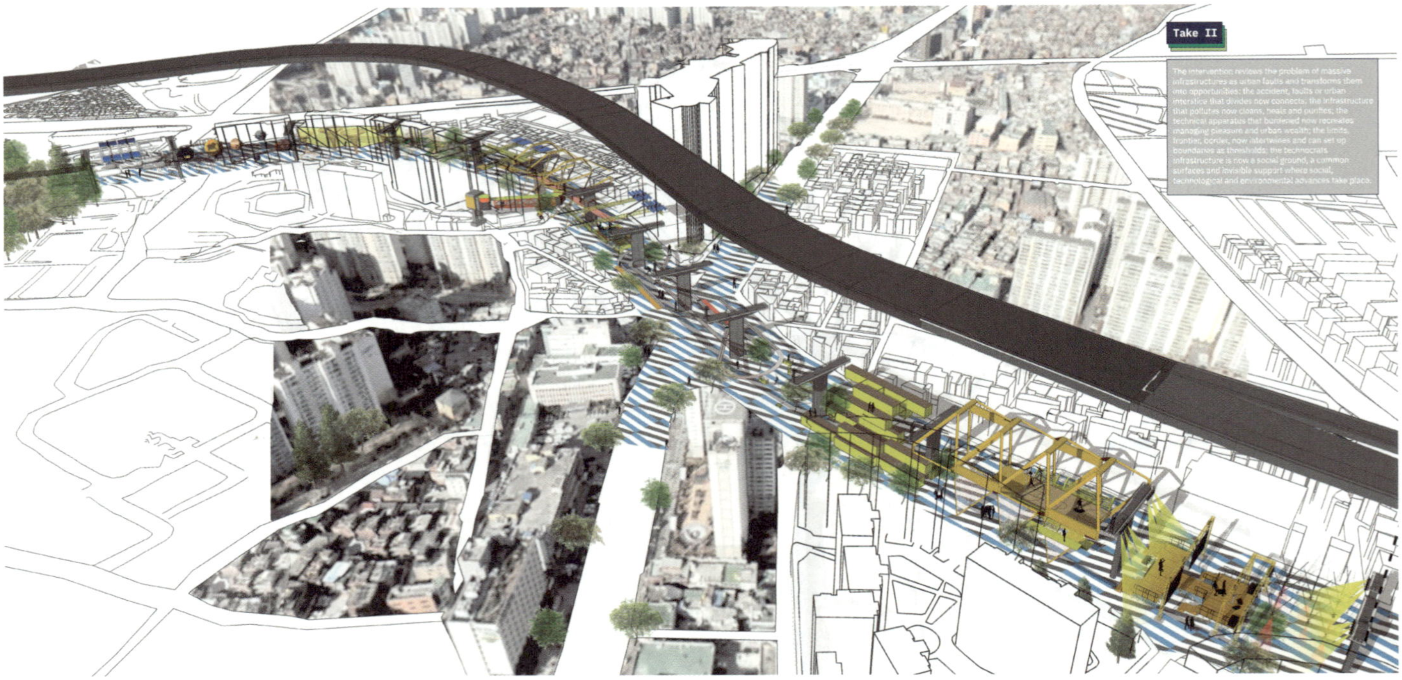
Take II
The intervention reviews the problem of massive infrastructures as urban faults and transforms them into opportunities: the accident, faults or urban interstice that divides now connects; the infrastructure that pollutes now cleans, heals and purifies; the technical apparatus that burdened now recreates managing pleasure and urban wealth; the limits, frontier, border, now intertwines and can set up boundaries as thresholds; the technocrats infrastructure is now a social ground, a common surfaces and invisible support where social, technological and environmental advances take place.

Architectural structures are fundamental bodies constructed from the repetition of parts, components and systems, coherently assembled by means of organizational patterns. The patterns contain figures that create structuring logics. The regularity of the figure is based on repetition and periodicity. It is combined by duplicates, in some cases related with invariance, that is, without changes or modifications. They can also be variables, based on scale, morphological and proportional variations, movements or exchanges. They are the result of applying these operations or transformations into geometric forms, systems, equations; other material objects or abstract entities.

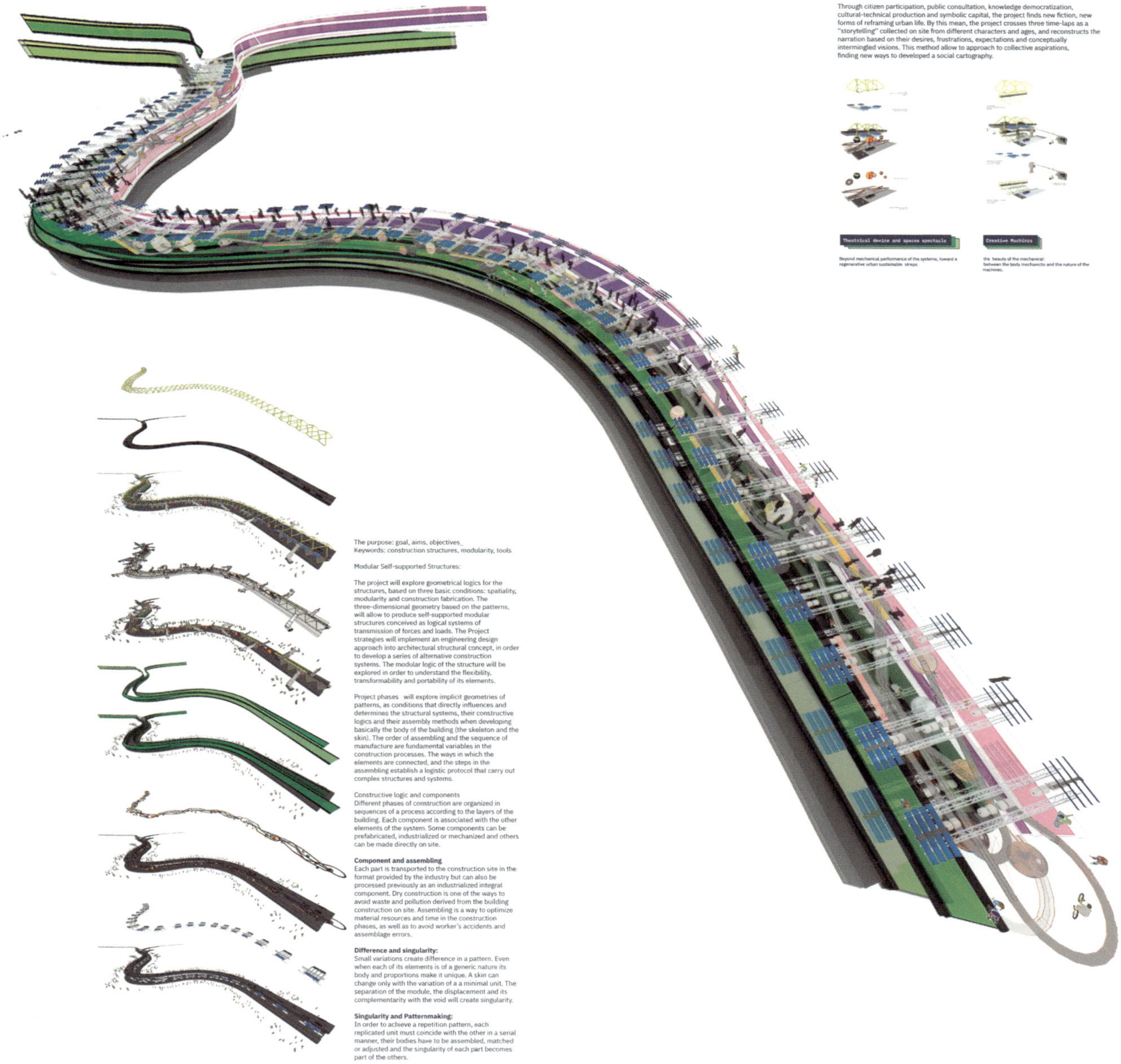

Take III

Through citizen participation, public consultation, knowledge democratization, cultural-technical production and symbolic capital, the project finds new fiction, new forms of reframing urban life. By this mean, the project crosses three time-laps as a "storytelling" collected on site from different characters and ages, and reconstructs the narration based on their desires, frustrations, expectations and conceptually intermingled visions. This method allow to approach to collective aspirations, finding new ways to developed a social cartography.

Theatrical device and spaces spectacle

Beyond mechanical performance of the systems, toward a regenarative urban sustainable streps.

Creative Machines

the beauty of the mechanical:
between the body mechanichs and the nature of the machines.

The purpose: goal, aims, objectives_
Keywords: construction structures, modularity, tools

Modular Self-supported Structures:

The project will explore geometrical logics for the structures, based on three basic conditions: spatiality, modularity and construction fabrication. The three-dimensional geometry based on the patterns, will allow to produce self-supported modular structures conceived as logical systems of transmission of forces and loads. The Project strategies will implement an engineering design approach into architectural structural concept, in order to develop a series of alternative construction systems. The modular logic of the structure will be explored in order to understand the flexibility, transformability and portability of its elements.

Project phases will explore implicit geometries of patterns, as conditions that directly influences and determines the structural systems, their constructive logics and their assembly methods when developing basically the body of the building (the skeleton and the skin). The order of assembling and the sequence of manufacture are fundamental variables in the construction processes. The ways in which the elements are connected, and the steps in the assembling establish a logistic protocol that carry out complex structures and systems.

Constructive logic and components
Different phases of construction are organized in sequences of a process according to the layers of the building. Each component is associated with the other elements of the system. Some components can be prefabricated, industrialized or mechanized and others can be made directly on site.

Component and assembling
Each part is transported to the construction site in the format provided by the industry but can also be processed previously as an industrialized integral component. Dry construction is one of the ways to avoid waste and pollution derived from the building construction on site. Assembling is a way to optimize material resources and time in the construction phases, as well as to avoid worker's accidents and assemblage errors.

Difference and singularity:
Small variations create difference in a pattern. Even when each of its elements is of a generic nature its body and proportions make it unique. A skin can change only with the variation of a a minimal unit. The separation of the module, the displacement and its complementarity with the void will create singularity.

Singularity and Patternmaking:
In order to achieve a repetition pattern, each replicated unit must coincide with the other in a serial manner, their bodies have to be assembled, matched or adjusted and the singularity of each part becomes part of the others.

700
160
150
140
130
120
110
100
90
80
70
60
50
40
30
20
10
0 m
-10
-20
-30
-40

요시하루 츠카모토

Yoshiharu Tsukamoto

용산 바디 컬쳐 클럽

본래 지형의 모습이 용의 형상을 닮았다고 용산이라는 이름이 붙었다. 용산은 풍수지리적으로 서울을 지켜주는 역할을 했으며, 서울 도심과 한강에 인접해 있어서 서울의 중요한 녹색자원이자 경복궁-용산-한강으로 연결되는 중요한 도시 축을 형성해 왔다. 하지만, 이 상징적인 장소는 도시 근대화 과정에서 경의중앙선(구 경원선)(1911), 이촌지역 매립개발(1960년대 후반), 강변북로(1970년), 동작대교(1984년)로 이어지는 교통인프라에 의해 영역이 분리되어 용산 공원에서 한강의 수변공간까지 보행자의 접근이 어려운 상황이다.

우리 디자인의 목표는 교통 인프라(서빙고로, 강변북로, 경의중앙선)의 일부 혹은 전부를 지중화하여 보행자의 영역을 확보하고, 용산에서 한강 수변 공간까지 접근성을 쉽게 만듦으로써 용산 공원과 한강 사이의 공간에 활력을 되찾아주는 것이다. 햇볕과 비를 막아주지만, 전철과 자동차의 소음이 있는 동작대교의 아래 공간 환경을, 서울 시민들을 위한 암벽등반, 테니스 벽치기, 배드민턴, 스케이트 및 댄싱 등의 다양한 바디 컬쳐의 공간으로 탈바꿈시키려 한다.

Yongsan Body Culture Club

Yongsan has its name from the dragon-like hills, a natural green resource beside the curving river of Hangang. The Yongsan protected the city of Hanyang which is the old name of Seoul in terms of Feng Shui. Due to its proximity to the city and the Hangang water front, the connection between Palace - Yongsan - Hangang became an important axis of Seoul. However, with modernization of the city, this symbolic area was divided by transportation infrastructures – the Gyeongui-jungang Line (1911), the developent of Ichon collective housing by reclamation of the river(1960s), the Gangbyeon Expressway (1970) and finally the Dongjak Bridge(1984) – which created a barrier causing poor pedestrian accessibility from Yongsan Park to the Hangang water front. Our design goal is revitalizing the connection between the Yongsan Park and the Hangang water front by clearing the ground level for pedestrians through undergrounding the traffic infrastructure and improving accessibility from Yongsan Park to the Hangang water front. The spaces under the bridge are shaded from the sun and sheltered from the rain but affected by noise from the trains and the cars. This condition is suitable for appropriation by various 'body cultures', such as wall climbing, playing wall tennis, badminton, basketball, skateboarding and dancing.

요시하루 츠카모토는 아틀리에 바우와우의 공동 창립자이자 동경공업대학 건축대학원의 교수로 재직 중이다. 아틀리에 바우와우와 도쿄공업대학의 츠카모토 연구실은 다양한 도시 리서치("메이드 인 도쿄", "보이드 메타볼리즘"), 건축학적 민족지학("창을 순례하다"), 디자인 프로젝트("BMW 구겐하임", "레이크사이드 댄서 클럽" 등)의 활동을 해 오고 있다.

Yoshiharu Tsukamoto is a co-founder of Atelier Bow-Wow and professor at the Graduate school of Architecture and Engineering at Tokyo Institute of Technology. Atelier Bow-Wow and Tsukamoto laboratory at Tokyo Tech have worked on various urban research projects ("Made in Tokyo"⊠"Void Metabolism" etc.), Architectural Ethnography("Window Scape1, 2, 3") and design practices ("BMW Guggenheim Lab", "Lakeside Dancers Club", etc.)

First site analysis and the final proposal

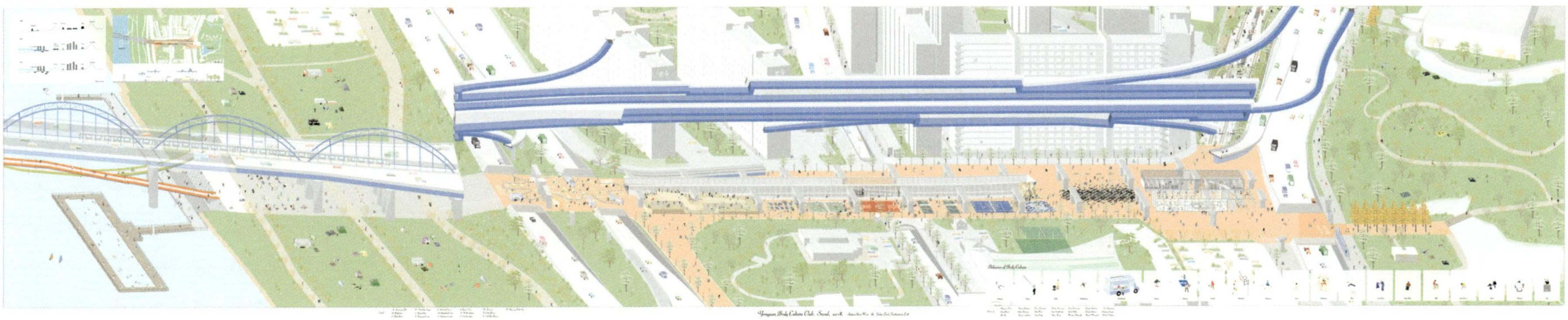

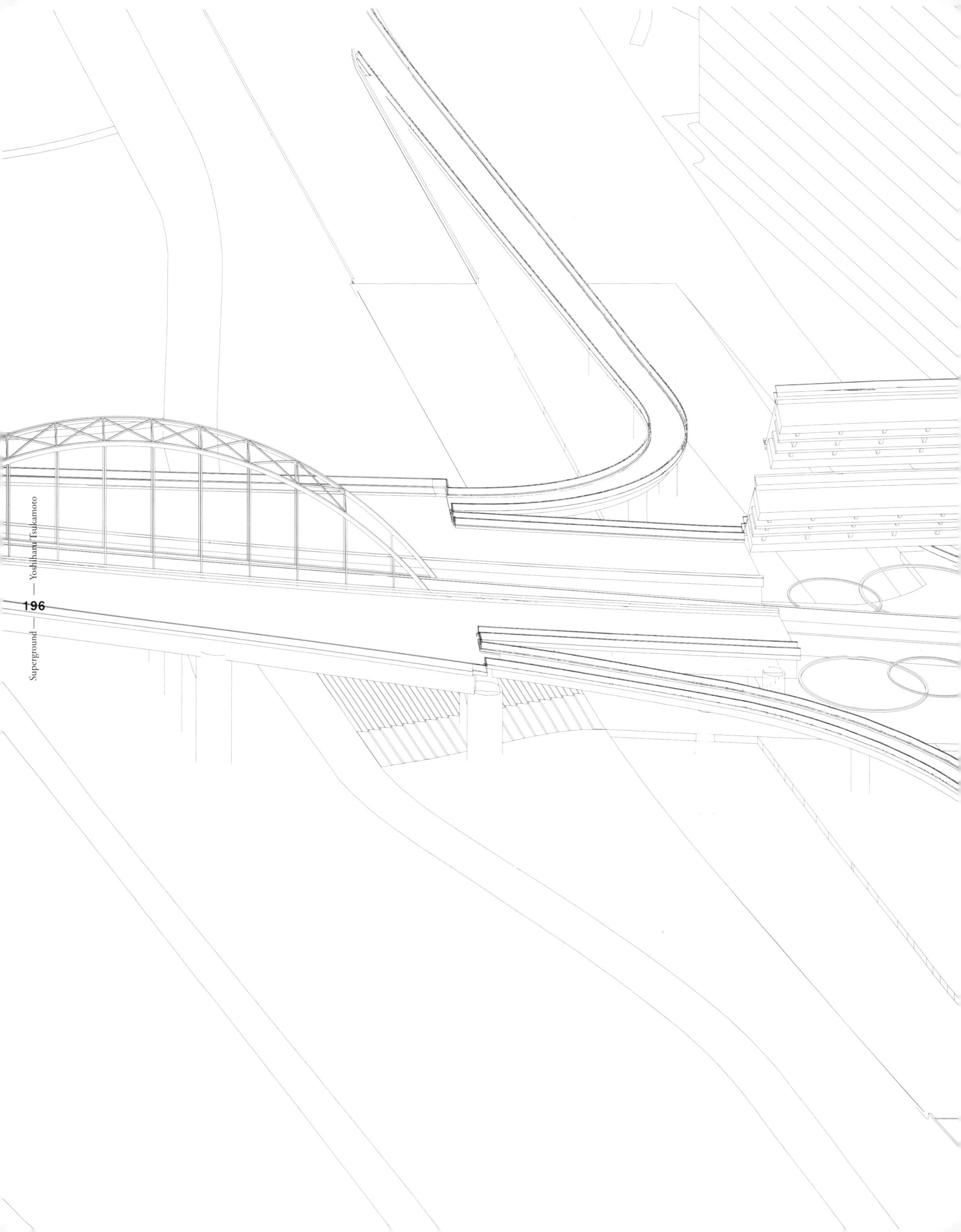

700
160
150
140
130
120
110
100
90
80
70
60
50
40
30
20
10
0 m
-10
-20
-30
-40

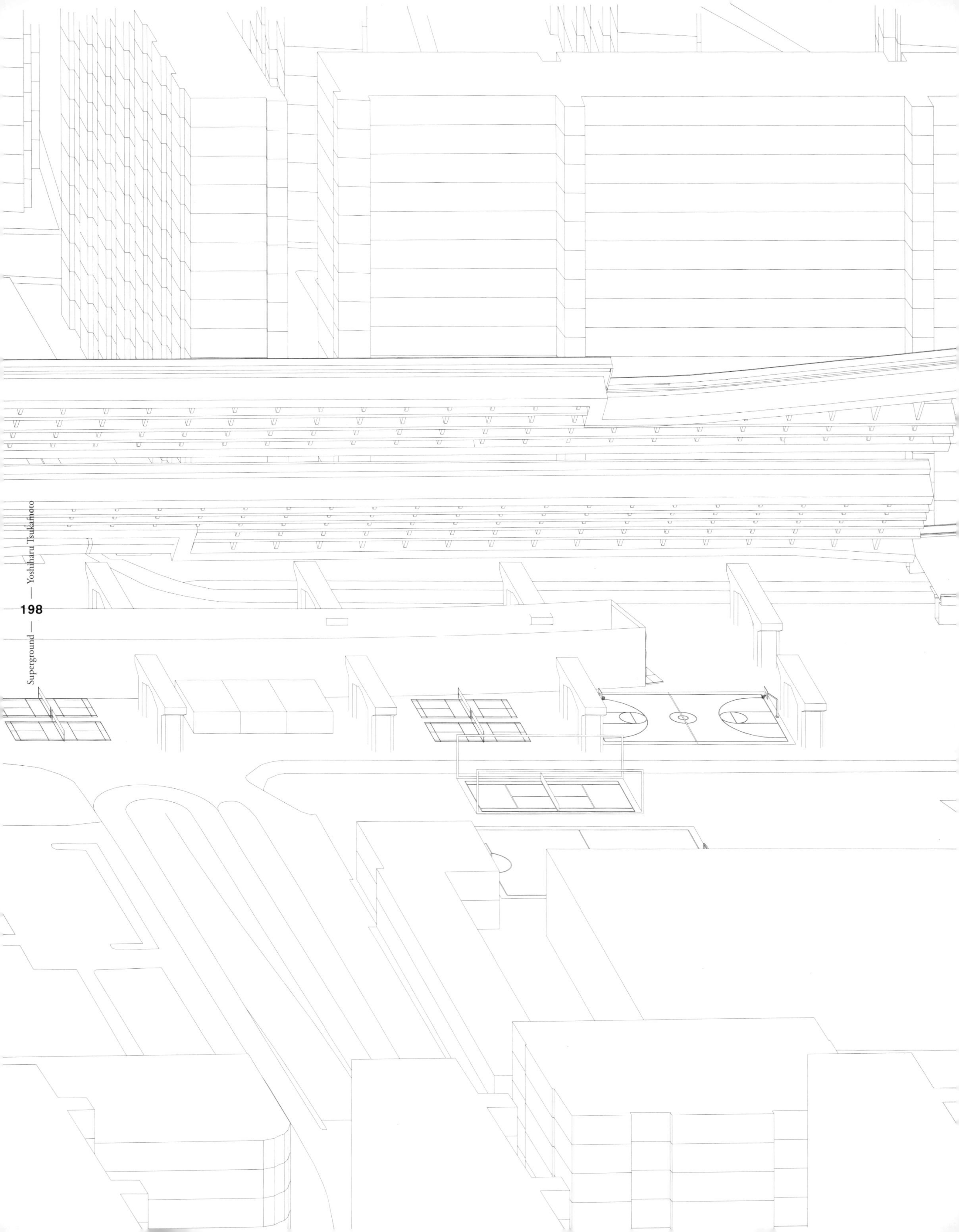

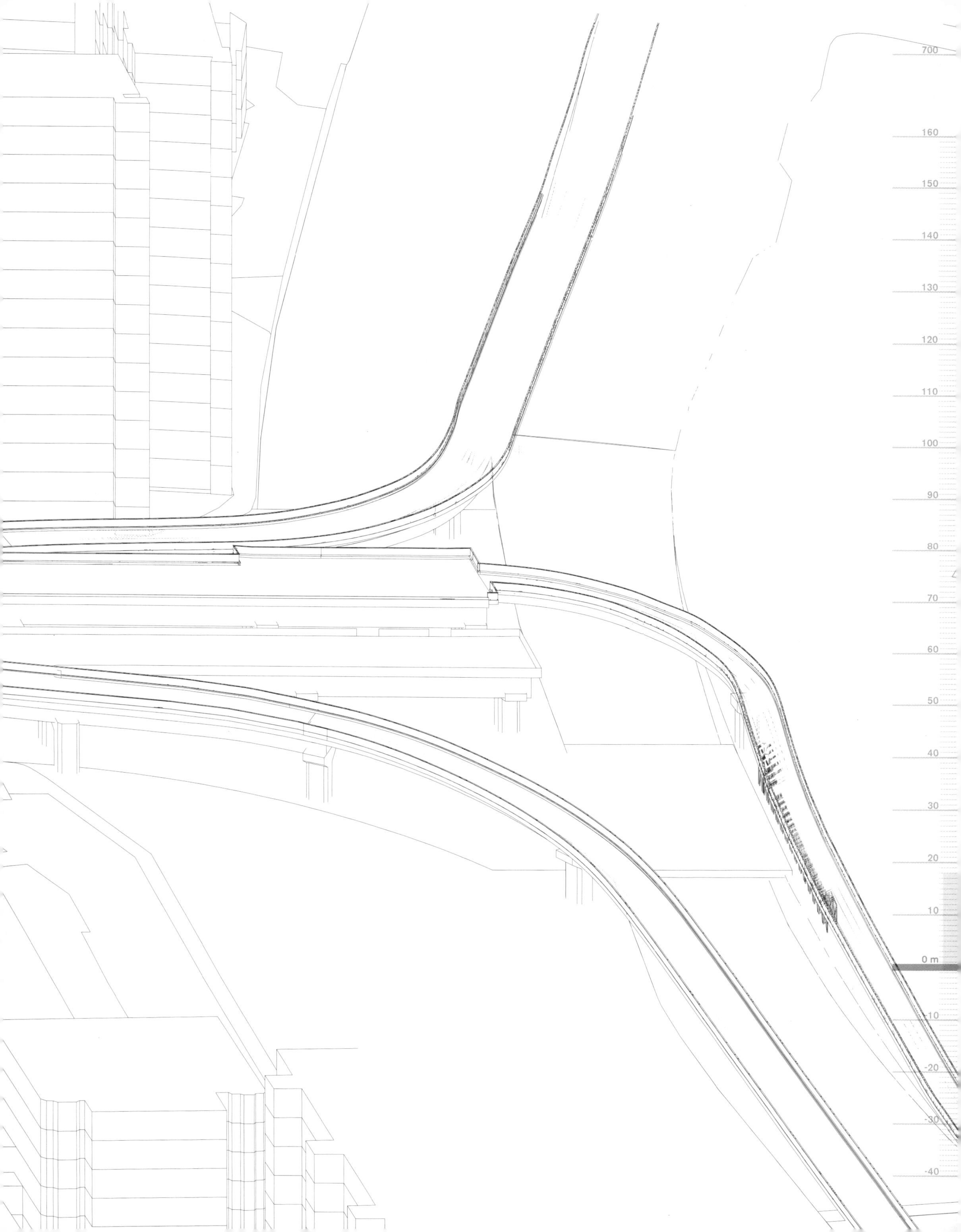
700
160
150
140
130
120
110
100
90
80
70
60
50
40
30
20
10
0 m
-10
-20
-30
-40

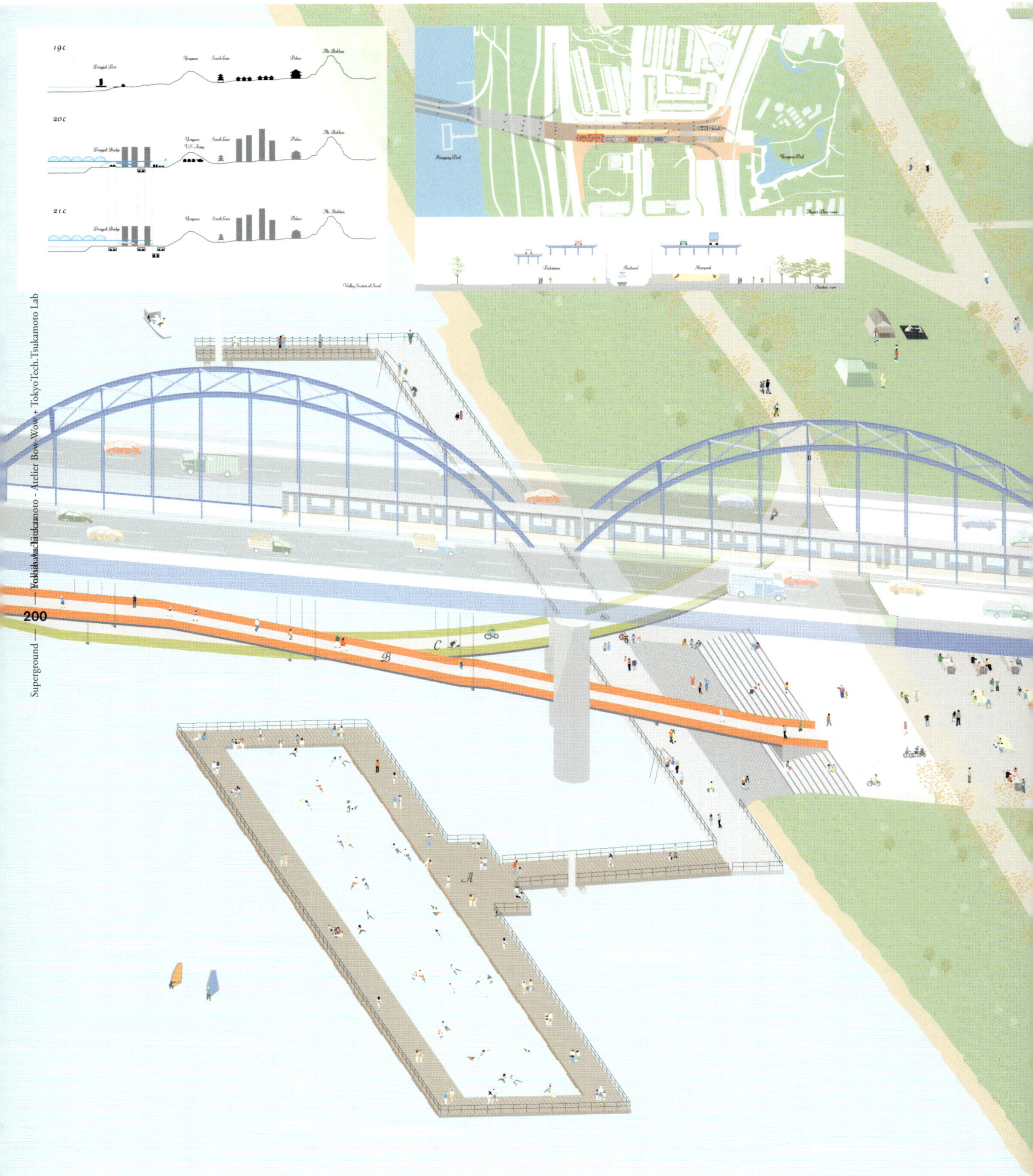
19c
Dongjak Port
Yongsan
South Gate
Palace
Mt. Bukhan
20c
Dongjak Bridge
Yongsan
U.S. Army
South Gate
Palace
Mt. Bukhan
21c
Dongjak Bridge
Yongsan
South Gate
Palace
Mt. Bukhan
Valley Section of Seoul
Hangang Park
Yongsan Park
Master Plan
Pedestrian
Railroad
Skatepark
Section
A
B
C

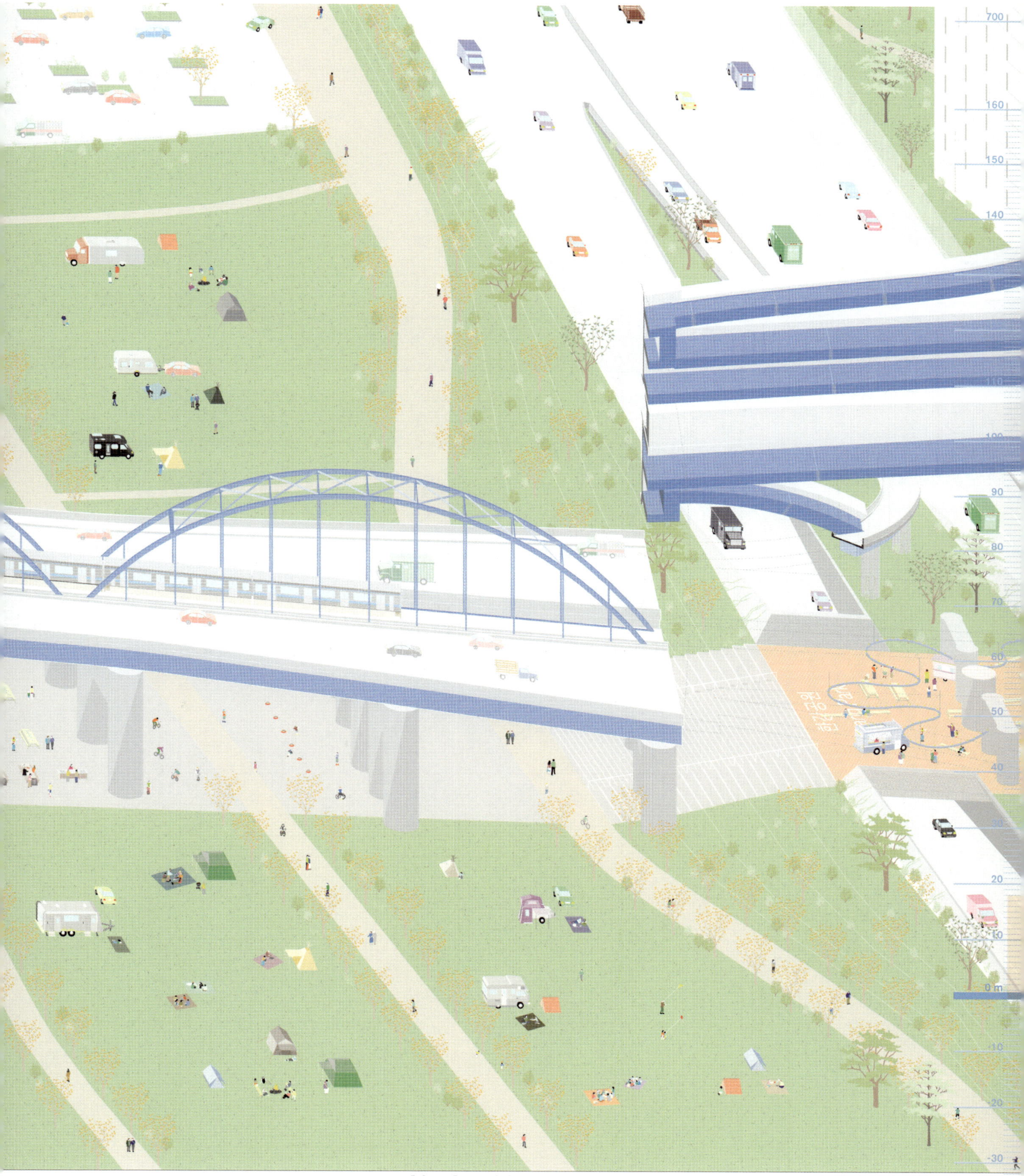

Legend

A. Swimming Pier
B. Pedestrian
C. Bike Road
D. Chandelier Square
E. Skate Park
F. Pingpong Court
G. Gateball Court
H. Basketball Court
I. Badminton Court
J. Tennis Court
K. Wall Climbing
L. Outdoor Gym
M. Fountain
N. Club House
O. Old Rail Road
P. Yongsan Park Gate

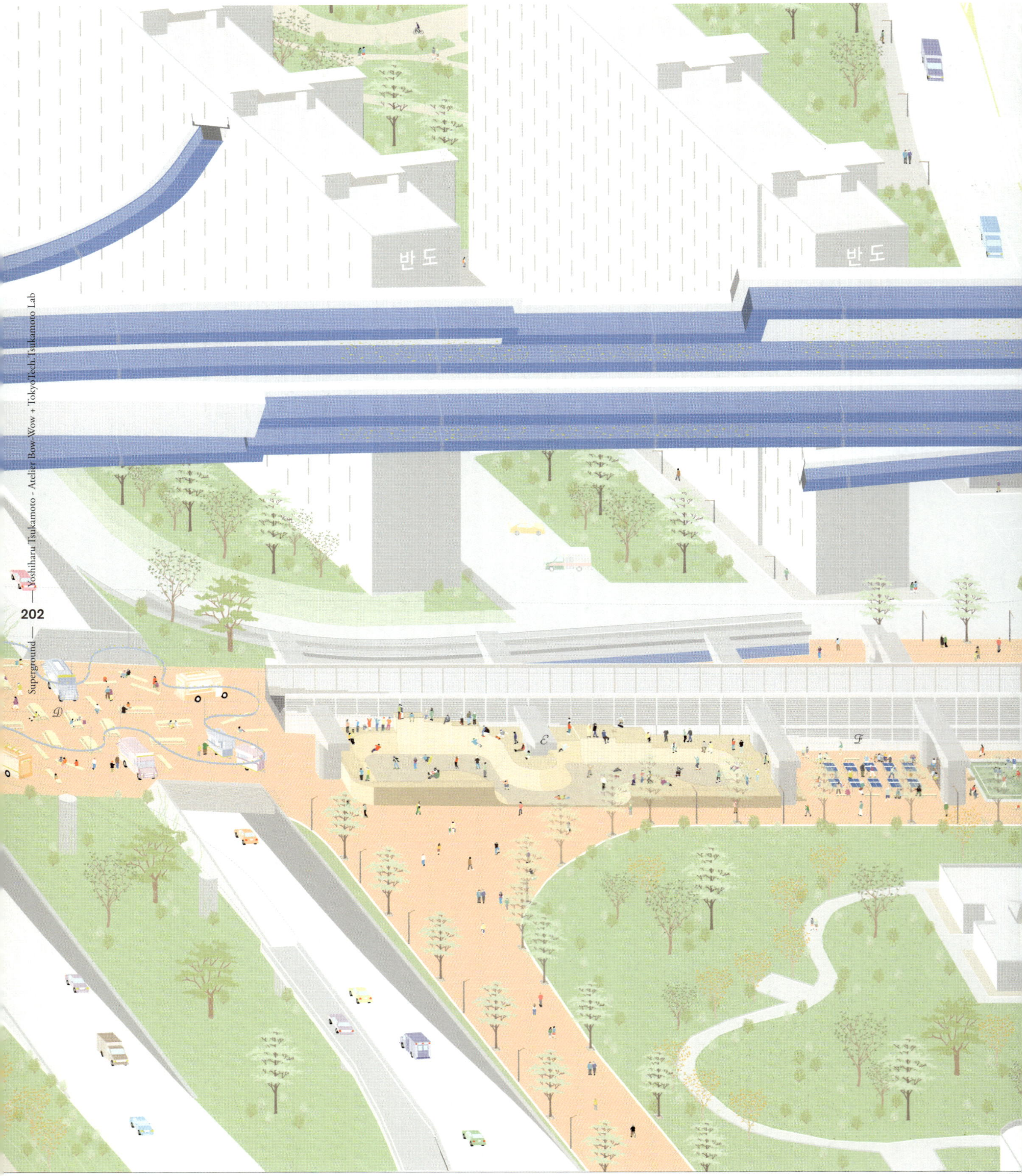

Yongsan Body Culture Club, Seoul, 2018, Atelier Bow-Wow & Tokyo Tech, Tsukamoto Lab.

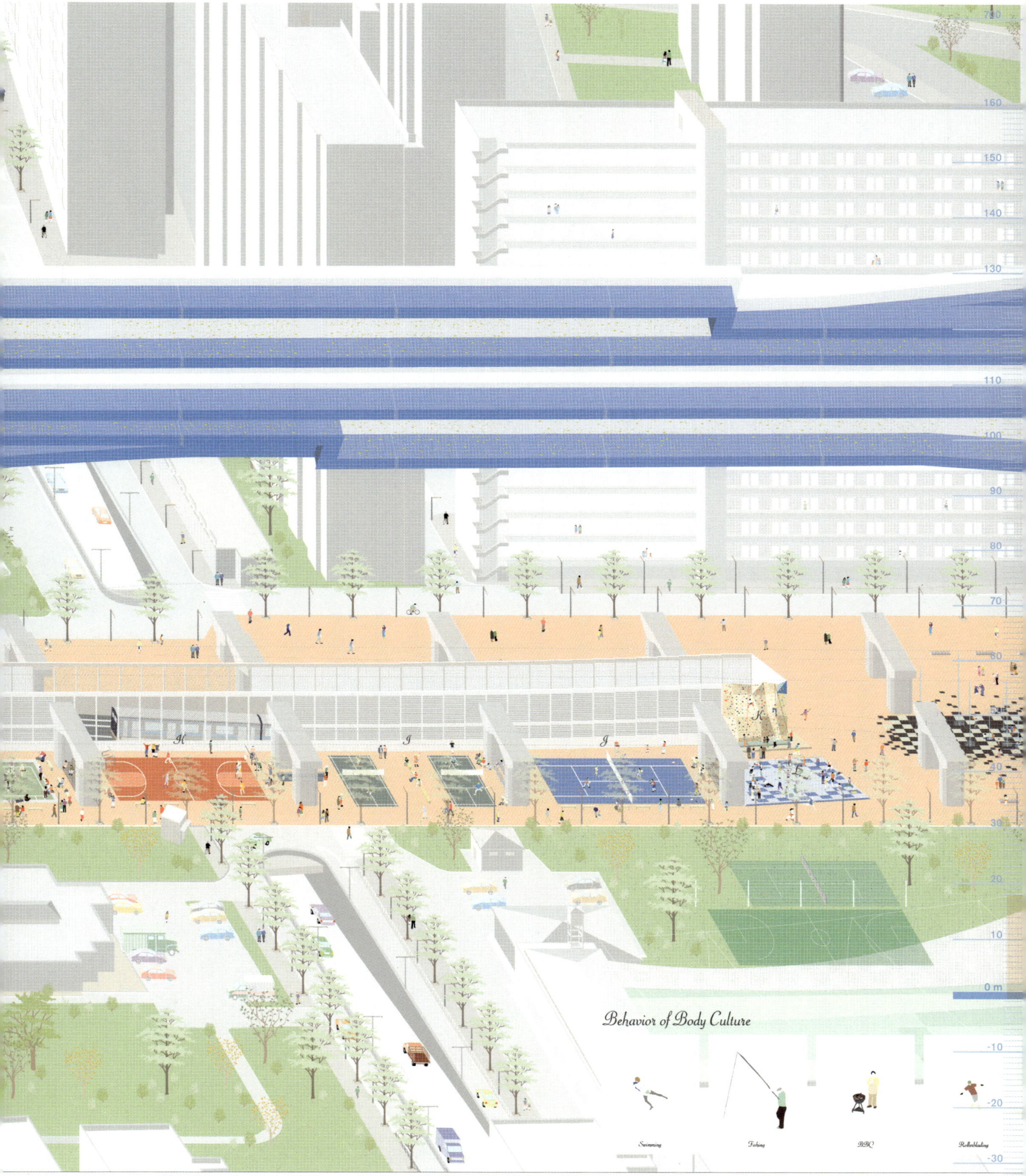

Drawn by

Hyunsoo Kim
Ivan Bonev
Hu Shi
Amena Rahman
Selma Shimura
Agnes Lundberg
Clara Havström
Kai Wen
Kan Tong
Shohei Kunisawa
Kai Kashibuchi
Shino Hagio
Sana Toumatsu
Daiki Chiba
Wataru Moriwaki
Kazuki Tanaka
Hiroki Kiyoto
Miyuki Watanabe
Ari Maruyama
Davina Iwana
Hofer Valentin

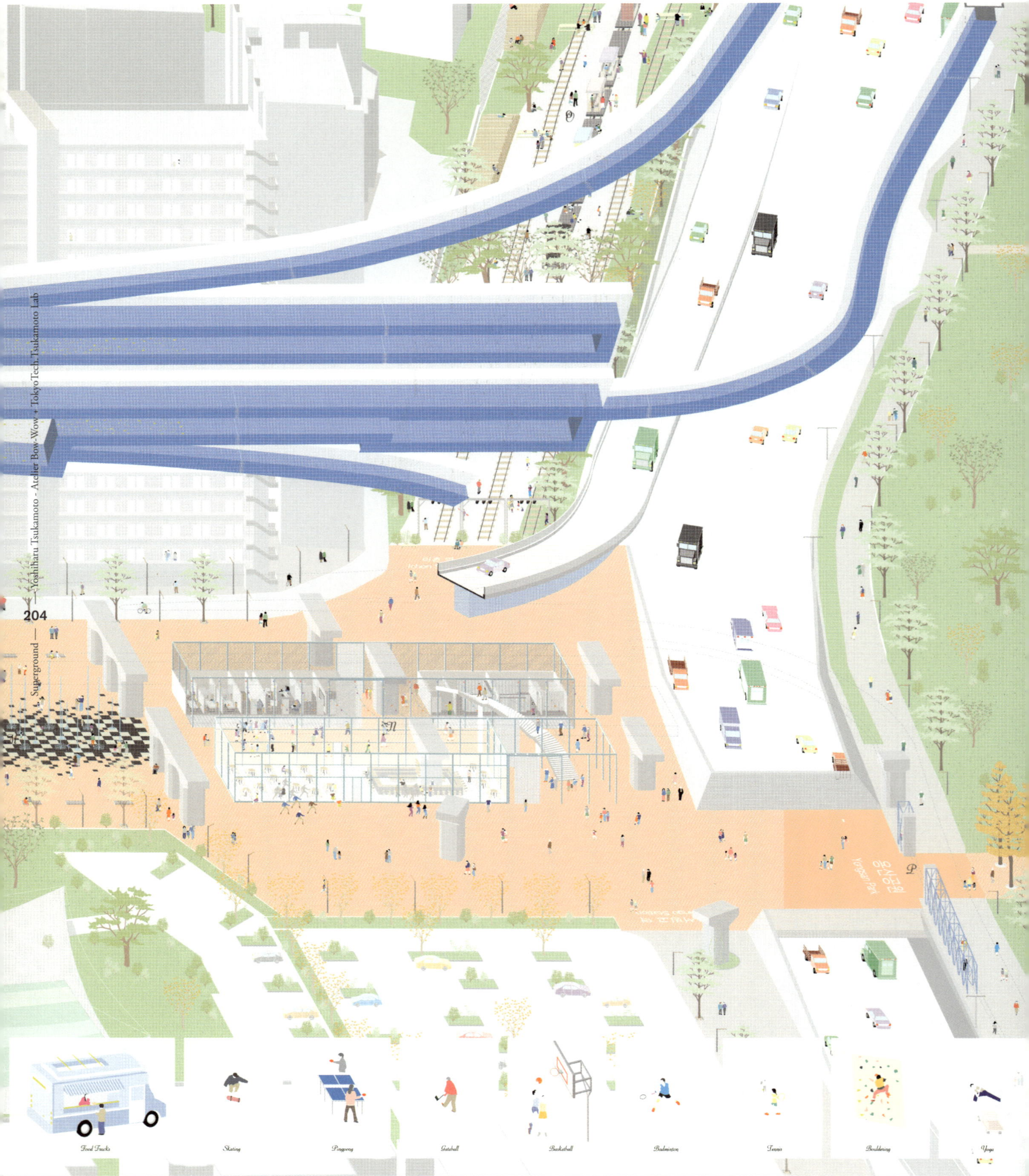
Food Trucks
Skating
Pingpong
Gateball
Basketball
Badminton
Tennis
Bouldering
Yoga

700
160
150
140
130
120
110
100
90
80
70
60
50
40
30
20
10
0 m
-10
-20
-30
-40
Social Dance
Street Music
DJ
Street Dance
Tattoo
Massage
Bar

NL 건축사무소

NL Architects

영등포 프리웨이

지난 수십 년 동안 서울이 폭발적 성장을 이룰 때 인프라스트럭쳐들은 큰 역할을 했다. 다발처럼 엮인 간선도로는 많은 공공공간을 차지하고 있고, 도시는 근육조직 같은 고속도로에 둘러싸여 있다.
영등포 로터리는 서울에서 가장 복잡한 교통 요지 중 하나다. 수많은 도로가 보행자들이 접근할 수 없는 섬 같은 '사각지대'를 형성하고 있다. 이 거리를 되찾을 수 있을까? 이 잃어버린 공간에 거주할 수 있는 방법이 있을까? 새로운 연결고리를 구축하면 어떨까?

프로젝트는 주요 전제를 공유하는 세 가지 제안으로 구성되어 있다. 서울의 경우 도로가 차지하는 면적이 어마어마하다. 소중한 지상 공간이 '해방'될 수 있는 방식으로 도로 체계를 ' 재편'하면 어떨까?

1--- "고속 로터리 가속기"는 모든 방향의 도로가 같은 면을 공유함에 따라 결과적으로 차량들이 서로 충돌하고 교통 체증이 발생하는 혼잡한 교차로의 우회도로를 형성해준다.

2--- "계곡의 숲"은 도로 아래 땅을 파내 현재의 교통체계가 만들어낸 고립 지역들을 다시 연결해준다.

3--- "여의도광장다리"는 도로들을 적층형 ' 간선도로' 형태로 재편해 소중한 지상 공간을 자유롭게 한다. 8차선 도로는 8층 '건물'이 된다. 기존 다리는 생동감 있는 체육공원으로 전환한다.

Yeongdeungpo Free Ways

In the explosive development of Seoul in the past decades` infrastructure played a crucial role. Bundles of highways define much of the public space. The city is wrapped in muscle tissue of motorways. The Yeongdeungpo Rotary is one of the busiest traffic nodes in Seoul. The myriad of lanes forms an impenetrable atoll for pedestrians, a 'dead zone'. Can we 'claim back the streets'? Can we find ways to inhabit this lost space? Can we establish new connections?

The project consists of three interventions that share a central premise. In Seoul the amount of space occupied by roads is enormous. Can we 'remix' the road system in such a way that valuable space at ground level can be 'liberated'?

1— A Rapid Rotary Accelerator creates a bypass for the overcrowded crossing, where all directions share the same plane and as a consequence cars run into each other and traffic jams form.

2— The Valley Forest re-connects the isolated patches that are formed by the traffic tissue by excavating the soil below the roads.

3— Yeoeuido Square Bridge. Regrouping the car lanes into a stacked 'highway' frees up valuable space at ground level. An 8 lane road becomes an 8 story 'building'. Former bridge turns into a lively sports venue.

NL 건축사무소는 도시 생활 활성화를 목표로 하며, 우리가 생활하고 일하는 방식에 대한 대안을 찾고자 지속적인 탐구를 진행 중이다. 어떻게 하면 사람과 사람 사이의 소통을 증진할 수 있을까? 이들은 건축을 우리가 사는 세상의 경이로운 복잡성을 연구, 발견, 재구성하는 사유의 과정이라고 여긴다. 평범함을 아름다움으로 응축해내거나 일상에서 숭고함을 추출해낼 수 있을까? 암스테르담 Bijlmermeer 의 초대형 아파트 단지 Kleiburg 재건축 프로젝트로 2017년 EU 미스 반 데어 로에 상을 받았다.

NL Architects aspires to catalyze urban life. The office is on a constant hunt to find alternatives for the way we live and work. How can we intensify human interaction? We understand architecture as the speculative process of investigating, revealing and reconfiguring the wonderful complexities of the world we live in. Can we compress banality into beauty; squeeze the sublime out of the obvious? For the renovation of Kleiburg, a super-sized apartment block in the Bijlmermeer, Amsterdam, NL Architects were granted the EU Mies van der Rohe Award 2017.

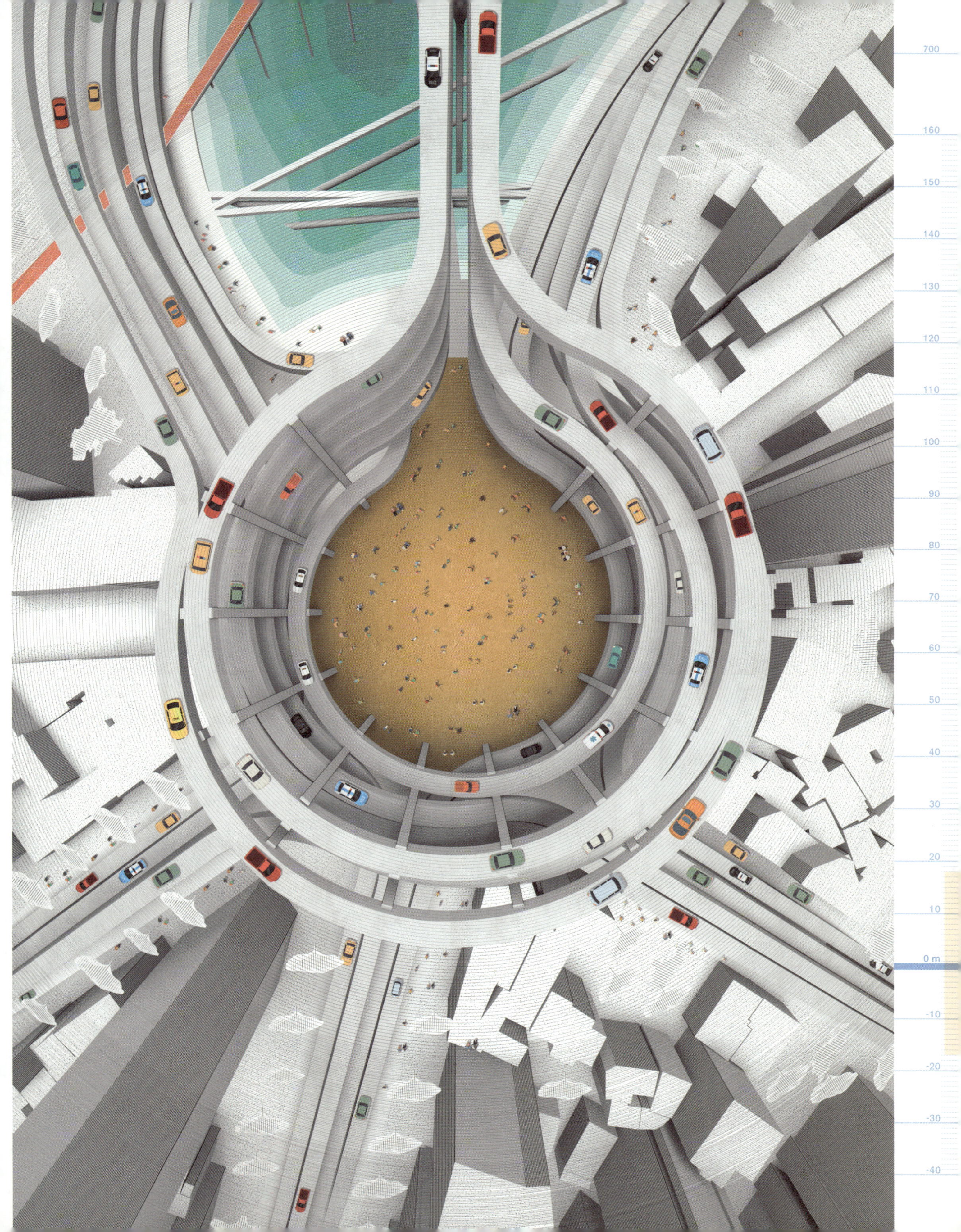
700
160
150
140
130
120
110
100
90
80
70
60
50
40
30
20
10
0 m
-10
-20
-30
-40

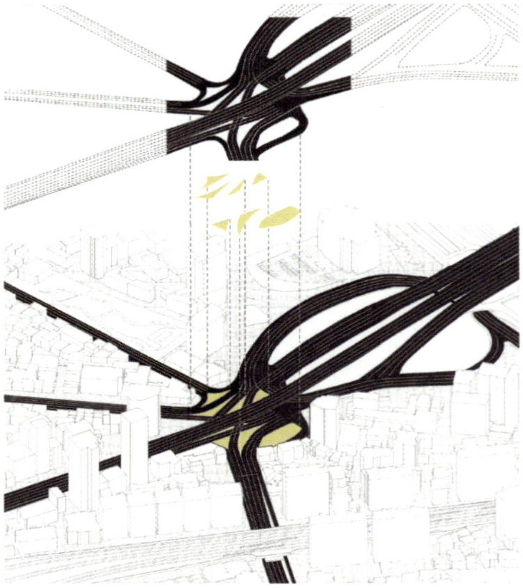
at the Yeongdeungpo Rotary all directions share the same plane

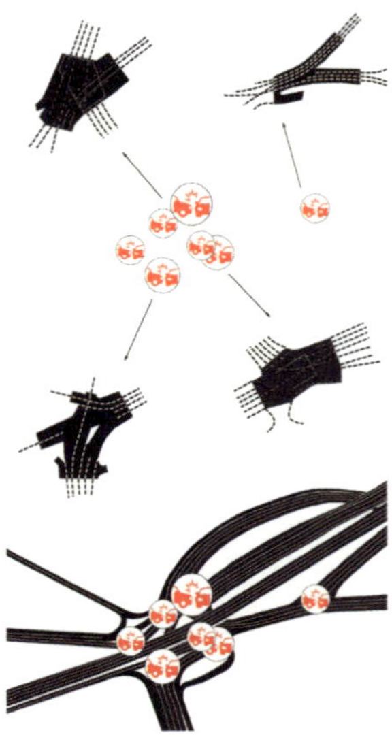
as a consequence cars run into each other, often literally, traffic jams form

isolated patches that are formed by the traffic tissue

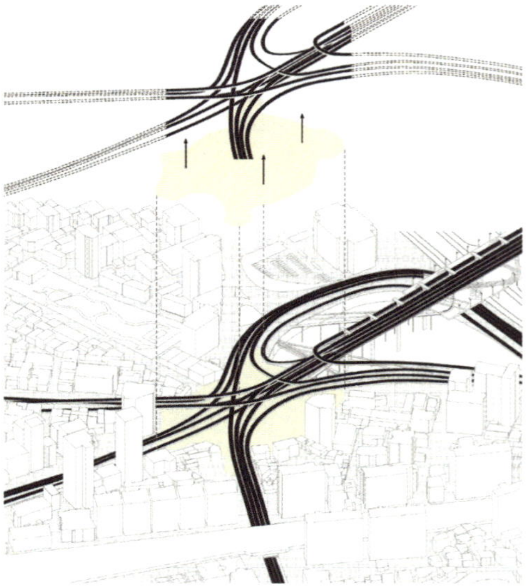
untangling the systems in multiple arteries based on transit will relieve the knot

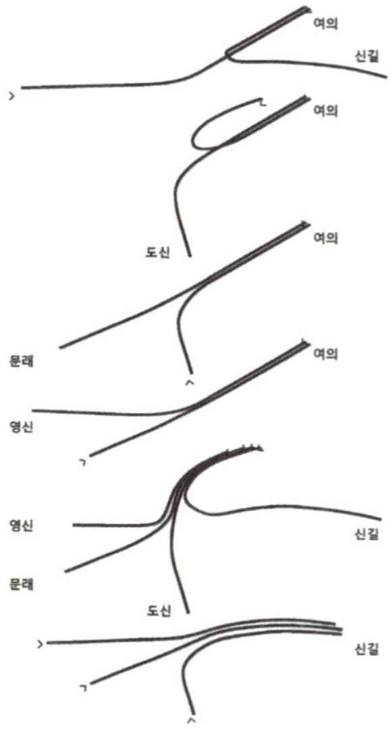

single lanes for single destinations

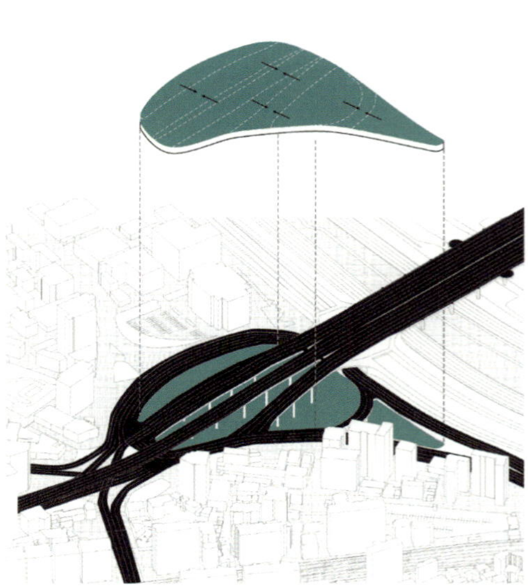
reconnecting isolated patches by excavating the soil below the roads

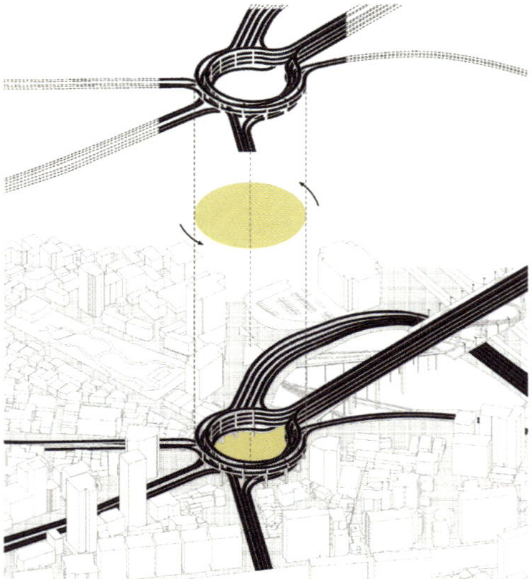
the multilayered rotary defines space; it creates and urban room, a circular arena, a round square

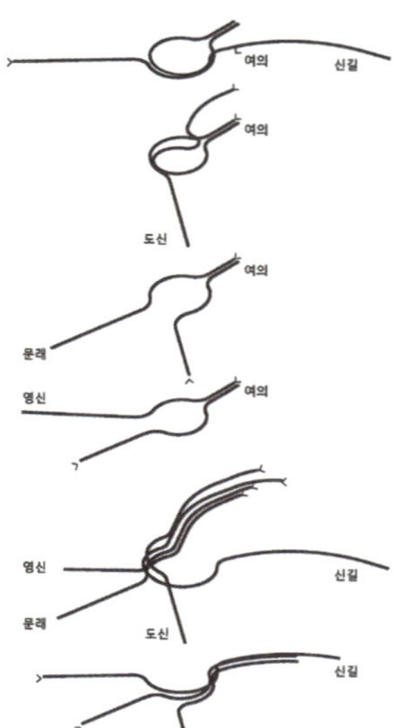

unravel the complexity with its inherent resistance into a streamlined, simple, smooth flow

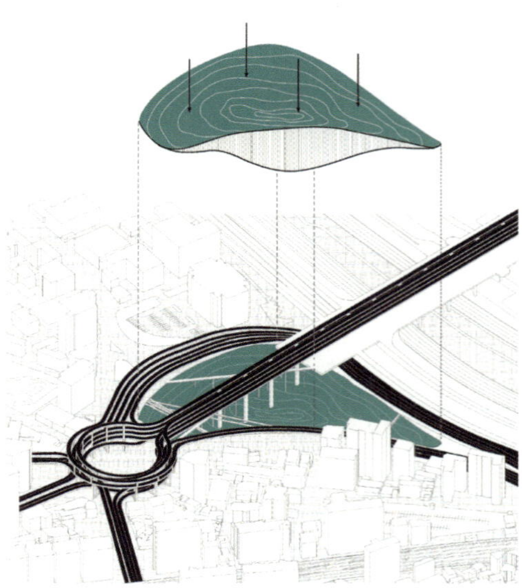
a beautiful sunken landscape emerge, a 3 dimensional pocket park

buffer zones have a limited natural and social diversity

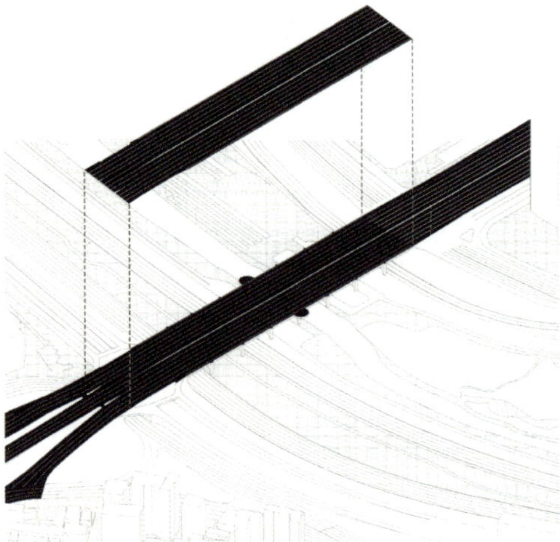

highway bridge defines a character of the public space

can we create a biotope to fit both infra and man?

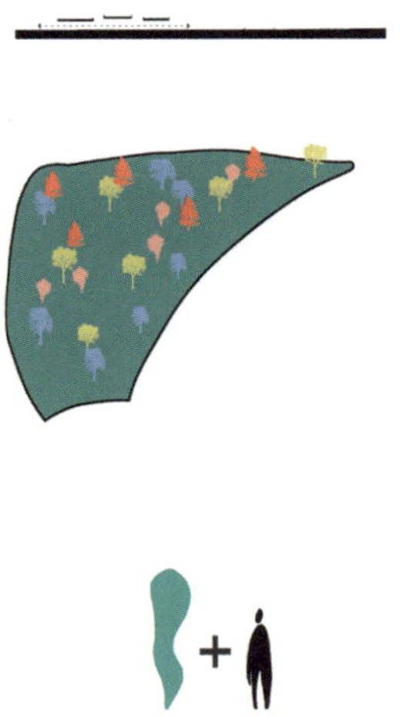

united green patch bring the man to enjoy the piece of urban nature

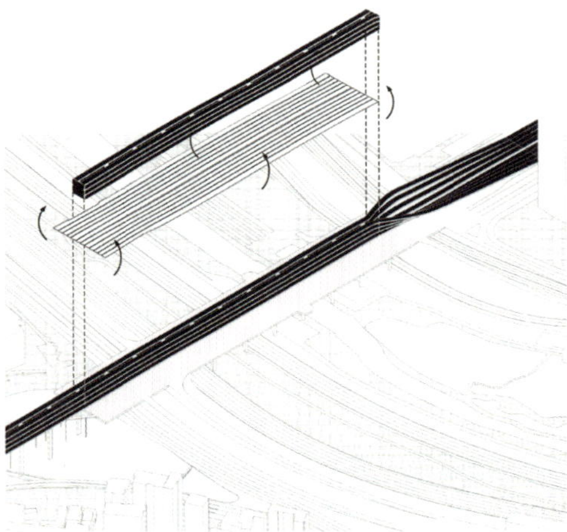

re-grouping the car lanes into a stacked 'highway', the 8-lane road becomes a 4 storey 'building'

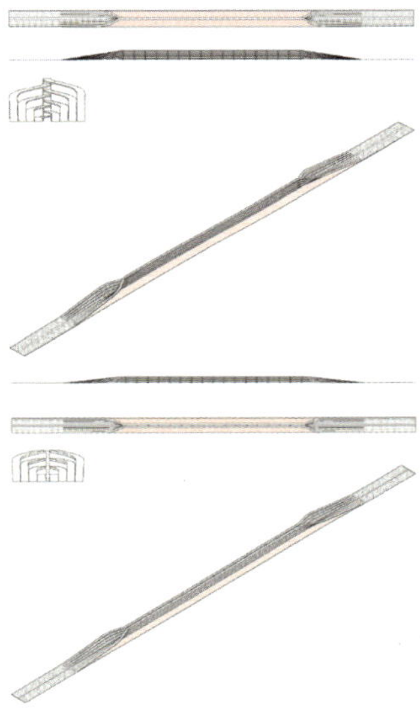

exploring the possible profile of a 'vertical higway'

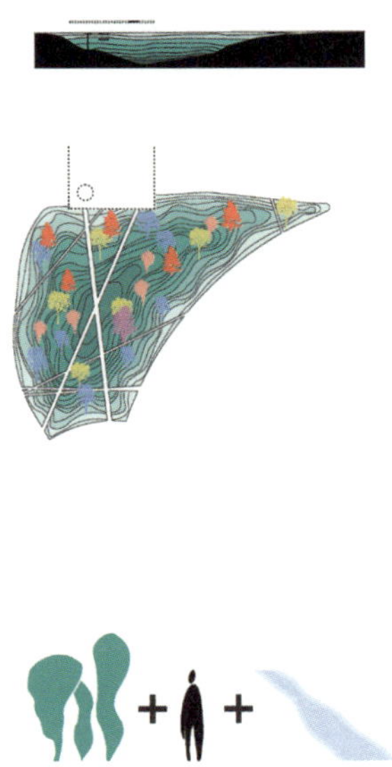

diversification of nature creates a truethfull gem

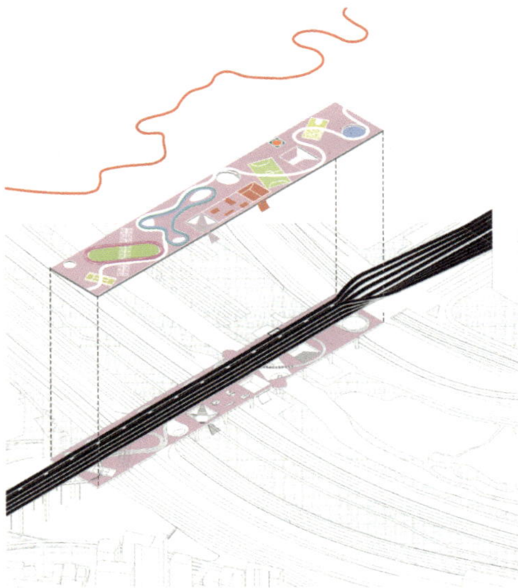

by stacking the lanes the current bridge can be fully pedestrianized

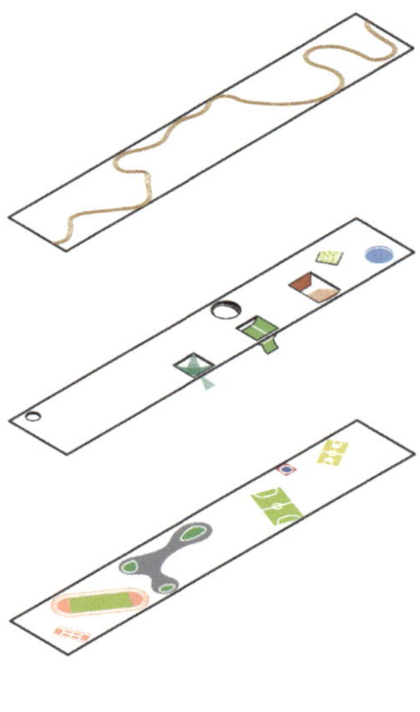

it becomes an elongated plaza, a podium for sports that ties together Yeoeuido and Yeongdeungpo

site subjugated by a transit network system

urban core established within a new pedestrian area

greenery anclaves broken to an unaccesible buffer zones

unused spaces united to form a distinct anclave of nature

local connectivity crippled and detached

all the local activities connected into a seemless network

THE RAPID ROTARY ACCELERATOR (OR THROUGH TRAFFIC CATALYSER)

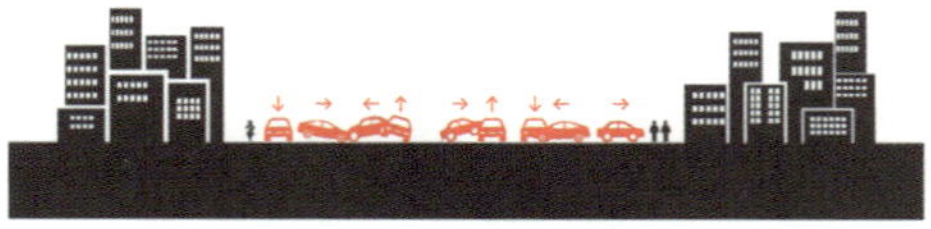
phase 1 - an overcrowded plane

phase 2 - untangling the road systems

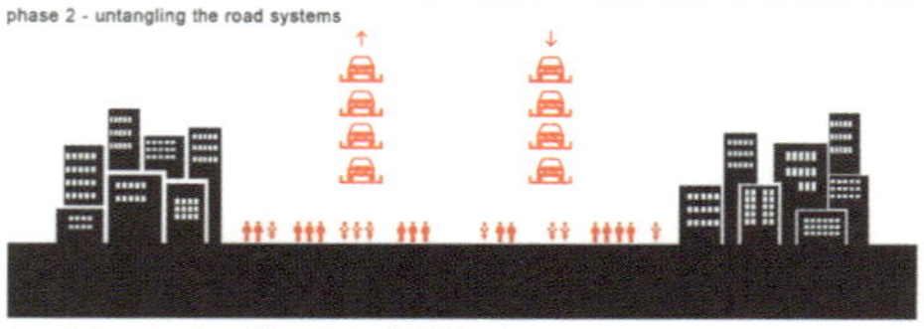
phase 3 - formation of a multilayered rotary that defines the space

THE VALLEY FOREST (OR THE BIG DIG)

phase 1 - roads isolates the green patches

phase 2 - excavating the soil below the roads to re-connect isolated elements

phase 3 - a beautiful sunken landscape emerges under the higway now placed on pillars

THE YEOEUIDO SQUARE BRIDGE

motorway, the muscle tissue of Seoul, defines city's public spaces

stacking a 8-lane road to create an 4 storey 'building'

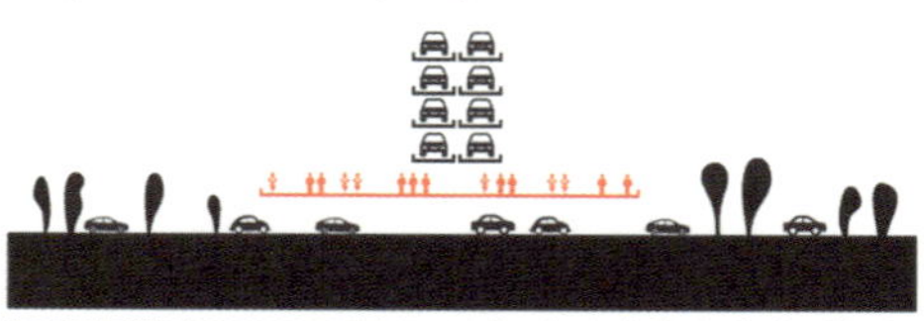
former traffic bridge becomes an elongated placa, a podium of sports, that ties together Yeoeuido and Yeongdeungpo

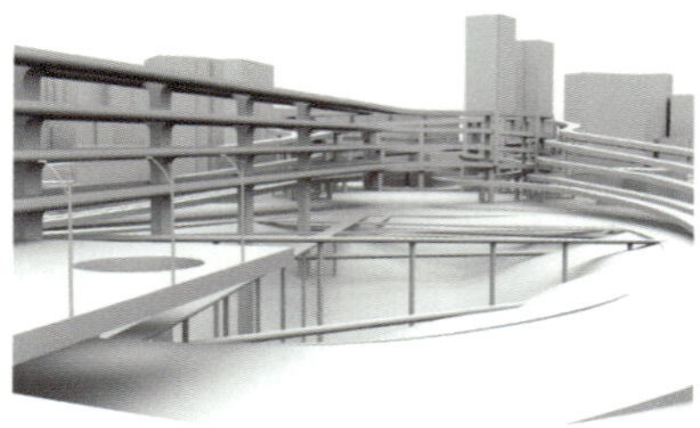

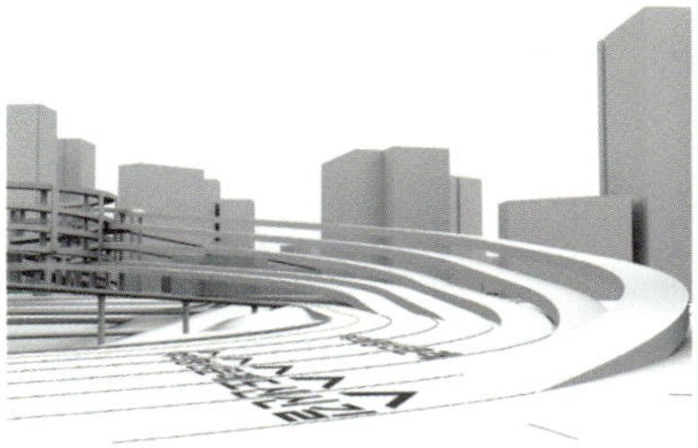

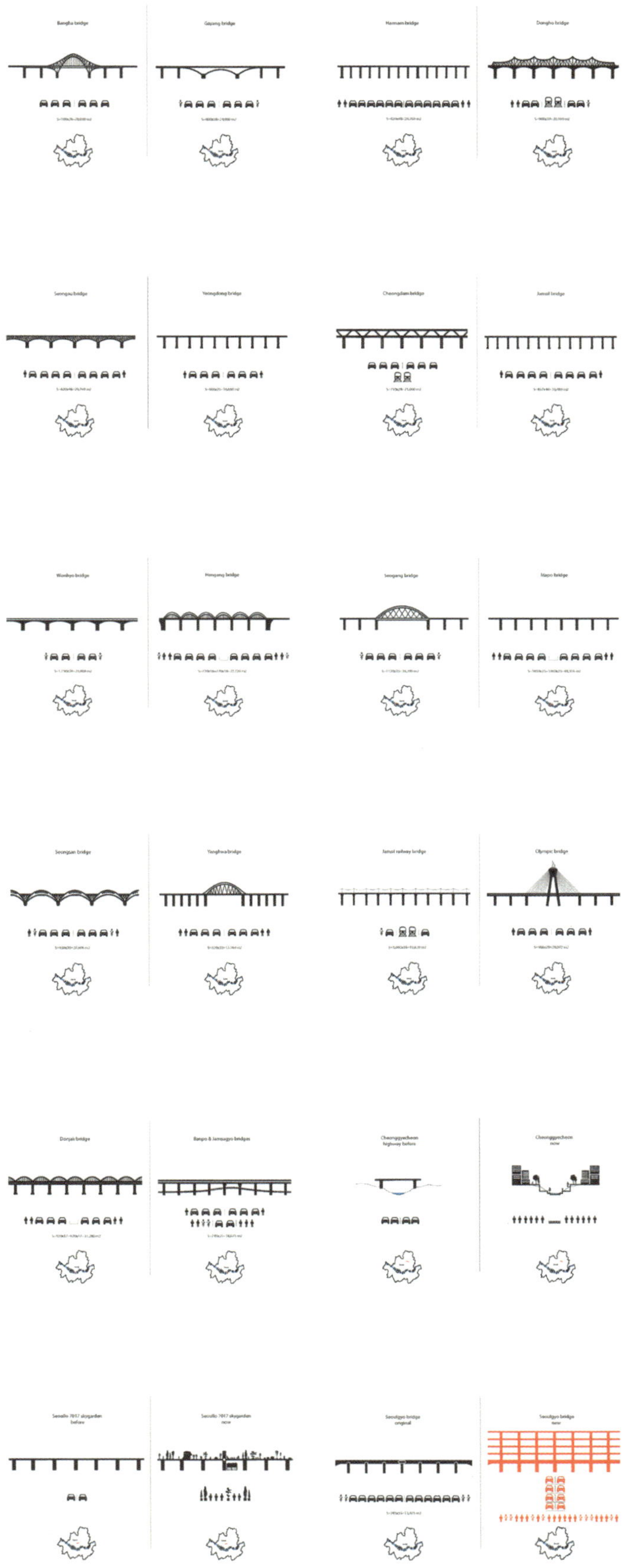

700
160
150
140
130
120
110
100
90
80
70
60
50
40
30
20
10
0 m
-10
-20
-30
-40

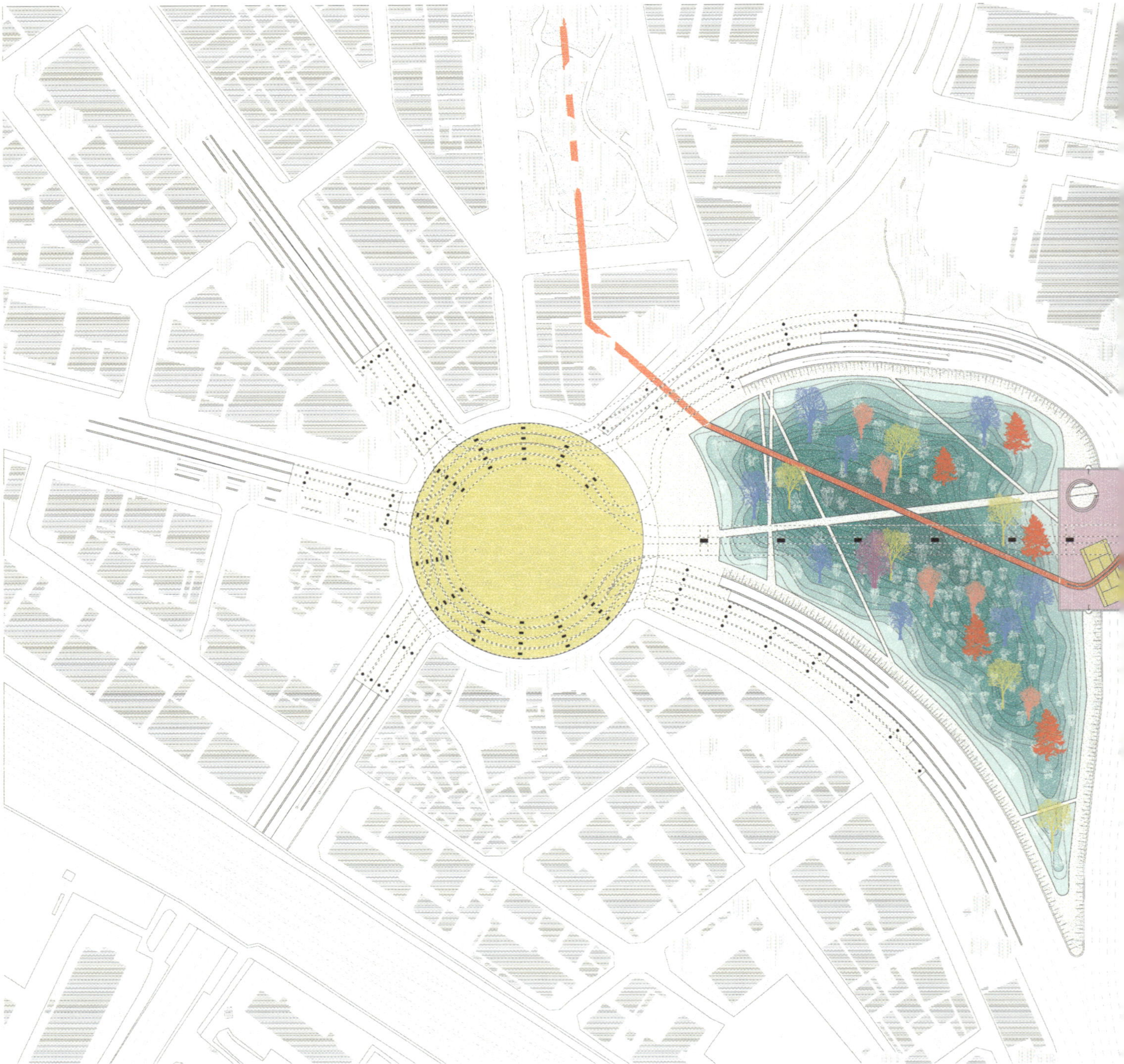

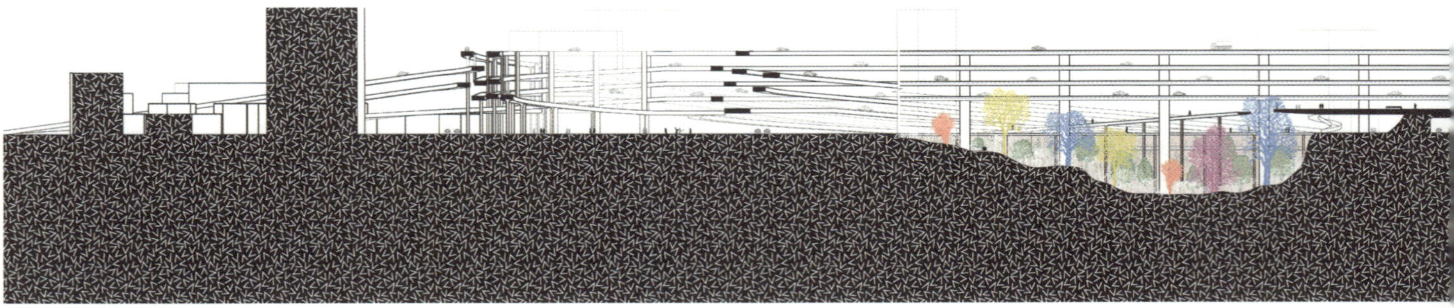

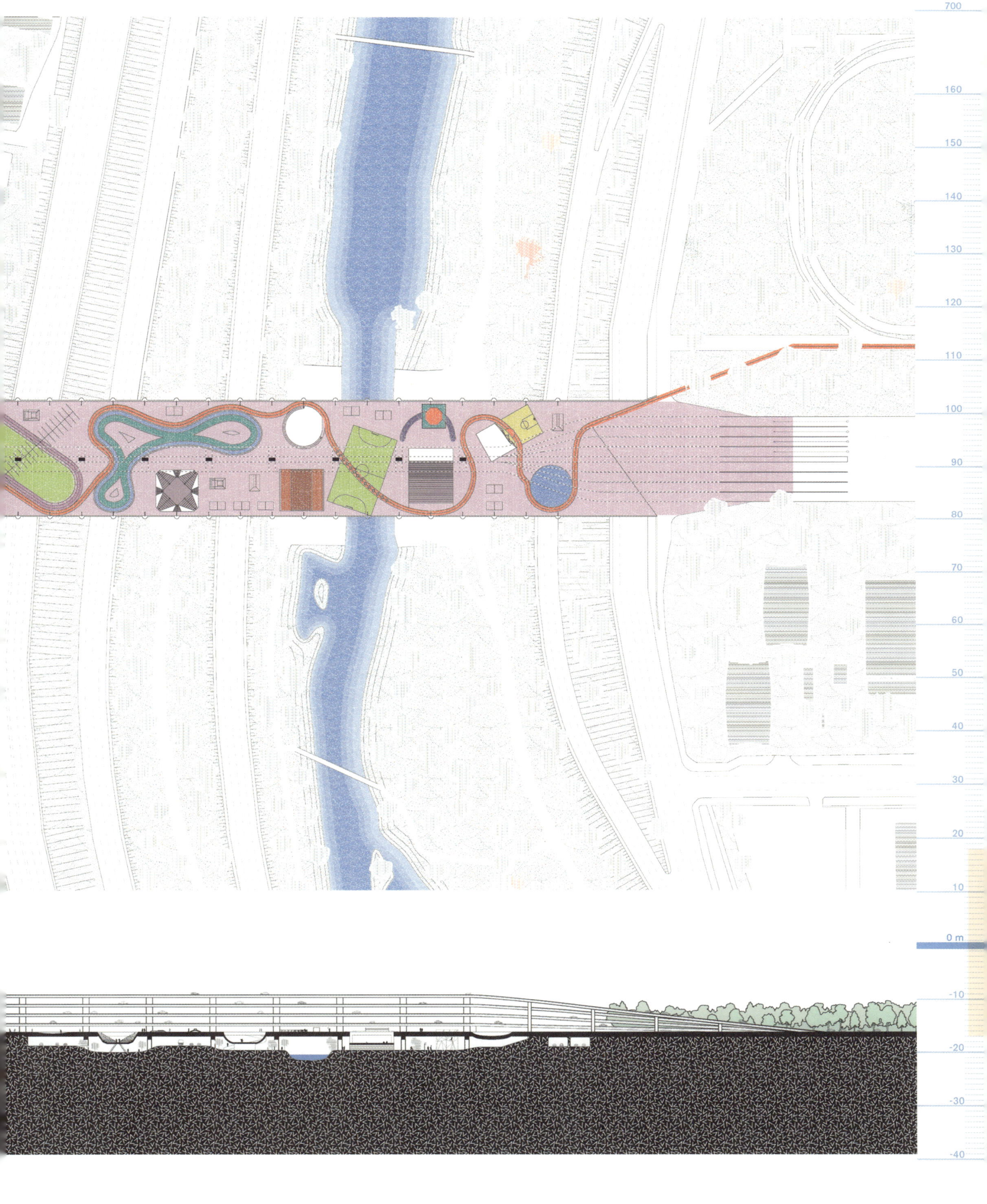

700
160
150
140
130
120
110
100
90
80
70
60
50
40
30
20
10
0 m
-10
-20
-30
-40

700
160
150
140
130
120
110
100
90
80
70
60
50
40
30
20
10
0 m
-10
-20
-30
-40

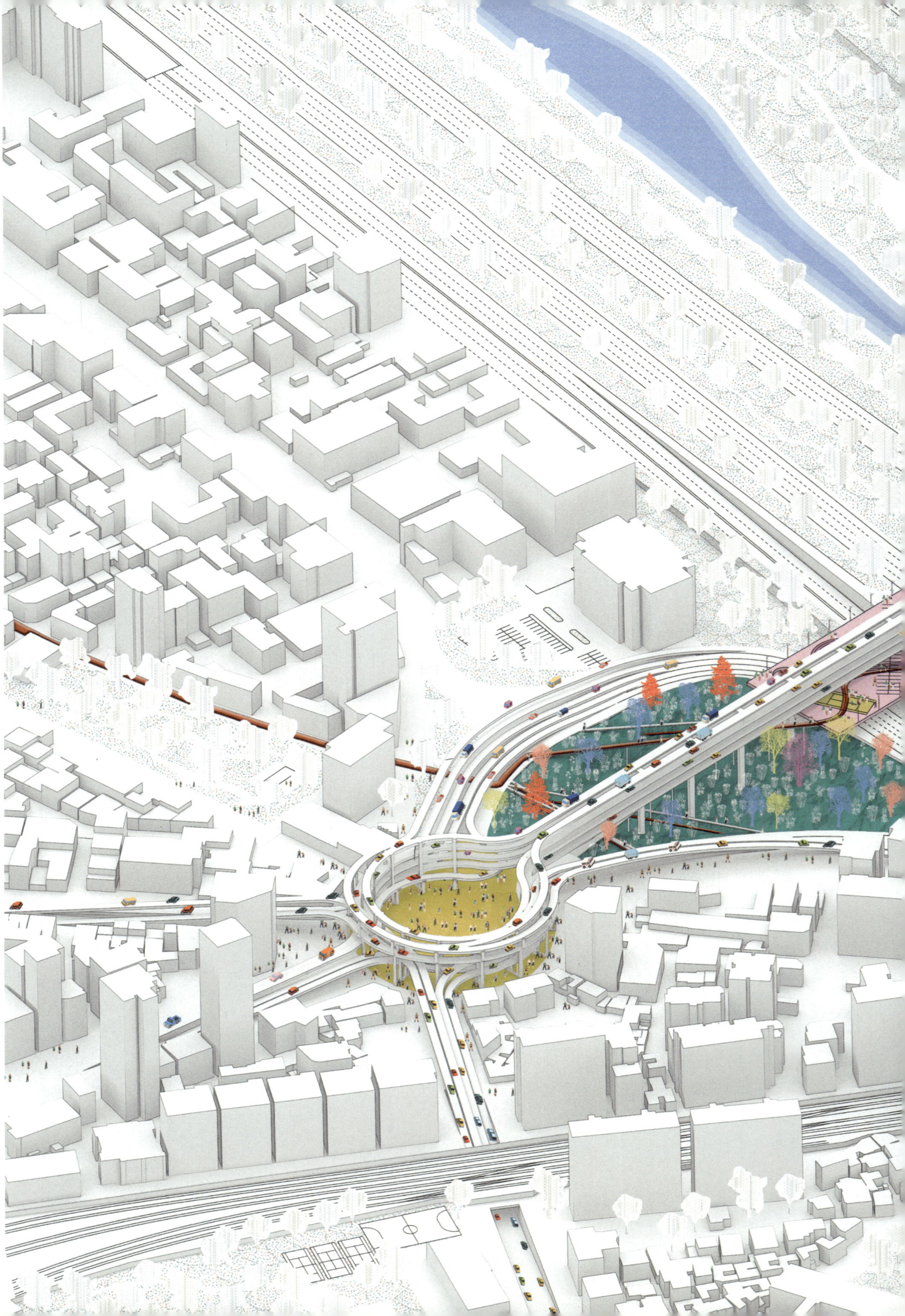

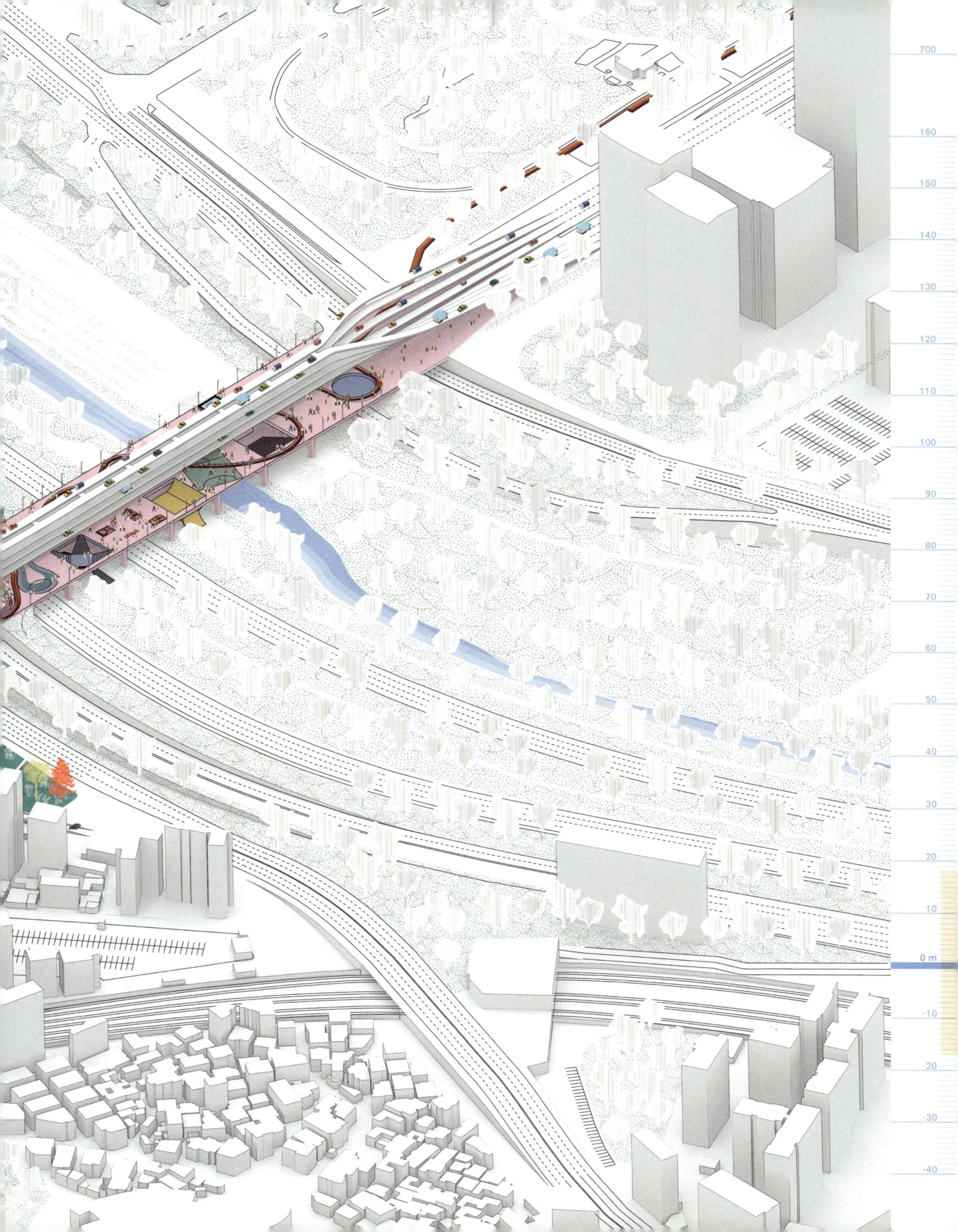
700
160
150
140
130
120
110
100
90
80
70
60
50
40
30
20
10
0 m
-10
-20
-30
-40

페데리코 소리아노 + 돌로레스 팔라시오스

Federico Soriano + Dolores Palacios

마포중첩경관기계

친환경 기계의 기능적이고 생산적인 구조와 물재생센터 네트워크가 뒷받침하는 일련의 생산적, 체계적 생태계를 만들 것을 제안한다. 이 자연 친화적 복합단지는 한강, 수변 산책로, 서울 도심 사이에 자리 잡은 도시와 자연의 연결고리다. 생산적 생태계는 자연공원의 기반시설을 도시가 필요로 하는 오락 프로그램, 시설에 재정적 도움을 주고 건축 복합체의 유지관리를 가능하게 해주는 사적 영리 기능과 결합한다. 일부 프로그램은 도시가 새로운 활동 공간이 필요할 경우 다른 프로그램으로 대체할 수 있다. Mapo Stackedscape Machine은 도시 체계적 기계로, 생산적 도시 풍경, 정원, 인프라스트럭쳐, 건축 그사이 어딘가에 속한 장치, 현재 생활 양식을 규정해주는 기계화된 에덴동산, 콘크리트로 구현한 건축적 이상향, 고속도로 형태의 한강 수변 산책로의 연장 보행로이자 살아있는 구조물이다.

Mapo Stackedscape Machine

Our proposal builds a set of productive and programmatic ecosystems, supported by the working and production diagrams of the eco-machines and by the network of water treatment systems. This natural complex is the urban–natural connection between the Han river, the riverside promenade, and the built centre of Seoul. The productive ecosystems combine the support–basis of a nature park with the leisure programs the city needs at each point in time, and the private profit-based uses that can provide financial support to the complex while warranting the maintenance of the architectural compound. Some of the programs could be substituted by other programs if the city should ever need a space for these new activities.
Mapo Stackedscape Machine is a civic programmatic machine; it is a productive urban landscape; it is a device somewhere between a garden, an infrastructure, and architecture; it is a mechanical Eden that defines our present lifestyle; it is a concrete architectural utopia; it is an pedestrian extension of the river Han's promenade with the geometry of a motorway; it is a living structure.

페데리코 소리아노와 돌로레스 팔라시오스는 스페인 마드리드에 기반을 둔 건축가다. 1992년 건축사무소 S&Aa를 설립했다. 건축박사를 보유하고 있으며, 마드리드의 여러 대학에서 정교수로 활동 중이다. 잡지 “Fisuras de la cultura contemporanea”의 편집자이며, 2010년 건축그룹 “Movimiento Encoger”를 설립했다. 주요 프로젝트로는 빌바오의 Euskalduna Jauregia, Bilbao 시청, Pza Bizkaia, 라 팔마의 Fuente Santa 온천, 말라가의 오디토리움이 있다.

Federico Soriano and Dolores Palacios are architects based in Madrid, Spain. In 1992 they founded S&Aa, architectural office. They are full professors and Ph doctor architect in different Universities in Madrid. Editors of Magazine *“Fisuras de la cultura contemporánea”*. In 2010 they founded *“Movimiento Encoger”*, shrinking architecture group. Main projects: Euskalduna Jauregia, Bilbao; Bilbao Urban hall; Office Building Pza Bizkaia, Bilbao; Thermal spa Fuente Santa, La Palma and the Málaga Auditorium.

-40
-30
-20
-10
0 m
10
20
30
40
50
60
70
80
90
100
110
120
130
140
150
160
700

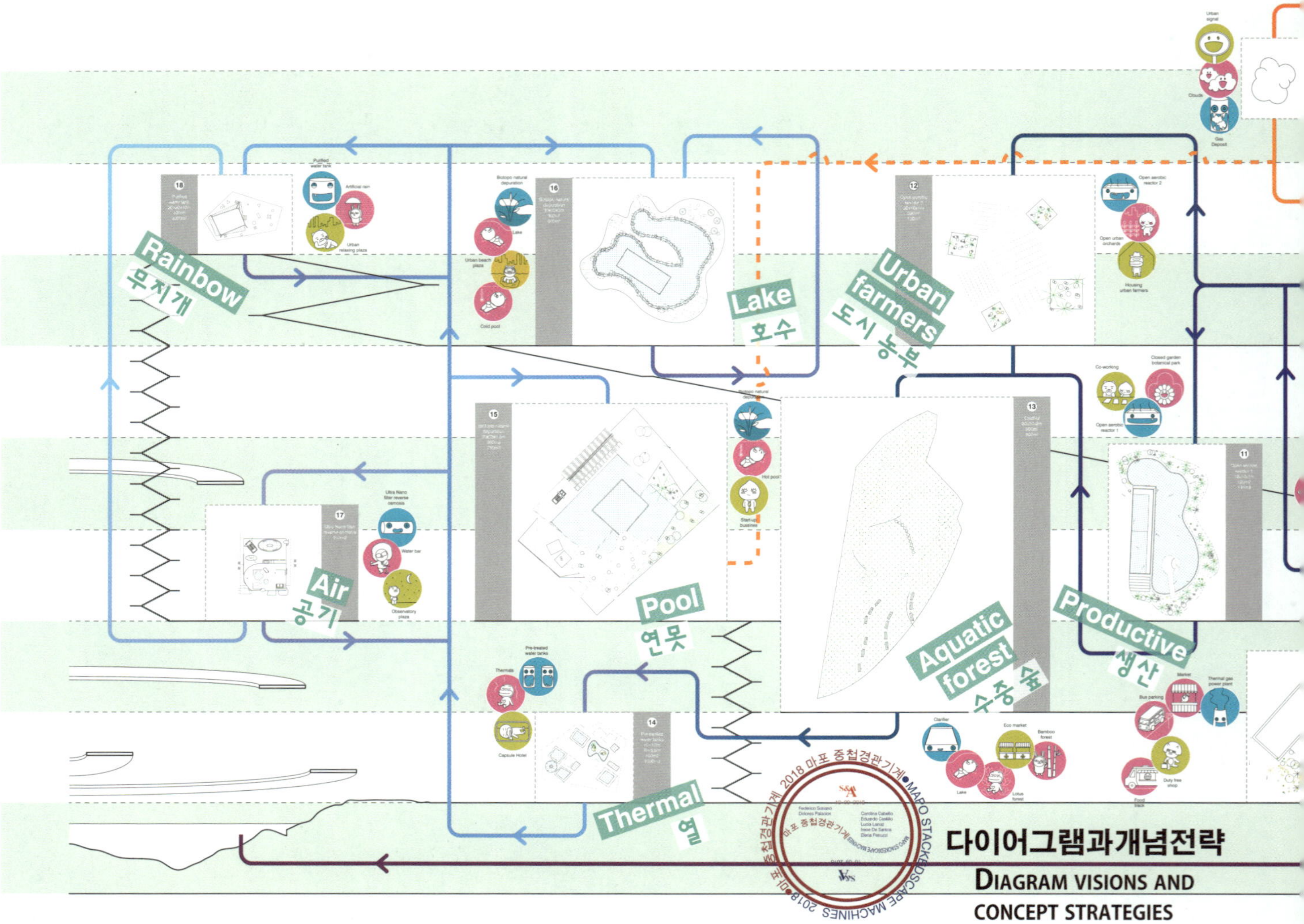

다이어그램과개념전략

DIAGRAM VISIONS AND CONCEPT STRATEGIES

다이어그램

이 건축 및 도시 작업 구성은 다음 세 가지 다이어그램을 따른다. 공간 다이어그램은 도시에서부터 한강으로, 그리고 가장 낮은 레벨에서 높은 레벨로 건축 프로그램들을 분산한다. 이 방향은 선형으로, 마포대로 1길에서부터 70번 국도와 한강 수변공간으로 이어지는 공공/인프라 관계를 따른다.
기술 다이어그램은 가장 오염된 폐수에서부터 정화된 식수까지 물의 흐름을 구성한다. 도시의 가장 높은 부분에서부터 강에 이르기까지, 낮은 지점에서 가장 높은 부분까지, 가장 더러운 물에서부터 높은 곳에 위치한 가장 정화된 물까지 그 방향은 선적이다. 이 다이어그램에서는 다른 프로그램에서 사용할 수 있는 바이오가스 저장소와 열변환소도 있다.
일반 다이어그램은 앞의 두 다이어그램을 통합하며, 실질적으로 이 프로젝트의 평면과 단면이 된다. 사람과 물, 양쪽 모두의 흐름을 보여준다. 공공과 이윤 기반의 프로그램들은 기존 인프라 및 자연 처리 시설과 혼합되어 있다.

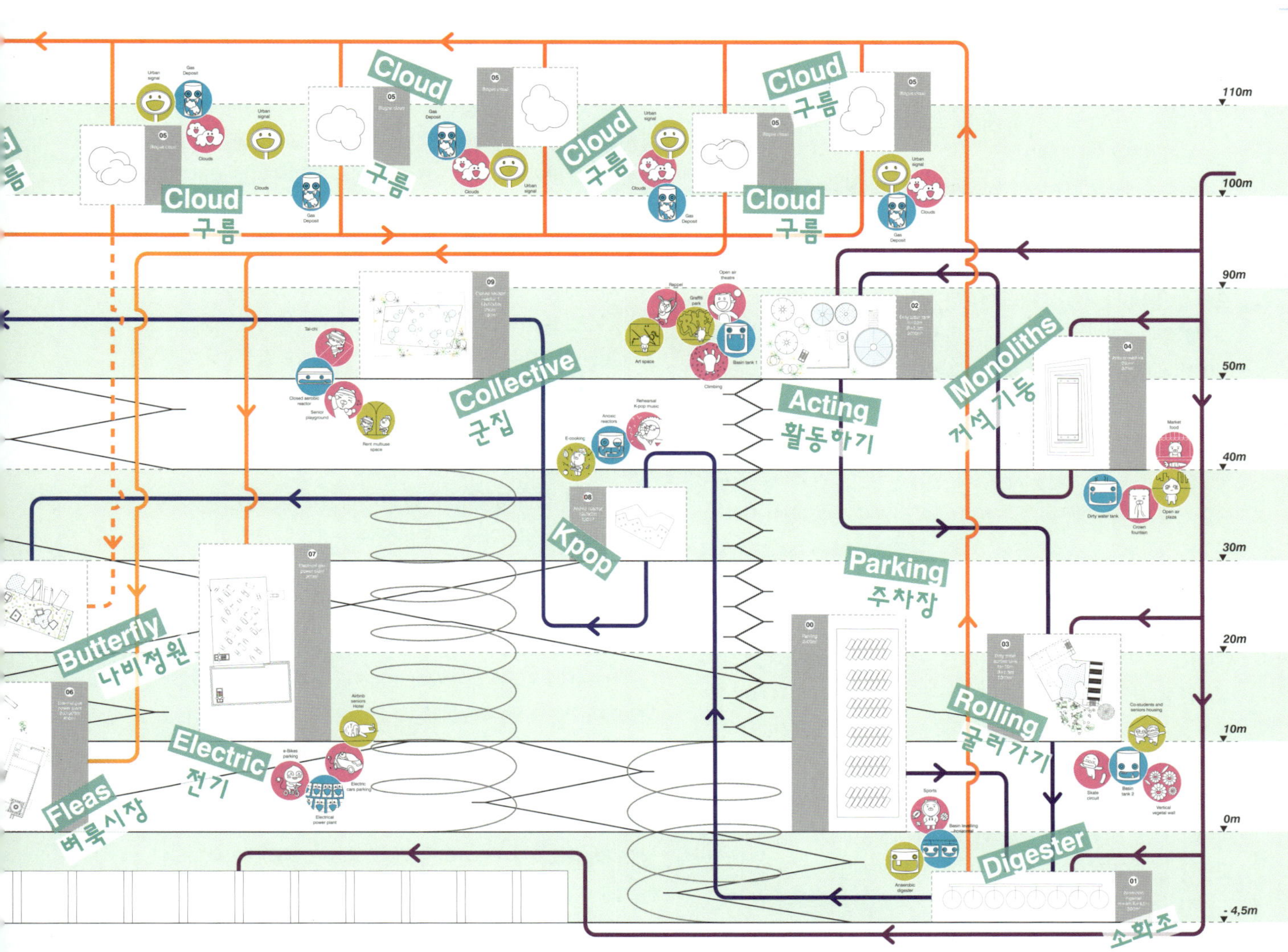

Diagrams

The organization of this architectural and urban artifact follows three specific diagrams.

The spatial diagram distributes the architectural programs from the city to the Han river and from the lower to the highestlevels. Its direction is linear and it follows a public/infrastructure relation from Mapo-daero 1-gil street towards the right, motorway 70, and Han river promenade.

The technical diagram organizes the water flows, from the most polluted wastewater to the purified drinking water. Its direction is linear from the highest part of the city to the river, and from the lower to the highestpart. That is, from the dirtiest to the most purified, the higher the deposit. In this diagram are also the biogas deposits and the thermal transformation stations to be used in the other program circuits.

The general diagram integrates the two previous ones and is in fact a plan and cross-section of the project. The flows shown are both of liquids and of people. The public and profit-based programs have been hybridized with the existing infrastructure and the natural treatment plant.

프로그램. 인프라 프로그램, 공공 프로그램, 생산 프로그램

프로그램은 특정 생태계 안에서 세 개가 하나의 그룹을 이룬다. 각 프로그램은 인프라 프로그램, 공공 프로그램, 생산 프로그램의 세 카테고리 중 하나에 속한다.

인프라 프로그램은 자연적인 물 관리와 정화를 위한 생태기계로, 장마 기간 중 우수 저장과 하수 처리를 위한 저장소들을 담고 있다. 이는 이 복합단지의 기반이 되는 프로그램으로, 기본적이고 전형적인 도시 설치물이다. 선형 수로와 연속된 개방형 저장소와 폐쇄형 저장소들로 이루어져 있으며, 작동 방식은 간단하다. 첫 번째 부분은 장마철이나 예기치 못한 홍수가 닥칠 경우 물로 가득 차는 물 처리 및 저장 시설로 이루어져 있다. 3m 높이에는 현재 영역을 덮는 개방형 저장소, 보다 높은 층에는 폐쇄형 저장소들이 위치하며, 저장소의 벽들은 여가 프로그램들을 지원한다. 전체 용량은 백만 리터로 현재 용량과 동일하다. 새로운 프로그램을 도입하면서 저층부에서 사라진 용량은 상층부의 개방형 저장소가 대신 메운다. 이들은 저장과 처리를 위한 저장소로 연결되며, 여기에서 처리 과정이 시작된다. 이들은 밀폐된 폐쇄형 저장소이다. 물은 이곳에 도착하기 전에 고체 이물질을 걸러내는 여과기와 생분해가 불가능한 물질을 걸러내는 금속망이 설치된 탱크를 통과한다. 두 저장소는 관으로 연결되어 있고, 가능한 때에 용수를 활용해 오수를 다음 처리 단계로 일정하게 흘려보낸다. Imhoff 탱크는 바닥의 이물질과 생물학적 분해가 가능한 침전물이 혐기성 박테리아에 의해 분해되는 곳이다. 이 과정에서 발생한 바이오가스는 이 계획안의 위쪽에 위치한 떠 있는 확장 가능한 덮개에 모인다. 일단 이 과정이 끝나면, 처리된 물들은 존 토드의 생태기계의 자연정화과정으로 이어진다. 폐쇄형 탱크와 개방형 탱크들로 구성되었으며, 선형 수로로 연결되어 있다. 하루에 약 40,000리터를 처리할 수 있다. 첫 번째 탱크 그룹은 무산소 반응로인데 이곳에서는 무산소 환경 하에 오수를 저어 탱크 속 용해성 이물질 제거를 촉진하는 유익한 미생물의 성장을 자극한다. 그다음 탱크 그룹은 폐쇄형 유산소 반응로이고, 이곳에서는 기포 확산기가 아래쪽에서 이물질에 공기를 주입하고, 표면에 설치된 바이오필터는 부식성 가스나 용해성 이물질을 걸러낸다. 이 탱크는 개방 탱크로 열이 제어되는 환경에 위치해야 한다. 세 번째 그룹의 탱크는 개방된 유산소 반응로이다. 표면의 식물이 뿌리를 통해서 물로부터 영양분을 얻고 산소를 다시 생성하기 위하여 유기물을 처리한다. 다음 탱크들은 이전과 같은 방식으로 작동하는 두 번째 유산소 반응로인데, 다만 물의 품질을 회복시키는 데 도움이 되는 다른 종류의 식물들이 있으며, 물고기나 곤충과 같은 유익한 유기체들이 있다. 이 탱크들은 외기에 면해 있다. 마지막 탱크 역시 외기에 면한 것으로, 마지막 침전물이 발생하는 곳에서 물을 정화하는 역할을 한다. 남아있는 바닥의 모든 이물질을 모아서 다시 한번 처리하기 위하여 펌프를 통해 수로 안으로 보낸다. 정화된 물은 재사용을 위한 중수 저장소에 저장된다. 여전히 많은 부유물을 함유하고 있어서 공원이나 정원 용수나 청소 목적으로 사용할 수 있다. 자외선 처리 장치가 달린 두 번째 생태기계는 수영장, 호수, 여가 활동 등에 안전한 물을 위한 정화 과정을 제공한다. 세 번째 수로는 저장소 물의 일정량을 정수해 바, 레스토랑, 그 외 정확한 품질 평가가 필요한 프로그램들에서 사용하기 위한 물들을 제공한다.

시스템의 초기단계에서 물의 일부가 재활용되면서 수영장이나 호수를 유지하기 위한, 생태기계와 별도로 진행되는 층이 있다. 물의 일부는 (화학물질이 없는) 생물학적 자갈 여과 과정, 소위 "자연적 수영장"으로 불리는 과정을 거쳐 처리된다. 수로는 물이 지속적이고 일정한 흐름을 유지할 수 있도록 크고 작은 다양한 크기의 자갈들을 물이 흐르는 방향으로 겹겹이 쌓아 놓은 웅덩이들을 지나도록 유도한다. (니트로소모나스, 니트로박터 속에 해당하는) 박테리아는 이곳의 다공질 구조에 자리를 잡고 서식하며 천연 여과 및 정수 층을 형성한다. 웅덩이나 연못의 물은 폭포를 통해 산소와 공기를 공급받는다.

물이 펌프가 설정해준 속도로 여과장치를 통과하면 깨끗해진 물이 아래쪽에서 수영장으로 돌아온다.

공공 프로그램은 주 인프라 시설과 연계된다. 공원과 정원의 경관을 참고하여 생태기계가 만들어낸 경관과 환경 조건들 속에서 나타난 동선이나 휴식을 위한 공간들은 서울 시민들이 서로 소통할 수 있고 즉흥적 공공 활동을 수용할 수 있는 열린 공공공간이 될 것이다. 공공 프로그램은 도시와 한강 수변공간을 연결한다.

생산 프로그램은 생산성과 이윤에 기반을 둔 민간 프로그램으로, 앞의 프로그램을 보완하거나 복잡성을 더한다. 이들은 민간 기업의 도심 복합시설에 대한 재정적 참여나 지원을 가능하게 한다.

생산 프로그램에는 상업, 주거, 여가, 숙박 등의 기능이 포함된다.

결과적으로 이 세 가지 핵심 프로그램은 일반적 정원보다 훨씬 입체적이며 녹색의 살아있는 풍경 위에 중첩된 도시 생태계의 밑바탕을 형성하게 된다.

Programs. Infrastructure program, public program, productive program.

The programs are grouped in sets of three in a specific ecosystem. Each program belongs to one of the three categories: infrastructure program, public program, or productive program.

The infrastructure program is a system holding the deposits for rainwater and sewage water regulation during the rainy season, with a natural water treatment and purification eco-machine. This is the base program of the complex, and a basic and paradigmatic urban installation. The way it works is quite simple, based on a linear circuit and a series of closed or open-air deposits. Its first part consists of the regulation and storage deposits, which will fill up over the rainy season and during any flash floods. They are open deposits, which cover the current area at elevation 3.00, or closed ones, located on higher floors and whose walls will support the leisure programs. The total planned capacity will be of one million liters, identical to the current volume. The cubic meters that disappear on the lower levels due to the inclusion of new programs are substituted with the open deposits on the higher levels. They all connect to the storage and treatment deposits, where they begin the treatment process. These are closed and sealed deposits. Before reaching these however, the water goes through a tank with a set of filters that separate solid waste, with an accessible metal screen that filters non-biodegradable solids. The two deposits are connected by pipes, using regulation water when available and evenly distributing the waste water to then channel it towards the following treatment stage. This is an Imhoff tank, where the sludge and biodegradable parts sediment at the bottom to be decomposed by anaerobic bacteria. The biogas produced during this process is collected in the expandable floating covers located above the proposal. Once the process is complete, the treated water continues its way towards the natural purification process in John Todd's eco-machines. These are a series of different closed and open tanks, connected in a linear circuit that is able to process up to 40 thousand liters a day. The first group of tanks is the anoxic reactor where the effluent is stirred in an oxygen-free environment in order to stimulate the growth of beneficial microorganisms that accelerate the elimination of dissolved waste in these closed tanks. The following set of tanks is the closed aerobic reactor where bubble diffusers aerate the effluent from below and a biofilter, planted on the surface, reduces any corrosive gases and dissolved waste. This is an open tank that needs to be placed in a thermally-controlled environment. The third group of tanks is the open aerobic reactor where the surface plants process the waste in order to obtain nutrients and reestablish oxygen in the water through their root systems. The next set of tanks is a second aerobic reactor operating in the same way as the previous, only that this tank holds different plant species and other beneficial organisms such as fish and insects that help restore the water quality. In this case, it is an open-air tank. The last tank, also in the open air, is the water clarifier where the last sedimentation occurs so that any remaining solids can be collected from the bottom and pumped back into the circuit to be processed once more. This water is stored in a greywater storage tank to be reused. It will still contain many nutrients, and it can be used for the associated park and garden irrigation purposes and for the cleaning of the complex. A second eco-machine with ultraviolet treatment will offer clean purification to produce safe water for swimming pools, lakes, leisure activities, etc. From the clean water storage deposit, a third circuit will further purify a certain amount of this water for its use in the bar, restaurant, and programs requiring precise quality assessment. There is a parallel layer of eco-machines to maintain the swimming pools and lakes as part of this water is recycled at the beginning of the system, although some of the water is treatedvia biological gravel filtering processes (with no chemical products) sometimes called "natural swimming pools". This circuit has the water flow through pools where there is a stratified layering of gravels, of different grain sizes, from larger to smaller grains in the direction of the current, in order to guarantee a constant and uniform flow. Bacteria —of the genus nitrosomonas and nitrobacter— deposit onthis porous substrate and colonize it, creating a natural filter and treatment layer. The water is aerated and oxygenatedin these pools and ponds by means of waterfalls and cascades. Once the water flows through the filters at the speed set by the pumps, the clean water returns to the swimming pools from below.

The public program is the one associated to the main infrastructure. Taking a landscape of parks and gardens as a reference, the circulation and rest areas —in contact with and making the most of the landscape and environmental conditions generated by the eco-machines— are thought of as open public spaces that enable interactions between the citizens of Seoul and the possibility of hosting unplanned public activities. The public program connects the city and its center with the Han river promenade.

The productive program is a private program, productive or profit-based, that complements or adds layers of complexity to the previous ones. It offers financial intervention and support from private companies to the urban complex. These include the sectors of commerce, residence and housing, leisure, hospitality, etc. The three main program areas are integrated into a triad of urban ecosystems, stacked on a green living landscape that is much more complex than a simple garden.

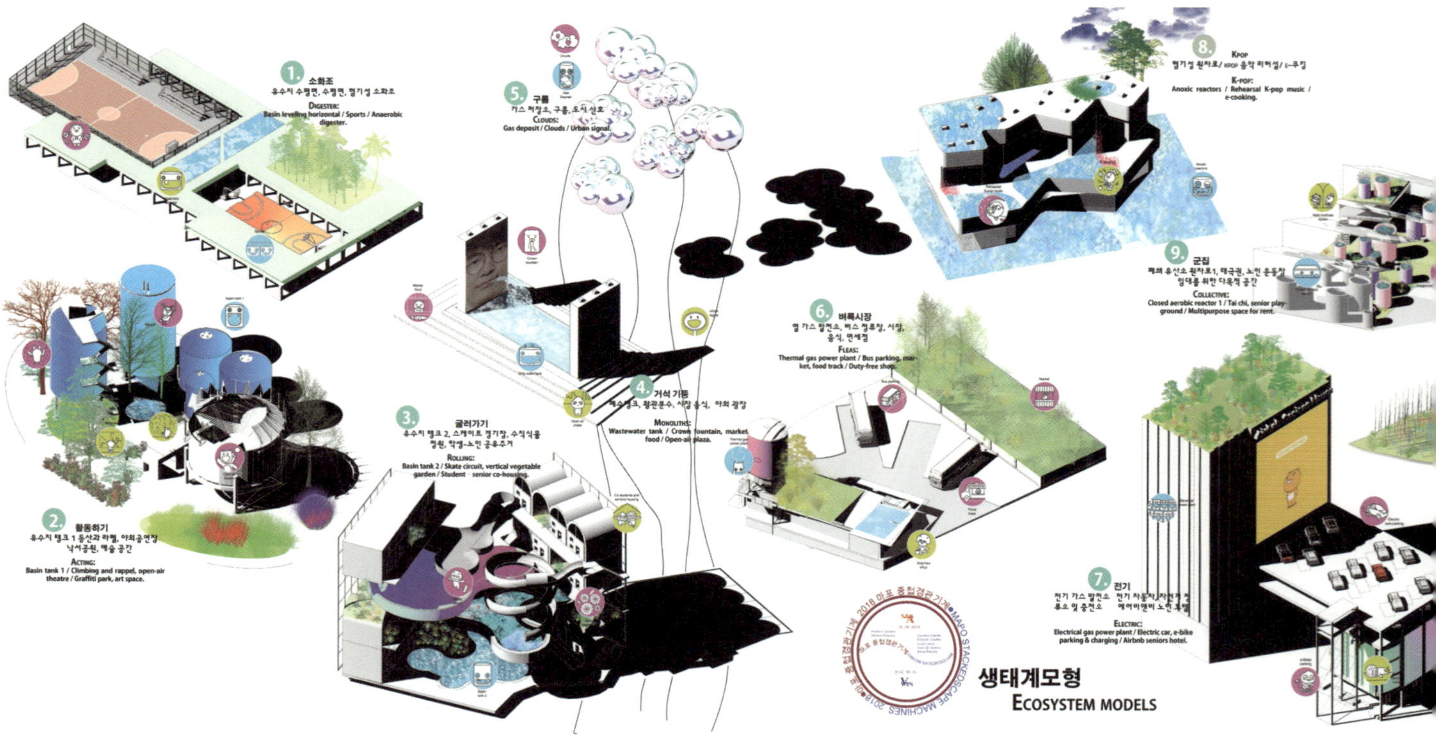

8개의 생태계는 이전의 분류에 따라 세 개의 다른 프로그램 중 하나와 결합되며 디자인되었다. 18개의 생태계와 관련된 건축적 프로그램은 다음과 같다.

1. 소화조 : 유수지 수평면/ 스포츠/ 혐기성 소화조
2. 활동하기 : 유수지 탱크1/ 등산과 라펠, 야외 공연장/ 낙서 공원, 예술 공간
3. 구르기 : 유수지 탱크 2/ 스케이트 경기장, 수직적인 식물 정원/ 학생-노인 공유주거
4. 거석 기둥 : 폐수 탱크/ 왕관분수, 시장 음식/ 야외 광장
5. 구름 : 가스 저장소/ 구름/ 도시 신호
6. 벼룩시장 : 열 가스 발전소/ 버스 정류장, 시장, 푸드트럭/ 면세점
7. 전기: 전기 가스발전소/ 전기 자동차, 자전거 정류소 및 충전소/ 에어비앤비 노인 호텔
8. K-pop : 무산소 반응로/ K-pop 음악 리허설/ e-쿠킹
9. 군집 : 폐쇄형 유산소 반응로 1/ 태극권, 노인 운동장/ 임대를 위한 다목적 공간
10. 나비숲 : 폐쇄평 유산소 반응로 2/ 나비 숲/ 전자 도서관
11. 생산 : 개방형 유산소 반응로 1/ 폐쇄형 식물원 공원/ 공유 작업공간
12. 도시 농부 : 개방형 유산소 반응로 2/ 열린 도시 과수원/ 도시 농부 주택
13. 수림 : 정화기/ 호수, 연꽃, 대나무 숲/ 생태 시장
14. 열 : 미리 처리된 물탱크/ 스파/ 캡슐 호텔
15. 연못 : 비오톱 자연정화/ 뜨거운 연못/ 스타트 업 비즈니스
16. 호수 : 비오톱 자연정화/ 차가운 연못, 호수/ 도시 해변 광장
17. 공기 : 역삼투 초나노 필터/ 워터 바/ 전망 광장
18. 무지개 : 정수 물탱크/ 인공 강우, 무지개/ 도시 휴식 광장

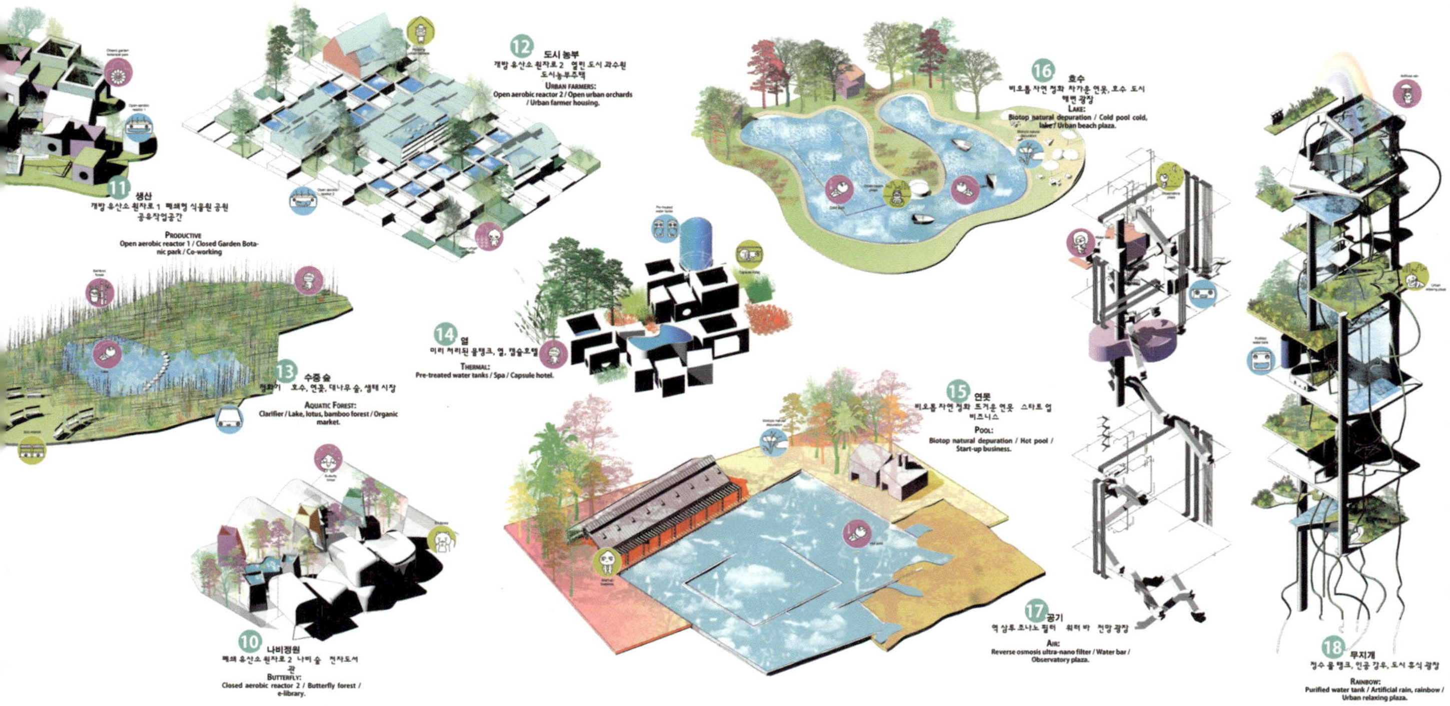

18 ecosystems have been designed, integrating each one of the three different programs according to the previous classification. The 18 ecosystems and their associated architectural programs are as follows:

1. Digester: Basin leveling horizontal / Sports / Anaerobic digester.
2. Acting: Basin tank 1/ Climbing and rappel, open-air theatre/ Graffiti park, art space.
3. Rolling: Basin tank 2 / Skate circuit, vertical vegetable garden / Student–senior co-housing
4. Monoliths: Wastewater tank / Crown fountain, market food / Open-air plaza.
5. Clouds: Gas deposit/ Clouds/ Urban signal.
6. Fleas: Thermal gas power plant / Bus parking, market, food track / Duty-free shop.
7. Electric: Electrical gas power plant / Electric car, e-bikeparking / Airbnb seniors hotel.
8. K-pop: Anoxic reactors / Rehearsal K-pop music / e-cooking
9. Collective: Closed aerobic reactor 1 / Tai chi, senior playground/ Multipurpose space forrent.
10. Butterfly: Closed aerobic reactor 2/ Butterfly forest / e-library.
11. Productive: Open aerobic reactor 1 / Closed botanicalgardens / Co-working.
12. Urban farmers: Open aerobic reactor 2/ Open urban orchards/ Urban farmerhousing
13. Aquatic Forest: Clarifier / Lake, lotus, bamboo forest / Organic market.
14. Thermal: Pre-treated water tanks/ Spa / Capsule hotel
15. Pool: Biotponatural depuration/ Hot pool / Start-up business
16. Lake: Biotponatural depuration/ Cold pool cold, lake/ Urban beach plaza.
17. Air: Reverse osmosis ultra-nano filter / Water bar/ Observatory plaza
18. Rainbow: Purified water tank/ Artificial rain, rainbow/ Urban relaxing plaza.

레벨플랜과 프로그램
PLANS AND PROGRAMS

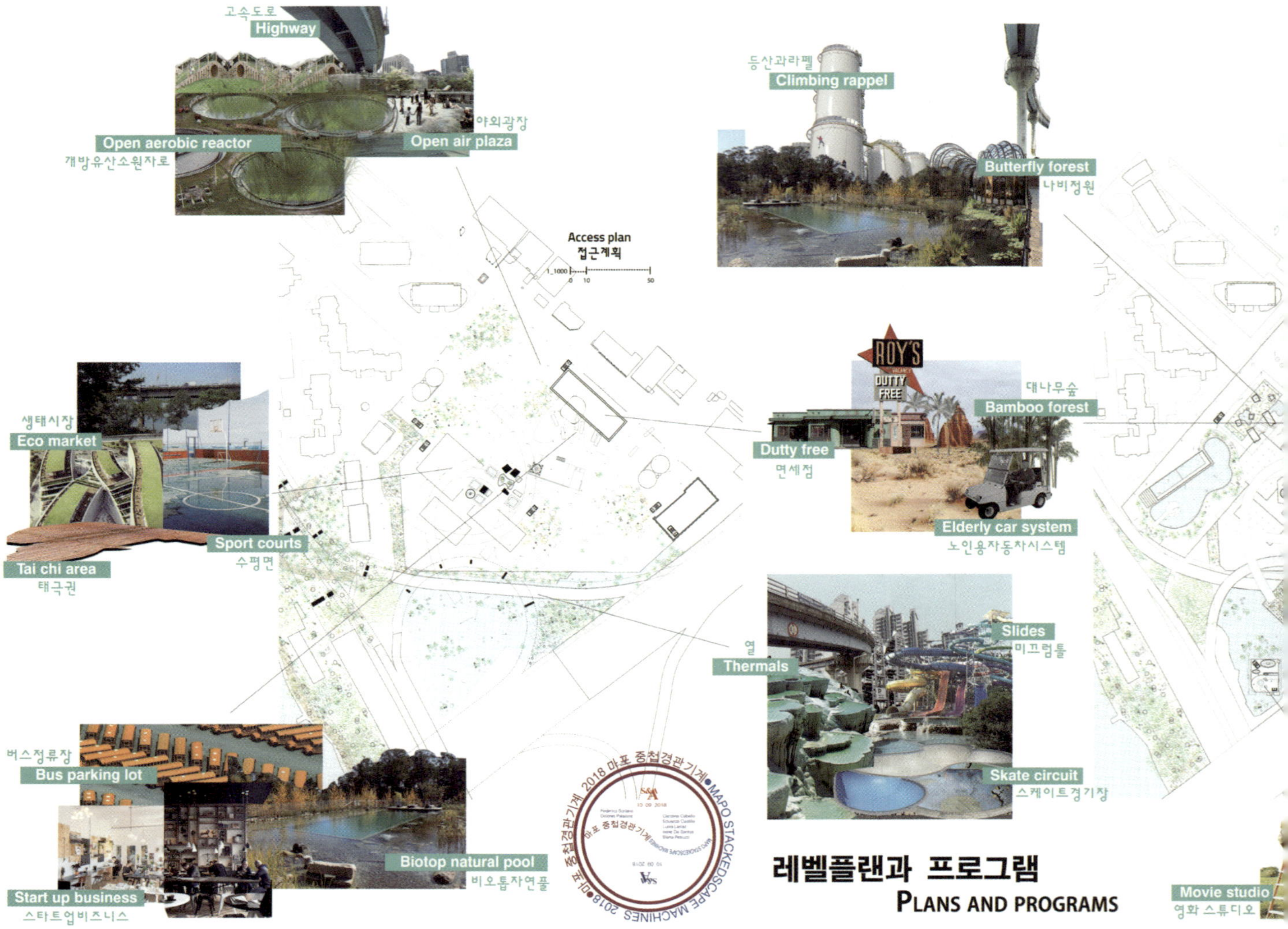

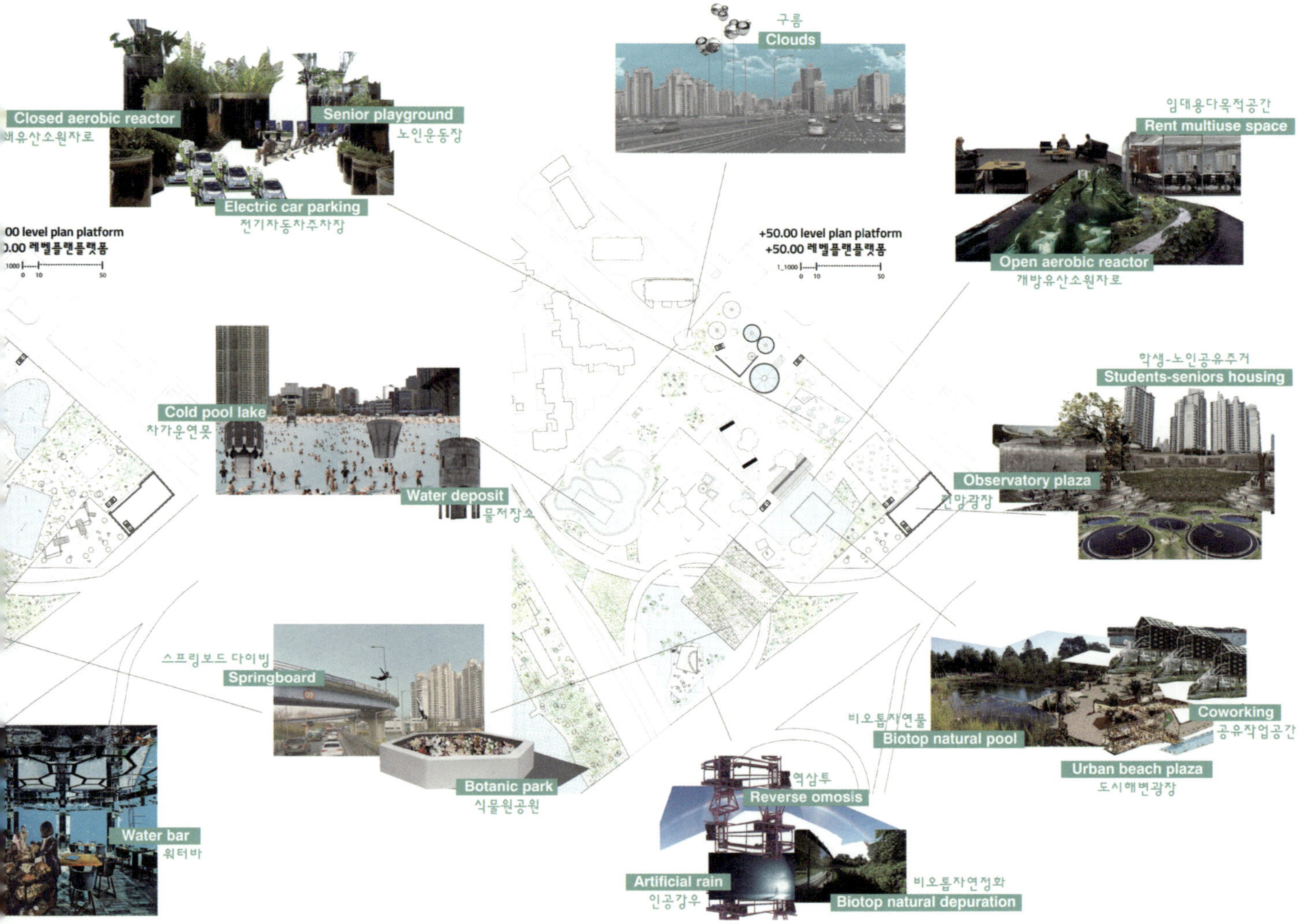

구름
Clouds
Closed aerobic reactor
폐유산소원자로
Senior playground
노인운동장
Electric car parking
전기자동차주차장
임대용다목적공간
Rent multiuse space
Open aerobic reactor
개방유산소원자로
00 level plan platform
0.00 레벨플랜플랫폼
+50.00 level plan platform
+50.00 레벨플랜플랫폼
Cold pool lake
차가운연못
Water deposit
물저장소
학생-노인공유주거
Students-seniors housing
Observatory plaza
전망광장
스프링보드 다이빙
Springboard
Botanic park
식물원공원
비오톱자연풀
Biotop natural pool
Coworking
공유작업공간
Urban beach plaza
도시해변광장
역삼투
Reverse omosis
Water bar
워터바
Artificial rain
인공강우
비오톱자연정화
Biotop natural depuration

700
160
150
140
130
120
110
100
90
80
70
60
50
40
30
20
10
0 m
-10
-20
-30
-40

700
160
150
140
130
120
110
100
90
80
70
60
50
40
30
20
10
0 m
-10
-20
-30
-40

중랑 고강도 공원

중랑 공원은 새로운 유형의 고밀도 도심 공원으로서 거대하고 밀집된 도시 인구가 자연을 맛볼 수 있도록 자연환경을 인공적으로 강화하였다. 기존 물 관련 인프라 시설은 이러한 시설이 지원하는 도시의 자연 보호구역 개발을 위한 최적의 조건을 제공한다.
대지의 지형은 약 1,100Ha 규모의 평지로 이루어져 있고, 평탄한 대지와 경계부의 홍수 방지용 제방이 특징이다. 북쪽으로는 도시 조직과 경계를 이루며, 이는 추후 확장되어 공원 경계부를 통합할 것이다. 평평한 부지는 수면으로부터 10.5m 높이에 자리 잡고 있으며, 부지의 서쪽과 남쪽, 동쪽 면은 홍수 방지용 제방으로 둘러싸여 있는데 제방 상부는 수면으로부터 18.5m 높이에 이른다.

대중교통 시설
대지의 서쪽으로는 청계천이, 남쪽과 동쪽으로는 중랑천이 지나며, 물 정화 시설로 사용되어 왔기 때문에 대중교통망으로부터 소외되어 왔다. 가장 가까운 전철 역은 2호선 용답역과 5호선 장안평역이다.
도로 시설 역시 개발이 잘 되어 있지 않다. 주변 도로들은 홍수 방지용 제방 위에 위치하며 차들이 많이 다니지 않고 있다.

High-Intensity Park Jungnang

Jungnang Park is proposed as a new type of high-intensity urban park, where natural conditions are artificially intensified to produce an enhanced milieu capable to deliver nature to a large and dense urban population. The existing water-related infrastructure provides an optimal condition for the development of a natural reserve in the city, supported by the water-related infrastructure.
Jungnang topography is currently shaped as a flat surface of approximately 1,100Ha, characterized by its flatness and the presence of a peripheral berm which acts to prevent flooding of the site. To the north it limits with a consolidated urban fabric which will be extended to consolidate the park edge. On the West, South and East sides the flat surface of the site, sitting approximately around +10.5m above the water, is surrounded by a berm topping at +18.5m above water level which prevents the flooding of the site.

Public transport infrastructure
The site, which is bordered on the West by the Cheonggyecheon Stream and on the South and East by the JungnangcheonStream has been long deprived of public transport, given its use as a large water-purifying facility. The closest rail stations are Yongdap on the Line 2, and Janghanpyeong on the Line 5 of Seoul Metropolitan Underground system.
The road infrastructure is also very underdevelopped on the site, mostly limited to a peripheral road of very low capacity, running on top of the peripheral flood-protection berm.

AZPML은 런던과 뉴욕에 본사를 둔 국제적인 사무소로 2011년에 전 FOA의 파트너였던 Alejandro Zaera Polo가 설립하였으며, 2013년 이후 Maider Liaguno와 파트너를 이루고 있다. AZPML은 프로그램과 지역을 넘나들며, 기술 혁신과 뛰어난 디자인을 지형을 결합하며 건축과 도시설계의 혁신을 추구한다. 지리나 유형에 있어서 다양한 프로젝트들을 진행해왔으며, 모든 상황에서 잠재성을 극대화하고자 한다. 모든 디자인 문제에 있어서 효율성과 표현 사이의 연속성 속에서 형태와 재료의 특별함을 추구한다.

AZPML is an international practice, based in London and New York. AZPML was born in 2011 as a legacy practice of FOA, after its dissolution, and follows former FOA's partner Alejandro Zaera-Polo, in partnership with Maider Llaguno since 2013. AZPML architecture has a commitment to innovation in architecture and urban design, combining technical innovation with design excellence across programs and geographies. The practice engages with a variety of geographically and typologically diverse projects, seeking to maximize the potentials of every situation, and to identify the formal and material specificities of every design problem, in a seamless continuity between efficiency and expression.

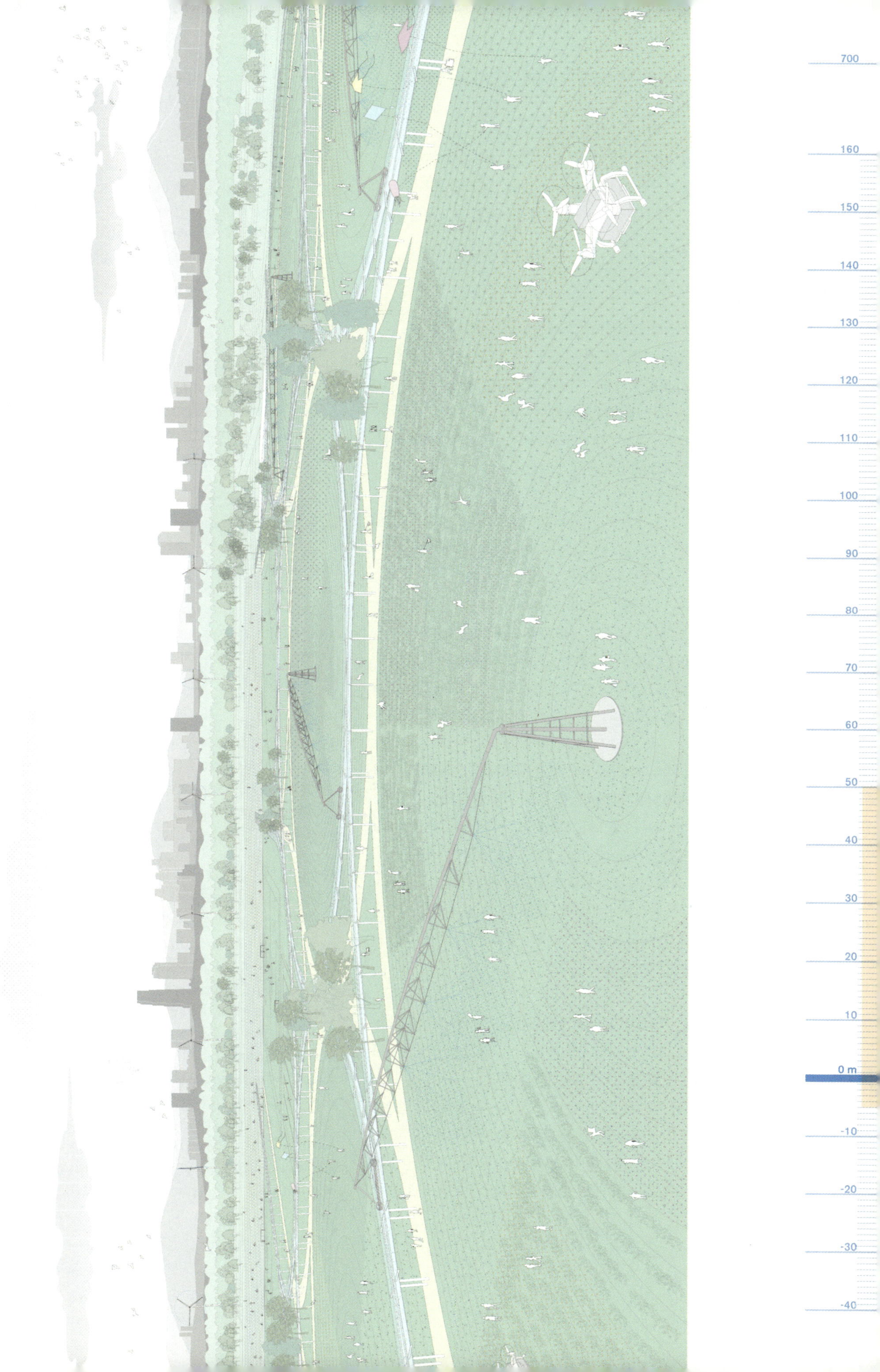

700
160
150
140
130
120
110
100
90
80
70
60
50
40
30
20
10
0 m
-10
-20
-30
-40

이 대지는 두 갈래의 동부간선도로가 중랑천의 한쪽으로 합류하는 지점에 위치한다.

대지와 성수동 및 송정동으로 이어지는 도로를 계획하여 앞으로 대지로 접근성을 개선할 수 있을 것이다. 그러나 새로운 공원을 더욱 잘 활용하기 위해서는 대중교통 시설이 확충될 필요가 있다고 생각한다.

1// 물의 도시

대지 북쪽의 격자망을 고밀도의 반폐쇄형 블록으로 통합할 것을 제안한다. 이 블록은 가로 배치를 정의하고 내부에는 녹지 공간을 갖는데, 이곳에서 도시의 미세 기후들을 환경적으로 조절하기 위하여 건물들로부터 수집된 빗물들을 사용할 예정이다. 물은 생태수로에서 자연적으로 정화되며 아르헨티나 멘도자처럼 운하망을 통해서 내부 중정과 도로의 식생을 위해 사용된다.

우리가 제안하는 도시 조직은 기본적으로 표준형 상업 및 주거 유형을 사용하되 서울 주거 단지에서 흔히 볼 수 있는 일반적인 "공원 안 타워" 유형 대신, 가로와 내부 녹지 공간의 경계가 없는, 더 "유럽적"인 공간 구성을 반영하도록 한다. 도시 필지의 블록들은 체계적으로 자연 환기가 될 수 있도록 내부 공간의 깊이를 15m 이하로 하여 에어컨디셔닝 수요를 최소화한다. 이러한 도시 조직은 전적으로 자연 환기와 복사시스템에 순응하며, 공기조화설비는 추후 규제를 통해 감소할 것이다.

건물의 입면은 상층부에서 자연적인 습도를 유지하기 위하여 우수를 모을 수 있는 식물이 심어진 테라스를 둔다. 남는 물은 바로 중정의 연못으로 흘러 들어가서 저장되고 정화되어 다시 수로로 흐른다. 도시 조직은 대지 용도를 사전에 결정하지 않고, 시장 상황에 따라 블록 내에서 주거 및 상업 기능을 수용할 수 있도록 제안한다. 우리는 도시 밀도가 높을 때, 즉 용적률이 4배 이상일 때 기반시설 투자비 회수에 더 유리할 뿐 아니라 이곳 시설들의 상시적 활동성 유지에 필요한 인구 밀도를 확보할 수 있다고 생각한다.

공원의 북쪽에는 고밀의 도시적 경계를 만들고자 하였다. 이를 위하여 공원을 따라 최소 12층에서 최대 30층 높이의 지붕선을 만들고, 공원 경계의 필지에는 보다 높은 용적률을 지정하였다.
공원 북쪽 부지 중 지하 물 정화 시설의 상부에는 공원 가장자리에 인접한 새로운 광장을 둘러싼 도시 생태를 위한 새로운 복합단지를 제안한다. 이 복합단지는 도시 미세 기후를 향상시키기 위해 필요한 도시 기술을 개발하고 이에 대한 논의를 활성화할 것이다. 새로운

The site is adjacent to the merging of the two directions of the Dongbu Expressway to one side of the Jungnangcheon Stream.

A denser peripheral infrastructure connecting the site to Seoungsu and Songjeong-Dong District have been planned and will provide better accessibility to the site in the future. However, we think that it will be necessary to expand the public transport infrastructure to optimize the use of the new Park.

1 // Water city

We propose to consolidate the grid north of the site with a high-density fabric of semi-closed blocks which define the street alignments while enclosing green spaces inside the blocks, where the stormwater collected from the buildings will be used as an environmental regulator for the urban microclimate. Water will be naturally purified in biosweals and used to densely vegetate the internal courtyards and the streets through a net of canals like the ones that exist in Mendoza (Argentina).

The urban fabric we propose is based on standard commercial and residential typologies but with a more "European" layout which delimits the streets and the internal green spaces, rather than following the customary "towers in the park" which is often seen in residential developments in Seoul. The urban plots will with blocks which allow systematically for natural ventilation of the interior spaces (<15m deep) to minimize the need for air-conditioning systems to climatize the buildings. This fabric will be entirely climatized by natural ventilation and radiation systems, and air-based climatization will be discouraged from the buildings through subsequent regulation.

The building facades will follow a specification to provide a substantial number of water-retaining surfaces, with a regulation on vegetated terraces which will collect stormwater to maintain natural humidity in the fabric at a higher level. The excess water will be directed toward the courtyard ponds, when it will be stored and purified, to be returned to the aquifer. We propose to use a fabric which does not determine land uses a priori, but which is flexible enough to accommodate residential or commercial functions indistinctively, sometimes forming residential or commercial campuses in the blocks, depending on market drivers. We believe a higher density of the fabric, over 4 FAR will not only be better to recoup theinvestment on infrastructure, but also always provide enough density of population to keep the facilities active.

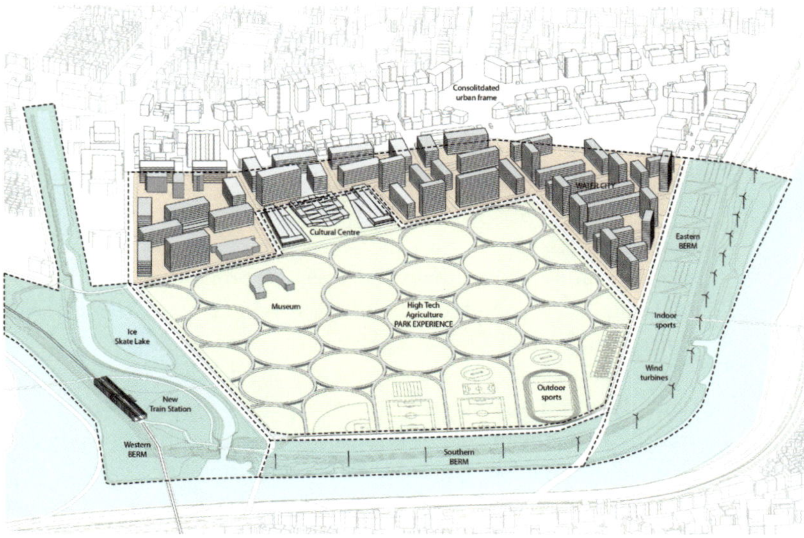

AXONOMETRIC VIEW OF JUNGNANG

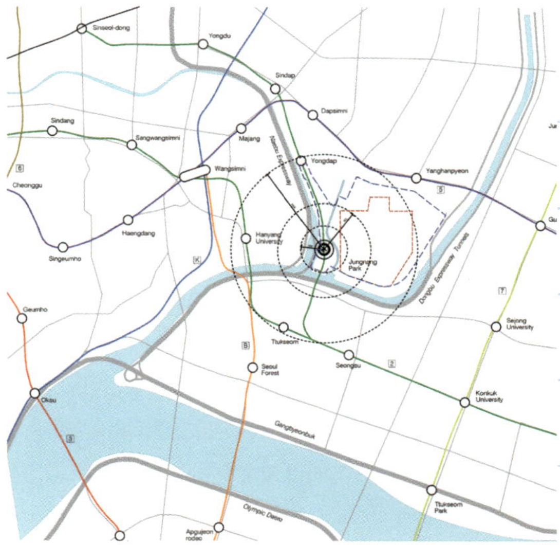

DIAGRAM OF THE MAIN TRAFFIC NETWORK

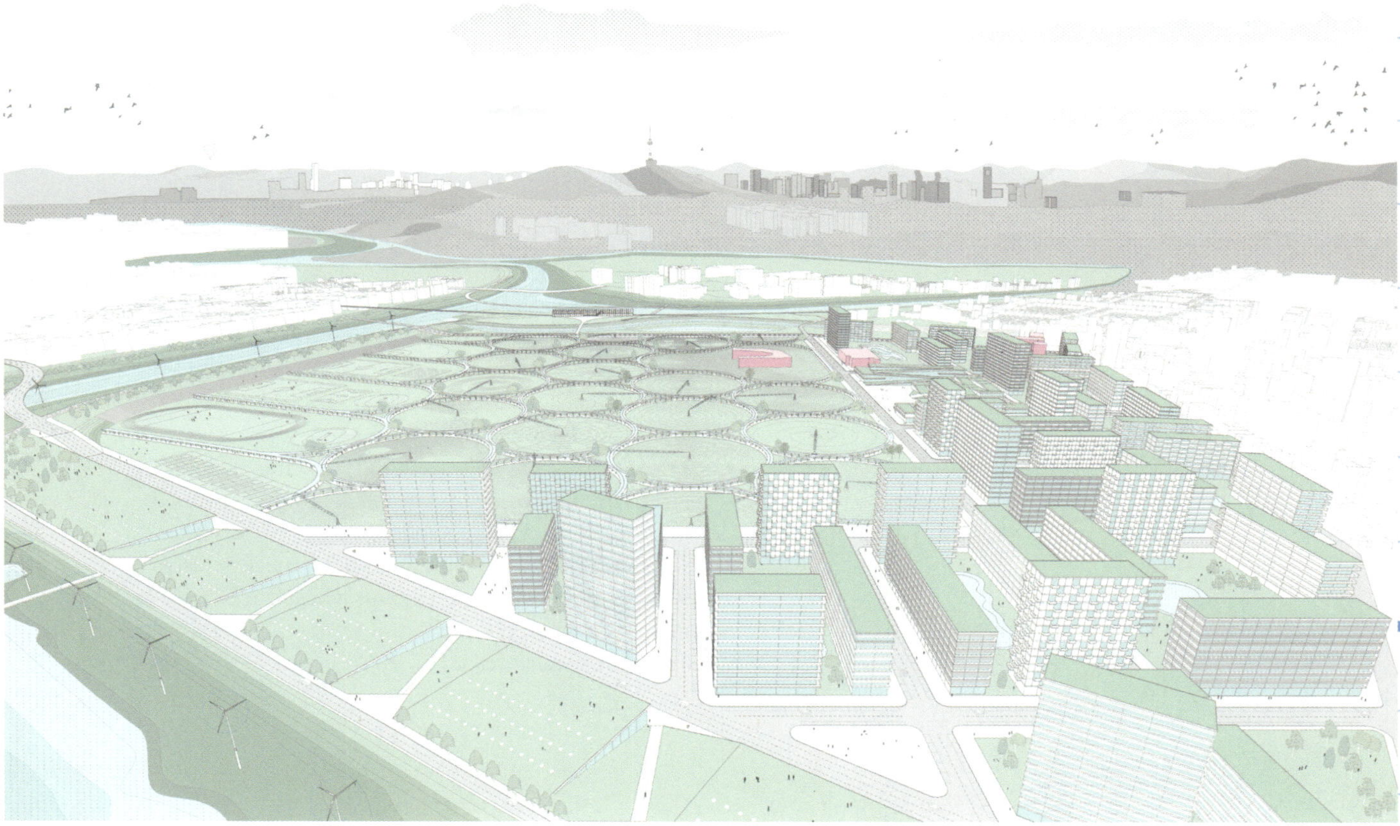

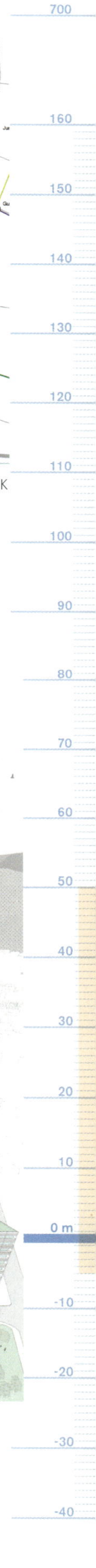

서울의 도시기술센터는 공기 오염, 수공학, 에너지 소비, 도시 녹화, 도시 교통 등의 분야를 다룰 수 있을 것이다. 이 센터는 박물관, 컨퍼런스 시설, 오디토리움, 전시 공간, 작업 공간과 이 분야에서 일하는 회사들의 창업지원 공간들을 포함할 수 있다. 물 정화 시설 위에 위치한 입지로 인하여, 건축물들은 슬래브를 통해 전달될 구조적인 문제들을 고려하여 저층으로 이루어질 것이다.

2// 도시 지형으로서 프로그램이 있는 제방

부지를 둘러싼 홍수를 방지하기 위한 제방은 18.5m 높이를 유지하며 높이의 차이를 이용하여 다양한 프로그램들을 배치하여 공원 지형에 일종의 극장성을 도입하며 차별화된 인프라 공간으로 전환된다.

a. 서쪽 경계에는 현재 차량기지 플랫폼 하부에 위치한 지하 수로를 복원할 것을 제안한다. 하천은 복원되어 구불거리는 생태수로로 다시 계획되며, 이곳에서 우수는 저장되고 자연적으로 정화된다. 또한 물의 순환과 자연정화 시스템을 보여주는 교육 시설로도 활용된다. 새로 조성된 조경 공간은 서쪽으로 물 정화 시설 상부 공원을 확장하며, 이 곳에서는 큰 나무와 식생이 자연 토양 위에서 자랄 수 있다. 생태수로에는 하천의 물을 자연적으로 정화할 수 있는 식물을 심고, 하천을 따라 우수를 이용한 연못이 형성되어 여름에는 수상스포츠, 겨울에는 아이스 스케이트 링크로 사용될 수 있다.

We have shaped the fabric to create a dense urban border on the North side of the park to create an urban façade to the park. To create this effect, we have set the cornice line along the park at a minimum height of 12 story's, and a maximum of 30, and assigned a higher FAR to the plots limiting to the park.

On the North edge of the park, above part of the underground water-purifying facilities, we propose to locate a new complex dedicated to Urban Ecology, surrounding a new square, adjacent to the Park edge. The complex will be dedicated to foster the development and discussion of urban technologies dedicated to improve the urban microclimate. Air pollution, hydrology, energy consumption, urban vegetation, and urban mobility are some of the areas of knowledge that the new Seoul Centre for Urban Technology will try to host. The centre will include a museum, conference facilities and auditoria, exhibition spaces and workspaces and incubators for companies working in this sector. Due to its location over the water-purifying facilities, the buildings will be low rise to avoid problems with structural transfer through the slab.

2 // The Programmed Levee As An Urban Topography

The flooding protection berm surrounding the site will be kept at +18.5 and converted into a differentiated set of infrastructures which will exploit the difference in levels to locate a diverse set of programs, introducing some theatricality to the park topography:

a. On the Western edge of the park we propose to unearth the culverted stream of Cheongdaero, which lies underneath the current train depot plat¬form. The stream will be unearthed and redesigned as a meandering reed¬bed where the stormwater will be stored and naturally purified, setting up an educational facility to illustrate the water cycle and the natural purifica¬tion systems. This newly landscaped surface will extend the park above the water-purifying facilities to the west, onto an area where large trees and vegetation can be planted onto natural soil. The reedbed will be planted with vegetation capable to naturally purify the water in the stream, and a stormwater pool has been created alongside the stream as a reservoir which can be used as a watersports pond in the summer and as an ice-skating rink in the winter season.

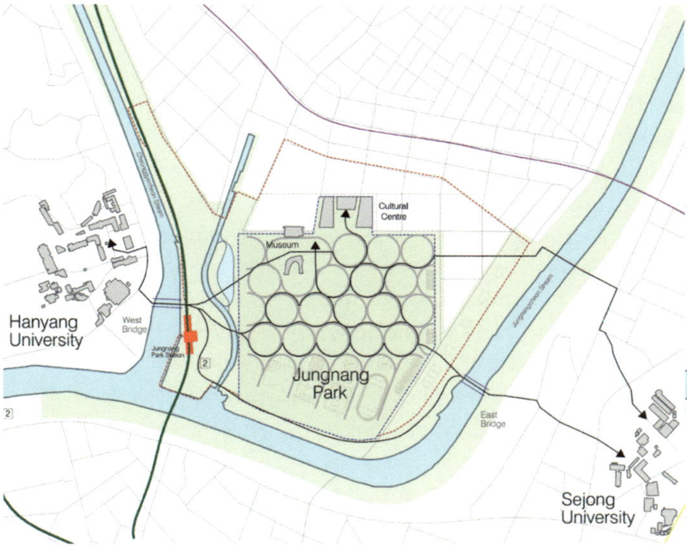

DIAGRAM OF PEDESTRIAN CONNECTIONS

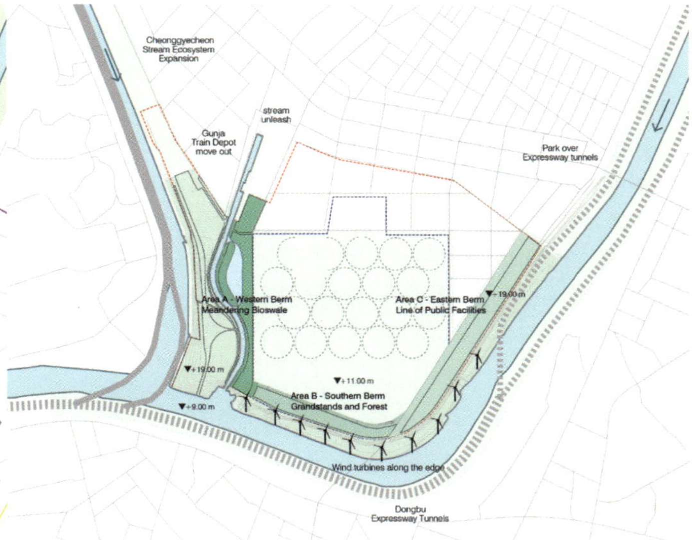

DIAGRAM OF THE GREEN BELT

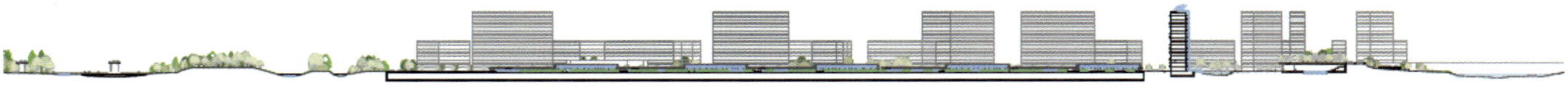

LONGITUDINAL SECTION

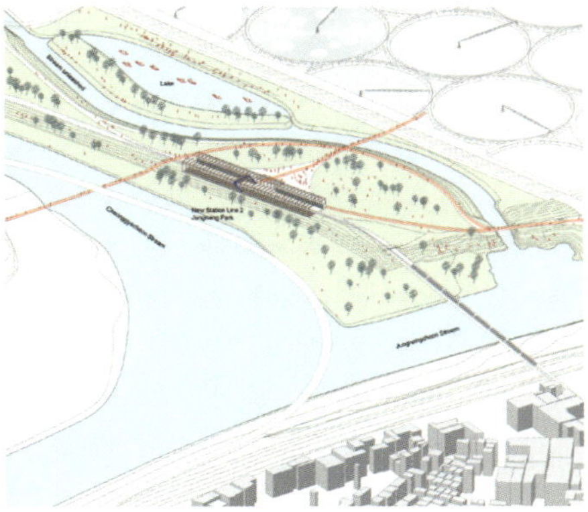

AXONOMETRIC VIEW A-MEANDERING BIOSWALE

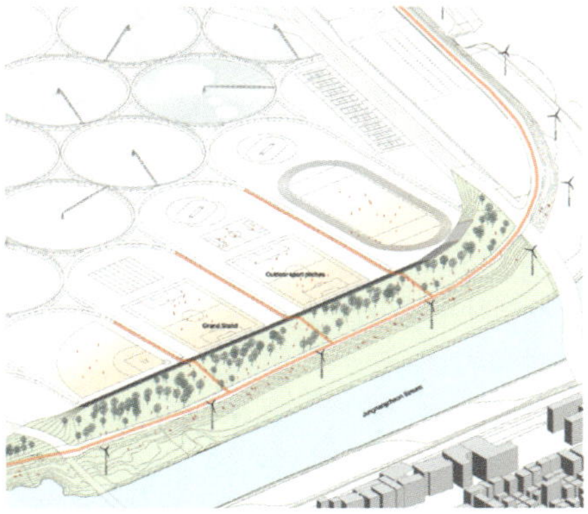

AXONOMETRIC VIEW B-TOPOGRAPHIC SOLUTION

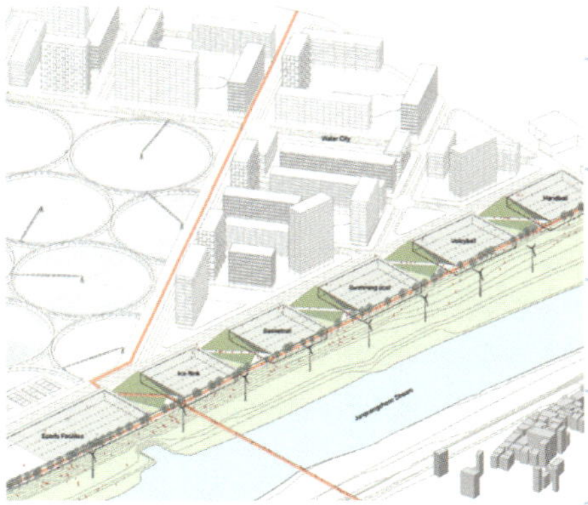

AXONOMETRIC VIEW C-LINE OF PUBLIC FACILITIES

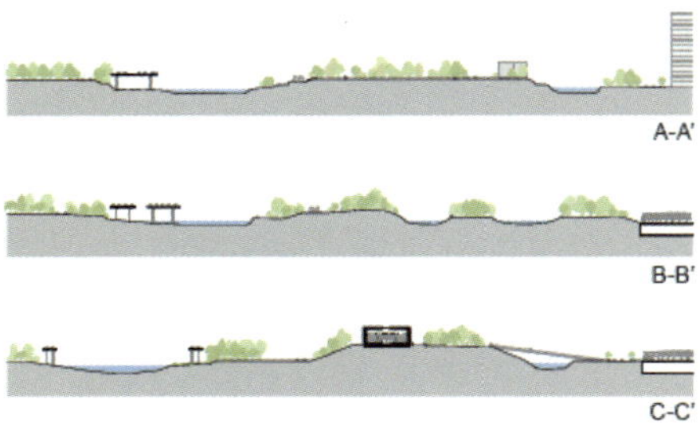

SECTIONS A-MEANDERING BIOSWALE

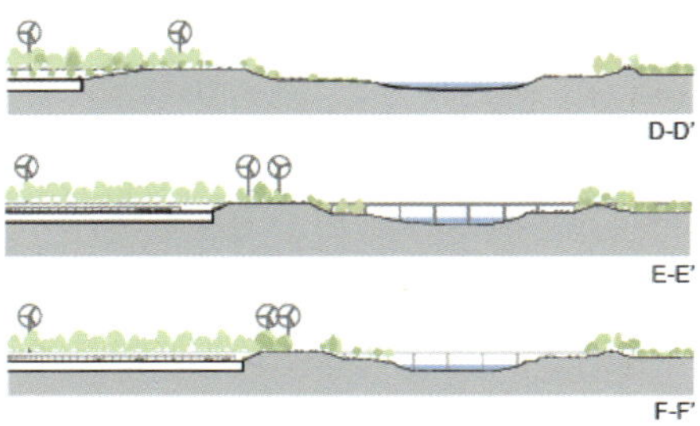

SECTIONS B-TOPOGRAPHIC SOLUTION

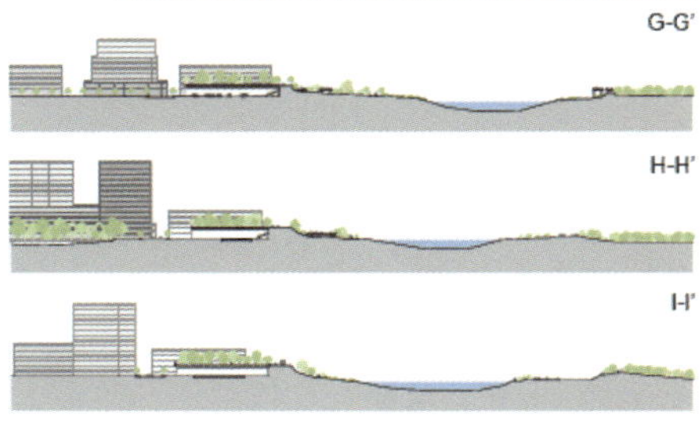

SECTIONS C-LINE OF PUBLIC FACILITIES

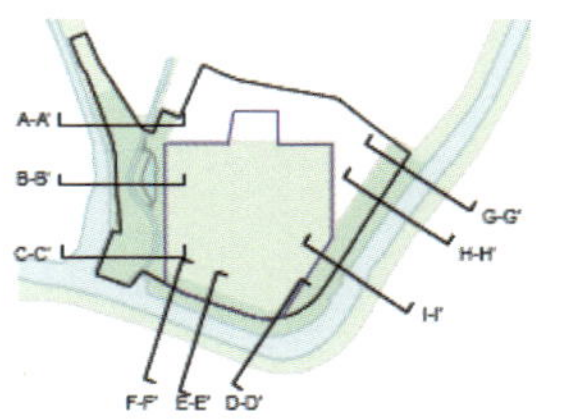

b. 새로운 하천의 반대편인 공원의 남서쪽에 위치한 제방에는 "중랑공원" 지하철역을 신설할 것을 제안한다. 이 지하철역은 지하철 2호선 용답역과 성수역 사이에 위치하며 이로 인하여 매우 적은 비용으로 더 많은 공공 접근이 가능하다. 이 대지는 오래도록 물 정화시설로 사용되었기 때문에 대중교통망으로부터 소외되어 왔다. 도시 인프라의 새로운 기능을 고려할 때, 중랑 공원은 더 많은 교통 시설이 필요하다. 용답역과 성수역 사이의 거리가 매우 멀다는 사실에 주목하여, 새로운 공원 인프라를 위한 정류장을 도입하는 것이 필요하다고 생각한다. 역은 제방 상부 높이인 18.5m 높이에 위치한다. 이는 전체적인 공원 인프라의 유리한 점을 제공하며, 새로운 시설을 위한 이상적인 입구가 될 것이다.

c. 제방의 남쪽 경계는 두 레벨의 연결을 위한 지형적 해법이 될 수 있는 긴 관중석을 둔다. 장애인 램프, 계단, 사람들이 앉아서 공원을 바라볼 수 있는 좌석 등 다양한 지형적 장치들이다. 관중석에는 테라스로 이루어진 화분들에 나무를 심어서 이곳에 앉아 있는 사람들에게 그늘을 제공할 수 있도록 한다. 이러한 지형으로 인하여, 사람들은 10.6m 높이에 위치한 지하화된 물 처리 시설 상부 플랫폼에서 벌어지는 각종 야외 공공 행사나 스포츠 경기를 관람할 수 있다. 거대한 관중석은 새 수변공원의 경계에 극적인 효과를 줄 것이다.

d. 수변공원의 동쪽 경계는 스포츠의 여가를 위한 일련의 공공시설들을 제안하는데, 강의 제방 높이에서 지붕을 설치하여 이들을 덮는다. 지붕에는 식물을 심어 제방에서 강변으로 이어지는 조경 공간의 연속성을 확보한다. 제방의 공원 경사는 물 정화 시설의 플랫폼 상부 10.5m 높이 지점과 제방 상부 18.5m 높이 지점 사이를 연계하는 다양한 지형적 해법으로 처리될 것이다. 또한 이 시설들의 지붕은 공원으로 흐르는 우수를 모으기 위한 일련의 경사로를 형성한다.
홍수 방지를 위해 물 정화 시설 주변 경계는 현재의 제방 +18.5m 높이를 유지하도록 한다. 만약 제방 안쪽 경사를 다양하게 처리한다면, 강가의 경사로에는 맹그로브와 같은 토착 강변 수종들로 이루어진 연속적인 수변 산책로를 조성할 수 있을 것이다.
강둑의 높은 풍속을 이용하기 위하여 제방 상부 높이에는 산책로를 따라 풍차들을 배치한다. 공원 시설 유지관리에 필요한 에너지를 공급해줄 뿐 아니라 공원에 끊임없이 움직이는 기계들로 이루어진 인공 생태계 이미지를 부여해줄 것이다.

b. On the other side of the new stream we propose to use the berm on the South-west of the park to locate an additional subway station, "Jungnang Park," on the Line 2 between Yongdap St. and Seoungsu St. to produce ad¬ditional public accessibility at a very small cost. The Jungnang site has been traditionally detached from the public transport infrastructure, given its use as a water-purifying infrastructure. With the new function as an urban infra¬structure, Jungnang Park will require additional transport facility. Realizing that the distance between Yongdap St. and Seoungsu St. is very large, we be¬lieve that the introduction of a new stop serving the new park infrastructure will be necessary. Located at the top level of the Berm at +18,50, the station will offer a vantage point of the overall park infrastructure, an ideal entrance to the new facilities.

c. The South edge of the berm will feature a long grand stand as a topographic solution to bridge both levels through a multiplicity of topographic devices, including ramps for disabled access, stairs and stands for people to sit and contemplate the park spectacle. Terraced planters will allow trees to grow on the stand surface to provide shade to the people sitting on the stepped topography. From this topography the public will be able to watch a variety open-air public events and sports making use of the platform over the buried water-purifying facilities at level +10,50. The grandstand will introduce a theatrical effect on the edge of the new water park.

d. The Eastern edge of the waterfront park is proposed as a line of public facilities for sports and leisure, which will be covered at the level of the river berm. The roofs will be vegetated in continuation of the berm land-scape toward the river slope. The park slope of the berm will be treated with a multiplicity of topographic solutions to articulate between the +10.5 level of the platform over the water plant, and the 18.5m level at the top of the berm. The roof of these facilities will also form a series of water-collection slopes bringing storm water down to the park for collection.

To protect the peninsula from flooding, all the edges around the water facilities will remain at +18.50, the current level of the perimeter berm. If the inner slope of the levee will be differentially treated, the river slope will be treated as a continuous waterfront promenade with indigenous riverfront species such as reeves and mangroves.
Exploiting the higher wind speed along the riverbed we will also locate an array of windmills to alongside the promenade, on the top level of the berm. Other than supplying the energy needed for the maintenance of the park facilities, these will create an image of the park as an artificial ecology of constantly moving devices.

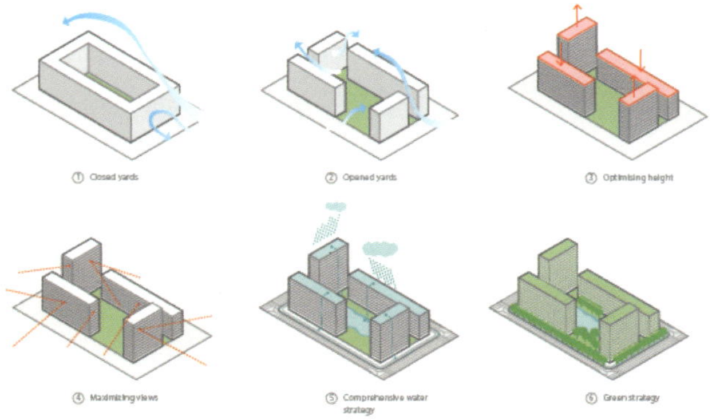

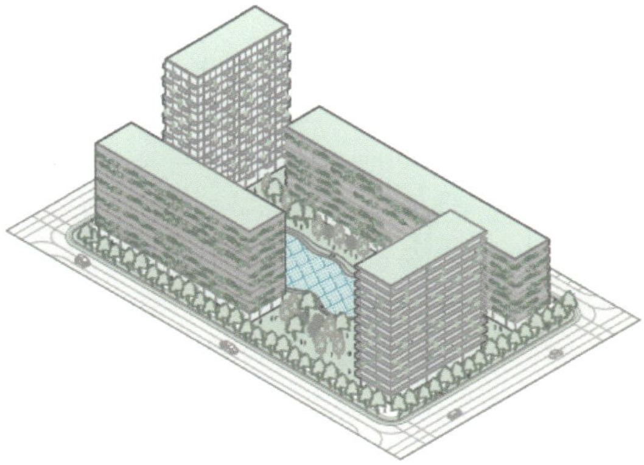

AXONOMETRIC VIEW OF THE WATER CITY TYPOLOGY B

PLANS AND ELEVATIONS OF THE GREEN TYPOLOGIES

PLANS AND ELEVATIONS OF THE GREEN TYPOLOGIES

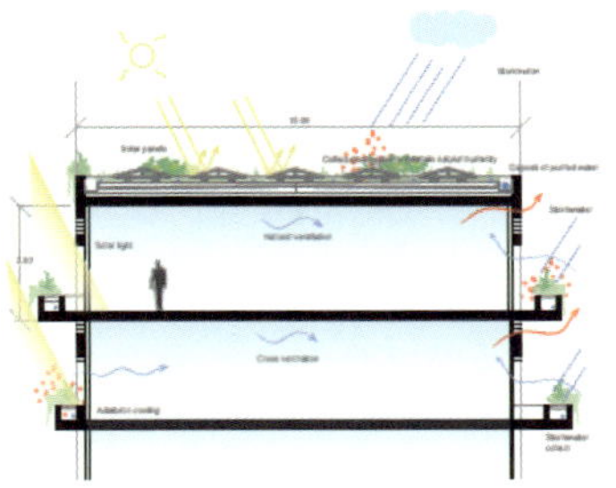

WATER CITY ENVIRONMENTAL PERFORMANCE

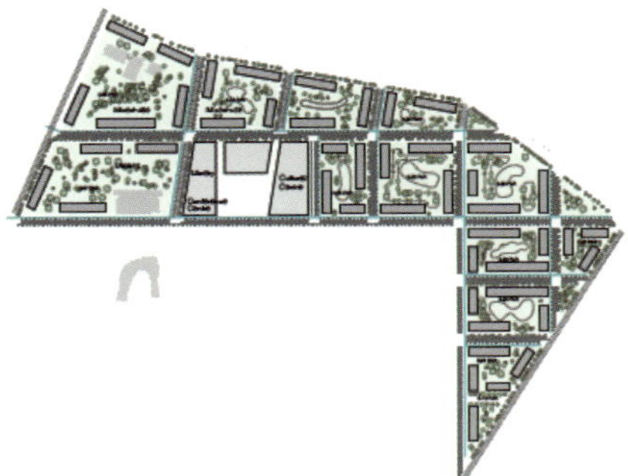

NATURAL COURTYARDS

Our proposal for the site includes three main operations on the Jongnang site:

3// 스테로이드(Steroid) 효과를 적용한 공원

물 정화 시설의 슬래브 상부는 강 옆에 자리한 남쪽 경계에는 스포츠 시설을 위한 공간을 두고, 집약 농업 시설의 공중 관개 시스템에서 영감을 얻은 고밀도 인공 자연 지역으로 사용할 것을 제안한다. 새 공원이 평평한 콘크리트 슬래브 위에 들어선다는 사실을 고려할 때 이곳에는 큰 나무들을 심을 수 있는 토양을 둘 수 없다. 대신 지피 식물, 농업 작물, 덤불 등을 심어서 슬래브 상부를 녹지 공간으로 만들고자 한다. 관개 시스템을 지상과 분리함으로써 시스템 자체가 멋진 볼거리가 될 수 있도록 한다. 공원 작물에 물을 주기 위한 시스템을 지상에 두는 대신 지면으로부터 8m 높이에 위치하여, 잘 보일 수 있도록 하였다. 자동화되고 거대한 규모로 머리 위에서 회전하는 살수기를 사용하여 집중적으로 식생을 관리한다. 64m 길이의 회전 날개는 중앙의 타워를 중앙으로 회전하는데이 타워를 통해 지하 시설로부터 물이 공급된다.

살수기 날개의 움직이는 끝부분은 고가 트랙에 위치하며, 이는 공공 캐노피의 뼈대가 된다. 캐노피는 공원 안의 길을 햇빛이나 비로부터 보호하는 역할을 한다. 이러한 구조는 공중 살수기 구조와 보행로 사이의 충돌을 방지해준다. 회전 반경을 따라 설치된 공중 캐노피는 인공 작물들이 심어진 원 주위로 주요 길들을 형성한다. 새 공원은 콘크리트 슬래브 위에 조성되기 때문에 조경에 나무를 사용할 수 없으며, 대신 인공적인 캐노피들이 그늘을 제공하고 사람들이 공원을 사용하는데 방해하지 않도록 회전하는 살수기가 8m 높이 위에 있을 수 있도록 한다.

공중 살수기는 다양한 종의 씨앗 뿌리기, 특수 비료 살포, 기타 작물 관리 등에도 사용할 수 있어 공원은 서울의 변화하는 자연에 대한 요구에 따른 지속적인 재구성이 가능하다.

공중에서 회전하는 농업용 로봇들은 앱을 통한 디지털 정보 시스템으로 관리 및 연결되어 시민들이 공원의 지속적 변화에 직접 관여할 수 있도록 한다.

본 제안은 디지털 운영 방식에 기반하여 광범위한 활용이 가능한 프로그램 공원이다. 녹지와 얕은 수공간은 마치 도시 이벤트처럼 번갈아 꽃을 피우는 다양한 식물들 속에서 생생할 것이다. 물 정화 시설 위의 얕은 토피층을 덮은 조경은 공중에서 회전하는 농업 살수기를 통해 물을 공급받으며 이는 그곳에서 자라는 작물은 다양하고 빠르게 변화시킬 것이다. 시간의 흐름에 따라 도시의 리듬에 반응하며 그 어느 때보다 복잡한 도시 생태의 부분으로 자연 시스템의 풍부함을 강화할 것이다.

중랑공원은 역동적이며 끊임없이 변화를 이어갈 것이다. 이는 아름다운 정원이라기보다 초고밀도 도시 환경 속 인공 자연과 어우러진 새로운 문화 공동체로 계획되었다. 공원은 살아있고, 시민들과 소통하며, 사람들을 자신의 늘 새로운 일상 속으로 안내하는 웹사이트 운영을 통해 매일 자신을 업데이트한다. 공기, 물, 에너지, 식물은 도시 자연의 새로운 한 부분으로 완전히 다시 구성될 것이다. 자연은 도시 이벤트가 될 것이다.

중랑공원은 새로운 유형의 도심 공원의 원형(prototype)이자 19 세기에 완성된 현시대 도심 공원 모델의 대안, 고밀도 도시 환경 속의 인공화된 자연을 활용한 공원으로 자리 잡을 것이다.

3 // Vegetating The Slab: A Park On Steroids

The top of the water treatment plant slab is proposed to be used partially for sports facilities along the South edge, next to the river, but also as a high-intensity artificial nature, inspired by the overhead water irrigation systems we can find in intensive agriculture. Given the fact that the new park will be located on top of a flat concrete slab, we will not be able to provide substantial earth layer to sustain large trees. Instead, we are proposing to use groundcovers, agricultural crops and bushes to provide the green cover on the slab. We have decided to detach the irrigation system from the ground to turn it into a spectacle by itself. Instead of locating the water on the ground, we are using agricultural irrigation systems to water the park crops, placing the water at 8m above the ground surface, and making it visible. Automated, large-scale, pivoting overhead watering sprinklers will allow tomaintain intensive vegetation through overhead irrigation. The 64m long revolving bridges will be pivoting around central towers where the water will be supplied from the underground facility.

The moving end of the sprinkler bridges has been located on an elevated track which will be also the backbone of a public canopy, providing a systemof sun-shaded and rain protected paths through the park. This will allow to avoid the collision between the hovering sprinkler beams and the pedestrian paths. The elevated canopies, following the rotating ends will form the primary path web in the new park, around the circles of artificial crops. As the new park lies on a concrete slab, the trees will have to be limited as a landscape feature, so these artificial canopies/rails will provide shadow and cover while enabling the rotating sprinkler beams to hover 8m above the surface of the park, avoiding interference with people using the park.

These hovering sprinkler beams can also be used to seed the ground and add fertilizers and other crop manipulations enabling a constant redesign of the park to suit Seoul's changing needs for nature.

The overhead pivoting agricultural robots will be managed and connected to digital information systems via apps which will enable the citizens to participate directly in the constant redesign of the park.

Our proposal is a programmed park of intensive use and extensive maintenance, digitally managed, where meadows of grass and superficial water bodies will be animated by alternated blooming of different crops, treatedas urban events. The landscaping of the shallow soil layer over the water-purifying facility will be irrigated from overhead pivoting agricultural sprinklers, enabling quick transformations of the crops, in time to react to the rhythms of the city, intensifying the richness of natural systems as part of an ever more complex urban ecology.

Jungnang Park will be dynamic and in constant transformation. Rather than a beautiful garden, we imagine it as a new cultural enclave to experience an artificial nature in a very dense urban condition. A park that is alive, that communicates with the citizens and that it updates itself daily through amanaging website that involves people in its always changing routines. Air, Water, Energy and Vegetation will become entirely reconfigured into this new piece of urban nature. Nature will become an urban event.

Jungnang Park will become a prototype for a new type of urban park, alter-native to the current models of urban parks as conceived in the XIX century, a park which will exploit the artificialization of nature in a dense urban environment:

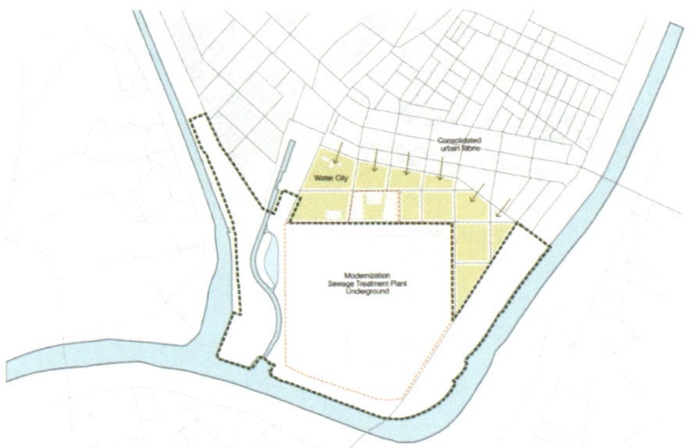

URBAN FABRIC

WATER

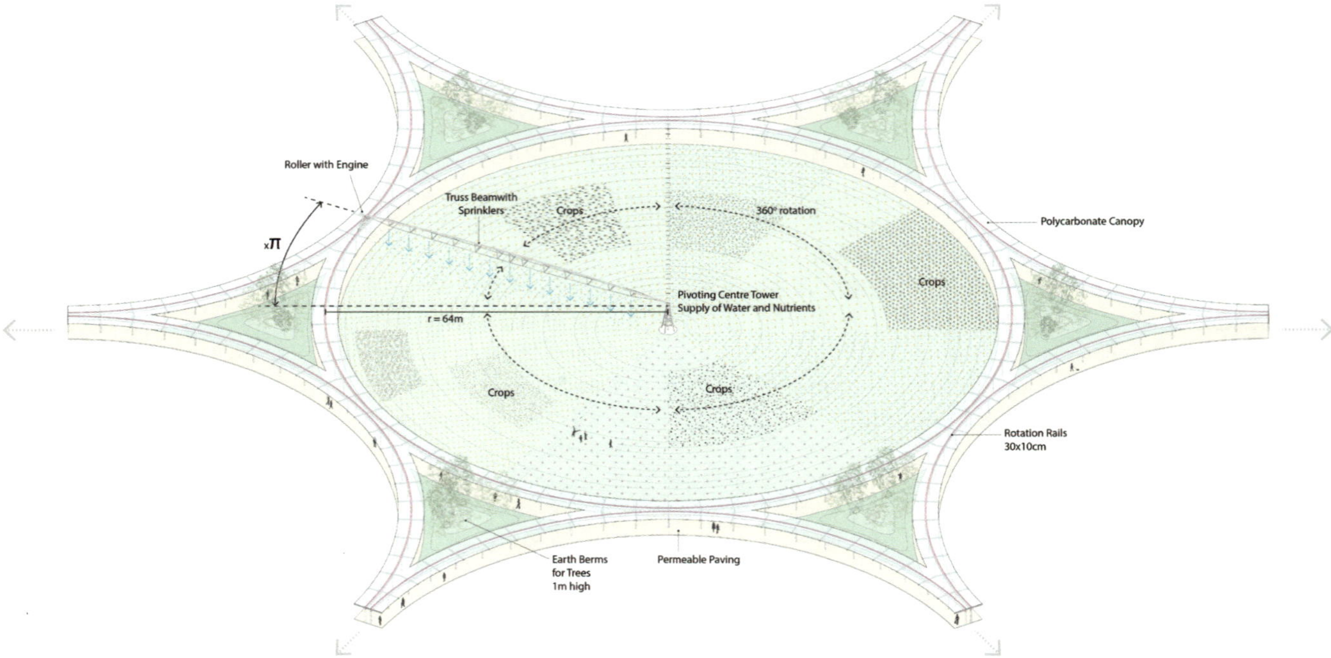

AXONOMETRIC VIEW OF THE FUNCTIONING OF THE SYSTEM

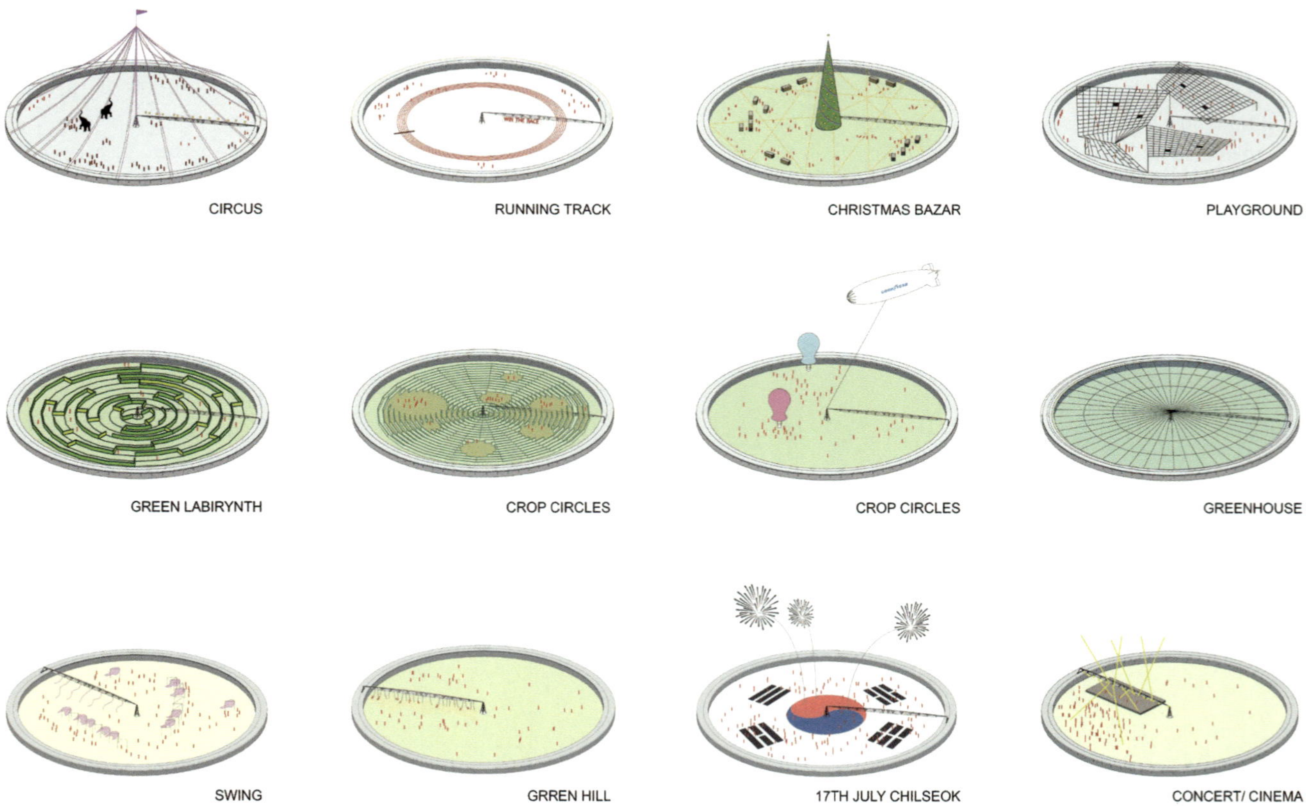

VEGETATING THE SLAB

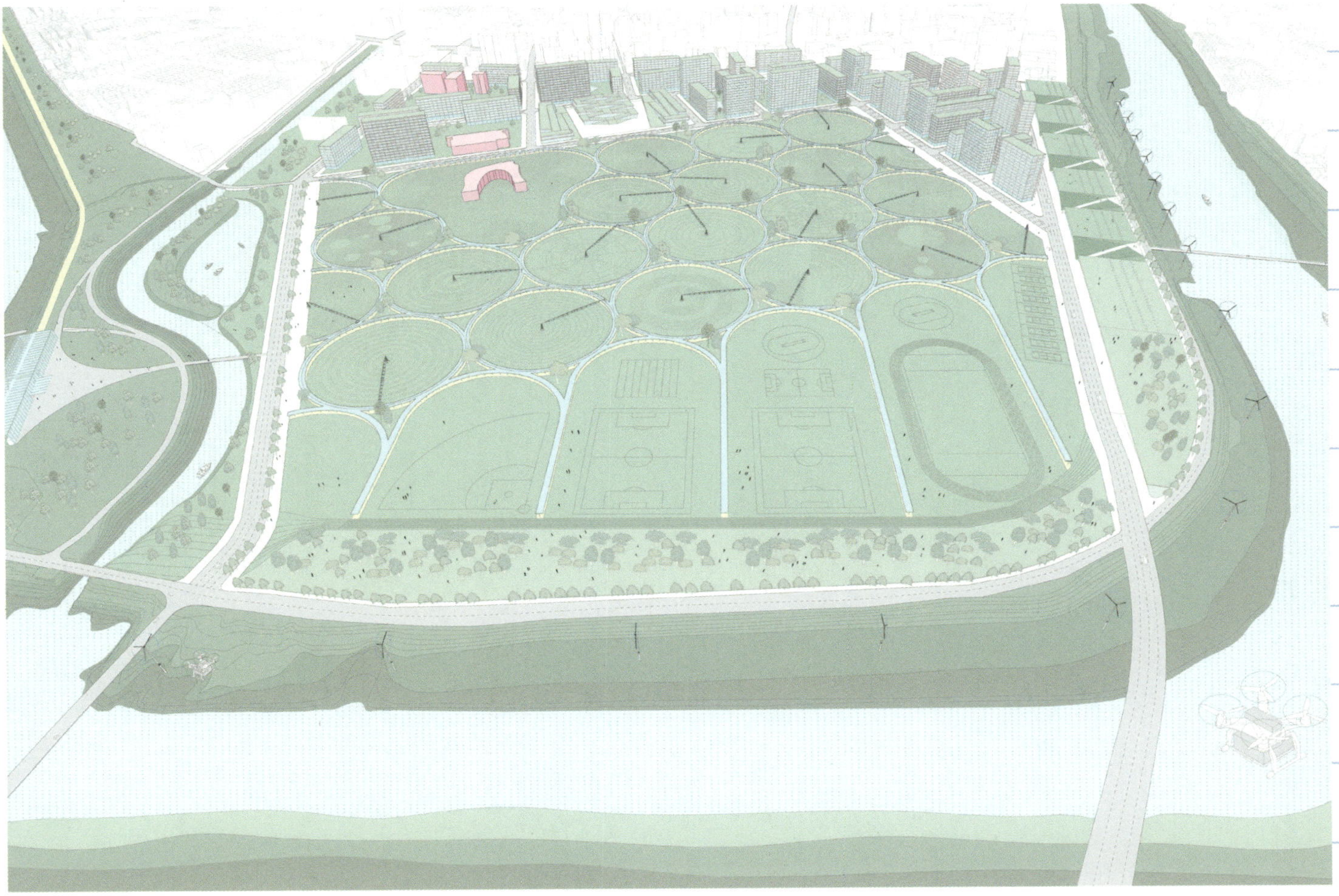

700
160
150
140
130
120
110
100
90
80
70
60
50
40
30
20
10
0 m
-10
-20
-30
-40

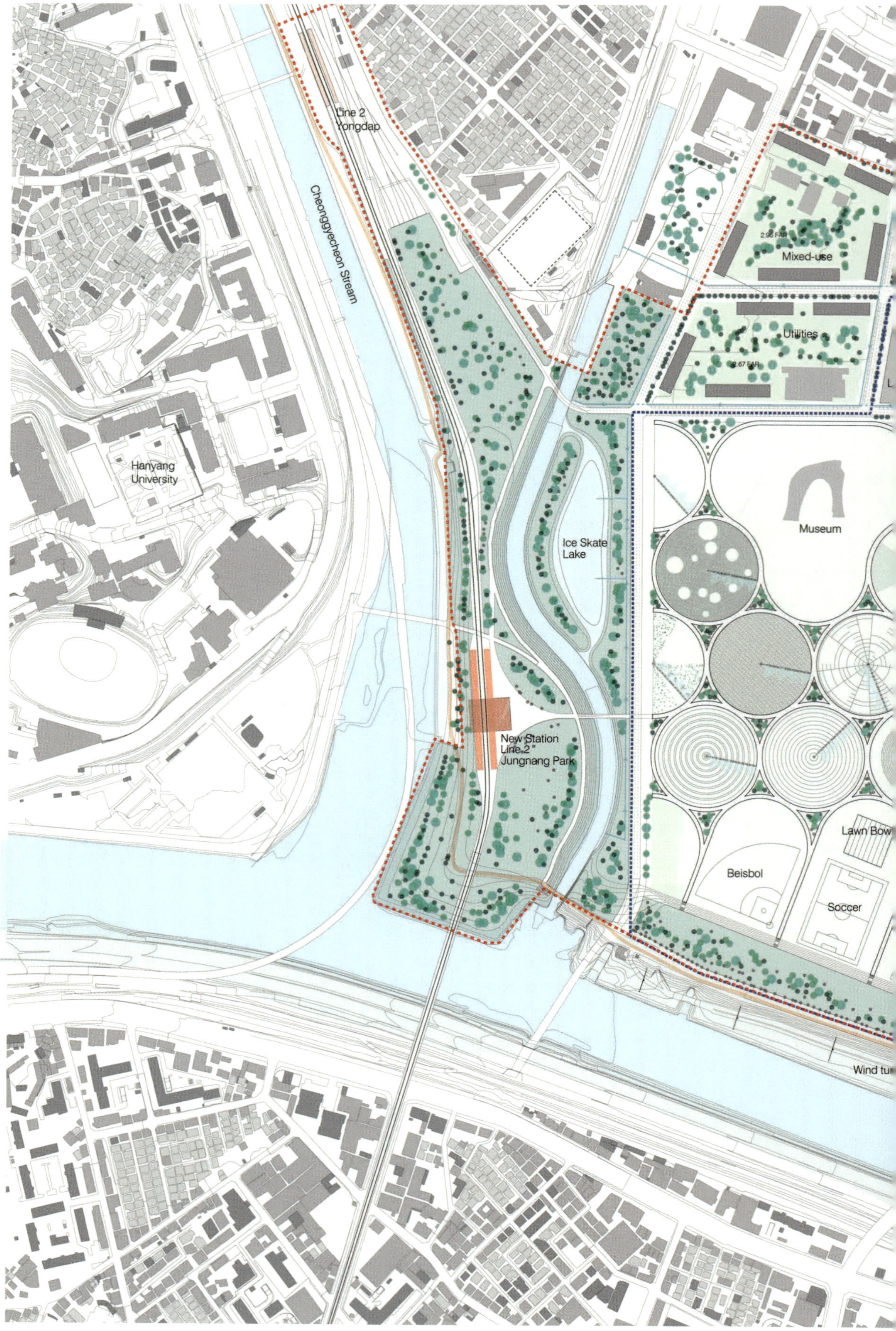
Line 2
Yongdap
Cheonggyecheon Stream
Hanyang
University
Mixed-use
Utilities
Museum
Ice Skate
Lake
New Station
Line 2
Jungnang Park
Lawn Bow
Beisbol
Soccer
Wind tu

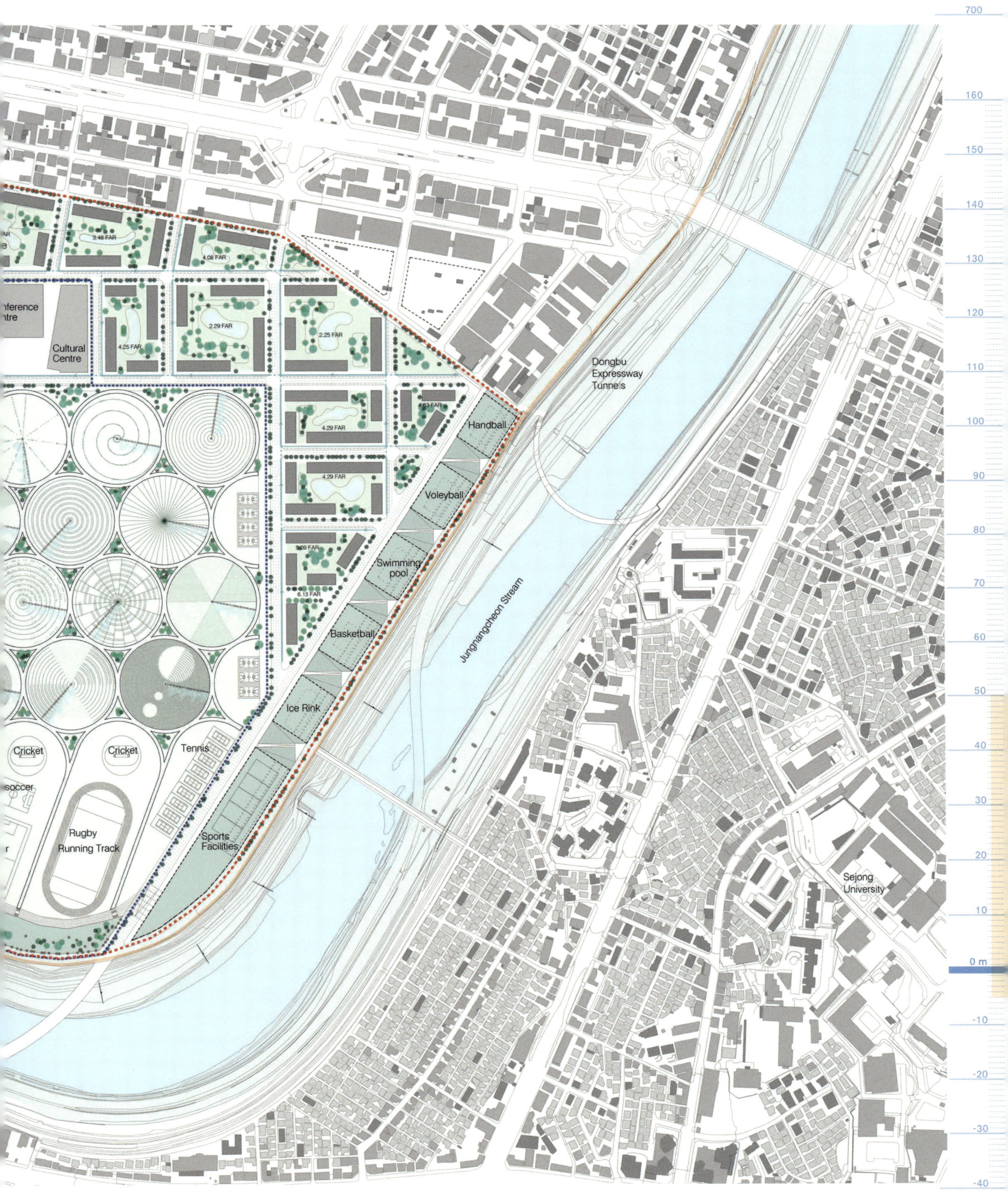
3.48 FAR
4.08 FAR
Cultural Centre
4.25 FAR
2.29 FAR
2.25 FAR
Dongbu Expressway Tunnels
4.63 FAR
Handball
4.29 FAR
4.29 FAR
Volleyball
5.09 FAR
Swimming pool
6.13 FAR
Jungnangcheon Stream
Basketball
Ice Rink
Cricket
Cricket
Tennis
soccer
Rugby Running Track
Sports Facilities
Sejong University
700
160
150
140
130
120
110
100
90
80
70
60
50
40
30
20
10
0 m
-10
-20
-30
-40

Go-Up 건축사무소

Go-Up Architects

어반 마운틴 파크: 걸을 수 있는 표면

물로부터 보호하는 것만이 아니라 수변 공원을 계획 부지에 끌어들여 사용자들이 항상 쉽게 접근할 수 있고 연결될 수 있는 도시 공공공간을 만들고자 하였다. 열려있고 가벼운 표면으로 덮여 있는 확장된 공원은 실내외의 다양한 스포츠를 위한 공간이 될 수 있으며, 또한 강과 이 지역을 연결하기 위한 공간이 될 것이다.
이 지역에서 물의 중요성을 강조하기 위하여, 몇몇 곳에 물로 된 광장을 두었는데, 안전을 위한 도구이면서, 풍경에 대한 시지각을 바꿀 수 있는 요소이다.
공원의 지붕이면서, 타워를 에워싸며, 길이면서 건물인 스킨은 이 프로젝트에서 생명력이 있는 요소이다. 산의 실루엣을 연상하게 하면서 동시에 걸어서 올라갈 수 있는 구조물처럼 생각하게 한다.

Urban Mountain Park: a Walkable Skin

The project, in addition to being an infrastructure of water protection, is designed to bring the riverside park into the planning area with the aim to create an urban public space always accessible and connected from the users. The extensive park, open and covered by a light skin, will be a place where you can practice many sports both outdoors and indoors, but mainly it shall be a space that connects the entire neighborhood with the riverfront.
In order to emphasize the importance of the water in this area, we decided to include several water-squares that have both the functions of the safety tools and items that can modify the visual perception of the landscape.
The skin that we are going to place as roof of the park, that surrounds the tower, the paths, the buildings, is the vibrant element of the project. It recalls the silhouette of a mountain, and we like to think of it as a walkable and climbable structure.

Go-Up 건축사무소는 Nicola Camessa와 Paolo Raffetto가 이탈리아 제노바에서 2015년에 설립했다. Go-Up은 도시 경관, 공공 영역 및 거주자 및 사용자의 일상 생활에 대한 건축의 영향에 초점을 맞춘 매력적인 공간에 대한 연구를 추구한다. 연구를 기반으로 하는 접근법은 건축, 도시, 조경 디자인 분야에서 사회적, 환경적 통합과 건물의 영향에 중점을 두고 공간적 혁신을 추진한다.

Go-Up architects was founded in 2015 by Nicola Canessa and Paolo Raffetto in Genoa, Italy, after another project involving them and other partners since 2008. Go-Up pursues a fascination investigative spatial research focusing on the urban landscape, the public realm, and the influence of architecture on the everyday lives of its inhabitants and users. Our research-based approach drives spatial innovation in the fields of architecture, urbanism and landscape design, with a strong focus on the social and environmental integration and impacts of buildings.

700
160
150
140
130
120
110
100
90
80
70
60
50
40
30
20
10
0 m
-10
-20
-30
-40

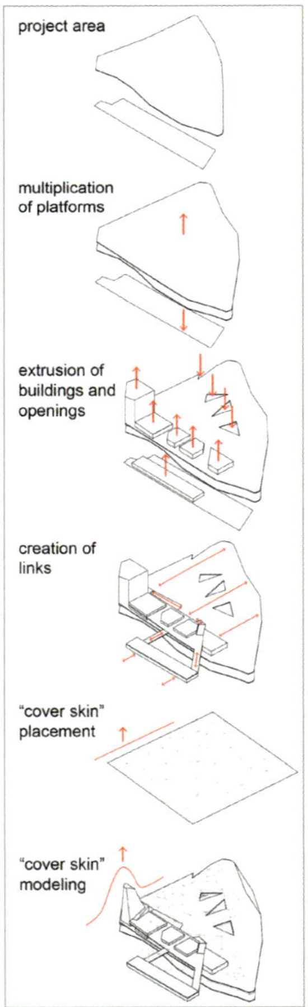

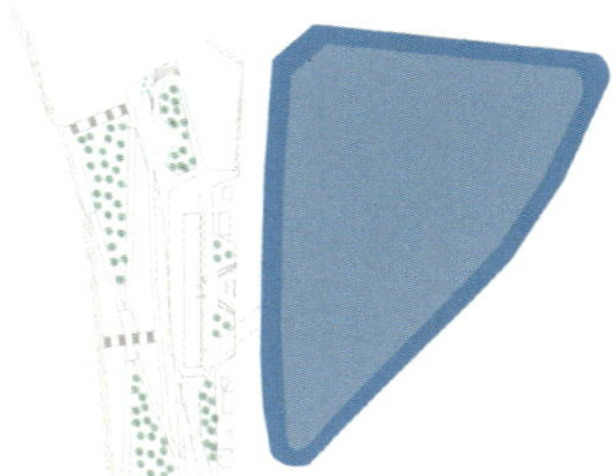

NEW RETARDING BASIN

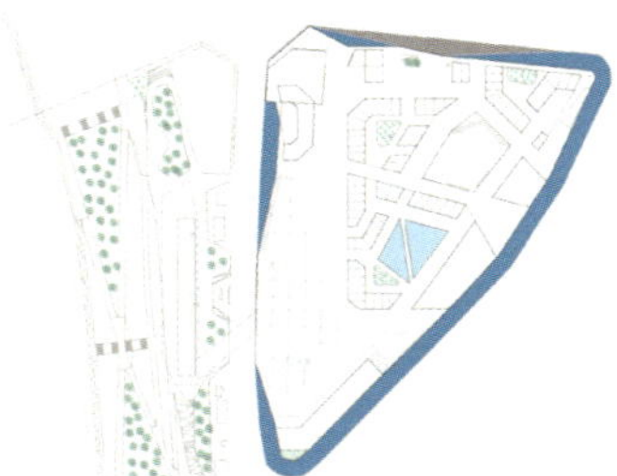

COMMERCIAL PLAN WITH FLEXIBLE SPACES AND WATER SQUARE

SEMI-COVERED PARK WITH CONVIVIAL SPACES AND OPENINGS ON THE UNDERLYING COMMERCIAL LAYER

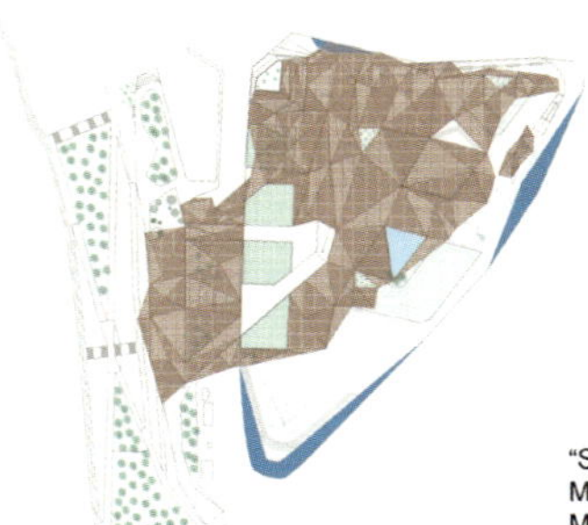

"SKIN" PARTLY MADE OF MICRO-PERFORATED MATERIAL AND PARTLY GREEN. Still under evaluation the hypothesis of making it walked on some parts.

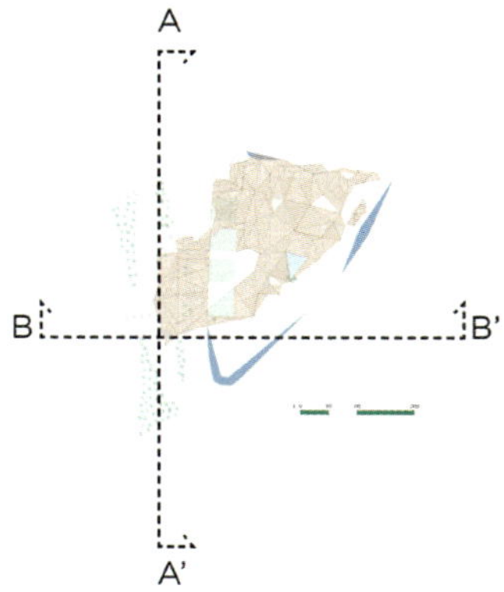

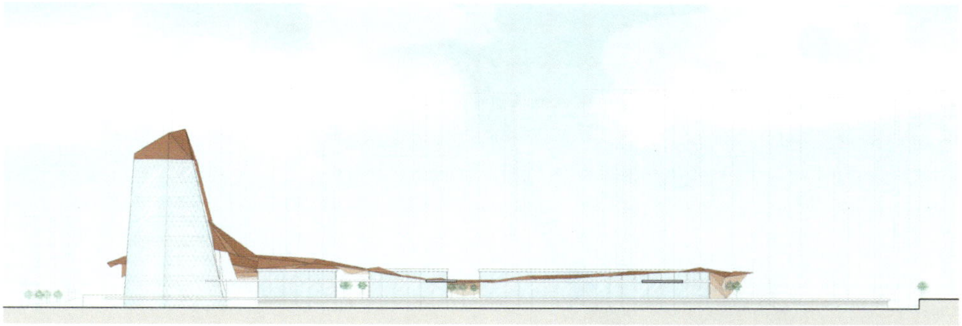

SECTION A-A'

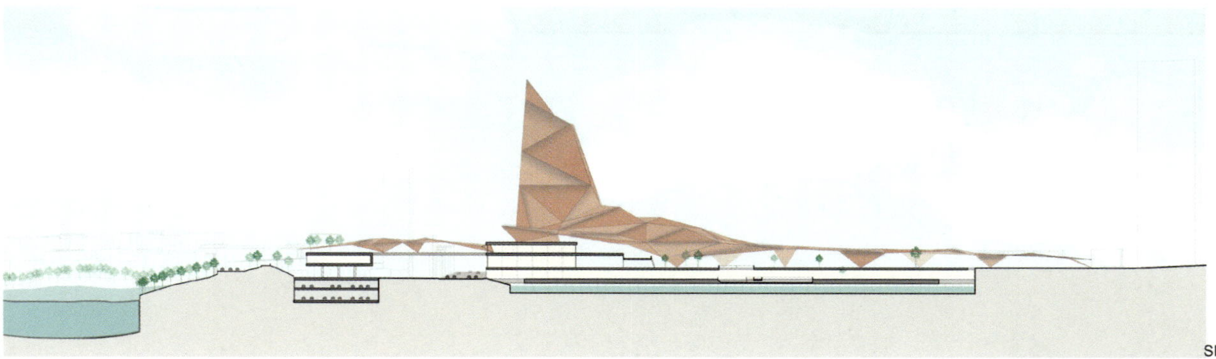

SECTION B-B'

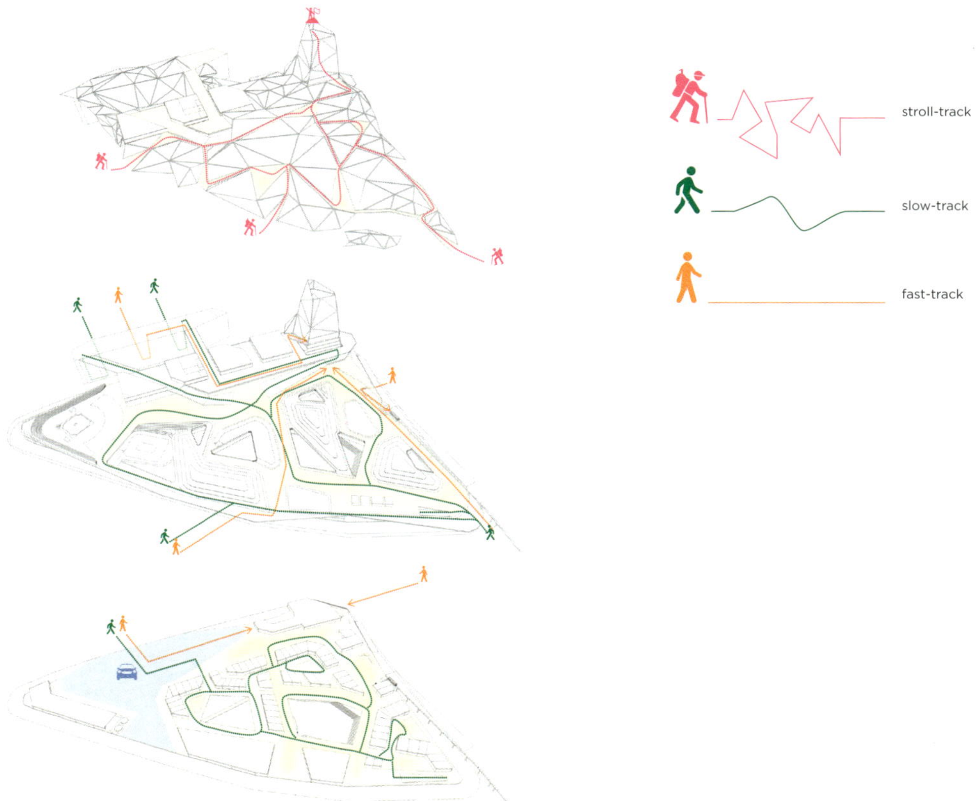

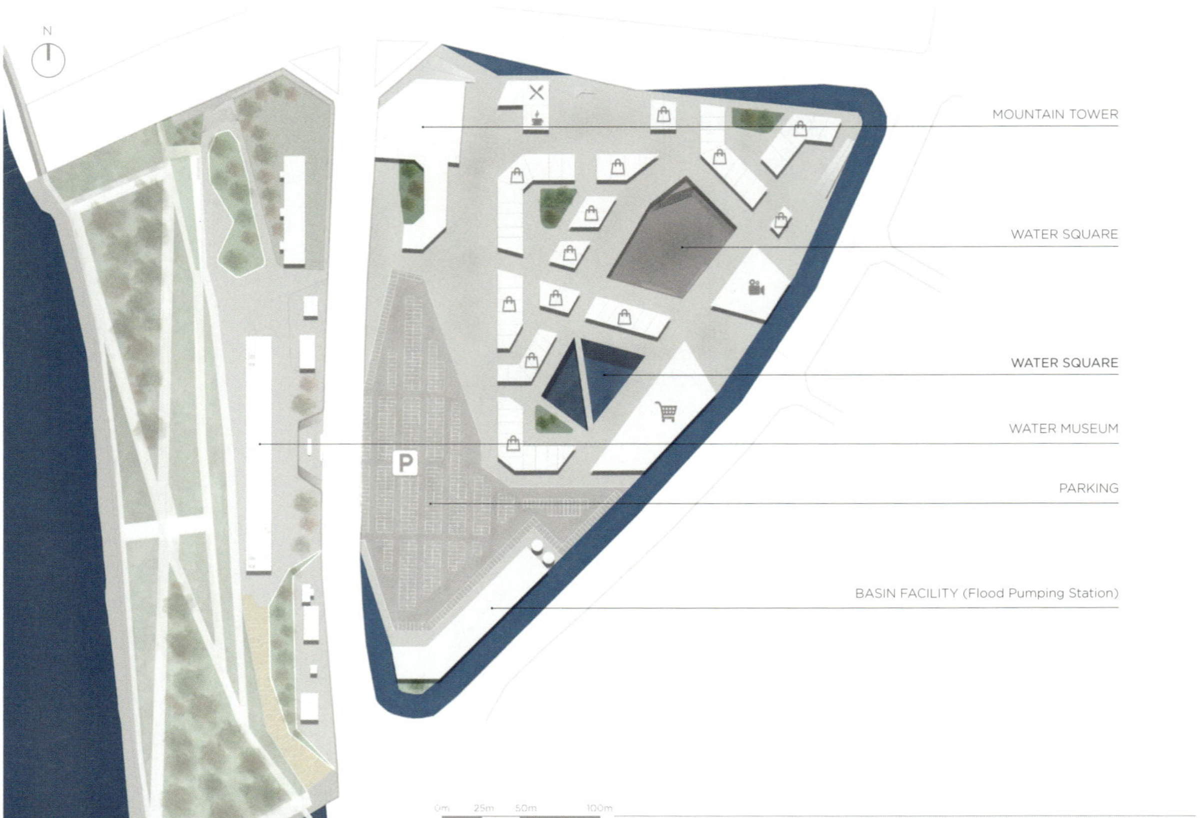

GROUND FLOOR

PEDESTRIAN ACCESS, PARKING AND COMMERCIAL AREA

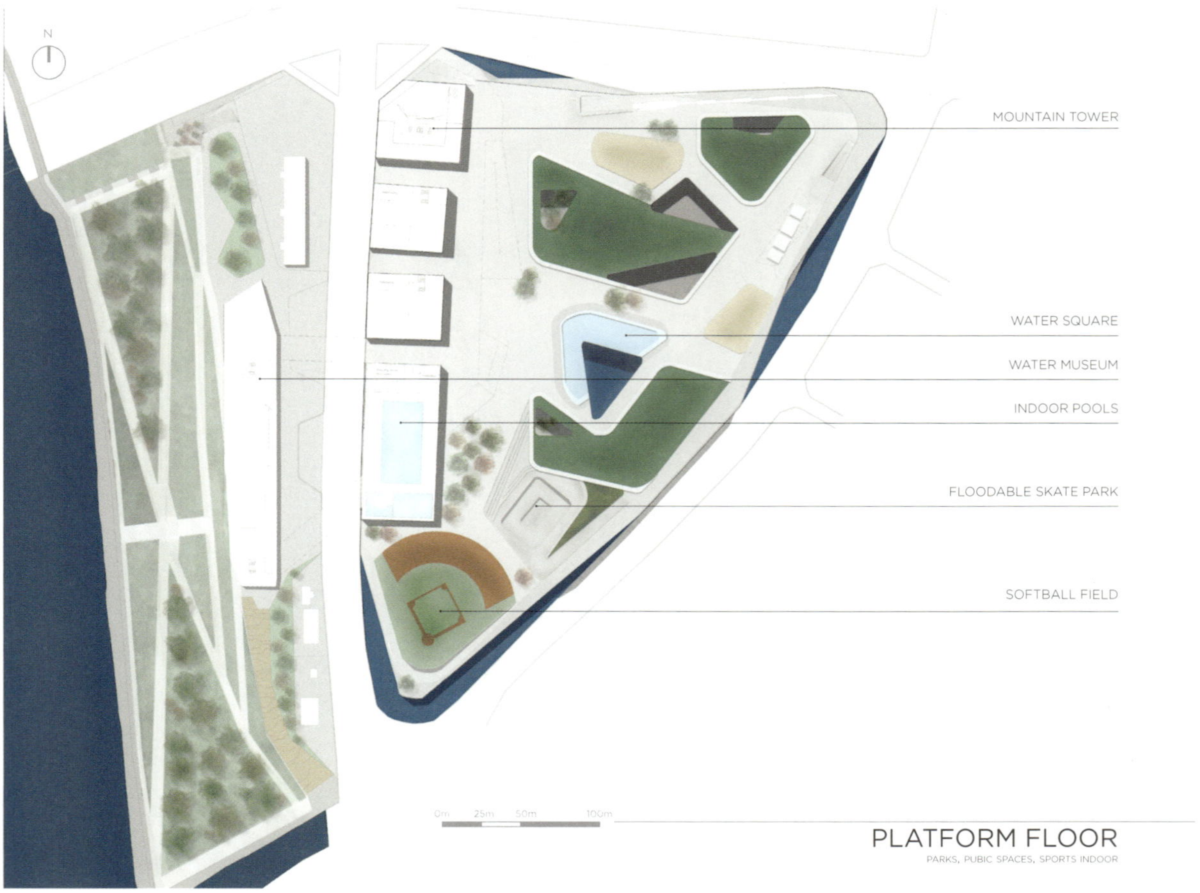

PLATFORM FLOOR

PARKS, PUBIC SPACES, SPORTS INDOOR

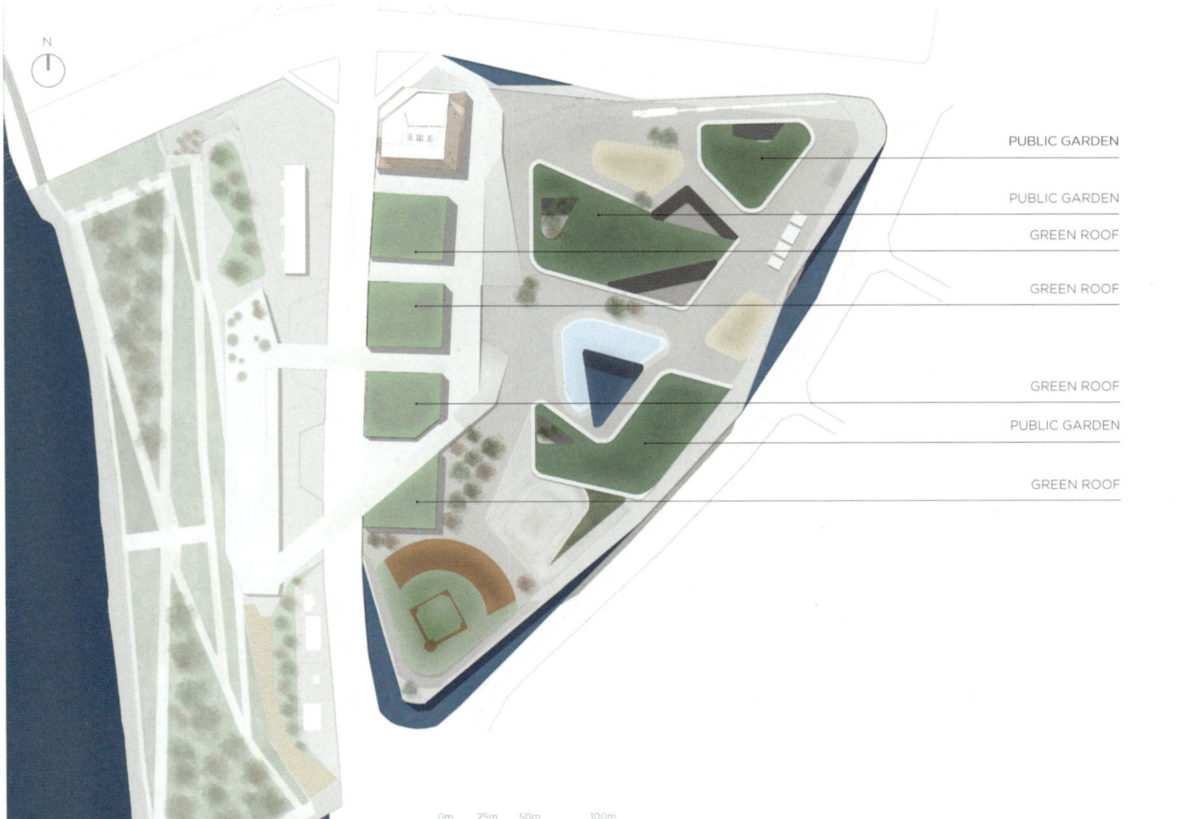

CONNECTION FLOOR

RAMPS, WALKWAYS

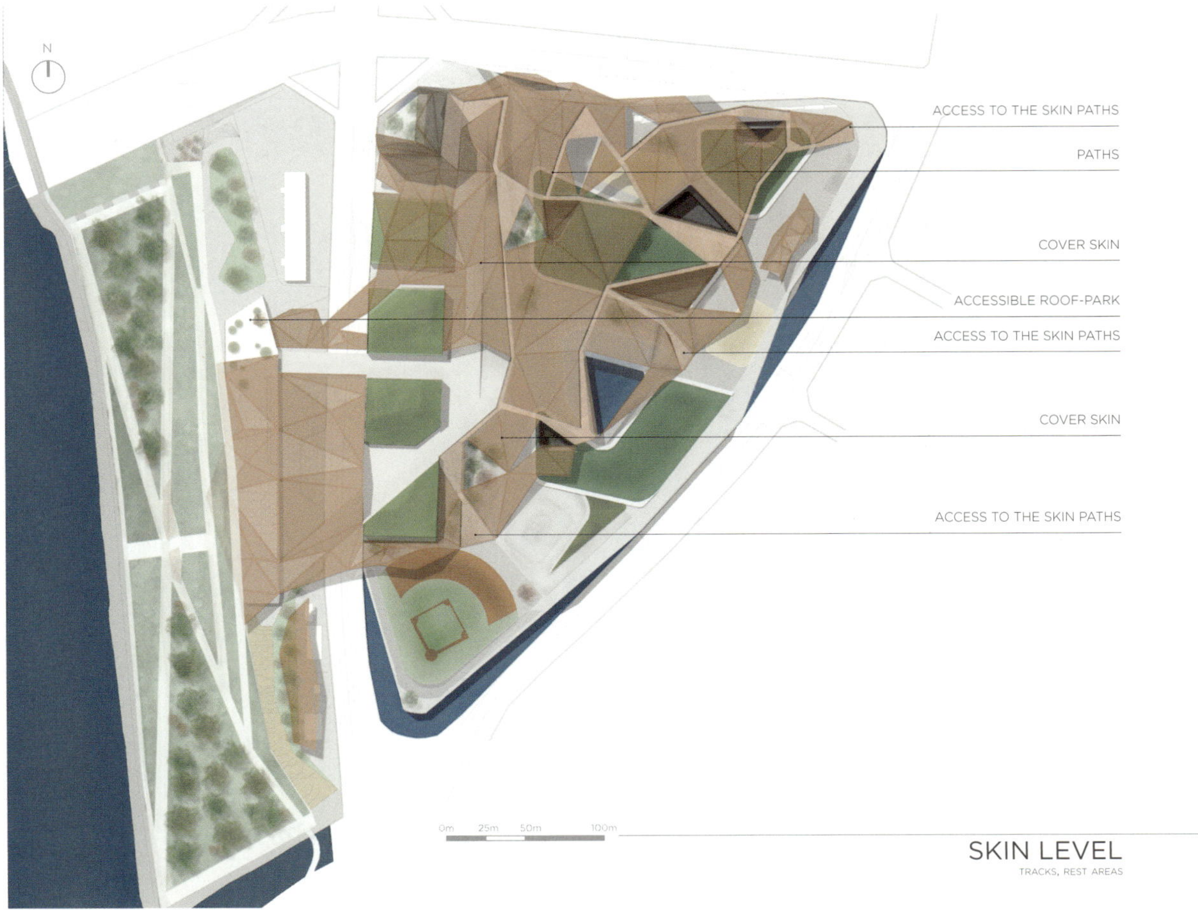

SKIN LEVEL

TRACKS, REST AREAS

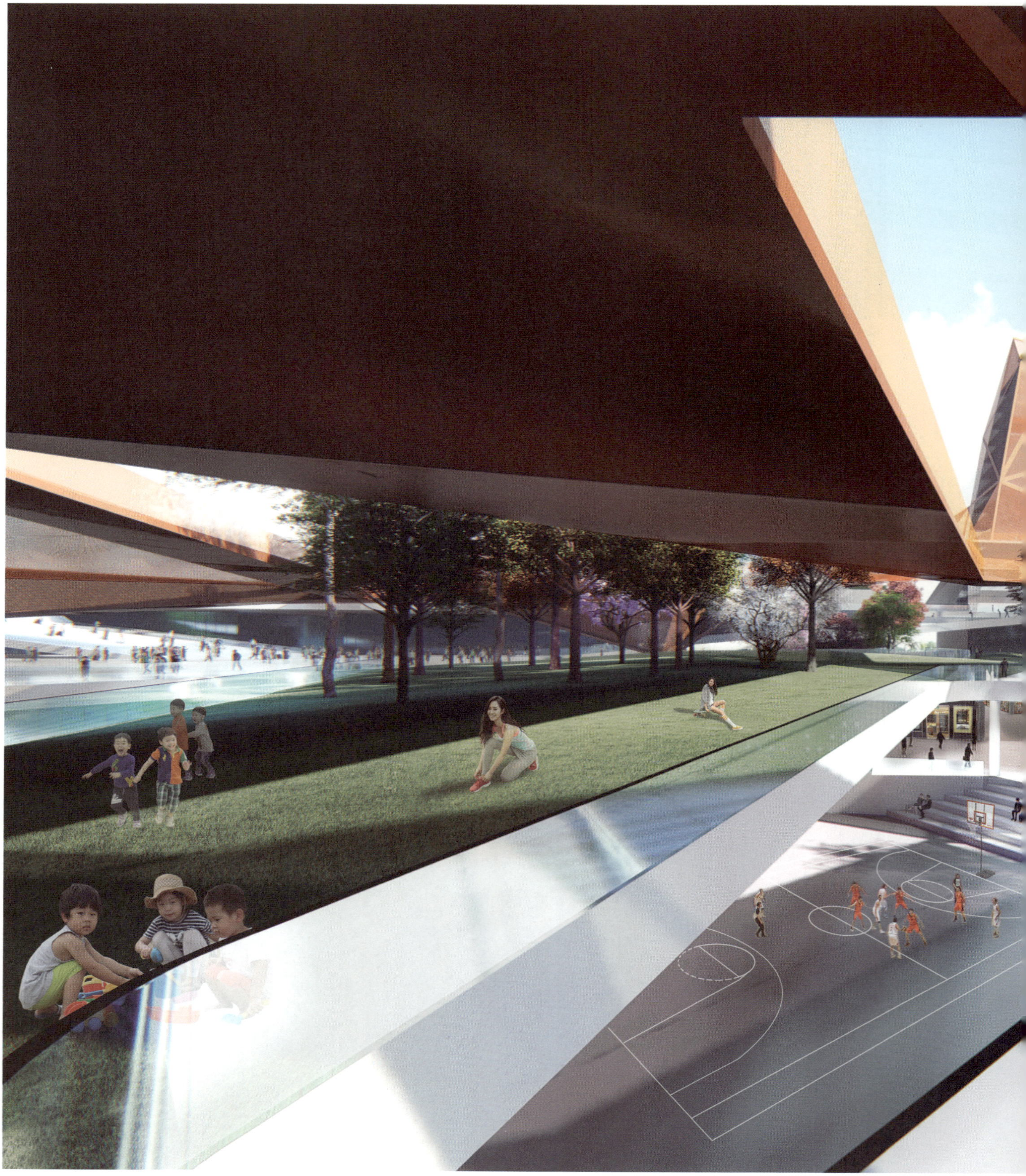

700
160
150
140
130
120
110
100
90
80
70
60
50
40
30
20
10
0 m
-10
-20
-30
-40
MERCI HIVER

700
160
150
140
130
120
110
100
90
80
70
60
50
40
30
20
10
0 m
-10
-20
-30
-40

700
160
150
140
130
120
110
100
90
80
70
60
50
40
30
20
10
0 m
-10
-20
-30
-40

신혜원

Haewon Shin

복합서식지 : 삶의 복합성을 디자인하다

서울은 자연 요소와 인문적 요소, 사유지와 공유지, 전통적 주민 생활 시설과 기술 기반 산업시설과 상업 공간, 기억과 현재와 잠재적 미래 시간이 공존하는 복합 거대 도시다. 망우리 저류조 공원은 한국 최초의 대형 공동묘지인 망우리 공동묘지에 터 잡은 공원으로서, 20세기 초 이래 서울이라는 복합 거대 도시의 변천 과정·성격을 압축적으로 보여주는 독특한 복합서식지다. 망우리 저류조는 상습침수지역인 중랑구 일대의 수해 대비를 위해 만들어진 도시기반시설이지만, 평소에는 체육시설로 사용되는 주민 생활편의시설이며 커뮤니티 공간이 그 표면 형상을 이룬다. 주변은 망우산을 품은 거대한 공동묘지로서 많은 예술가와 독립운동가 등 역사적 인물들이 묻혀 있으며, 산은 용마산·봉화산으로 이어지고 산책로가 조성된 서울 둘레길의 일부이다. 이러한 요소들이 어우러져 이 공간은 하나의 유기적 시민공원을 이루고 있다.

이 프로젝트는 망우리 저류조 공원이 지닌 복합서식지로서의 의미를 충분히 이해하여, 그 맥락에 맞는 복합적 공간 전략을 세우려는 기획이다. 도시기반시설이 어떻게 효율적이고 미학적으로 생활 편의적 커뮤니티를 포함할 수 있으며, 인문적 요소와 자연환경을 공존시키는 효율적·다층적·응축적 공간이 어떻게 가능할 것인가가 포인트다. 더불어 '묘지'라는 시설이 도시의 삶과 자연스럽게 공존할 수 있는 시각 전환에 대한 고민을 개입시키고 있다. 이를 위해 주민 접근성이 떨어질 뿐만 아니라 자연 훼손을 야기할 수 있으며, 자연과 인공과의 경계를 불필요하게 뚜렷이 확정하는 산 정상 지역에 공공시설을 짓는 일은 가급적 피하며, 진입로에 이미 있는 저류조 시설들을 적극적이고 응축적으로 활용한다는 기본 전략을 채택한다.

Urban and Natural Multi-Habitat: Designing the Complexity of Life

Seoul is a complex city that contains multiple dualities such as those of natural components and humanist components, private lands and public lands, traditional residential facilities and industrial and commercial spaces based on technology, and the past and the present. The Mangwoo reservoir site is a park space located on the Korea's first large public cemetery site; as a "multi-habitat" it demonstrates in a condensed manner the mixed-use nature and development of the large metropolitan city that is Seoul. Though the Mangwoo site is an urban infrastructure meant to prevent flood damage in the constantly flooded region of Jungnang-gu, it is daily used by the nearby community as the site of sports amenities. The surrounding region is known as the resting place of many historical artists and political leaders and linked to the Yongma Mountain and the Bongwha Mountain as part of Seoul's Dulle-gil trail system. All of these aspects form harmony to create a truly communal and organic park space.

The project is to understand the full meaning of the Mangwoo reservoir site as a "multi-habitat" and maximize its potential according to its context. The key is to have the urban infrastructural facility effectively and aesthetically embrace communal amenities while being in harmony with humanist and natural components of the site. Moreover, the program of cemetery may involve switch in perception regarding its coexistence with the life in city. To fulfill the goal, the basic strategy is to avoid public construction on top of the mountain that would lead to natural damage and unnecessary divide between the natural and the artificial, let alone the issue of accessibility, and actively utilize existing reservoir facilities near the access road.

신혜원은 로컬디자인 대표이며, 건축설계, 도시연구, 공공프로젝트 기획 및 전시, 교육 등 다양한 분야에서 활동하는 건축가다. 홍콩중문대학조교수, 한국예술종합학교 겸임교수를 지냈으며, 서울시 공공건축가, 젊은 건축가상, 대한민국 공공디자인대상 최우수상을 수상했다. 베니스, 런던, 베를린, 멜버른 등 다수의 국제전시에 참여했다.

Haewon Shin is a representative of lokaldesign, an architect who works in various fields such as architectural design, urban research, public project planning, exhibition, and education. She was a professor at Hong Kong University of China, and an adjunct professor at the Korea National University of Arts, and a public architect of Seoul. She received the prize for a Young Architect and the best award for Korean public designs. She participated in many international exhibitions such as Venice, London, Berlin and Melbourne.

700
160
150
140
130
120
110
100
90
80
70
60
50
40
30
20
10
0 m
-10
-20
-30
-40

과거 History

강소천
1915–1963
아동문학가

계용묵
1904–1961
소설가

권진규
1922-1973
조각가

김말봉
1901-1962
소설가

이중섭
1916-1956
화가

장덕수
1895-1947
언론인

조봉암
1898-1959
진보당 당수

지석영
1855-1935
의사

김상용
1902-1951
시인

김이석
1915-1964
소설가

김호직
1905-1959
영양학자

노필
1927-1966
영화감독

최백근
1914-1961
정치인

최신복
1906-1945
아동문학가

최학송
1901-1932
소설가

한용운
1879-1944
애국지사

문일평
1888-1936
언론인

박승빈
1880-1943
변호사

박인환
1926-1956
시인

박찬익
1884-1949
애국지사

사이토 오토사쿠
1866-1936
산림관료

아사카와 다쿠미
1891-1931
민예연구가

이인성
1912-1950
화가

김영랑
1903-1950
시인

방정환
1899-1931
아동문학가

설의식
1900-1954
소설가

오긍선
1879-1963
의사

오세창
1864-1953
애국지사

이기붕
1896-1960
국회의장

임방울
1904-1961
국악인

채동선
1901-1953
작곡가

박길룡
1898-1943
건축가

유상규
1897-1936
애국지사

이광래
1908-1968
극작가

이영민
1905-1954
야구선수

이영준
1896-1968
국회의원

차중락
1942-1968
가수

함세덕
1915-1950
극작가

송진우
1889-1945
언론인

나운규
1902-1937
영화인

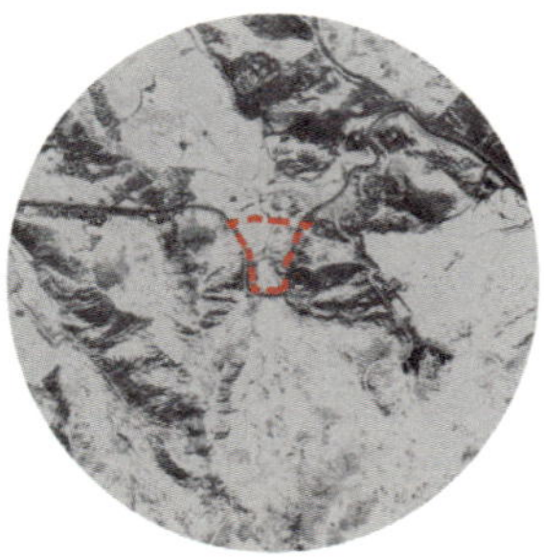

1945

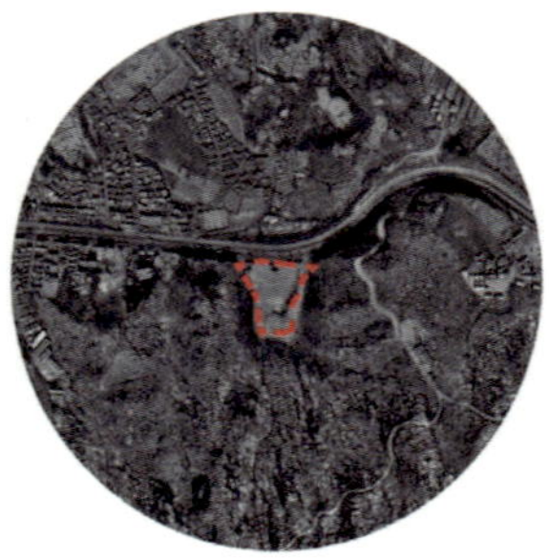

1980

2012

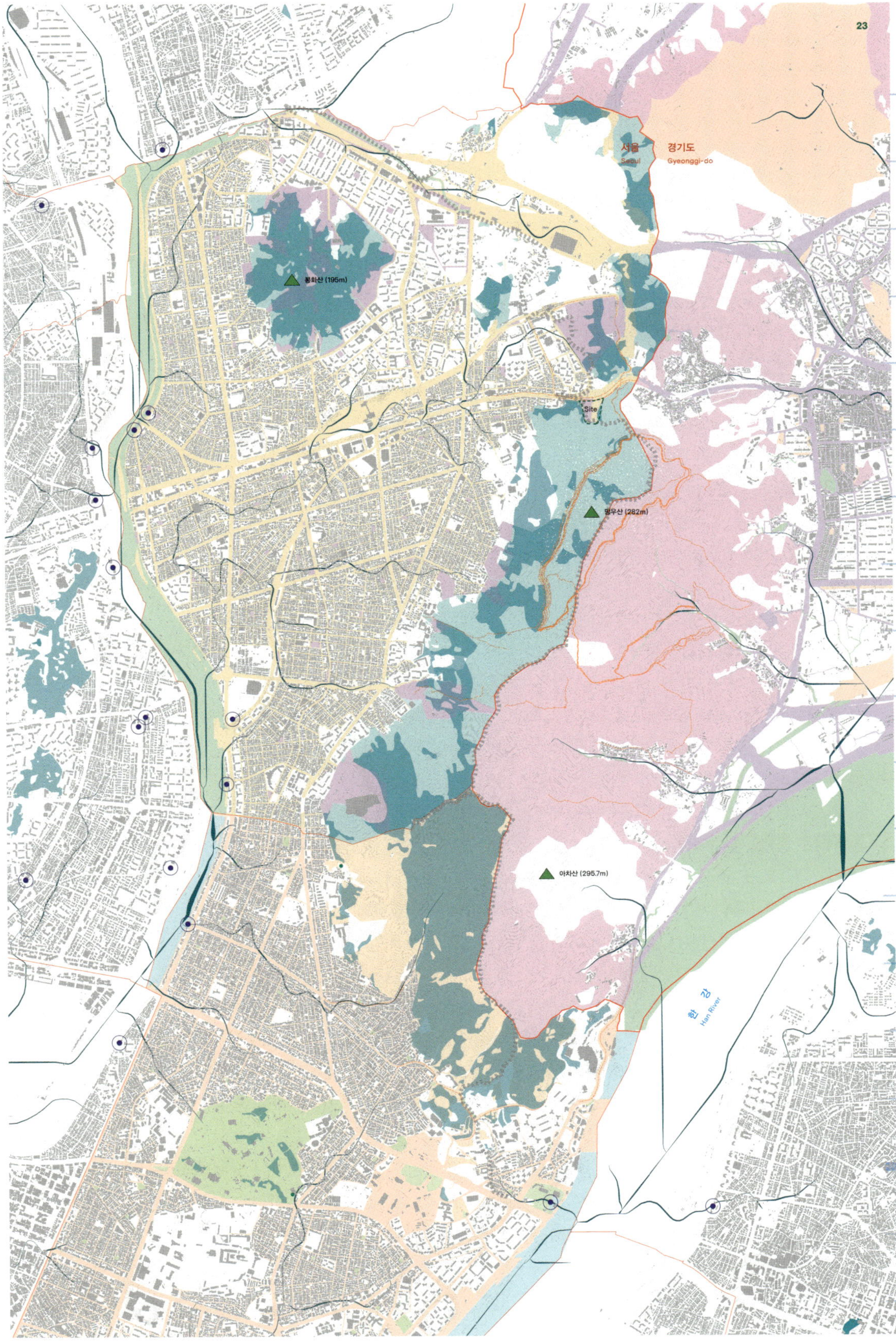
서울
Seoul
경기도
Gyeonggi-do
봉화산 (195m)
Site
망우산 (282m)
아차산 (295.7m)
한 강
Han River
Index
자연림
Natural Forest
자연녹지 공원
Natural Green Park
산 (서울 지역)
Mountains
비오톱 1등급 (서울 지역)
1st Class Biotop (Seoul Area)
산 (구리)
빗물 펌프장
Flood Pump Station
서울 둘레길
Seoul Walking Trail
행정 경계
Administration Border
빗물 길
Drainage Path
자전거 트랙
Bicycle Track
대상지
Site
700
160
150
140
130
120
110
100
90
80
70
60
50
40
30
20
10
0 m
-10
-20
-30
-40

시민도시 서울은 서울의 미래 가치를 표현하는 기본적 도시 비전이자 서울의 역사적 현재를 구성하고 있는 문화적·정치적 정체성이다.' 시민도시 서울은 권리 주체로서의 시민과 공동체에 대한 책임 주체로서의 시민이라는 현대 개인의 정체성을 도시적 입장에서 적극 수용한다. 이를 위해 서울시는 도시의 공동체성을 회복하고, 자연과 인간이 함께 온전한 활력을 회복하며, 지속가능한 삶을 도모하기 위한 공존 원칙으로서 응축-공유도시, 생태-인문도시라는 기본 원칙을 확보한 바 있다. 여기에서 '응축'은 서울이라는 도시를 여러 층위의 복합성·가변성·교차성·횡단성·다중심성으로 이해하며, 도시 집중성 문제를 밀도 높은 기술혁신을 통해 대응한다는 뜻이다. '생태-인문' 도시는 자연과 삶의 인공적 요소를 분리된 것으로 이해하지 않으며, 그 둘이 밀접한 연관 속에 있다는 사실을 자각한다. 이때 서울이라는 도시는 다른 도시와의 관계를 통해 더 큰 삶의 맥락과 연결되며, 지구적 시야에서 생명공동체의 일부를 이룬다. 서울을 이해하는 이런 기본 관점에 따라, 서울시는 이 관점을 관철하기 위한 열 가지 도시 전략을 선정한 바 있다. 복합서식지, 다층적 경계, 참여형 시민도시, 총체적 공간생태계, 재도시, 시민중심 관광, 역동성 있는 문화유산 등 열 가지 패러다임이 이에 해당한다.(≪시민도시 서울 기초조사≫, 2018)

'슈퍼그라운드'는 '시민도시 서울'의 정체성에 기반하여 만들어진 열 가지 패러다임을 가상적인 형태로 실현해 보고, 이러한 도시 전략에 부응하는 적절한 형상을 제안해 보는 도시디자인 시뮬레이션 프로젝트이다. '망우리 저류조 공원'은 이 중에서 '복합서식지'라는 패러다임을 프로젝트 전략 구상의 주요 원칙으로 삼는다. 서울은 자연 요소와 인문적 요소, 사유지와 공유지, 전통적 주민 생활시설과 기술기반 산업시설과 상업 공간, 기억과 현재와 잠재적 미래 시간이 공존하는 복합 거대 도시이다. 망우리 저류조 공원은 한국 최초의 대형 공동묘지인 망우리 공동묘지에 터 잡은 공원으로서, 20세기 초 이래 서울이라는 복합 거대 도시의 변천 과정과 현재 성격을 압축적으로 보여주는 독특한 복합서식지다. 망우리 저류조 공원은 상습침수지역인 중랑구 일대의 수해 대비를 위해 만들어진 도시기반시설이다.(2004) 저류조는 기습 폭우시 빗물을 일시 저류했다가 서서히 방류하는 수해 예방 및 치수 안전 도구를 말한다. 현재 망우리 저류조 공원은 홍수의 우려가 발생하지 않는 평소에는 주민 생활편의시설로 이용되고 있다. 저류조 상부에 생기는 평평한 공간을 테니스, 야구, 게이트볼, 배드민턴 등의 체육시설로 만들어 사용하고 있는 것이다. 이는 망우리 저류조 표면이 평소에는 주민 커뮤니티 공간의 형상을 하고 있으며, 가장 중요한 기능 역시 그 지점에 있다는 것을 뜻한다. 망우리 저류조 공원을 '공원'이라는 입장에서 이해할 때 주목해야 하는 것은, 그 주변이 용마산˙봉화산으로 이어지는 산책로의 입구로서 서울 둘레길의 일부가 된다는 사실이다. 시민들은 대부분 저류조 공원을 통해 산책로로 진입하며, 자전거 라이더들에게 이 길은 자전거 라이딩의 주요 코스로 꼽힌다. 도시 서울, 나아가 현대 한국의 형성과 관련하여 역사적이면서도 문화적인 차원에서 망우리 저류조 공원이 갖는 가장 강력한 인상은, 무엇보다도 이곳이 '망우리 공동묘지'의 입구라는 점이다. 1933년 일제식민지 시절 조성되기 시작한 망우리 공동묘지는 도시기획 차원에서 이루어진 한국 최초의 현대 도시공동묘지이며, 현재 서울에서 가장 규모가 큰 공동묘지이다. 1973년 2만8500여 기로 묘지가 만장된 후, 다른 묘지로의 이장 등을 통해 현재는 8,424기가 남아 있지만, 대규모 도시 공동묘지로서 '망우리'라는 장소가 지닌 상징성은 여전히 이 지역을 규정하는 강력한 이미지이자 정체성이다. 공동묘지로서 특기할 만한 사실은 이곳에 왕족 명온공주, 화가 이중섭, 조각가 권진규, 최초의 영화감독 노필, 시인 한용운과 박인환, 독립운동가 오세창, 건축가 박길룡, 작가 방정환, 작곡가 채동선 등 많은 예술가와 독립운동가 등 역사적 인물들이 묻혀

Mangwoo Reservoir site takes the paradigm of "Urban and Nature Multi-Habitat" as the main principle of the strategy. Urban and Nature Multi-Habitat is a complex habitat where natural elements and urban elements form a harmony. It addresses the concept of Complexity, ecological-humanistic harmony, the symbiosis between different aspects of the site.

Seoul is a mega-complex city where diverse natural elements and artificial objects intermingle. There are private lands and public lands, and civic spaces exist as common spaces that link and mutually include those two spheres. In addition, traditional facilities for daily life and digital facilities based on science and technology coexist. The complex relationality of Seoul, where memories of the past, everyday life in the present, and the sphere of the potential future coexist, manifests itself in many key areas at the same time. Through the coordination and democratic control of elements encompassed by these areas under the principle of respect for living beings, Seoul can be turned into a complex habitat equipped with the power of viability and coexistence.

In this context, we are questioning the new territorial articulations, and their demands of urban re-naturalization, the enhanced value of the landscape factor and a new environmental land-use specified in the given brief. The main approach is to have the urban infrastructural facility embracing communal amenities in a condensed way while being in harmony with humanist and natural components of the site.
The Mangwoo reservoir site is on the outskirt of Seoul located right next to Korea's first large public cemetery site, Mangwoo Cemetery. As a "Multi-habitat", it demonstrates the mixed-use nature and a type of development of a large infrastructure in the city of Seoul. Though the Mangwoo site is an urban infrastructure meant to prevent flood damage in the region of Jungnang-gu, it is daily used by the nearby community as the site of sports amenities.

Mangwoo Reservoir Park is an urban infrastructure facility designed as a flood prevention in Jungnang-gu area. The reservoir temporarily stores rainwater during heavy rain water surge and discharges it gradually. As a typical typology of these reservoir concrete structure, public facilities are placed mostly sports facilities used by neighboring residents. For Mangwoo's reservoir case, it is built on the site of existing sports facilities. Currently, there are tennis, soccer, inline skating, gate ball, and badminton field on the site. These sports facilities above the reservoir act as an important space for community gathering but have poor accessibility, especially when as the site is located on the border of a mountain, cemetery on one side and the highways on the other side.

Mangwoo Reservoir site is also at the edge of the promenade that leads to Mount Yongma and Mount Bonghwa as part of Seoul's Dulle-gil trail system.

700
160
150
140
130
120
110
100
90
80
70
60
50
40
30
20
10
0 m
-10
-20
-30
-40

있다는 사실이다. 이 사실은 망우리 공동묘지가 일반적 공동묘지와는 달리 죽음의 역사성과 기억의 현재성을 시간적으로 환기하며, 특별한 인문적 공간으로서 존재할 수 있는 가능성을 시사한다. 슈퍼그라운드, 〈망우리 저류조 공원 | 복합서식지〉는 망우리 저류조 공원이 지닌 복합적 특성을 응축도시, 생태-인문도시라는 원칙 하에 이해하고, 도시기획 전략의 바탕을 '복합서식지'라는 상기 패러다임 아래 접근해 보려는 프로젝트이다. 이 프로젝트에서 핵심은 도시기반시설이 어떻게 효율적이고 미학적인 차원에서 생활편의적 커뮤니티를 일상적으로 포함하면서도, 도시 재난대비시설이라는 특수 기능을 효과적으로 구현할 수 있는가 하는 문제이다. 그뿐만 아니라 인문적 가치를 내포한 공동묘지와 쾌적한 산책로가 있는 산이라는 자연환경을 어떻게 공존시킬 것인가 하는 문제도 개입되어 있다. 또한 현재 한국사회의 문화적 인식에 근거한다면, 대표적인 도시 혐오시설로 인식되는 공동묘지를 어떻게 생활의 한 요소로 이해시킬 수 있을까 하는 어려운 시각 전환적 과제도 내포되어 있다.

그러나 다른 관점으로 보면, 망우리 저류조 공원 일대가 지닌 자연환경의 친근성, 이미 자리 잡은 도시편의적 요소와 접근성, 인문적 잠재성을 감안할 때, 이러한 복합서식지가 지닌 다양한 요소들은 도시 기획의 방법론적 전환에 따라 '시민도시 서울'의 새로운 공동체 디자인의 중요한 전환 사례가 될 수도 있음을 암시하고 있다. 이 프로젝트는 이를 위해 과거 혐오시설로 여겨지던 망우리 공동묘지 일대를 오히려 이 지역의 새로운 관계성을 여는 다층적 경계로 구성할 것을 제안한다. 기존 망우리 저류조 공원은 공간의 다층성을 물리적이면서도 상징적으로 도입하는 응축 공간으로 디자인되며, 이 공간을 오가며 사용하는 다양한 시민들을 모으고 다른 차원의 공간으로 인도하고 분배하는 게이트로서의 역할을 분명하게 수행하도록 디자인된다. 생활편의시설이라는 현재성과 형이하학, 공동묘지라는 형이상학, 주변을 둘러싼 산이라는 자연적˙경관적 요소, 산책로와 자전거길이라는 공간연계적 성격, 도시방재시설이라는 기능성, 역사적 인물들과 조우하는 기억과 인문적 요소 등을 동시적으로 드러나게 하고, 겹치게 하며, 공존시키는 다층적 디자인이 필요하다. 이를 위해 주민 접근성이 떨어질 뿐만 아니라 자연 훼손을 야기할 수 있으며, 자연과 인공과의 관계를 뚜렷이 확정하는 산 정상 지역에 공공시설을 짓는 일은 최대한 피하며, 진입로에 이미 있는 저류조 시설들을 적극적이고 응축적으로 활용하는 다층적 디자인을 구조적으로 지향한다. 공중에서 보았을 때, 이 구조는 망우산의 일부처럼 보일 뿐만 아니라, 이미 망우산의 일부가 되어 있는 공동묘지의 한 지표면처럼 디자인된다. 이 프로젝트에서는 기존 저류조 시설의 상부에 묘지를 방문하는 사람들을 위한 방문자 센터와 주차시설 그리고 인근 지역 주민을 위한 실내 운동공간과 커뮤니티 공간, 망우리 역사문화관을 배치하였다. 또 그 상부 옥외에는 야외 농구장, 배드민턴장, 족구장, 게이트볼장, 달리기 트랙, 산책길, 공원 등의 기존 실외 프로그램들을 더욱 응축하여 녹색 경관의 일부로 녹아들도록 재구성하였다. 공동묘지에 묻힌 망자가 경관의 일부가 된 복합구조물을 '자연스러운' 시선으로 산 위에서 내려다볼 수 있는 디자인이 가능할까. 그것은 아마도 산과 도시, 자연과 인공, 삶과 죽음, 생활편의적 기능과 인문적 요소들을 구획 짓지 않으며, 이 지역 전체를 하나로 통합하는 전략을 궁극적인 디자인 목표로 삼는 방향일 것이다.

The most notable aspect about the park is that it is the entrance to the 'Mangwoo Cemetery', especially in the historical and cultural aspects of urban Seoul and the formation of modern Korea. Mangwoo reservoir park's unique identity as a gate is also related to the cemetery which is a heritage with historical and cultural richness. Created in 1933 during Japanese colonial rule, Mangwoo cemetery is the first modern public graveyard planned in urban scale and is still the largest in Seoul. Fully interred with 28,500 graves in 1973, though it remains 8,424 today followed by constant displacements the identity of Mangwoo area is still determined as a large-scale urban cemetery in Seoul.

Superground, Mangwoo Multi-habitat is seen with the principle that the complex nature of the Mangwoo Reservoir Park is a condensed city and an ecological-human city. The key to this project is how urban infrastructures can effectively implement the special functions of urban disaster prevention facility while incorporating everyday life of the communities. There is also a question of how to coexist with the environment of a cemetery that still is associated with a negative connotation as an element of life with humanistic value, and the surrounding mountain and trails in symbiosis relationship.

The project proposes the Mangwoo reservoir site to be composed of multi-layered boundaries that open up new relationships in the surrounding context. It is strategically planned as a condensation space that physically and programmatically introduces the multi-layered platforms that act as a gateway to summon and distribute various users through the site. It is a place of active public facilities with an information center and the gateway to the cemetery and the surrounding mountains, linking to the promenades on the existing concrete tank for rainwater detention. Multi-layered ground simultaneously exposes, overlaps, and coexists with the programmatic elements and the surrounding landscape.

This approach then deters encroaching the natural landscape with added public facilities with parking, and access roads for cars that have already disconnected and separated territories between nature and urban and residents and visitors. The proposed Superground is a composite structure that is part of the landscape, compilation of mountains and cities, nature and artifacts, life and death, living amenities and human factors, and a complex habitat where natural elements and urban elements form a harmony.

● 전략 Strategy

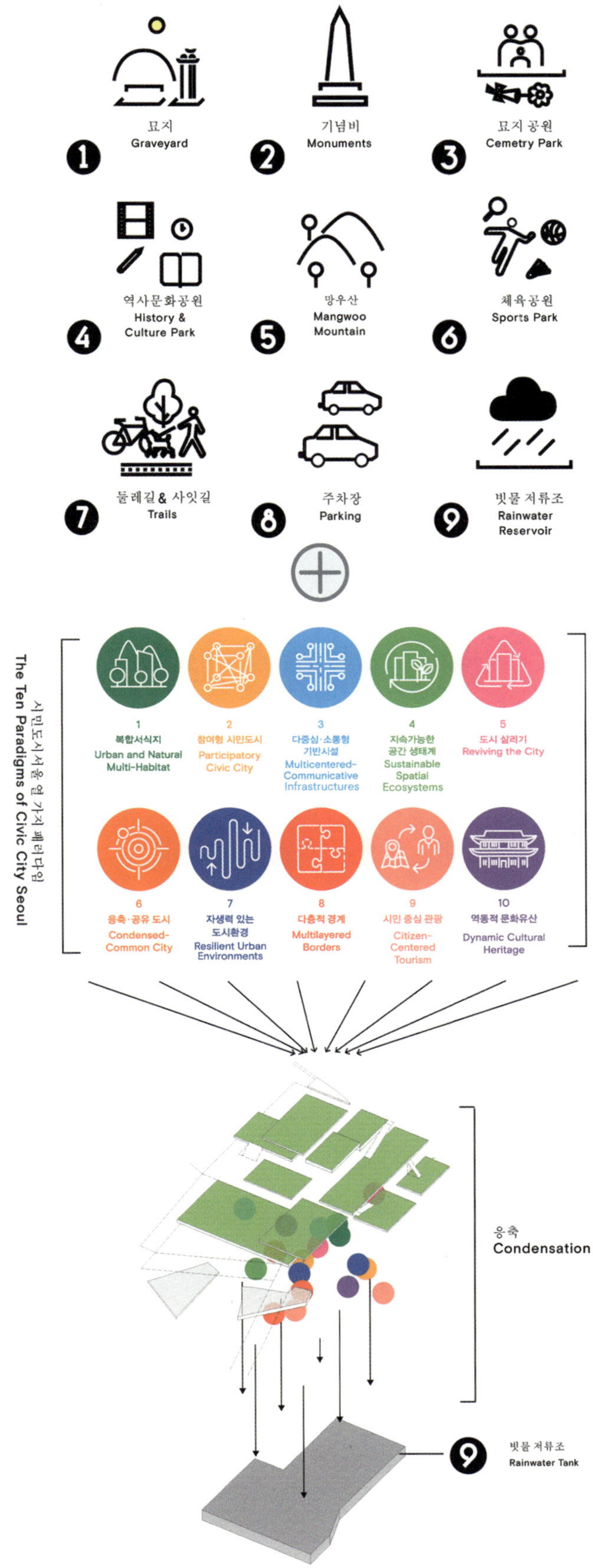

묘지
Graveyard
1
기념비
Monuments
2
묘지공원
Cemetry Park
3
역사문화공원
History & Culture Park
4
망우산
Mangwoo Mountain
5
체육공원
Sports Park
6
둘레길& 사잇길
Trails
7
주차장
Parking
8
빗물저류조
Rainwater Reservoir
9
시민도시서울 열 가지 패러다임
The Ten Paradigms of Civic City Seoul
1
복합서식지
Urban and Natural Multi-Habitat
2
참여형 시민도시
Participatory Civic City
3
다중심·소통형 기반시설
Multicentered-Communicative Infrastructures
4
지속가능한 공간 생태계
Sustainable Spatial Ecosystems
5
도시 살리기
Reviving the City
6
응축·공유 도시
Condensed-Common City
7
자생력 있는 도시환경
Resilient Urban Environments
8
다층적 경계
Multilayered Borders
9
시민 중심 관광
Citizen-Centered Tourism
10
역동적 문화유산
Dynamic Cultural Heritage
응축
Condensation
9
빗물저류조
Rainwater Tank

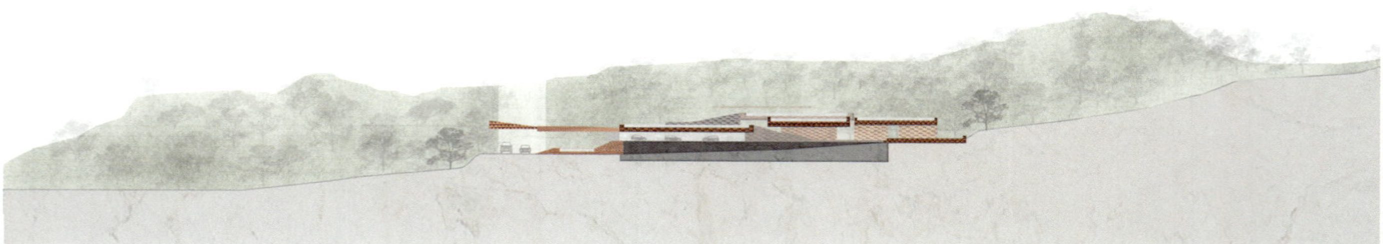

×57.6
×59.6
×62.5
×64.4
×58.8
×65.5
×64.1
×58.2
×59.5
×60.8
×58.4
×60.7
×63.5
700
160
150
140
130
120
110
100
90
80
70
60
50
40
30
20
10
0 m
-10
-20
-30
-40

700
160
150
140
130
120
110
100
90
80
70
60
50
40
30
20
10
0 m
-10
-20
-30
-40

언더그라운드

서울
새로운 땅의 풍경

UNDERGROUND

SEOUL
NEW *GROUNDSCAPES*

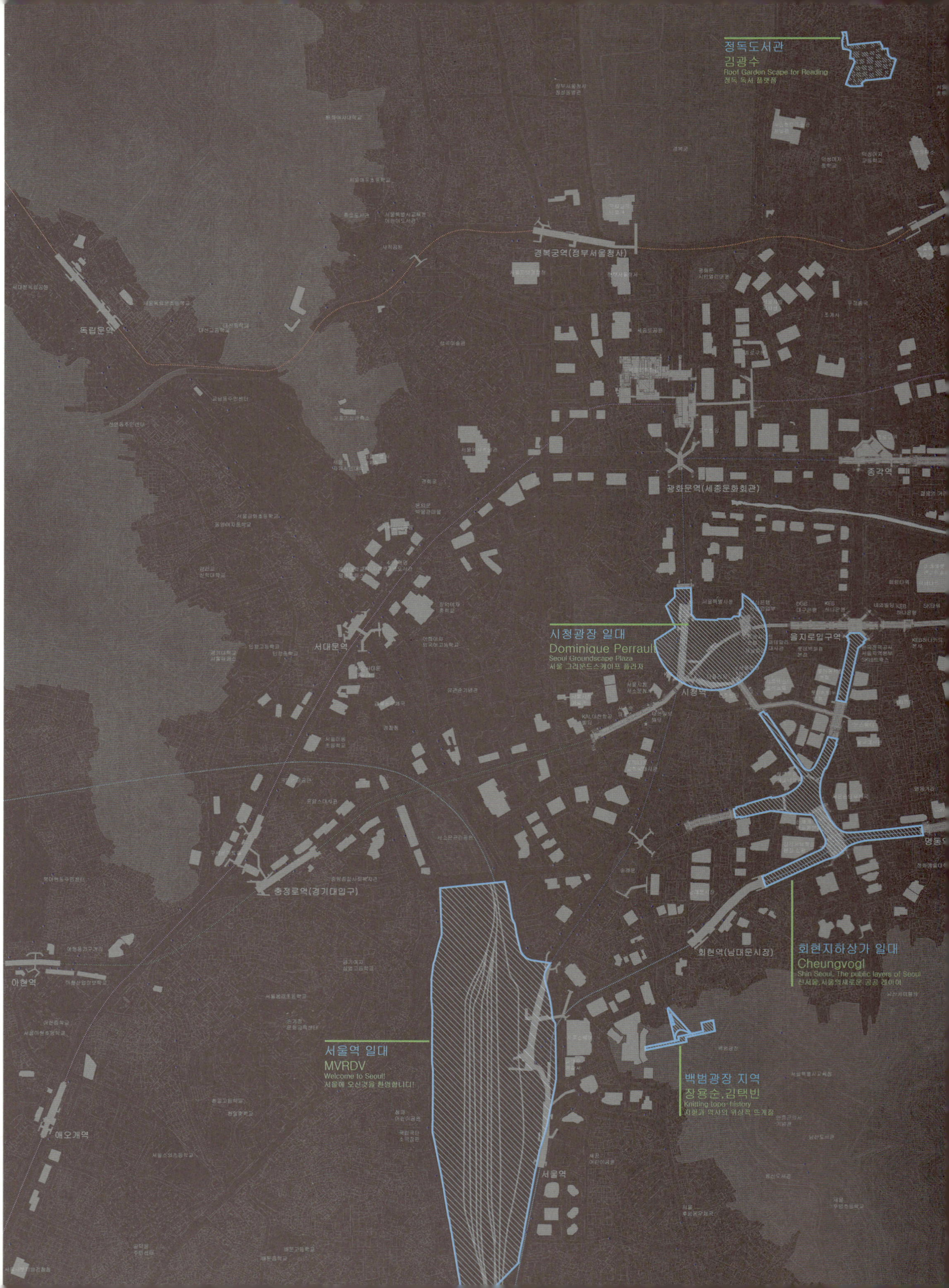

정독도서관
김광수
Roof Garden Scape for Reading
정독 독서 플랫폼
경복궁역(정부서울청사)
독립문역
광화문역(세종문화회관)
종각역
서대문역
시청광장 일대
Dominique Perrault
Seoul Groundscape Plaza
서울 그라운드스케이프 플라자
시청역
을지로입구역
충정로역(경기대입구)
회현역(남대문시장)
회현지하상가 일대
Cheungvogl
Shin Seoul, The public layers of Seoul
신서울, 서울의새로운 공공 레이어
아현역
서울역 일대
MVRDV
Welcome to Seoul!
서울에 오신것을 환영합니다!
백범광장 지역
장용순,김택빈
Knitting topo-history
지형과 역사의 위상학 뜨개질
애오개역
서울역

혜화역
창신역
동대문 성곽공원
modostudio
UN-interrupted City
연속된 도시
종로4가
Kees Christiaanse
Jongro Connector
종로커넥터
동묘앞역
종로3가역(탑골공원)
종로5가역
동대문역
종로3가역
훈련원공원
SOA
Vessels
베셀즈
을지로4가역
을지로3가역
을지로4가
Terminal 7
Seoul Chronicle: Veins
서울 연대기:흐름
동대문역사문화공원역
신당역
충무로역
청구역
동대입구역
약수역
9개 대상지
현재 지하공간
지상 공간

모도스튜디오

modostudio

연속된 도시

1978년, 그러니까 40년 전, modostudio는 로마에서 "Roma Interrotta (로마인터로타)"라는 전시회를 개최하였다. 지오반바티스타놀리(Giovan Battista Nolli)가 그린 유명한 로마 지도에서 영감을 얻은 이 전시회는 로마의 도시 상태와 콜린로우(Collin Rowe), 알도로시(Aldo Rossi), 로버트벤투리(Robert Venturi), 제임스스털링(James Stirling)과 같은 저명한 건축가들에 의해 12가지의 다채로운 프로젝트로 전시되었다. 그 전시회는 도시 프로젝트의 아이콘으로 기억되고 있으며, 현재의 도시개발을 분석하는 방법 및 도시 규모를 보존하며 일관된 개발을 창출하는 솔루션의 척도가 되었다.
근현대 서울의 믿기지 않는 빠른 성장은 옛 도시생태를 바꾸었고 도로 체계의 단절을 초래하였다. 여전히 도시의 곳곳에 이질적인 요소들을 유지하고 있는 이러한 도시의 구성은 중단되고 끊겨 있다. 동대문지역은 중단된 도시 패턴의 명확한 사례다. 교차로 하나 안에 있는 이 지역은 도시의 중추점으로서 동대문, 시장, 도시공원, 문화적 건물, 그리고 두 지하철역을 잇는 지하 보도까지도 설계가 가능하다.

UN-interrupted city

In 1978, fourty years ago, was held in Rome the "Roma Interrotta" Exhibition. The exhibition, which took inspiration from the famous Rome map drawn by Giovan Battista Nolli in 1748, was investigating the condition of the city of Rome and its interruped process of transformation through 12 different projects proposals by prominent architects such Colin Rowe, Aldo Rossi, Robert Venturi, James Stirling. That exhibition has become an icon of the urban project, how to analyze the urban condition of a city and the possible solutions to create a coherent development preserving the urban scale. The incredible rapid growth of the city of Seoul in the recent past has modified the original urban pattern which is now characterized by a strong urban discontinuity. The composition of the city which still mantains some heterogeneous patterns in different areas of the city, in many parts seems interrupted, discontinuous.
Dongdaemun gate area is a clear example of an interrupted urban pattern. An extreme vital node of the city, which in a single crossroad, is able to host a series of incredible valuable elements: the Dongdaemun gate, the Market, the Naksan park, a cultural building, and, at last, an underground passage connected to two different metro lines.

모도스튜디오는 로마에 위치한 건축, 도시계획 그리고 조경디자인을 아우르는 회사다. 2006년 말, 파비오 시비넬, 로베르토 로란티 그리고 조지오 마토치아 세 명의 건축가들에 의해 설립되었으며 세계적인 건축가들과 오랜 협업 후 많은 공모전과 건축상을 수상하였다.
모도 스튜디오는 그간 문화시설, 기업의 사옥, 사무공간, 주거 건물 그리고 조경작업들을 수행해 왔다. 모도스튜디오의 파트너들인 세 건축가들은 2008, 2013, 2016 그리고 2018년에 Cornell대학교에서 학생들을 가르쳤다. 또한 2010년에서 2016년까지 InArch의 대학원과정에서 지속가능한 디자인을 그리고 IED(European Institute of Design in Rome)에서 2011년에서 2015년까지 건축설계를 가르쳤다.

modostudio | cibinel laurenti martocchia architetti associati, located in Rome, is a multidisciplinary practice of architecture, urban planning and landscape design. Established at the end of 2006 by three principal architects, Fabio Cibinel, Roberto Laurenti, and Giorgio Martocchia, after many years of collaborating with internationally acclaimed architects modostudio was awarded and shortlisted in many international architectural competitions. Along the years the office completed research and cultural buildings, industrial headquarters, office workplaces, residential buildings and landscaping. Modostudio partners have been teaching architecture at Cornell University, architecture faculty in 2008, 2013, 2016 and 2018, sustainable design at Inarch postgraduate master between 2010 and 2016 and architectural design at IED - European Institute of Design in Rome between 2011 and 2015.

modostudio

위에서 언급한 요소들은 상생할 수 없으므로 도시 패턴의 중대한 단절을 초래하며 특히 단절 시에 대한 인간의 인식을 발생시킨다. 이 지역은 주변 지역의 여러 독립적인 요소들 간의 소통을 증진시키고 용이하게 해주는 중추적인 기반시설이 필요하다.
또한 이 지역은 도시의 여러 층위 사이의 연결을 강화할 필요가 있다. 우리의 접근방식은 이 지역에 도시의 재생을 촉진시키는 데에 도움을 줄 수 있도록 여러 도시 요소들 사이의 단절을 해결할 수 있는 디자인을 제안하길 원한다. 우리는 도시의 공공영역이 다양하게 경험될 수 있는 수준 높고 매력적인 공간으로 만들기를 원한다.

The above mentioned elements are not able to dialogue togheter, creating a strong discontinuity in the urban pattern and mostly in the human perception of an interrupted city. The area needs of a new infrastructural spine able to facilitate and implement the dialogue of the indipendent elements of the surroundings.
The area needs also to reinforce the connections between the different layers of the city. Our approach wants to make a design proposal able to solve the disconnection between the different elements of the area helping the activation of a urban regeneration. We want to make the public urban space a quality and attractive space which can be experienced in many different ways.

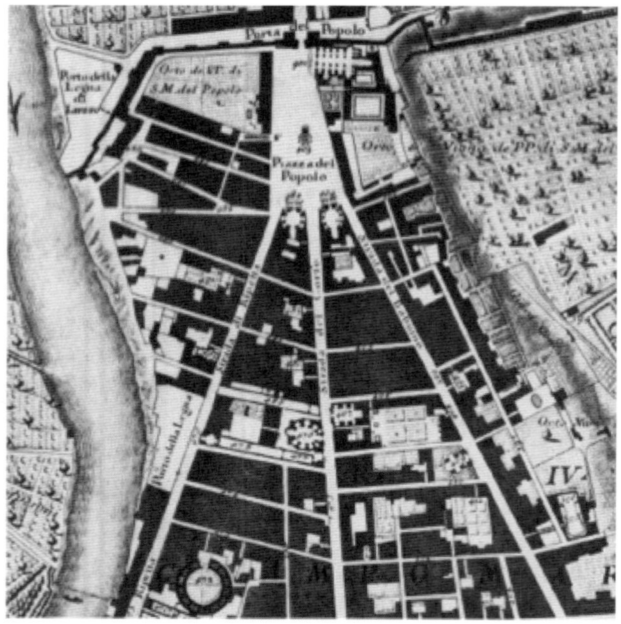

아무리 방 하나하나가 그 자체로 아름답다고 하더라도 연속된 방들만으로는 집을 만들 수 없듯이 개별적으론 훌륭한 건축물들만 가지고서는 도시를 만들 수 없다. 그런 개별적인 요소를 묶어주는 연속성이 필요하다. 구체적으로, 궁전, 교회, 가로, 광장 등은 서로 인접한 요소들을 고려해야 한다. 그들은 각자 홀로 존재할 수 있는 것들이 아니다. 이는 "미완의 시"를 의미한다. – 브루노제비, 1971 ("Saper vedere la città", 도시를 바라보는 법)

The Continuum City

"A series of rooms, even if each is beautiful in itself, does not form a house; a series of buildings, even though splendid individually, does not set up a city. We need a bond of interdependence, the continuum. But, to make it concrete, every element, palace, church, avenue, plaza, must refer to the adjacent ones. Each element has to renounce to its autonomy. This means: the poetics of the unfinished"
Bruno Zevi, Roma 1971 from "Saper vedere la città"

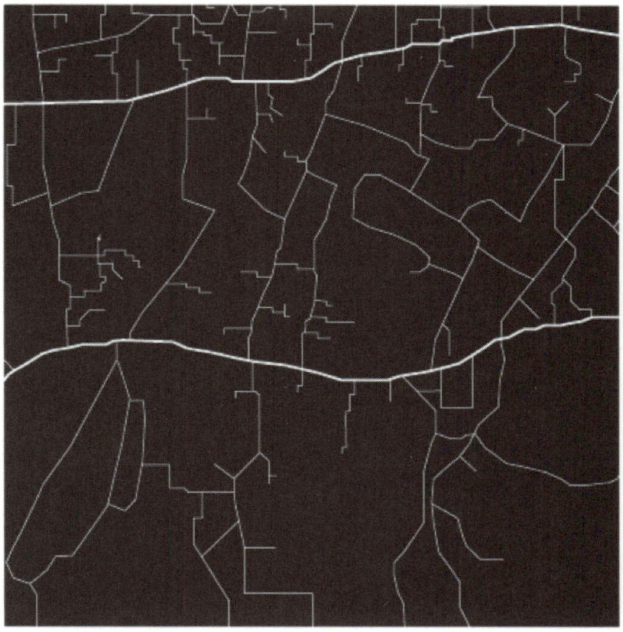

Continuum City
Seoul typical historical urban pattern

Dis-Continuum
Seoul actual urban pattern

Urban grid A grid as reference

Dis-Continuum Streets as element of disconnection

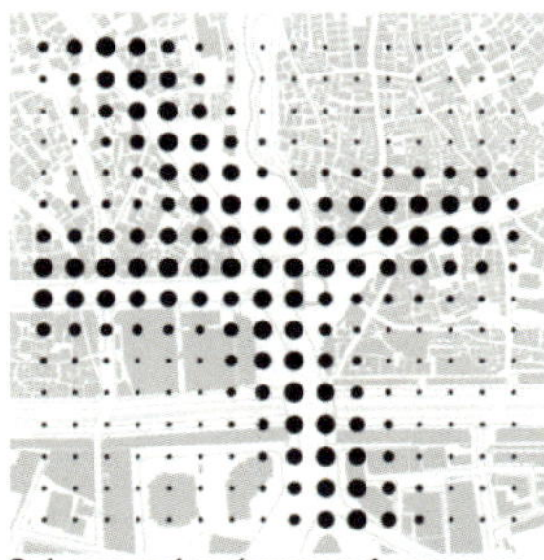

Subway and underground passages
A spine for new urban connections

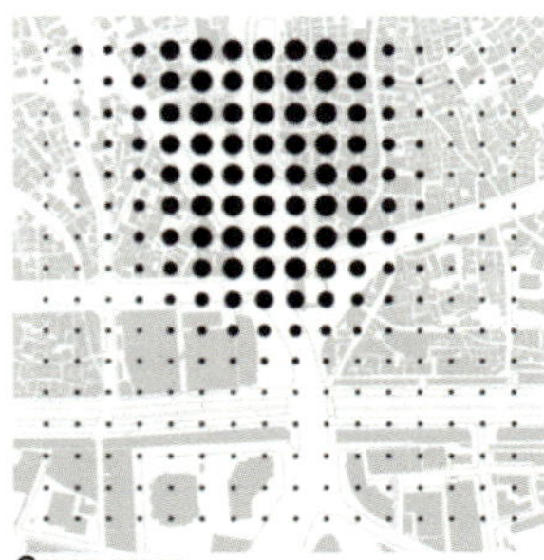

Green areas
Naksan Park, a green area to implement

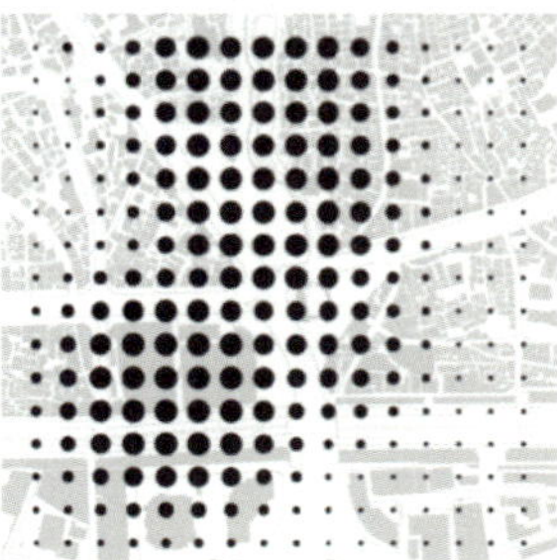

Superimposition
A new multi-layer urban density

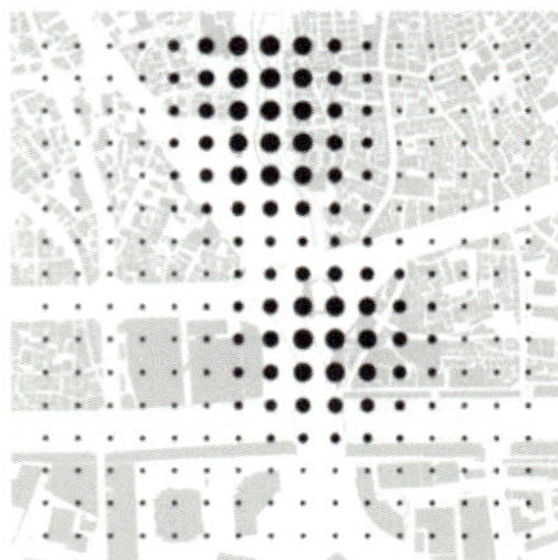

Historical values
Dongdaemun Gate and City Wall

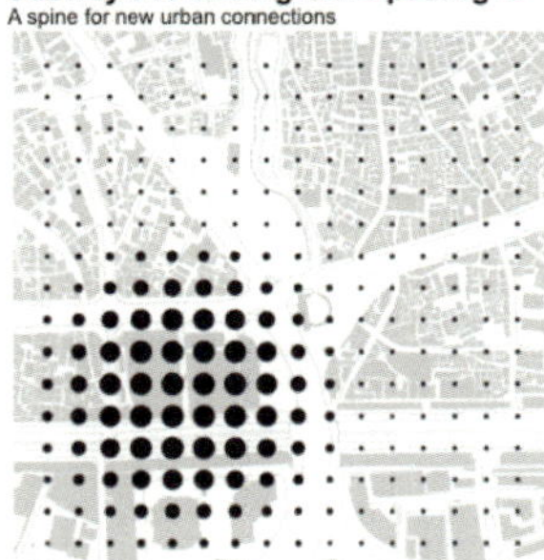

Market area
Dongdaemun Market, a valuable urban element

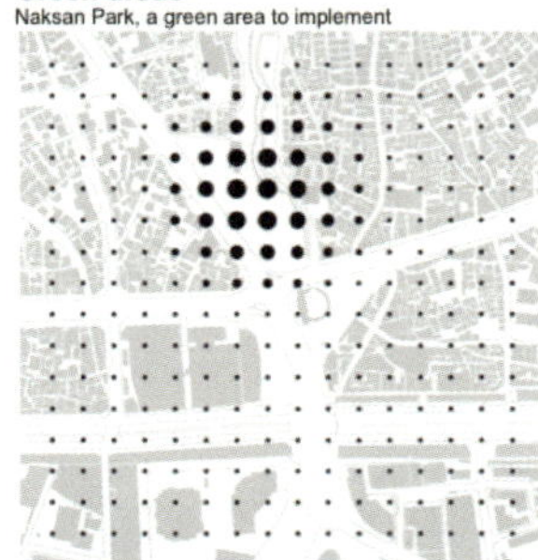

Cultural values
Seoul City Wall Museum and Design Foundation

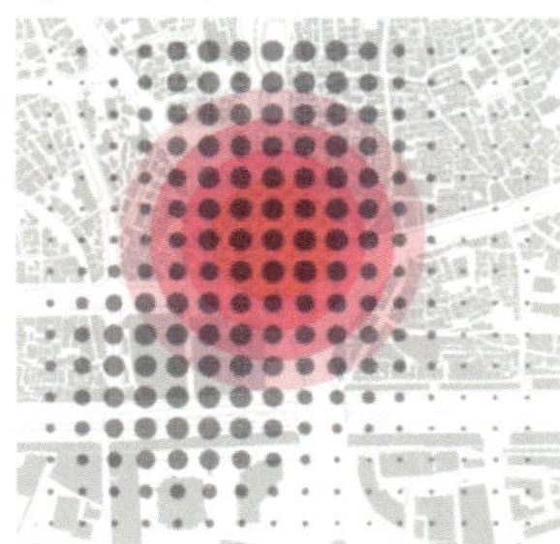

Multi-layer centrality
A new multi-layer space for a participatory life

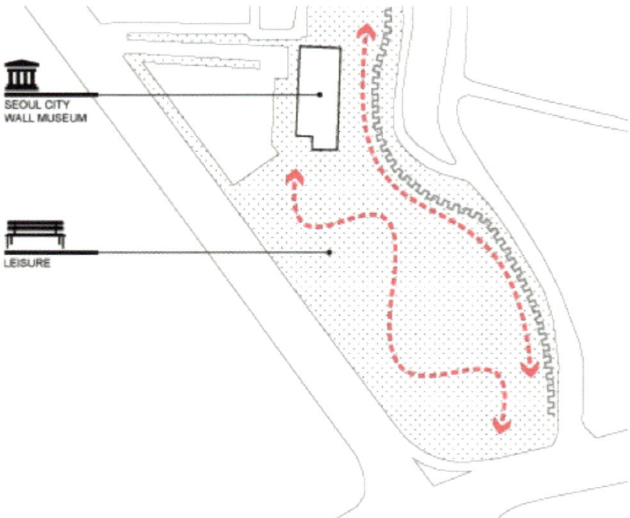

Park level - actual

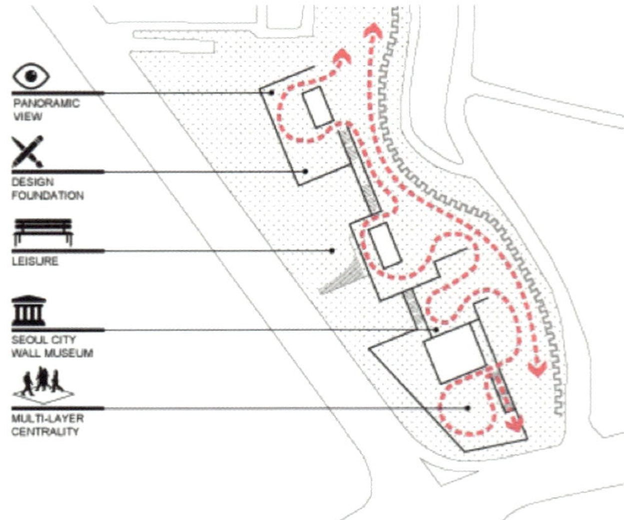

Park level - project

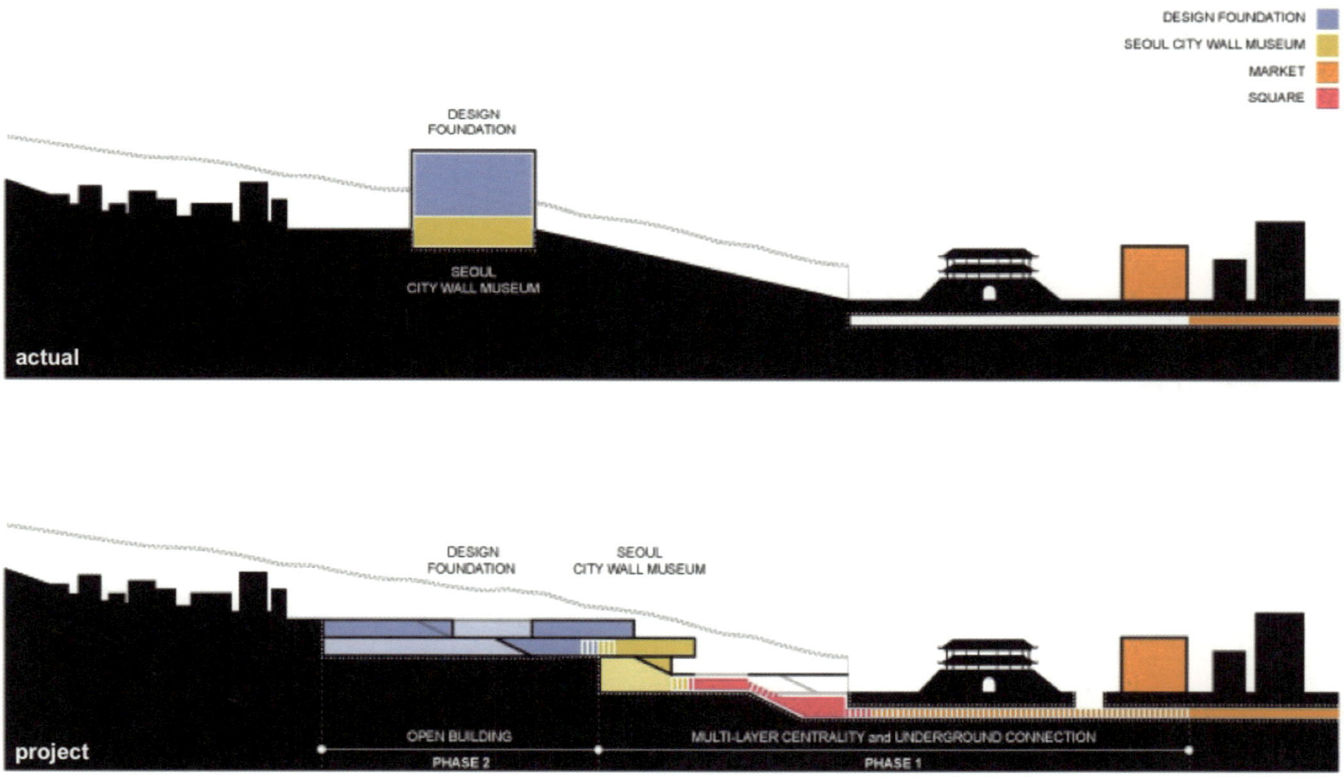

Functions as a continuum

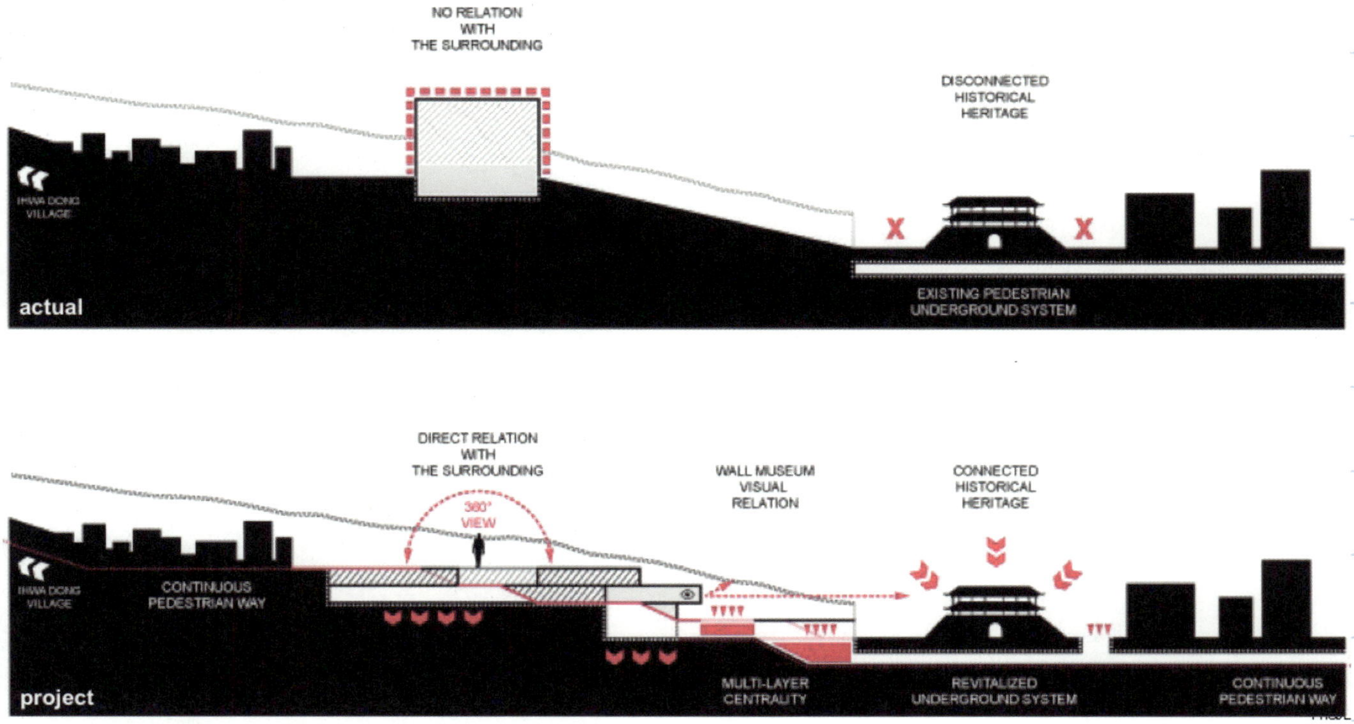

Urban re-activation

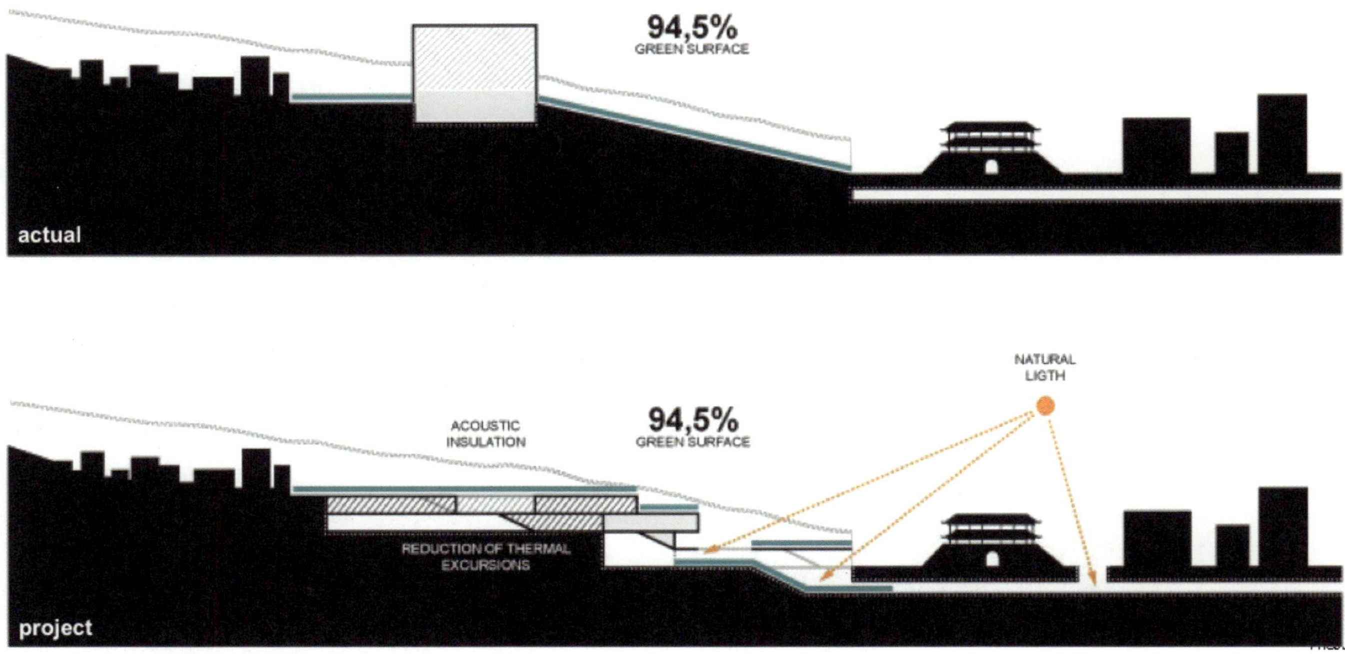

Urban green preservation

GROUND LEVEL

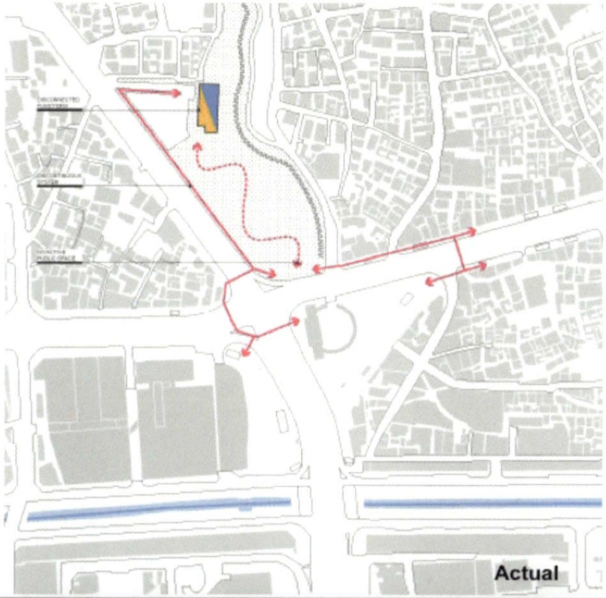

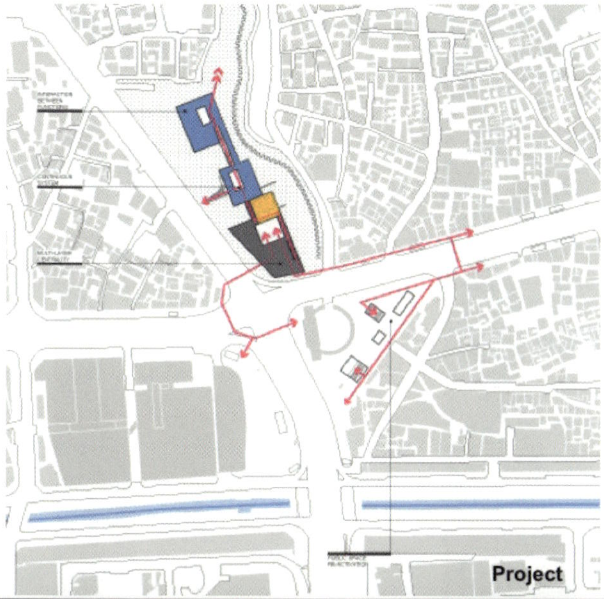

UNDERGROUND LEVEL

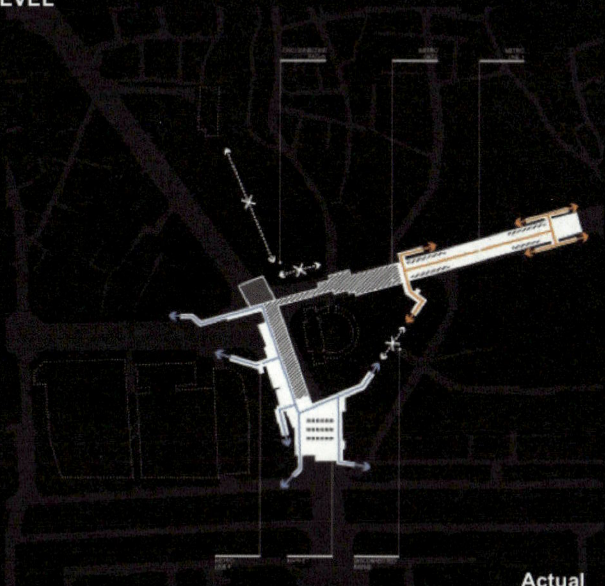

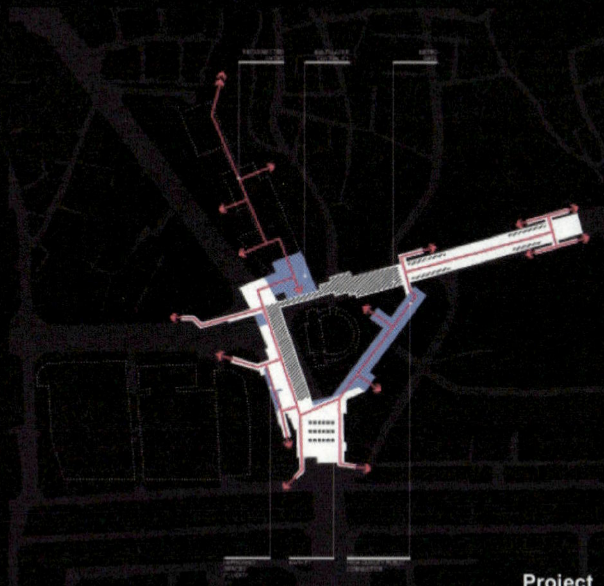

Functions and levels

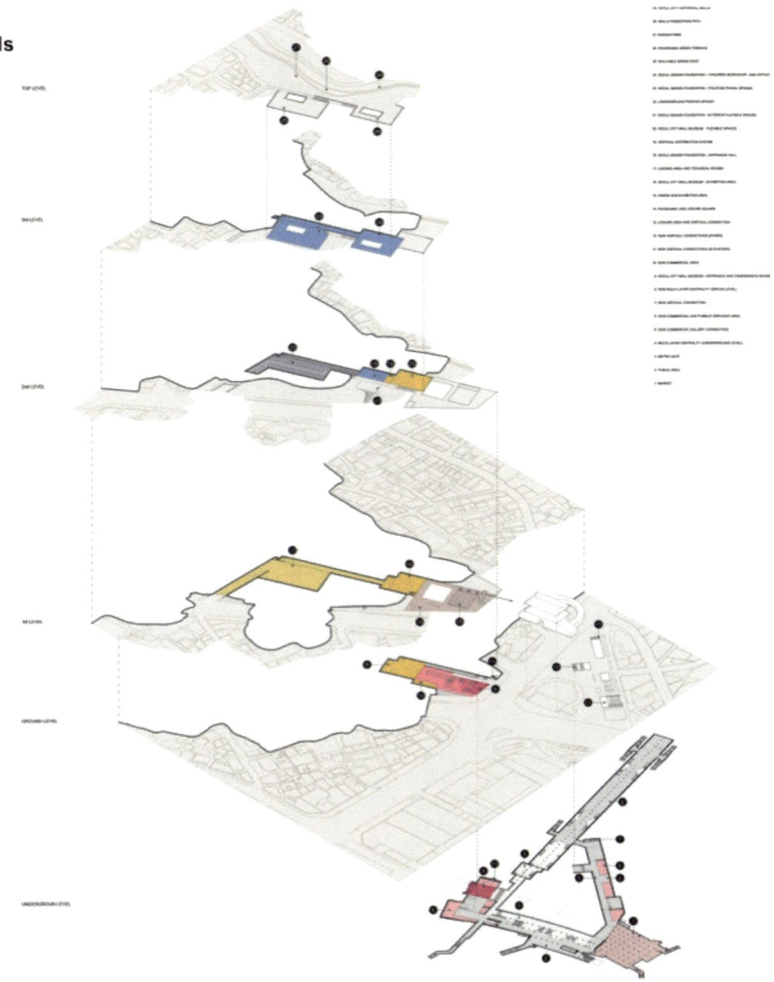

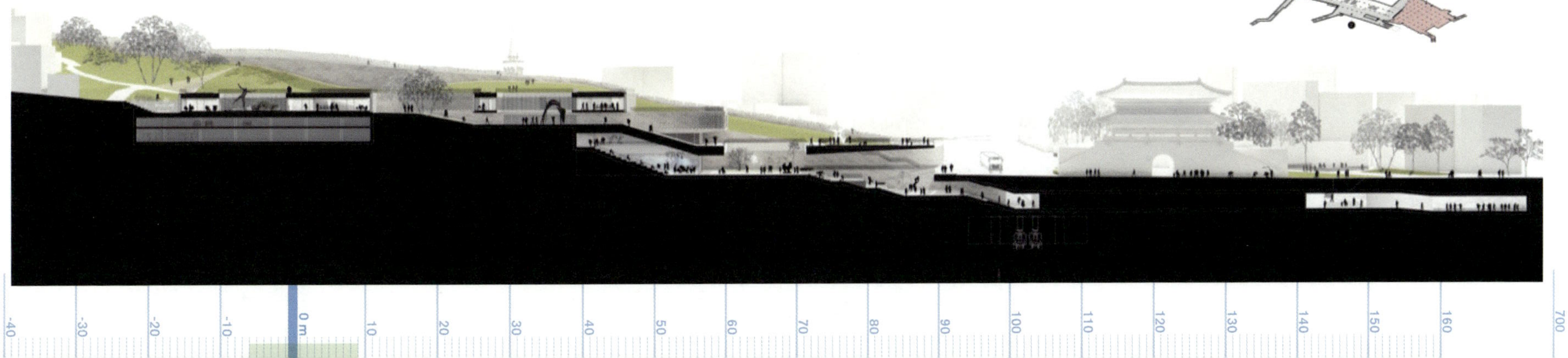

Seoul Metro
동대문역
한양도성박물관
Seoul City Wall Museum

한양도성박물관
Seoul City Wall Museum
SEOUL

한양도성박물관

700
160
150
140
130
120
110
100
90
80
70
60
50
40
30
20
10
0 m
-10
-20
-30
-40

베셀즈

총면적 1만 6,732㎡의 훈련원 공원은 을지로 일대의 밀집된 도시조직 내에 거의 유일하게 비워진 공간이다. 상당히 넓은 면적의 땅이 건축 행위 거의 없이 남아 있는 이유는 역사적으로 공공건축이 위치했기 때문이다. 조선시대 병사를 양성하는 훈련원[원래 훈련관]이 있던 곳이다. 1392년 현재 동대문디자인 플라자 인근에 조성되었다가, 1466년에 지금의 장소로 이전되었다고 한다. 일본에 의한 주권 피탈의 과정 중 대한제국의 군대가 해산되면서, 1907년 군사기관의 역할을 다하게 된다.
그 후 경성사범학교, 서울대학교 사범대학, 헌법재판소, 시설관리공단의 주차장 등이 차례로 이 터를 차지하다가 1997년 공원으로 바뀌었다. 기존의 주차장은 지하로 옮겨서 유지하되, 지상에는 녹지와 식생, 운동시설 등이 자리하고 있다.
이 공영주차장은 주로 동대문시장 일대의 소상공인과 패션업계의 종사자들을 위한 도시의 인프라[infrastructure]로 작용하고 있으며, 주변에 관광호텔이 들어서면서 관광버스의 주차장으로도 활용되고 있다.
5개 층의 주차장 중 지하 1~2층은 2006년 '서울패션벤쳐타운'이라고 하는 메이킹 스페이스(making space)로 전환되었으며, 지하 3~5층만이 주차장으로 유지되고 있다. 서울패션벤쳐타운의 지하 1층은 두 개의 다리를 통해서 을지로 지하상가로 연결되어 있다.

Vessels

The Hullyeonwon Park, with a total area of 16,732 m², is the only space left empty within the dense urban fabric of the Euljiro area. This considerably large area of land still remains undeveloped due to the historical presence of public facilities. There used be a military training center of the Joseon Dynasty called "Hullyeonwon" (orignially called "Hullyeonkwan"). Before, it had been built near the site of the Dongdaemun Design Plaza in 1392 and then was moved to the present site in 1466.
It was decommissioned as a military institute in 1907 during the process of colonization by Japan, as the armies of the Korean Empire were dissolved. After that, the site was occupied by the Kyungsung Normal School, Seoul National University's College of Education, the Constitutional Court, a parking lot of Seoul Facilities Corporation in turn, and finally became a public park in 1997. The previous parking lot went underground, and now the ground is covered by multiple green spaces, vegetation and sports facilities.
This public parking lot serves as the infrastructure of the city for small business owners and fashion industry workers mainly in the Dongdaemun Market, as well as for tour buses that utilize new tourist hotels nearby. The first and second levels of the five-floor basement car parking were transformed into a 'making space' called the "Seoul Fashion Venture Town" in 2006, leaving from the third to fifth levels as the only underground parking.

SoA는 2010년 서울에서 설립되어 도시와 건축의 사회적인 조건에 대한 분석을 통해 다양한 스케일의 구축환경에 관한 작업을 진행하는 젊은 건축가 그룹이다. 현대적인 삶에 대한 이해를 바탕으로 그것이 더욱 풍요로와질 수 있는 건축의 새로운 가능성을 믿고 추구한다. 오송 바이오밸리 마스터플랜 국제공모(2011), 부산 중앙광장 국제 공모(2010) 등에 입상하였고, 우포 자연도서관(2013), 남가좌동 공유주택 The Rabbit (2015), 성평등도서관(2015)을 통해 2015년 문화체육관광부와 새건축사협의회가 주최하는 '젊은 건축가상'을 수상하였다. 2015년 현대카드와 뉴욕현대미술관(MOMA) 국립현대미술관(MMCA)이 주관하는 '젊은 건축가 프로그램'(YAP)의 우승자로 선정되었으며, 당선작 '지붕감각(Roof Sentiment)'을 통해 2016년 ≪아키텍추럴 리뷰(Architectural Review)≫가 주관하는 Emerging Architecture Award의 파이널리스트로 선정되었다. 같은 해에 제주도의 '생각이섬' 프로젝트로 김수근문화재단이 주최하는 김수근건축상 프리뷰상을 수상하였다.

SoA, established in Seoul in 2010, is a group of young architects working on built environments of various scale through analysis of the social conditions of urbanism and architecture. Based on understandings of modern life, SoA believes and seeks the potential of architecture to improve it. SoA won the Korean Young Architects Award hosted by the Ministry of Culture, Sports and Tourism and Korea Architects Institute in 2015 for Upo Museum of Nature (2013), Namgajwadong the Rabbit Share House (2015), and the Gender Equality Library (2015). They won the grand prize of 'Young Architect Prize (YAP)' in 2015 hosted by Hyundai Card, MOMA, and MMCA. SoA also won the Preview Prize of Kim Swoo Gweun Architectural Award sponsored by Kim Swoo Geun Foundation for 'Sayou: Living And Thinking In Architecture' in the same year.

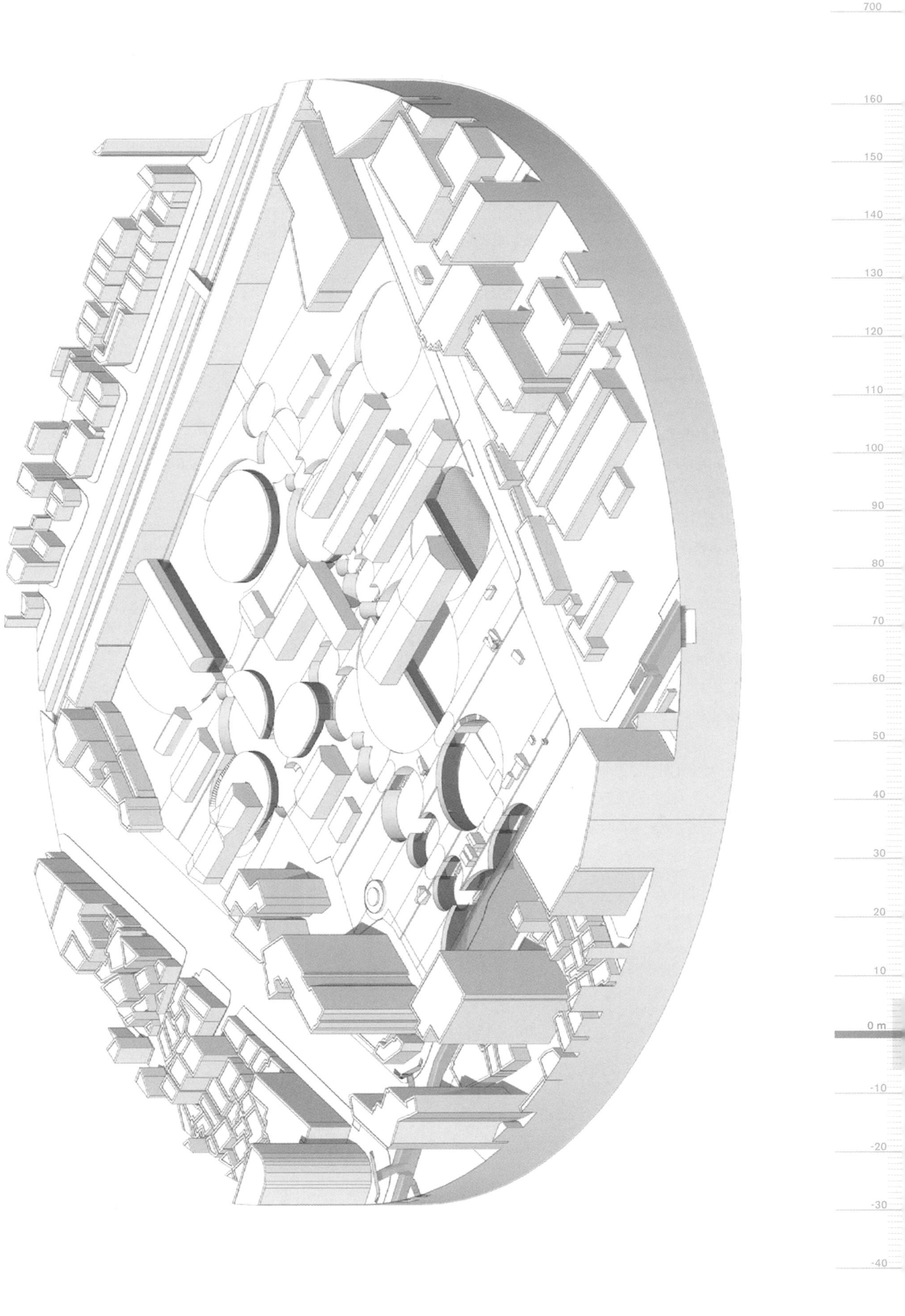
700
160
150
140
130
120
110
100
90
80
70
60
50
40
30
20
10
0 m
-10
-20
-30
-40

본 제안은 훈련원공원 하부의 지하시설물을 도시적 연결을 위한 입체적 매개요소로 재구성하는 프로젝트이다. 이를 위해서 광화문에서 동대문까지 3.3km에 이르는 을지로 지하공간에 인접한 땅 중에서 세운상가를 제외하고 유일하게 을지로와 청계천을 엮을 수 있는 이 땅의 잠재력을 높이는 데 집중한다.

디자인의 방향은 다음과 같다.

첫째, 훈련원 공원 지하를 도시 내 면적인 요소로 바꿔준다. 훈련원 공원은 을지로 지하공간과 약 170m 정도 연접하고 있다. 남쪽의 대지 전체가 지하공간과 맞닿은 것이지만, 두 개의 다리로만 제한적으로 연결되어 있다. 을지로 지하공간과 사이트 사이의 전면적인 개방을 통한 다각적인 연계 방식을 모색한다.
둘째, 훈련원 공원과 공원의 지하를 시각적/물리적으로 연결할 수 있도록 한다. 제한적인 수직 동선 외에는 감춰진 공원지하 공간을 지상으로 드러냄으로써, 을지로 지하상가, 미 극동공병단 부지, 평화제일 시장 등 부지 주변의 주요 장소의 맥락에 닿게 한다. 훈련원 공원을 평범한 근린공원이 아닌 도시적 프로그램과 연결된 적극적인 공공공간으로 활용한다.
셋째, 훈련원 공원과 유사한 역사와 성격을 가진 북쪽의 미 육군 극동공병단 부지까지 대지의 연속으로 파악한다. 미 육군 극동공병단 부지는 약 4만2614㎡로, 미군부대가 평택으로 이전하면서 국고로 반환된 땅이다. 이로써 서울역부터 동대문까지 지하의 수평적 연결과 을지로에서 평화시장까지 지상의 수직적 연결이 가능해진다.
넷째, 훈련원공원과 미 육군 극동공병단 부지를 하나의 대지로 고려하여, 을지로에서 청계천까지 약 300m 되는 거리를 지하공간부터 지상공간까지 점차적으로 연결하도록 한다. 청계천이라는 서울의 지상 수평축을 을지로 지하상가라고 하는 지하의 수평축으로 자연스럽게 연결되도록 한다.
다섯째, 청계천 변에 있는 평화시장과 훈련원 하부의 의류 제조 공간(서울패션벤쳐타운)을 엮어줌으로써, 생산과 소비의 공간을 연속하게 한다.

The first basement level of the Seoul Fashion Venture Town is connected to the Euljiro Underground Mall through two bridges.

Our project proposes to reorganize underground facilities in the lower part of the Hullyeonwon Park as a three-dimensional mediator of urban connection. To do this, we focus on increasing the potentiality of this site, which indeed provides the last opportunity except for the Sewoon Plaza to connect the Euljiro area and the Cheonggyecheon while being adjacent to the Euljiro underground space of 3.3km from Gwanghwamun to Dongdaemun.

The direction of the design is as follows.

First, the underground space of the Hullyeonwon Park is turned into the city's surface element. The Hullyeonwon Park runs tangent for about 170meters with the Euljiro underground space, with which the whole southern side of the park is in contact but in fact connected by only two bridges. We seek various ways of linking by fully opening up the site unto the Euljiro underground space.

Second, we intend to connect the park with its underground space both visually and physically. Except for the restricted vertical circulation spaces, the underground spaces will be actively brought up to ground and connected to the context of other major sites around our site, such as the Euljiro Underground Shopping Center, the US Army Corps of Engineers Far East District, and the Pyunghwa Market. The park will serve as an active public space that connects with urban programs rather than stay an ordinary neighborhood park.

Third, the Hullyeonwon Park can be seen as continuing to the site of the US Army Corps of Engineers Far East District, which shares similar history and character as the park. The US Army Corps of Engineers Far East District of 46,614m^2 has been returned to the Korea Governmentwhen the US base moved to Pyeongtaek. This makes possible the horizontal connections of the underground spaces from the Seoul Station to the Dongdaemun area and the vertical linking of the ground areas from the Euljiro to the Pyunghwa Market.

Fourth, by considering the park and the military base as a single site, we gradually connect the underground and the overground along the 300 meter street from the Euljiro to the Cheonggyecheon. We will make a natural connection between the Cheonggyecheon, the horizontal axis on the ground of Seoul, with the Euljiro Underground Shopping Center, the horizontal axis of the underground.

Fifth, the combination of the Pyunghwa Market, which is adjacent to the Cheonggyecheon, with the Seoul Fashion Venture Town, which is the clothing manufacturing workshop under the park, will hold the spaces of production and consumption together.

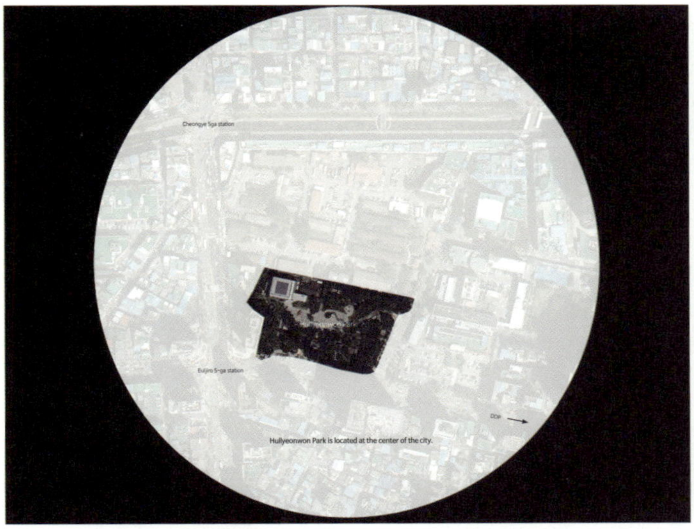
Cheongye 5ga station
Euljiro 5-ga station
DDP
Hullyeonwon Park is located at the center of the city.

Pyeonghwa fashion market

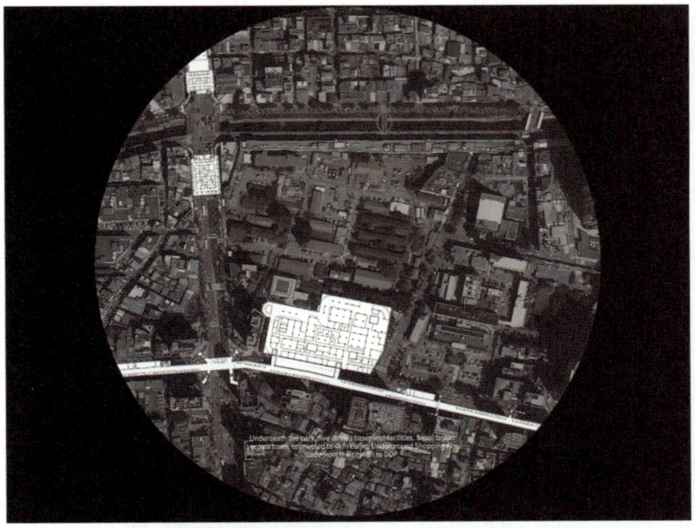
Underneath the park, five stories basement facilities.

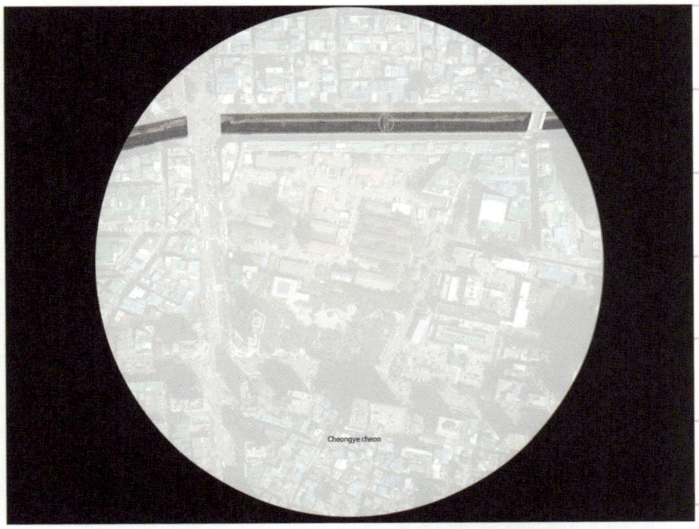
Cheongye cheon

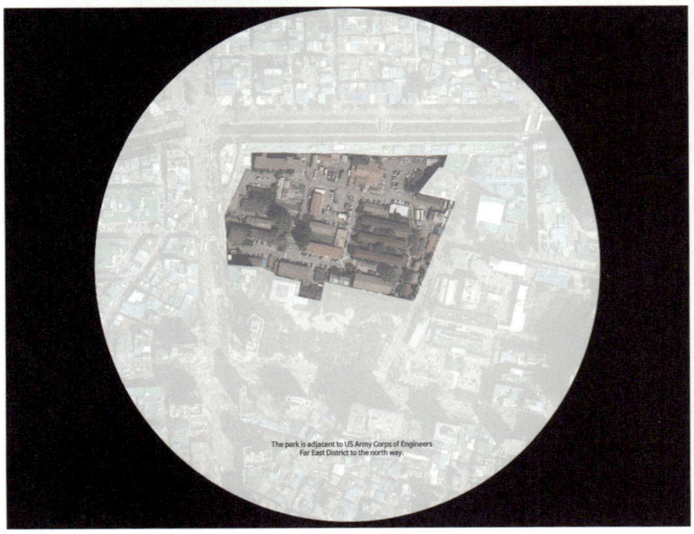
The park is adjacent to US Army Corps of Engineers
Far East District to the north way.

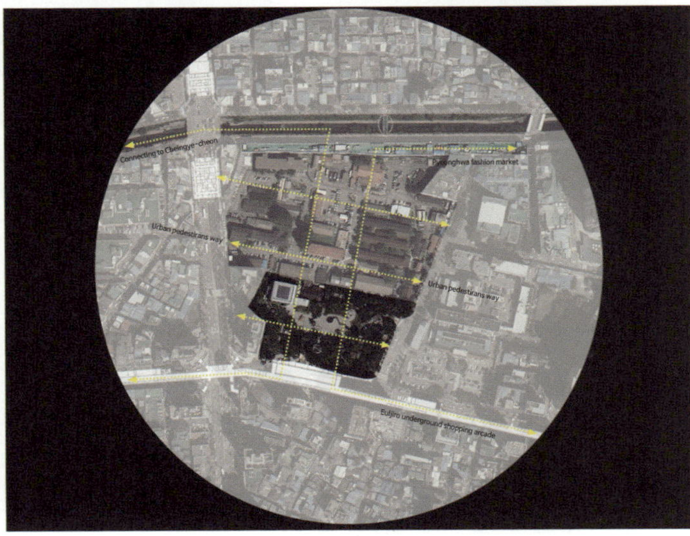
Connecting to Cheongye-cheon
Pyeonghwa fashion market
Urban pedestrians way
Urban pedestrians way
Euljiro underground shopping arcade

마지막은 이 제안의 목적이기도 하다.

훈련원 공원 지하 1~2층에 있는 '서울패션벤처타운'은 동대문 일대의 패션 산업 네트워크의 일부이지만, 물리적인 연계는 떨어진다. 기존의 공영주차장의 공간 조직을 그대로 둔 채 '서울패션벤처타운'으로 일차원적으로 전환했기 때문이다.

하지만 훈련원 공원은 북쪽으로 평화시장까지 확장이 가능한 곳으로, 생산과 소비, 지하와 지상의 입체적인 결절이 가능한 땅이다. 이 제안은 지하에 묻혀 있는 생산 플랫폼을 기획과 소비의 네트워크와 연결시키는 것이다. 근 미래에 비워질 미 공병단의 건물들을 활용하여 기획과 디자인의 스튜디오가 입주함으로써 지하의 생산 공간을 지원하도록 하고, 이 협업의 결과물이 평화시장과 을지로 지하상가에서 소비되도록 유도하는 것이 이 프로젝트의 목적이다.

The last is also the goal of this proposal.

The "Seoul Fashion Venture Town" located on the first and second basement levels of the park is part of the fashion industry network of the Dongdaemun area, though in poor physical connection. Such separation is due to hasty and one-dimensional conversion of the existing public parking lot into the "Seoul Fashion Venture Town" without changing any of the spatial organization.However, the Hullyeonwon Park can indeed expand to the Pyunghwa Market to the north, which can potentially become the three-dimensional hub of production and consumption and underground and overground. Our proposal is to connect the underground production platform to the network of planning and consumption. The project aims to support the underground production space by repopulating the previous buildings of the US Army Corps of Engineers Far East District as planning and design studios, and to promote the result of this collaboration to be consumed in the Pyunghwa Market and the Euljiro Underground Shopping Center.

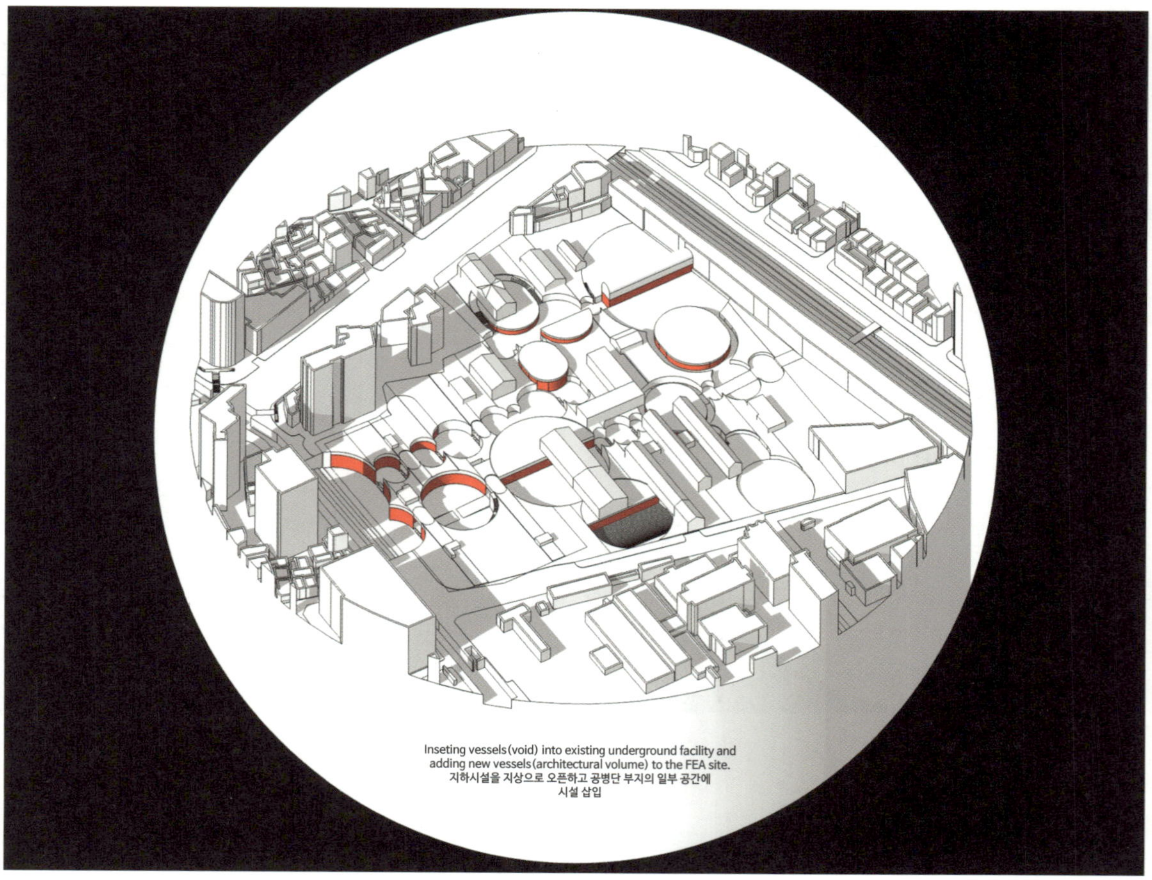

Inseting vessels(void) into existing underground facility and adding new vessels(architectural volume) to the FEA site.
지하시설을 지상으로 오픈하고 공병단 부지의 일부 공간에 시설 삽입

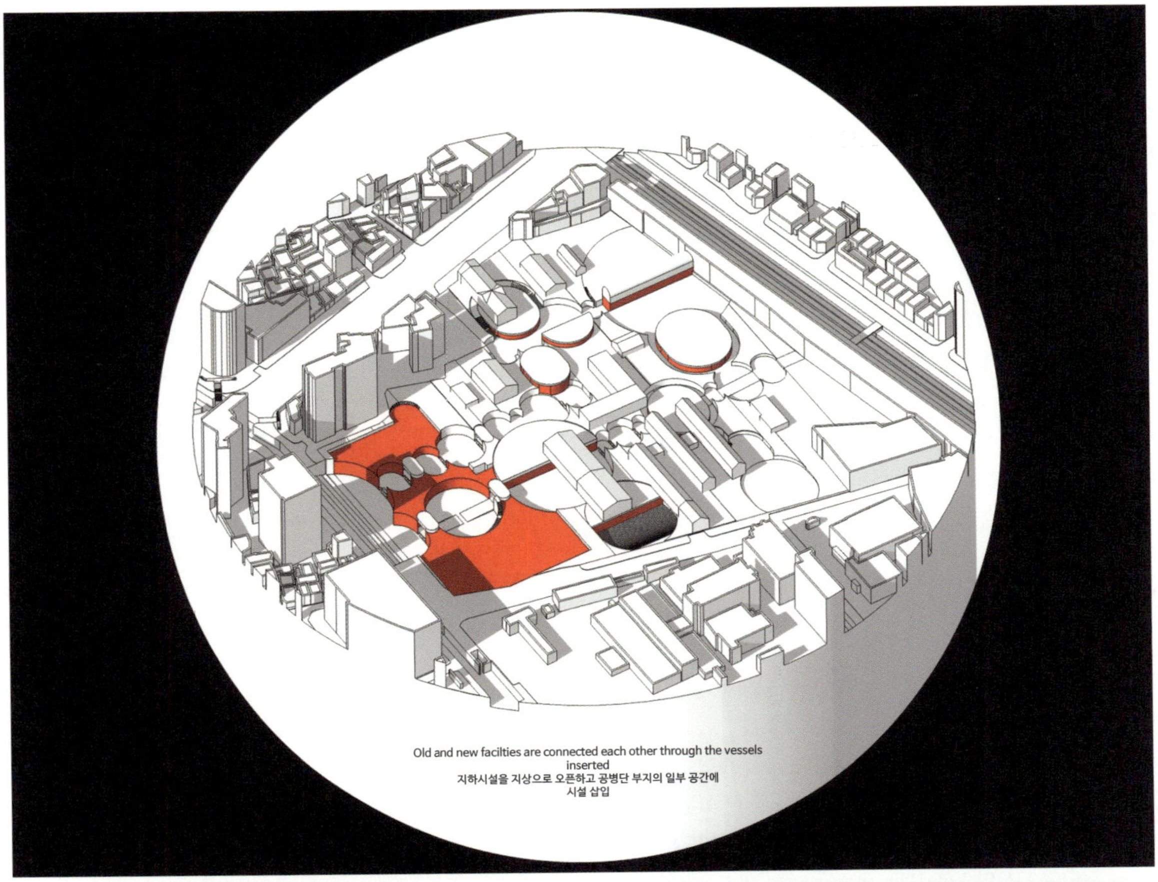

Old and new facilties are connected each other through the vessels inserted
지하시설을 지상으로 오픈하고 공병단 부지의 일부 공간에
시설 삽입

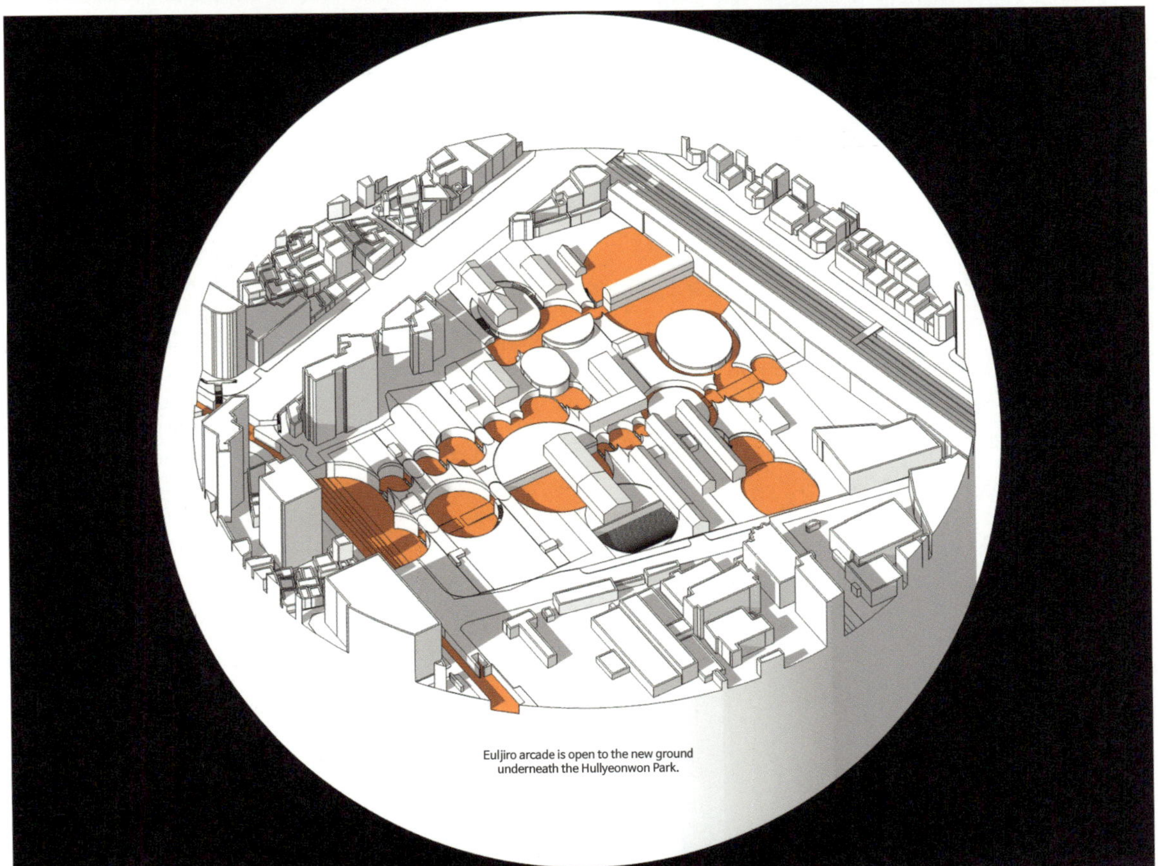

Euljiro arcade is open to the new ground underneath the Hullyeonwon Park.

Vessel

'용기 형태의 비워진 공간[Void-Vessel]'을 대지에 수직적으로 삽입함으로써, 160m x 87m의 크기의 지하 공간을 내외부가 상호작용하는 도시적인 맥락 안으로 끌어들인다. 이때 비워내는 공간은 지하 1층~3층까지 그 깊이가 다양하며, 지하에 수직적인 아트리움의 기능을 하게 된다. 특히 을지로 지하상가에 면해있는 부분은 약 20m와 40m 되는 반원형의 외부 아트리움을 형성함으로써, 지하에서 훈련원 땅을 입면으로 드러내게 한다.
주차장의 단위 모듈을 경계로 남북방향으로 연속 병치되는 Void-Vessel은 을지로와 청계천을 연결하는 흐름을 만든다.
Void-Vessel은 기존의 지하 시설과 다양한 방식의 단면적 관계를 만들어내며 점진적으로 남과 북의 지하-지상을 연결한다. 즉 을지로 지하상가에서 시작된 지하 3층 깊이의 바닥으로부터 공병단 부지를 지나 평화시장, 청계천에 이르는 다양한 레벨의 수직적 외부 공간이 연속되도록 한다.
이는 또한 다양한 크기로 병치되면서 기존 지하시설의 8.4m x 8.4m 모듈이 가진 경직된 레이아웃에 균열을 내며 서로 다른 스케일의 감각과 공간적인 표정을 만들어낸다.
지하가 있는 훈련원 부지에서는 서로 다른 크기의 Vessel이 겹쳐지면서 Vessel의 수평적인 확장이 일어난다. 이때 한쪽의 Vessel은 Void-Vessel이며, 다른 쪽은 건축-Vessel 타입이다.
건축-Vessel 타입은 지상의 공원 프로그램을 수용하거나 필요한 또 다른 공공 프로그램이 들어가는 곳이다. 기존의 공원 시설들이 이곳에 수용됨으로써, 공원은 자연스럽게 지하로 연결되게 된다.
미 극동 공병단 부지에서는 Void-Vessel은 기존의 병영 건물들과 연계가 된다. 부지 내에 있던 기존 건물을 통해서, 지하로 내려갈 수 있는 구조를 만드는 것이다. 또한 지하의 굴착으로 인해 필요한 보강 구조를 Void-Vessel이 수행하게 된다. 이곳은 기획자나 디자이너의 워크숍으로 상정했다. 이로써 생산과 소비를 중재하는 동선을 형성하게 된다.
베셀즈(Vessels)는 기존의 지하시설이 가지고 있는 폐쇄적인 구조에 단순한 조작을 더함으로써 좁고 긴 지하상가, 빛이 들지 않는 지하 업무공간의 공간 경험을 재구성하는 것을 넘어, 도시의 중요한 장소와 시설이 상호 확장되도록 하는 효과를 갖게 될 것이다.

Vessel

'Void-Vessel' that is vertically inserted into the ground will invite a 160m x 87m underground space into the flexible and interactive urban context. Here, the depth of the space to be emptied varies from the first to the third basement levels, which will function as a vertical atrium in the basement. Especially, the part facing the Euljiro Underground Shopping Center will make a semicircular outdoor atrium of about 20 meters and 40 meters, exposing the elevation of the park site in the basement.

The Void-Vessels juxtaposed in the north-south direction against the boundary of the unit modules of the parking lot create connective flows between theEuljiro and the Cheonggyecheon. They create various cross-sectional relationships with existing underground facilities, gradually connecting the underground and the overground from the north to the south. In other words, they will connect the vertical outer spaces of various levels ranging from the third basement level of the Euljiro Underground Plaza to the US military Base, the Pyunghwa Market, and the Cheonggyecheon.

Juxtaposed in various sizes, they will make cracks in the rigid layout of the existing 8.4m x 8.4m modules of the existing underground facilities, creating a variety of spatial effects and a senseof different scales.

At the site of the Hullyeonwon Park with its underground space, vessels expand horizontally due to the overlapping vessels of different sizes. Here, one part of Vessel is made of the Void-Vessel and the other is an Architecture-Vessel type. The Architecture-Vessel type accommodates the programs of the park on the ground and other public programs. Accommodating existing park facilities in the Architecture-Vessel, it naturally connects the park to the underground.

The Void-Vessel is linked to the existing barrackson the site of the military base. A structure leading to the basement is made possible by the existing building on the site. Void-Vessel also plays the role of reinforcement structure necessary to excavation work. This is planned as workshops for promoters and designers. This will form the intervening circulation that mediates the production and consumption.

The Vessels will make the city's important places and facilities expand interactively as well as restructure the experiences of long and narrow underground shopping malls and underground working spaces through simple manipulations of the closed structures of the existing underground facilities.

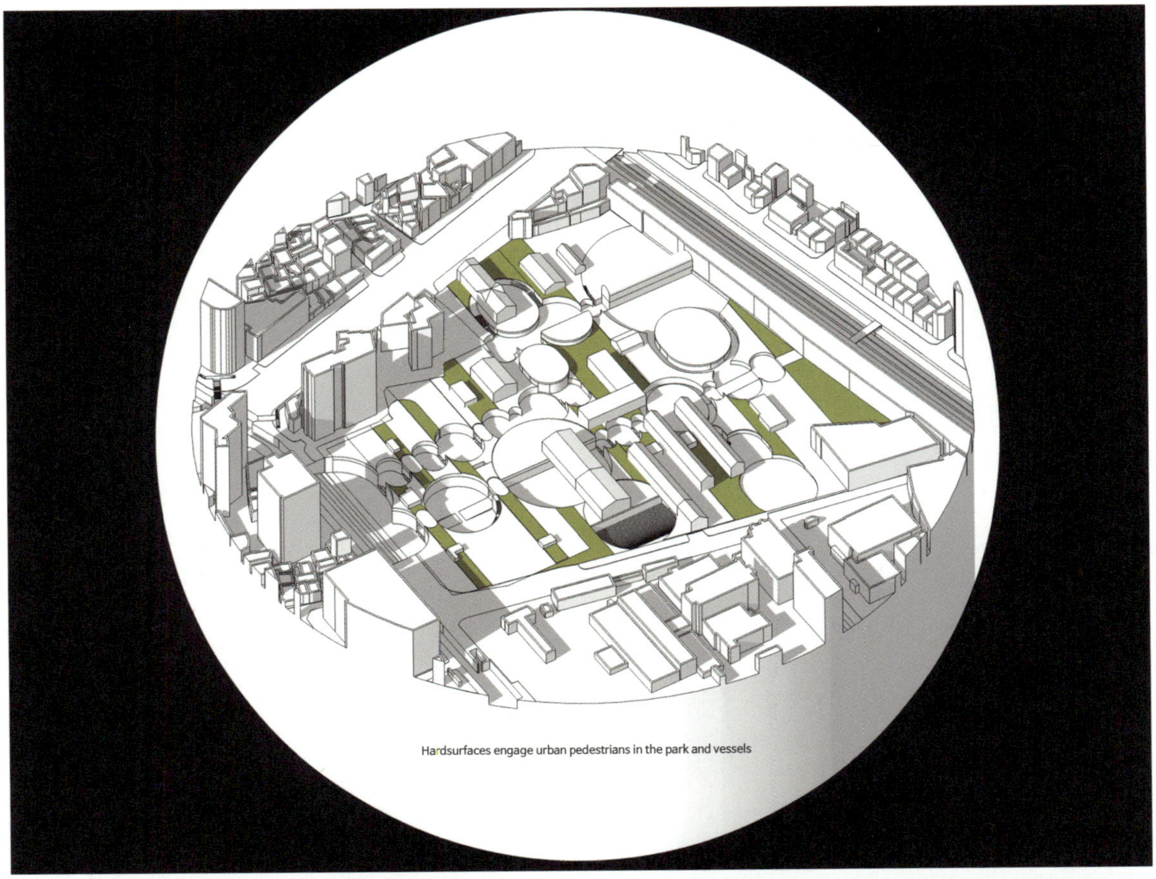

Hardsurfaces engage urban pedestrians in the park and vessels

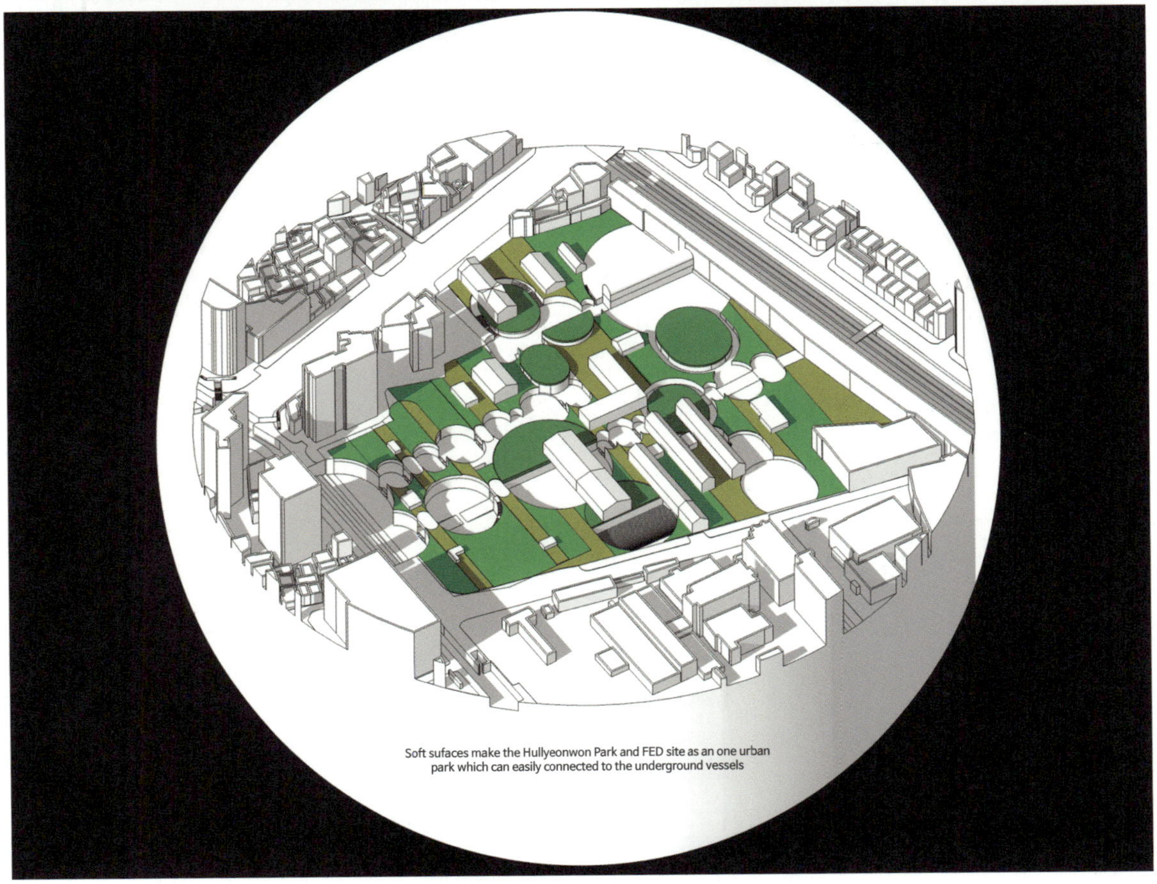

Soft sufaces make the Hullyeonwon Park and FED site as an one urban park which can easily connected to the underground vessels

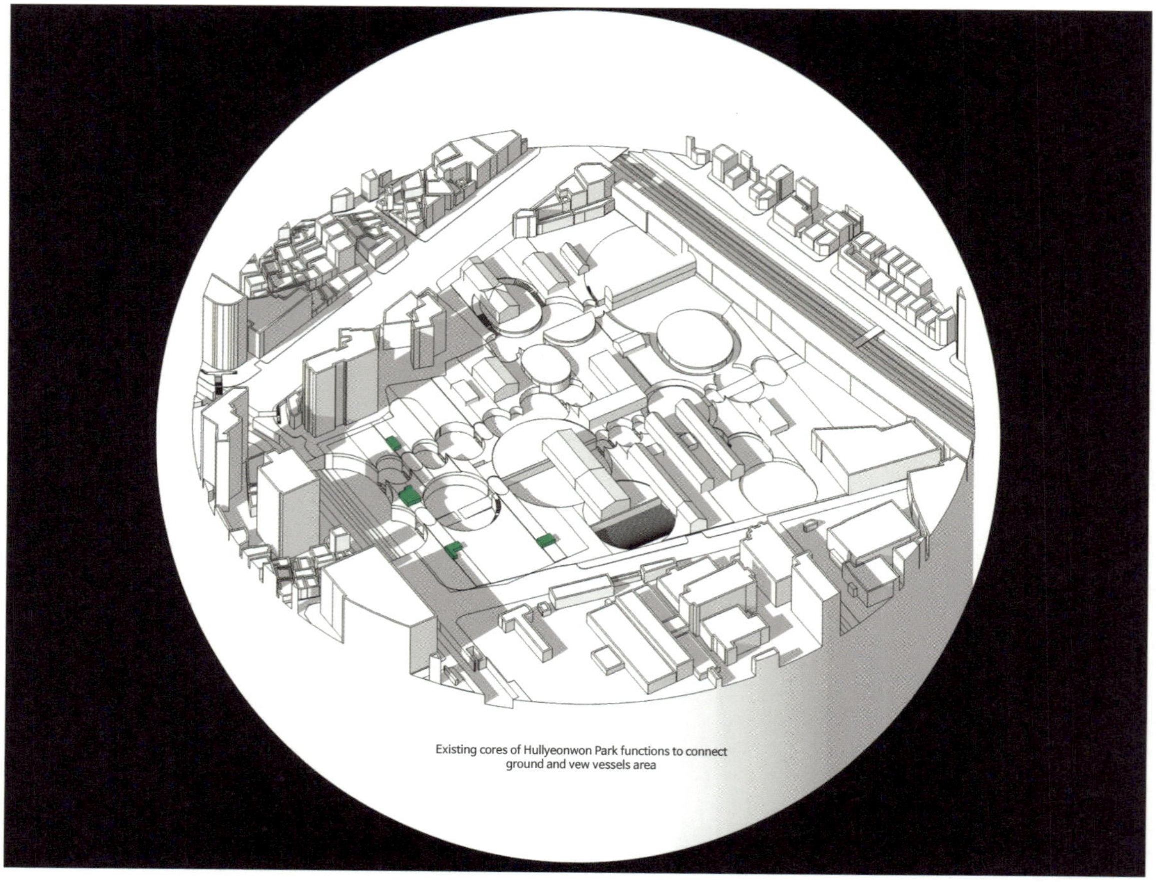

Existing cores of Hullyeonwon Park functions to connect ground and vew vessels area

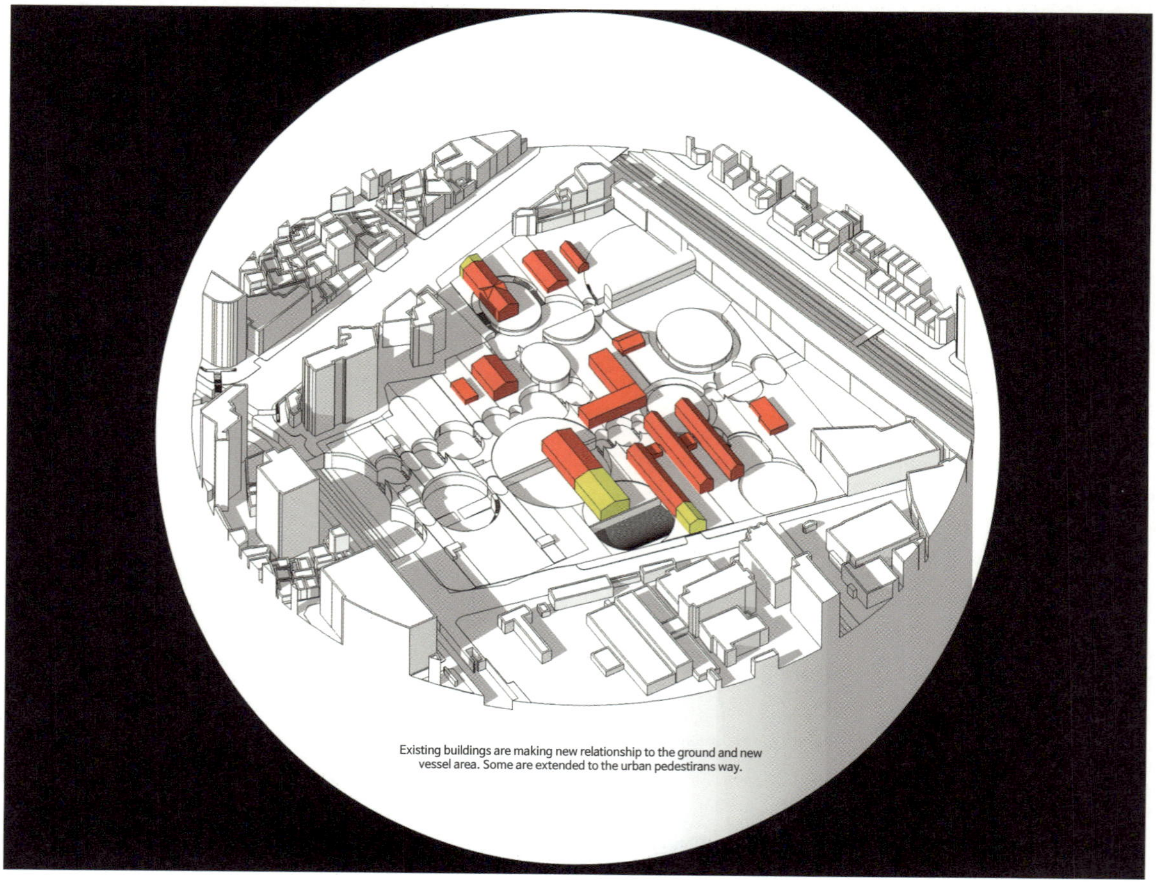

Existing buildings are making new relationship to the ground and new vessel area. Some are extended to the urban pedestirans way.

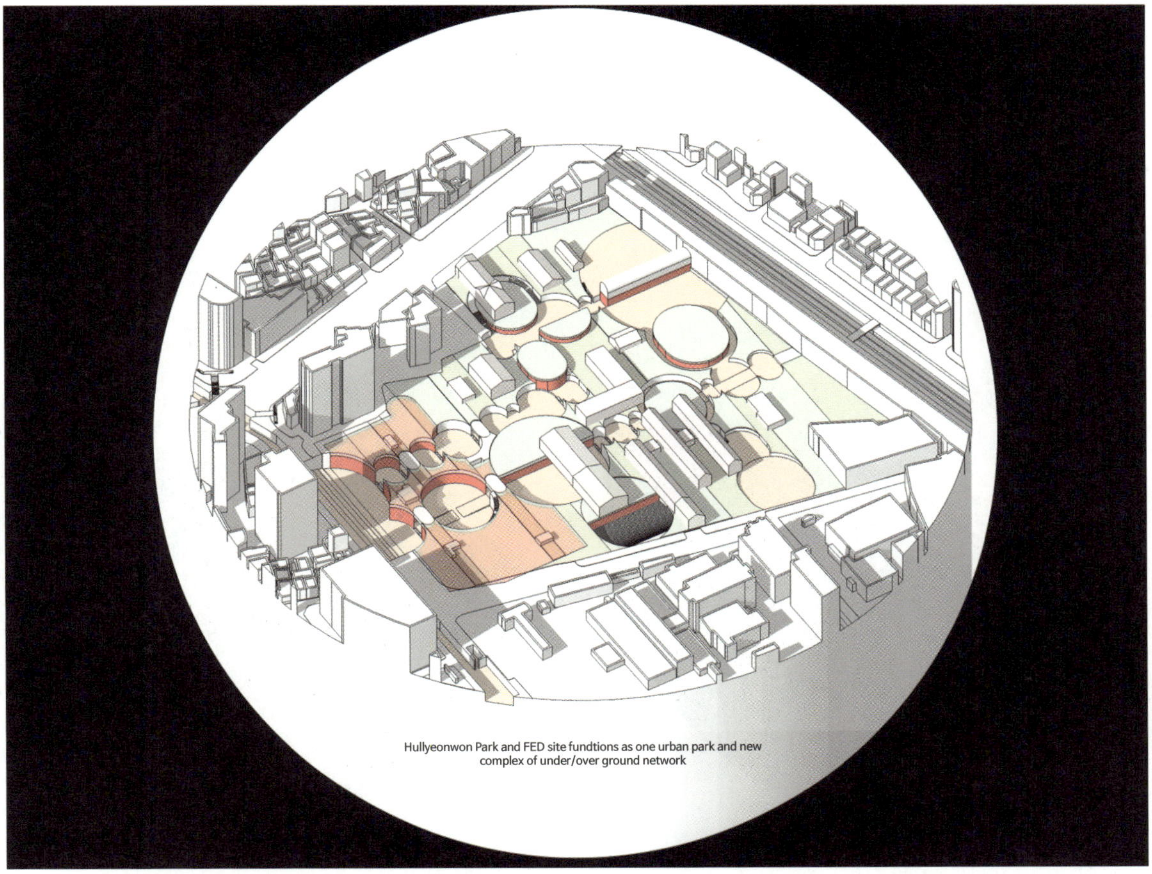

Hullyeonwon Park and FED site fundtions as one urban park and new complex of under/over ground network

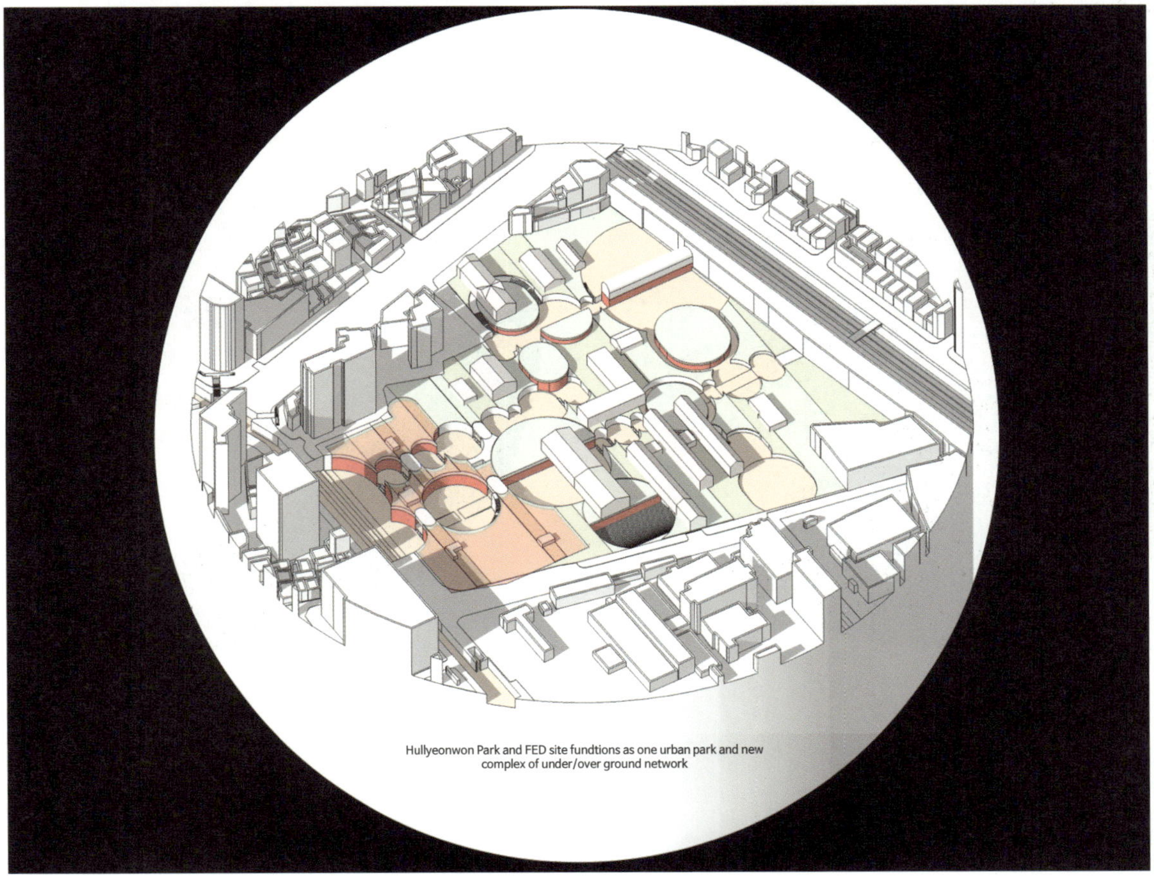

Hullyeonwon Park and FED site fundtions as one urban park and new complex of under/over ground network

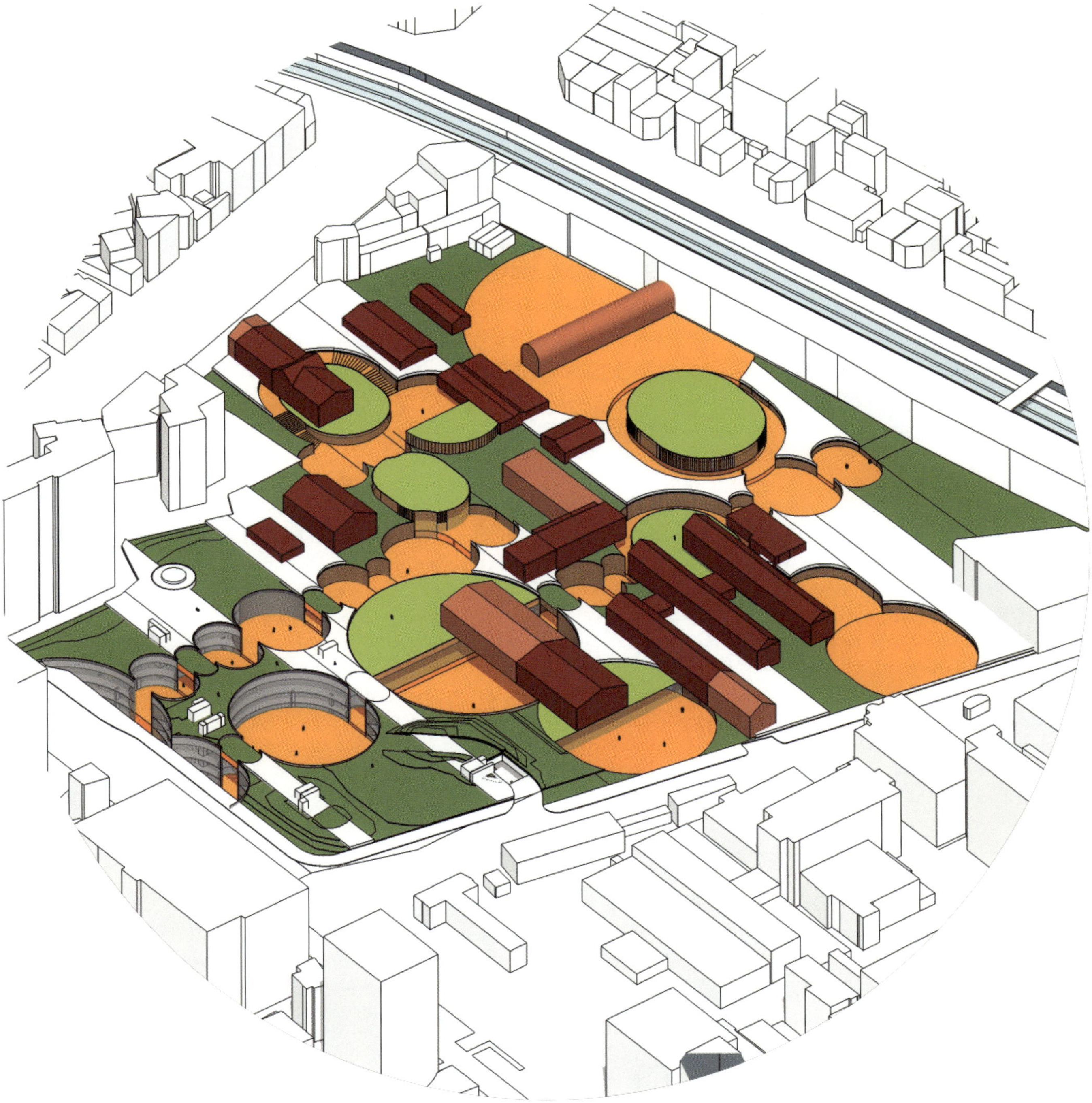

700
160
150
140
130
120
110
100
90
80
70
60
50
40
30
20
10
0 m
-10
-20
-30
-40

김택빈+장용순

Taekbin Kim + Yong-Soon Chang

지형과 역사의 위상적 뜨개질

1. 지형의 복원
이 대지는 과거부터 있었던 자연 지형이 일제 강점기에 도로 건설을 통해서 파헤쳐지고 훼손되었으며 성곽은 끊어져 버린 단절의 역사를 담고 있다.
우리는 파헤쳐진 지형과 끊어진 성곽을 복원하고 지형의 연속적인 흐름을 회복하려 한다 두 개의 인공대지의 평평한 부분은 새로 삽입되는 기준면이 되어서 다양한 레벨로 지상과 지하를 가로지르면서 끊어진 동선들을 연결한다.
삼각형의 경사광장은 지형을 연속적으로 연결하고 지형과 도로에 의해서 단절되었던 보행자 동선을 뜨개질하듯이 다시 연결해준다 도로와 성벽에 의해 끊어져 있던 동선들을 데크와 지하공간을 통해서 연결하고 지하에 위치한 선큰 마당과 다양한 시설들은 도시의 여러 레벨과 연결되면서 활력을 제공한다.

2. 성벽의 복원
지형이 단절되고 도로가 들어서면서 서울 성곽은 단절되어 있다. 지형을 복원하는 경사광장을 만들고 그 위에 서울 성곽을 복원하여 기억과 흔적의 연속성을 회복한다.
경사 광장 위에 복원되는 서울 성곽은 형태를

Knitting Topo-history

1— Restoration of terrain
This site contains the history of discontinuities where the natural landscape from the past was destroyed by the construction of the road during the Japanese colonial period. and the rampart broke.
We are restoring the revealed terrain and the cut rampart and trying to restore the continuous flow of the terrain.
The flat part of the two artificial grounds becomes the newly inserted side and connects the circulation across the ground and the underground at various levels. The triangular sloping square continuously connects the terrain and reconnects like a knitting of the pedestrian severed by the topography and road. Connect the circulation that had been cut off by roads and walls through the deck and the underground space, the underground Sunken garden and various facilities are connected with several levels of the city and provide vitality.

2— Restoring the Fortress Wall
The terrain is cut, the road enters and Seoul Fortress Wall is cut off. Make a sloping square to restore the terrain, restore the Seoul Fortress Wall to restore the continuity of memory and traces on it.
Seoul Fortress Wall restored on the sloping square does not reproduce the shape as it is, but restores the Seoul rampart in a figurative way in the form of plates and canopy tilted by 45 degrees.
The tilted plates wall has a different sense of opening depending on the

---

김택빈은 이_스케이프 건축사사무소를 운영하고 있다. 홍익대학교 건축학과와 동 대학원을 졸업하고, 건축, 환경, 경관에 관심을 두고 다양한 작업을 실천하고 있다. 대표작으로는 세운상가 활성화 공공공간 도시재생 국제공모 당선 및 설계, 스킵 퍼즐 하우스, 대진 등대 문화 공간, 남해 전망대 등의 작업이 있으며, 마포 석유 비축기지 국제현상에서 가작을 수상하였다.
장용순은 서울대학교 건축학과를 졸업하고 동 대학원에서 석사학위를 받았다. 파리 베르사이유 건축 대학교를 졸업한 뒤 자크 리포 설계 사무실과 건축사 사무소 기오헌에서 건축 실무를 익히고 프랑스 국가 공인 건축사 (DPLG) 자격을 취득하였다. 파리 8대학 생드니 철학과에서 알랭 바디우의 지도로 철학과 건축, 도시를 아우르는 공부를 하여 「현대 건축과 도시론의 철학적 토대」라는 논문으로 박사 학위를 받았다. 현재 홍익대학교 교수로 설계와 이론을 가르치면서 새로운 건축과 도시, 철학, 영화에 대한 꿈을 꾸고 있다.

Kim Taekbin, President of E_SCape Architects. Graduated from Hongik University and the Graduate School of Architecture. Practicing various tasks with respect to Architecture, Environment and Landscape. Representative works are Winning the international competition for Re-Structuring SeunsanggaCitywalk and completion of the project, Skipped Jigsaw House, Daejin Lighthouse Cultural Facility, Namhae Observatory, and awarded honorable mention for the international competition for Rehabilitating Mapo Oil Depot into a Cultural Depot Park.

Chang Yongsoon, professor of architecture in Hongik University, graduated from Seoul National University, practiced in Atelier d'architecture Jacques Ripault and Kiohun Architect and Associates and earned his PhD with the thesis 'Philosophical Foundations of Contemporary Architecture and Urbanism' supervised by Alain Badiou in the Department of Philosophy of Université Paris-VIII. He wrote 'The Philosophical Adventure of Contemporary Architecture', a work of four volumes, and designed the re-structuring of the SeunsanggaCitywalk project and KB Rockstar Youth Step project.

-40
-30
-20
-10
0 m
10
20
30
40
50
60
70
80
90
100
110
120
130
140
150
160
700

그대로 재현하는 것이 아니라 45도로 기울어진 판들과 캐노피의 형태로 서울 성곽을 은유적 방식으로 복원한다.
기울어진 판들로 벽은 보는 각도에 따라서 개방감이 달라지며 완전히 폐쇄되지도 완전히 개방되지도 않은 현대적 벽이 된다.
은유적 성벽 옆에는 벤치와 보이드가 있어서 벤치에 앉아서 지상을 내려다 볼 수 있고 도로를 지나면서도 인공대지 위에 지나가는 성벽을 느낄 수 있다.

3. 역사의 켜(layer)
이 대지는 여러 시대의 역사의 켜가 중첩되어 있다. 일제강점기, 김유신, 안중근, 김구, 서울성곽, 근대화의 흔적들이 겹쳐져 있다.
우리는 지상과 지하 공간들을 연결하면서 잘 알려지지 않았던 이런 역사를 부각시킬 수 있는 건축적이고 상징적인 장치들을 설치한다.
두 개의 큰 선큰 마당은 고요함 속에서도 역사의 흔적을 느낄 수 있는 공간이다. 선큰 마당에는 김구, 김유신, 서울성곽, 남산 등의 역사를 전시하며 선큰 마당 주변의 지하공간에는 전시실, 세미나실 등이 위치한다. 선큰 마당에서 도시의 여러 방향으로 나갈 수 있다.
인공대지의 하부에는 카페와 휴식공간이 위치하고 카페 내부 지하공간의 넓은 계단을 통해서 선큰 마당으로 접근할 수 있다. 넓은 계단은 공연, 강연, 북카페로 다양하게 활용될 수 있다.
건물은 도시적 가로의 연속성을 살려주면서 지형의 흐름을 따라가면서 배치되며 건물 상부의 데크는 산책로 레벨과 자연스럽게 연결된다.
두 개의 지하공간은 지하에서 서로 연결되고 지상과 밀접하게 연관되어 있어서 평평한 인공대지나 계단을 통해서 도시의 다양한 레벨을 연결한다.
이 제안은 지형과 역사를 복원하면서 과거와 현재, 인공과 자연, 지하와 지상을 가로지르는 3차원적인 입체적 공간을 만드는 작업이다.

angle of viewing, and it becomes a modern wall that is not completely opened even if it is completely closed.
Next to the figurative castle wall there are benches and voids, you can sit on the bench and look down on the ground, you can feel the castle walls passing over the artificial earth while passing through the road.

3. Historical layer
This site contains layers of history of several periods. The Japanese colonial period, Kim Yu-sin, Ahn Jung-geun, Kimgu, Seoul Fortress Wall, traces of modernization overlap.
We will connect a ground and an underground space and install a structurally symbolic device that can emerge such history, which was not well known.
Two big Sunken plazas are spaces where you can feel traces of history, even in silence. In the Sunken, history such as Kim Yu-Sin, Namsan, Kimgu and Seoul Fortress Wall is displayed, and an exhibition room, a seminar room, etc. are located in the underground space around the Sunken garden. You can go to some direction of the city in the Sunken garden.
At the lower part of the artificial land, cafes, Libraries and rest area are arranged, and you can access the Sunken plaza through the stairs which is wide in the underground space inside the cafe. A wide stairs can be utilized diversely in performances, lectures, and book cafe.
Buildings are arranged keeping the continuity of the urban side while keeping track of the topography while the deck at the top of the building is naturally connected with the walking track level.
The underground spaces are linked each other and closely related to the ground to connect various levels of the city through a flat artificial ground or stairs.
This proposal connects two underground spaces that undertake restoration of the topography and history, the past and present, artificial and nature, work to create a three-dimensional system and space traversing the underground and the ground are mutually connected underground.

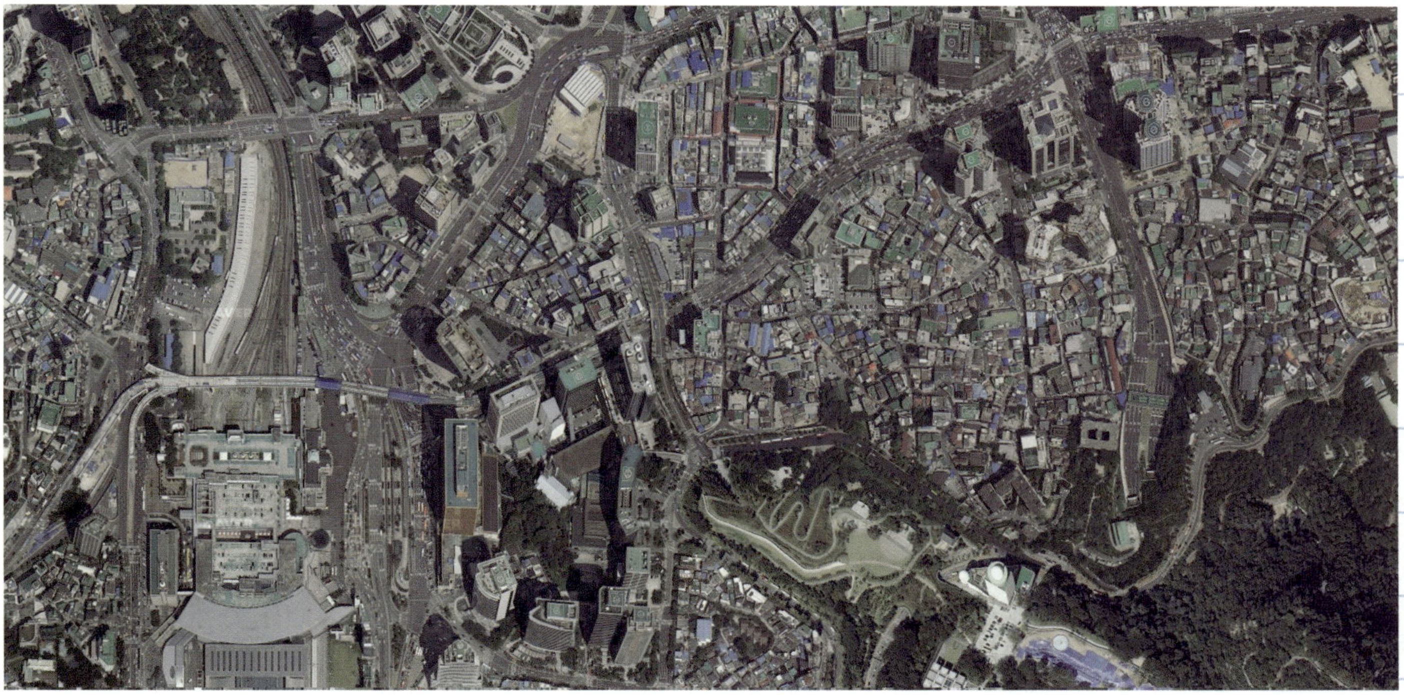

항공 사진 (2018년)

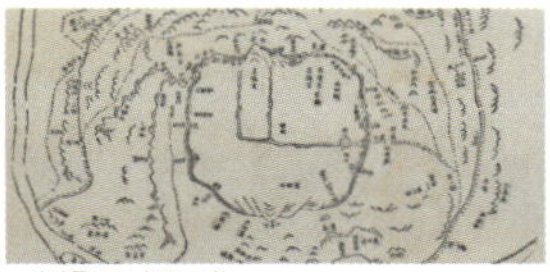

사산금표도 (1765년)

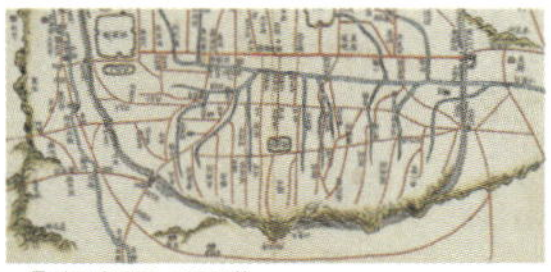

동여도 (1856-1872년)

대동여지도 (1861년)

조선 교통 전도 (1910년)

조선 신궁 진입 계단

조선 신궁 근경 (1925년)

동식물원 (1971년)

동식물원 철거 이후 (2006년)

서울 도시 계획 공원 (1962년)

서울 도시 계획 공원 (1965년)

남산 제모습 찾기 전체 계획도

회현지구 조성 계획도

지역의 역사

일제강점기

일제는 1910년 이 대지에 30만 평(990,000㎡)에 이르는 '한양공원'을 조성하였으며 1920년 '조선신사'가 들어섰다. 1925년에 '조선신사'는 '조선신궁'으로 승격했다. 면적은 12만7900여 평(422,811㎡)에 달했다. 지금의 '백범광장'에서 서울시 교육연구정보원, '안중근 기념관' 일대가 조선신궁 경내였다. '숭례문'에서 '남산' 입구에 이르는 진입로와 많은 계단, 광장과 단을 조성하였고, 옛 '남산식물원' 자리까지 총 14개의 건물을 배치하였다

조선신궁

신토라는 이름의 가장 높은 신중이 서울 남산 중간에 일제 강점기 한국 식민통치의 상징으로 일제에 의해 지어졌다.

동식물원

해방 후 '조선신궁'은 철거되고 그 자리에는 스키장이 들어섰다. 1960년대에는 '남산' 어린이 놀이터'가 있었으며 1968년 '남산식물원'을 건립하였고 1971년까지 2~4호 관을 차례로 설치하였다

국회의사당

1958년 국회는 '남산'에 국회의사당을 짓겠다고 발표하고 현상공모를 하였다
당선안은 '조선신궁' 부지를 그대로 이용하였고 어린이 놀이터 부지는 진입광장으로 '백범광장' 부지는 녹지로 조성하고 현재의 '안중근 의사 기념관'과 '남산' 도서관 부지에 국회의사당 본관을 짓는 계획이었다
이 사업은 1961년 5.16 군사 정변으로 중단되었다

김유신 동상

1969년에 시청 앞에 건립되었다가 1971년 지하철 공사로 인해서 '남산'으로 이전하였다
이 동상은 신라시대 '김유신'과는 관련이 없는 곳에 서 있지만 1969년 당시 공화당 집권층과 애국선열 조상 건립 위원회가 '김유신'을 통해 무엇을 말하고자 하였는지를 알 수 있는 중요한 동상이다.

History Wall

Japanese colonial period

In 1910, Japan established "Hanyang Park" ranging from 300,000 pyeong(990,000☒) to the site, and "Joseon Shinsa" entered in 1920. 'Joseon Shinsa" was promoted to "Joseon Shingung" in 1925. The area reached 129,700 pyeong(422,811☒). At the current "Baekbeom Plaza", the Seoul Metropolitan Education Research Information Center, "Ahn Jung-geun Memorial Museum" were in the precincts of the Joseon Shingung. They built access road and a lot of stairs, plazas and steps from the "Sungnyemun Gate" to the entrance of "Namsan" and arranged a total of 14 buildings up to the old "Namsan Botanical Garden" location.

Joseon Shingung:

A shrine with the highest shrine's place called Shinto shrine, which Japan built at the middle of Namsan in Seoul as a symbol of Korean colonial rule in Japanese colonial period.

Zoological and botanical garden

After the liberation, the "Joseon Shingung" was removed and in the 1960s when the ski slope was in place, there was "Namsan Children's Playground",and in 1968 "Namsan Botanical Garden" was constructed, and by the year 1971 it installed in order of No. 2-4 buildings.

Houses of Parliament

In 1958, the National assembly announced that it will make a parliament building in Namsan, and promoted architectural competition.
The winning work used site of the 'Joseon Shingung' as it was, and proposed the area for the children's playground as an entrance plaza, the "Baekbeom Plaza" as green space, and the current "Ahn Jung-geun Memorial Museum" and Namsan Library site as the main building of the Houses of Parliament. This project was suspended by 5.16 military coup in 1961.

Kim Yu-sin Statute

It was built in front of the city hall in 1969, but in 1971 moved to Namsan by subway construction. This statue is unrelated to the place and the place is not related to Silla Dynasty nor Kim Yu-sin himself, but it is important that you can know what Republican regime of 1969 and the patriotic ancestral construction committee would like to say via Kim Yu-sin statue.

'이승만' 동상

1956년에 조선신궁이 있던 자리에 '이승만 대통령'의 동상이 건립되었다. '이승만 동상'은 1955년 '이승만 대통령 80회 탄신축하위원회'의 발의로 세워졌다. 부지면적 3000평(9900㎡)에 높이 25m 규모로 건립된 당시 세계에서 가장 큰 동상이었다. 1960년 4·19 혁명 이후 8월에 '이승만 동상'은 철거되었다.

'백범 동상'

1969년 '이승만 동상'이 있던 자리에 '백범 동상'을 '백범 김구' 사업 협회에서 건립하였다.
'이승만 동상' 자리가 원래 1949년 '김구'가 암살된 후 '백범김구선생 동상' 봉립추진 위원회에서 김구 동상을 건립하려던 자리였다. 그 자리에 김구가 아닌 '이승만의 동상'이 들어섰다가, 20년 후에 결국은 '김구의 동상'이 세워진 것이다.

서울 성곽

조선은 '남산'을 남쪽의 외적을 막는 자연의 방패로 삼아 태조 5년(1396년) '도성축조'를 시작하였다. '세종', '문종', '광혜군', '숙종', '영조' 때에 도성개축 공사를 실시하였다.
'일제강점기'에 많은 부분이 도로와 옹벽에 의해 훼손되었으며 현재는 2009년 발굴조사를 토대로 2011-12년 '남산르네상스 회현 자락 복원사업' 의 결과로서 '남산' 끝자락을 여러 토막으로 끊어놓았던 옹벽을 헐고 도로를 덮어, 옛 '남산' 어린이 놀이터로부터 '백범광장'을 거쳐 서울 과학전시관 남산 분관까지 자연스럽게 이어지는 능선이 복원되었고 무너진 옛 성곽 일부가 제 모습을 찾게 되었다.

안중근 기념관

1970년 기와지붕을 얹은 콘크리트 양식으로 건립된 구 '안중근 기념관'을 헐고 '하얼빈' 의거 100주년을 맞아 국민성금으로 새롭게 건립된 '안중근 기념관'은 부부 건축가 '임영환', '김선현'에 의해서 12인의 단지동맹을 상징하는 12개의 반투명 유리 상자가 투과하는 부드러운 빛과 전이공간으로 설계되었고 2010년 문을 열었다.

Rhee Syngman Statue

A statue of President Rhee Syngman was founded in the place where the Joseon Shingung was in 1956.
Rhee Syngman Statue was built on the initiative of President Rhee Syngman 80th birthday celebration committee in 1955. The statue of Lee Seongman was removed in August after the 1919 4.19 revolution, which was the largest statue in the world at the time when it was constructed with a scale of 25meters high on the site area of 3,000pyeong(9,900⊠).

'Baekbeom Statue'

In 1969, 'Baekbum statue" was constructed in the places where "Rhee Syngman Statue" was founded by Kimgu Association. The site was originally planned to build Kimgu statue by "Baekbeom Kimgu Statue Promotion Committee" after Kimgu was assassinated in 1949. There was no Kimgu on the spot but "Rhee Syngman statue" entered, but in 20 years, finally "Kimgu statue" was built.

Seoul Fortress Wall

Joseon made Namsan as a shield of nature to prevent the enemy of the south and began conducting conductive construction for the 5th year of King Taejo (1396). Sejong, Munjong, Gwanghaegun, Sukjong, Yeongjo renovation work was carried out.
A lot of parts were damaged by the road and the retaining wall in the days of the Japanese colonial period, and now based on the excavation survey in 2009, as a result of the "Namsan Renaissance Hwihyun restoration project" in 2011-12. It breaks the retaining wall cut into multiple writings, overwrites the road, goes from the old Namsan children's playing field to Baekbum Plaza through Seoul Science Exhibition Hall Namsan Branch naturally connected ridgeline is reconstructed and collapsed old Castle Some have found their figure.

Ahn Jung-geun Memorial Museum

In 1970, the former "Ahn Jung-geun Memorial Hall" built on a concrete form with a roof tile was built, celebrating the 100th anniversary of Harbin's enactment, the newly constructed Ahn Jung-geun Memorial Museum, donated by the people, is designed by the architects, Lim Younghwan and Kim Sun-hyun. Opened in 2010, designed to soft light and transition space through which twelve translucent glass boxes symbolizing the twelve amputation alliances.

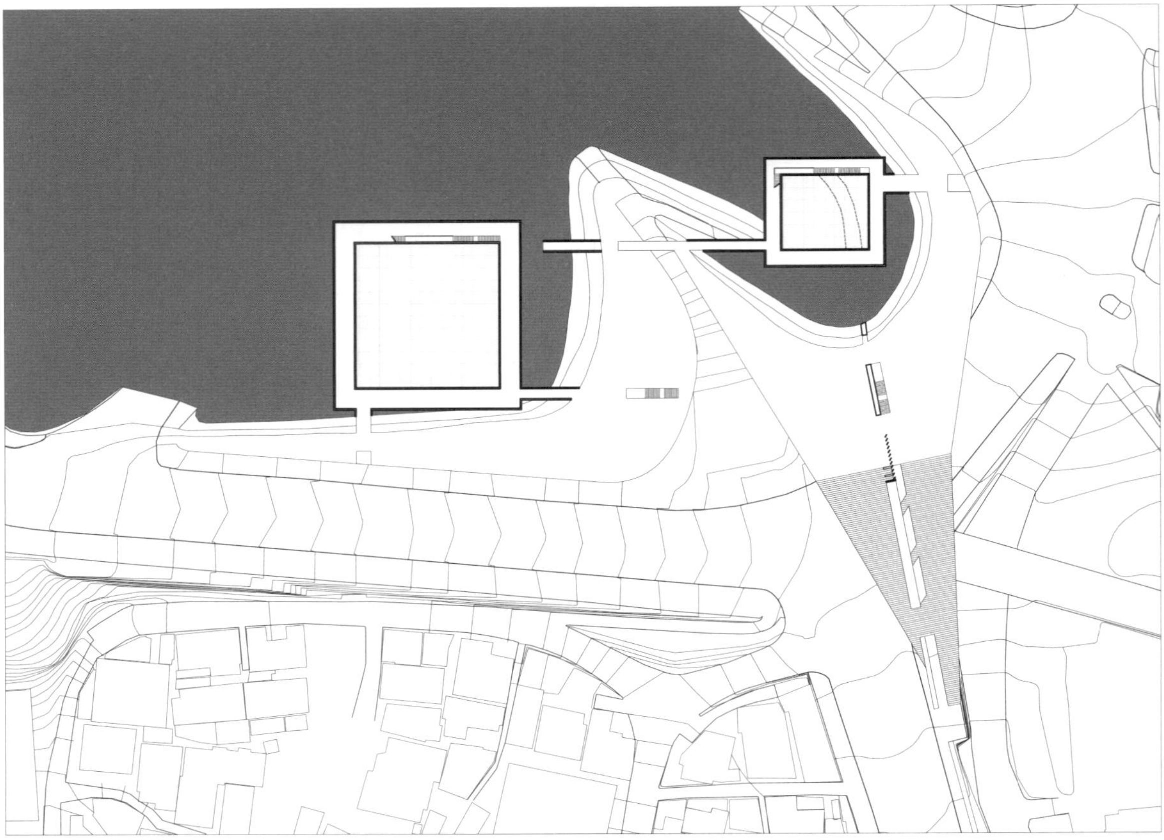

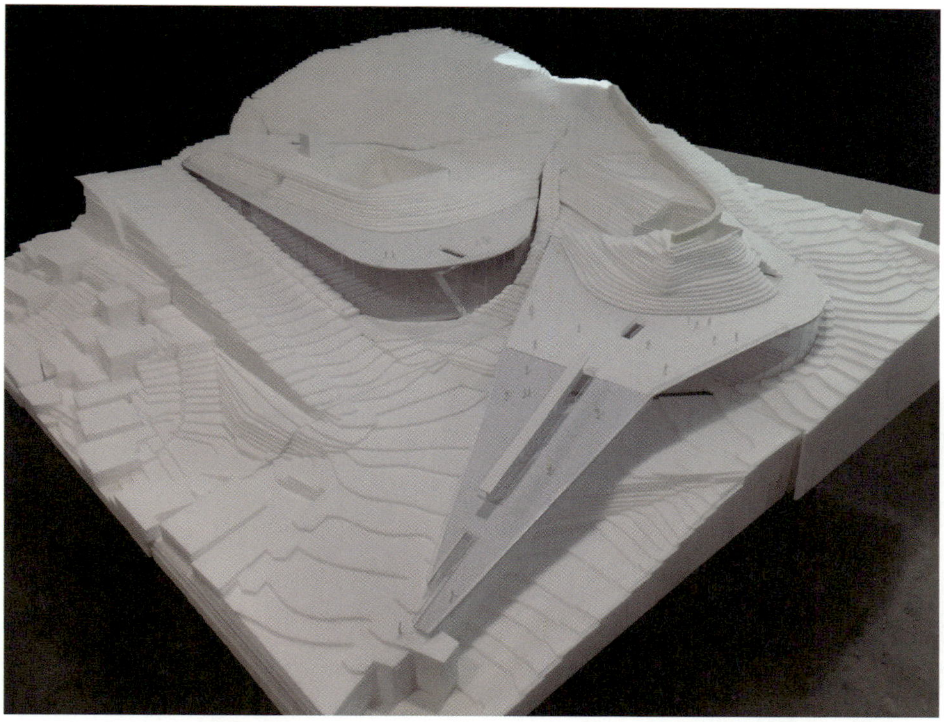

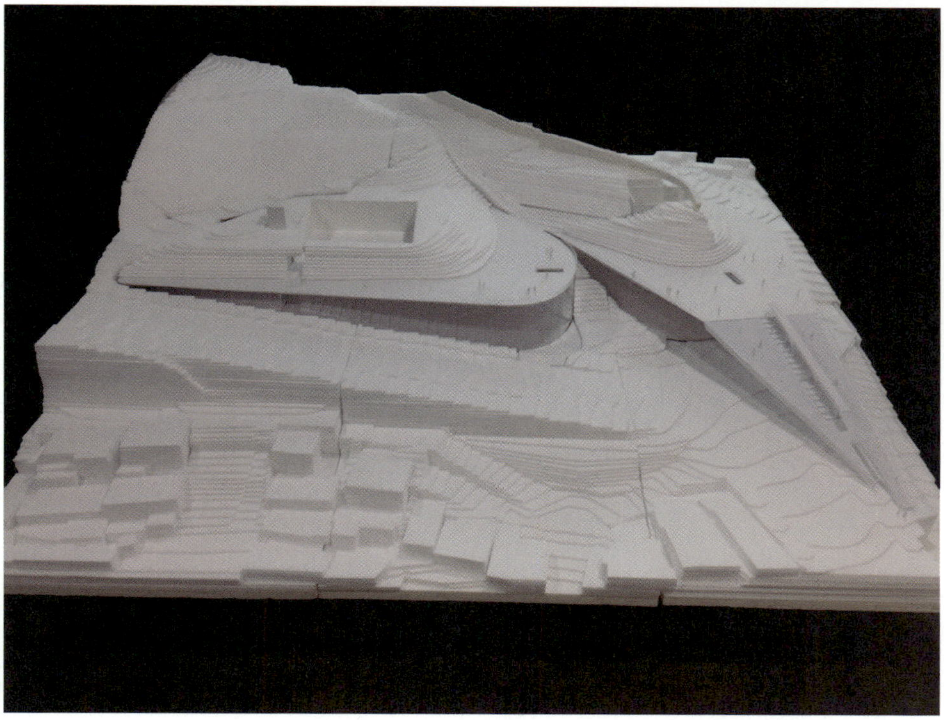

700
160
150
140
130
120
110
100
90
80
70
60
50
40
30
20
10
0 m
-10
-20
-30
-40

700
160
150
140
130
120
110
100
90
80
70
60
50
40
30
20
10
0 m
-10
-20
-30
-40

케이스 크리스티안제

Kees Christiaanse

종로 커넥터

건설 가능한 대지가 점점 부족해짐에 따라 수많은 탑이 하늘로 솟아오르고, 그 반대 방향 즉, 지하에는 새로운 기능 공간들이 조성되고 있다. 지하공간의 이미지는 주로 어둠, 환기가 잘 안 되는 환경, 불안한 터널, 지하철역, 주차장 등과 연결되어 왔지만, 아시아권과 최근 유럽 지역에서 특히 기차역을 중심으로 개발된 지하공간들은 수용 가능한 도시 공간 유형으로 인정받고 있다. 그 예로 몬트리올 Ville Souterraine, 교토 중앙역, 도쿄 시부야, 싱가포르 마리나 베이 등이 있으며, 취리히 중앙역, 암스테르담 중앙역 같은 소규모 지하 기차역도 그에 속한다.

지상층, 중간층, 지붕으로 구성되어 있는 이들은 3D 도시를 구성하는 미래적 요소라고 할 수 있다. 레벨들을 터널, 가로, 다리 또는 지붕을 활용해 수평적으로 연결하는 경우가 많아지고 있는데 이는 마리나 베이의 복잡한 지하 보행 네트워크에서도 볼 수 있다. 밀도 높은 아시아 도시들의 협소한 공간에서는 공공공간을 가로 밑, 지상, 지붕의 세 가지 형태로 확장하는 전략이 환영받고 있다.

역사를 살펴보면 도시는 정책적으로나 디자인적으로나 2차원적 "초질서(hyper-order)"에 종속되어 있었다. 도시 공간에 있는 대부분의 것들은 단순히 차곡차곡 쌓아 올린 것이 아니었다. 오히려 그것들은 서로 맞닿아 있었다. 지구 표면이 평평하기 때문에 사물들 역시 서로 맞닿아 있을 수밖에 없었기 때문이다. 이러한 상황에서 벗어나기 위한 다소 온건한 해법이 지난 세기 특히, 전후 기간에 개발되었다. 그리고 오늘날 거대 도시의 고밀 중심지들은 상업시설과 결합된 3차원적 공공공간 네트워크의 장점을 발견하게 되었다.

지하공간은 기후의 영향을 덜어줄 수도 있다. 서울의 경우 여름 기온이 40° C에 이르는 일이 점점 흔해지고 있다. 지하는 냉방에 필요한 추가 에너지 소비량이 적다. 신기술은 지하공간을 더 안락한 곳으로 만들어줄 수 있다. 예를 들어 유리섬유 다발은 에너지 소비 없이 자연광을 공급해주고 새로운 형태의 자연 환기를 가능하게 한다. 이러한 기술을 활용한다면 쾌적한 지하공간을 구축할 수 있을 것이다. 또한 예술 작품으로 채워져 있고, 광장과 이벤트 시설, 정원과 수공간이 있는 파티오 등을 갖춘 지하 공공공간을 조성할 수도 있다.

아울러 지하공간은 통합형 물류, 배달 시스템, 기술 기반시설, 폐기물 수거, 지역 냉방 설비 등에 점점 더 많이 활용되고 있다. 기존 지하 터널을 활용한 새로운 형태의 도시 물류 시스템의 예로는 스위스의 "cargo sous terrain" 프로젝트, 엘론 머스크의 하이퍼루프(Hyperloop) 등이 있다. 물류의 지하화는 지상 교통 압력을 해소해주고 운송의 자동화를 쉽게 해준다. 터널에는 다른 교통수단의 간섭이 없기 때문이다.

싱가포르 주롱 호수 지역을 위한 KCAP의 마스터플랜에서 모든 형태의 교통과 기반시설을 아우르는 통합형 지하 네트워크는 건물 지하 레벨을 통해 여러 지하철역과 고속철도 연결망을 연계함으로써 일반 가로 레벨을 '활동적 움직임'(걷기, 자전거)과 공공공간에 내어준다.

케이스 크리스티안제는 델프트 공대 건축 및 도시설계학부를 졸업했다. 1980년 OMA에 입사해 1983년 파트너가 되었다. 1989년 로테르담에 현재의 KCAP Architects&Planners로 발전한 자신의 스튜디오를 설립했다. 1990년 쾰른에 공동으로 ASTOC Architects and Planners을 설립하고 2002년까지 파트너로 활동했다.

케이스의 작업은 복잡한 상황에 얽혀 있는 도시 문제 해결과 도시화 유도에 초점을 맞춘다. 케이스는 대학 캠퍼스 개발, 옛 산업, 철도, 항구 지역 활성화 전문가이며, 해외 여러 국제 도시 개발 사업을 감독했다.

지금까지 케이스는 늘 교육과 연구를 KCAP에서의 자신의 작업과 결합하고, 그를 통해 풍성한 성과를 얻어냈다. 1996년부터 2003년까지 베를린공과대학에서 건축 도시설계학부 교수로 활동했고, 2003년부터 2018년까지 스위스취리히연방공과대학(ETH)의 건축 도시설계학부 확장으로 재직했다. 2010년부터 싱가포르 미래도시연구소(FCL)와 협력하고 있으며, 2013년 싱가포르 기술디자인 대학(SUTD) 건축디자인학부 외부 자문위원회 위원장으로 임명되었다.

2009년 케이스는 "열린 도시. 공존의 디자인(Open City. Designing Coexistence)"이라는 주제로 열린 제4회 로테르담 국제 건축비엔날레(IABR)의 감독으로 활동했다. 건축, 도시계획 관련 수많은 저서와 에세이를 집필하기도 한 케이스는 여러 상을 수상했으며, 건축 분야에서의 특별한 공로를 인정받아 '2016 RIBA International Fellowship' 평생공로상을, 건축환경 개선을 위한 지속적이고 혁신적인 노력을 인정받아 'ARC17 Oeuvre Award'을 받았다.

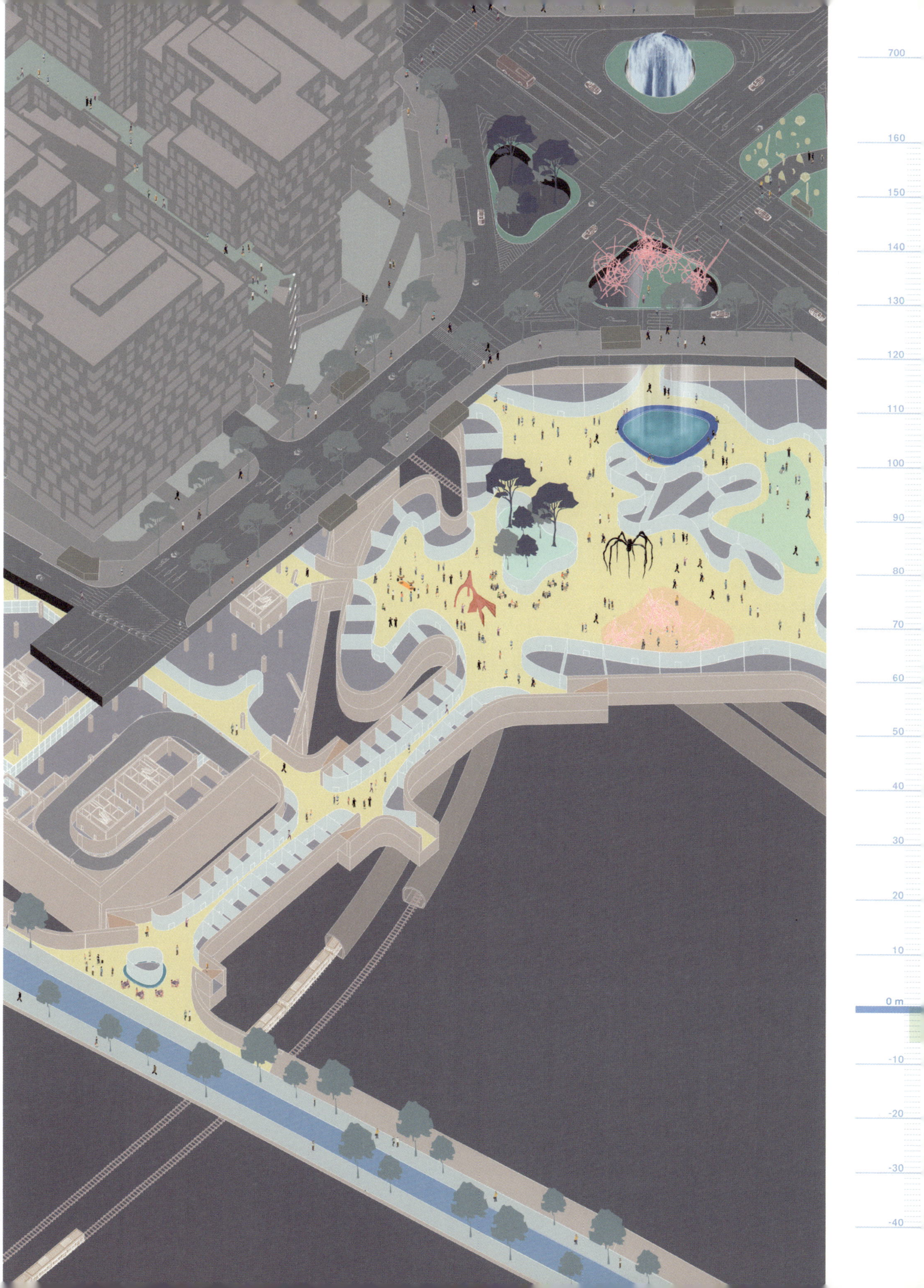
700
160
150
140
130
120
110
100
90
80
70
60
50
40
30
20
10
0 m
-10
-20
-30
-40

Jongno Connector

As constructible land is becoming scarce, not only are many towers soaring into the skies, but also new functional space is increasingly created in the opposite direction: underground. While the image of underground spaces has been mostly associated with dark, badly-ventilated, insecure tunnels, metro stations, and parking garages, the underground space in the Asian context, and recently also in European developments specifically around railway stations, is gradually transforming into an accepted urban typology. Examples are the Ville Souterraine in Montréal, Kyoto central station, Shibuya Tokyo or Marina Bay in Singapore, but also smaller underground railway station areas such as at Zurich's main station and Amsterdam Central Station.
Together with the ground, middle and roof levels, they are the upcoming features of a 3D city. Increasingly, levels are connected horizontally by tunnels, streets, bridges or even complete roofs, as the intricate underground pedestrian network of Marina Bay shows. In the crammed spaces of dense Asian cities, the tripling of public space below the street, on the ground and on the roofs provides a welcome solution.
Historically, both in politics and in design, cities were guided by a 2D "hyper-order". Most things were simply not on top of each other in urban space, rather they were adjacent. As the surface of the earth is flat, things could not be anything but organized next to each other. The rather modest take-off from this condition developed during the last century, mainly in the post-war period. Today, dense centralities in large agglomerations have discovered the virtues of 3D organized public space networks in combination with commercial development.
Underground spaces may also mediate climatic nuisances: 40° C summers have become more and more common in Seoul. Underground, little extra energy is required to keep spaces cool. New technologies can make underground spaces more comfortable, as for instance large glass fibre bundles providing daylight without using energy, and new forms of natural ventilation. With such technologies, we can make underground spaces enjoyable. We can create an urban public space underground adorned with art, comprising plazas, event spaces, and patios with gardens and water.
In addition, underground space is increasingly used for integrated logistics, delivery systems, technical infrastructure, waste collection, and district cooling plants. New types of city logistics using the existing underground tunnels, for example the "cargo sous terrain" project in Switzerland, or Elon Musk's Hyperloop. Moving logistics underground eases the pressure on traffic in the streets and makes automated transport much easier, because in the tunnels, no other modes of mobility interfere.
In KCAP's master plan for Jurong Lake District in Singapore, integrated underground networks for all mobility and infrastructure types connect the different subway stops and high-speed railway network with the basement levels of building blocks, in order for the regular street level to be reserved for 'active mobility' (walking and cycling) and public space.

Kees Christiaanse studied architecture and urban planning at TU Delft. In 1980 he joined the Office for Metropolitan Architecture (OMA) and was appointed partner in 1983. In 1989 he founded his own company, now KCAP Architects&Planners, in Rotterdam. In 1990 he co-founded ASTOC Architects and Planners in Cologne and was partner until 2002. Kees focuses in his work on urban assignments in complex situations and on guiding of urban processes. He is an expert in the development of university campuses and in the revitalisation of former industrial, railway and harbour areas and is a supervisor of several international urban developments.
Throughout his career Kees has always combined teaching and research with his professional work within KCAP, which has generated fruitful cross-fertilisations. From 1996 until 2003 he held a professorship for architecture and urban planning at the Technical University of Berlin. From 2003 until 2018, he has been chair of the Architecture and Urban Planning Institute of Swiss Federal Institute of Technology (ETH) in Zurich. Since 2010, he has been involved in the Future Cities Laboratory (FCL) in Singapore. In 2013, he was appointed Chairperson of the External Advisory Board of the Architecture and Design Department of the Singapore University of Technology and Design (SUTD).
In 2009, Kees was curator of the 4th International Architecture Biennale Rotterdam (IABR) with the title "Open City. Designing Coexistence". He is author of a multitude of books and essays about architecture and urban planning. Kees has received numerous honours among others the lifetime award '2016 RIBA International Fellowship' for his particular contribution to architecture and the 'ARC17 Oeuvre Award' for his lasting and innovative contribution to the improvement of the built environment.

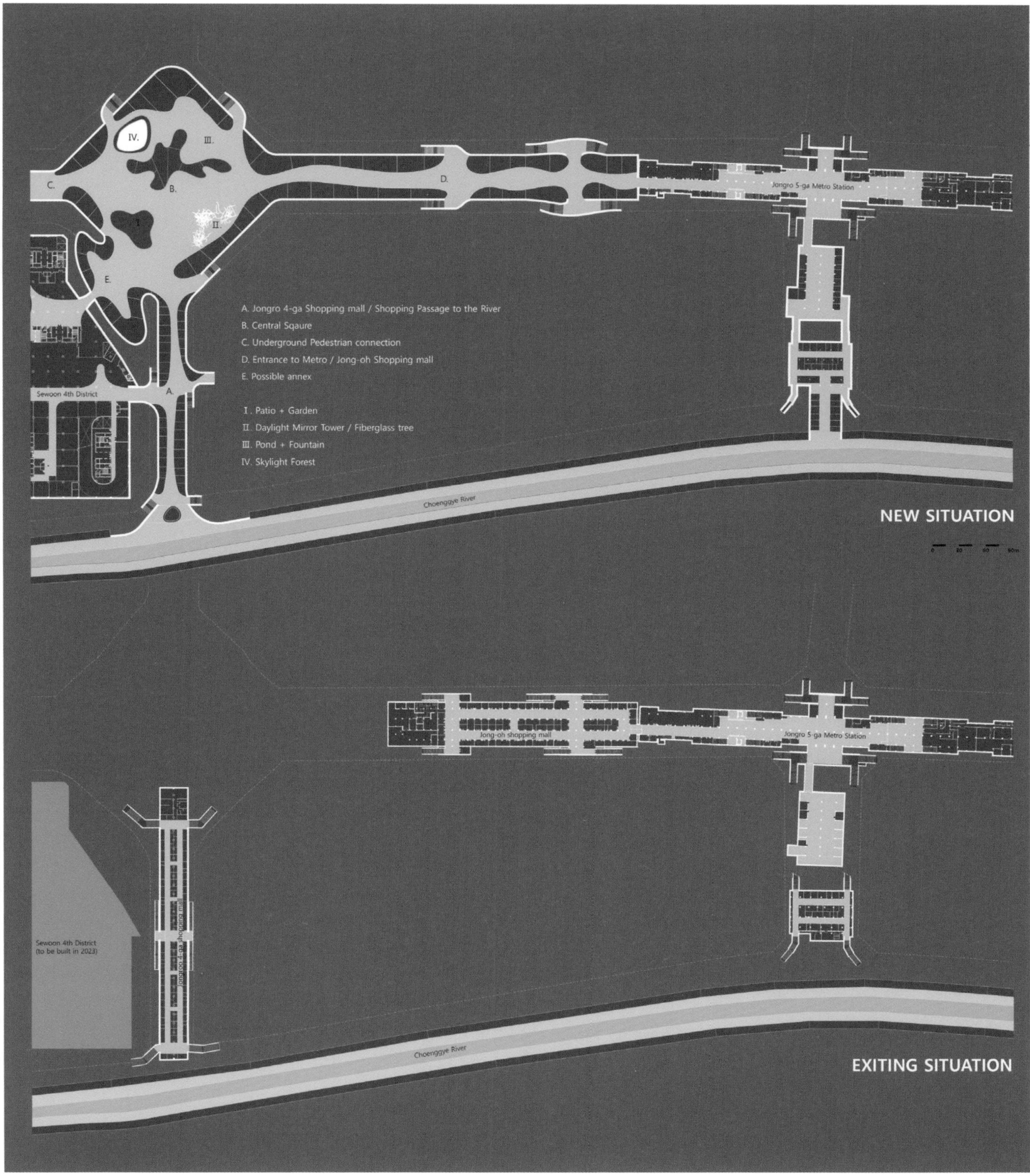

IV.
III.
C.
B.
D.
I
II.
E.
Jongro 5-ga Metro Station
A. Jongro 4-ga Shopping mall / Shopping Passage to the River
B. Central Sqaure
C. Underground Pedestrian connection
D. Entrance to Metro / Jong-oh Shopping mall
E. Possible annex
I. Patio + Garden
II. Daylight Mirror Tower / Fiberglass tree
III. Pond + Fountain
IV. Skylight Forest
A.
Sewoon 4th District
Choenggye River
NEW SITUATION
Jong-oh shopping mall
Jongro 5-ga Metro Station
Jongro 4-ga shopping mall
Sewoon 4th District
(to be built in 2023)
Choenggye River
EXITING SITUATION

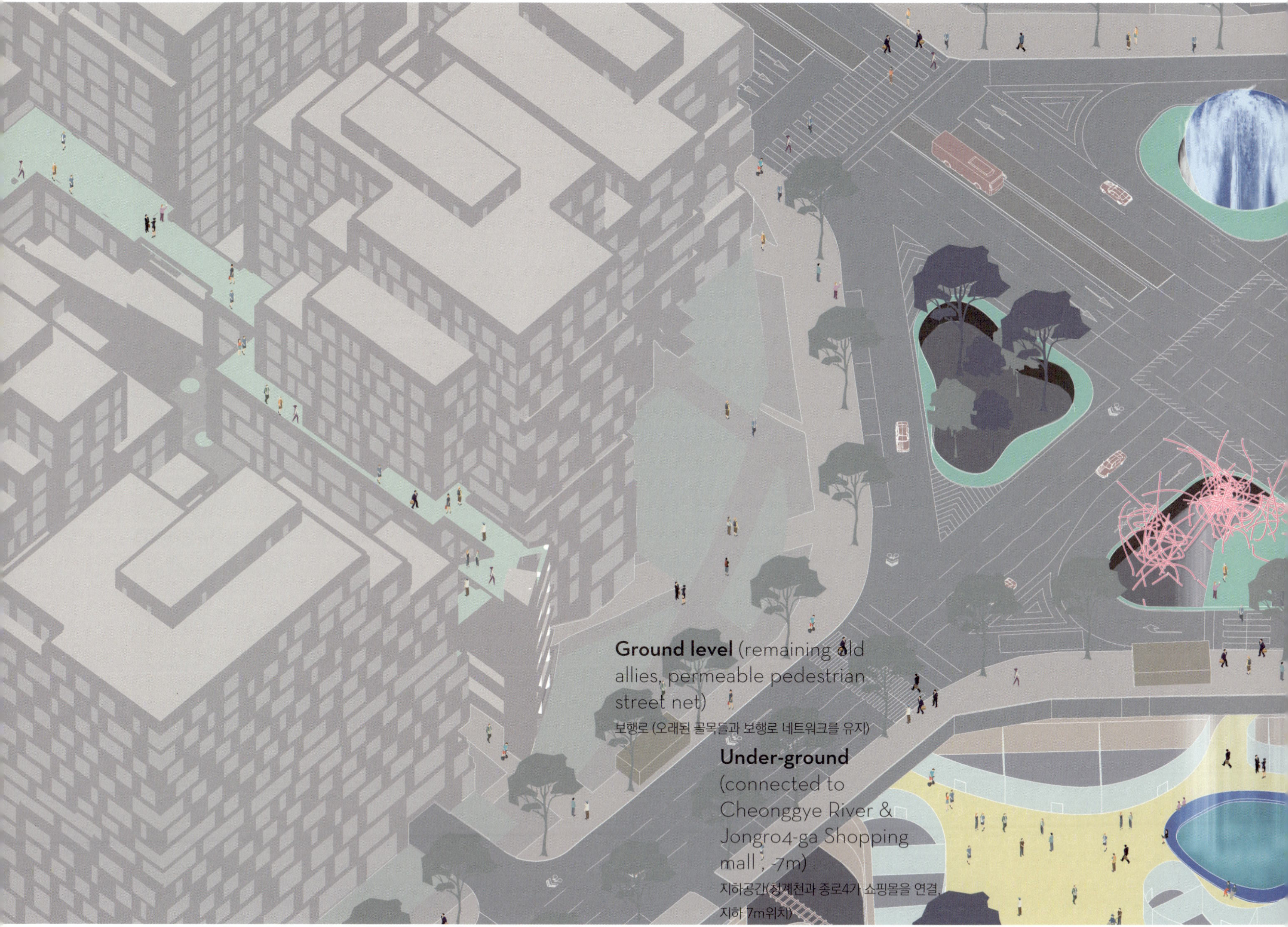
Ground level (remaining old allies, permeable pedestrian street net)
보행로 (오래된 골목들과 보행로 네트워크를 유지)
Under-ground (connected to Cheonggye River & Jongro4-ga Shopping mall ; -7m)
지하공간(청계천과 종로4가 쇼핑몰을 연결, 지하 7m위치)

▼Traffic islands to the urban park
(Transformed into the pedestrian connector as well as sculpture parks)
교통섬에서 도시 공원으로(건널목과 연계된 조각공원으로 변화)

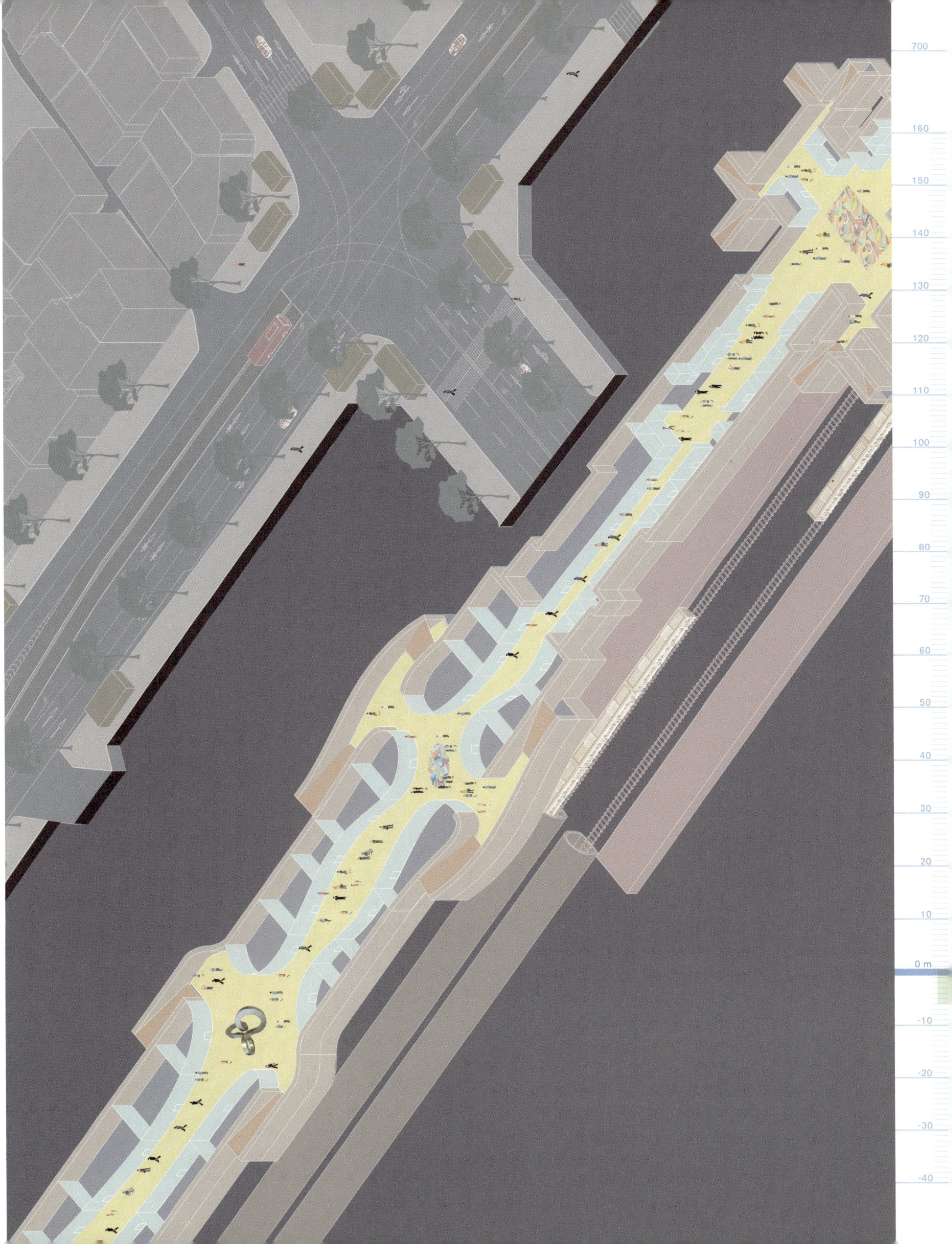
700
160
150
140
130
120
110
100
90
80
70
60
50
40
30
20
10
0 m
-10
-20
-30
-40

1. 안마당

1. PATIO

안마당은 작은 정원으로 조성되고 유리로 둘러싸여 있다.

A patio with a little garden on the underground level surrounded by glass.

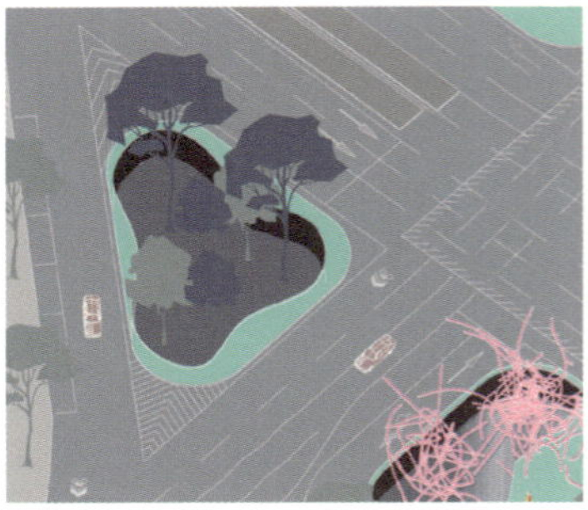

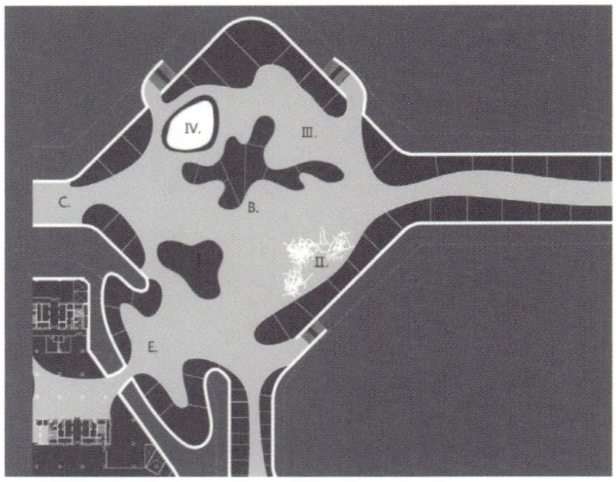

2. 유리 타워/ 유리섬유 나무

2. AYLIGHT MIRROR TOWER/ FIBERGLASS TREE

주간에 햇빛을 지하공간까지 끌어들이는 유리섬유 나무 조형물

A daylight tree of glassfibre providing another daylight sculpture

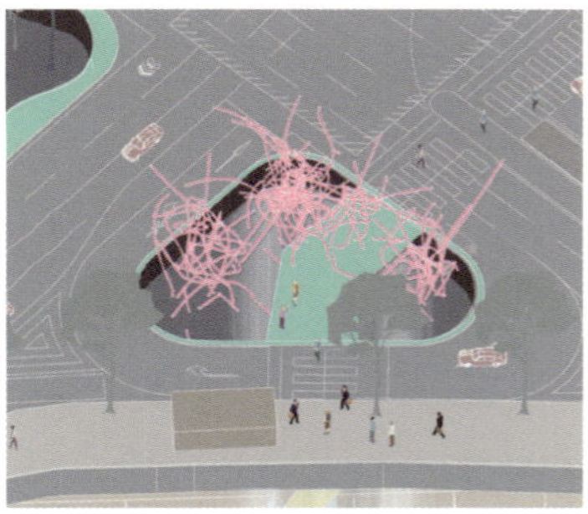

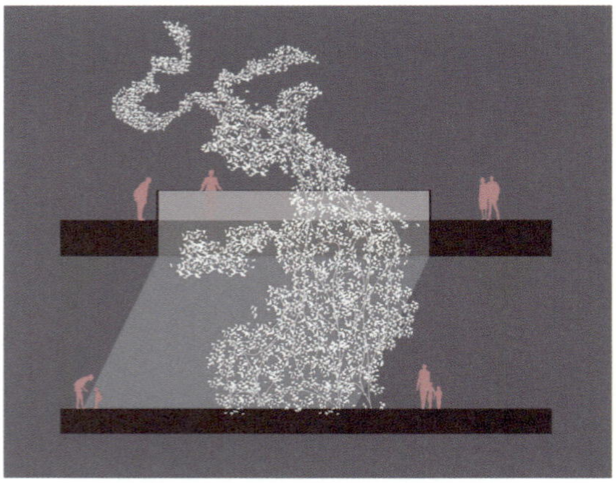

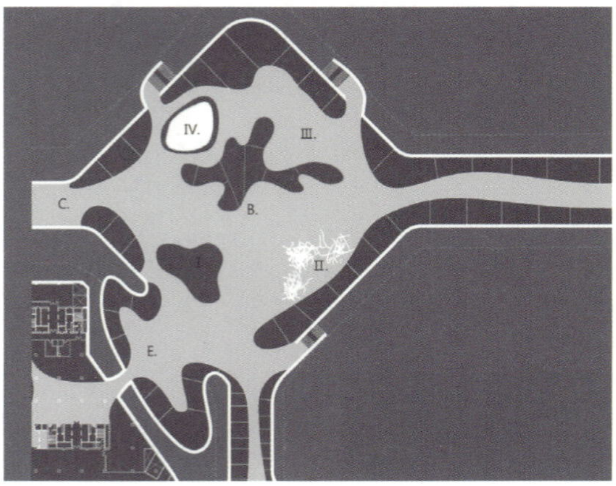

3. 천창: 숲

3. SKYLIGHT FOREST

지하에 다양한 형태로 햇빛을 보내주는 다양한 크기와 형태의 천창들

A collection of skylights of different shape, forming a daylight sculpture under the groun

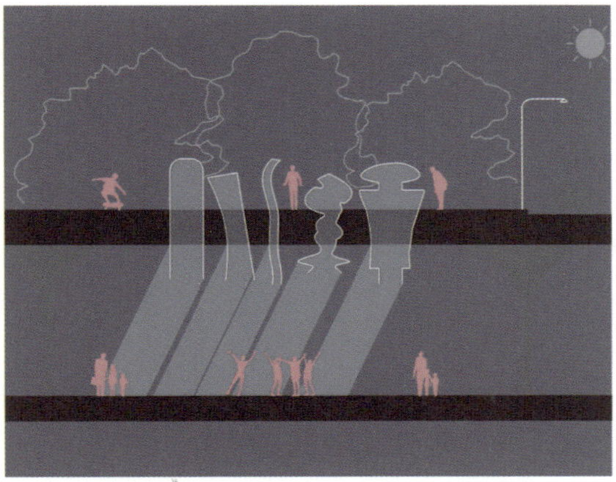

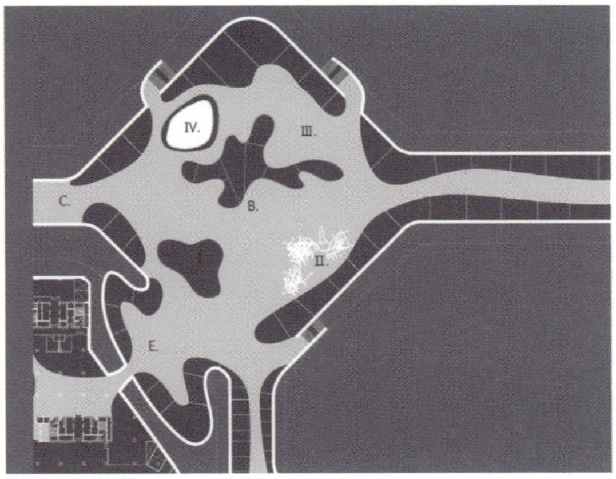

4. 연못+분수

4. POND + FOUNTAIN

벤치가 있는 지하 연못으로 물이 흘러가는 구 모양의 분수인 '물-사과'

A 'water-apple' in the form of a spheric fountain from which water runs down to an underg-ound basin with benches

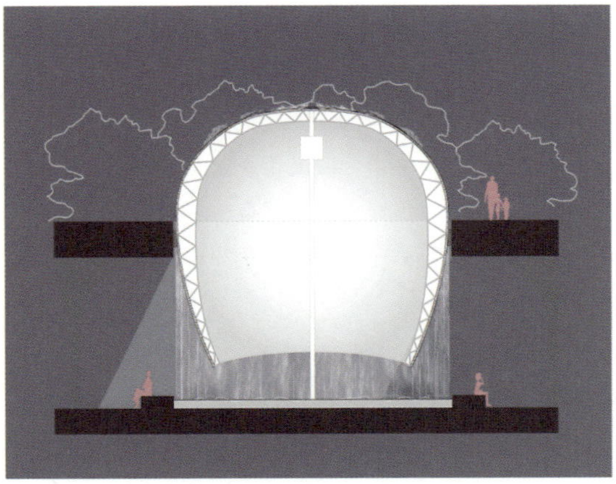

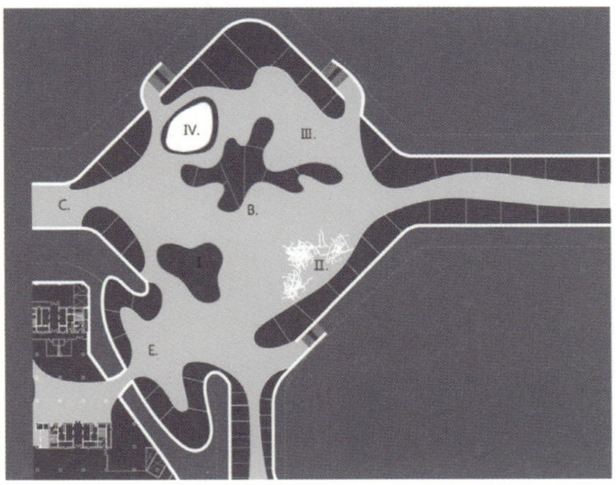

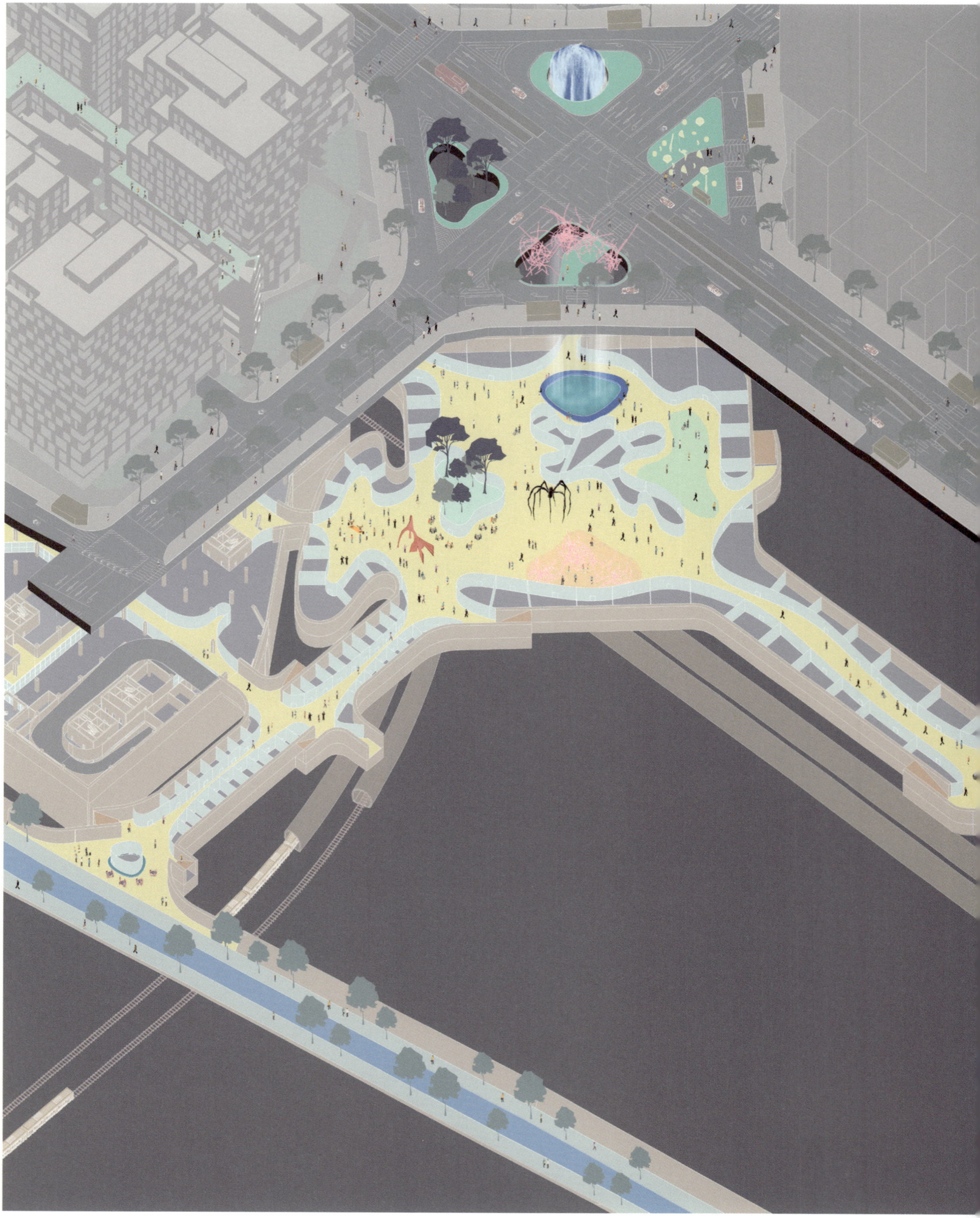

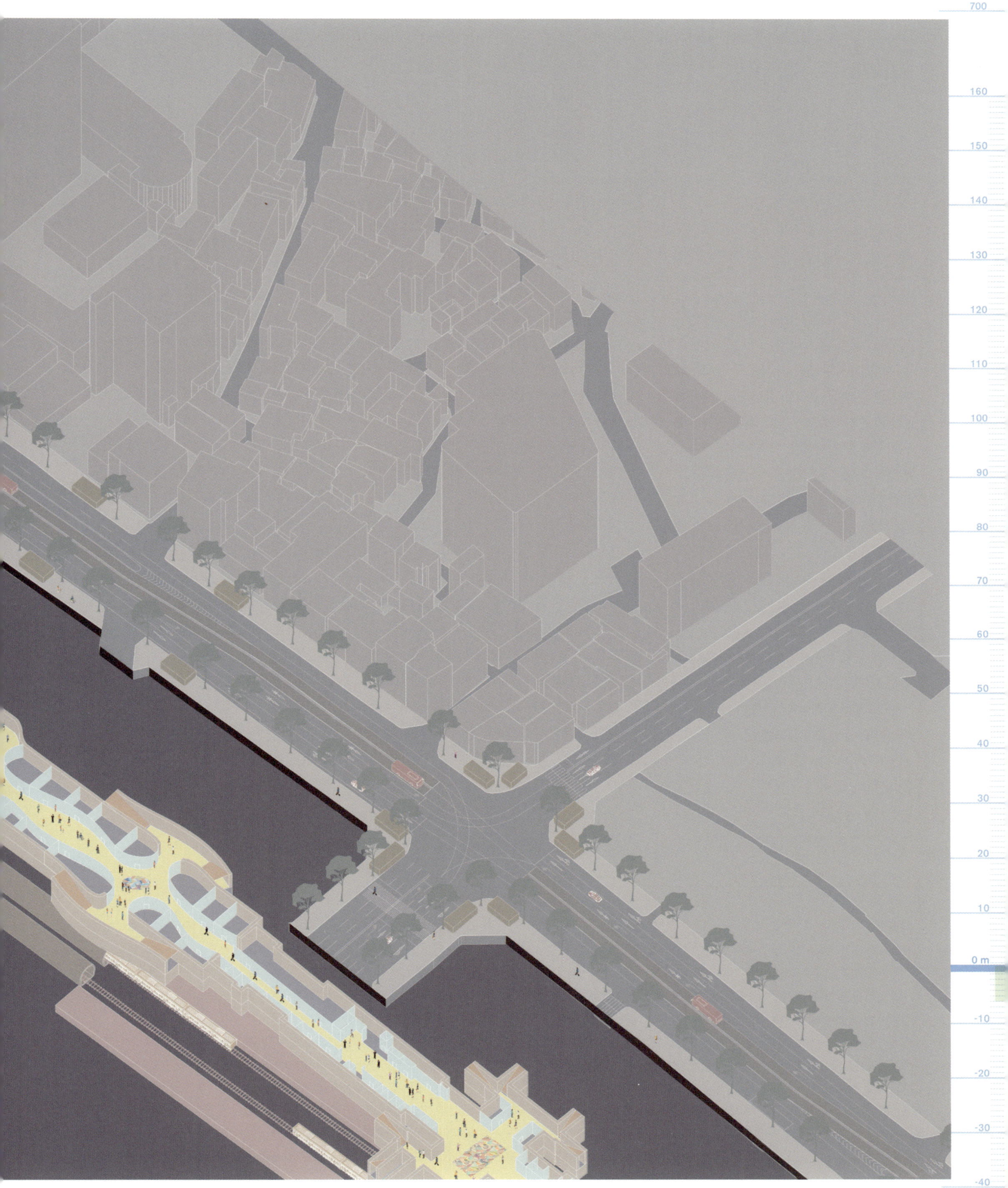
700
160
150
140
130
120
110
100
90
80
70
60
50
40
30
20
10
0 m
-10
-20
-30
-40

김광수
studio_K_works

정독 독서 플랫폼

본 대상지가 위치한 곳은 서울의 고성인 경복궁과 창덕궁 사이의 오래된 한옥거주지(북촌)에 위치해 있다. 이곳은 과거 고등학교가 위치해 있던 장소로서, 1977년에 도서관으로 변경되어 현재까지 쓰이고 있다. 근래에 들어 본 도서관의 주변 지역은, 오래된 서울의 한옥을 체험하기 위해 상당히 많은 유동인구들이 드나드는 곳이 되었으며, 주변에 작은 규모의 상점이나 카페, 레스토랑들이 많이 들어섰다. 그리고 인근의 국립현대미술관과 아트선재센터 등의 문화시설들 및 경복궁, 국립민속박물관 등과 함께 서울시민 및 관광객들이 수시로 방문하는 지역이 되었다.

하지만, 현재의 정독도서관 부지는 최대 8m의 높은 축대에 의해서, 주변 지역의 유동인구 동선 및 도시 활동의 맥락과 상당히 단절되어있다. 이러한 이유로, 이곳은 정독도서관 이용자들의 휴게공간 구실만을 하는 등, 부지가 가진 커다란 잠재성에 비하면 그 활용도 및 인지도가 무척 떨어지는 실정이다.

정독도서관 부지는 밀도가 높은 주변 지역에 비해 상당한 오픈스페이스를 확보하고 있으며, 이곳은 정독도서관만을 위한 장소가 되기보다는 주변 지역의 도시활동을 적극적으로 포괄하는 열린 공공의 영역이 될 필요성이 높아 보인다. 또한 이곳은 대규모의 시설이 들어서더라도 기존 주변 지역의 소규모 고밀도의 도시조직이 훼손되지 않고 상생할 수 있는 방법의 모색이 절실한 곳이며, 기존의 정독도서관 오픈스페이스가 제공하는 탁월한 개방감과 서울 시가지를 한눈에 담을 수 있는 우수한 경관을 유지할 수 있는 방법을 고안하는 것도 무척 중요한 이슈로 등장한다고 본다.

본 안은 정독도서관이 있는 북촌 특유의 성격(골목길과 소규모 건물 스케일 등)을 이어받으며 기존의 정독도서관 부지가 가지고 있는 오픈스페이스의 감각을 유지할 수 있는 방법을 고안하는 것에 중점을 두었다. 그리고 이러한 방안이 지하층과 적극적으로 연계되며, 동선, 채광, 활동가시성 등이 성취될 수 있는 방법을 고민하였다.

제안하는 프로그램은 '책'을 중심으로 한 교류활동과 서적, 문화예술관련 중고상품거래를 위한 플랫폼 및 공원이다.

본 안의 루프레벨은 기존의 부지 레벨보다 살짝 들어 올려져, 서측으로는 경복궁과 인왕산, 남측으로는 남산과 시가지 전경, 동측으로는 가회동 한옥마을과 창덕궁 능선 그리고 북측으로는 북악산의 전경들이 360도로 펼쳐지는 우수한 경관을 갖게 된다. 또한 기존의 오픈스페이스 감각을 유지하되, 각 건물 메스의 루프는 소규모로서 적당한 위요감과 함께 책을 주제로 한 '독서가든'이 형성된다. 각각의 옥상 독서가든은 서로 다른 물리적 형상과 특징적인 화초류 가드닝의 주제를 가지고 형성된다. 그리고 그 하부에 교류를 위한 다양하고 개별적인 실내공간이 존재하고 지하로 내려갈수록 중고서적 거래 및 개가식 도서관을 위한 넓은 플랫폼 공간이 등장하게 된다. 이곳은 지하공간이지만, 선큰 공간과 각 건물 레벨의 단차에 의해서 자연채광, 환기 및 동선의 연계 등이 이루어지게 된다.

이러한 방법을 통해서 본 안은 루프가든과 지하 공간을 함께 아우르는 또 하나의 대지를 형성하며, 책을 주제로 공원화되고 명소화된 루프-스케이프를 제안한다.

김광수
- studio_K_works 대표 / 집담공간 CURTAINHALL 공동대표
- 전 이화여자대학교 교수
- 예일대학교 건축대학원 석사졸업, 연세대학교 건축공학과 학사 졸업

김광수는 협업을 지향하며 다양한 장르의 전문가, 대중, 공간 사용자들의 관계성을 유도하는 디자인과 건축 작업에 관심을 보이고 있으며, 뉴미디어 매체로 인한 사회성과 인지성의 변화 그리고 도시/건축 환경의 변화를 주목하고 있다.

2004년 베니스비엔날레 건축전에서 '방들의 가출(City of Bang, Venice Biennale, 2004)'이라는 주제로 한국사회의 아파트와 방 문화현상을 조사 전시한 바 있으며, 핀란드 국립미술관(Museum of Cultures, Helsinki, 2007), 오스트리아 국립미술관(Museum of Cultures, Vienna, 2013), 독일 아데스 겔러리 등에도 그의 프로젝트가 초대되어 전시를 한 바 있다. 지역협업을 중심으로 작업한 철원 양지리의 'DMZ 철새타운'은 대한민국공간대상 장관상을 수상하기도 하였으며 최근에는 쓰레기소각장을 문화시설로 재생하는 '부천아트벙커 B39'를 설계하여 주목을 받기도 하였는데 이는 2018 대한민국 공공건축 대상을 수상하기도 하였다.

주요 작업으로는 '100개의 알 수 없는 방(2008)', '순천_빈집프로젝트(2006)', '판교주택(2017)', '연대 앞 창작놀이센터(2016)', '광주시민회관 재조성사업(2011)', '달로문학관은 달로문학관입니다(2009)', '백사마을 주거지보존사업(2014), '부천아트벙커 B39(2018)' 등이 있으며 공저로는 '제주현상'(2016), '철새협동조합'(2012), 'Stadebauwelt_City of Bang'(2008), '느림의 도시_순천'(2007), 'Germany-Korea Public Space Forum'(2005) 등이 있다.

700
160
150
140
130
120
110
100
90
80
70
60
50
40
30
20
10
0 m
-10
-20
-30
-40

Jeongdok Reading Platform

This project is located in the Korea's traditional Hanok residential area called "Bukchon" between Gyeongbokgung and Changdeokgung, two of the old palaces of Seoul. There used be a high school on the site, which was transformed into a library in 1977. Recently, the surrounding area of the library has been attracting thousands of tourists to experience old Hanok with a lot of flourishing small shops, cafes and restaurants. Along with cultural facilities such as the National Museum of Modern and Contemporary Art, the Art Sonje Center, Gyeongbokgung Palace and the National Folk Museum of Korea, this area has become a frequently visited tourist attraction in Seoul. However, the high embankment of up to 8 meters is currently isolating the site from the active circulation of floating populations and the context of urban activities in the surrounding area. This has rendered the site only as the resting place for the Jeongdok Library users with very limited usage and awareness considering its great potential.

Having secured a very large open space compared to the densely populated surrounding area, the site seems more apt to serve as an open public area that can encompass urban activities for the surrounding area rather than just for the Jeongdok Library.

On the other hand, this area urgently requires finding a measure to enable large facilities to coexist with small-scale high-density urban tissues without giving damage to the surrounding area, and the issue of devising a way to excellently keep openness and the view towards the outstanding landscape of Seoul's downtown from the existing Jeongdok Library is also emergent.

This proposal focuses on devising a method to inherit the unique characteristics of Bukchon, the site of the Jeongdok Library, such as various alleyway and small scales of buildings and to maintain the sense of openness in the site. Also, much thought has been put into figuring out ways to actively link the proposal with the basement and implement proper circulation, lighting, and visibility of activities.

The proposed program entails a platform and park for communicative activities focused on books and trading of secondhand culture and art works.

The rooftop of the proposal is raised slightly above the site, which provides excellent scenic view of 360 degrees; Gyeongbokgung and Inwangsan to the west, Namsan Mountain and the city area to the south, Gahoedong Hanok Village and the ridge of Changdeokgung Palace to the east, and the panorama of Bukaksan Mountain to the north.

Keeping the existing sense of openness, the roof of each building mass forms book-themed 'reading garden' of small scale with a proper sense of enclosure. Each rooftop reading garden has a different physical shape designed with the characteristic theme of plant gardening. A wide variety of individual spaces for exchanges are planned below them, and a vast platform space for used book trading and open access library is placed at the lower level. Though they are situated underground, sunken space and different levels of each building provide them with natural light, ventilation, and circulation.

Applying such methods to the site, this proposal suggests the creation of a roofscape that forms an extra ground that covers the roof garden and the underground space, thereby transforming the site into a park and a tourist attraction characterized by the theme of books.

Kim Kwangsoo is the CEO of studio_K_works / Co-CEO of CURTAINHALL, Former Professor, Ewha Womans University and Master's degree from School Architecture, Yale University, bachelor's degree from Architectural Engineering, Yonsei University

Kim Kwangsoo has participated in the projects of design and architecture which facilitate relationship between experts, public and space users from various fields, and has paid attention to the change of the characteristics of society and perception and urban and architectural environment caused by new media.

He held an exhibition based on research about the phenomenon of apartments and room culture in Korean society under the theme of 'City of Bang, Venice Biennale (2004)' in Venice Biennale of Architecture 2014, and invited exhibitions in many museums including Museum of Cultures in Helsinki in 2007, Museum of Cultures in Vienna in 2013, and Ades Gallery in Germany. He won the Minister Prize of the Good Place Award for 'DMZ Migratory Bird Town' focused on local cooperation in Cheorwon Yangjiri, and his recent regeneration project 'Bucheon Art Bunker B39' which transformed a garbage incineration plant into cultural facility attracted public attention and he received the grand prize of 2018 Public Building Awards of Korea thanks to the project.

- 북악산과 인왕산의 산세에 감싸인 장소에 놓여있음
- 경복궁 및 시가지 보다 높은 지대에 위치

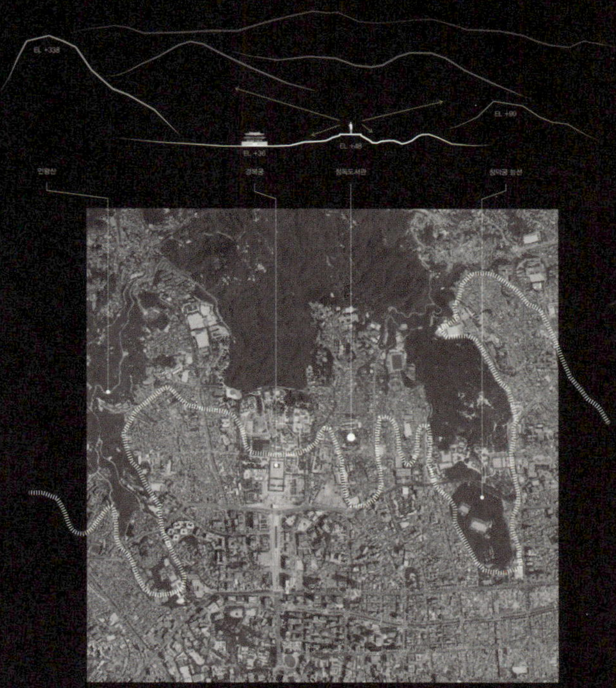

- 작은 스케일의 도시한옥과 신축건물이 혼재하는 화동에 위치
- 건물들이 밀집되어 있는 도시조직 한 가운데 탁 트인 오픈스페이스를 갖고있음

정독도서관 주변 가로 현황

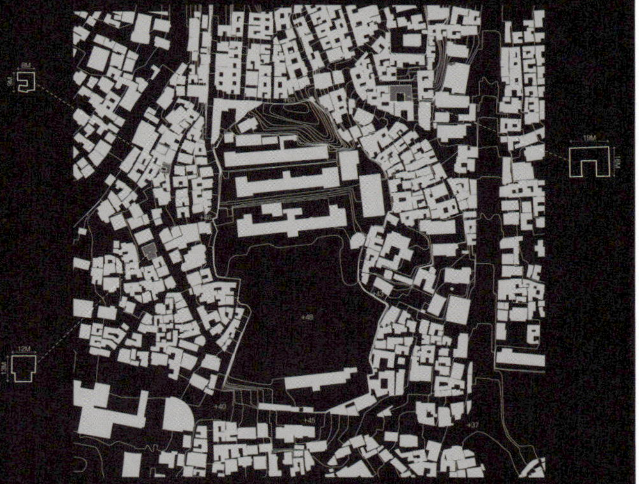

program keyword = 독서문화

'책' 을 중심으로 한 교류활동, 개가식 도서관 및 중고서적거래 플랫폼

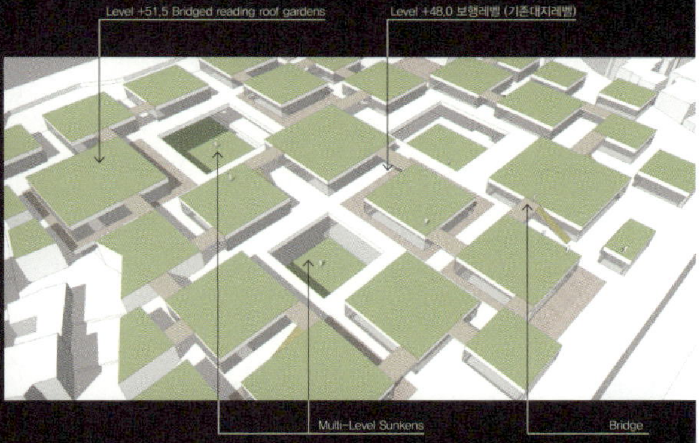

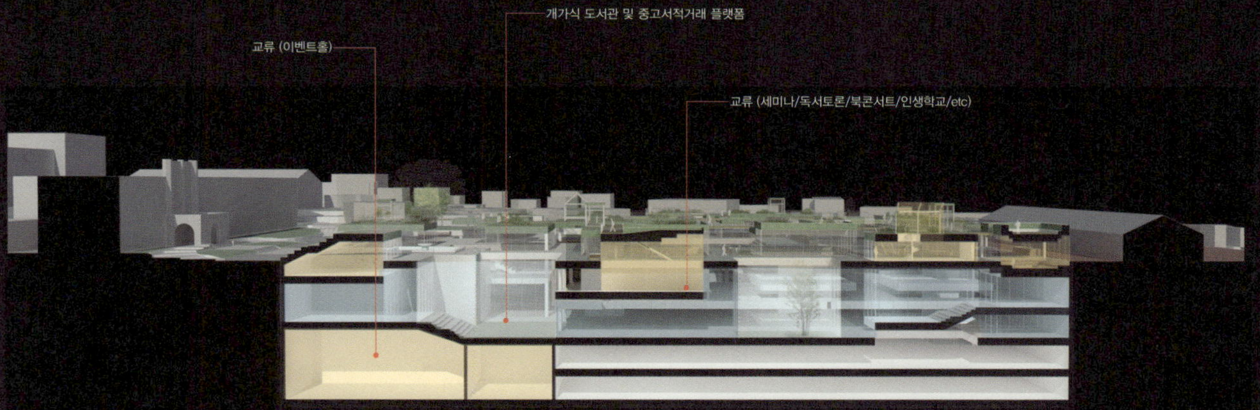

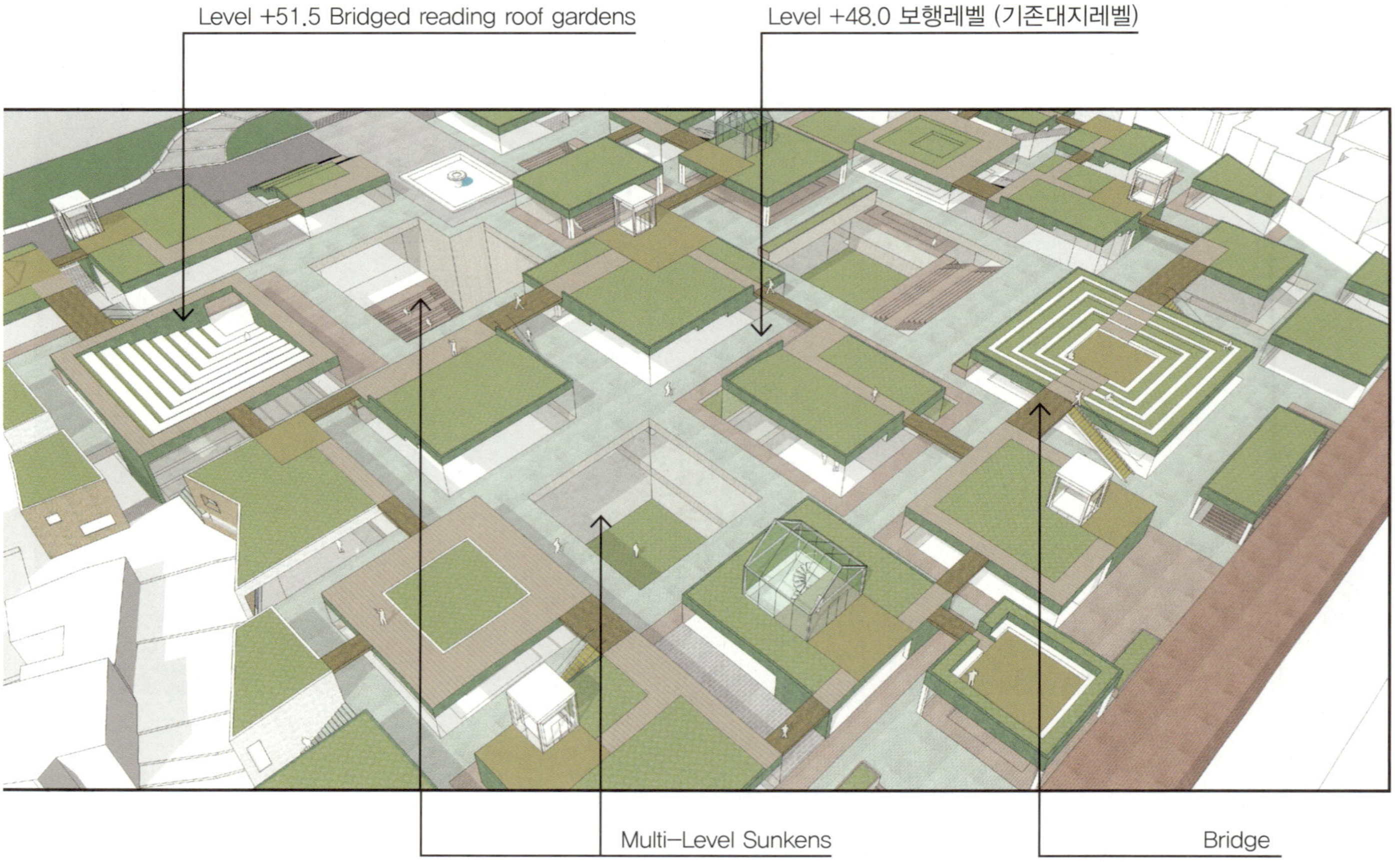
Level +51.5 Bridged reading roof gardens
Level +48.0 보행레벨 (기존대지레벨)
Multi-Level Sunkens
Bridge

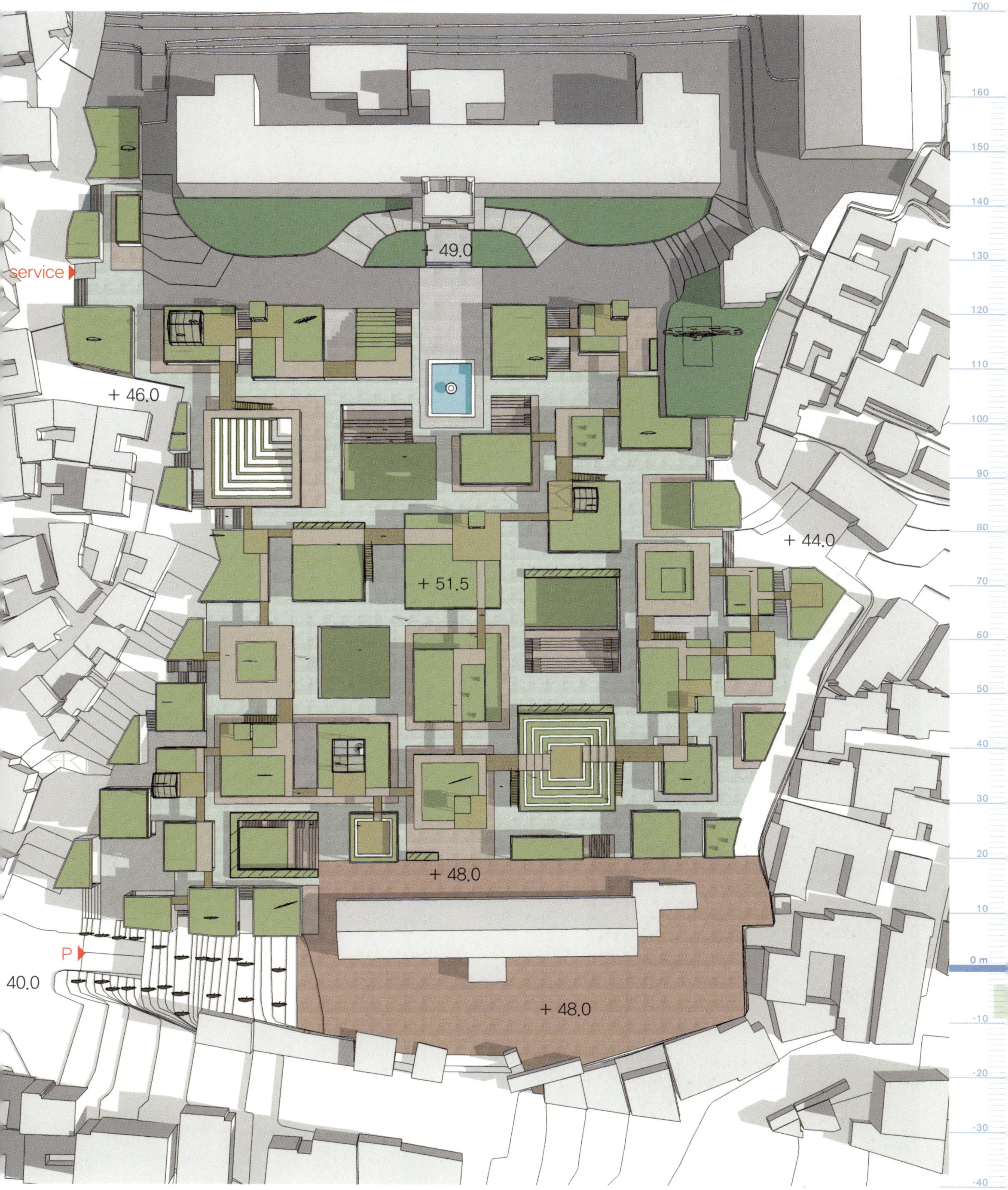

service
+ 49.0
+ 46.0
+ 44.0
+ 51.5
+ 48.0
P
40.0
+ 48.0
700
160
150
140
130
120
110
100
90
80
70
60
50
40
30
20
10
0 m
-10
-20
-30
-40

루프브릿지와 코어

– 북촌 특유의 골목길 경험이 대상지 내로 확장되도록 길을 따라 변화하는 다양한 레벨의 진입부 계획

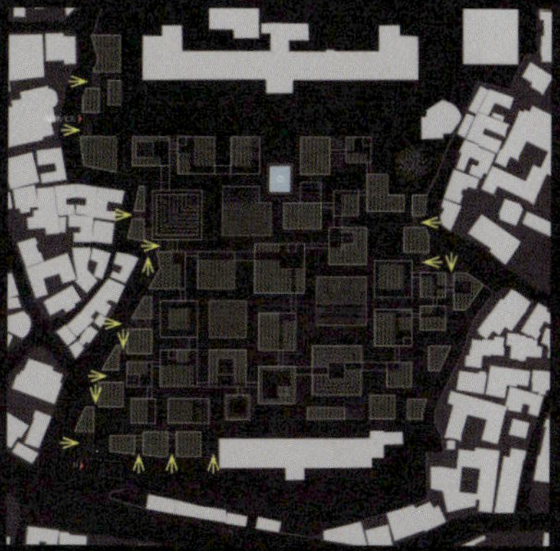

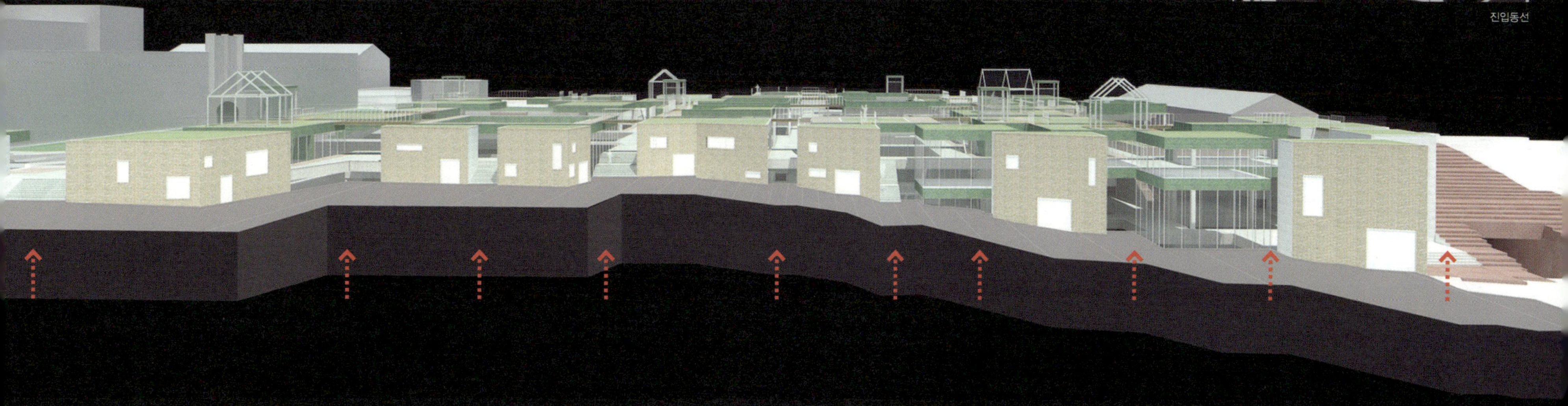

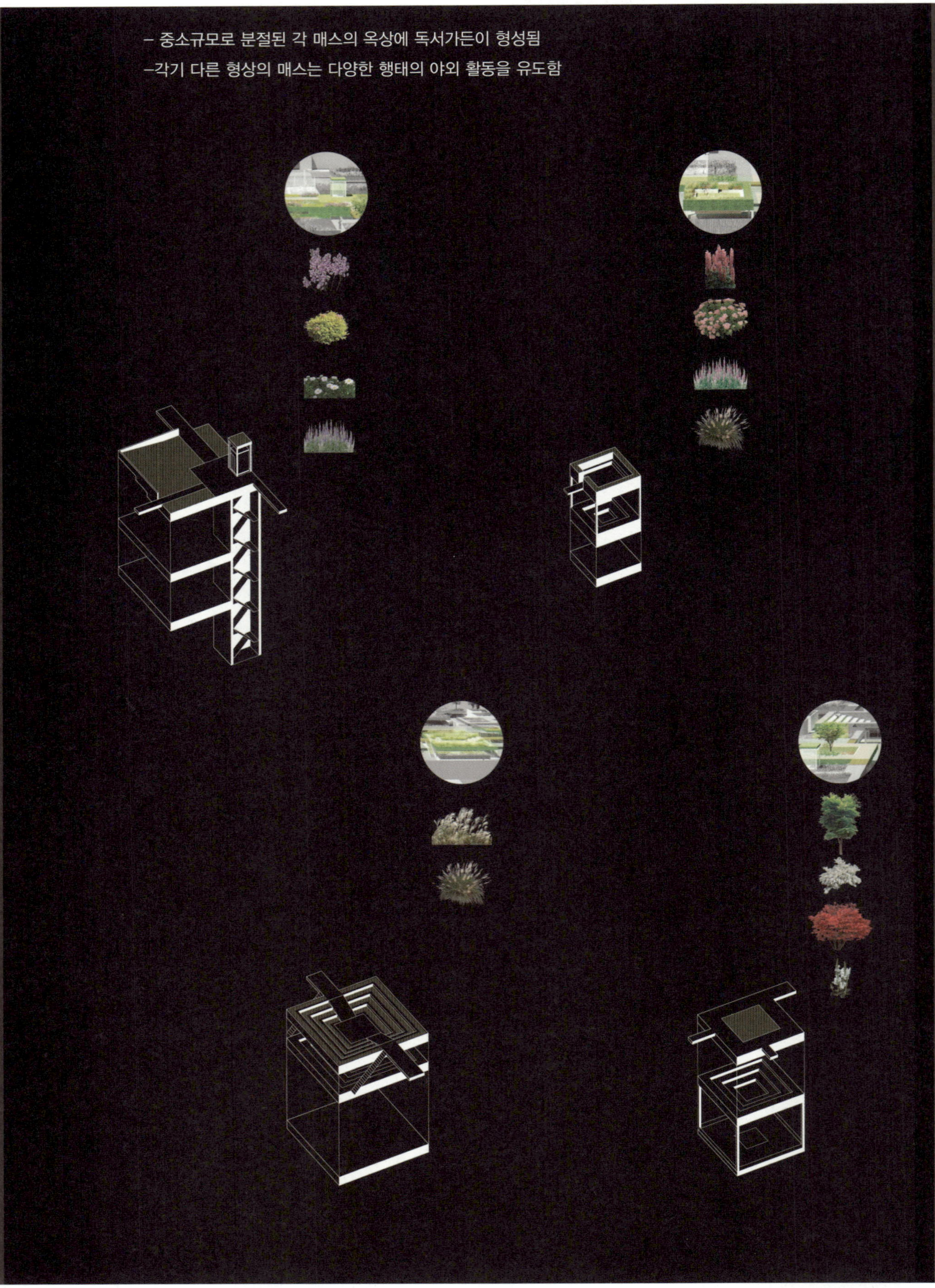
– 중소규모로 분절된 각 매스의 옥상에 독서가든이 형성됨
–각기 다른 형상의 매스는 다양한 행태의 야외 활동을 유도함

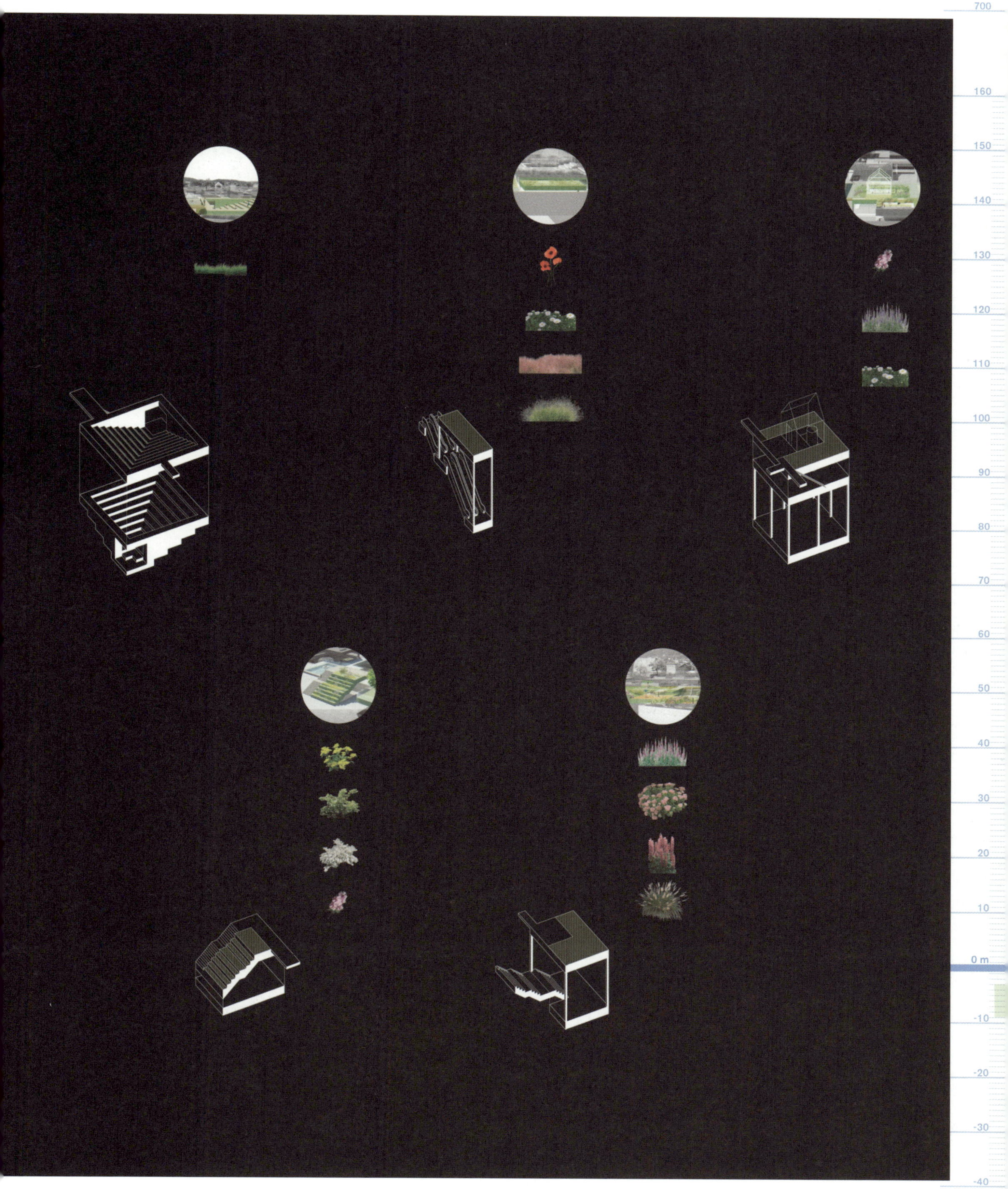
700
160
150
140
130
120
110
100
90
80
70
60
50
40
30
20
10
0 m
-10
-20
-30
-40

– 층간의 레벨차에 의해 형성되는 틈과 선큰들은 내외부 활동의 가시성을 이루고 공존감을 제공함

내외부 활동 가시성

– 선큰과 층간레벨차로 인해 밝고 개방감있는 지하같지 않은 지하공간을 형성

700
160
150
140
130
120
110
100
90
80
70
60
50
40
30
20
10
0 m
-10
-20
-30
-40

청보글

Cheungvogl

신서울, 서울의 새로운 공공 레이어

기존 지하공간을 재개발하고 서울 도심 지하 연결망으로 확장하는 일은 서울의 거대 교통망 아래 존재하는 유휴 부지들을 다시 연결함으로써 도시 조직에 새롭고 확장된 켜를 더해줄 것이다. 이 새로운 공공의 켜는 지하공간 체계가 지상의 가로나 도시 경관과 직접적 상관관계를 맺을 때 비로소 도시 조직 안에서 작동할 것이다. 지하공간 활성화 사업은 도시 생활 양식이나 도시 맥락과의 관계성에 많은 영향을 받을 것이다. 하지만 이번 사업의 총체적 개발 전략은 도시 외곽에 강남 같은 새로운 업무 및 상업지구를 개발하도록 이끈 지가 상승의 여파로 정체되어 있던 도심 지역의 활성화에 도움을 줄 것이다. 한편 이 지역 도시 상업 공간 개발에 대한 최근의 무관심은 지난 수십 년 동안 잠자는 숲속의 공주와 같은 상태에 있던 도심 지역이 지닌 가능성을 재발견 또는 재개발할 수 있는 여지를 남겨 놓았다. 이러한 맥락에서 이번 지하공간 개발 사업은 단순한 개발 사업이 아닌 서울 도심 공간을 위한 활력소가 될 것이다.
새로 개발된 지하공간은 기존 지하철역과 지하철 연결망을 이용하는 통근자를 비롯해 수많은 사람들이 방문하게 될 것이며, 지하철역과 다양한 지하철 노선 사이의 새 연결망이 편리함을 더해주는 지하철 시스템의 혜택을 누릴 수 있을 것이다.

서울 도시 생활에 필수적인 통행로라는 개념을 뛰어넘어 더 큰 발전을 이루려면 지하공간을 도시 조직 내 주요 결절점과 연결하거나 그곳을 향해 개방하고, 해당 지역과 그 주변의 도시 가로 풍경에 변화를 몰고 올 수 있는 도시적, 문화적, 사회적 교류와 소통의 장을 형성해야 한다. 이 새로운 공공의 켜는 지상 공간의 활성화 여부에 많은 영향을 받을 것이다.

도심 배양기

지하공간과 가로 풍경을 가장 극명하게 분리하는 것은 시각적, 물리적 연결 고리의 부재인데 이는 심리적 경계와의 분리감을 증폭한다.
지하공간의 흐름을 가로 레벨에 추상적으로 투사해주는 조형물은 내외부 공간 사이에 중간지대를 형성하는 한편 주요 교차로에 랜드마크를 조성해주며 지하 네트워크의 존재를 알리고, 목적지나 명소의 형태를 빌어 멀리서 방향을 안내해준다.
입구에 이르러 조형물은 키가 더 커지고 밀도가 상승하며 인구의 흐름을 지상과 지하 풍경 사이의 주요 지점으로 유도한다.
조형물들은 딱딱한 도시 조직에 다양한 각도의 새로운 감각을 불어넣어 주며 도시 명소나 매개물, 랜드마크가 되거나 도시 맥락의 흐름 안팎에 물리적 간섭을 일으키거나 기존 도시 패턴과 개인의 자유 사이의 경계를 무너뜨린다.
미지의 존재와 눈에 보이지 않는 것은 호기심을 불러일으키는 법이다. 공공연하게 합리적 패턴을 따르지 않으며, 외견상 비합리적으로 보이는 추상적 형태의 건축적 매개물은 새로운 감각을 낳는 도심 배양기가 된다.
그리고 신서울이라는 매개물은 사업 대지와 회현, 명동, 시청을 연결해주고 동시에 대지 주변의 크고 작은 가로들을 통해 시각적 연계성을 구축해내며 그를 통해 지하의 새로 확장된 공공의 켜를 향해 흐르는 일종의 중력장을 만들어낸다.

청보글은 주디청과 크리스토프 보글에 의해 2008년 설립된 건축설계사무실이다. 기획 본사는 홍콩에 위치하며 중국과 독일에 지사를 두고 있다. 현재 홍콩과 중국, 대한민국, 일본, 독일 그리고 미국에 프로젝트를 진행중이다. 최근에는 서울 여의나루 페리터미널 마스터플랜의 국제 현상설계에 당선되었다.
청보글의 작품은 예술과 과학 그리고 철학간의 끊임없는 연계를 모색한다. 그들의 감성과 이성에 대한 동시적 분석은 건축의 가치와 품질을 유지시킨다. 그들의 사고가 매우 합리적이고 생산적이며 효율적인 결과를 달성하는 것에 집중하며 이를 지향하고 있지만 그들의 작업은 시민들을 감성적으로 어루만지고 연계하는 특정한 종류의 미묘한 감각에 대하여 이야기한다. 그것들은 시간과 함께 디자인의 중요한 부분으로 맞물려 공간의 맥락 안에서 새로운 해석과 경험을 형성한다. 시간의 질은 만족감으로 측정된다. 시간과 건축과 예술 그리고 문화간의 안무는 인문학적 가치의 청보글 철학의 핵심적인 믿음이자 원동력으로서 그들의 열정과 헌신이다.
건축을 만들어 냄으로서 그들의 작업은 "시적인 실용주의"를 표방하며 과학을 예술과 융합하고 예술과 건축을 융합하고 건축을 공간의 시적인 감응에 융합한다.

700
160
150
140
130
120
110
100
90
80
70
60
50
40
30
20
10
0 m
-10
-20
-30
-40

Shinseoul, The Public Layers of Seoul

Urban Activator

The redevelopment of the existing underground spaces and the extension to a connected system beneath the city center of Seoul will provide the urban grain with an extended new layer by reconnecting the unoccupied ground beneath the city's extensive traffic network. This new public layer will only function within the urban fabric if the underground system stands in direct correlation with the overground streetscape and cityscape.
The reactivation of the underground development project will largely depend on the interlink with the city life and context. In return, the ambition of the holistic development will feedback to the reactivation of the city center, which has been halted due to increasing property prices, leading the development of alternative business and commercial districts in the outer districts, such as Gangnam. Subsequently, the recent unattractiveness for urban and commercial development in the area has now created opportunities for rediscovery and redevelopment potentials in the city center, which had been left in a state of sleeping beauty in the past decades. In these means, the development of the underground layer will become more than a development in itself, but an urban activator to central Seoul.
The new redeveloped underground system will receive large numbers of visitors in form of commuters through the connection to the existing metro stations and will benefit the subway system with the convenience of newly created interlinks between stations and different subway lines.
To develop the system further, away from a mere thoroughfare to an integral part of Seoul's city life, the underground system will have to connect and open up to central nodes within the urban grain, creating places of urban, cultural and social relevance and interest, which will result in transformation of the city's streetscape in these areas and beyond. The new underground public layer will largely depend upon the simultaneous activation of the overground.

Urban Incubator

The aspect which generally separates underground spaces from the streetscape most is the lack of visual and physical connection, which amplifies the disconnection into a psychological barrier. The introduction of a sculptural installation that abstractly identifies the footprint of the underground space on street level, creating an intermediate zone between the inside and outside while establishing landmarks at strategic intersections, indicating the existence of the underground network and offering orientation in form of destinations and attractions from afar.
At entry points, the sculptural installation heightens and densifies, directing human flow towards gravitation points of the development between the over-and-underground landscapes.
The sculptural installations, creates new perceptions from different angles within the rigid urban grain, becoming attraction, intervention, landmark and physical interruption in and to the rhythm of the urban fabric, breaking barriers between the existing city pattern as well as in individual freedom. The unknown and the unseen create curiosity. The seemingly irrational intervention of architecture in form of abstraction, which does not apparently follow rational patterns, becomes the urban incubator of a new perception.
The intervention of Shinseoul physically connects the site with Hoehyeon, Myeong-dong and City Hall while creating a visual connection through major and minor streets surrounding the site, creating a gravity field towards and into the new underground public layer extension.

Cheungvogl is an architecture practice founded by Chui Lai Judy Cheung and Christoph Hoelscher Vogl in 2008. The creative team is based in Hong Kong with site offices in China and Germany. The practice is currently working on projects in Hong Kong, China, South Korea, Japan, Germany and the United States. Recent projects include the winning design for the international competition of the Yeoui-Naru Ferry Terminal and master plan in Seoul.
Their works consistently explore connections between art, science and philosophies. Their simultaneous analysis of sensual and rational thinking is pertinent in creating values and qualities to architecture. While their thinking is focused and directed on achieving highly rational, productive and efficient results, their work speaks of a specific kind of subtle sensitivity that touches and connects people emotionally. Their engagement with 'time' as an integral part of the design palette forms new interpretations and experiences within the context of space. Quality of time is measured by contentment. The choreography between time, architecture, art and culture is their passion and commitment, with humanistic values being the core belief and driving force of Cheungvogl's philosophy.
Through the making of architecture, their works amalgamate science into art; art into architecture; architecture into the poetics of space, manifesting the idea of "Poetic Pragmatism".

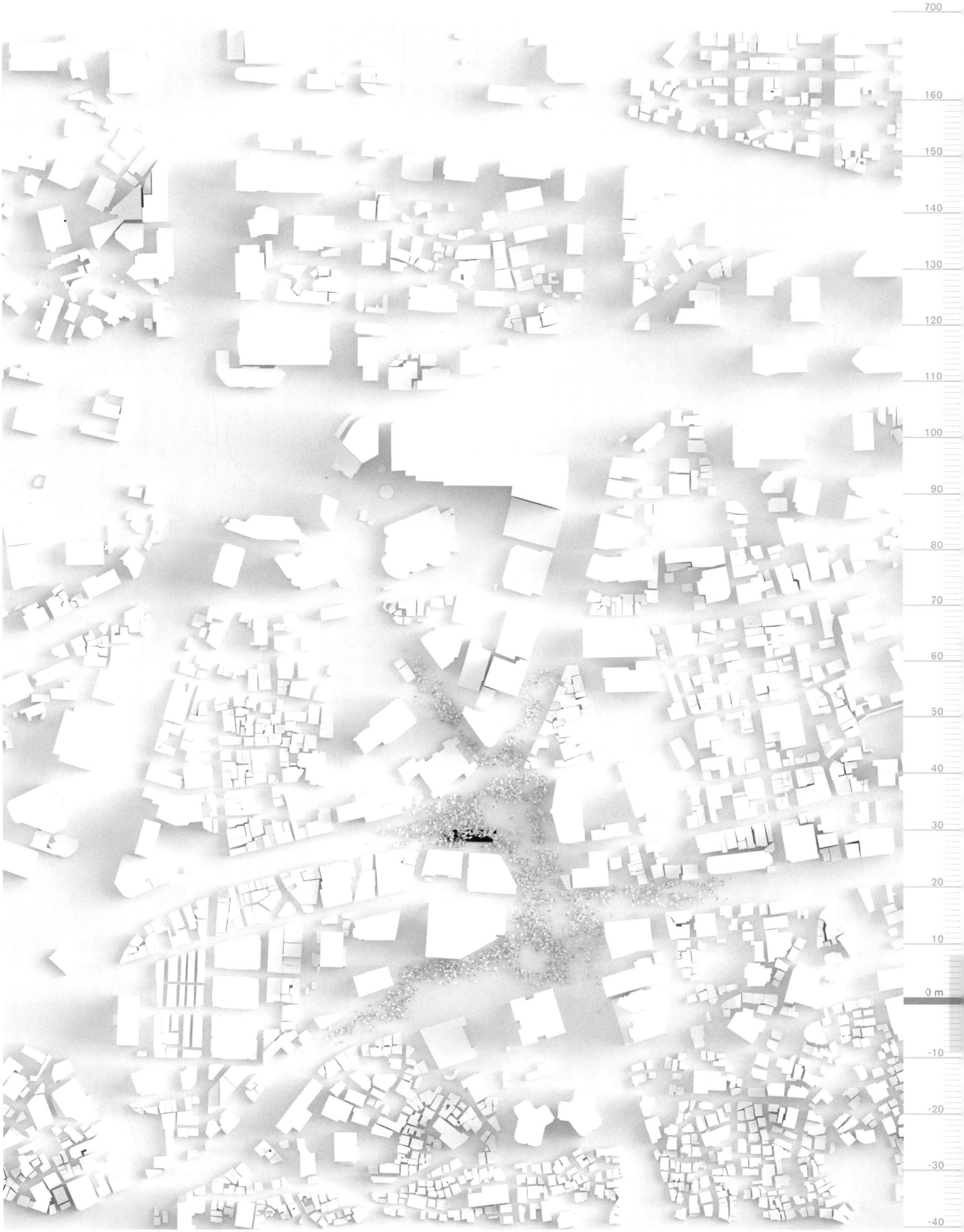

700
160
150
140
130
120
110
100
90
80
70
60
50
40
30
20
10
0 m
-10
-20
-30
-40

평면 확장기 – 도시의 켜를 연결하다

도시 조직 내 주요 교차점의 고밀화된 조형물 지대 아래에서는 가로 풍경이 커다란 순환형 경사로의 유기적인 흐름에 따라 지하층으로 잠겨 들어가는데, 이 경사로는 도시 조직이 넓고 빛으로 충만한 공공공간을 향해 열리는 지점에서 가로 레벨과 지하 도시 층을 자연스레 연결해준다.

가로 레벨은 지하공간으로 부드럽게 흘러 들어가고, 대지 주변의 건축 매스들과 극명한 대조를 이루는 연속적인 연결 고리를 여러 켜와 오브제 사이에 만들어내는 완만한 파형 풍경으로 여러 레벨을 통합한다. 이러한 과도적 층 구성은 지상과 지하 레벨 사이의 물리적, 시각적 단절을 극복하고, 완만한 경사가 이어지며 다양한 레벨 사이의 매개가 되는 새로운 공간으로 도시 경관을 자연스럽게 확장해준다.

중앙 결절지의 지상 공간에는 다양한 크기의 개방구들이 점점이 박혀 있어 자연 채광과 환기를 가능하게 하고, 도시 광장을 가로 레벨 아래의 공공의 켜까지 확장해준다.

신세계 백화점과 연결된 출입구와 서울중앙우체국과 한국은행 앞의 공공 광장은 지상과 지하 사이에 자리한 융합의 장이 되어 새로운 공공의 켜와 주요 보행자 동선을 주변 영역 안에 담아내도록 계획되었다. 출입구 위의 움직임들은 밀집된 조형물 아래에서 다양한 날씨 상황을 피할 수 있다. 지상 레벨에서 공공공간과 더불어 엘리베이터, 에스컬레이터, 계단 등의 수직 연결 장치를 품고 있는 전면 파빌리온은 지상과 지하 사이의 시각적, 물리적 경계를 더 무너뜨려 준다.

본 지하 공간 재개발 계획은 부족하게 주어진 공간적, 구조적 여건 내에서 공간과 기능을 새로 정의하는 데 초점을 맞추고 있다.

새로 확장된 영역의 지하공간은 구조적 경간이 더 넓고 2층 높이 층고를 지닌 공간을 향해 열려 있고, 통근자 동선을 기존과 동일한 레벨에 유지하는 한편 주요 시설 주변에 행사, 전시, 체육 활동, 집회 등을 위한 넓은 공간을 조성해준다. 상층부는 도시 지하에 이르면 보행자 동선과 테라스를 품은 채 도로를 따라 상점과 카페, 식당을 펼쳐 놓은 반공공형 가로 풍경으로 바뀌는데 이러한 풍경은 신세계 백화점까지 이어진다. 기존 네트워크 사이사이에 새로 형성된, 2층 높이 층고를 지닌 공간들은 상업 시설들 사이의 문화적, 사회적 연결 고리가 되어 해당 시설들을 새로운 지하 도시 광장으로 바꾸어 놓는다.

기본 목표는 순환형 경사로의 개방구들을 최대한 활용해 도시 하부 흐름을 따라 지하와 지상을 연결함으로써 물리적 교차점과 시각적 연계성을 구축해 진정한 의미에서 도시의 공공의 켜들을 통합하는 것이다. 이때 수직 교차점들은 햇빛으로 가득한 공간이자 가로 풍경으로의 확장이 된다.

Surface Multiplier - Connecting the city layers

Underneath the densified areas of the sculptural installation at significant junctions within the urban fabric, the streetscape submerges with the underground layer through smooth transition of large circular ramps, which seamlessly connecting the street level with the lower ground city layer at points where the urban grain opens up to larger light filled public spaces.

The street level gently unfolds into the underground spaces, unifying the different levels by gentle undulating landscape, which naturally creates a continuous connection between the layers and stands in stark contrast to the building masses surrounding the site. The transitional layering overcomes both, the physical and the visual disconnection between overground and subterranean levels and extends the cityscape seamless into the new development, where gentle slopes continue to mediate between different levels. At central nodes, the ground is punctuated with openings of different sizes to allow daylight and natural ventilation to extend the city squares into the public layers below street level.

The entry points to Shinsegae Department Store as well as the public square in front of Korea Post Headquarters and Bank of Korea are designed to form the new melting points between over-and-underground, merging the new city public layer with the main pedestrian flow into its adjacent areas. Hovering over the entry points, movements are sheltered from weather conditions under the densified sculpture. At ground level, entrance pavilions, containing public spaces, vertical connections of lifts, escalators and stairs further break down the visual and physical barriers between under-and-overground.

The redevelopment of the existing underground is focused on the redefinition of space and its usage within the given narrow spatial and structural parameters.

Within the new extensions, the underground opens up into double height volumes with wider structural spans, maintaining commuters flow at the same existing level, while creating large spaces for events, exhibitions, sports activities and communal gathering points around attractions. The upper tier transforms into an intermediate public streetscape below the city, containing pedestrian flows and terraces, lining the traffic with retail, cafes and restaurants which extends into the adjacent Shinsegae Department Store. The newly created double height spaces between the existing network systems will form cultural and social relevant interlinks between the commercial developments, transforming these spaces into the new underground city squares.

The main aim is to connect the underground with the overground on its path beneath the city at as many points as possible through openings of circular ramps, which do not only provide physical intersections, but also visible connections to truly merge the public layers of the city. The vertical intersections become natural light filled spaces and extension to the streetscape.

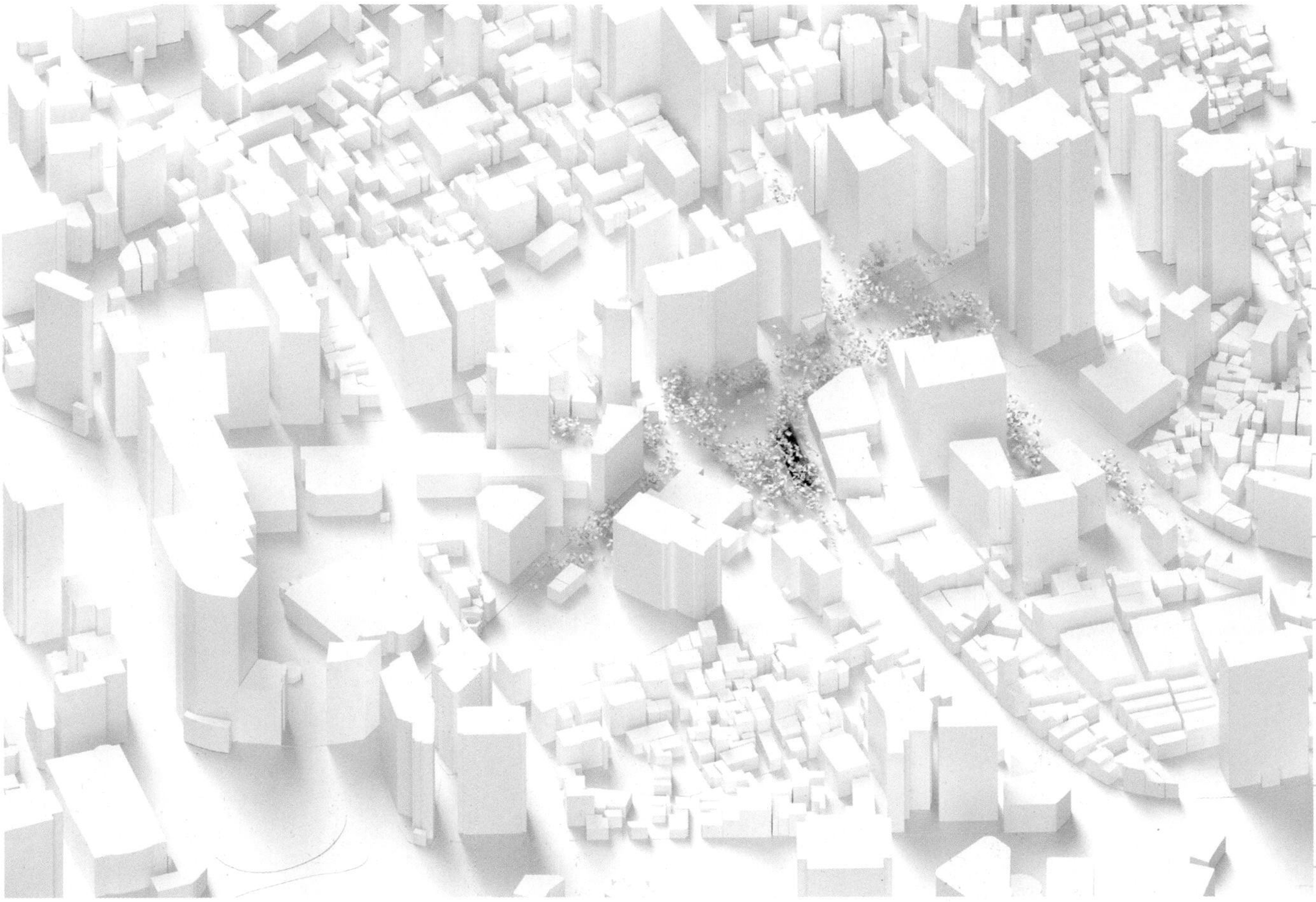

서울을 위한 공공의 켜

서울의 지하공간은 그 위 가로 레벨의 복제물이 아닌, 삶의 모든 영역을 아우르는 건강하며 종합적인 도시 맥락 안에 존재하는, 도시 생활의 연장이다. 도시계획은 그곳에 정착한 사회의 반영이자 전체 공동체와 개인 모두에게 중대한 영향 요인이다. 도시 개발의 장기적 성공 여부는 기존 맥락을 고려한 활성화와 상호작용 그리고 경제성, 사회 문화적 맥락, 공동체의 필요 사이의 세밀한 균형잡기에 달려있다. 도시 재생 전략과 해당 지역 공동체 사이에서 균형을 이루는 신서울은 도시가 지닌 물리적, 인간적 켜들의 연결 고리를 다양한 차원에서 재활성화하고 확장한다. 또한 다양한 분야를 아우르는 '슈퍼-타이폴로지(Super-Typology)'의 한 형태로서 기존의 도시 개발 전략을 삼차원적 도시계획으로 발전시킨다. 위계와 기능성에 기반을 둔 맥락 속에서 모호한 어긋남이 초래한 변화는 서로가 없으면 규범과 자유가 존재하지 못하는 건강한 사회의 균형을 되찾아준다. 여기서 제안하는 새로운 도시 공간은 기존 맥락과의 조화와 대립 위에 세워진다. 재생이란 뿌리와의 단절이 아닌 미래에 대한 질문에서 시작되는 것이다.

The Public Layers of Seoul

The underground layer of Seoul is not a replica of the street level above, but an extension to the city life, which as in any healthy and holistically grown urban context covering all aspects of life. City planning is not only a reflection of the inhabiting society, but the main influence on the community as a whole as well as on the individuals. The long term success of the development is highly dependent upon the positive activation and interaction with its existing context and sensitively balancing the economic figures, social and cultural relevance and communal needs.

Creating a balance between urban renewal strategies with its inhabiting communities, Shinseoul reactivates and expands the connection of physical and humanistic layers of the city in multiple levels. Shinseoul, as a form of interdisciplinary "Super-Typology" moves the urban development strategy beyond three dimensional spatial city planning. In a context derived from hierarchies and functionality, the disruption created by abstract nonconformity reinstates the balance of a healthy society, in which regulation and freedom cannot exist without one another. The new urban intervention is built upon coherence and confrontation with the existing. Renewal does not happen in isolation from its roots, but in question of its future.

ong-dong Station Extension
Korea Post Tower Link
Shinsagae Link
Ho

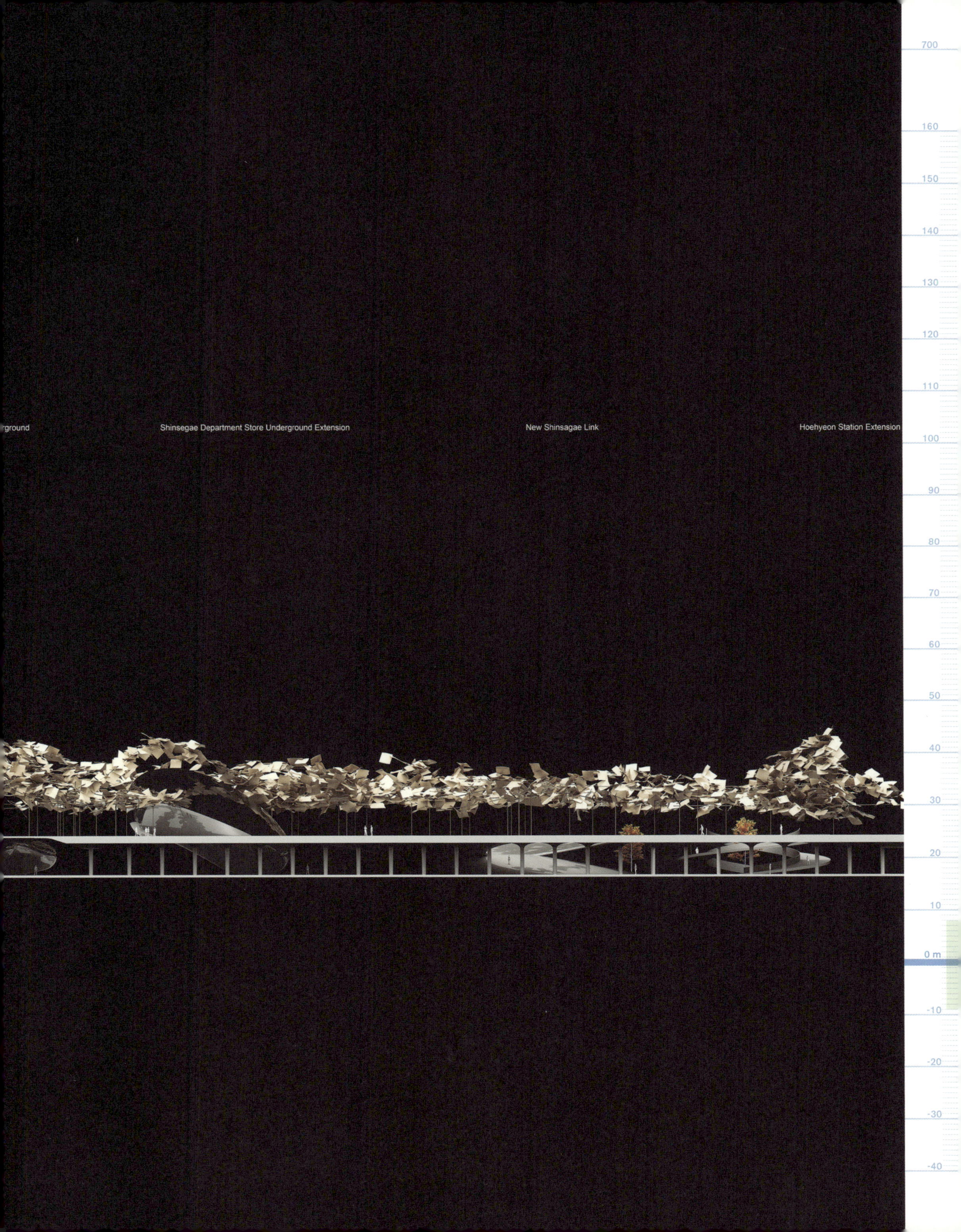
rground
Shinsegae Department Store Underground Extension
New Shinsagae Link
Hoehyeon Station Extension
700
160
150
140
130
120
110
100
90
80
70
60
50
40
30
20
10
0 m
-10
-20
-30
-40

www.ilogen.com
1588-9988
700
160
150
140
130
120
110
100
90
80
70
60
50
40
30
20
10
0 m
-10
-20
-30
-40

700
160
150
140
130
120
110
100
90
80
70
60
50
40
30
20
10
0 m
-10
-20
-30
-40

터미널 7

Terminal 7 Architects

서울연대기: 정맥

1394년 조선이 도성을 지금의 서울로 이전할 당시 조선의 창업자와 그의 학자 관료들은 네 개의 산으로 둘러싸여 있고 동서로 강이 흐르는 대지를 선택했다. '청계천'과 같은 방향으로 흐르는 '을지로'는 '종로'와 나란히 서울을 동서로 가로지른다. 옛 도성에는 남북으로 지나는 도로가 거의 없었다. '묵사동천길'은 작은 개천을 따라 이어지는 오래된 길로, '을지로 4가' 근처에서 '청계천'과 만난다.
서울이 근대화를 거치는 동안 옛길 위에는 더 넓은 새 도로가 건설되었다. '배오개길'은 남북으로 곧장 뻗어 나가다 '을지로 4가' 교차로에서 '을지로'와 만난다. 1980년대 말 차량 교통 개선을 목적으로 서울에 수많은 교통섬이 조성되었다. 그러나 편리해진 교통은 보행자의 안전을 앗아갔다. '을지로 4가' 교차로에는 네 개의 삼각 교통섬이 모퉁이마다 자리하고 있다.
을지로 4가 주변에서는 서울 옛길의 흔적을 많이 찾을 수 있다. 도시 블록은 현대적 도로를 기준으로 나뉘어져 있지만 블록 안쪽으로 들어가 보면 옛길들이 블록 내부를 정맥처럼 연결하고 있다.
서울 중심부에는 조명 산업이 매우 활성화되어 있다. 전자 산업은 서울을 남북으로 가르는 거대 구조물인 '세운광장'의 북쪽 지역에 자리 잡고 있다. 기계 산업은 '청계천' 남쪽부터 '을지로' 북쪽 전자 산업지대 아래까지 밀집되어 있다. 도시 블록 내부의 옛길은 조명 산업의 소통을 가능하게 해주었다. 인쇄 산업 지역은 도시의 남서에서 북서 방향으로 여러 블록에 걸쳐 이어져 있다. 인쇄 산업 지역이 이렇게 분산되어 있는 것은 인쇄 작업이 여러 단계를 거치기 때문이다. 최초 디자인에서 인쇄 후처리 단계 사이에는 수많은 전문 업체가 존재한다. 옛길은 블록 내부의 그 작은 업체들을 연결하고, 그들 사이의 상호작용을 돕는다.
옛 서울 동대문 주변 전통시장은 옛 도로를 따라 도시의 남서쪽으로 확장되었다. '동대문시장'은 '신진시장'과 '광장시장'까지 이어진다. 그리고 옛 도로 '묵사동천길'을 따라 이어지던 시장은 남쪽으로 방향을 틀어 '방산시장'과 '중부시장'에 이른다.
시청에서 DDP까지 뻗어 있는 을지로는 인쇄 산업의 흐름과 '방산시장'과 '중부시장' 사이의 흐름을 단절시킨다. 을지로 지하상가는 을지로와의 연결이 제한되어 있고 따라서 지상의 역동성에서 유리되어 있다.
본 제안은 지하공간을 통해 옛길들을 연결하고 지상과 지하 사이의 단절을 최소화하는 것을 목적으로 한다. 지상의 역동적 흐름은 새 개방구를 통해 지하상가까지 이어진다.
을지로 4가 교차로에서는 로터리가 고립된 교통섬을 대체하고 광장을 중앙에 자리하도록 한다. 원형 로터리 주위의 완만한 경사는 차량 소음을 줄여주고, 로터리에 채광정을 삽입해준다. 광장 주변 풍경과 원형 개방구의 돌출부는 지하상가의 자연채광을 극대화해준다.
남쪽에서 시작된 인쇄골목은 을지로에서의 단절을 극복하고 북쪽의 포장골목까지 이어진다. 개방구는 닫힌 지하공간에 햇빛을 공급해준다. 지하를 통한 수직 연계는 인쇄 산업의 흐름을 지하까지 연결해준다.
'중부시장'과 '방산시장'의 활동은 을지로에서 단절되고, 제한적인 지하 연결 상태는 지하상가를 고립시키고 말았다. 옛길을 따라 이어지는 아트리움은 지하의 여러 레벨을 통합하고, 시장의 흐름을 지하상가로 끌어들인다.
지상과 지하 사이의 출입구와 연결로는 단절된 두 시장을 하나로 묶어주고 지상의 활동을 지하상가로 확장해준다. 서울의 근대화기에 살아남은 옛 도로들은 지하로 다시 연결되어 도시의 정맥 역할을 한다. 도시가 간직한 실제적 기억은 순차적으로 재구성되고 '서울연대기'로 다시 서술된다.

터미널 7 아키텍츠는 건축 디자인이 사회와 개인 모두를 변화시킬 수 있다고 믿는다. 또한 기존 맥락에 대한 연구를 바탕으로 아이디어를 개발하고, 새로운 기술을 접목한 건축 디자인을 제안한다.
설립자이자 소장 조경찬(AIA, LEED AP BD+C)은 자신의 풍부한 경험을 터미널 7에 나누어 주었다. 컬럼비아 대학 건축대학원에서 건축석사 학위를 받기 전에 그는 고려대학교에서 사회학을, 한국예술종합학교에서 건축을 공부하며 건축과 사회에 대한 기본적인 이해를 쌓았다.
또한 조경찬은 뉴욕 라파엘 비놀리 아키텍츠에서 8년 동안 다양한 프로젝트를 거치며 건축가가 되기 위한 수업을 받았다. 2015년 뉴욕에 터미널 7 아키텍츠를 설립했고, 2016년 한국 사무소를 열었다. 터미널 7의 소장으로서 그는 다양한 프로젝트의 설계를 진행했으며, 한국예술종합학교에서 고급설계스튜디오를 강의하고 있다.

700
160
150
140
130
120
110
100
90
80
70
60
50
40
30
20
10
0 m
-10
-20
-30
-40

Seoul Chronicle: Veins

When the capital of Joseon was relocated to modern-day Seoul in 1394, the founder and his scholar-officials choose the site where four mountains are surrounded, and the stream flows from west to east. Following the direction of 'Cheonggyecheon' stream flow, 'Euljiro' is crossing Seoul from west to east along 'Jongno'. There were few streets running from south to north in old city. 'Muksadongcheon-gil' was one of old streets along the small stream, which merges to 'Cheonggyecheon' nearby 'Euljiro 4-ga'.

During the modernization of Seoul, new widen road was built over old streets. 'Baeogae-gil' runs straight from south to north, and meets 'Euljiro' at 'Euljiro 4-ga' junction. In late 1980's, the thousands of the traffic island was installed in Seoul for the purpose of the better flow of the car traffic. The convenience of the car traffic jeopardizes the safety of the pedestrians. There are four triangle traffic islands each corner of 'Euljiro 4-ga' junction.

Many traces of old streets of Seoul can be still found around Euljiro 4-ga area. The city block is divided by the modern road, but if you step into the inside of the block, old streets connects the interior of the block like the vein.

The lighting industries are very active in the center of Seoul. The electric industry is developed along the north of 'Sewoon plaza', the mega-structure which runs Seoul from south to north. The machinery industry is crowded from the south of 'Cheonggyecheon' to the north of 'Euljiro' below the electric industry. The old street inside of the block made the interaction of the lighting industry possible. The printing industry expands several blocks from the south west to the north east of the city. The expansion of the printing industry was due to the multiple processes of the printing. From the initial design to the after treatment of the printing, there are tens of different specialized companies. The old road connects these small companies inside the block and helps the mutual connection between specialized companies.

The traditional market around the east gate of the old Seoul was expanded to the south west of the city also along the old road. The east gate market, 'Dongdaemun market' expands to 'Shinjin market' and 'Gwangjang market'. Along the old road, 'Muksadongcheon-gil' the market turns to south, and reaches to 'Bangsan market' and 'Jungbu market'.

Running from the city hall to DDP, Euljiro disconnects the flow of the printing industry and the market between 'Bangsan' and 'Jungbu'. Euljiro underground mall has limited connection to the Euljiro, and is isolated from the vivid of the ground.

The proposal is to connect the old streets through underground space, and reduce the disconnection between the ground and underground. The vivid flow of the ground continues to the underground mall with the new openings.

At the Euljiro 4-ga junction, the roundabout replaces the isolated traffic islands and enables to located the plaza in the center. The slight slope around the circle cuts the noise of cars and inscribe the circle light well. The landscape around the plaza and the section profiles at the circular opening maximize the natural light into the underground mall.

The print alley from the south continues to package alley to the north in spite of the disconnection at Euljiro. The openings give the natural light into the closed underground. The vertical connection through the underground continues the flow of the printing industry to the underground.

The activity at 'Jungbu market' and 'Bangsan market' disconnected at the Euljiro, and limited connection to underground isolated the underground mall. The atriums along the old streets integrate the difference levels in underground, and introduce the flow of the market into the underground mall. These gates and connection from the ground to the underground enables to merge two disconnected markets and also expands the activity of the ground to the underground mall. The old roads survived during the modernization of capital city now re-connected through the underground, and works as the vein in the city. The factual memory of the city reorganizes in order, and re-written as 'Seoul Chronicle'.

Terminal 7 Architecture understands that architectural design work can transform the society as well as individuals. We make the idea through the research of the existing conditions, and propose the architectural design solution with new technology.

As principal and founder, K-Chan Zoh, AIA, LEED AP BD+C, brings a broad range of experience to Terminal 7 Architects. Before receiving his professional Mater of Architecture degree from Columbia University, Graduate School of Architecture, Planning and Preservation, Zoh studied Sociology in Korea University and Architecture in Korea National University of Arts, where formed his foundation understanding of architecture and society. He worked eight years in Rafael Vinoly Architects in NYC, where he trained as an architect through number of projects. In 2015, Zoh founded Terminal 7 Architects in New York, NY and 터미널7아키텍츠 건축사사무소㈜ in Seoul, Korea in 2016. As a principal of T7, Zoh designed various project and teaches advanced design studio in Korea National University of Arts.

700
160
150
140
130
120
110
100
90
80
70
60
50
40
30
20
10
0 m
-10
-20
-30
-40

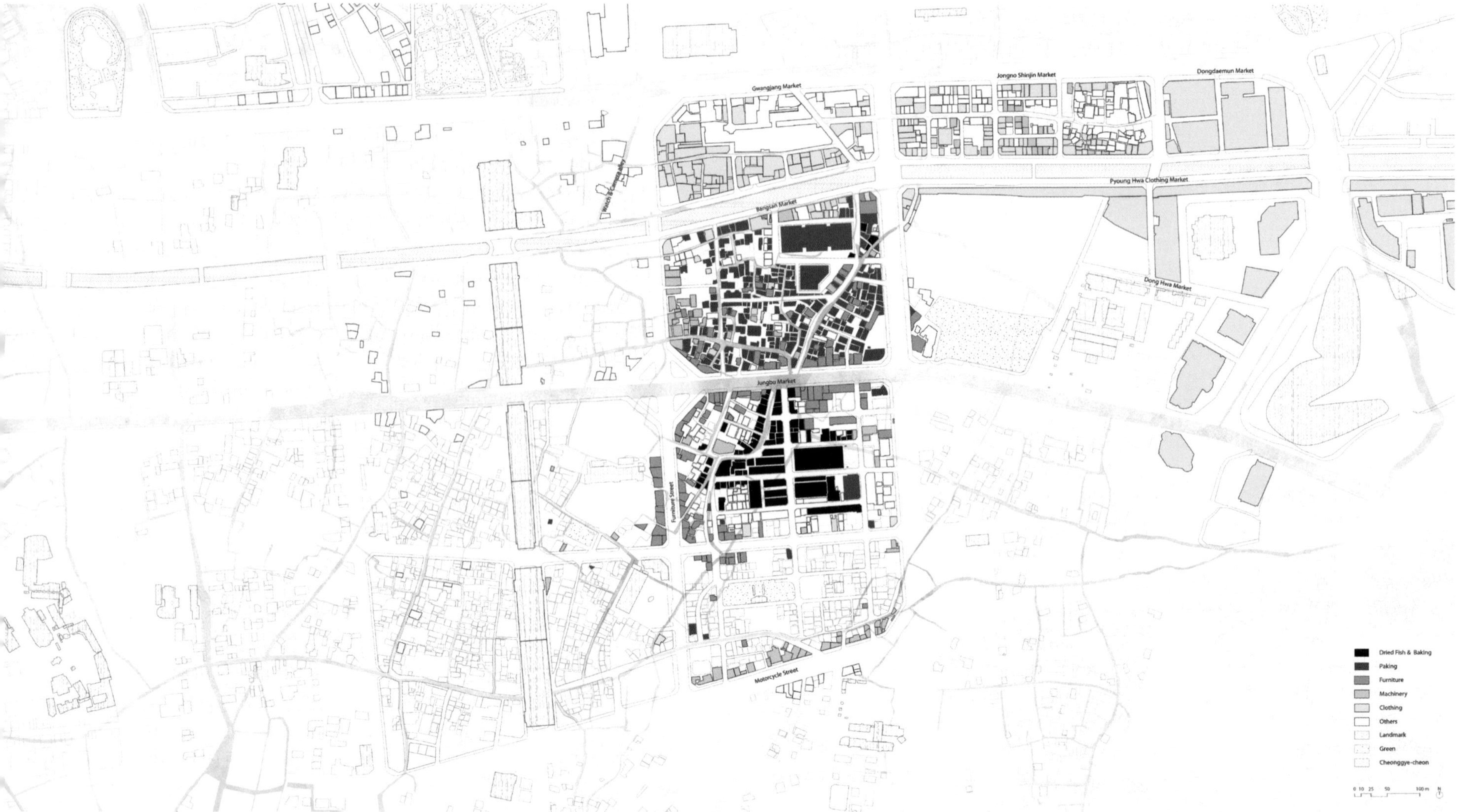
Gwangjang Market
Jongno Shinjin Market
Dongdaemun Market
Pyoung Hwa Clothing Market
Bangsan Market
Watch & Camera Alley
Dong Hwa Market
Jungbu Market
Furniture Street
Motorcycle Street
Dried Fish & Baking
Paking
Furniture
Machinery
Clothing
Others
Landmark
Green
Cheonggye-cheon
0 10 25 50 100 m
N

700
160
150
140
130
120
110
100
90
80
70
60
50
40
30
20
10
0 m
-10
-20
-30
-40

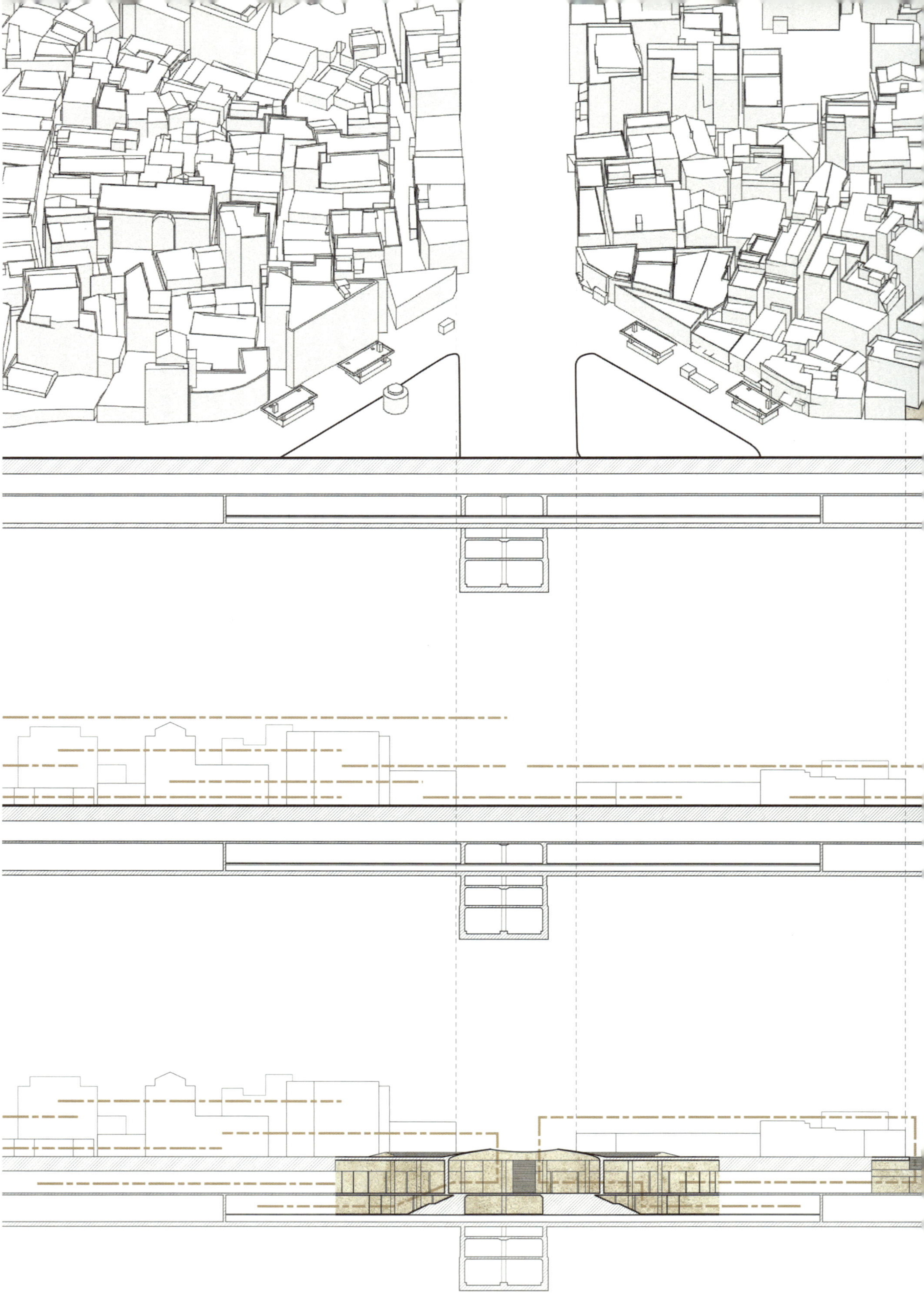

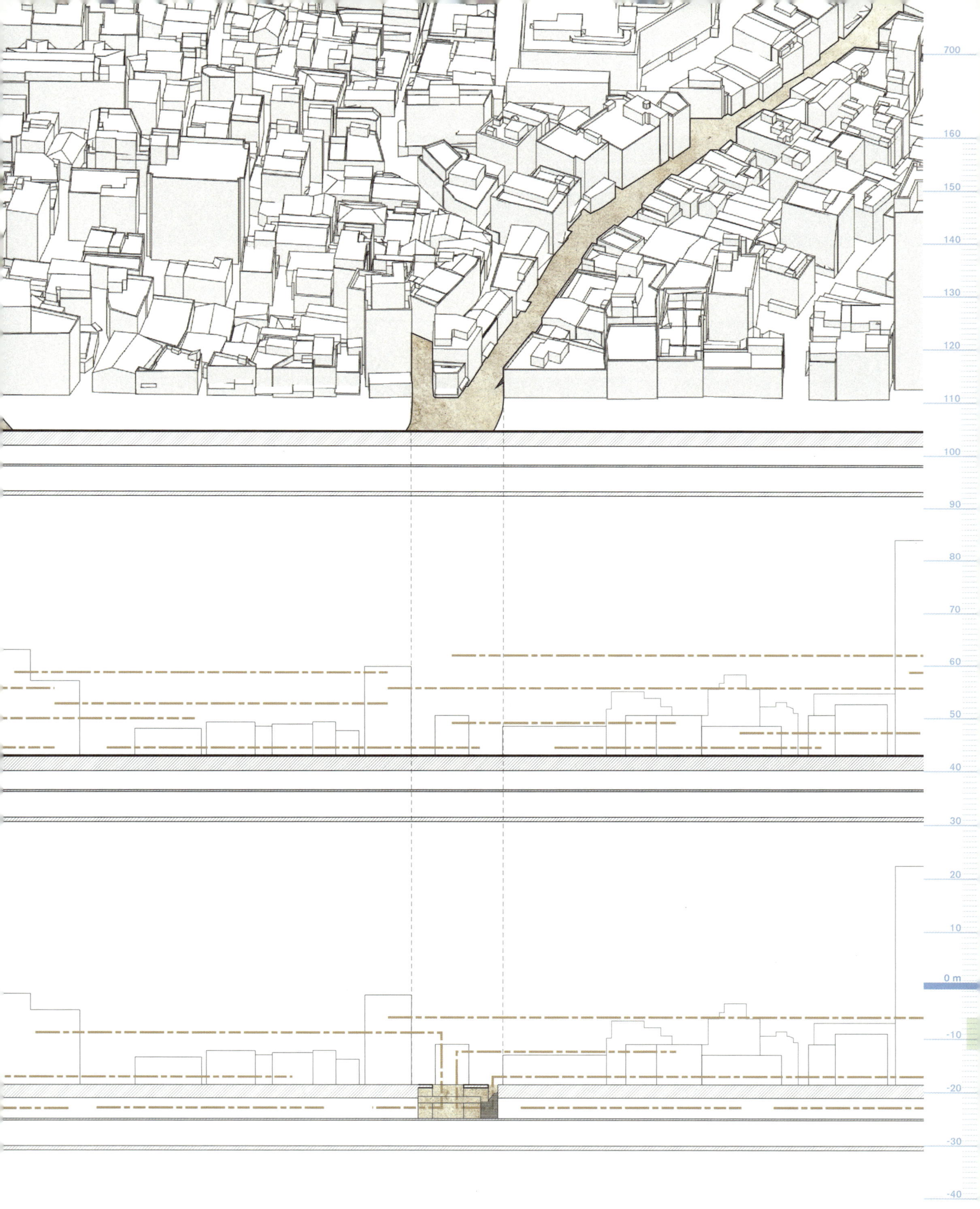

700
160
150
140
130
120
110
100
90
80
70
60
50
40
30
20
10
0 m
-10
-20
-30
-40

EXISTING CONDITION

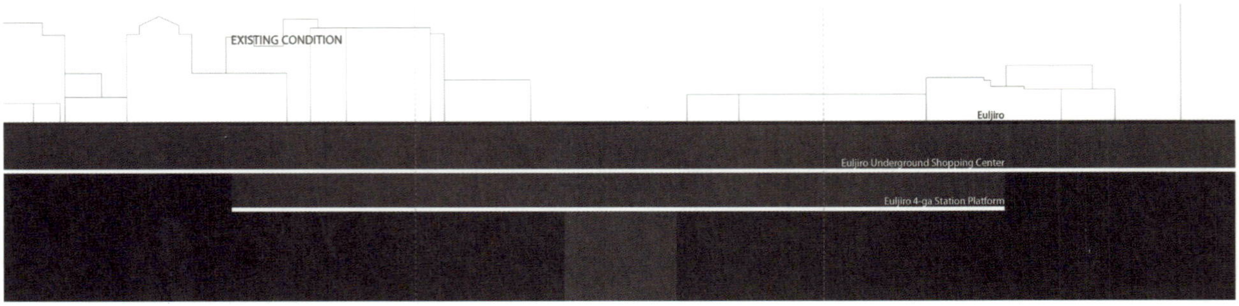

DESIGN PROCEDURE

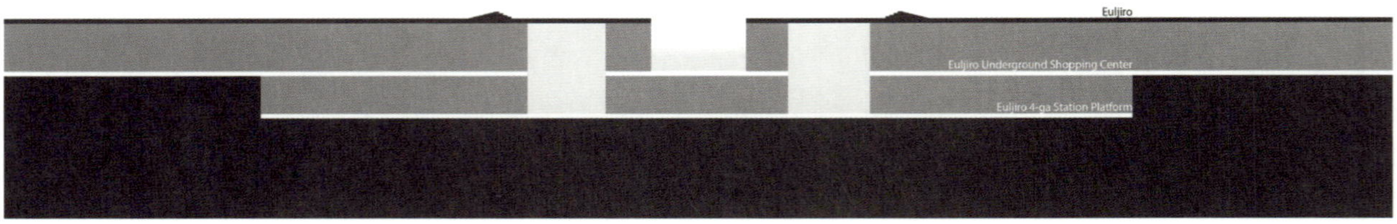

DESIGN PROPOSAL

EXISTING CONDITION

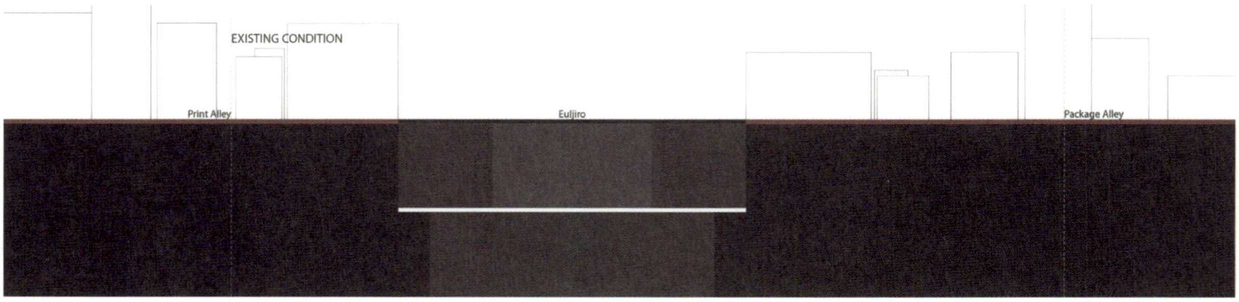

DESIGN PROCEDURE

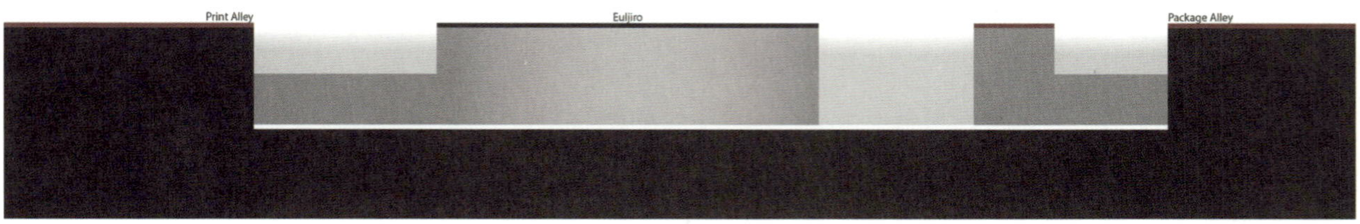

DESIGN PROPOSAL

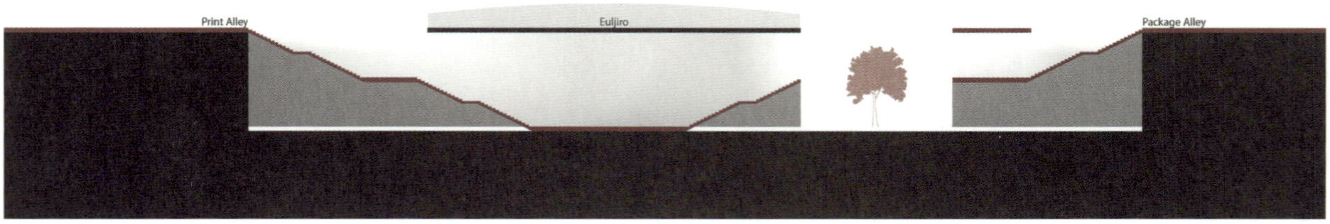

EXISTING CONDITION

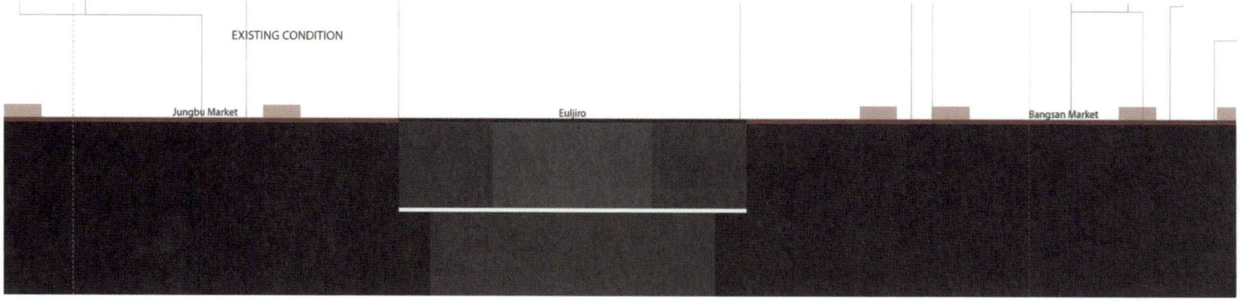

DESIGN PROCEDURE

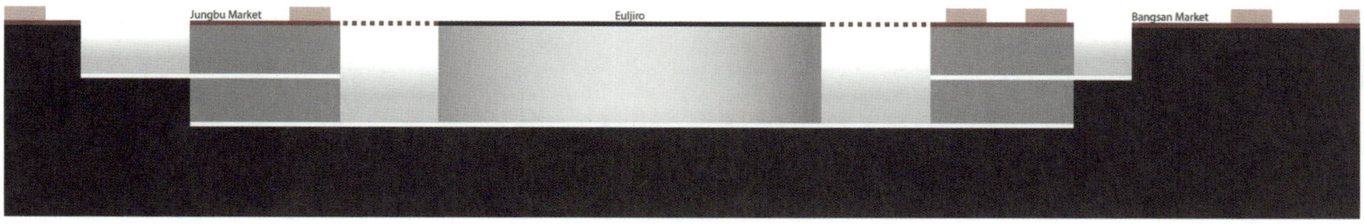

DESIGN PROPOSAL

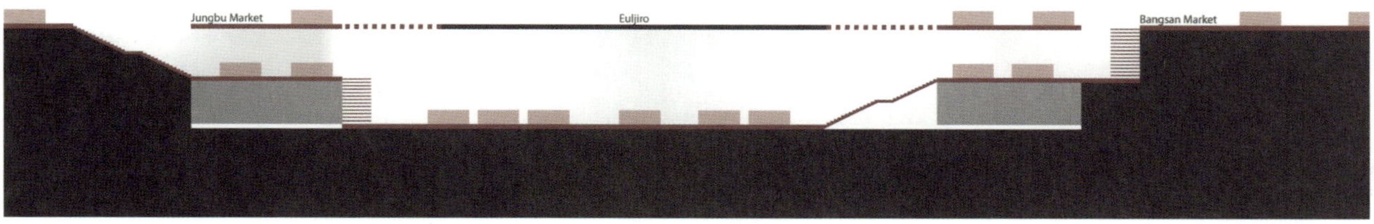

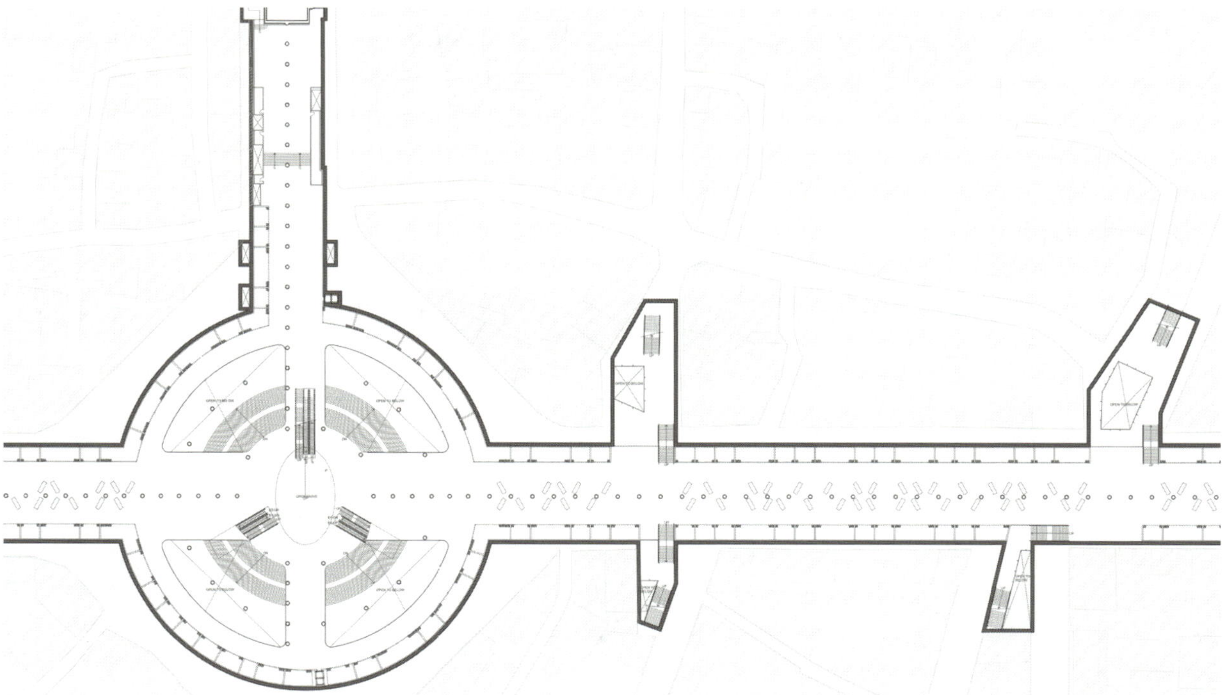

웰컴 투 서울!

MVRDV의 제안은 서울의 철도 중심지인 서울역에 초점을 맞추었다. 서울역은 세 가지 점에서 지하공간을 개선하기 위한 최적의 후보였다. 첫째, 서울 지역의 GTX 고속철도망 도입은 서울의 중앙역을 다시 획기적으로 개발할 수 있는 기회를 마련하였다. 둘째, 현재 서울역과 주변부의 구성은 서울 도심을 두 부분으로 나누고 있다. 이 지역의 대로와 높은 벽과 건물들은 동서를 분리시켜서 이곳을 도보로 지나가는 것을 매우 어렵게 하는데 이는 개선이 필요한 실정이다. 마지막으로, 이 프로젝트는 서울역의 북쪽 끝에서 철로를 가로지르는 MVRDV가 기존에 수행한 프로젝트인 서울로7017 하늘정원의 자연스러운 연장으로 구상하였다.
서울로7017은 1970년대부터 자동차 전용 고가도로라는 자동차 기반의 구조물을 공원으로 만들어 보행자에게 돌려줌으로써 서울역으로 접근을 용이하게 하고 즐길 수 있게 하려는 대범한 시도였다. 이것이 서울로 1.0이었다면 현재 진행 중인 서울로 2.0은 이 구역의 보행자 마스터플랜을 만들기 위해 지역 건축가 및 주민들과 협력하여 이 보행자 시설을 주변 지역으로 확장하는 것이다. 서울의 새로운 지하 공간을 구상해 달라는 요청은 MVRDV에게 다음 단계를 생각할 수 있는 기회가 되었다. 그렇다면 서울로 3.0이란 무엇인가? 이 보행자 중심의 구상에서 가장 중요한 것은 무엇인가? MVRDV는 이 제안을 통해서 서울이 가치 있는 지하공간을 만들어낼 수 있는 방법과 함께 지하공간의 조정을 통해서 지상 공간을 크게 개선할 수 있는 방법을 보여주고자 하였다.
MVRDV의 디자인은 우선 지면에서 철로를 걷어내고 기존 지하철 노선 아래로 재배치하고자 한다. 새로운 철도 선로와 지표면 사이의 공간은 높이 22.5m, 폭 380m의 광대한 지하 홀 공간을 만들기 위해 개방함으로써 아래쪽의 기차와 홀 공간의 동쪽 가장자리를 따라 지나가는 지하철로 접근할 수 있다. 또한 이 홀은 극장, 도서관, 상점, 레스토랑 및 체육관을 포함한 공공 편의시설을 수용한다. 기존 선로의 양쪽에 있는 자동차도로도 제거하여 역사 홀의 바닥에서 10m 위에 있는 밀폐된 튜브를 따라 통행하도록 지하에 재배치한다.
지면에서 철도와 도로를 걷어내면서 1925년

MVRDV는 위니 마스, 야콥 판 레이스, 나탈리 드프리스가 1993년 설립하였다. 네덜란드의 로테르담에 본사를 두고 전 세계를 대상으로 모든 지역의 현대 건축과 도시 문제에 대한 해법을 제공하고 있다. 우리는 고도의 공동 연구에 기반을 두고 프로젝트 설계 초기의 창작과정부터 수많은 분야의 고객, 이해 관계자 및 전문가를 포함하여 진행한다. 이에 따라 우리의 도시와 경관이 보다 나은 미래를 향해 발전할 수 있도록 본보기가 되는 획기적인 프로젝트를 만들어왔다.
MVRDV의 작업은 전세계에서 전시하고 출판되면서 수많은 국제적인 상을 수상하였다. 250 명의 건축가, 디자이너 및 도시설계자는 엄격한 기술적, 창의적 조사를 수반하는 여러 분야의 공동 설계과정을 통해서 프로젝트를 진행한다. MVRDV는 BIM으로 작업을 진행하며 사내에 공식적인 BREEAM 및 LEED 평가팀을 보유하고 있다.
MVRDV의 독창적인 디자인 접근 방식으로 만든 제품은 모든 유형과 규모의 건물에서부터 도시계획, 비전, 수많은 출판물, 설치 및 전시회에 이르기까지 다양하다. 준공작으로는 하노버에서 개최된 세계 엑스포 2000의 네덜란드 파빌리온, 로테르담의 주택과 상점을 결합한 마켓홀, 암스테르담 실로담 집합주택; 헤이그 이펜부르그 주택 및 도시계획, 로테르담 디덴빌리지옥상 주택 확장, 도쿄 자이어 부티크 쇼핑 센터; 스피케니스 공공 도서관; 노르웨이 오슬로의 국제 은행 본부; 마드리드의 상징적인 미라도르와 셀로시아 주택 등이 있다. 로테르담의 공공 예술 창고, 파리 중심부의 복합용도건물 변경, 뉴욕과 심천의 복합 고층건물, 네덜란드, 프랑스, 중국, 인도 및 여러 나라에서 다양한 주택 프로젝트 등을 현재 진행중이다.
우리의 연구 중심의 접근방법은 델프트 공과대학과 함께 운영하는 독립 싱크탱크이자 연구소인 더와이팩토리가 잘 보여주는데, 이 연구소는 미래 도시를 구상하면서 건축과 도시 분야의 화두를 제공한다. MVRDV는 자신들의 작품과 개념에 대한 선언을 담은 FARMAX(1998) 출간 후 MetaCity / Datatown (1999), Costa Iberica (2000), Regionmaker (2002), 5 Minutes City (2003), KM3 (2005), Spacefighter (2007) 및 Skycar City (2007), The Vertical Village (With Why Factory, 2012) 및 준공작을 모아 놓은 첫번째 단행본인 MVRDV Buildings (2013년 발간, 2015 년 개정판) 등을 발간했다.

700
160
150
140
130
120
110
100
90
80
70
60
50
40
30
20
10
0 m
-10
-20
-30
-40

완공, 1981년 역사적인 랜드마크로 지정된 원래 서울역 건물을 제외한 이 지역에 남아있는 모든 건물을 제거하면 지상의 공간은 서울 도심부의 새로운 대형 공공 공원으로 바뀌게 된다.
공원의 조경 디자인은 지하의 기차역에 있는 사람들에게 이 지역의 역사를 보여주는 거대한 스테인드글라스 천장으로 조성하려고 구상하고 있다. 철거된 건물의 외곽선과 한때 이곳을 따라 흐르던 강에서 가져온 경로를 결합하거나 새로운 공원의 가장자리에서 중요한 지점 간을 직접 연결하는 직선 경로를 따라 공원을 횡단하는 길을 조성한다. 이 경로 사이의 공간에서 여러 가지 색깔의 유리는 아래에 있는 홀에 빛을 도입한다. 유리 광장에 끼워 넣은 화분에 지지되어 있는 나무는 지상에 있는 사람에게는 그늘을 제공하고 지하에 있는 사람에게는 빛을 제공함으로써 두 공간 모두에게 최상의 것을 제공한다.
MVRDV의 설계안에서 2011년에 문화 시설로 개조된 오래된 서울역사는 향상된 가시성과 접근성 덕분에 새로 조성된 공원 환경의 혜택을 받게 된다. 한편 새로운 삶을 시작하게 될 서울로 7017 스카이 가든은 보행자 동선에서는 중요성이 줄어들겠지만 지상과 새롭게 연결되면서 공원을 조망하는 전망대로서 더욱 매력적인 곳이 될 것이다. 디자인의 마지막 요소는 공원의 북쪽과 남쪽 끝에 세워질 일련의 탑의 형태로 도시적인 밀도를 이곳으로 다시 도입한다. 이 탑들은 대상지의 기존 건물과는 달리, 공원의 경로가 이루는 네트워크 형태에 따라 보행자의 접근을 우선적으로 다룰 것이다.
예정된 GTX 철도망 외에도 또다른 철도 계획이 서울역 개발을 매우 중요하게 만드는 역할을 할 수 있는데 바로 북한과의 연결이다. 이러한 계획이 계속 진행된다면 서울은 섬처럼 고립된 남한만의 네트워크 중심에서 북한, 러시아만이 아니라 유럽에서 온 여행객들을 위한 한국의 관문으로 탈바꿈할 것이다. 이같은 희망적인 미래에서 어느 편이 더 나을까? 차로 꽉 막힌 채 평범하고 제대로 계획되지 않은 건물의 좁은 공간을 따라서 방문자들을 이동하게 하는 것인가, 아니면 세계에서 가장 독특한 도시 공원 중 하나로 장식된 세계에서 가장 멋진 기차역 중 하나에서 그들을 환영하는 것인가? 서울에 오신 것을 환영합니다.

MVRDV was founded in 1993 by Winy Maas, Jacob van Rijs and Nathalie de Vries. Based in Rotterdam, the Netherlands, we have a global scope, providing solutions to contemporary architectural and urban issues in all regions of the world. Our highly collaborative, research-based design method involves clients, stakeholders, and experts from a wide range of fields from early on in the creative process. The results are exemplary, outspoken projects that enable our cities and landscapes to develop towards a better future.
The work of MVRDV is exhibited and published worldwide and has received numerous international awards. Two hundred and fifty architects, designers and urbanists develop projects in a multi-disciplinary, collaborative design process that involves rigorous technical and creative investigation. MVRDV works with BIM and has official in-house BREEAM and LEED assessors.
The products of MVRDV's unique approach to design vary, ranging from buildings of all types and sizes, to urban plans and visions, numerous publications, installations and exhibitions. Completed projects include the Netherlands Pavilion for the World EXPO 2000 in Hannover; the Market Hall, a combination of housing and retail in Rotterdam; the Silodam Housing complex in Amsterdam; the Ypenburg housing and urban plan in The Hague; the Didden Village rooftop housing extension in Rotterdam; the Gyre boutique shopping center in Tokyo; a public library in Spijkenisse; an international bank headquarters in Oslo, Norway; and the iconic Mirador and Celosia housing in Madrid.Current projects include a public art depot in Rotterdam, the transformation of a mixed-use building in central Paris, mixed-use high-rises in New York and Shenzhen, and a variety of housing projects in the Netherlands, France, China, India, and other countries.
Our research-oriented approach is exemplified by The Why Factory, an independent think tank and research institute that we run together with the Delft University of Technology, which provides an agenda for architecture and urbanism by envisioning the city of the future.MVRDV first published a manifesto of its work and ideas in FARMAX (1998), followed by MetaCity/Datatown (1999), Costa Iberica (2000), Regionmaker (2002), 5 Minutes City (2003), KM3 (2005), Spacefighter (2007) and Skycar City (2007), The Vertical Village (with The Why Factory, 2012) and the firm's first monograph of built works MVRDV Buildings (2013, with an updated edition published in 2015).

Welcome to Seoul!

MVRDV's proposal took Seoul Station, the main railway hub of the city, as its focus. The station area was a perfect candidate for an underground intervention, for three reasons. Firstly, the introduction of the GTX high-speed rail network in the Seoul region makes it an opportune moment for a significant redevelopment of the city's main station. Secondly, the current configuration of the station and its surroundings splits the centre of Seoul in two; the area's highways, high walls, and assemblage of buildings separate east from west, making crossing on foot almost impossible, and are begging for improvement. Finally, the project was imagined as a natural development of an existing MVRDV project, the Seoullo 7017 skygarden, which crosses the railway tracks at the northern end of the station.

Seoullo 7017 was a brave attempt to make the station area more accessible and enjoyable by returning a piece of car-based infrastructure, a raised highway from the 1970s, to pedestrians in the form of a park. That was Seoullo 1.0. Seoullo 2.0, which is currently underway, extends this pedestrian infrastructure into the surrounding neighbourhoods by working with local architects and residents to create a pedestrian masterplan for the district. The request to envision a new, underground piece of Seoul became a chance for MVRDV to consider what comes next. What is Seoullo 3.0? What would the apotheosis of this pedestrian-focused vision be? With the proposal, MVRDV therefore aimed to show not only how Seoul could create underground spaces of value, but also how those underground interventions could offer significant improvements to the ground level.

MVRDV's design begins by removing the railway tracks from ground level and relocating them below the existing metro line. The space in between the new railway tracks and the surface would be opened up to form a vast underground station hall, 22.5 metres high and 380 metres wide, giving access to the trains below and the metro running along the eastern edge of the hall.This hall would also be filled with public amenities, including a theatre, a library, shops, restaurants, and gyms. The highways on either side of the existing tracks would also be removed and relocated below ground level, travelling through enclosed tubes suspended 10 metres above the floor level of the station hall.

With the railway tracks and roads removed from ground level, all of the remaining buildings in the area – with the exceptionof the original station building, which was completed in 1925 and designated a historic landmark in 1981 – would be removed, turning the ground level into a large new public park in the centre of Seoul.

The landscape design of the park is envisioned as a gigantic stained glass ceiling displaying the history of the site to those in the station below.

Paths through the park are created by combining outlines of the demolished buildings and the course taken by the river that once flowed through the site, as well as straight paths that provide direct shortcuts between important points on the edge of the new park. In the spaces between these paths, colourful glass allows light to enter the hall below. Trees will be supported in pots embedded into these glass plazas, giving the best of both worlds: shade for the people at ground level, and light for the people below.

In MVRDV's proposal, the old station building, which was converted into a cultural complex in 2011, will benefit from its new park setting thanks to its increased visibility and accessibility. The Seoullo 7017 skygarden, meanwhile, will begin a new life, becoming less crucial for pedestrian movement, but more appealing as a viewing point over the park, enabled by new connections with the ground level.The final element of the design reintroduces urban density to the site in the form of a series of towers set in the northern and southern ends of the park. Unlike the buildings currently on the site, these would prioritise pedestrian access, conforming to the shape of the park's network of paths.

In addition to the planned GTX network, another railway plan could serve to make the development of Seoul Station critically important: the connection to North Korea. If such plans go ahead, Seoul will be transformed from a central hub of an insular South Korean network into a gateway to South Korea for travellers from North Korea, Russia, and even Europe. In this hopeful future, which would be better: to funnel visitors through an unremarkable and poorly-planned cluster of buildings choked by cars – or to welcome them in one of the world's most spectacular train stations, topped with one of the world's most unique city parks? Welcome to Seoul!

LAYERS

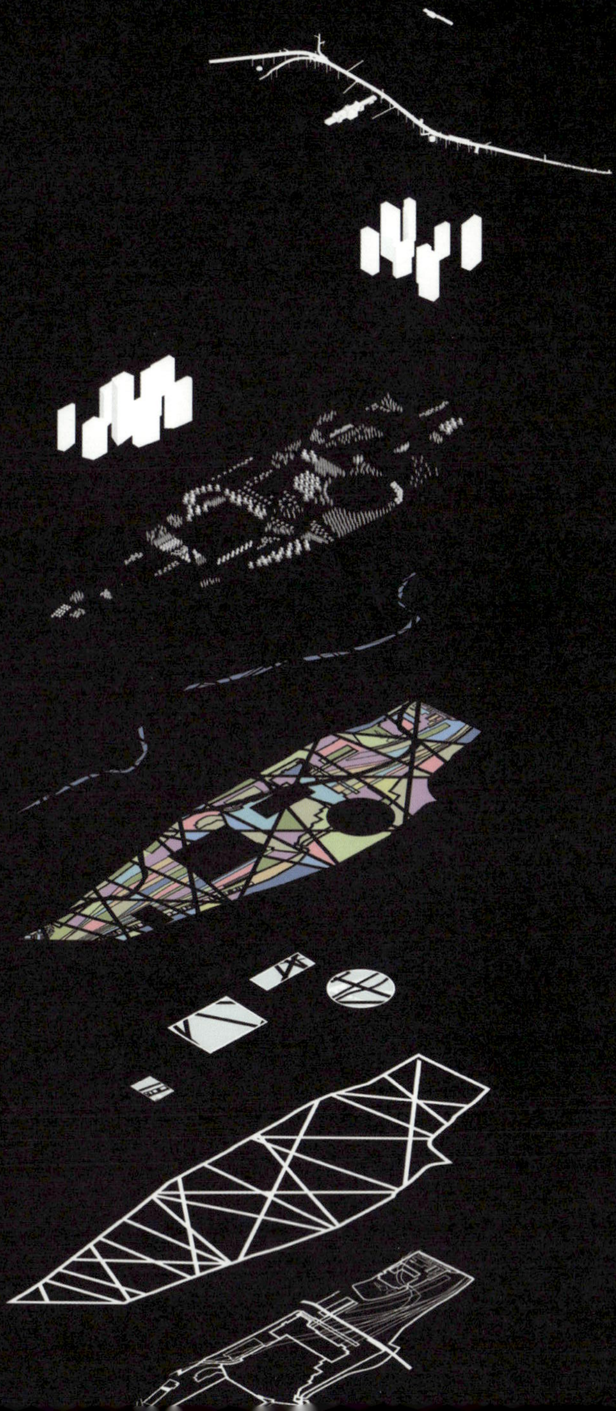
seoullo 7017 서울로 7017
seoul station 서울역
handmade shoe street 수제화거리
new buildings 신규건물들
landscape 조경
old water stream 옛 물길의 흔적
transparent floors 투명 바닥
plazas 광장
shortcuts 지름길
tracing lines of old buildings 옛 건물의 흔적들

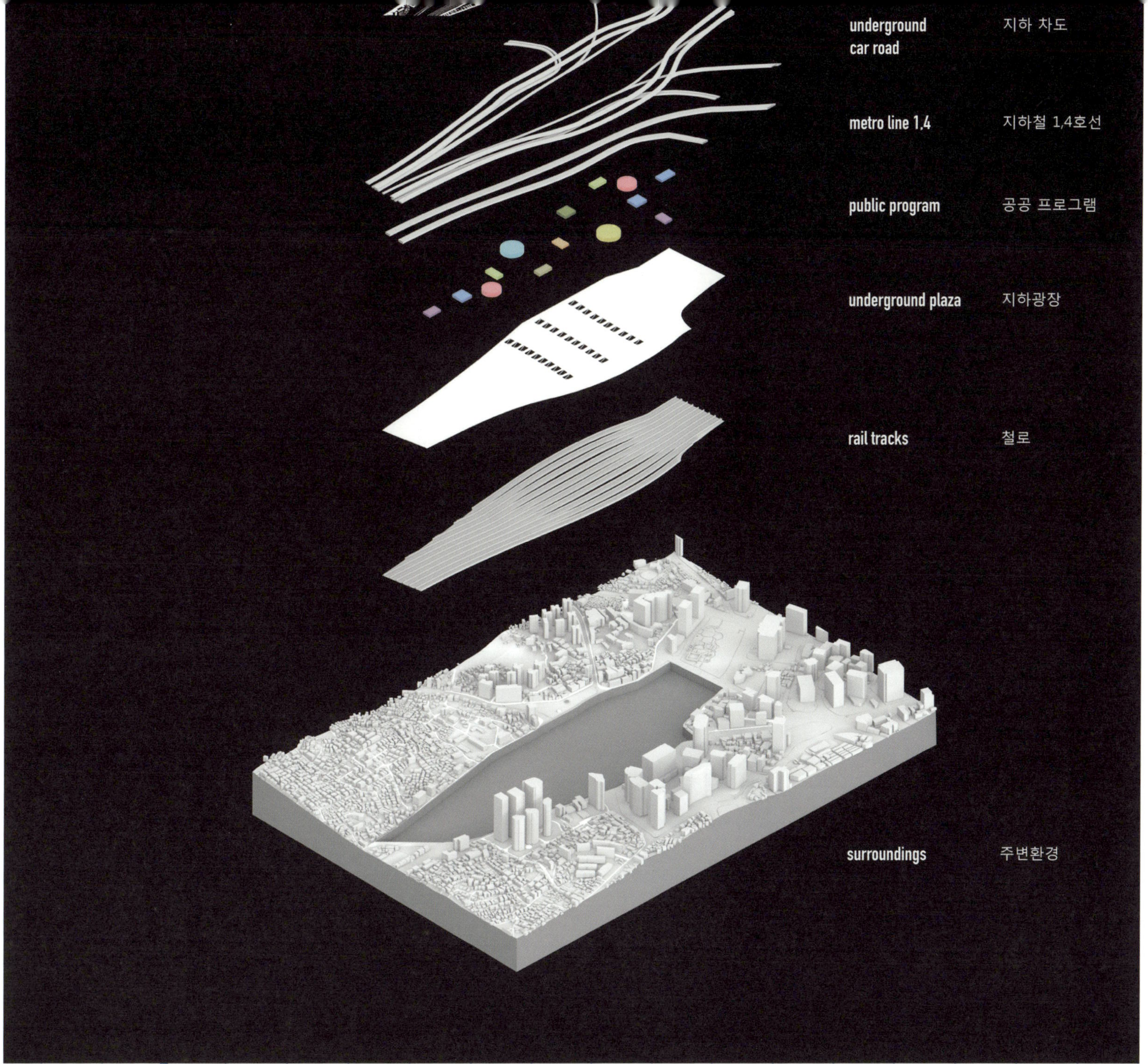
underground car road
지하 차도
metro line 1,4
지하철 1,4호선
public program
공공 프로그램
underground plaza
지하광장
rail tracks
철로
surroundings
주변환경

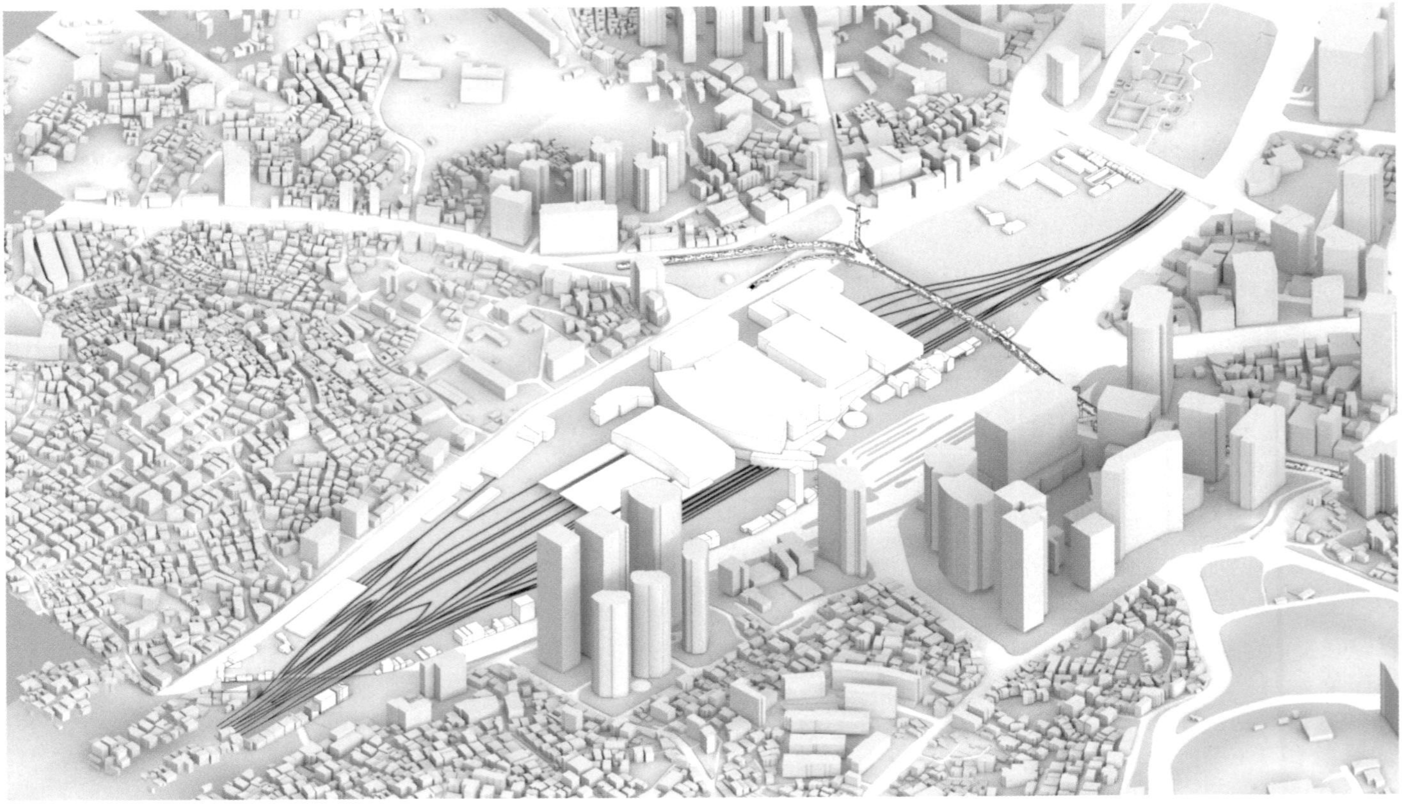

Existing 현황

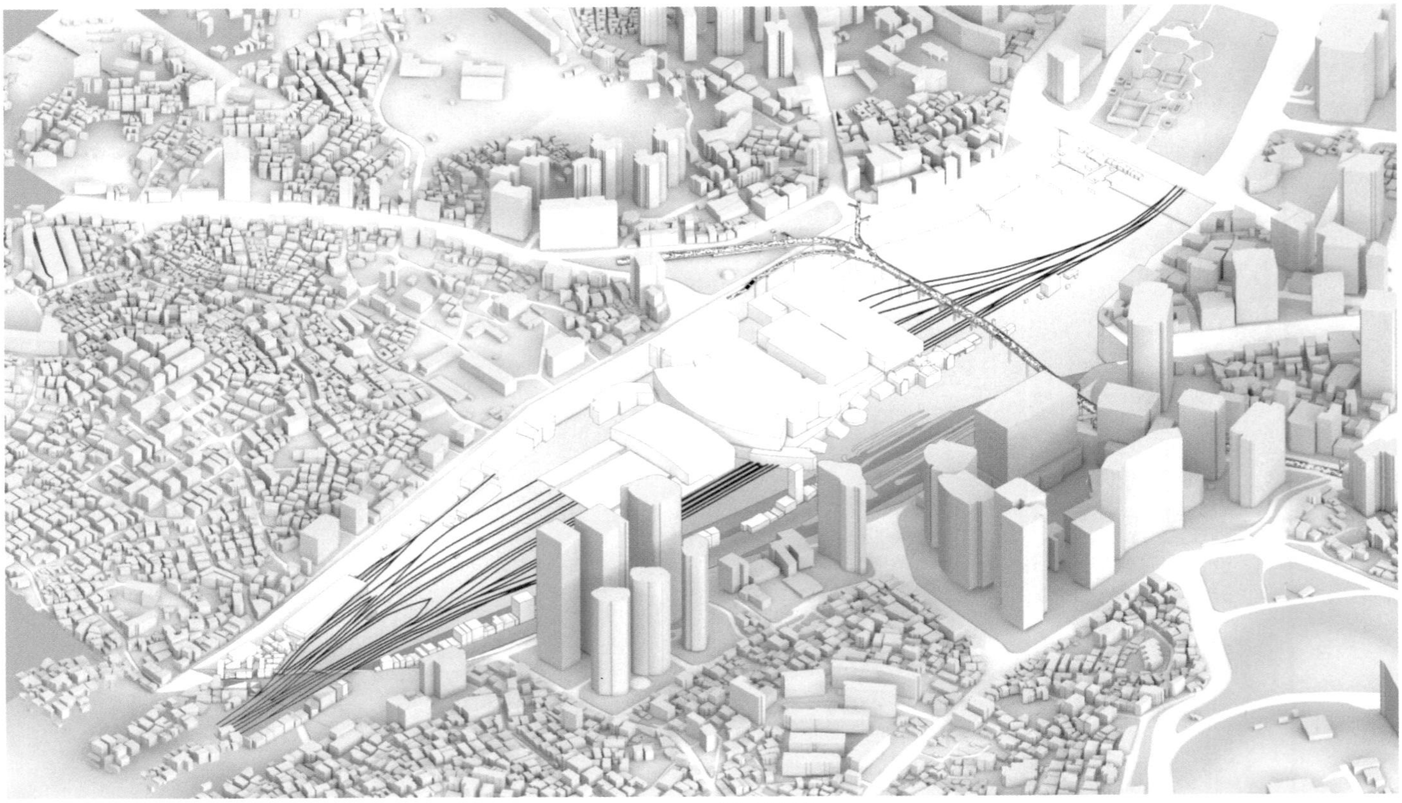

Excavate 지하 파내기

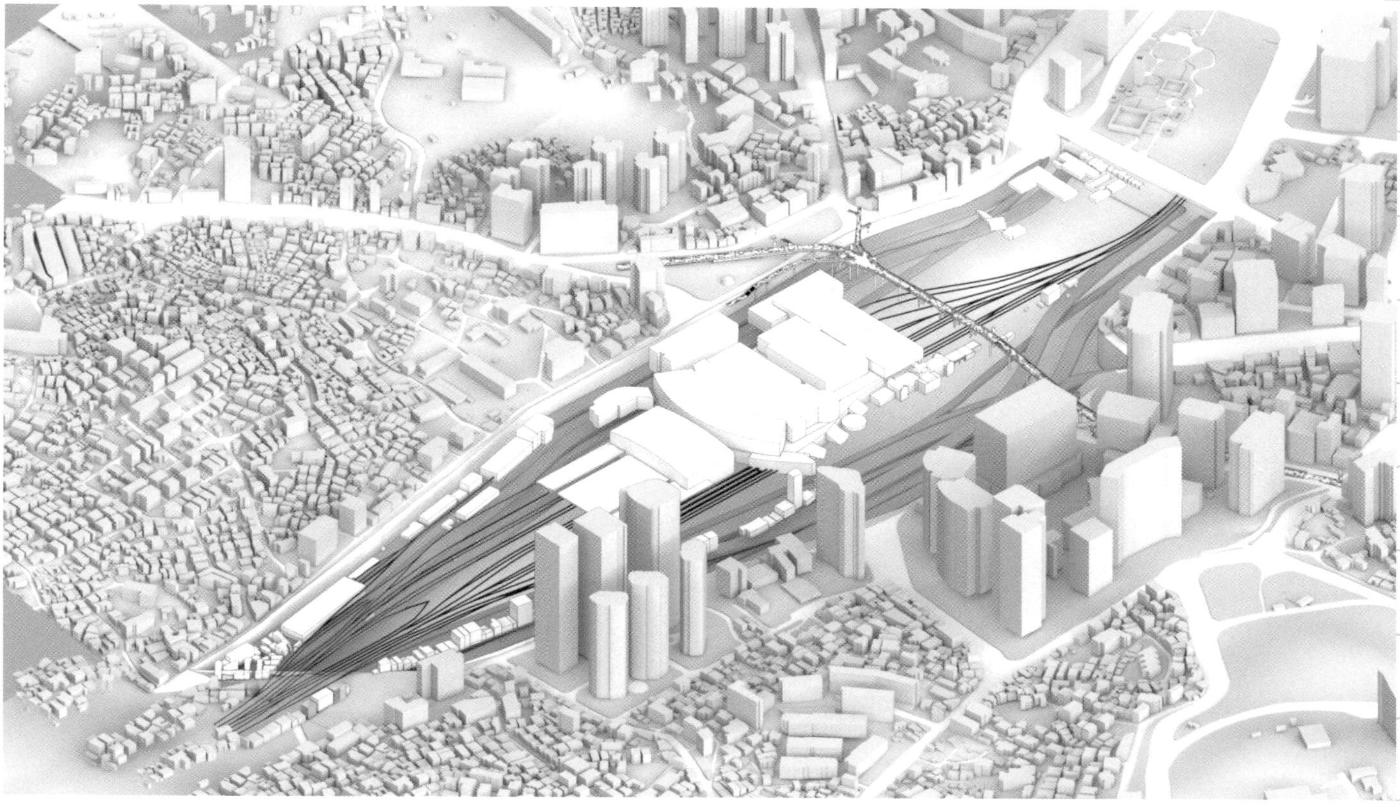

Move car road to underground 도로 지하화 하기

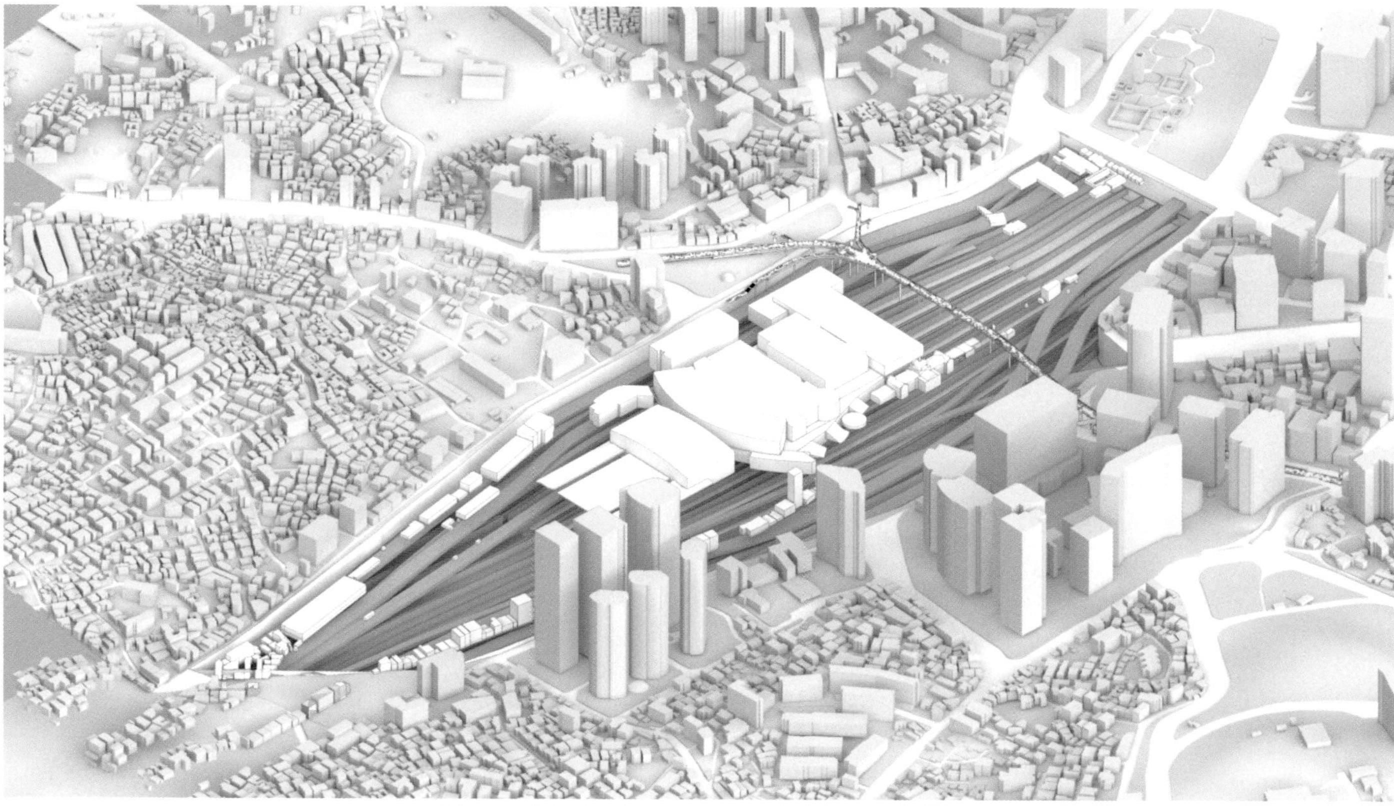

Move rail tracks to underground 철로 지하화 하기

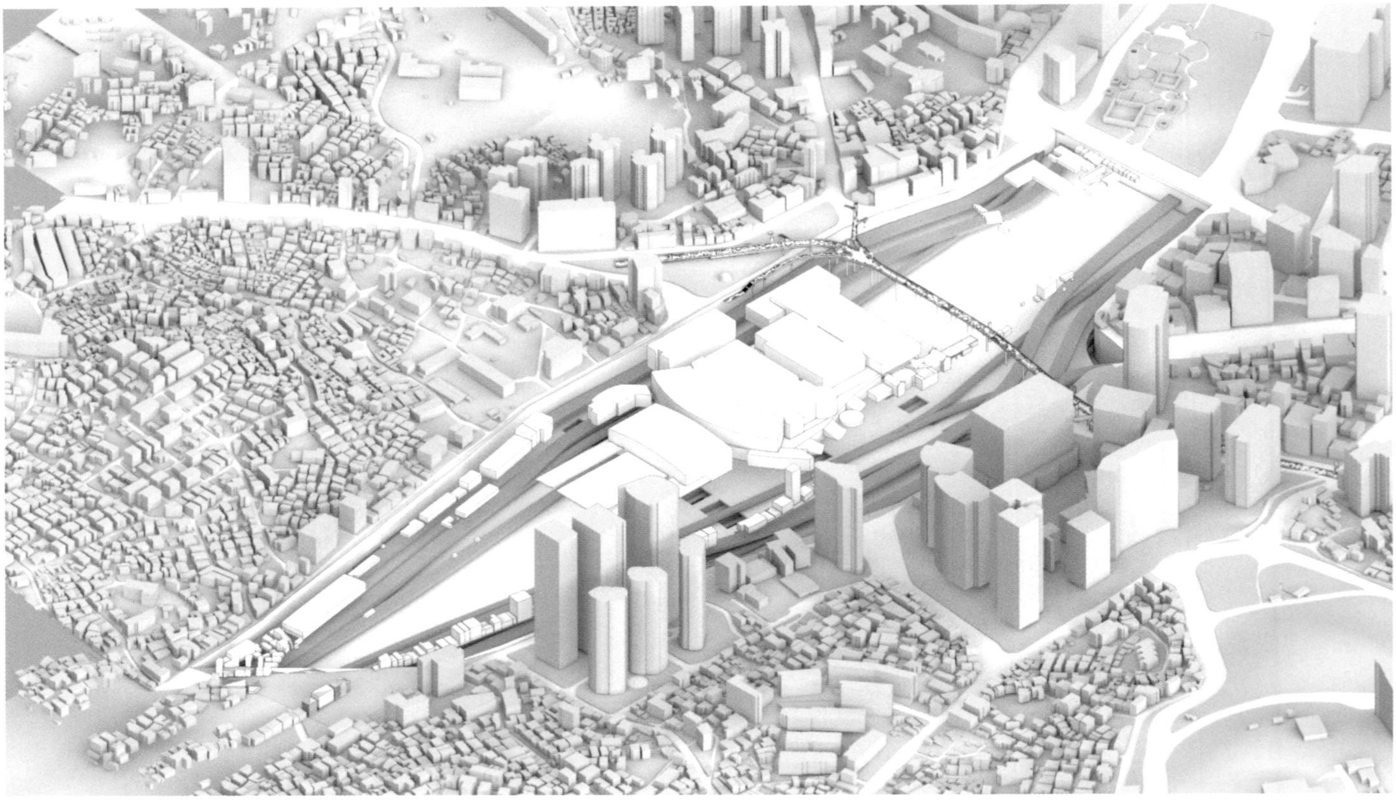

Add underground plaza 지하 광장 만들기

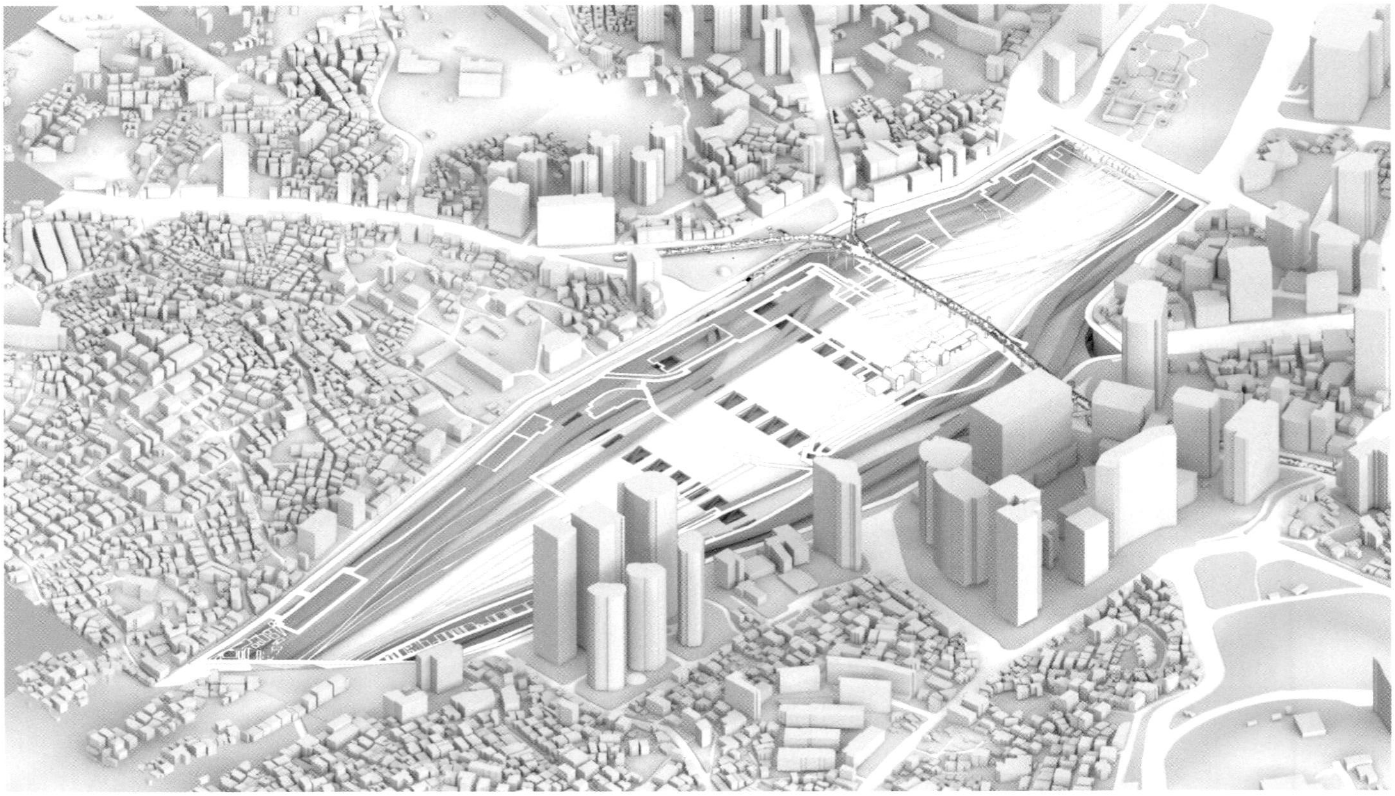

Trace buildings 건물 흔적 남기기

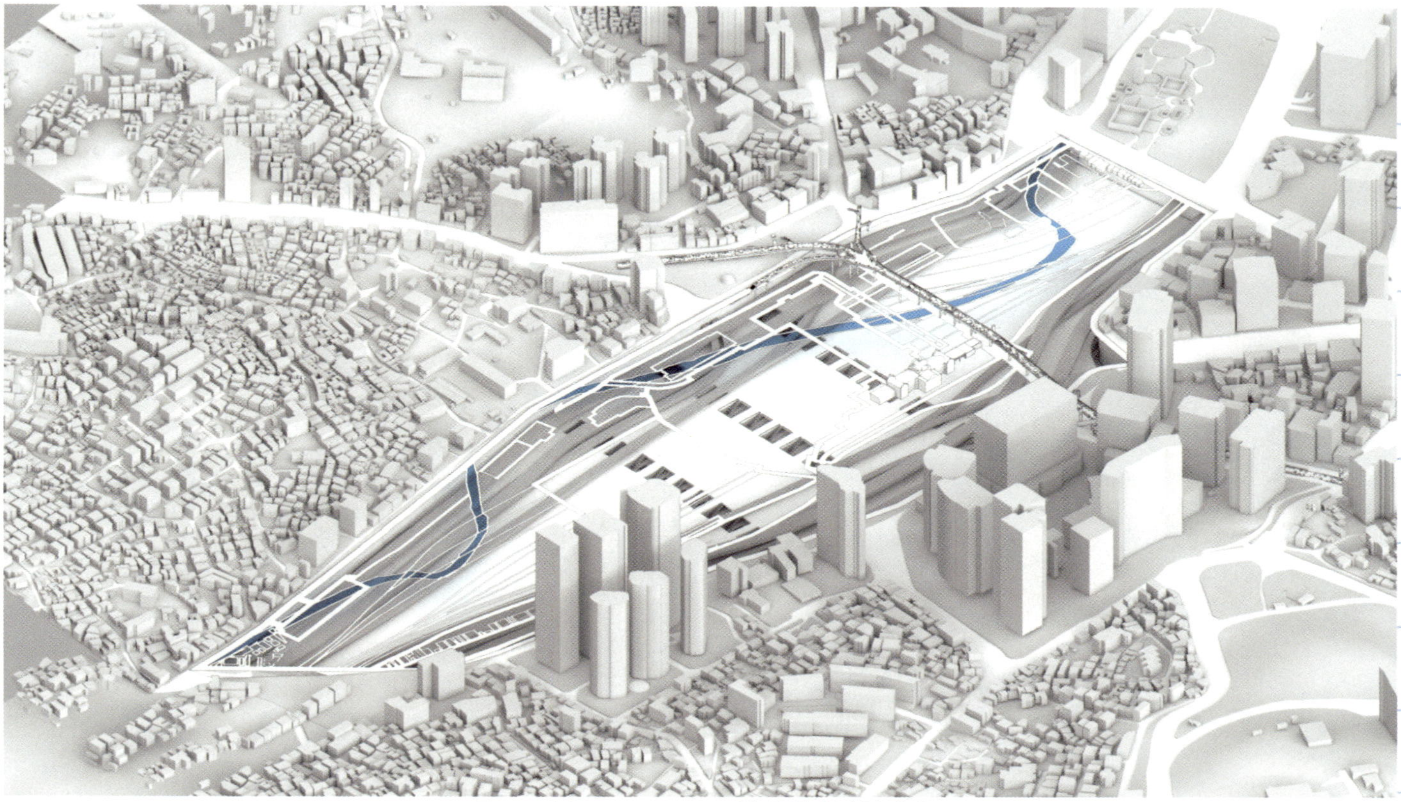

Trace old water stream 옛 물길 흔적 남기기

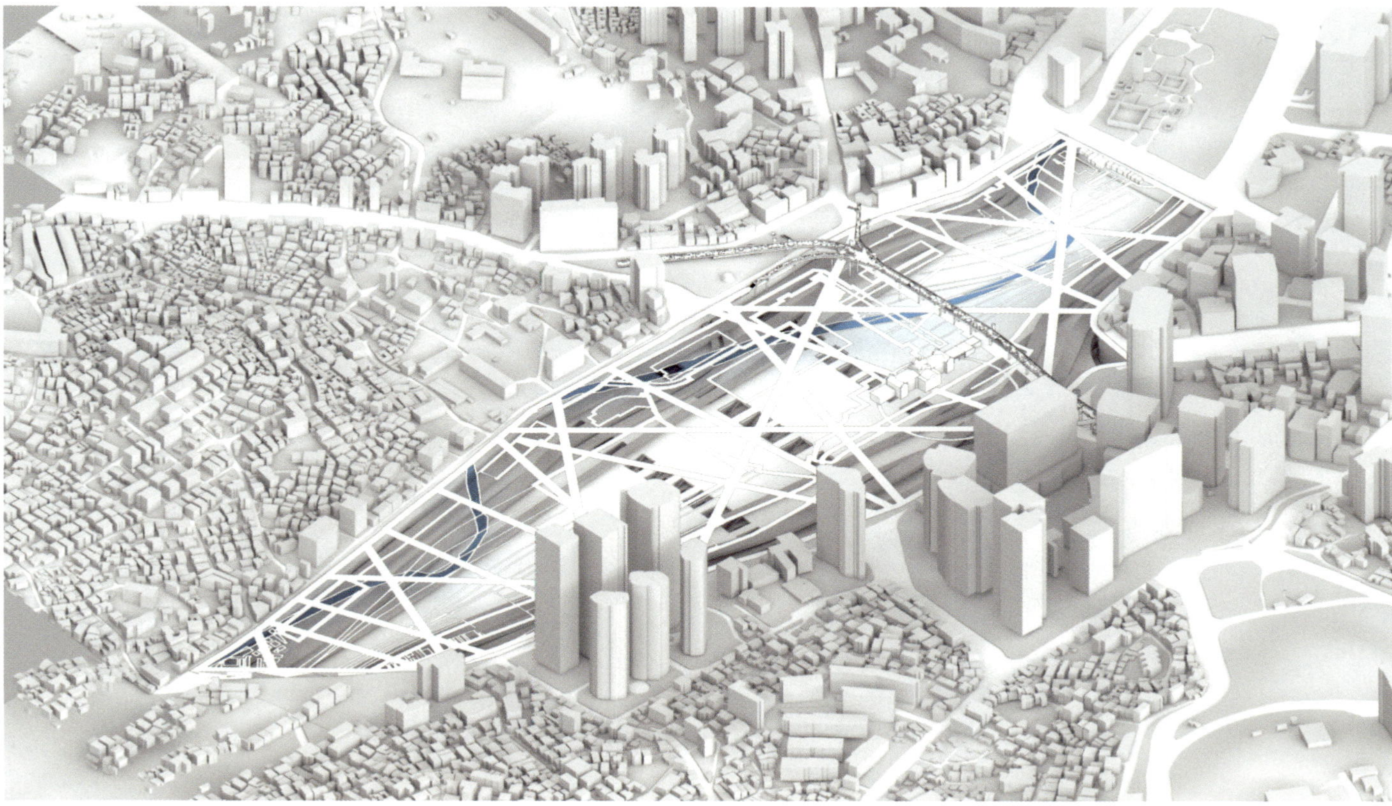

Make shortcuts 지름길 만들기

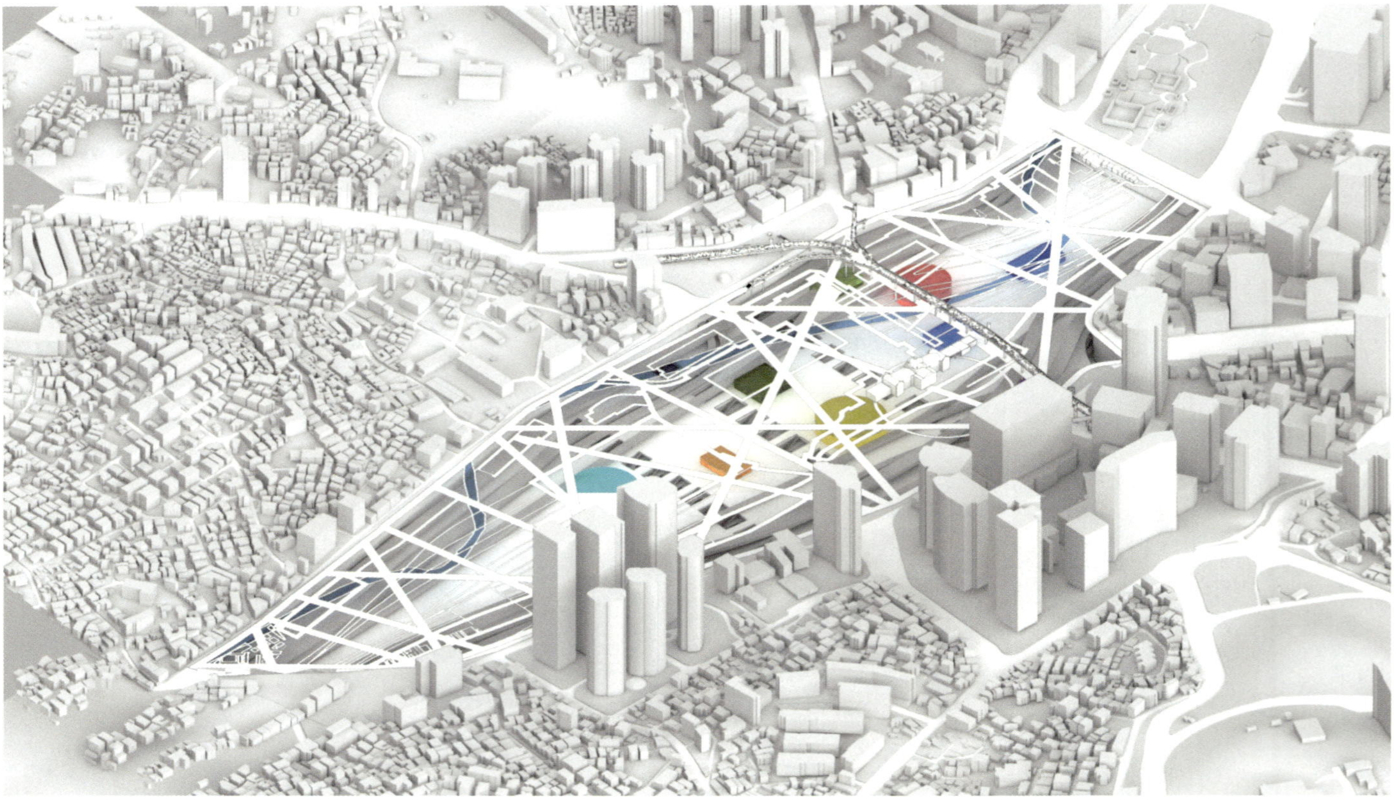

Add public program 공공 프로그램 추가하기

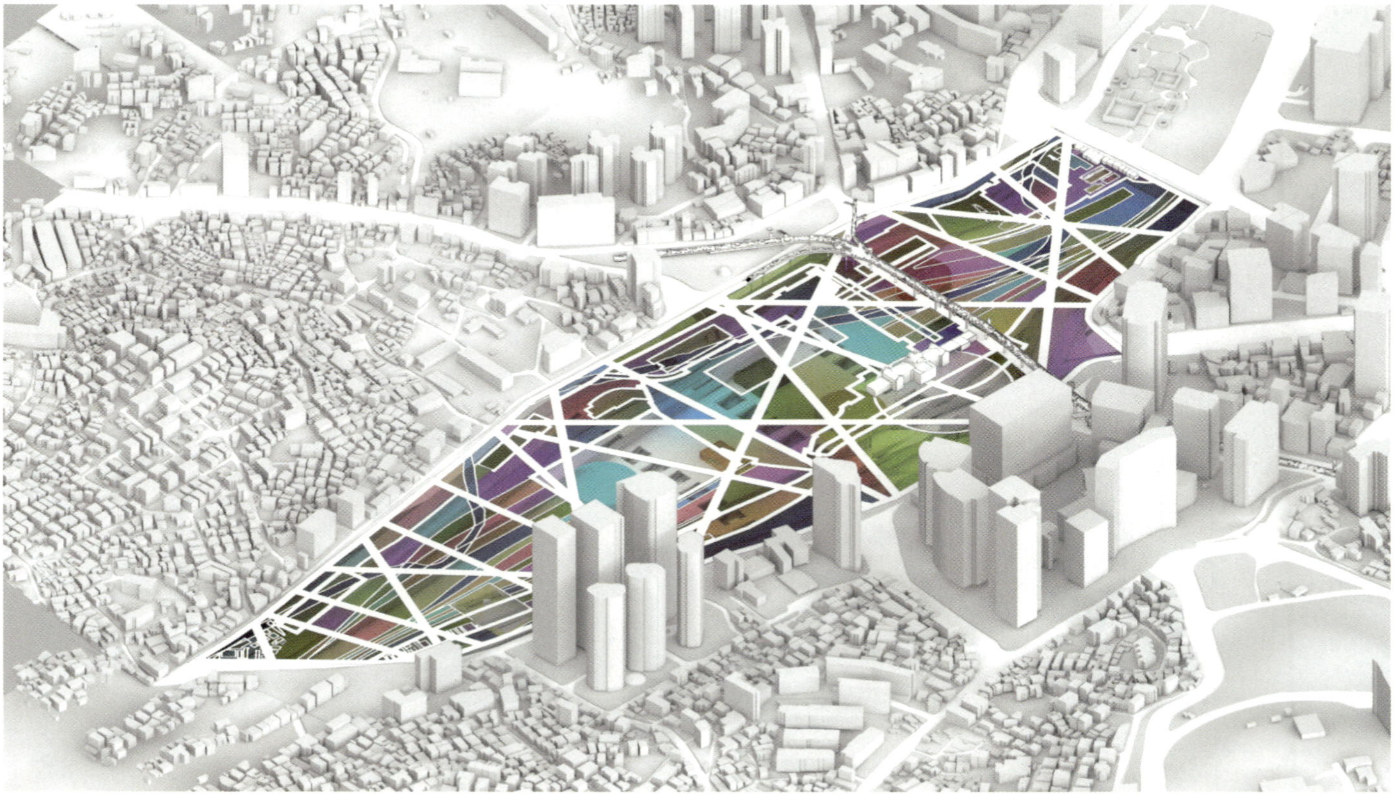

Add transparent floor 유리 바닥 추가하기

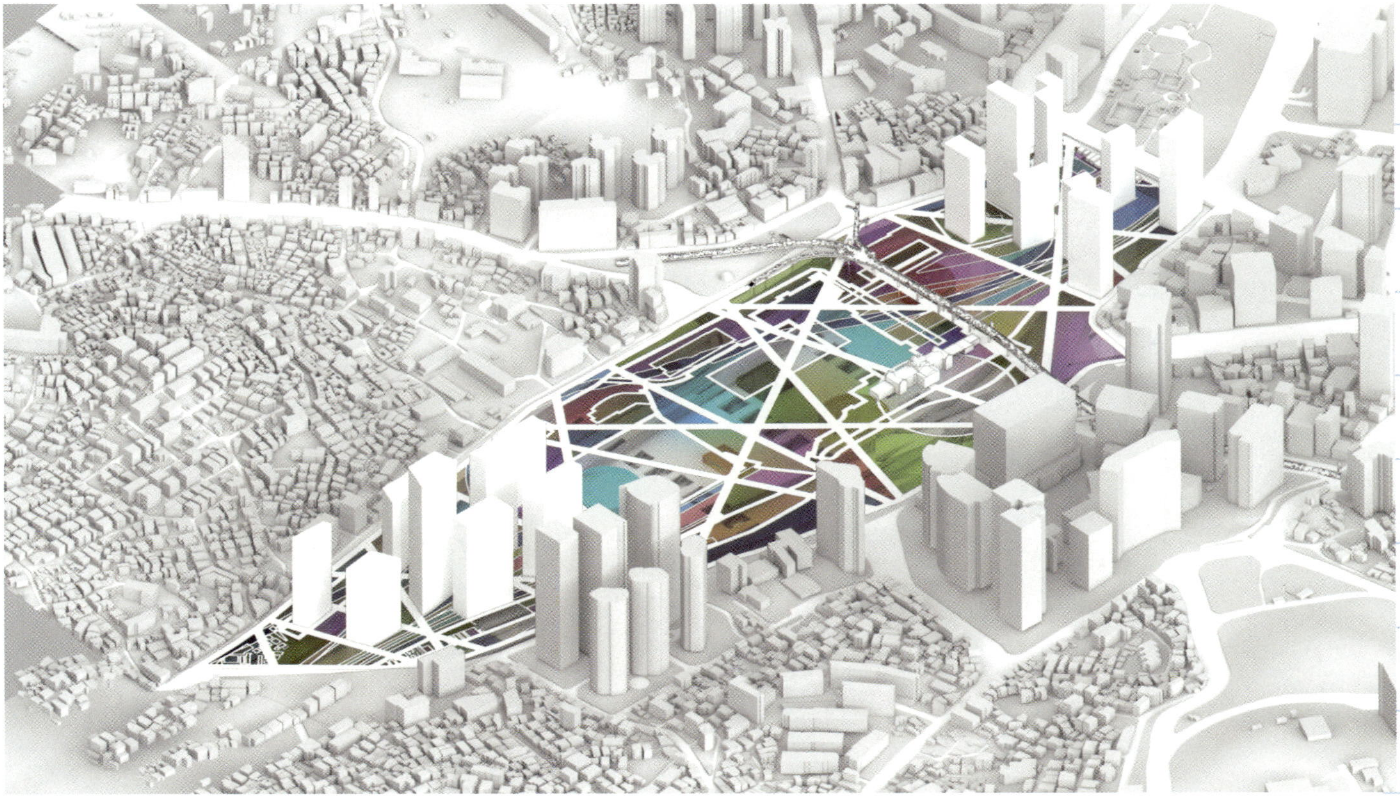

Add new towers 신규 건물 추가하기

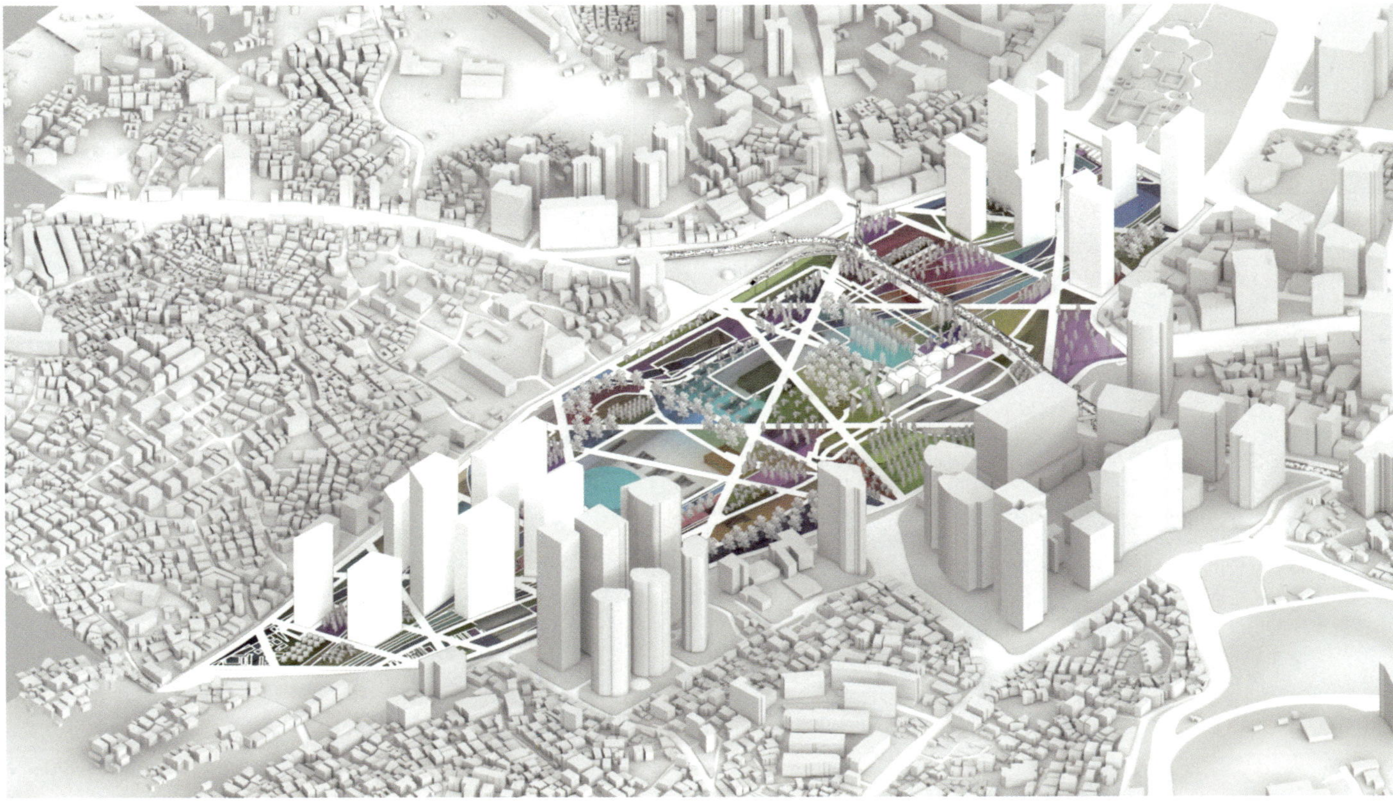

Add landscape 조경 추가하기

SHINHUNG
SILOAM
SAUNA
700
160
150
140
130
120
110
100
90
80
70
60
50
40
30
20
10
0 m
-10
-20
-30
-40

도미니크 페로

Dominique Perrault

서울 그라운드스케이프 플라자

서울의 중심부는 과묵한 랜드마크이자 대지 깊숙이 뿌리를 내리고 있는 놀라움의 공간이다. 도시 내 유서 깊은 흐름의 교차점에 자리 잡고 있는 서울광장은 광대한 도시의 심장, 도시 중력의 중심을 구성한다. 대지의 상징적 가치, 도시 조직의 밀도와 복합성, 기존 기반시설의 복잡성은 주어진 환경을 일관성 있는 공간으로 바꾸어 놓을 수 있는 해법을 요구하고 있다.
지상 시설은 고요하고, 거의 비어 있으며, 현재 도시 형태 그리고 만남과 회합의 장이자 현대판 아고라인 소중한 대지의 대중적 가치를 철저히 존중한다. 동심원 형태로 이어지는 보도는 보행자 친화를 추구하는 새로운 서울의 상징인 공공 광장 개념을 강조해준다.
하나는 광장 중앙에 있고 다른 하나는 덕수궁 정원에 있는 두 개의 간결한 형태는 광장을 유유히 가로지르도록 이끄는 초대장이 된다. 대지 표면을 매끈하게 잘라낸 듯한 두 흐름은 대지미술 작품처럼 보이며, 고요하고 정중한 랜드마크와 대지에 뿌리내린 새로운 풍광을 구성한다.
지하에서는 전혀 다른 세계가 펼쳐진다. 서울의 어두운 터널들과 달리 이곳 내부는 햇빛을 가득 머금은 채 공공의 켜를 확장해주는, 새로 발굴된 볼륨과 프로그램이 노출된 기반시설과 공존하는 독특한 분위기를 연출해낸다.
제안 시설은 땅속 깊이 뻗어 나가며 건물들이 뿌리를 내리게 하고, 지하공간에 기능적이거나 보조적이거나 기술적이지 않은 목적을 부여한다. 이 새로운 건축물은 지하 주거 공간을 제공해주고, 도시적이고 건축적이며 시적인 역동성을 창출해내며, 사용자는 지하 깊은 곳, 그라운드스케이프에서 자연의 빛과 공기를 맛볼 수 있다.

Seoul Groundscape Plaza

The heart of the heart of Seoul is a quiet landmark, an unexpected territory rooted deeply into the ground.
Situated at the intersection of the city's historical axis Seoul Plaza constitutes the heart of the heart of the metropolis, the center around which the city gravitates. The symbolic relevance of the site, the density and complexity of the urban fabric, and the intricacy of the existing infrastructure, call for a solution capable of transforming the given reality into a coherent territory.
Above ground the project is silent, almost absent, radically respectful with the current urban morphology and with the popular character of the precious site, a contemporary agora for gatherings and congregations. A continuous pavements of concentric circles reinforces the idea of public plaza, a symbol of a renewed Seoul, which aims to become more pedestrian friendly
Two apparently simple gestures, one at the center of the Plaza, its counterpoint at the gardens of the Deoksugung Palace, serve as discrete invitations to smoothly penetrate into the territory. Appearing as clean cuts on the surface of the ground both movements come off as land art interventions, they constitute a quiet and respectful landmark, a new horizon rooted in the ground.
Below ground a different universe comes to life. In contrast to the dark tunnels of Seoul, the interior spaces are flooded with natural light creating a unique atmosphere, a device in which coexist unveiled infrastructures with newly excavated volumes and programs that multiply the layers of public space.
The proposal reaches deep into the soil, letting buildings take root and giving a purpose for the underground space that is neither functional, nor logistical or technical. This new architecture offers underground living spaces and creates a dynamic that is at once urban, architectural and poetic, where users can experience natural light and air, deep into the ground, in the Groundscape.

Dominique Perrault는 프랑스 건축가이자 도시 계획가입니다. 또한 광범위한 관점에서 건축을 연구하는 종합 연구 플랫폼인 DPAx와 지하의 새로운 비전인 '지상 풍경 (Groundscape)'에 대한 연구를 포함하여 건축 어휘를 재창조하는 연구 및 혁신 개발 실험실인 DPA Lab의 창립자입니다. 그는 1992년 도시 계획에 대한 은메달과 1996년 Mies van der Rohe Prize를 수상한 프랑스 국립 도서관 디자인으로 세계적인 건축가로 명성을 날리면서 2010년에 그는 그의 모든 작품에 대해서 프랑스 건축 아카데미로부터 금메달을 수상, 또한 그는 2015 PraemiumImperiale Laureate for Architecture로 지명되었습니다. 프랑스의BibliothèqueNationale de France에 추가로 그의 주요 프로젝트에는 베를린의 올림픽 벨로드롬 및 수영장, 룩셈부르크의 유럽 연합 재판소 확장, 마드리드의 올림픽 테니스 경기장이 포함됩니다. 그는 서울의 ECC (이화 캠퍼스 단지)로 지하 건축물에 대한 그의 표현과 신념을 향상시키는 건축물들이 있습니다. 도시 연구 프로젝트에는 2024년 파리의 올림픽 빌리지 (Olympic Village)와 2040년까지의 파리의 번창하는 역사적 중심지의 미래를 반영하는 프랑스 공화국 대통령이 의뢰한 도시 연구인 "Ile de la Cité"가 포함됩니다.

Dominique Perrault is a French architect and urban planner. He is also the founder of DPAx, a multidisciplinary research platform exploring architecture from a wider perspective, and DPA Lab, a laboratory of research and innovation developing processes that reinvent the vocabulary of architecture including his research on 'Groundscape' as a new vision of underground. He became world known for the design of the French National Library, distinguished with the Silver medal for town planning in 1992 and the Mies van der Rohe Prize in 1996. In 2010 he was awarded the gold medal by the French Academy of Architecture for all his work. He was named as the 2015 PraemiumImperiale Laureate for Architecture. Along with the BibliothèqueNationale de France, his main projects to date include the Olympic Velodrome and Swimming Pool in Berlin, the extension of the Court of Justice of the European Union in Luxembourg, the Olympic Tennis Stadium in Madrid. With ECC (Ewha Campus Complex) in Seoul, he adds another architecture enhancing his manifest and belief in underground architecture.
Urban research projects include the Olympic Village – Paris 2024 and the"Mission Ile de la Cité," an urban study commissioned by the president of the French Republic that reflects upon the future of the thriving, historical center of Paris from now until 2040.

700
160
150
140
130
120
110
100
90
80
70
60
50
40
30
20
10
0 m
-10
-20
-30
-40

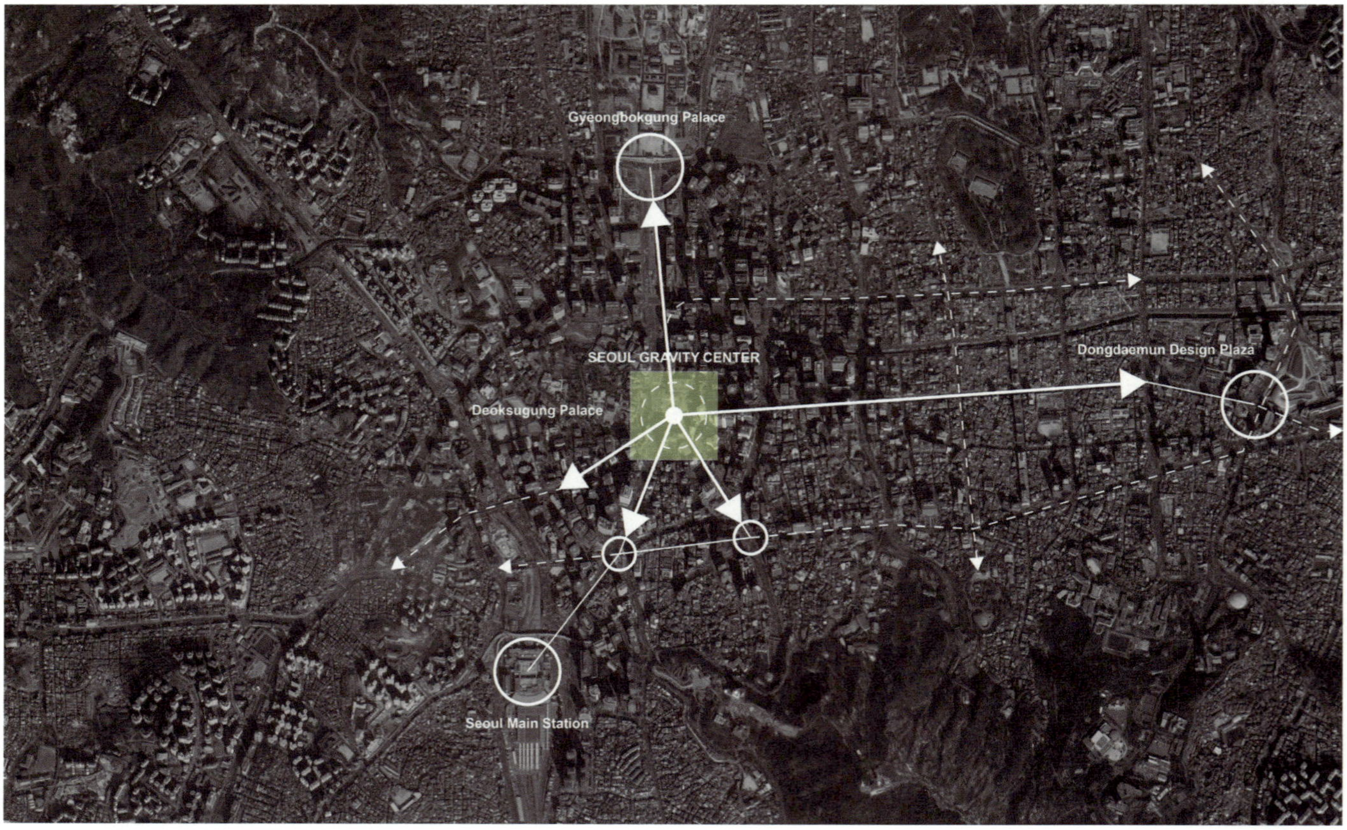
Gyeongbokgung Palace
SEOUL GRAVITY CENTER
Dongdaemun Design Plaza
Deoksugung Palace
Seoul Main Station

URBAN FARM
CITY ADMINISTRATION OFFICES
CITY LIBRARY RING
HOTEL FACILITIES
CULTURAL FACILITES
PERFORMING ARTS CENTER
SUBWAY
STORAGE FACILITIES
DRONE RACE
ACADEMIC FACILITES
FITNESS CENTER
DEOKSUGUNG MUSEUM
DESIGN SCHOOL
CIRCULAR FOOD COURT
CINEMA
GRAND PIAZZA
CO-WORKING
SHOPPING MALL
FLEY MARKET
OFFICE SPACE
SCULPTURE GARDEN
THEATRE
COMERCIAL GALLERY
SWIMMING POOL
CONCERT VENUE
CONFERENCE CENTER
UNDERGROUND BABYLON GARDENS

700
160
150
140
130
120
110
100
90
80
70
60
50
40
30
20
10
0 m
-10
-20
-30
-40

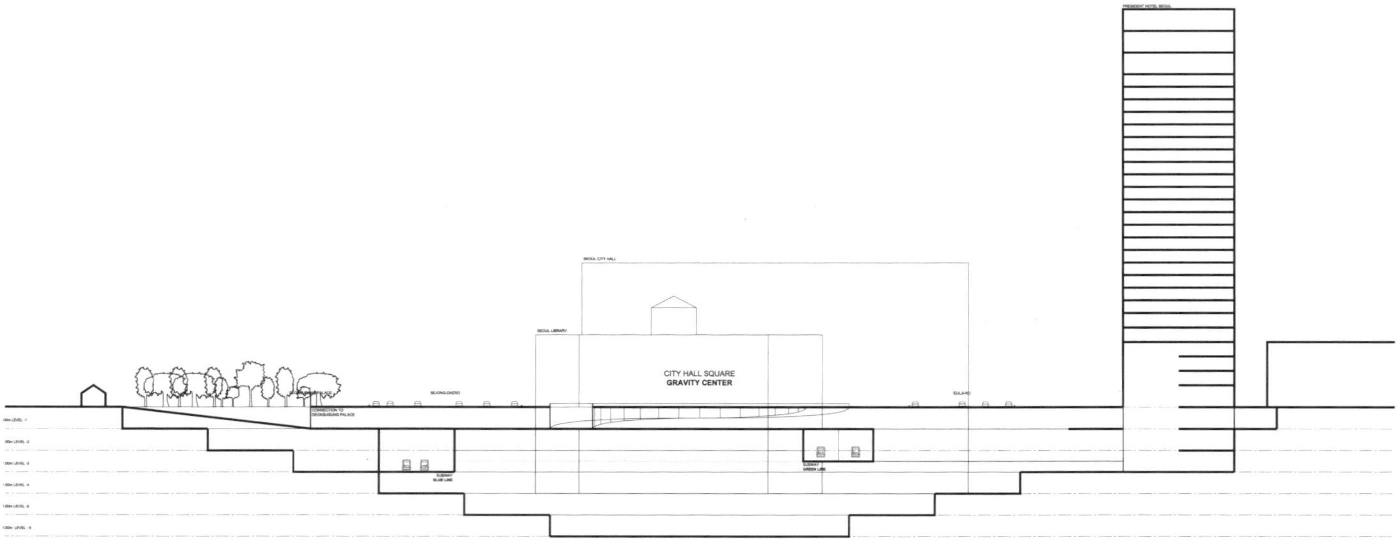
CITY HALL SQUARE
GRAVITY CENTER

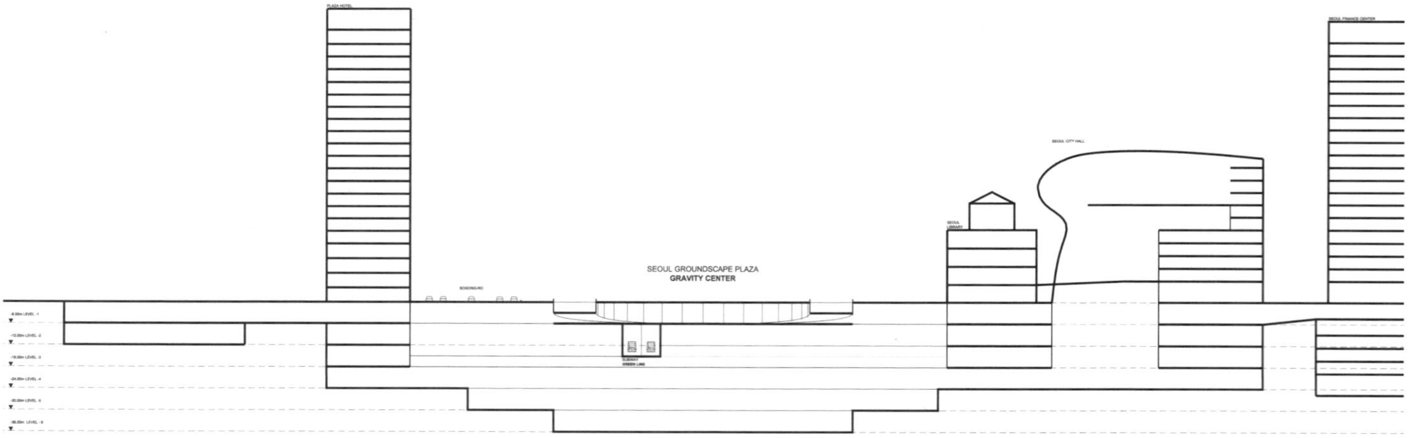
SEOUL GROUNDSCAPE PLAZA
GRAVITY CENTER

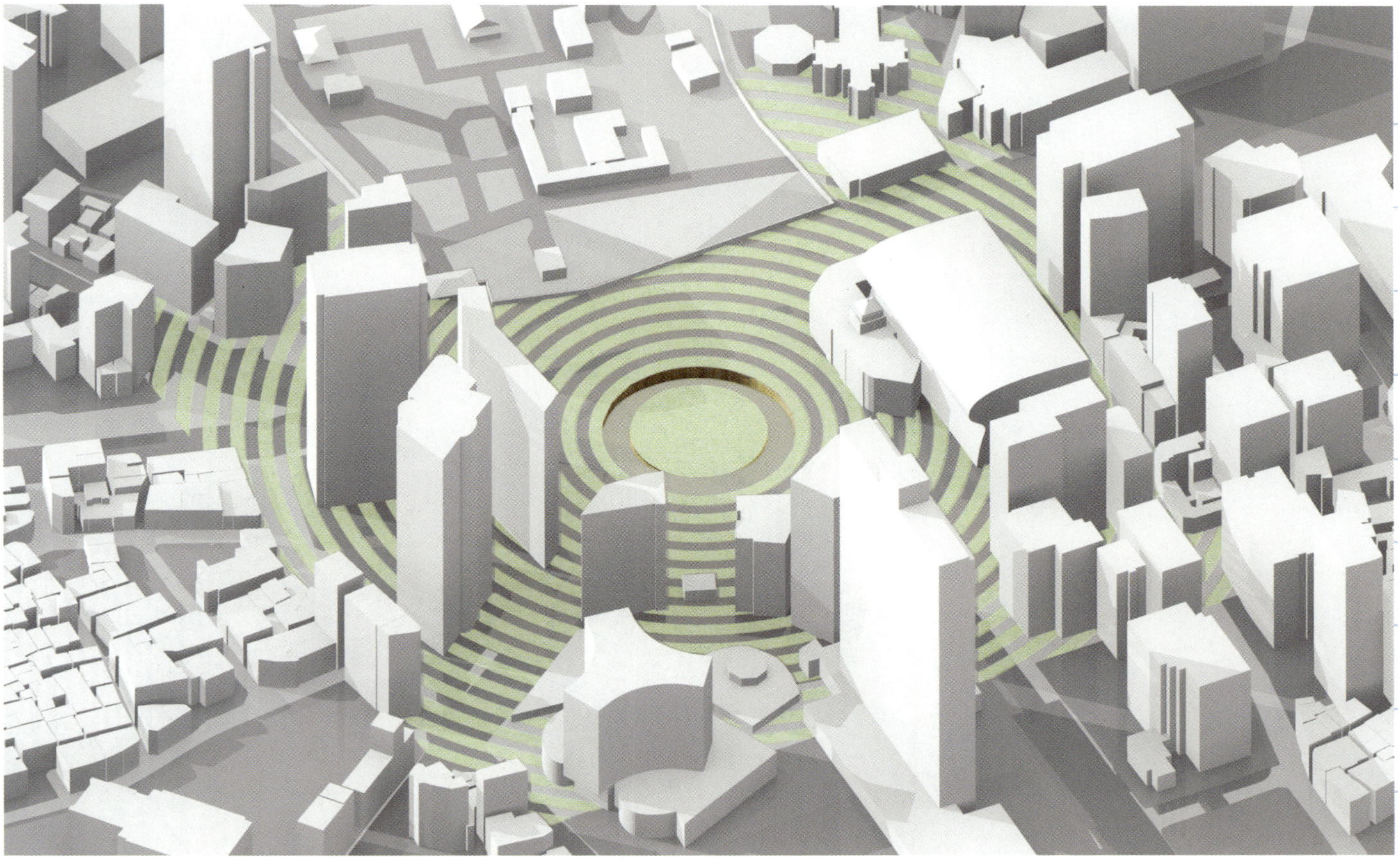

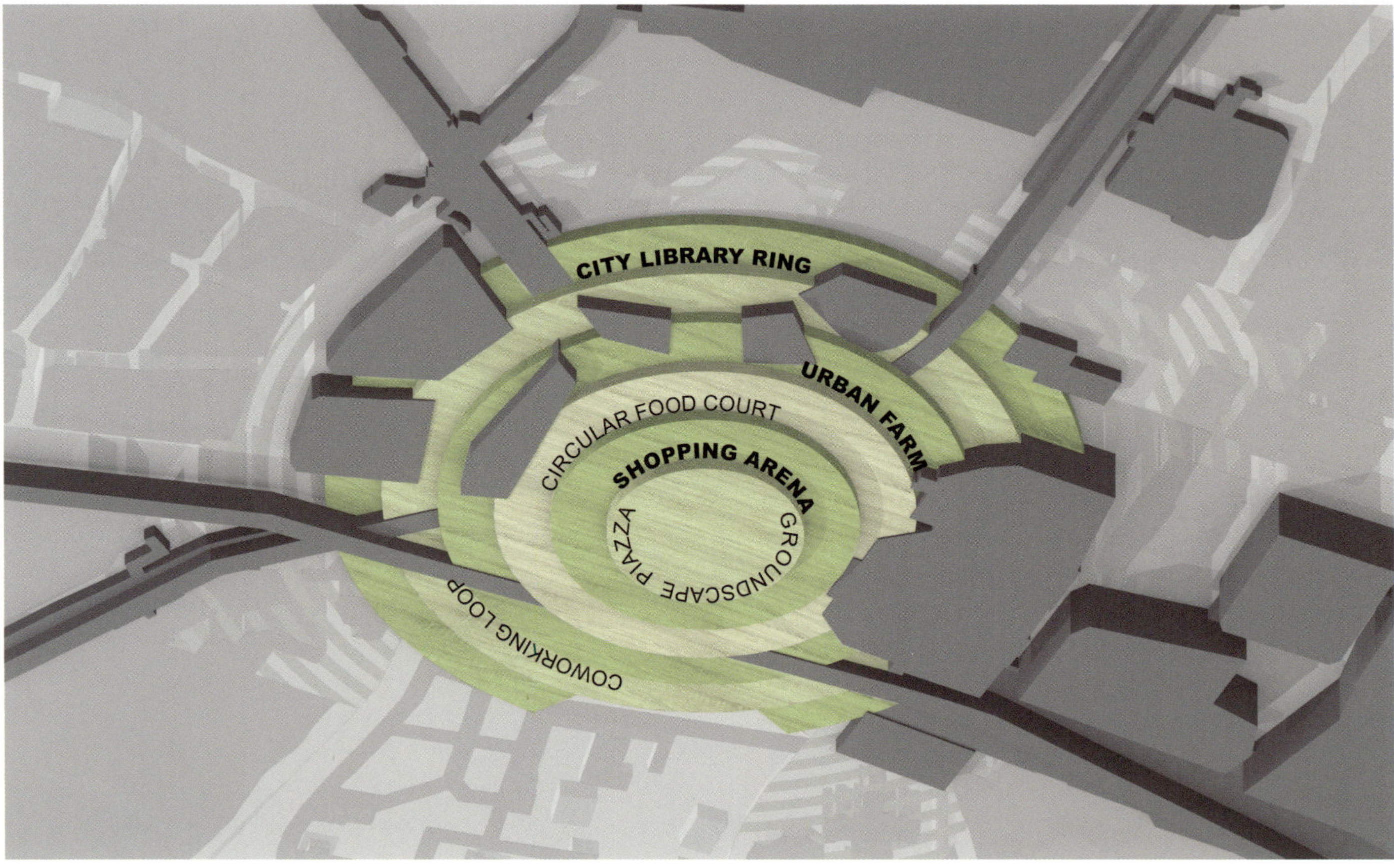
CITY LIBRARY RING
URBAN FARM
CIRCULAR FOOD COURT
SHOPPING ARENA
GROUNDSCAPE PIAZZA
COWORKING LOOP

700
160
150
140
130
120
110
100
90
80
70
60
50
40
30
20
10
0 m
-10
-20
-30
-40

700
160
150
140
130
120
110
100
90
80
70
60
50
40
30
20
10
0 m
-10
-20
-30
-40

700
160
150
140
130
120
110
100
90
80
70
60
50
40
30
20
10
0 m
-10
-20
-30
-40

서울신문
KOREANA
HOTEL

700
160
150
140
130
120
110
100
90
80
70
60
50
40
30
20
10
0 m
-10
-20
-30
-40

SUPERGROUND

찰스 왈드하임과 어바니제이션오피스 | Charles Waldheim with Office for Urbanization
프로젝트 리드 Project Lead: Jeffrey S. Nesbit
팀 Team: Aziz Barber, 김민규 (Mingyu Kim), Xun Liu, 여석민 (Seok Min Yeo)
연구 파트너 Research Partner: Eric de Broche des Combes, Luxigon, Paris

---

토포텍 1 | Topotek 1
디자인 리드 Design Lead: Martin Rein-Cano
프로젝트 리드 Project Lead: Chiara Feliz Di Palma
건축 Architect: 최혜진 (Hye Jin Choi)
조경 Landscape Architect: Zoe Hochstein-Morran

장윤규 | Yoon gyoo Jang
장윤규 (Yoon gyoo Jang), 운생동 (UnSangDong architects)

스튜디오 푹사스 + 라몬 프랫 홈스 | Studio FUKSAS + Ramon Prat Homs
Studio FUKSAS (Massimiliano Fuksas, Doriana Fuksas), Ramon Prat Homs (urbanNext)
조민석 | Minsuk Cho
조민석 (Minsuk Cho), 매스스터디스 (Mass Studies)
팀 Team: 강준구 (Junkoo Kang), 구재승 (David Koo), 이성훈 (Nathaniel Lee), 김보라 (Betty Kim), 석치환 (Cihwan Seok), 정대인 (Daein Cheong)

프란시스 솔러 | Francis Soler
Francis Soler with Paolo Mezzalama (It's), Michel Desvigne Paysagiste

---

에두아르도 아로요 | Eduardo Arroyo- NO.MAD Arquitectos SLP
Eduardo Arroyo, Alfonso Navarrete, Aurora Donoso

윌리 뮐러 | **Willy Müller – IAAC Urban Science Lab**
Willy Müller
팀 Team: Jordi Vivaldi, Giovanna Carnevalli, Rim Youssef, Ani Urquizo

---

김찬중 | Chanjoong Kim
김찬중 (Chanjoong Kim), 더시스템랩 (THE_SYSTEM LAB)
팀 Team: 이지훈 (Jeehoon Lee), 한상옥 (Sangok Han), 강민식 (Minsik Kang), 정호승 (Hoseung Jung), 왕탄 (Tan Wang)

이은영 | Eunyoung Yi
이은영 (Eunyoung Yi), Yi Architects

승효상 | Seung H-Sang
승효상 (Seung H-Sang), 이로재 (Iroje Architects and Planners)
팀 Team: 이동수 (Dongsoo Lee), 이규빈 (Kyubin Lee), 최보 (Bora Choi), 안기현 (Kihyun Ahn), 김대홍 (Daehong Kim)

알레한드로 하이엑 콜 | Alejandro Haiek Coll (Lab.pro.Fab)
Alejandro Haiek Coll, The public Machinery
팀 Team: Nashira Covarrubia, Enrique Henriques, Daniela Rodriguez, Alexandra Montes, Irina Urriola,
영상/애니메이션 (Video Team / Animation): Alvaro Leon / Coma y Punto, Cristina Escribano, Oscar Vergara, Miguel Angel Sainero / Alexander Wright
모형 Models: Research Institute of Sweden.

요시하루 츠카모토 | Yoshiharu Tsukamoto
Yoshiharu Tsukamoto
팀 Team: 김현수 (Hyunsoo Kim), Ivan Bonev, Hu Shi, Amena Rahman, Selma Shimura, Agnes Lundberg, Clara Havström, Kai Wen, Kan Tong, Shohei Kunisawa, Kai Kashibuchi, Shino Hagio, Sana Toumatsu, Daiki Chiba, Wataru Moriwaki, Kazuki Tanaka, Hiroki Kiyoto, Miyuki Watanabe, Art Murayama, Davina Iwana, Hofer Valentin

---

NL 건축사무소 | NL Architects
Pieter Bannenberg, Walter van Dijk, Kamiel Klaasse
팀 Team: Nazar Gresko, Mathieu Landelle, Conor Denison, Jane Lee, Zofia Wojdyga

---

페데리코 소리아노 + 돌로레스 팔라시오스 | Federico Soriano + Dolores Palacios
팀 Team: Carolina Cabello Sanchez,
Eduardo Castillo Vinuesa, Lucia Larraz Pérez, Irene de Santos, Helena Petruzzi. 렌더 Renders: ARC Shadow Corp.
번역 Translators: Daniel Lacasta Fitzsimmons (영어/English)

AZPML
팀 Team: Alejandro Zaera-Polo, Maider Llaguno-Munitxa, Ivaylo Nachev, Carlos Orihuela, Rubén Gayarre del Cerro, Maria Herrera, Raul Zurera
조경 Landscape Architect: Arquitectura Agronomía, Teresa Gali

Go-Up 건축사무소 | Go-Up Architects
Nicola Canessa, Paolo Raffetto
팀 Team: Carlotta Crosa di Vergagni, Maddalena Piccini, Marta Barile, Sara Amielli, Matteo Doglio
연구 Research: Gic-Lab Reserch Team, Matilde Pitanti, Gi-orgia Tucci, Alessia Ronco Milanaccio, Francesca Vercellino

---

신혜원 | Haewon Shin
신혜원 (Haewon Shin), 로칼디자인 (lokaldesign)
팀 Team: 이소영 (Soyoung Lee), 최승아 (Seungah Choi)
표지디자인 Cover Design: Hwaran Yoo (유화란)

UNDERGROUND

모도스튜디오 | modostudio
Cibinel Laurenti Martocchia architetti associati
팀 Team: Cibinel, Roberto Laurenti, Giorgio Martocchia, Daria Fimmanò, Giulia Mangiola
타임랩스 Time-lapse: 김지원 (Ji Won Kim), Apinan Chanabun
SoA Studio
팀 Team: 강예린 (Yerin Kang), 이치훈 (Chi Hoon Lee), 이재원 (Jae Woen Lee), 이정연 (Jeongyeon Lee)

김택빈+장용순 | Taekbin Kim + Yong-Soon Chang
김택빈 (Taekbin Kim, 이스케이프 Escape), 장용순 (Yong-Soon Chang, 홍익대학교 Hongik Univ.)
팀 Team: 박근이 (Geun-e Park), 유예지 (Yeji Yoo), 임혜진 (Hye-Jin Lim), 양혜선 (Hyeseon Yang), 정세영 (Se-Young Chung), 허이서 (Iseo Heo), 박가영 (Ga-Young Park)

케이스 크리스티안제 | Kees Christiaanse
Kees Christiaanse (founder of KCAP Architects&Planners)
팀 Team: Yi Chien Liao, 김병우 (Byoungwoo Kim), Murtada Al-Kaabi, 박혜리 (Hyeri Park), 유나호 (Yoo Na Ho)

김광수 | studio_K_works
김광수 (Kwangsoo Kim)
팀 Team: 한주희 (Ju-Hee Han), 구혜민 (Hyemin Gu), 서도현 (Dohyeon Seo)

청보글 | Cheungvogl
Cheungvogl
팀 Team: Judy Cheung, Christoph Vogl, K Nakamura, Mui Tang, Piers Christensen

---

터미널 7 | Terminal 7 Architects
조경찬 (K-Chan Zoh)
팀 Team: 채민혁 (Minyuk Chai), 백설아 (Seola Baek), 김재연 (Jaeyeon Kim)

MVRDV
Winy Maas (MVRDV)
팀 Team: Wenchian Shi, 이교석 (Kyo Suk Lee), 석대희 (Daehee Suk), Chi Zhang, 이동민 (Dongmin Lee), 이슬 (Seul Lee)

도미니크 페로 | Dominique Perrault
Dominique Perrault
팀 Team: Gaëlle Lauriot-Prevost, Ignacio Ferrer, 이윤희 (Yoonhie Lee), Richard Nguyen, 성소오 (So-oh Sung)
모형 Modeling: ING Model Company

김영준 서울대학교에서 건축을 공부했다. 공간사와 이로재, OMA(로테르담)에서 경험을 쌓은 후, 1998년부터 YO2 설계사무실을 운영하고 있다. 자하재(뉴욕 MOMA 소장), 일산 허유재 병원, 행정복합도시 현상설계(공동1등), 논현동 ZWKM 사옥 등의 작업을 진행하면서, 한국 예술종합학교, 마드리드 유러피안 대학, 메사추세츠 공과대학 등에서 강의했다. 파주 출판도시의 건축코디네이터이고 서울시 2대 총괄건축가였다.

Young Joon Kim studied architecture at Seoul National University. After working at Space Group, Iroje, OMA(Rotterdam), he has been running his own firm YO2 since 1998. JaHaJae Residence(Acquired and exhibitted at MOMA, NY), HerYooJae Hospital, Korea New Administrative City Competition(First Tier Prize), ZWKM Buildings are the main works among various projects between architecture and urbanism. He taught at Korean University of Arts, European University of Madrid, Massachusetts Institute of Technology. He is a Coordinator of Paju Book City, and a City Architect of Seoul(2016-2018).

마뉴엘 가우사 나바로 (1959년 바르셀로나, 스페인 출생)은 PHD 건축가이자 비평가, 저자이다.
2017년부터 현재까지 제노아 대학(Università degli Studi of Genova)의 DAD-UNIGE의 정교수이자 도시디자인 학장으로 재직 중이다. 동대학에서 2008년에서 14년까지는 부교수로, 2014년에서 2017년까지는 건축 및 도시디자인의 정교수로 재직하였다. 또한 2015년 이후 현재까지 도시 및 디자인의 박사과정 프로그램의 디렉터이자 코디네이터이다.
2012년에서 2015년까지 바르셀로나 IAAC((Institut d'Arquitectura Avançada de Catalunya) 센터 장으로 재직했다. 현재는 이 센터의 공동 창립자이자 석좌교수로서 이론 및 언드밴스드 널리지 분야의 주임 교수이자 과학 위원회의 멤버이다.
악타 출판사와 건축, 조경 도시디자인 사무소인 악타 건축사무소의 창립멤버(2000)이자 주요고문(2008년 이후)이다.
2000년에는 프랑스의 건축 아카데미 메달(Médaille de l'Académie d'Architecture de France)을 받았다.

Manuel Gausa Navarro (Barcelona, Spain,1959) is a PHD architect and critic, author of several publications.
From 2017 he has the Chair of Urban Design as Full Professor at DAD-UNIGE, Università degli Studi of Genova) where from 2008 to 2014 he was Associate Professor of Design and from 2014 to 2017 he was Full Professor of Architecture and Landscape Design and where he is from 2015 Director-Coordinator of the ADD (PHD Program in Architecture and Design)
From 2012 to 2015 he was Dean of the IAAC (Institut d´Arquitectura Avançada de Catalunya, Barcelona) centre where, as Co-founder and Senior Professor, is now Lead Professor in Theory and Advanced Knowledge and Member of Scientific Comity.
Founding Member (2000) and Principal Advisor (from 2008) of Actar Publishers and Actar Arquitectura, office of architecture, landscape and urban design.
In 2000 he was honoured with the Médaille de l´Académie d´Architecture de France.

슈퍼그라운드
서울 새로운 땅의 풍경
언더그라운드

SUPERGROUND
SEOUL NEW GROUNDSCAPES
UNDERGROUND

발행일	2019. 11.
발행처	서울특별시
발행인	박원순 서울특별시장
발행부서	서울특별시 도시공간개선단
주소	서울시 중구 세종대로 110
주관	서울특별시 도시공간개선단
기획	김영준((전)서울특별시 총괄건축가) 마뉴엘 가우사(제노아대학교)
코디네이터	언더그라운드 이영석(어반인덱스랩) 슈퍼그라운드 신은기(인천대학교) 최태산(더워크샵)
운영	양근보, 이진아(㈔서울건축포럼)
디자인	ACTAR PUBLISHERS
편집/인쇄	하나
ISBN	979-11-6161-731-2 93530
발간등록번호	51-6110000-002108-01
가격	25,000원

Published in November 2019
Published by Seoul Metropolitan Government
Publisher Wonsoon Park, Mayor Seoul Metropolitan Government
Production Dept. Urban Space Improvement Bureau
Address: 110 sejongdaero, Jung-gu, Seoul

Department in charge: Urban Space Improvement Bureau

Curators:
Young Joon Kim (Second City Architect Seoul)
Manuel Gausa (UNIGE-University of Genoa)

Coordination:
UNDERGROUND: Youngseok Lee (urbanindexlab)
SUPERGROUND: Eungee Cinn (Incheon National University), Taesan Choi (theWorkshop)

Managed by Keunbo Yang, Jina Lee (Seoul Architecture Forum)

Designed by ACTAR PUBLISHERS
Edited/Printed by HANA

ISBN 979-11-6161-731-2 93530
GPRN 51-6110000-002108-01

Price 25,000 won

서울특별시 SEOUL METROPOLITAN GOVERNMENT I·SEOUL·U 너와 나의 서울